THE DORSEY SERIES IN SOCIOLOGY

EDITOR ROBIN M. WILLIAMS, JR. *Cornell University*

Crime, correction, and society

ELMER HUBERT JOHNSON

Professor of Sociology
Center for the Study of Crime, Delinquency, and Corrections
Southern Illinois University at Carbondale

1974 Third Edition
THE DORSEY PRESS Homewood, Illinois 60430
IRWIN-DORSEY INTERNATIONAL London, England WC2H 9NJ
IRWIN-DORSEY LIMITED Georgetown, Ontario L7G 4B3

Third Edition

First Printing, January 1974
Second Printing, December 1974
Third Printing, May 1975

ISBN 0–256–01418–3
Library of Congress Catalog Card No. 73–77022
Printed in the United States of America

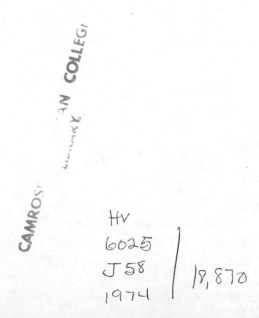

To
Elmer Daamgaard Johnson
and
William McKinley Holmes

Preface

This book emerges from my long-standing belief that criminological theory is the greatest resource for those people who carry out the vital and difficult work of law enforcement, the courts, and corrections. Although recognizing the glaring inadequacies of the contemporary system of criminal justice, I have great respect for the many dedicated persons who have accepted formidable responsibilities in this unwieldy and, in many respects, obsolete system. This respect was developed in the course of my sharing some of these responsibilities for a time as a parole officer and later as assistant director of an American prison system. Following this practical experience, I returned to my teaching of sociology with the desire to communicate to students the rich experiences I had had in relating theories to the fascinating practice of criminology. *Crime, Correction, and Society* is my instrument for encouraging students to develop a feeling for theoretical issues.

This third edition surpasses the previous editions in demonstrating the relevance of theories to practice. I have endeavored to carry out concurrently the explanation of crucial ideas and the description of the real worlds of crime and criminal justice. For example, Chapter 8 traces the conflicting goals of contemporary practice to the earlier dispute between the classical and positive schools, and Chapter 11 relates various theories to social reform and intervention. I have continued to orient the reader to the practical issues of law enforcement, criminal justice, and criminology. Greater effort has been made to organize description around concepts such as institution, system, role, community, and so on.

The result is an improved organization of the book as a whole and greater clarity in presentation. To guide the reader, each section of the book has a preface and each chapter a final summary. The recent criminological literature has been carefully explored and brought into play to keep the book abreast of the remarkable changes underway in criminology. Each chapter has a list of references in addition to those cited in the footnotes.

Although the field of corrections continues to be an important part of this book, I have oriented the third edition more toward the criminal justice system as a whole. The coordination of law enforcement, and the functions of the courts, jails, and corrections is an urgent necessity in an urban society relying especially on the formal controls upon which the apparatus of criminal justice depends. In evaluating the workings of each of these components and their coordination with one another, the careful observer finds many inconsistencies and much organizational malfunctioning. However, emotional denunciation of these failures is a poor substitute for understanding of the basic causes of crime and the complex issues involved in strengthening the effectiveness of criminological practice. I have accepted the responsibilities of the constructive critic to offer suggestions for improving undesirable conditions. My hope is that criminological workers, present and future, who read this book will find it useful in strengthening the value of their efforts.

Prefaces to the first two editions cited my debts to several persons. In addition, I acknowledge the vital editorial contributions to this edition of Alvin Rudoff, John R. Stratton, Kenneth Venters, and Robin M. Williams, Jr. Gloria Reardon provided exceptional support as copy editor. Finally, in typing manuscript, the following persons conferred the tribute of identifying this book as their own. Margaret Camarato, Jacqueline Goepfert, Jill Johnson, Darnecea Moultrie, Lorraine Townsend, and Pearl Whited.

December 1973   ELMER H. JOHNSON

Contents

and compliance models. Exchange and the strategy of conflict. Differential influences of legal sanctions.

Part I
Introduction

Crime arouses intense popular interest. We will endeavor to channel this interest into a systematic study of human behavior, particularly the social framework that gives order to the behavior of individuals.

The study of crime, correction, and society will be initiated by inquiring: What is criminology? What is crime? What are the dimensions of the crime problem? The answers to these questions must be tentative. This entire book can provide only an introduction to this single aspect of man's most interesting problem: himself.

1

Crime and criminology

Every citizen is, in a sense, a victim of crime. Violence and theft have not only injured, often irreparably, hundreds of thousands of citizens, but have directly affected everyone. Some have been afraid to use public streets and parks. Some have come to doubt the worth of a society in which so many people behave badly. Some have become distrustful of the Government's ability, or even desire, to protect them. Some have lapsed into the attitude that criminal behavior is normal human behavior and consequently have become indifferent to it, or have adopted it as a good way to get ahead in life. Some have become suspicious of those they conceive to be responsible for crime: adolescents or Negroes or drug addicts or college students or demonstrators; policemen who fail to solve crimes; judges who pass lenient sentences or write decisions restricting the activities of the police; parole boards that release prisoners who resume their criminal activities.[1]

The high priority assigned by the American people to the social problem of crime is indicated by this statement of the President's Crime Commission. While public concern over crime and criminals sometimes is based on faulty premises, as Chapter 2 will indicate, the dimensions of the crime problem in urbanized society do merit great concern.

Criminal law reflects the fundamental values of a given society, and violations of that law are symptomatic of the society's sociocultural organization. Thus criminology, in the course of confronting the riddle of criminal behavior, also provides a means of studying society and qualifies as a particularly useful survey course in the social sciences. As higher education attempts to improve the relevancy of teaching and research to public issues, criminology is taking its place as an academic specialization that combines theory and application.

[1] President's Commission on Law Enforcement and Administration of Justice, *The Challenge of Crime in a Free Society* (Washington, D.C.: U.S. Government Printing Office, February 1967), p. 1.

3

DISTINGUISHING THE CRIMINOLOGIST

The first use of the term "criminology" is credited to Paul Topinard, a French anthropologist, in 1879.[2] The suffix "ology" refers to "a science" or "branch of learning," and the term implies a scientific study of crime or criminals. In the 18th and early 19th centuries, however, writers in the field were less concerned with scientific analysis than with such humanitarian aspects as the application of punishment. Their writings, as Hermann Mannheim notes, were closer to the tradition of humane letters than to science. They were devoted to penology rather than the broader range of topics represented by the criminology which emerged later.[3]

Criminology, for our purposes, includes two separate but interdependent fields: scientific study and criminological practice. Both are concerned with the causation of criminal behavior, criminal behavior itself, societal reaction to crime, and prevention of lawbreaking. And both, ideally, are based on the principles of science.

The criminologist: Theory in practice

If the term "criminologist" is to be useful, it must be able to distinguish a group of specialists on the basis of specified characteristics. Although the primary orientation of this book is toward the applied field, theoretical criminology is indispensable as the foundation for meaningful practice. Without the intellectual thrust of relevant theories, the practitioner does not qualify as a genuine criminologist.

Policemen, correctional officers, and other criminological workers have laid claim to the title of criminologist because they have direct experience in coping with criminals in action. Criminals, usually in the status of prisoner or former criminal, may even claim to be criminologists because they have directly experienced both the development of their own "criminal personality" and the personal significance of being exposed to the workings of the system of criminal justice. An analogy would be the psychoanalyst who undergoes psychoanalysis as part of his training. However, because the objectivity and analytic skills of the scientist are also marks of the criminologist, it is neither necessary nor sufficient that he personally undergo the phenomena he studies or with which he is supposed to deal.

Direct experience, of course, is a valuable ingredient in the expert knowledge of any field of practice, but the *interpretation* of events dis-

[2] William A. Bonger, *An Introduction to Criminology*, trans. Emil Van Loo (London: Methuen & Co., Ltd., 1936), p. 1. The early identification of criminological studies with physical anthropology was continued by the preference of Havelock Ellis for the term "criminal anthropology"; see Ellis, *The Criminal*, 4th ed. (New York: Charles Scribner's Sons, 1910), p. 31.

[3] Hermann Mannheim (ed.), *Pioneers in Criminology* (Chicago: Quadrangle Books, 1960), pp. 1–2.

tinguishes the expert from others who also undergo relevant experience. The student of criminology is likely to have great interest in the dynamics of personality which are inaccessible to direct observation by the researcher but underlie the development and expression of criminality. The feelings of those exposed to the procedures and sanctions of criminal justice are important data for criminological research; at the very least, they provide a means of measuring the efficiency of penal policies in preventing or correcting criminality. Nevertheless, emotions are not sufficient for reliable understanding of criminal behavior.

As a basis for distinguishing a group of criminological experts as criminologists, there must be intellectual discipline in the application of a specialized body of knowledge and an ethical commitment to community service beyond individualistic self-interest. In law enforcement, courts, and corrections, the call for "professionalism" entails promotion of these qualities in personnel. For the professor of criminology and the researcher, the scientist's role and the scientific method impose similar qualifications.

The principles of science underlie both fields of criminology, scientific study and criminological practice. While the practitioner may not engage in research or regard himself as a scientist, ideally he is a consumer of research, trained in the knowledge and techniques it tests, and he exhibits those characteristics of the scientist that are relevant to his practice.

Characteristics of science

Science endeavors to accumulate verifiable knowledge systematically and to subject this knowledge to the kinds of interpretation that will enable man to continue to push back the frontiers of ignorance regarding the workings of his world. As a special kind of observer, the scientist proposes expert guesses about the answers to questions he or his colleagues have uncovered and attempts to test these hypotheses against evidence. Because his predecessors have taken care that their discoveries are based on truth, not unsubstantiated opinion, the contemporary scientist has some established facts as a platform from which to launch his probing. Through this accumulative process, the total body of reliable knowledge is progressively enlarged.

In gathering information, the scientist selects from a host of items those that are relevant to his hypothesis, which is a statement of the relationships he believes exist between the various bits of information. The information considered and the design of the study are selected to rule out the effects of variables other than those whose relationships he is testing. Thus the scientist tries to control the conditions of his experiment so that his conclusions will be more reliable than those available to the casual observer, being aware that the manner of selecting among items and his own expectations may color his results. As a *scientific* observer, he is charged with obligations to be accurate, precise, and objective so that his conclusions express fact rather than "proving" a particular predetermined outcome.

Theories are the tools of science. By lending order to the observation and recording of information, they enable the observer to select intelligently and with a sense of priority among the tremendous number and variety of informational bits that are available in even the most "obvious" events. His knowledge of the theories of his field of study provides the scientist with an orientation toward the events he will observe and forms a basis for formulating the hypotheses that lend direction to his investigation. As the products of verifiable conclusions, theories provide a means of inserting discoveries into the accumulated body of knowledge. The carefully precise terms promote meaningful communication among colleagues.

By definition, therefore, the criminologist has the characteristics of the scientist. He is a trained, intellectually disciplined, and *objective* observer who fits his interpretations into a body of systematically accumulated theories. Criminological research demonstrates these characteristics, as developed in Chapter 3.

We have noted above that direct experience alone, no matter how relevant, does not qualify a criminological practitioner or a criminal as a criminologist. The emotions stirred by personal experience are possibly raw material for research, but they obstruct the gathering of objective and verifiable information. If, however, in addition to their direct experiences, they employ the theoretical knowledge, trained observation, and systematic objectivity characteristic of criminology as a science, those directly involved with the problem of crime can so qualify.

CRIMINOLOGICAL SCIENCES

The criminological sciences are manned by academic and research specialists who seek to develop bodies of meaningful theories and reliable information through application of the methods of science to the study of crime.

A collection of criminological sciences

Theoretical criminology is a collection of criminological sciences rather than a single autonomous science. The studies of crime causation involve every facet of human behavior, including societal responses to criminal behavior. If criminology were defined as an independent, self-contained discipline, it would have to be capable of handling all the problems of man as an individual and as a socially organized creature. Although the majority of the participants in an international symposium[4] expressed a preference for the definition of criminology as an autonomous science, they did not fail to recognize the absence of the unique clinical and experimental methods that would characterize such a discipline.

Internationally, criminology is found within a multiplicity of academic structures and is subject to the conflicting claims of biology (linked with physical anthropology), law, psychology, and sociology. Similar heterogeneity is found in the United States, but here sociology is dominant. The history of American criminology is intimately related to the struggles of sociology in earlier decades to establish a distinct identity among the social sciences.[5]

The earlier sociological interest in criminology expressed a rather simplistic and reformist orientation toward social problems. In the 1930s, a three-year survey of criminology and criminal justice presented a number of conclusions which suggest the shortcomings of criminology as a science at that time. The report claimed that there was no scientific knowledge in the fields of criminology. Descriptions of the processes and institutions of criminal justice were deemed of little practical utility. Criminology depends in large part upon the subject matter of psychology and sociology, and the conclusion then was that these lacked theory and research methodology.[6] In retort, one critic indicated the authors of this study had mistaken the nature of a science of society and were too pessimistic about possibilities of doing any scientific work in the social studies.[7]

After this period of minimal scientific performance, most sociologists withdrew from both the reformist orientation and from practical concerns. "Pure" research and the development of abstract principles for their field of study drew the primary attention of sociologists in general. The few sociologists with an interest in criminology, as Chapter 9 will show, devoted themselves largely to criticism of psychological and psychiatric attempts to explain criminal behavior rather than to the development of

[4] Denis Carroll and Jean Pinatel, "Report on Teaching of Criminology," in *The University Teaching of Social Sciences: Criminology* (Paris: UNESCO, 1957), p. 15. For arguments that criminology should be considered an independent science, see Marvin E. Wolfgang, "Criminology and the Criminologist," *Journal of Criminal Law, Criminology and Police Science*, 54 (June 1963): 155–62.

[5] Stanton Wheeler, "The Social Sources of Criminology," *Sociological Inquiry*, 32 (Spring 1962): 139–59; Walter C. Reckless, "American Criminology," *Criminology*, 8 (May 1970): 4–20; Richard Quinney, *The Problem of Crime* (New York: Dodd, Mead & Co., 1970), pp. 43–100; Gilbert Geis (ed.), *White-Collar Criminal* (New York: Atherton Press, 1968), pp. 1–6; C. Wright Mills, "The Professional Ideology of Social Pathologists," in Mark Lefton, James K. Skipper, Jr., and Charles H. McCaghy (eds.), *Approaches to Deviance* (New York: Appleton-Century-Crofts, 1968), pp. 3–23.

[6] Jerome Michael and Mortimer J. Adler, *Crime, Law and Social Science* (New York: Harcourt, Brace & Co., 1933), pp. 390–91.

[7] Joseph Mayer, "Toward a Science of Society," *American Journal of Sociology*, 39 (September 1933): 159–93.

sociological theories oriented toward criminology. With some exceptions, psychiatrists ignored explanations competing with their own. American law schools exhibited little interest in criminology or the social sciences. In short, criminology occupied a marginal and uncertain status in the worlds of academia and practice which has continued to be an influence today.

Marginal status of criminologists

In his study of the development of criminology in Europe and the United States, Leon Radzinowicz was impressed by its universal characteristics. Even in the most advanced countries, extremely limited support has been given to the scientific study of crime. Nevertheless, those dedicated to its study have demonstrated undaunted resilience "in the face of persistent indifference or scarcely veiled scepticism." The dedication of some of them has been rewarded by the effects certain criminological ideas have had on even very traditional systems of criminal justice.[8]

Skepticism of academic criminology has been expressed by both practitioners and members of the academic community. The opposition of a sizable proportion of practitioners stems from suspicion of intellectual abstractions, distrust for the rigorous testing of traditional practices and previously unexamined assumptions, and doubts that academic people understand the problems of such things as police work on the streets or supervision of prison cell blocks. Academic criminologists are likely to be seen as strange beings who appear briefly on the work sites of practitioners, express unfamiliar ideas in a weird jargon, and then return to their "ivy-covered towers" to meditate over their findings in pleasant isolation from the harsh realities of crime control.

Scientists on and off the campuses also tend to be skeptical of the worth and appropriateness of the work of academic criminology and research. Many scientists believe productive pursuit of verified truth requires concentration on systematic development of knowledge in their own discipline because they feel specialization has advantages over diffusive study of the many facets of a social issue. If theoretical criminology has any unity, Stanton Wheeler says, it rests in a common concern for criminological issues by academic specialists drawn from diverse disciplines, not in distinctive concepts and forms of analysis shared by criminologists as such. Concern for criminological issues raises the difficulties of multidisciplinary study which requires understanding of a variety of concepts—a formidable task compared with the framing of research issues appropriate to a scientist's own discipline. Wheeler also notes that the theoretical criminologist places special emphasis on formulating the-

[8] Leon Radzinowicz, *In Search of Criminology* (Cambridge, Mass.: Harvard University Press, 1962), p. vii.

ories that are relevant to criminological issues, which makes him particularly responsive to short-run opinion.[9] The diversion of the applied researcher's interest into short-run, practical issues (recruitment of police personnel, evaluation of prison educational programs, analysis of bail practices, and so on) also raises the possibility that pursuit of objective truth will be undetermined by loyalty to those establishments of criminal justice within whose ideology he becomes socialized in the course of research.

The criminologist is likely to question the reality of the idealized image of the "pure" scientist standing aloof from the crosscurrents of changing social conditions in an unwavering pursuit of truth. If objectivity can be maintained in analysis, the academic criminologist might argue, theoretical concepts are tested severely by their exposure through applied research to the social reality they are supposed to explain. Further, the range of criminological topics permits both multidisciplinary studies in which the interests of several disciplines converge and analysis from the perspective of a single discipline.

Later developments

The years between the two world wars were the germinal phase in which criminological studies in the United States began to transcend European influence. With its uniquely sociological bent, American criminology abandoned its previous clumsy imitation of the biological and juristic orientations of criminology in western Europe. Radzinowicz notes that "American criminology, an almost unknown newcomer, established itself firmly amidst the sociological and social sciences and achieved an academic recognition which has continuously been denied it in almost every other country."[10] A remarkable growth in volume of criminological papers and maturity of work can be found in the relevant American journals. The literature cited in this book, especially in Chapter 10, is further testimony.

Evidence of a new vigor for criminology is attested to by an unprecedented rapprochement between the law and the social sciences[11] and between psychiatry and sociology.[12] The increased level of governmental funding of criminological research and action programs indicates substantial recognition by legislators and governmental executives that community interests call for innovative measures to be taken to correct serious

[9] Wheeler, "The Social Sources of Criminology," pp. 139–59.

[10] Radzinowicz, *In Search of Criminology*, pp. 114–18.

[11] See the relatively new journal, *Law and Society Review*, as one tangible bit of evidence.

[12] The growth of community psychiatry and of the psycho-social model of mental illness provides relevant examples; see Chapter 9, pp. 222–23.

defects in the administration of criminal justice. Perhaps the most encouraging development is the growing partnership of action agencies and higher education.

With approval, Edwin M. Schur cites a gradual shift of criminological studies away from individual-centered approaches that view crime in terms of heredity, physical characteristics, and so on. The trend is toward analysis of the ways in which an individual's position in society—his socioeconomic status, place of neighborhood residence, family situation, and primary group affiliations—contribute to his involvement in crime.[13] This represents increasing recognition that efforts to identify distinct individual characteristics marking "the criminal" have been neither productive of significant findings nor useful for criminological policy making. The trend is toward recognition that crime is patterned behavior, and its patterns intersect in many ways the institutional patterns of the overall society.

In keeping with this development, this book will trace the patterns of criminal behavior within society's systems of norms, statuses, and institutions. It will endeavor to relate criminological theories to criminological practices and to the operation of the system of criminal justice which constitutes the formal control structure of society. It will place prevention, control, and correction of crime within the context of the environment of the community served by the system of criminal justice operating in it.

CRIMINOLOGICAL PRACTITIONERS

Applied criminology is carried on by a loose confederation of practitioners in law enforcement agencies, criminal courts, probation and parole programs, prisons, juvenile training schools, private and public welfare agencies, and various crime prevention programs.

Coordination of "people work"

The broad organization within which this confederation of practitioners operates has been described as "the criminal justice system" because ideally the work of each agency would be effectively coordinated with the work of the other agencies. In reality, as demonstrated in Chapter 12, the performance of these agencies fails to qualify as a genuine system. Recent developments, at any rate, have produced an unprecedented demand that agents of criminal justice coordinate their activities within the total "people work activities" of the community. The increasing complexity of society that has been wrought by industrialization and urbanization necessitates greater coordination of criminological work with that

---

[13] Edwin M. Schur, *Our Criminal Society* (Englewood Cliffs, N.J.: Prentice-Hall, Inc., 1969), pp. 8–9.

of agencies not concerned solely with criminal justice. Unprecedented efficiency in carrying out the host of responsibilities of police, courts, and correctional agencies is called for.

Coordination of these activities can be promoted by appropriate design of agency structures, but ultimately it depends on the personnel who man these agencies. It is especially important because of the unusual degree of discretion called for in decision making by those in the lower levels of the organizational hierarchy of law enforcement, probation, prison, and parole agencies. Some of the practitioners in these positions are distributed over a wide geographical area difficult to supervise from a central headquarters, and all have intimate and persistent contacts with those they process. Unit decisions must form comprehensible patterns if the activities of the criminal justice system are to make sense.

An ideal occupational system

Coordinated performance of the diverse tasks of criminal justice calls for an *occupational system* through which, ideally, dedicated individuals would be recruited for each properly designed position. They would be trained in relevant knowledge and skills and motivated to perform their assigned tasks to advance the ultimate purposes of the organizational plan for criminal justice. A fundamental weakness of American criminal justice administration is the lack of an occupational system that is of such quality as to assure the achievement of its vital functions. We will discuss these matters in more detail when considering their relevance to technical competence in the operation of correctional institutions.[14]

The "people work" of all phases of criminological practice calls for intelligent direction by a professional elite and direct supervision of personnel by technical careerists. There must also be systematic performance by criminological workers who have the most continuous and intimate contacts with the people being served or processed by the agency. The professional elite is qualified in the knowledge of theoretical criminology and has bonds with colleagues which can link applied and theoretical criminology. The technical careerists, characterized by technical competence and a commitment to their field of practice as a life's work, give substance to the abstract principles and policies advanced by the elite. In carrying out detailed tasks at the lower levels of agency structure, criminological workers are most directly concerned with the ultimate outcome of abstract principles as applied to the realities of daily interactions with one another and with clients.

Later chapters will demonstrate a manpower crisis in criminal justice administration that is characterized by an insufficient supply of properly

[14] See Chapter 17, pp. 428–31.

Figure 1–1. Training for "people work" in corrections.

To further understanding of typical reactions of inmates to recurrent situations in correctional institutions, employees of the Federal Bureau of Prisons participate in role-playing sessions at the Bureau's Staff Training Center, El Reno, Oklahoma.

trained and managed personnel, regardless of the particular activity. Proposals for reform almost always call for improved education and training to produce a larger, more reliable supply of skillful, dedicated, and ethical staff members capable of working effectively with citizens and offenders as individuals. To curb the excesses of bureaucracy, these workers would ideally balance self-initiative and organizational conformity so that systematic work activities would be tailored to the individual qualities and needs of clients. If their work is to have impact in reducing the volume of criminal behavior, they must understand the theoretical principles by which initiative in decision making is practiced without jeopardizing the achievement of the ultimate goals of their agency.

From the perspective of employees, criminological practice must provide an occupational system that would justify their personal commitment to this work. Ideally, their energies would be enlisted in sustained support of organized programs because the system provides attractive economic and psychic rewards, a dependable route for promotion through demonstration of relevant competence, and a set of principles which justifies their response to the call for public service. The harsh reality is that applied criminology has been deficient in these characteristics. Several developments indicate that improvements may be under way. Action agencies have had some success in raising salary scales, reducing the adverse effects of the granting of jobs as rewards for service to political parties, and introducing professional standards into criminological work. Impetus for personnel reform has also come from increased federal funding, greater public awareness of the manpower crisis, growing recognition by agencies outside criminal justice that they share common interests with those in the field, and the hesitant but increasing interest of higher education in preparing students for careers in criminal justice.

The role of higher education

The university has a key role to play in the development of the confederation of criminal justice practitioners. It has the necessary resources of theoretical concepts and trained personnel, and its intellectual storehouse holds many "skeleton keys" with which to unlock answers to persistent difficulties. The university also has the institutionalized function of providing competent and constructive criticism of traditional practice. Teaching prepares students for criminological careers, and competence of practitioners is upgraded by short-term institutes.

Illustrative of increasing interest in the mobilization of university resources are the studies of the President's Crime Commission and the Joint Commission on Correctional Manpower and Training. Their reports suggest the mounting dissatisfaction of criminological administrators with current conditions and the awakening interest of higher education in playing a more active role in the preparation of personnel for careers in applied criminology.[15]

Developments underway in higher education hold prospects for a breakthrough in overcoming the intellectual sterility and unquestioning acceptance of bankrupt philosophies that has characterized criminological practice. The isolation of criminological practices from changes underway in other kinds of "people work" and the handicaps of an incomplete and inadequate career system are also being dealt with at the university level. A remarkable number of academic programs has been introduced in the past decade, especially among two-year community colleges. Because these programs often lack properly qualified instructors and adequate grounding in relevant theories, much improvement is necessary before their potential can be realized.[16]

In-service training conducted by action agencies is a useful way to orient recruits, upgrade and keep current the practical knowledge of employees, and introduce changes in policies and procedures. However, such programs frequently suffer from an emphasis on empirical knowledge without proper grounding in relevant theories. To remedy this, cooperation with institutions of higher education would be particularly useful.

Academic training is of four types:

1. Schools of social work envisage correctional work as essentially clinical and nonauthoritarian in nature.
2. Sequence of courses within departments of sociology attempt to educate future law enforcement and correctional practitioners in a program usually designed primarily to prepare students for careers in sociology per se.
3. Programs within schools of public administration, social welfare, public safety, police science, psychology, and political science usually involve a core curriculum without integration of criminological knowledge and experience with the theoretical studies.
4. Independent specialized programs are advocated to overcome the shortcomings of other programs—criminology does not mesh with any single behavioral science, and the generic approach of traditional

[15] For analysis of the implications for corrections, see Kenneth Polk, *The University and Corrections: Potential for Collaborative Relationships* (Washington, D.C.: Joint Commission on Correctional Manpower and Training, 1969).

[16] Elmer H. Johnson, "One Answer to Manpower Needs of Applied Criminology: Associate in Arts Degree," *Police*, 12 (May–June 1968): 52–56; Charles L. Newman and Dorothy Sue Hunter, "Education for Careers in Law Enforcement: An Analysis of Student Output 1964–67," *Journal of Criminal Law, Criminology and Police Science*, 59 (March 1968): 138–43; Charles A. Tracy, "Survey of Criminal Justice Subject-Matter Baccalaureate Programs," *Journal of Criminal Law, Criminology and Police Science*, 61 (December 1970): 576–79.

departments does not provide training in the settings in which theoretical principles are to be applied.[17]

Programs based on a single discipline assume that criminology is not a primary, self-contained discipline because its subject matter involves the full range of the social and behavioral sciences. Through intensive study within a particular discipline, the student is supposed to gain the theoretical knowledge which characterizes the genuine professional. However, this form of curriculum organization does not permit integration and coordination of the total body of criminological theory, because members of each discipline regard crime and criminals as merely a specialized issue within their particular generic approach. Consequently, the various theoreticians are isolated from one another to the detriment of the development of the interdisciplinary approach essential to criminology.[18]

A CRUCIAL ISSUE: WHAT IS CRIME?

Although it eludes clear or conclusive answers, the question "What is crime?" lies at the base of criminological studies and criminal justice administration. The task of theoretical criminology is to investigate crime, criminality, and society's responses to crime. The definition of crime therefore determines the boundaries which distinguish the subject matter of criminology from the area of social deviance or other scientific studies. The occupational specialization of criminological practitioners concerned with the work of preventing, controlling, and correcting criminal behavior is tied to the validity of the distinctions made between criminals and noncriminals.

Legal and social definitions

Under the *legal definition* of crime, criminal behavior differs from other forms of social deviance in that it is in violation of the criminal laws promulgated by a political authority and subject to punishment adminis-

[17] Julian Roebuck and Paul Zelhart, "The Problem of Educating the Correctional Practitioner," *Journal of Criminal Law, Criminology. and Police Science,* 56 (March 1965): 45–53; Peter Lejins, "Aspects of Correctional Personnel Training as Viewed by a College Professor," *Proceedings, 85th Annual Congress of Corrections, American Prison Association, 1955;* Walter C. Reckless, "Training the Correctional Worker," in Paul W. Tappan (ed.), *Contemporary Correction* (New York: McGraw-Hill Book Co., 1951), p. 40; Alfred C. Schnur, "Pre-Service Training," *Journal of Criminal Law, Criminology and Police Science,* 50 (May–June 1959): 30; J. S. Lobenthal, "Proposals for Correctional Education and Training," *Prison Journal,* 40 (April 1960): 3–12.

[18] F. Ferracuti and M. W. Wolfgang, "Clinical vs. Sociological Criminology: Separation or Integration?" *Excerpta Criminologica,* 4 (July–August 1964): 407–10; Gordon Trasler, "Strategic Problems in the Study of Criminal Behavior," *British Journal of Criminology,* 4 (July 1964): 422–42.

tered by agents of the state. In strictly confining the definition of crime to the limits of the criminal law, the classical school of criminology[19] placed emphasis on the crime, not the criminal. The principle of "no crime without a law" was intended to curb the barbaric and arbitrary administration of courts in the early 19th century.[20]

In the last half of the 19th century, the positive school[21] transferred attention from the crime to the criminal in efforts to apply scientific methods to the study of the criminal. One member of this school, Raffaele Garofalo, defined "natural crime" as conduct which offends the basic moral sentiments of pity (repugnance to acts which produce pain) and probity (respect for property rights of others). Because behavior that is defined as criminal by the laws of some societies is approved of in others, he rejected the legal definition and substituted as a standard the evolution of basic moral sensibilities. Supposing the moral sense of a people to be transmitted from generation to generation, he saw the moral sense to be either "the effect of psychological heredity alone" or "the effect of such heredity combined with the imitative faculties of the child and the influence of family tradition." Criminals were explained as "psychic anomalies—exceptions similar to physical monstrosities" who, "in the absence of a better explanation," are attributed to atavism.[22]

This primitive version of a *social definition* of crime was given a sounder position when Thorsten Sellin advocated the substitution of conduct norms for legal crimes.[23] Seeing criminal laws as part of the larger body of norms, Sellin found the legal definition of crime especially vulnerable to variability in time and place because the legal norms depend on the character and interests of the groups with the political power to influence the enactment of criminal laws to safeguard the social values they treasure. As the values of the dominant group are modified and as the vicissitudes of social growth revise the power structure, the conduct norms embodied in the criminal law lose their congruence with the moral ideas of the day. This variability, Sellin argues, renders legal norms unsuitable for research. Instead he recommends the selection and classification of data independently of their legal form.

Conduct norms are found wherever there are social groups and are not necessarily embodied in law. Sellin would place criminological research in the study of conduct norms in general, with less attention to the legal labels attached to crime. Furthermore, conduct norms acquire valid-

[19] See Chapter 8, pp. 172–74.

[20] Clarence Ray Jeffery, "The Historical Development of Criminology," in Mannheim, *Pioneers in Criminology,* p. 367.

[21] See Chapter 8, pp. 169–71.

[22] Raffaele Garofalo, *Criminology* (Boston: Little, Brown & Co., 1914), pp. 9, 23, 31.

[23] Thorsten Sellin, *Culture Conflict and Crime* (New York: Social Science Research Council, 1938), pp. 21–25, 30, 40–45.

ity in groups to the extent they are incorporated in the personalities of members of the group. Therefore, Sellin points to what he regards as the crucial element distinguishing criminals from noncriminals: the degree of sensitivity of a person to the pressure of group opinion, which is dependent on his intellectual grasp of the norm and on the extent to which it has emotional significance to him. The weaker the person's sensitivity and the more negative his feelings toward the given norm, the more likely he is to be a violator.

Evaluation of the alternatives

In spite of its inadequacies, the legal definition has been recommended by many writers as the best means of delimiting the subject matter of criminology by differentiating criminals from noncriminals. Clarence Jeffery supports the legal definition on three grounds. First, criticism of the concept confuses the criminal act with the label of criminality; the official definition of a given act as criminal is a different matter than explaining that behavior in the given individual. This issue will be taken up in the next section. Second, because all norms are relativistic, both the social and legal definitions suffer inadequacies as timebound and culturebound measures of crime patterns. Finally, since laws are conduct codes, they also can be analyzed as norms.[24]

Although suggesting an excessive faith in the quality of the decision-making procedures of courts, Paul W. Tappan makes several apt points. He notes that the legal definition provides a means for determining qualification for criminal status on the basis of conviction for a crime; safeguards for individuals are provided by the due-process model of court operations. He also argues that since laws are products of sociocultural forces, they can be revised to coincide with changing conditions.[25]

To expand the concept of crime to include nonlegal norms, Shlomo Shoham warns, is highly precarious and problematic because this projects criminology into the broader subject of social deviance.[26] If criminology were considered an autonomous science, the boundaries of its subject matter would have to be determined by the legal definition of crime to avoid laying claim to the entire range of nonconformity—a claim challenged by students of family disorganization, alcoholism, mental illness, and other forms of deviance.

We prefer the definition of criminology as a collection of sciences encompassing specialists in the study of crime and societal reactions to

[24] Clarence Ray Jeffery, "The Structure of American Criminological Thinking," *Journal of Criminal Law and Criminology,* 46 (January–February 1956): 670.

[25] Paul W. Tappan, "Who Is the Criminal?" *American Sociological Review,* 12 (February 1947): 96–102.

[26] Shlomo Shoham, "The Norm, the Act, and the Object of Crime as Bases for the Classification of Criminal Behavior," *International Journal of Social Psychiatry,* 11 (Autumn 1965): 273.

crime and involving examination of legal norms within the context of all norms. This perspective would permit use of the social definition of crime when pertinent to the hypothesis being tested.

The relative merits of the legal and social definitions should be assessed according to their use. For personnel of the criminal justice system, the legal definition delineates the population with which they work. The criminological researcher would prefer either the social or legal definition, depending on the nature of his study topic, but he need not be limited to official data based on the legal definition. He might turn to self-reporting of offenses committed by respondents or complaints by crime victims who did not inform the police. For either the practitioner or the theoretical criminologist, the application of the legal definition has defects, which have been described above. As George W. Wilbur says, however, the real question is not whether the legal conception is good, but whether it is good enough.[27]

Distinction of behavior and definition

In referring to theoretical criminology, George B. Vold placed his finger on the nub of the difficulty. Because crime and criminality lie in the area of deviant behavior, or behavior that is considered improper and forbidden, criminology has a dual problem in explaining criminal behavior. The theories must account for behavior *as behavior* and for the *definitions* by which specific behavior comes to be considered criminal or noncriminal.[28] Thus criminology is caught in a dilemma because the very definition of certain behaviors as criminal is a product of group norms. Do criminals differ from noncriminals in behavior or characteristics as individuals, or are these apparent differences only the outcome of the legal definitions whereby certain behaviors or group characteristics are singled out for imposition of the criminal law?

Ideally, the body of criminal law has been extracted from the larger body of norms characteristic of a given people. Because certain values are especially cherished in a given society, particular norms have received the reinforcement of the criminal justice system through enactment of criminal laws. A "good" law is supposed to receive popular support and general compliance because it coincides with public conceptions of right and wrong. Presumably, the enacters and enforcers of laws represent a general consensus of public opinion as to where the interests of the community as a whole lie. In this case the legal norms would be a proper extraction from the larger body of norms and cultural traditions which

[27] George W. Wilbur, "The Scientific Adequacy of Criminological Concepts," *Social Forces,* 28 (December 1949): 168.

[28] George B. Vold, *Theoretical Criminology* (New York: Oxford University Press, 1958), pp. v–vi.

lend order to the community. The criminal laws would be satisfactory measuring sticks for determining which persons are criminal, how many of them there are in the community, and to whom the agents of criminal justice should direct their specialized attention.

Because legal norms have proved to be inadequate as such measuring sticks, criminological theorists and practitioners have great difficulty in distinguishing criminals from noncriminals. The individuals classified under any legal crime category are so included in the course of their transactions with other persons, including criminological authorities. The classification constitutes the assignment to the individual of a criminal *status,* with little real regard for the uniquely criminal qualities of the lawbreaker and his behavior.[29] Official reports tell us nothing about how shoplifters, rapists, and other legal categories of arrested persons differ in behavior from noncriminals. The official statistics based on these legal categories include only that proportion of all offenders remaining after the elimination of similar offenders not reported to the police, not arrested, not tried, not convicted, and so on. In the course of this chain of events, the decisions to include or exclude individuals from the crime category are strongly influenced by many factors extraneous to criminality itself.

Austin Turk has summarized the weaknesses of legal norms as behavioral measuring instruments. Somewhere, at some time, some culture has tolerated what we call murder of one's parent, incest, or other abhorrent "crimes." Further, the legal-offense categories are inefficient in marking the differences in total behaviors between noncriminals and those officially labeled as "criminals." Both criminals and noncriminals engage in behavior which, at least technically, is defined as criminal: perverted sex practices, manipulation of others to serve selfish purposes, displays of violence, and so on. No matter how objective participants in an event may be, the report of a "crime" will suffer from selective and differential perceptions of witnesses, victims, suspects, and agents of criminal justice; the definition of a given act as criminal entails many possibilities of error. The behavior of even the "genuine" criminal includes both tolerable and intolerable elements. The definition of the individual as a criminal exaggerates his criminality and underestimates his compliance with accepted norms because grossly criminal behavior, in the long term, is rare. Criminal statistics based on arrests or convictions are inadequate samples of the full universe of criminal behavior because most criminal acts do not come to the attention of authorities, and not all such acts known to authorities receive the equivalent punishment that would be required if enforcement were constant and universal.[30]

---

[29] Austin T. Turk, *Criminality and Legal Order* (Chicago: Rand McNally & Co., 1971), pp. 8–10.

[30] Ibid., pp. 10–18.

MORALS AND CRIMINOLOGY

Probably since the time man first developed a sense of morals, there has been a belief that crime is in violation of some universal and permanently valid moral law, of which criminal law is but an imperfect and vacillating reflection. Dissatisfaction is frequently expressed with the way criminal law functions. Somehow the "true criminal" is not affected in the way some persons think he should be.

Probing the reasons for this dissatisfaction reveals that this conception of crime is colored by ideas of sin and immorality. Acts of religious sacrilege, indecency, and vice have been and are subjected to criminal law. A vice is a moral fault or failing which is directed primarily against one's self. Alcoholism, drug addiction, gambling, homosexuality, and prostitution are among those vices that have become subject to criminal law.

Distinction between public and private interests

Employment of the criminal law in attempts to control such forms of behavior erodes distinctions between public and private interests. The public interest is involved when the means of gratifying vices have major adverse effects on society. Crime syndicates draw a large share of their revenue from illicit operations in gambling, liquor, narcotic drugs, and prostitution. Widespread sexual irregularity may undermine family life. Excessive gambling, alcoholism, and drug addiction may drain family finances. The deviant may turn to crime as a means of getting money to support his vice. The vice victim's behavior and physical appearance may shock aesthetic and moral sensibilities of the public.

On the basis of the separation of private and public morality, the British parliamentary committee chaired by Sir John Wolfenden urged minimization of statutory laws controlling and penalizing both heterosexual and homosexual activities. The Wolfenden report contended that the law should confine itself to those activities which offend against public order and decency or expose the ordinary citizen to what is offensive and injurious. This view is consistent with the common-law tradition that a person's privacy is safeguarded by law against illegal search and seizure and wiretapping. In a society with diverse subcultures, a neat balance must be maintained between private choice and public policy, if both individual freedoms and social order are to be safeguarded.[31]

Distinction between illegality and immorality

Criminal statutes have been applied against conduct which outrages certain moral sentiments. The general morals of the community are

[31] Joseph Fletcher, "Sex Offenses: An Ethical View," *Law and Contemporary Problems*, 25 (Spring 1960): 245–57.

supposed to be safeguarded by laws against sending obscene material through the mails, indecent theatrical performances, business on Sunday, and so on. Morality by comparison is a heritage of 19th-century efforts of religiously motivated reformers to suppress drinking, family nonsupport, and other behaviors not consistent with the moral standards of influential groups.

Conceptions of vice as a "sin" come in several varieties. In one view, vice is entirely a matter of immoral behavior, with little attention given to psychological, cultural, and physiological factors. A second recognizes the individual's loss of control over his vice but holds him responsible for exposing himself to the risk. In a third view, the "sin" is attached to the abuse, as opposed to the use, of drugs or alcohol. In other views, sin is seen alternatively as the individual's selfishness, any hindrance to development of a healthy personality, a pathological condition in society, or "original sin." Howard Clinebell, Jr., sees a fallacy in the assumption that emphasis on the individual's personal culpability will make him more responsible and more moral. Increasing the guilt load only enhances the strength of the alcoholic's compulsion, his defensiveness, and his inaccessibility to help.[32]

Effects of enforcement of morals

If all such acts are treated as crimes, there is a danger of engulfing society in an anarchy of personal moralities or imposing the morality of a politically powerful minority on all its members.

When the criminal law becomes the means of expressing moral condemnation, serious difficulties result in a diverse culture such as ours. In the absence of universal condemnation of the "immoralities," great disparities occur in the application of criminal laws. Enforcement exaggerates differences in behavior and motivations of those subject to legal penalties and those not so subject. Alcohol is consumed under some social circumstances which are consistent with approved values. Abortion may be stimulated by economic inability to provide adequately for additional children as well as by fear of the consequences of extramarital sex activity. Further, repressive laws erode the distinction between morally disapproved conduct and conduct imperiling the public order. The drug user is less likely to receive the medical and psychological rehabilitation he requires when the law defines him as a criminal along with those who traffic in dangerous drugs. In the face of a desperate demand for forbidden services, legal prohibitions can create circumstances favorable to the development of illicit enterprises.[33]

[32] Howard J. Clinebell, Jr., "The Ethics of Alcoholism," in Raymond G. McCarthy (ed.), *Drinking and Intoxication* (Glencoe, Ill.: Free Press, 1959), pp. 331–36.

[33] Edwin M. Schur, *Crime without Victims* (Englewood Cliffs, N.J.: Prentice-Hall, Inc., 1965); Alfred R. Lindesmith, *The Addict and the Law* (Bloomington:

In a pluralistic culture, rules of groups differ according to social class and ethnic, occupational, racial, age, and similar subcultural groups. Legal rules do not necessarily correspond with the rules of these groups. The legal and moral norms are enforced formally by groups in social positions that afford the necessary weapons and power. Therefore, deviant individuals are subjected to legal and moral rules not of their own making and not necessarily consistent with their own views.

When an individual is defined as a deviant, he is cut off from participation in conventional groups. No longer is he "respectable." Regardless of his qualities or attitudes apart from his vice, he is subjected to the standardized treatment accorded the occupant of the deviant status. While his previous routine may have meshed reasonably well with social arrangements of family, work, and neighborhood activities, his new status interferes with them. At this point, he may move to the next stage in development of a stable deviant career—he may find common interests with deviant groups organized around activities defined as a vice.[34] He accepts a deviant subculture for the sake of the rationalizations it supplies for this vice, the solutions it offers for carrying it out with a minimum of difficulty, and, perhaps, the fellowship. Increasingly, he now conforms to the vice image. Consequently, when a vice is defined as either "criminal" or "sinful," risk is increased that the incidental rule violator will be confirmed in his deviance and that the hope of reclaiming him for "respectable" society will be lost.

The efficiency of law enforcement is determined to a large degree by the extent to which community mores support the legal norms. Whereas community mores universally support police action against traditional crimes such as murder and theft, this is less true in respect to laws regulating morality. In a pluralistic culture, the treatment of immoralities as crimes invites the imposition of the morality of a politically powerful minority on all groups. When the criminal law runs counter to the traditions of minorities, administration of justice becomes entangled in the difficulties of coercing substantial numbers of respectable citizens to conform to rules they regard as unnatural and unreasonable. The gathering of evidence is complicated when law enforcement officials are portrayed as "snoopers" and persecutors under cover of the law. In vices involving personality maladjustments, debates whether the deviant is to be treated as a patient or a criminal complicate consistent enforcement of laws.

Ordinary law enforcement techniques are ineffective in combating prostitution, homosexuality, gambling, narcotics traffic, and illegal sale of alcohol. The client for such goods and services does not qualify as a

---

Indiana University Press, 1965), pp. 283–86; Granville Williams, *The Sanctity of Life and the Criminal Law* (New York: Alfred A. Knopf, Inc., 1957).

[34] Howard S. Becker, *Outsiders: Studies in the Sociology of Deviance* (New York: Free Press of Glencoe, 1963), p. 37. Becker has been identified with the so-called "labeling school," which is discussed in Chapter 10 below, pp. 258–64.

victim of crime because he is a willing buyer in cooperation with a willing seller. To obtain evidence under these circumstances, the police agency may employ informers, frequently involving itself in relationships with known criminals. The major traffickers in vice usually evade detection, whereas the client-victims and "small fry" criminals are more likely to be arrested. Ironically, reduction in the supply of illicit alcohol and drugs may raise prices and attract other criminals to such traffic.

The reliance on law enforcement to deal with vice results in a repetitive cycle of arrest, short-term incarceration, and release which burdens police, courts, and jails with a large and continuous flow of people with personality problems. This revolving-door policy poses serious problems for administration of law enforcement, courts, and jails. It has, for example, contributed further to the deep-seated dependency of many chronic inebriates.[35]

SUMMARY

In initiating the exploration of crime and its associated problems, this chapter described the nature and interrelationships of the theoretical and practical branches of criminology, emphasizing the vital contributions of science to both. The complexity of this application of science was suggested in considering the definition of crime, a matter crucial to delineation of the bounds of criminology and to the effects of criminal law on the lawbreaker. The stigmatization of the offender will be a frequent theme in the following pages; here the matter was related to the unanticipated consequences of using the law to enforce morals. The analysis suggests the importance of controlling our own moral judgments as we pursue elusive truths in our study of crime and criminals and their control.

FOR ADDITIONAL READING

Akers, Ronald L. "Problems in the Sociology of Deviance: Social Definitions." *Social Forces,* 46 (June 1968): 455–65.

Brereton, George H. "The Importance of Training and Education in the Professionalization of Law Enforcement." *Journal of Criminal Law, Criminology and Police Science,* 52 (May–June 1961): 111–21.

Chapman, Dennis. *Sociology and the Stereotype of the Criminal.* London: Tavistock Publications, 1968.

Frank, Benjamin, and Pappas, Nick. *Targets for In-Service Training.* Washington, D.C.: Joint Commission on Correctional Manpower and Training, 1967.

[35] David J. Pittman and C. Wayne Gordon, "Criminal Careers of the Chronic Drunkenness Offender," in David J. Pittman and Charles R. Snyder (eds.), *Society, Culture, and Drinking Patterns* (New York: John Wiley & Sons, Inc., 1962), p. 537; Jacqueline S. Wiseman, *Stations of the Lost: The Treatment of Skid Row Alcoholics* (Englewood Cliffs, N.J.: Prentice Hall, Inc., 1970).

Fuller, Richard C. "Morals and the Criminal Law." *Journal of Criminal Law and Criminology,* 32 (May–June 1942): 624–30.

Germann, A. C. "Scientific Training for Cops?" *Journal of Criminal Law, Criminology and Police Science,* 50 (July–August 1959): 206–10.

Johnson, Elmer H. "Personnel Problems of Corrections and the Potential Contribution of Universities." *Federal Probation,* 31 (December 1967): 57–61.

Quinney, Richard. *Crime and Justice in Society,* pp. 1–30. Boston: Little, Brown & Co., 1969.

Saunders, Charles B., Jr. *Upgrading the American Police: Education and Training for Better Law Enforcement.* Washington, D.C.: Brookings Institution, 1970.

Szabo, Denis. "Criminology and Criminologist: A New Discipline and a New Profession." *Canadian Journal of Corrections,* 5 (January 1963): 28–39.

Tadeusz, Grygier. "Education for Correctional Workers: A Survey of Needs and Resources." *Canadian Journal of Corrections,* 4 (July 1962): 137–51.

Trends and impact of crime

Crime is a perennial public issue because threats to personal safety and property imperil everyone's fundamental interests. The dangers of crime to society stimulate a keen interest in the offender and, more fundamentally, in the study of criminology. To provide background for this study, this chapter presents basic information on the volume and characteristics of offenses. It discusses the parameters of the impact of crime on society and considers crime control in the context of a society that is increasingly characterized by an urban way of life.

CRIMES MEASURED BY ARRESTS

The volume of arrests made by law enforcement agents attests to the great size of the crime problem in the United States. Even so, we can only guess at the actual number of arrests made each year, because the most reliable and complete count of arrests is based on voluntary reporting to the Federal Bureau of Investigation by only a portion of the total law enforcement agencies.

Peter Lejins points out that the FBI's *Uniform Crime Reports,* as a "house organ" of the police, is interested primarily in offering statistics on police work.[1] As the most complete collection of data on the incidence of crime, however, these reports attract a wide audience. They demonstrate clearly that law enforcement is a formidable task, as Table 2–1 shows. In 1971 the personnel of 5,649 agencies made almost seven million arrests, if arrests for suspicion and all other offenses except traffic are included. Table 2–1 omits arrests for suspicion and all other offenses except traffic, thereby producing a rate of 3,888 arrests for every 100,000 persons in the jurisdictions of these agencies. Note that, because an unknown number of persons were arrested more than once in 1971, it is not known how many *individuals* were arrested.

[1] Peter P. Lejins, "Uniform Crime Reports," *Michigan Law Review,* 64 (April 1966): 1016–17.

TABLE 2–1

Arrests by offenses for 5,649 police agencies submitting statistical reports to Federal Bureau of Investigation, 1971

Offenses charged	Number of arrests	Percentage distribution	Arrests per 100,000 population
Total crimes	6,043,178	100.00	3,887.6
Crimes against persons			
Criminal homicide:			
Murder, nonnegligent			
manslaughter	14,549	.24	9.4
Manslaughter by negligence ...	2,768	.05	1.8
Forcible rape	16,582	.27	10.7
Aggravated assault	140,350	2.32	90.3
Other assaults	307,107	5.08	197.6
Other sex offenses	50,695	.84	32.6
Crimes against property			
Larceny-theft	674,997	11.17	434.2
Burglary, breaking-entering	315,376	5.22	202.9
Automobile theft	130,954	2.17	84.2
Vandalism	121,850	2.02	78.4
Robbery	101,728	1.68	65.4
Fraud	95,610	1.58	61.5
Stolen property, receiving, etc. ...	75,516	1.25	48.6
Forgery, counterfeiting	45,340	.75	29.2
Arson	11,154	.18	7.2
Embezzlement	7,114	.12	4.6
Crimes suggesting personal disorganization			
Drunkenness	1,491,782	24.69	959.7
Disorderly conduct	621,057	10.28	399.5
Driving intoxicated	489,545	8.10	314.9
Narcotic drug laws	400,606	6.63	257.7
Liquor laws	231,192	3.83	148.7
Runaways	204,544	3.38	131.6
Weapons: possessing, etc.	114,569	1.90	73.7
Curfew, loitering violations	101,943	1.68	65.6
Gambling	86,698	1.43	55.8
Vagrancy	80,180	1.33	51.6
Offenses against family, children ..	56,456	.93	36.3
Prostitution, commercialized vice .	52,916	.88	34.0

Source: Federal Bureau of Investigation, *Crime in the United States: Uniform Crime Reports—1971* (Washington, D.C.: U.S. Government Printing Office, 1972), pp. 116–17. Offenses not included in above table: suspicion (54,374); all other offenses except traffic (869,270). Population covered by data is estimated to be 155,446,000.

To facilitate analysis, the various offenses have been classified into crimes against persons, crimes against property, and crimes suggesting personal disorganization. Although criminals are feared most because of the physical injury they may inflict on their victims, the greatest proportion of arrests (65 percent) was for crimes suggesting personal disorganization; drunkenness and disorderly conduct accounted for 35 percent. Crimes against property represented 26 percent of all arrests; robbery, holding the greatest potential threat to the physical safety of victims, accounted for less than 2 percent. Although arrests for crimes against persons were almost 9 percent of the total, criminal homicide and forcible rape, the most serious of these offenses, represented less than 1 percent of all arrests.

Crimes against persons

Because in our scale of values the risk of death or physical harm ranks as a great threat, crimes against persons are regarded with concern. In its evaluation of the threat of crime, the public gives high priority to violence and is more tolerant of crimes against property. The President's Crime Commission found a third of the survey respondents did not feel safe walking alone at night in their neighborhoods. In police precincts studied in Boston and Chicago, 20 percent of the citizens wanted to move because of crime in their neighborhoods, 82 percent always kept their doors locked at night, and 37 percent kept firearms for protection.[2]

Nevertheless, crimes of violence represent only a modest share of the total police workload. The chances of an average individual being the victim of criminal homicide, forcible rape, or even robbery are less than those of being victimized by an accident or inadequate medical care. Further, the chances of being the victim of a violent crime vary according to the individual's place of residence and the nature of his relationships with his friends and family. To a high degree the offender is likely to be a member of the victim's family or at least previously known by the victim, rather than a stranger. The President's Commission on Crime in the District of Columbia studied arrest statistics of District police for 1961–65. Most of the murderers were known to the victim as a spouse (27 percent), relative (10 percent), or acquaintance (40 percent). The victim-offender relationship for aggravated assault was spouse (10.7 percent), another relative (10 percent), acquaintance (51.9 percent), neighbor (8.4 percent), or a stranger (19 percent). Two thirds of the rape victims were attacked by persons with whom they were at least casually acquainted.[3]

Crimes against property

One of several major concepts on which the American economy is based is that of property as a collection of rights, responsibilities, and duties associated with intangibles and material objects. Property rights

[2] President's Commission on Law Enforcement and Administration of Justice, *Task Force Report: Crime and Its Impact—An Assessment* (Washington, D.C.: U.S. Government Printing Office, 1967), pp. 87–88.

[3] *Report of the President's Commission on Crime in the District of Columbia* (Washington, D.C.: U.S. Government Printing Office, 1966), pp. 42, 53, 76. For further discussion of the sociocultural characteristics of homicide and forcible rape, see Chapter 7 below.

exist in the possession, use, and control of economic goods. Competition occurs when individuals are motivated by their culture to strive for goods and other rewards. In this competition, the social order is maintained; those who fail acknowledge the winner's success by abandoning their claim. Property crimes undermine the social order because they represent violation of this principle and the use of an illegitimate means of gaining rewards, thus challenging the efficacy of the legitimate motivational system. Nevertheless, such crimes reflect the success of this system in that they stimulate a demand for the economic rewards sought by adherents of the legitimate norms.

The outrage of the middle class against certain property crimes is prompted by more than loss of property alone. Breaking into a building is different from shoplifting because the burglar is also illegally present in a building; his invasion of the territorial rights of other persons may also threaten their physical security. The middle-class respect for property may be more injured by the property destruction of a vandal than by outright theft.[4]

Of larceny-theft arrests reported to the FBI in 1971, 18 percent were from automobiles, 19 percent were of automobile accessories, 17 percent were stolen bicycles, and 16 percent were from buildings. Shoplifting represented 10 percent, purse-snatching 3 percent, and pocketpicking 1 percent of larceny-theft arrests.[5]

The relatively high incidence of automobile theft is a reflection of the high social value placed on this product of our technology. The highest rates appear in the most heavily populated areas, indicating the urban nature of the offense. In 1971, 72 percent of these arrests were of persons less than 21 years of age, with 53 percent being less than 18 years of age.[6]

Robbery has the qualities of a crime against persons in that it is pregnant with violence. Along with burglary, it can be perpetrated by professionals, with careful planning and efficient execution. The greatest possibility of violence lies in perpetration by amateurs capable of recklessness.[7] Vandalism and arson, which represent malice more than acquisitiveness, have high proportions of juvenile offenders. The relatively low incidence of embezzlement reflects the difficulty of discovering offenses concealed within routine business transactions. Furthermore, such offenses take place only in positions of trust which offer the protection against stern law enforcement that is afforded "respectables."

[4] Thorsten Sellin and Marvin E. Wolfgang, *The Measurement of Delinquency* (New York: John Wiley & Sons, Inc., 1964), pp. 218–25.

[5] Federal Bureau of Investigation, *Crime in the United States: Uniform Crime Reports, 1971* (Washington, D.C.: U.S. Government Printing Office, 1972), p. 22.

[6] Ibid., p. 29.

[7] Everett DeBaum, "The Heist: The Theory and Practice of Armed Robbery," *Harper's Magazine*, 1197 (February 1950): 69–77. See Chapter 7 below for further analysis of robbery.

Crimes suggesting personal disorganization

Personality disorganization has been defined as a failure of the individual to organize his life for the efficient, progressive realization of his fundamental interests.[8] The high incidence of arrests for crimes related to personality disorganization is interpreted by some as a sign of moral weakness, but it also indicates the degree of reliance placed on the criminal law as a by-product of moral condemnation of antisocial behavior that is not strictly criminal. The bulk of these arrests represents attempts to control the vices of drunkenness, drug use, and gambling. Others attempt to deal with family disorganization. Arrests for disorderly conduct, vagrancy, and curfew and loitering violations bring criminal justice to bear on transgressions against middle-class conceptions of respectability and self-responsibility. The high incidence of all such arrests indicates the heavy burden they place on the system of criminal justice. The implications of the problems raised will be discussed in Part IV of this book.

The large number of arrests for drunkenness forces the machinery of justice to cope with a complex medical, psychiatric, and moral problem with few resources other than punishment or social stigmatization. Arrests for driving while intoxicated tend to cross socioeconomic class lines because of the special peril of such offenses. Arrests for disorderly conduct, vagrancy, liquor laws, weapons, gambling, and offenses against the family or children show a greater class correlation because of the subtle influences of social class as a causal factor in crime and because of class differentials in the probability that criminal sanctions will be applied. Prostitution and commercialized vice involve social class, too, but the strength of the mores and the relationship of these offenses to organized crime must also be considered.

The startling increase in arrest rates for drug offenses, from 43.7 per 100,000 population in 1966 to 257.7 in 1971, merits special attention. At the turn of the century, as Alfred Lindesmith and John Gagnon note, drug addiction attracted little notice as a social problem and had little relationship with a criminal underworld. Middle-aged, middle-class women were heavily represented in the addict population of that time. As addiction has assumed its present concentration among males, blacks, the lower social classes, and the younger age groups, suppressive law enforcement tactics against drug abuse have been introduced. Lindesmith and Gagnon argue that these tactics have produced the present characteristics of drug users. With the shutting off of legitimate supplies of drugs, a lucrative market for criminal organizations emerged in large cities—especially port cities—which favored the spread of drug addic-

---

[8] W. I. Thomas and Florian Znaniecki, *The Polish Peasant in Europe and America,* 2 vols. (New York: Alfred A. Knopf, Inc., 1927), pp. 1128–29.

tion among those segments of the urban population with access to illicit supplies.[9]

Aside from the effects of more rigorous application of suppressive measures, the increase in the size of the drug-using population has been produced by the interaction of certain characteristics of drug-prone persons with the social structure of their communities. The high rates among adolescents and young adults are associated by Charles Winick with the frustrations of their stage in the life cycle which lead to problems of school, sexual adjustment, vocational choice, and establishment of a family.[10] A study of drug-epidemic areas found them to be characterized by high concentrations of racial minorities, wives separated from husbands, low income and educational attainment levels, unskilled job status, and other qualities of slums.[11]

The spread of drug use within the ghetto and ranging outside it has been attributed to the congeniality of certain subcultural values to drug use. Harvey Feldman cites the ideological seedbed of ghetto street gangs which confer high prestige on the "stand-up cats" who first use drugs and are admired for their daring, predilection for excitement, and toughness.[12] There is evidence that some middle-class youth in high schools identify marijuana use with the collegiate way of life.[13] In colleges, marijuana use has been found more prevalent among students who adhere to a nonconventional, "hang-loose" ethic that sees the campus as a place of political freedom with a comfortable bohemian atmosphere.[14]

THE ECONOMIC IMPACT OF CRIME

The numbers and characteristics of offenses are only one facet of the effects of crime in the United States. Estimates of the economic impact of crime run into scores of billions of dollars. The President's Crime Commission estimated this impact at $21 billion (see Table 2–2), to indicate a rough order of magnitude, but the figures are probably conservative. The

[9] Alfred R. Lindesmith and John H. Gagnon, "Anomie and Drug Addiction," in Marshall B. Clinard (ed.), *Anomie and Deviant Behavior* (New York: Free Press, 1964), pp. 163–65, 171–74.

[10] Charles Winick, "Epidemiology of Narcotics Use," in Daniel M. Wilner and Gene O. Kassebaum (eds.), *Narcotics* (New York: McGraw-Hill Book Co., 1965), pp. 9–10, 16.

[11] Isadore Chein et al., *The Road to H: Narcotics, Delinquency, and Social Policy* (New York: Basic Books, 1964), pp. 14, 26–27.

[12] Harvey W. Feldman, "Ideological Supports to Becoming and Remaining a Heroin Addict," *Journal of Health and Social Behavior*, 9 (June 1968): 131–39.

[13] Armand L. Mauss, "Anticipatory Socialization toward College as a Factor in Adolescent Marijuana Use," *Social Problems*, 16 (Winter 1969): 357–64.

[14] Edward A. Suchman, "The 'Hang-Loose' Ethic and the Spirit of Drug Use," *Journal of Health and Social Behavior*, 9 (June 1968): 146–55; James T. Carey, *The College Drug Scene* (Englewood Cliffs, N.J.: Prentice-Hall, Inc., 1968).

Figure 2–1. Part of the cost of crime.

Paralyzed for life as a result of a criminal act, this citizen represents the impact of crime on victims—a cost which until recently has gone unrecognized by criminal justice. Hawaii is one of seven states providing compensation to victims and dependents of deceased victims of criminal actions, under conditions specified by legislation.

elusiveness of the factors contributing to such estimates calls for caution in their use. Four factors affect the size of the crime bill:[15]

1. *The loss of productive labor that is diverted to meeting the challenge of crime.* This would include law enforcement and criminal court personnel, insurance men, burglary alarm makers, and so on. The potentially useful labor of criminals also is lost. Estimation of such loss encounters some troublesome questions: How well are criminals qualified by their physical and mental abilities and by their skills and motivations to assume legitimate employment? Is the economy prepared to offer productive employment for court and police personnel no longer involved in crime control?

2. *Economic waste caused by crime.* Property is destroyed or its value diminished because of crime. The cost includes a hidden charge for insurance, plant protection, allowances for expected theft, and the portion of the tax bill which goes to pay for governmental programs directed against crime. On the other hand, there are crimes that reduce waste. For example, businessmen on occasion have invited racketeering as a means of reducing unrestrained competition. Furthermore, the costs of crimes do not fall with equal impact on all citizens. Some unknown portion of the costs of robberies, burglaries, and hijackings is absorbed by manufacturers and distributors to keep their prices competitive.

3. *Transfer of money and property from victim to criminal.* Analysis of this effect is complicated by its relationship to the redistribution of national income. The loss to the victim is obvious, but what is the effect on society as a whole? It may be that the total immediate consumption of income is increased by crime through the transfer of wealth from those who would withhold it from the market to those who immediately purchase goods and services.

4. *Expenditures for crime control and care of offenders and their dependents.* These include the costs of administering the systems of law enforcement, justice, and correction. Some of the costs of caring for the indigent also would be charged to this item, but some of these services would be required even if crime could be abolished: traffic control, tracing of lost persons, and handling of crowds, for example. Prisoner labor reduces the burden of prison operations to the taxpayer. Probation and parole programs contribute indirectly to community and family integration and to the alleviation of personal problems. These services would be shifted to other welfare programs if not needed for crime control.

Table 2–2 challenges several popular assumptions. Police statistics suggest that robbery, burglary, larceny, and automobile theft comprise the major share of property crimes, but other property crimes impose a much heavier burden. Employee theft, embezzlement, and other business

[15] E. R. Hawkins and Willard Waller, "Critical Notes on the Cost of Crime," *Journal of Criminal Law and Criminology,* 46 (January–February 1956): 657–72.

TABLE 2–2

Estimated economic impact of crime and related expenditures (millions of dollars)

Crimes against persons		$ 815
Homicide	$ 750	
Assault and other	65	
Crimes against property		3,932
Unreported commercial theft	1,400	
Robbery, burglary, larceny $50 and over, auto theft	600	
Embezzlement	200	
Fraud	1,350	
Forgery and other	82	
Property destroyed by arson and vandalism	300	
Other crimes		2,036
Driving under influence	1,816	
Tax fraud	100	
Abortion	120	
Illegal goods and services		8,035
Narcotics	350	
Loansharking	350	
Prostitution	225	
Alcohol	150	
Gambling	7,000	
Public law enforcement and criminal justice		4,212
Police	2,792	
Corrections	1,034	
Prosecution and defense	125	
Courts	261	
Private costs related to crime		1,910
Prevention service	1,350	
Prevention equipment	200	
Insurance	300	
Private counsel, bail, witness expenses	60	
Total		$20,940

Source: President's Commission on Law Enforcement and Administration of Justice, *The Challenge of Crime in a Free Society* (Washington, D.C.: U.S. Government Printing Office, February 1967), p. 33.

crimes are at such a volume as to raise questions concerning the sharp differentiation of adjudicated offenders from so-called noncriminals. Although homicide makes up only a small fraction of arrest statistics, its economic impact is greater than commonly supposed. Driving under the influence of alcohol, an offense generally given inadequate attention, exacts an even heavier economic burden. The toll of syndicated crime is dominant, especially in gambling, a crime that elicits an ambivalent public reaction. The expenditure of over $4 billion for public law enforcement and criminal justice would be interpreted by some as evidence of a growing willingness to invest in innovative responses to crime. The President's Crime Commission reported that police and, especially, corrections costs are rising rapidly, but the bulk of the costs go into personnel and nontreatment activities such as traffic control and maintenance of prisoners.

THE SOCIAL-PSYCHOLOGICAL IMPACT OF CRIME

Although the size of the total crime bill is uncertain, the financial burden obviously is high. The social and psychological consequences of crime are further justification for concern: the fear of potential and actual victims, the effects of suspicion and hostility on relationships between citizens, the weakening of some individual's faith in moral values, and the economic insecurity created for families of victims and of imprisoned offenders.

Hyperemotional reactions and conflicting opinions

Because crime and criminals often are reacted to hyperemotionally, the study of relationships between public opinion and the facts related to the causes and control of crime is complicated. "The criminal" may be described as a monster or pictured as a hunted animal or the helpless victim of brutality. These emotional variations are reflected in crime fiction. One story describes the resourcefulness of the clever criminal in outwitting the police and the courts. Another presents the heroic figure of the fearless policeman risking his life and using his wits to overcome the vicious criminal. Often public attention to the issue ends with the clang of prison gates.

For most people, attitudes about crime trends, the causes of crime, and the operation of the criminal justice system are derived largely from vicarious sources rather than from direct experience of personal victimization. This experience of being robbed or assaulted is infrequent, but *imagined* victimization plays a large part in public attitudes. Crimes on the street are envisaged as a threat beyond the level of risk for the life situation of the particular respondent that comparisons of crime rates would indicate.[16] These concerns call for immediate, uncomplicated solutions, and the causes of what is envisaged as "dangerous" criminal behavior are therefore likely to be attributed to the "nonhuman" qualities of criminals. Suppressive measures are favored because they seem to hold better prospects for quick solutions without all the complexities of a long-term study of the many psychological and sociological factors in criminal behavior.

The complexity of public attitudes is indicated by inconsistency in even such matters as supporting a policy of rigorous law enforcement. Studies have indicated that citizens regard as least serious many of the offenses receiving the heaviest penalties in court,[17] that they believe

[16] Jennie McIntyre, "Public Attitudes toward Crime and Law Enforcement," *Annals of American Academy of Political and Social Science,* 374 (November 1967): 36–41.

[17] Arnold M. Rose and Arthur E. Prell, "Does Punishment Fit the Crime? A Study in Social Valuation," *American Journal of Sociology,* 61 (November 1955): 247–59.

white-collar offenses are punished insufficiently,[18] and that they have little knowledge of what goes on behind prison walls.[19] There are great differences in opinion as to whether or not severe punishment deters crime or the system of criminal justice is efficient.[20] An interesting paradox, John Conklin finds, is that there is less active support for law enforcement in communities in which the official crime rates are high than in those where they are low. He cites three possible explanations: fear of crime may paralyze citizens; lack of public support through the reporting of crimes to the police may favor criminals; or, in crime-prone areas, citizens may try to avoid adverse penalties from offenders or neighbors because of involvement with the police, who are held suspect by the local subculture.[21]

History provides reasons to doubt hyperemotional images of a current unprecedented crime wave and contentions that contemporary Americans particularly tend to be criminalistic. The extent of criminality in previous ages appears to be underestimated in such charges. Laxities in business honesty and general disregard for the law were major characteristics of our frontier era.[22] Several authors have described the general lawlessness of the early years of various metropolises.[23] After examining early American history, Daniel Bell concludes that in the United States there probably was less crime in 1960 than there was 100, or 50, or even 25 years earlier.[24] There were widespread complaints about crime waves and the "mollycoddling" of criminals in earlier decades when procedural safeguards for civil rights for suspects received less attention.[25]

[18] Donald J. Newman, "Public Attitudes toward a Form of White-Collar Crime," in Gilbert Geis (ed.), *White-Collar Criminal* (New York: Atherton Press, 1968), pp. 287–93; Don C. Gibbons, "Crime and Punishment: A Study in Social Attitudes," *Social Forces,* 47 (June 1969): 391–97.

[19] Don C. Gibbons, "Who Knows What about Corrections?" *Crime and Delinquency,* 9 (April 1963): 137–44; John Galliher, "Attitudes of Missouri Citizens toward the State Prisons," *Criminology,* 8 (November 1970): 239–50.

[20] Don C. Gibbons, Joseph F. Jones, and Peter G. Garabedian, "Gauging Public Opinion about the Crime Problem," *Crime and Delinquency,* 18 (April 1972): 134–46; *The Public Looks at Crime and Corrections* (Washington, D.C.: Joint Commission on Correctional Manpower and Training, 1968).

[21] John E. Conklin, "Criminal Environment and Support for the Law," *Law and Society Review,* 6 (November 1971): 247–59.

[22] Mabel A. Elliott, *Crime in Modern Society* (New York: Harper & Bros., 1952), p. 272.

[23] Herbert Ashbury, *Gangs of New York* (New York: A. A. Knopf, Inc., 1928); Herbert Ashbury, *Gem of the Prairie* (New York: Alfred A. Knopf, Inc., 1940); Carl Bridenbaugh, *Cities in Revolt: Urban Life in America, 1743–1776* (New York: Alfred A. Knopf, Inc., 1955); Robert Bruce, *1877: Year of Violence* (New York: Bobbs-Merrill Co., Inc., 1959); Philip Taft, "Violence in American Labor Disputes," *Annals of American Academy of Political and Social Science,* 364 (March 1966): 127–40; and Irving Werstein, *July 1863* (New York: Julian Messner, Inc., 1957).

[24] Daniel Bell, *The End of Ideology* (Glencoe, Ill.: Free Press, 1960), p. 137.

[25] Yale Kamisar, "When the Police Were Not 'Handcuffed,' " in Donald R. Cressey (ed.), *Crime and Criminal Justice* (Chicago: Quadrangle Books, 1971), pp. 46–57.

Effects of hyperemotionalism: Drugs and alcohol

The employment of criminal sanctions against drug abuse and alcoholic overconsumption is a prime example of the consequences of hyperemotional evaluations and oversimplified explanations for legally prohibited behavior. The mythology of the "drug fiend," which emerged in the United States soon after the Civil War, conveys an impression of perversion and implies a threat to civilization, reinforced by suggestive references to "dope parties" and "vicious crimes."[26] Heroin, cannabis, and hallucinogens are popularly described as treacherous and demoniacal in power, tempting use through a false promise of pleasure. Richard Blum suggests that this notion of pleasure motivates a particularly strong rejection of drug abuse in a society dominated by the norms of work and self-discipline. Where moderation is the rule, the "chemical mystique" draws forth the same suspicion as the ecstasy and orgiastic frenzies of the religious mystic.[27] The passivity and nonproductivity of the addict are "un-American" in these respects.[28]

The emotionality and exaggeration of this mythology may have blocked reasonable assessment of the functions and effects of drugs when administered under competent medical supervision to achieve clearly specified medical purposes.[29] Heated debates over use of drugs under less controlled conditions tell us more about the values of the contending parties than such crucial matters as what kinds of drugs are involved, how frequently they are used, and under what social-psychological conditions they are taken. Erich Goode suggests the broad dimensions of the value conflicts involved by pointing out that drug users tend to give priority to irrationality over logic, bursts of insight over logical thought, and "creative experience" over traditional forms of behavior. Their opponents are likely to assume, without possession of pertinent facts, that drug use inevitably precipitates crime, immorality, and mental breakdown.[30] Between these extreme positions would be the evaluation of the effects of drug use which, for certain drugs under persistent and uncontrolled conditions, can involve grave risks.

[26] Lawrence Kolb, *Drug Addiction* (Springfield, Ill.: Charles C Thomas, 1962), pp. 152–66.

[27] Richard H. Blum, "On the Presence of Demons," in Richard H. Blum and Associates, *Society and Drugs* (San Francisco: Jossey-Bass, Inc., Publishers, 1969), pp. 332–34.

[28] Edwin Schur, "Attitudes toward Addicts: Some General Observations and Comparative Findings," *American Journal of Orthopsychiatry,* 34 (January 1964): 80–90.

[29] Louis Lasagra, "Addicting Drugs and Medical Practice: Toward the Elaboration of Realistic Goals and the Eradication of Myths, Mirages, and Half-Truths," in Daniel M. Wilner and Gene O. Kassebaum (eds.), *Narcotics* (New York: McGraw-Hill Book Co., 1965), pp. 5, 62–63.

[30] Erich Goode, "Marijuana and the Politics of Reality," *Journal of Health and Social Behavior,* 10 (June 1969): 83–94.

A similar value conflict between asceticism and the search for pleasure is expressed in attitudes toward beverage alcohol. Raising the glass in good fellowship draws favor, but ascetics suspect the contents of the glass to be subverting to moral duty, work efficiency, and psychological equilibrium.[31] The moral abhorrence of drunkenness today is less strong than that of drug abuse, possibly because the production and distribution of alcoholic beverages form both a significant and legitimate business enterprise and a source of tax revenues. Further, the public drinking house has become a social institution, serving a variety of functions dependent on the particular clientele and their place in the social structure. The downtown cocktail lounge offers attractive surroundings in which businessmen can conduct transactions and maintain occupational affiliations. The neighborhood tavern provides a setting for integrating the lives of workers and, sometimes, their families. The skid-row bar has been suspected as a meeting place of criminals, but it also serves as a center for social life.[32]

The association of alcohol and drug abuse with crime is often offered as a justification for resorting to law enforcement to control them. Such justifications may be parenthetical to criminology in that they emphasize not crime but the offending of public taste and disturbance of peace by disorderly conduct, the necessity of protecting the health of either potential or actual users, or the imposition of the moral standards of politically dominant groups on the behavior of other groups. If possession of intoxicants or drugs and addiction, in and of themselves, are defined as crimes, however, the offenses of users can be related directly to behaviors associated with their use of alcohol or drugs. The least challengeable justification is the perpetration of crimes against persons and property as byproducts of alcohol and drug abuse.

Although there appears to be a recent increase in the proportion of drug addicts with criminal records prior to addiction, John O'Donnell believes this trend is a product of the way of life forced on the addict.[33] In urban areas where drug use is most prevalent, property crime is likely to be high, but the association of drug use and crime is complicated by the effects on both of the social conditions of the slum. Addicts tend to be arrested for nonviolent property offenses to a greater degree than do non-

[31] Abraham Myerson, "Alcoholism: The Role of Social Ambivalence," in Raymond G. McCarthy (ed.), Drinking and Intoxication (New Haven, Conn.: College & University Press, 1959), pp. 306–12.

[32] Marshall B. Clinard, "The Public Drinking House and Society," in David J. Pittman and Charles R. Snyder (eds.), Society, Culture, and Drinking Patterns (New York: John Wiley & Sons, Inc., 1962), pp. 270–92; David Gottlieb, "The Neighborhood Tavern and Cocktail Lounge: A Study of Class Differences," American Journal of Sociology, 62 (May 1957): 559–62; Julian Roebuck and S. Lee Spray, "The Cocktail Lounge: A Study of Heterosexual Relations in a Public Organization," American Journal of Sociology, 72 (January 1967): 388–95.

[33] John A. O'Donnell, "Narcotics and Crime," Social Problems, 13 (Spring 1966): 374–85.

addicts. Denying that greater prevalence of drug use produces an increase in those crimes not directly related to drug abuse, Isadore Chein et al. argue that the increase in property crimes is counterbalanced by fewer rapes, assaults, automobile thefts, and incidents of disorderly conduct.[34]

URBANISM AND CRIME RATES

With remarkable consistency, arrest rates for major crimes increase progressively with greater population size of cities (see Table 2–3). This consistent relationship demonstrates the point, frequently repeated in this book, that criminal behavior is a product of the sociocultural organization of the society, rather than society being the victim of the lawbreaker, as it is usually portrayed.

TABLE 2–3
Rates per 100,000 population for major crimes by size of cities

Population groups (thousands)	Murder, nonnegligent manslaughter	Robbery	Aggravated assault	Burglary, breaking-entering	Larceny-theft	Auto theft
Total cities	10.7	81.4	101.2	220.3	521.7	97.3
Over 250	19.0	154.7	141.1	275.9	527.9	145.0
100–250	11.2	71.6	115.2	247.5	598.8	95.2
50–100	6.1	41.8	76.1	196.7	559.8	81.8
25–50	4.9	35.2	63.4	180.1	558.1	65.2
10–25	3.7	21.1	62.3	155.8	461.4	50.9
Under 10	3.0	14.9	72.6	152.9	386.3	48.1
Ratio: over 250 to under 10	6.3	10.4	1.9	1.8	1.4	3.0
Rural areas	5.1	10.9	48.6	129.6	132.9	36.3
Ratio: Total cities to rural areas	2.1	7.5	2.1	1.7	3.9	2.7

Source: Federal Bureau of Investigation, *Crime in the United States: Uniform Crime Reports—1971* (Washington, D.C.: U.S. Government Printing Office, 1972), Table 24.

The interrelationships between urbanism and crime are analyzed in Chapter 10. Here discussion is limited to a variety of factors which are grouped for convenience under three categories: administration of justice, formal social control, and relative opportunities for crime.

It should be noted first, however, that while cities have exceeded rural areas in arrest rates for all of the selected major offenses, the ratio has varied among offenses. For example, the urban robbery rate is 7.5 times the rural robbery rate—the greatest difference shown on Table 2–3. Conversely, the rural tendency toward crimes against persons is indicated by the low ratios for criminal homicide and aggravated assault. The even

[34] Chein, et al., *Road to H*, p. 11.

lower ratio for burglary and breaking-entering, crimes sometimes entailing the invasion of residences, continues to lend an especially personal note to the threat of crime.

Although there are some breaks in the pattern, the rates for all crimes rise with increase in size of city. The effect of population size is suggested by the ratio of the rates for cities of over 250,000 residents to the rates of cities with less than 10,000 residents. Robbery has the highest ratio, with criminal homicide in second place. Crimes against property, except robbery, show less response to population size as a factor in stimulating the crime rate.

Regardless of size of city, larceny-theft rates were highest in arrest rates and burglary and breaking-entering ranked second. The largest cities record a particularly high rate for robbery, but for cities of other sizes aggravated assault and automobile theft compete for third and fourth places, and robbery takes fifth place. Criminal homicide has the lowest rate among the crimes listed in this comparison.

Administration of justice

Statistics on crime tend to underestimate crime in rural areas because they reflect intensity of police action, and law enforcement agencies are concentrated largely in urban areas. There is also a greater likelihood in rural areas that relatively minor offenses will be handled without resort to official action by agents of justice. In his sociological assessment of a small town, Albert Blumenthal reports that the very intimacy among townspeople which serves as a deterrent to lawbreaking creates peculiar difficulties for police officers. Public opinion does not support formal and objective enforcement of laws against neighbors who commit minor offenses.[35] The increased workload of the police in urban areas reflects a decline in tolerance for a given offense; the legal redefinition, as appropriate for police action, of forms of misconduct previously handled informally among neighbors; or the deterioration under urban conditions of the neighborhood controls that formerly handled minor transgressions without resort to the law. For example, the modern equivalent of the youthful rural prank of watermelon swiping is likely to be considered larceny-theft.

Changes in crime rates or the relative position of various classes of crime are being affected by a new willingness of victims to report crimes to authorities. For example, growing expectations of the poor and minority groups have increased their demands for adequate police protection, whereas formerly they tended to overlook reports of all but the most serious offenses.[36]

[35] Albert Blumenthal, *Small-Town Stuff* (Chicago: University of Chicago Press, 1932), pp. 188–89.

[36] President's Commission on Law Enforcement and Administration of Justice, *The Challenge of Crime in a Free Society* (Washington, D.C.: U.S. Government Printing Office, 1967), p. 25.

Because of the effect on arrest statistics of unreported crimes, the President's Crime Commission asked 10,000 households whether any member had been a victim of a crime during the past year, whether the crime had been reported to the police, and if not, why the incident was not reported.[37] The survey found the actual amount to be several times that reported to the *Uniform Crime Reports.* Forcible rapes were three and one half times the reported rate, burglaries three times, aggravated assaults and larcenies of $50 and over more than double, and robbery 50 percent greater. Only vehicle theft was slightly lower. Why were the police not notified of many crimes? The most frequent explanation was the belief that the police could not do anything, especially for malicious mischief, burglaries, and larcenies of $50 and over. The next most important reason given was that the offense was a private matter or that the victim did not want to harm the offender. This explanation was offered for at least half of the aggravated and simple assaults, family crimes, and consumer frauds. Fear of reprisal, though least often cited, was strongest in the case of assaults and family crimes. Failure to report varied from 90 percent of the consumer frauds to 11 percent of the automobile thefts.

Arrest rates may also show a spurious increase simply because kinds of transactions previously withheld from official records are now reported. This alone can indicate a "crime wave." The President's Crime Commission cites over a dozen major cities which experienced upsurges in official crime statistics after improvement in case disposal and recording of statistics.[38]

Unreported crimes may also be considered from the perspective of the offender. Studies that asked a selected sample of presumably law-abiding people to recall their behaviors that might have resulted in sentences if apprehended uniformly show that delinquencies or crimes are committed at all levels of society.[39] Studies of convicted and imprisoned offenders, however, reveal a skewing toward the lower socioeconomic classes, indi-

[37] President's Commission on Law Enforcement and Administration of Justice, *Task Force Report: Crime and Its Impact,* pp. 17–19; Fred J. Cook, "There's Always a Crime Wave," in Cressey, *Crime and Criminal Justice,* pp. 23–45.

[38] President's Commission on Law Enforcement and Administration of Criminal Justice, *Task Force Report: Crime and Its Impact,* pp. 22–23.

[39] For example, see John P. Clark and Eugene P. Wenninger, "Socio-Economic Class and Area as Correlates of Illegal Behavior among Juveniles," *American Sociological Review,* 27 (December 1962): 826–34; Robert Dentler and Lawrence J. Monroe, "Early Adolescent Theft," *American Sociological Review,* 26 (October, 1961): 733–43; Maynard L. Erickson and LaMar T. Empey, "Class Position, Peers, and Delinquency," *Sociology and Social Research* (April 1965), pp. 268–82; Martin Gold, "Undetected Delinquent Behavior," *Journal of Research in Crime and Delinquency,* 3 (January 1966): 27–46; Leroy C. Gould, "Who Defines Delinquency: A Comparison of Self-Reported Indices of Delinquency for Three Racial Groups," *Social Problems,* 16 (Winter 1969): 325–36; Fred J. Murphy, Mary M. Shirley, and Helen L. Witmer, "The Incidence of Hidden Delinquency," *American Journal of Orthopsychiatry,* 16 (October 1946): 686–96; Albert J. Reiss, Jr., and Albert L. Rhodes, "The Distribution of Juvenile Delinquency in the Social Class Structure," *American Sociological Review,* 26 (October 1961): 720–32.

cating differential handling of offenders by the screening process of criminal justice. Since he is more likely to be arrested and even more likely to be imprisoned again, the person with a previous criminal record and a low socioeconomic status is more likely to be included in official crime statistics. The selective process encourages underestimation of the prevalence of crime because it cloaks the transgressions of those in positions of respectability.

Urbanism and formal social control

The urban-industrial society has placed greater reliance on criminal law as a control technique, thereby extending the area of behaviors subject to being defined as criminal. As the scope of criminal law has been extended to encompass a greater number of behaviors, direct historical comparison has reflected unfavorably on contemporary society. With the rise of urban-industrial culture, formal control techniques have been employed in efforts to compensate for the declining effectiveness of the informal controls of the family and neighborhood. Duties of police have been extended beyond the area commonly considered to be the enforcement of criminal law. New laws and ordinances can be a factor in accelerating the rate of increase in demands for police services.

While urbanization and industrialism have tended to standardize behavior, so that critics of contemporary culture decry the forcing of individuals into mechanical conformity in dress, play, and thought, they have also tended to release the individual from the constraints of tradition. Mass production, population mobility, and mass education have extended the opportunities for individual choices in goods to be purchased, in the satisfactions to be sought through work and marriage, and in the personal aspirations to be sought. Diversity in behavior has been made possible through enlargement of personal choice and reduction of the influence of cultural traditions as constraints on individual behavior. Because of this greater diversity, the urbanite is freed to an important degree from the traditional constraints which were thrust upon him, regardless of his wishes or their significance and usefulness to him in his particular economic and social situation. This freedom from the controls of a tradition-dominated society releases energies for adaptation to new circumstances, but it also offers opportunities for extreme deviations that are forbidden by the criminal law. Therefore, although urbanization and industrialization have tended to standardize behavior, they have also increased the possibility of deviant behavior.

As the waves of migration from the country to the city and the Old World to the New created large urban clusters, the urban population has been drawn from diffuse cultural backgrounds. Because the migrant's personality was probably developed in a different culture, cultural tensions were increased, and he was partially released from the norms to which he had been socialized in childhood. Rapid technological change has also undermined the importance of family in determining social status. Conspicious consumption of wealth, exhibited in such status symbols as high-priced automobiles, large houses, club memberships, and mink coats, has become the principal means of acquiring prestige.[40]

In serving as an instrument of formal control in an increasingly urbanized social environment, law enforcement agencies are primarily peace preservation bodies as Harry Shulman points out. Their major functions are the protection of life, limb, and property on the streets, in places of public assemblage, and in private and commercial places entered illegally.[41] These agencies have little control in crimes of sex, intrafamily relationships, criminal syndicates, illegal behavior of otherwise legitimate business enterprises, and other violations of public policy. Because they have effective enforcement opportunities only for that behavior that is characterized as illegal, arrest rates—no matter how complete and accurate in describing police activities—do not capture the full scope of deviant behavior.

Population expansion can generate a larger number of crimes without qualitative change in the factors causing crime. The President's Crime Commission estimates that 40 to 50 percent of the total increase of *Uniform Crime Report* arrests between 1960 and 1965 could be attributed to increases in population and changes in the age composition of the population.[42]

Relative opportunities for crime

Population density favors the criminal because sheer numbers block the close personal relationships characteristic of rural groups. Spatial mobility also contributes to the anonymity of the city, protecting the criminal from detection, whereas the rural resident is subjected to closer observation by those who can identify him as a specific individual. The large number of people in a relatively small spatial area provides sufficient customers for organized crime as a business, even though there may be few customers per 1,000 population. Urban areas offer greater opportunities for theft and robbery because wealth is available in larger

[40] W. Lloyd Warner presents a clear analysis of changes in our status and class systems. See his *The Status System of a Modern Community*, Vol. II, Yankee City Series (New Haven, Conn.: Yale University Press, 1942).

[41] Harry Manuel Shulman, "The Measurement of Crime in the United States," *Journal of Criminal Law, Criminology and Police Science,* 57 (December 1966): 487–88.

[42] President's Commission on Law Enforcement and Administration of Justice, *Task Force Report: Crime and Its Impact,* p. 25. Also see Roland J. Chilton and Adele Spielberger, "Is Delinquency Increasing? Age Structure and the Crime Rate," *Social Forces,* 49 (March 1971): 487–93.

amounts, in more concentrated forms, and of a more portable nature than is usually found in rural areas.

Changes in the patterns of socioeconomic institutions may create new types of offenses or may favor the growth of certain types of offenses. The recent rise in bank robbery partially reflects the development of small, vulnerable banks in suburbs. The greater prevalence of large-scale, self-service retail establishments has aggravated the difficulties of controlling shoplifting because there is greater public tolerance of thefts from large organizations, and easy access to goods is provided.

SUMMARY

The study of crime, its causes, and the nature of efforts to control criminal behavior can be justified by the volume of crime, the economic burdens it imposes, and its social-psychological impact on members of the community. The incidence and nature of three major types of crime —crimes against persons, crimes against property, and crimes suggesting personal disorganization—were considered. Special attention was paid to their relationship to urbanization as a way of life.

The chapter to follow will be devoted to the many implications of the great volume of crime, the urban environment which has given rise to it, and the operations of the criminal justice system that has been developed to cope with it.

FOR ADDITIONAL READING

Beattie, Ronald H. "Problems of Criminal Statistics in the United States." *Journal of Criminal Law and Criminology,* 46 (July–August 1955): pp. 178–86.

Black, Donald J. "Production of Crime Rates." *American Sociological Review,* 35 (August 1970): 733–48.

Boggs, Sarah L. "Urban Crime Patterns." *American Sociological Review,* 30 (December 1965): 899–908.

Cipes, Robert M. *The Crime War.* New York: New American Library, 1968.

Ferdinand, Theodore N. "Demographic Shifts and Criminality: An Inquiry." *British Journal of Criminology,* 10 (April 1970): 169–75.

Harris, Louis. "Changing Public Attitudes toward Crime and Corrections." *Federal Probation,* 32 (December 1968): 9–16.

Girard, Paul J. "Burglary Trends and Protection." *Journal of Criminal Law, Criminology, and Police Science,* 50 (January–February 1960): 511–18.

Gould, Leroy C. "The Changing Structure of Property Crime in an Affluent Society." *Social Forces,* 48 (September 1969): 50–63.

Graham, Fred P. "A Contemporary History of American Crime." In Hugh Davis Graham and Ted Robert Gurr (eds.), *Violence in America,* pp. 485–504. New York: Bantam Books, 1970.

Kitsuse, John I., and Cicourel, Aaron V. "A Note on the Uses of Official Statistics." *Social Problems,* 11 (Fall 1963): 131–39.

Martin, J. P., and Bradley, J. "Design of a Study of the Cost of Crime." *British Journal of Criminology,* 4 (October 1964): 591–603.

Poveda, Tony G. "The Fear of Crime in a Small Town." *Crime and Delinquency,* 18 (April 1972), 147–53.

Robison, Sophia M. "A Critical View of the Uniform Crime Reports." *Michigan Law Review,* 64 (April 1966): 1031–54.

Rudoff, Alvin. "The Soaring Crime Rate: An Etiological View." *Journal of Criminal Law, Criminology and Police Science,* 62 (December 1971): 543–47.

Savitz, Leonard D. "Automobile Theft." *Journal of Criminal Law, Criminology, and Police Science,* 50 (July–August 1959): 132–43.

Turk, Austin T. "The Mythology of Crime in America." *Criminology,* 8 (February 1971): 397–411.

Wilson, James Q. "Crime in the Streets." *Public Interest* (Fall 1966): 26–35.

3

Research and
the search for meaning

The Presidential response to the riotous summer of 1967 was the appointment of a commission to conduct a crash study of the causes of violence and to make public policy recommendations. The murders of Martin Luther King, Jr., and Robert Kennedy prompted the President to name another commission to investigate causes of assassinations. While the membership of these commissions was made up of representatives of various groups, politicians predominated. The commissions did solicit the counsel of reputable social scientists, but their membership included none of those who had devoted their careers to careful study of such issues.

To many observers, it was surprising that it could seriously be believed that such crash projects could do anything more than take a *census of opinions* on what the causes and solutions were. In this connection, Hubert Blalock, Jr., asked: How is it possible to collect and analyze data for a genuine scientific study while under public pressure to produce a report before the next election, riot, or assassination? Do politicians really believe this is the way to conduct research, or is it merely a political gimmick to make the public believe something is being done?[1]

RESEARCH: GREAT NEED, LIMITED USE

Blalock's questions indicate the importance of methodological expertise if research is to be a means of meeting social crises. Research has great potentialities for providing information and interpretations that can be of value to the political leader, but this potentiality cannot be released through a quick study of "obvious" facts under intense public pressure for immediate action. "Law and order" as a political issue or heated controversies following a prison riot are unpromising situations for the

[1] Hubert M. Blalock, Jr., *An Introduction to Social Research* (Englewood Cliffs, N.J.: Prentice-Hall, Inc., 1970), pp. 3–5.

objective collection of relevant facts and reliable analysis of the pertinent criminological issues that should mark such research.

This chapter has three themes: the potentiality of research for lending direction to the criminal justice system; the difficulties of providing the conditions for meaningful research; and an orientation for the analysis of criminological theories and practices in later chapters.

President's Crime Commission

When crime is an unusually hot public issue, the appointment of blue-ribbon commissions is a frequent official response. The prominent recent example is the President's Commission of Law Enforcement and Administration of Justice, also known as the President's Crime Commission. The commission produced an array of summary reports, frequently cited in this book, which captured the key features of the crime problem, offered a number of highly general recommendations, and presented the findings of competent consultants on pertinent topics. Among its recommendations (see Figure 3.1) was a call for an expanded research effort and the creation of a better organizational scheme for operating criminal justice agencies as well as private and university units.

While the commission's recommendations at first glance appear very attractive, they offer little guidance in the difficult tasks of designing and

Figure 3–1. Recommendations for research

Recommendations of the President's Commission on Law Enforcement and Administration of Justice for research activities

Expanded research is essential for preventing crime and improving the effectiveness of criminal justice. It must be conducted by operating agencies; universities, foundations, and research corporations; private industry; and government institutes. It must look more carefully at the way the criminal justice system operates. Change need not wait upon the gaining of such knowledge; only through innovation and evaluation of operations can most of it be obtained.

The Commission recommends:

Criminal justice agencies such as state court and correctional systems and large police departments should develop their own research units, staffed by specialists and drawing on the advice and assistance of leading scholars and experts in relevant fields.

Substantial public and private funds should be provided for a number of criminal research institutes in various parts of the country.

Universities, foundations, and other private groups should expand their efforts in the field of criminal research. Federal, state, and local governments should make increased funds available for the benefit of individuals or groups with promising research programs and the ability to execute them.

A National Foundation for Criminal Research should be established as an independent agency.

Source: President's Commission on Law Enforcement and Administration of Justice, *The Challenge of Crime in a Free Society* (Washington, D.C.: U.S. Government Printing Office, 1967), pp. 275–77, 300.

implementing the kinds of research greatly needed by criminal justice agencies. The scope of the commission's survey of the problems of criminal justice denied its members the opportunity to undertake the quality of investigation which criminological research, as a subject for scientific study in itself, would require. Further, because they represented many constituencies, often in fundamental ideological disagreement on the nature of the "law and order crisis," commission members were forced into generalized statements in order to reach agreement on research recommendations. These ideological conflicts represent the chief barrier to the setting of specific goals for criminal justice administration. Without delineation of clear-cut goals for programs, the researcher lacks means of implementing studies that can answer the "why" and "how" questions raised by administrators. The vagueness of the commission's recommendations is in itself evidence that conditions in the fields of criminal justice, which aggravate the need for research, also explain the inferior quality of most criminological research.

The commission sponsored some useful short-term research to "mark out paths along which further exploration should proceed." This modest claim for its own research projects is evidence of an important point made by the commission: "The revolution of scientific discovery has largely bypassed the problems of crime and crime control," as demonstrated by negligible expenditures "for the kinds of descriptive, operational, and evaluative research that are obvious prerequisites for a rational program of crime control."

The commission continued:

It is true, of course, that many kinds of knowledge about crime must await better understanding of social behavior. It is also true that research will never provide the final answers to many of the vexing questions about crime. Decisions as to the activities that should be made criminal, as to the limits there should be on search and seizure, or to the proper scope of the right to counsel, cannot be made solely on the basis of research data. Those decisions involve weighing the importance of fairness and privacy and freedom—values that cannot be scientifically analyzed. But when research cannot, in itself, provide final answers, it can provide data crucial to making informed policy judgments.[2]

Versions of research

From the broadest perspective, two kinds of criminological research are involved: theoretical and applied. *Theoretical research,* conducted largely by universities and private institutes, seeks to develop general

[2] President's Commission on Law Enforcement and Administration of Justice, *The Challenge of Crime in a Free Society* (Washington, D.C.: U.S. Government Printing Office, 1967), p. 273.

principles through prolonged study, with little attention to any immediate, practical "payoff." The long-term development of criminology and
criminological practice is dependent on this kind of research. Without
establishment of fundamental truths about criminal behavior and societal
reactions to crime, both theoretical and applied criminologists will rely
excessively on philosophical speculation and untested opinions. Theoretical research, however, does not provide answers to the more immediate problems of administrators or the empirical questions that are also
worthy of objective study.

While *applied research* exhibits the objectivity of theoretical research
and employs scientific methods, it concentrates on more immediate issues
involving the goals and practices of action agencies. Applied research,
which is conducted by some action agencies as well as by universities and
private institutes, is of three types: operations research, correlational
analysis, and experimental research.[3]

Operations research is the employment of a scientific method to provide executive departments with a quantitative basis for decisions regarding operations under their control.[4] The methods may be those of theoretical research, but the research aim generally is limited to a concrete
problem of immediate concern. For example, the effectiveness of a one-
man patrol car may be compared with that of a two-man team, or several
prisoner vocational training courses may be compared in terms of size of
paychecks earned after release from prison.

Correlational research also employs scientific methods to guide managerial decision making, but the emphasis is on measurement over a period
of time. Large populations are studied objectively to determine long-term
trends. Answers are sought to such questions as: What are the characteristics of accused persons coming before the courts? Are they older than
those coming before it a decade ago? Are they more sophisticated as
criminals?

Experimental research is the most sophisticated and thorough application of scientific methods within an action program. It is theoretical research in terms of study design and the long-term significance of its findings to criminology as a social science. When such research is carried on
by employees of penal institutions as part of an action program, it also
is directed by practical purposes.

Growth, but short of need

A survey of research in American correctional institutions and research
institutes in 1960 found a large and increasing volume of studies, but,

[3] James A. McCafferty, "Four Steps to a Sound Correctional Research and Statistics Program," *Crime and Delinquency*, 8 (April 1962): 134–38.

[4] Elmer H. Johnson, "Latent Functions of an Administrative Statistical System
in Correction," *Proceedings, American Correctional Association, 1960*, pp. 291–96.

with a few exceptions, they were fortuitous and haphazard.[5] Today a more favorable assessment would be justified, but there is much room for improvement. Daniel Glaser cites the establishment of research units in the correctional systems of California, Wisconsin, Minnesota, and other states and in the Home Office of Great Britain, but he also reports on how research is suppressed and research units are diverted from evaluative studies into routine counting of prisoner populations and other agency business affairs.[6]

The political and social climate in the United States would appear to encourage research in human services. Disillusionment caused by the failure to solve social problems is accompanied by growing awareness of human needs, suggesting a willingness to test the outcome of established approaches and experiment with new ones. Some funding legislation requires program evaluation. Real collaboration between research and human service agencies, however, rarely has occurred. The literature on crime and delinquency, one study reports, reveals much research undertaken but small impact on practice.[7] In spite of a conviction of the need for collaboration, real difficulties must be overcome before any achievement can be noted beyond an expression of hope that research will be utilized with increasing effectiveness.

Several recent developments pointing to greater collaboration between research and service agencies have been noted by Denis Szabo. The public and authorities have become increasingly concerned about increasing crime rates and the appearance of new forms of criminality. As the costs of administering criminal justice have escalated, interest has intensified in making current procedures more effective, experimenting with new approaches, and devoting more attention to criminal justice as an aspect of social policy. Escalating governmental costs and limited tax revenues have aggravated the need for efficient administration of criminal justice; such agencies are in an inferior position when competing for funds with other governmental services such as highway construction and education. The universities are undergoing their own related crisis; under pressure to make education and research more relevant to the social problems of the day, they are producing a new breed of researchers oriented toward applied research.[8]

---

[5] Arthur L. Beeley, "The Prison as a Laboratory for the Study of the Offender," *American Journal of Correction,* 22 (July–August 1960): 22.

[6] Daniel Glaser, "Correctional Research: An Elusive Paradise," *Journal of Research in Crime and Delinquency,* 2 (January 1965): 1–11.

[7] David Twain, Eleanor Harlow, and Donald Merwin, *Research and Human Services: A Guide to Collaboration for Program Development* (New York: Research and Development Center, Jewish Board of Guardians, 1970), p. 1.

[8] Denis Szabo, in collaboration with Marc Leblanc and Andre Normandeau, "Applied Criminology and Government Policy: Future Perspectives and Conditions of Collaboration," *Issues in Criminology,* 6 (Winter 1971): 79–80.

WHAT RESEARCH CAN OFFER ACTION AGENCIES

The products of competent researchers can provide assistance to criminologists in three specific areas of service: guidance for policy makers, program evaluation, and the application of prediction as a basis for decisions.

Guidance for policy makers

From the perspective of applied criminology, social policy can provide a framework for action in which the goals are to prevent, control, or correct criminal behavior. Policy makers undertaking the achievement of these goals believe that the problems associated with crime can be overcome, or at least reduced, by some rationally designed and concerted action; they should not be left to unguided developments. At this point, there is a linkage between applied, policy-oriented research and theoretical criminology.[9]

The framing of policy decisions ideally follows an orderly sequence: appearance of a given problem; clarification of goals and ranking according to priority; listing of alternative problem solutions; analysis of the probable outcomes of each alternative action; and choice of the policy most likely to produce an outcome consistent with the goals. Reality often conflicts with this procedure, however, as Charles Lindblom points out. Policy makers encounter diffuse situations which do not present a single problem, or the difficulty is so symptomatic of underlying conditions that identification of the "real problem" is a formidable assignment.[10] Because "the crime problem" is a multifaceted phenomenon, as suggested, for example, by its relationship with urbanization (see Chapter 2), the demand for relevant principles and reliable information is great among policy makers.

Research is an invaluable tool to the policy maker in the tasks of program planning, development, implementation, and evaluation. Reliable information and advance testing of assumptions enable him to take into account the conditions of the environment as he seeks to reduce the discrepancy between these conditions and his goals. He is thus in a position to adjust his goals and their means of attainment to the limitations these conditions impose, and he is better prepared to develop an effective strategy and to gauge the probable impact on the population chosen as the target for change.

---

[9] This linkage of societal reactions to social problems is pointed out by Sarajane Heidt and Amitai Etzioni (eds.), *Societal Guidance: A New Approach to Social Problems* (New York: Thomas Y. Crowell Co., 1969), pp. 1–2.

[10] Charles E. Lindblom, *The Policy-Making Process* (Englewood Cliffs, N.J.: Prentice-Hall, Inc., 1968), pp. 12–14.

Program evaluation

The possibility that the treatment of offenders is an example of a tendency of present-day society to engage in activities which have no more support through reliable evidence "than the incantations of medicine men and the potions of witches" has been advanced by Leslie Wilkins. He calls for an examination of our assumed knowledge and beliefs in the field of corrections. "Perhaps where we know so little," he says, "we should not be anxious to try to do so much."[11]

Evaluation is intended to answer questions such as: What happened that would not have happened if a particular programmed intervention had not been initiated? Of all the existing or suggested strategies of intervention, which ones work the best? Theoretical criminology is concerned with such questions because of their implications for the development and testing of principles in the long run. Applied criminology presses for immediate and specific answers to what is going on in the present and the relatively immediate future. Intellectual curiosity is supplemented by an urgent need to know whether *this* is the best way to spend money and other resources and whether or not the "job" is being done. The increasing recognition by managers and funding agencies of the importance of evaluation is suggested by the appearance of manuals, articles, and books on how to measure the effects of the many projects designed to help Americans cope with the problems of urban society.[12]

The capacity of practitioners to subject their "precious" ideas to the harsh light of objective and searching criticism is severely tested by evaluation. This, and the fact that evaluative studies must cope with complex and interrelated factors, is suggested by a series of remarkable studies initiated by the California Department of Corrections.[13] A control group of imprisoned and paroled juveniles was compared with an experimental group released immediately on probation; after 24 months in the community, the probationers had a significantly better record under supervision. But the probationers averaged more known delinquent offenses, and the supervisors, because of their belief in community treatment, appeared to be more lenient toward the experimental group when the offense was of low or moderate severity. The superiority of probation was not established.

Another study compared later performance of men paroled after six

---

[11] Leslie T. Wilkins, *Evaluation of Penal Measures* (New York: Random House, 1969), p. 9.

[12] For example, see Joseph S. Wholey et al., *Federal Evaluation Policy: Analyzing the Effects of Public Programs* (Washington, D.C.: The Urban Institute, 1970).

[13] James Robison and Gerald Smith, "The Effectiveness of Correctional Programs," *Crime and Delinquency*, 17 (January 1971): 67–80.

months of imprisonment with that of parolees who had been in prison longer. When the expected performance was considered for all cases, the earlier release made no difference in outcome. Regardless of the "treatments" administered in prison, the likelihood of future offenses increases with lengthened confinement. A third study compared three groups of prisoners: those receiving counseling in small groups, those living in "community groups" in prison, and those receiving no counseling. Contrary to expectation, there were no significant differences in outcome among the groups. A fourth study tested the belief that a reduced caseload would increase the effectiveness of parole. Again outcome was not significantly different between 15-man, 30-man, and 90-man caseloads.

Nevertheless, these studies demonstrate that confinement, especially long-term confinement, has no advantages over more speedy return of the convicted offender to the community. In fact, the failure of small-caseload parole was reflective of the capacity of more intensive supervision to detect minor violations. Since the studies discount any differences in the efficacy of various treatment programs regardless of their differences in cost, James Robison and Gerald Smith, authors of the report on the studies, believe the choice comes down to how much punishment "we want to impose and the amount of money we are prepared to spend in imposing it."[14]

Prediction: Basis for decisions

The aim of science is to bring the future into the range of human understanding. In the control of delinquency and crime, valid theories are means of forecasting individual and group behavior and the probable outcome of contemporary events. At all stages of the criminal justice system, from arrest to parole, decisions must be made on what to do about an offender. These decisions involve estimates of the relationship between future outcomes and the qualities of the individual and the situations within which he will be placed.

Decision making becomes most difficult when a host of factors determines outcomes and when the situation does not provide high probability of either desirable or adverse consequences. In the gray area of uncertainty, scientific methods become a useful adjunct to the experience and intuition of competent decision makers. Prediction tables, based on the recorded behavior of similar offenders in past cases, provide calculated estimates of the chances that a particular offender will succeed on probation, parole, or any other program.

The usefulness of reliable prediction is suggested by its potentiality for relating vocational training in prisons to chances for job success of re-

14 Ibid., p. 80.

leased prisoners. Marshall Brenner objects to the usual study which compares the later reconviction rates of graduates of various treatment programs.[15] This measurement describes who is likely to return to prison but does not identify which prison practices or personal inadequacies contribute to return. Brenner suggests some more useful questions: Does group counseling improve the released offender's relationships with his peers at work? Does employment of prisoners in the community improve later ability to manage shopping, use of time, relationships with neighbors, and other routine aspects of the environment? Are the job skills learned in prison marketable in the community to which the prisoner returns? With answers to such specific questions, prison treatment programs could be based on valid predictions of the situation the released prisoner will face, the probable problems he will encounter, and what capacities and information he will need in order to cope with his own environment.

Another category of decisions involves the allocation of limited resources to deal with the crime problem at least cost and for maximum benefit. One example of the application of research is the proposal that the number of calls to the police be correlated with meteorological variables such as temperature and hours of daylight to enable police planners to adjust patrol deployment and officers' vacations.[16]

An example: The Silverlake Experiment

An attempt to unite the scientific functions of theory and research with the correctional functions of administration and intervention was the Silverlake Experiment, conducted by Boys Republic, a private institution for delinquents, and the Youth Studies Center of the University of Southern California. Selected aspects on this experiment[17] provide an example of the specific ways in which research can be used by service agencies. Such experiments and reports are relatively rare.[18]

The Boys Republic had followed the control model of juvenile insti-

[15] Marshall H. Brenner, "The Prediction of Vocational Success of Criminal Offenders," *Proceedings, American Correctional Association, 1970,* pp. 322–25.

[16] Nelson B. Heller and Robert E. Markland, "A Climatological Model for Forecasting the Demand for Police Service," *Journal of Research in Crime and Delinquency,* 7 (July 1970): 167–76.

[17] LaMar T. Empey and Steven G. Lubeck, *The Silverlake Experiment: Testing Delinquency Theory and Community Intervention* (Chicago: Aldine Publishing Co., 1971).

[18] Other examples include: Edwin Powers and Helen Witmer, *An Experiment in Prevention of Delinquency: The Cambridge-Somerville Study* (New York: Columbia University Press, 1951); Lloyd W. McCorkle, Albert Elias, and F. Lovell Bixby, *The Highfields Story* (New York: Henry Holt & Co., 1958); Elliot Studt, Sheldon L. Messinger, and Thomas P. Wilson, *C-Unit: Search for Community in Prison* (New York: Russell Sage Foundation, 1968); Gene Kassebaum, David A. Ward, and Daniel M. Wilner, *Prison Treatment and Parole Survival: An Empirical Assessment* (New York: John Wiley & Sons, Inc., 1971).

tutions: residential cottages; a four-year high school building and other physical features of a program of school and work; regimentation of daily activities; a male counselor and housemother at each cottage, with a small supervisory staff for overall custodial duties; and a "student government," used partially as a control device. When it became interested in developing a community-based program as an alternative, the Youth Studies Center entered into an agreement to participate in the selection of an organizational model based on relevant theory, to study the operational and organizational problems encountered in the implementation of the experiment, and to study the experimental model.

The experimental model drew on a number of theories of delinquency causation.[19] The original theorems were:

1. The lower the social class status of the juvenile, the higher the subsequent strain. *Strain* was defined as a disaffection from the norms of the institutions of the juvenile's community and the consequential rise of tension between him and the institutional system.
2. Decreased achievement results in increased identification with delinquent peers. *Achievement* was defined as attainment of goals, *through legitimate means,* that are endorsed and defined as important by society. For adolescents, this successful goal attainment would be in the family, school, and, to a lesser extent, work.
3. Increased strain results in delinquency.
4. The lower the social class, the higher the subsequent identification with delinquent peers.
5. Decreased achievement results in delinquency.

Because the evidence gathered in this study situation gave little support to the concepts of "social class" and "achievement," the theorems were revised to become:

1. Decreased institutional ties result in increased identification with delinquent peers.
2. Increased strain results in delinquency.
3. Decreased institutional ties result in delinquency. For our purposes, this revision demonstrates the usefulness of research in the reformulation of assumptions *before* policies are implemented.

Derived from these theorems, these principles of intervention were employed:

1. The delinquent group should be made the target of change. Pressures

---

[19] Prominent among the theories were those of Albert Cohen, Richard A. Cloward and Lloyd E. Ohlin, and the role-self theory presented in Chapter 10 below.

generated *within* the delinquent group were to enlist delinquents in the reformulation process.[20]
2. Social strain among delinquents should be reduced in a setting encouraging free expression of feelings, developing a sense of common group membership among both staff and juveniles, and providing rewards in excess of the rewards for adherence to delinquent roles.
3. Means for legitimate achievement by delinquents should be made available. The juvenile would be sponsored in a reformation role and would be provided effective linkage with the nondelinquent world.

The experimental group attended the local high school and returned to their homes in the community each weekend. The objective was to permit the delinquent some degree of freedom under circumstances favoring his reintegration into nondelinquent activities. The group was supposed to develop a subculture favorable to internalization of prosocial values in which prestige would be conferred by peers on those assuming the reformation role. Daily guided group interaction sessions were instituted as a mechanism for developing a sense of collaboration, a means of solving problems through group effort, and a source of treatment through social learning. Thus a reservoir of theories was applied to criminological practice to lend a sense of purpose to programmed activities.

Participants in the experimental program (experimental research group) and in the traditional Boys Republic program (control research group) were selected randomly from offenders in the county. Only repeat offenders, ages 15 through 17, were included. The only exclusions were serious sex offenders, narcotic addicts, and retarded and psychotic boys.

An indication of the usefulness of research in predicting behavioral outcome and evaluating the experimental model was the measurements based on runaway rates, completion of program, in-program failures, seriousness of law violations, and several projective tests that were provided. The net conclusion was that the experimental program was not more effective than the traditional program in reducing delinquency. In addition to a reliable evaluation, the research provided guidance on correcting the experimental model. For example, LaMar Empey and Steven Lubeck cite failures to recognize the crucial importance of dealing with family disorganization, to establish effective relationships with the local school, and to provide sufficient understanding of the outcomes of the traditional program. Because different boys probably react differently to various treatment programs, the researchers suggest that matching of types of offenders with types of programs would be a more promising use of correctional resources.[21] The pilot project made a contribution to the

---

[20] See Chapter 11, pp. 272–73, for analysis of the group as a medium of change.

[21] Empey and Lubeck, *Silverlake Experiment,* pp. 273–75.

accumulation of reliable knowledge by providing a basis for study of reasons for failure.

PREREQUISITES TO RESEARCH

To acquire the benefits of research, the action agency must provide certain conditions: a climate favorable to research, competent personnel, adequate financial support, and research equipment. John Mannering lists the elements of a favorable climate as a clear statement of agency goals by the top administration, a setting of priorities among possible research proposals for the most beneficial employment of limited resources, and the granting of freedom essential to scientific inquiry.[22]

Research competence

Because research is a highly technical business, applied criminology needs a larger supply of trained and experienced personnel than is now available for the design and implementation of studies. The following questions indicate some of the research issues requiring methodological expertise.

Can we be reasonably certain that the findings from a study of a specific group of offenders can be properly applied to other offenders? The answer depends on whether or not the specific group constitutes a *sample* (a smaller representation of a larger whole) of a universe (the "larger whole"; in this instance, all offenders). In selecting the study group, care would have been taken that they are typical of the larger whole for which the findings are sought. If the drawing of the sample justifies confidence that it is representative of the universe, there is reason to argue that the findings can be extended to the larger group. For example, if vocational training has certain benefits for only certain kinds of offenders in the sample, we are in a position to contend that these benefits will accrue to offenders in the community with similar characteristics and exposure to training.

How can we determine whether a given factor has a certain effect? For example, was the vocational training program responsible for the offenders abandoning their law violations? One method is to expose some offenders to the training *(experimental group)* and to give no such training to other offenders *(control group)* who are identical to the trainees in every other respect.

Can we be reasonably certain that only the factors studied determine the relationships discovered? *Random sampling* is based on the assump-

[22] John W. Mannering, "Developing Research Resources within the Correctional System," *Proceedings, American Correctional Association, 1959*, pp. 59–62.

tion that every event has an equal chance of being included in the study population. For example, all the persons in the universe of 1,000 juvenile offenders could be assigned a number from 1 to 1,000. A page of the telephone book is opened arbitrarily, the last three digits of the telephone numbers listed in order, and the juveniles with the selected numbers placed in the sample. Because each of the 1,000 juveniles had an equal chance of being chosen, it is assumed that the influences of factors other than those being investigated will cancel each other out.

If differences are found, does this prove that a relationship exists? Trained juveniles probably would differ from untrained juveniles simply because job success rates are unlikely to be identical even if training had no effect. Therefore, researchers require that the differences be greater than pure chance could produce. They must be "statistically significant."

Abstract and concrete thinking

Applied research may be impeded by opposition of practitioners arising from the differences between the abstract thinking of the scientist and the concrete thinking of the empiricist who relies on sensory experience and "common sense." The researcher's time-consuming attention to detail may arouse the antipathy of persons subjected to the processing of the criminal justice system and workers who must cope with the frustrations of dealing with lawbreakers in reality. They are unlikely to feel sympathetic toward the researcher's careful design of studies to assure unvarnished facts or his "nit-picking" analysis of interrelationships among variables. Their impatient concern for action *now* is supplemented by a faith in "common sense" which tells them that familiar formulas will solve the problem if effort is intensified: more education in the old mold; more patrol cars, equipment, and higher pay for policemen; more parks and baseball diamonds for delinquency-prone neighborhoods; more teachers, psychologists, and industries for prisons, without altering their organizational scheme; and so on. From this perspective, the call for further and more systematic research appears to be largely an excuse for withholding action and a diversion of precious money into studies which may only conclude that even more studies are necessary.

This impatience, while understandable, must be balanced against the long-term benefits of valid knowledge accrued through abstract thinking. Scientists seek general statements which link together a host of discrete events and thereby lend conceptual order to what otherwise appears to be a mass of unrelated occurrences. The thinking of the scientist is abstract in that he notes the common elements among events he classifies as similar on the basis of some *concept,* a mental image expressed by a term which captures the meaning of a particular relationship. Examples of concepts are "crime" as discussed in Chapter 1, "social status" in Chapter 5, and "social institution" in Chapter 6.

Through abstract thinking and the employment of concepts, the scientist can move beyond the confusing details of everyday experience and capture the intellectual significance of what he observes selectively. He can note the similarity in patterns he observes and the findings of previous research which might appear to be unrelated to his study. Thus the research project benefits from the accumulative nature of science and the theories that emerge through the progressive work of a body of scientific colleagues.

Favorable climate

Research requires what Scott Greer has called "a willing suspension of belief."[23] In studies conducted within a criminological agency, the investigator is ready to challenge the assumptions held sacred by the people who have made their work their career and the agency their occupational home. The researcher's persistent "why" questions create discomfort among those who have accepted traditions and routine practices as facts. His work requires a readiness to break with tradition and accept new ideas, especially among executives whose authority is essential to the establishment of an in-house research program and to the attitudinal reception of the data collectors in the field. This readiness is created by executive sensitivity to problems requiring research, an image of the potentiality for improvement in problematic situations, and a general experimental attitude acceptive of innovation, as noted by Rensis Likert and Ronald Lippitt.[24]

The need for a climate of acceptance is especially great in policy guidance because the design of a study must be to promote answers to questions relevant to the crucial issues. In designing his study, the research worker must know the specific goals of the administrators if he is to test the means proposed to achieve them. For example, parole may have the goal of reintegrating inmates into the community as fully participating citizens or, alternatively, of reducing the population of overcrowded prisons by releasing both low- and medium-risk inmates. The means may emphasize psychological and other forms of intervention that concentrate on strengthening the capacity of parolees to become fully participating citizens, or the use of surveillance techniques to maximize the protection of the community against further antisocial behavior among parolees. The significance of rule violations of intermediate seriousness would be evaluated differently against each of these alternative goals and means.

In a climate of research acceptance, agency executives recognize that

[23] Scott Greer, *The Logic of Social Inquiry* (Chicago: Aldine Publishing Co., 1969), p. 3.

[24] Rensis Likert and Ronald Lippitt, "The Utilization of Social Science," in Leon Festinger and Daniel Katz (eds.), *Research Methods in the Behavioral Sciences* (New York: Dryden Press, 1953), p. 582.

a question requiring research does exist. They are willing to discuss fully their goals and their choice of means with the researcher and solicit his advice early enough to enable him to contribute to the framing of testable questions. Finally, they will accept research conclusions that conflict with their expectations and hopes. Statements by executives that they "welcome" research frequently are not based on such acceptance. The delineation of goals in advance of research probably is the primary difficulty because they may not be able to define their specific objectives clearly. They also cannot control all the factors involved (for example, availability of funds, future decisions of their superiors, public responses, and so on) and lack crucial information on which to base a statement of goals. Realization of the latter deficiency is reflected in the executive's call for research.

The researcher in such a situation has several alternatives. He can guess at the specifics of generalized goals and means, thereby filling the vacuum with his own policy decisions—an action contrary to the ethical neutrality of the scientist. Or, as has been suggested, he can read many novels in his lonely office as he waits in vain for the policy makers to respond to his insistence that they define their goals fully.[25] The preferable action is for him to participate in the laborious processes of program development in at least a research advisory capacity. Thereby he can suggest ideas for experimentation, develop a data collection system, encourage rational assessment of conditions and issues, and finally design appropriate studies.[26]

Difficulties of collaboration

Social and behavioral scientists only recently have shown sustained, substantial interest in the activities of criminological agencies. When they have become involved, their interest frequently has been either of a reformist bent or motivated by a desire to use the agencies temporarily as laboratories for testing abstract principles. These principles are necessarily couched in technical language that is difficult to translate into terms that are understandable or useful to practitioners.[27]

On the other hand, criminological agencies, as compared with other social institutions, usually have been relatively inaccessible to social science research. The authoritarian nature of their functions for society has not been conducive to the spirit of free inquiry. Administrators have provided some entrée to researchers, however, as the growth of criminological

[25] Howard E. Freeman and Clarence C. Sherwood, "Research in Large-Scale Intervention Programs," *Journal of Social Issues,* 21 (January 1965): 17.

[26] Michael P. Brooks, "The Community Action Program as a Setting for Applied Research," *Journal of Social Issues,* 21 (January 1965): 31–34.

[27] The marginal status of the theoretical criminologist is also a problem which has become less salient in recent decades; see Chapter 1, pp. 8–9.

literature shows. The impediments to research lie not in direct opposition to the projects, but in slowness to recognize what incisive research is and the conditions it requires. Reluctance to expose closed systems to public attention also should be considered.

Emphasis on coercive measures to control crime diverts attention from the personality and social factors involved in the development of criminality, as well as from the nature of the criminological agencies themselves. When practitioners have applied theories in their work, they usually have taken an essentially clinical view of delinquency and crime which stresses the individual offender and takes the treatment program, the practitioner, and his agency as unchallengeable constructive factors.

Meaningful evaluation of programs can be handicapped by such false beliefs of action personnel as the ideas that evaluation cannot be added to an ongoing program or that informal self-evaluation by workers is sufficient. They may feel that a program with superior clients can arbitrarily claim success for its approach or that existing procedures for selecting clients are equivalent to random assignment to experimental and control groups. Discovery of unanticipated failures in a program may be seen as meaning that the evaluative study is also a failure, and the costs of research may be regarded as exceeding their usefulness to the agency.[28]

Weaknesses of much official data

In several respects the data routinely collected by agencies, when they do exist, are of doubtful quality for theoretical research and for much of the administrative research that is done. Too frequently, official statistics suffer from heterogeneity in unit of count, effects of accommodations in the course of daily administration, incomplete control over extraneous variables, fragmentation of data, expediency in collection, and paucity of information on behavior.

Criminal statistics generally lack homogeneity because of wide variation in the legal labels given a particular type of crime. Burglary in one judicial system may in another be a form of larceny or theft. Second, there is a lack of uniformity in the unit of count. Assume three men are tried on an indictment charging five gasoline station holdups. The unit of count might be one trial, three defendants, five holdups, or 15 offenses. Although statistics should reflect uniform and automatic enforcement of the law, agencies modify their reactions to offenders through accommodations to the problems of everyday administration. Police agencies lack resources for complete enforcement. Full, formal adjudication of all serious criminal cases would require greatly increased court staffs and other facilities. To ease this burden, the agencies of criminal justice are

[28] Gordon P. Waldo, "Myths, Misconceptions, and the Misuse of Statistics in Correctional Research," *Crime and Delinquency,* 17 (January 1971): 57–62.

willing to make concessions in sentencing or to reduce charges. The complex decision making required reduces the accuracy of the records of police and court business as indices of criminal conduct. For example, assault may be reduced to disturbing the peace, with the result that the actual incidence of assault is understated.

If crime rates are to be valid measurements, the influence of complicating and extraneous factors must be held constant or must be minimized. Thermometer readings do not measure room temperature in a useful way if ice is attached to the bulb at one time and a heating coil at another. Statistics are subjected to many influences extraneous to the desired purpose. Changes in police policies or an improvement in personnel and equipment can increase arrests without an upsurge in criminality. An atrocious crime may inflame public fear and anger, stimulating special legislation and sterner law enforcement and court action. Parents, school officials, and welfare agencies will deal informally with personality problems on some occasions; at other times, similar behavior results in formal criminal charges. The social class status of the offender and the reputation of his family may determine the choice between these alternatives.

Some agencies gather information; some do not. A complete and consistent statistical description of crime is lacking because there is little system in the methods employed and the types of data gathered. James McCafferty classifies criminal statistical operations as being "concentric" or "fragmented" or a compromise between the two.[29] In the "concentric" form, a central agency is responsible for the collection and presentation of all criminal and correctional statistics. In the "fragmented" form, each operating criminal or correctional agency collects data relevant to its activities. Police, courts, probation agencies, jails, prisons, juvenile training schools, and parole boards all collect bodies of statistics. Lack of coordination among these statistical systems prevents comparison of crime rates at the several stages of the penocorrectional process or the generation of a complete record of a career in crime. The problem of different units of count is aggravated. After tracing the development of a "concentric" collection system in California, Ronald Beattie describes studies on the careers of narcotic offenders, probationers, and released prisoners, in addition to annual reports on crime trends.[30]

Once the data are collected, it is often difficult to utilize them efficiently for purposes other than those envisaged originally. Bodies of data have been gathered routinely without careful assessment of the purposes of the data. For example, a law enforcement agency could count arrests in a

[29] James A. McCafferty, "Prisoner Statistics—National and State," *Proceedings, Social Statistics Section, American Statistical Association, 1960,* pp. 25–33.

[30] Ronald H. Beattie, "A State Bureau of Criminal Statistics," in Marvin E. Wolfgang (ed.), *Crime and Culture* (New York: John Wiley & Sons, Inc., 1968), pp. 169–86.

manner which would provide information on the age and occupation of the offender and the specifics of his offense in ways that would also be useful to courts and correctional agencies.

Labeling of the individual as a criminal is an administrative action. It is not necessarily descriptive of the etiology and motivation behind his behavior. Statistical data on crime usually tell something about administrative action (such as an arrest or granting parole) and the ranking of the offender within a continuum of some general population attribute (such as age). But rarely do criminal statistics, as routinely gathered, tell why the offense was committed or give information on the subtleties of the etiological background of the crime. Chapter 1 discussed this distinction between behavior and the definition of behavior as criminal.

Because of the weaknesses in much official data based on arrests, court dispositions, or prison admissions, researchers sometimes have developed other sources of basic information. Several approaches have been used in obtaining a more complete census of crimes perpetrated than is provided by agency files and official reports. A sample of respondents representing a cross-section of a selected population may be asked to list their law violations regardless of official apprehension. In a sample drawn from a given geographical area, citizens may be interviewed to determine the degree and quality of their victimization by criminals in a particular period of time. Department stores and other economic enterprises are sources of data on shoplifting, thefts by employees, and other losses to criminals. Insurance companies offer files on insurance claims. These approaches to data collection entail greater initiative and expenditure of resources than the use of official crime statistics and documents drawn from files of criminological agencies. They also cover only a segment of the total spectrum of criminal behavior. Nevertheless, they can afford superior control over the methodological difficulties outlined above—such as uniformity of count, concentration on behavior as distinct from administrative reactions to behavior, and minimization of the effects of factors extraneous to the research topic.

SUMMARY

The system of criminal justice is in particular need of the means for intelligent policy making and overall coordination that can be provided by competent employment of research methods. The shortage of research is due to very basic reasons inherent in the nature of the difficulties in administering criminal justice and the demanding conditions for meaningful research. Perhaps with excessive optimism, we see a trend toward fuller use of the potentialities of research, especially because of the greater need for effective management of an increasingly costly system of criminal justice. In raising important issues concerning criminological research and in offering a brief introduction to the characteristics of the scientific method, this chapter serves as an orientation to the discussions of criminological theories and problems of criminological practice that follow.

FOR ADDITIONAL READING

Caplan, Nathan. "Treatment Intervention and Reciprocal Interaction Effects." *Journal of Social Issues,* 24 (January 1968): 63–88.

Eynon, Thomas G. "New Roles of Research in Classification and Treatment." *Proceedings, American Correctional Association, 1970,* pp. 83–87.

Fosen, Robert H., and Campbell, Jay, Jr. "Common Sense and Correctional Science." *Journal of Research in Crime and Delinquency,* 3 (July 1966): 73–81.

Freeman, Howard E., and Sherwood, Clarence C. *Social Research and Social Policy.* Englewood Cliffs, N.J.: Prentice-Hall, Inc., 1970.

Gottfredson, Don M. "The Practical Application of Research." *Canadian Journal of Corrections,* 5 (October 1963): 212–28.

Hackler, James C. "An 'Underdog' Approach to Correctional Research." *Canadian Journal of Corrections,* 9 (January 1967): 27–36.

Johnson, Elmer H. "Correctional Research as a Bridge between Practice and Theory." *Canadian Journal of Corrections,* 10 (October 1968): 545–52.

Martin, John M. "Agency Research: To Be or Not to Be?" *Crime and Delinquency,* 15 (July 1969): 341–47.

Mathiesen, Thomas. "The Sociology of Prisons: Problems for Future Research." *British Journal of Sociology,* 17 (December 1966): 360–79.

Smith, Alexander B., and Bassin, Alexander. "Research in a Probation Department." *Crime and Delinquency,* 8 (January 1962): 46–51.

Special Commission on the Social Sciences of the National Science Board. *Knowledge into Action: Improving the Nation's Use of the Social Sciences.* Washington, D.C.: U.S. Government Printing Office, 1969.

Tifft, Larry A., and Bordua, David J. "Police Organization and Future Research." *Journal of Research in Crime and Delinquency,* 6 (July 1969): 167–76.

Waldo, Gordon P. "The Dilemma of Correctional Research." *American Journal of Correction,* 31 (November–December 1969): 6–10.

White, Mervin F., and Dean, Charles W. "Problems in Operationalizing Theoretical Ideas in Corrections." *Journal of Research in Crime and Delinquency,* 6 (January 1969): 87–98.

Part II

Sociocultural context and social control

Criminologists are concerned with: (1) lawmaking as a process whereby certain behaviors are defined as targets for the system of criminal justice, (2) the behaviors of individuals in conflict with the laws, and (3) societal reaction to crime as a means of protecting social interests and preventing future crimes. In investigating the setting of criminological issues within society, Part II provides details on topics that make criminology a particularly fascinating subject.

Chapter 4 locates criminology within the context of social control, seeing lawmaking as an attempt to utilize formal controls to supplement the informal controls of socialization, habit, and the ordinary spontaneous reactions of individuals and groups that operate to maintain the order essential to human life. The function of social control within the sociocultural environment is illustrated by the effect of tolerance on the administration of justice. Chapter 5 focuses on how the individual is fitted into this environment on the bases of his various statuses, which affect both the possibility of criminality and the response of society to transgressions. Chapter 6 moves from the individual to the social institutions that bind individuals and groups into a normative network to give order to society. Chapter 7 culminates the consideration of crime as a functional part of the broad social system by investigating patterns of criminal behavior.

4

Norms and criminology

Human society is only possible when individuals comply with its system of rules. Although there apparently still are some who believe that "criminals" are completely outside of and apart from society, the facts show that criminal behavior can only be understood as a part of the social order.

The function of norms, or authoritative standards, as a regulatory mechanism in society is the subject of this chapter. One section, centering around the concept of tolerance, particularly considers the pertinence of norms to the study of criminology.

NORMS AND THE SOCIAL ORDER

In his efforts to satisfy persistent needs for sustenance, shelter, companionship, sexual activity, and societal order, man has developed certain ideas, attitudes, and habits. Ages ago, man was at the mercy of his physical environment. Ever so slowly, he learned by observation and by chance how to extend his control over it. The ways of doing and thinking that were found to be effective have become part of the heritage of the human group. Each generation benefits from the past and adds its own unique experiences to the store of culture received from previous generations. In this way, man has created a sociocultural screen between himself and the natural environment and has provided himself with the tools necessary for adjustment to it.

Man as a normative being

Nonhuman societies are dependent upon heredity as the basis for cooperative behavior. The response of individuals is organized on the basis of an inherited tendency to react in a fixed manner to stimuli provided by other members of the group. Nonhuman societies are perpetuated through transmission of the genes.

Human societies, on the other hand, require learning of cultural patterns which afford a systematic network of mutual stimulus and response. Man's social system is perpetuated through learning. As an instrument of communication, language has enabled men to convey an idea of situations not experienced directly and has provided a means for prescribing appropriate behavior.

Communication and learning have afforded human society the unique characteristic of normativeness, allowing man to derive a double meaning from reality: the factual order of what *is* and the normative order of what *ought* to be.[1] The human being is born into a society organized on the basis of norms. Social relationships are regulated because many of the norms are backed up by *sanctions,* punishments and rewards of various kinds and degrees, applied through techniques of social control. Each human group is unified by the belief of its members that certain things and behaviors are desirable, admirable, proper, moral, or legitimate and that other things and behaviors are unfit, despicable, unbecoming, immoral, or illegitimate. Thus a *value* system is a major element of the cultural heritage of each group.

Social norms and social control

Social norms are rules of conduct which specify what human beings in a given culture should or should not do as members of the group. As a sociological concept, social norm is particularly useful in linking social and cultural factors. Social behavior fits certain patterns because the norms, as elements of culture, channel the doing and thinking inherent in social life. The element of *should* is vital; man is supposed to judge his own behavior and the behavior of others according to the standards accepted by the groups within which they associate with one another. "Should" also suggests that actual behavior may differ from expectations and that such discrepancies may be more frequent than usually believed. Group efforts to assure conformity to social norms (social control) are undertaken to assure the group's continued existence.[2]

Norms require certain actions (prescriptive function) and also prohibit other actions (proscriptive function). Sexual appetites, for example, are directed into marriage and away from rape. Some norms are characteristic of the society as a whole, and others are found among only certain groups. Patriotism and vocational ambition are supposed to be American norms, but tastes in dress among subcultures and expectations among specialized occupational groups vary greatly.

Sociologists usually classify norms under the concepts of folkways, mores, and laws. *Folkways* are customary and habitual ways of doing

---

[1] Kingsley Davis, *Human Society* (New York: Macmillan Co., 1949), p. 52.

[2] Judith Blake and Kingsley Davis, "Norms, Values and Sanctions," in Robert E. L. Faris (ed.), *Handbook of Modern Sociology* (Chicago: Rand McNally & Co., 1964), p. 456.

things in a particular group. They range from the friendly handshake to wedding etiquette. *Mores,* also customary and habitual, add the component of moral obligation to behave as expected for advancement of the general social interest. To the folkway of kissing is added the moral abhorrence applied to the wife caught in the arms of a friendly door-to-door salesman. As products of politically organized societies, *laws* are expressly enacted by legislatures or decreed by legitimate authorities and enforced by agents of the state. Folkways and mores operate within the fabric of daily life, whereas laws are consciously developed and deliberately enforced. Nevertheless, the effective law is consistent with and supported by the folkways and mores to enhance the probability of its observance.

Social control refers to the social forces that are brought into play to prevent or oppose deviance from norms considered vital to the effective functioning of the group. Individuals are supposed to accept the group's norms as measuring rods for behavior through operation of informal and formal controls. *Informal controls* rely on folkways, mores, and public sentiments operating more or less unconsciously within the environment of daily routines. The deviant is subjected to social pressures exerted by persons in his own group. The individual's conscience, composed of the social norms that have become part of his basis for evaluating himself, polices his own behavior and prevents and regulates deviance. *Formal controls* are deliberately formulated and consciously implemented by agencies specifically designed for the regulation of certain aspects of behavior. The official behavior of the policeman, as one of the agents of the criminal justice system, illustrates how the criminal law serves as the basis for the formulation and implementation of formal controls. He enforces the criminal law through arrest in clear-cut events, differentiated from the routines of daily life, which are specifically defined as calling for his official action as an authorized and specialized agent of organized society. His task performance involves application of force to other individuals without necessarily involving their sense of conscience.

Socialization and legitimacy

Learning and communication are essential to the operation of controls. *Socialization* aids the child in learning the norms of his culture through environmental contacts with parents, siblings, playmates, and other associates. His *culture* consists of all the knowledge, beliefs, values, norms, and technology developed in the history of his people. Although there are variations among cultures and each culture has potentialities for great differences among individuals in the manner in which its elements are combined and interpreted, socialization will produce patterns among personalities developed in a given sociocultural environment. In learning the cultural norms through communication with other persons as he seeks to gratify his personal wants and emotional needs and develops a personality fitting the pattern of his normative environment, the child becomes so subject to informal controls that the norms become *legitimate*. The child accepts the norms as binding on his own conduct, and the system of norms is thus legitimatized.

Through socialization, the child learns to perceive objects, events, and persons within frames of reference which are shared with members of his group. By placing less dependence on personal or unique evaluations of his world and learning to look at things in terms of group norms, he earns membership in groups and acquires a means of communicating with others. The acquiring of habitual frames of reference made up of group norms is encouraged by (1) a system of rewards and punishments supporting tendencies towards conformity, (2) the lack of competition from other norms in the child's immediate world, and (3) the dependence of the child on his elders for physical care and social guidance.

Norms are learned and brought to bear on human conduct through communication, the process by which a symbol is given a standardized meaning to enable interacting persons to have a more or less similar experience of it. This process requires that the communicating persons share a frame of reference. Man's perception of the world about him is highly selective, so that he experiences its nearly infinite stimuli through a psychological and sociological filter. A $10 bill, a child's smile, and a Congressional Medal of Honor are meaningful symbols of social values to Americans because we have learned to understand them within a social context. Man selects such symbols of social values out of a mass of stimuli and interprets them in terms of shared norms which make communication possible.

Values and social institutions

As criteria for the norms which constitute more specific rules of conduct, the basic values of a given culture are related to the typical thought patterns which shape the orientation of a people toward the world. *Values* have been defined by Robin Williams, Jr., as standards of desirability employed as criteria for preference or as justifications for proposed action in terms of "good" or "bad," "beautiful" or "ugly," appropriate or inappropriate, and so on. Broad value orientations of Americans include emphasis on personal achievement (especially in an occupation), strenuous activity, a curious conflict between humanitarianism and faith in rugged individualism, the desirability of material comforts, technological "progress," and a demand for both social order and personal freedom.[3]

When a set of norms "cohere around a relatively distinct and socially

[3] Robin M. Williams, Jr., *American Society: A Sociological Interpretation* (New York: Alfred A. Knopf, Inc., 1970), pp. 27, 452–98.

important complex of values," as Williams notes, the basis for a *social institution* is established. Among all cultural norms, institutional norms are distinctive in intensity of social sanctions, degree of agreement among group members that these norms should be supported and applied, and enforcement within definite social organizations.[4] The patterning of such norms around some human purpose is the basis of social institutions.

Examples of social institutions include the family, school, government, and private economic enterprise. Each can be compared to the blueprint for a house. As a comprehensive plan, the blueprint gives significance to each piece of wood, plastic, or metal making up the completed house. In the case of the family, the institutionalized norms form a pattern for regulating sexual relations, the behavior of man and wife toward one another, the manner of raising the children, and other matters related to the functions of family members in serving purposes essential to society. A set of guidelines channels the sex drive in support of society through criteria for selecting a mate and maintaining appropriate relationships between man and woman in the social statuses of husband and wife.

Each social institution contributes to the general social order by its support of common values and expected role performance. For example, in a stable society, families teach children to be competent employees of businesses and factories, dedicated participants in the affairs of schools and churches, and effective citizens within political institutions.

Collectively, social institutions, by design, are intended to provide a regularized normative structure within which social control can operate. Through the development of habits and the conditioning of attitudes in the course of socialization, the individual's behavior is channeled according to his statuses and roles within the structure of groups formed around a set of institutional norms. In relationships with other persons, he occupies a *social status*—his social position, such as father, university dean, head of an office staff, army private, and so on. Attached to each social status is a *social role,* a set of expectations against which performance in a given social position is evaluated. The norms of particular role-statuses are illustrated by expectations that a mother place the interests of her children ahead of her own, that a business executive be certain and competent in his decisions, that a military officer be courageous in the face of danger, or that a subordinate be punctual and obedient to instructions.

Social order in urban society

Tasks and responsibilities are allocated within a social scheme as a means of meeting social and individual needs through engendering cooperation among the groups composing society and the members of these

[4] Ibid., p. 37.

groups. This social scheme incorporates roles and statuses within the framework of social institutions. Informal and formal controls promote individual behaviors that are congenial to the social order essential to the functioning of the society within this scheme. This order is challenged at varying rates by changes in the social conditions experienced by the given society. The rate of social change is affected by such factors as growth and mobility of population, accessibility of the society to the insertion of new ideas from other cultures, development of technological systems for converting natural resources into products for human consumption, and degree of similarity among groups in the values emphasized in socialization of personality.

How is the social order maintained? The many possible answers may be grouped into two broad categories.[5] Most sociologists follow *order theories,* which emphasize a normative consensus derived from a shared culture and agreement on values that support a relatively persistent and stable structure. The social order is maintained by the capacity of society's members to understand one another and to act in concert in achieving common goals through common rules of behavior.

Conflict theories see society as a product of accommodations among continually contesting groups with opposing goals and perspectives. Force and constraint, maintained by the dominant group, produce a social stability as a sort of moving equilibrium among changing distributions of power, wealth, and status.

With the growth of an interdependent large-scale society that is highly advanced technologically, vast concentrations of power and complicated social mechanisms have been developed. These conditions add to the difficulties of maintaining social order through "natural" development and the persistence of normative consensus by means of socialization, habitual adherence to traditional values, and informal controls. More conscious engineering of consent is required. Through the employment of *power,* the chance is increased that an individual or a group will realize its own will in a communal action, even against the resistance of others who are participating in the action.[6]

Power implies differential access of men and groups to its elements: public esteem, capacity to influence others through persuasion or coercion, possession of financial resources and knowledge, and occupancy of positions of authority in community organizations. Criminology is concerned with how power operates in society to influence the probability of

[5] Ralf Dahrendorf, *Class and Class Conflict in Industrial Society* (Stanford, Calif.: Stanford University Press, 1959), pp. 157–62; John Horton, "Order and Conflict Theories of Social Problems as Competing Ideologies," *American Journal of Sociology,* 71 (May 1966): 701–21, including commentaries of Bert N. Adams and Robin M. Williams, Jr.

[6] Max Weber, *From Max Weber: Essays in Sociology,* trans. Hans H. Gerth and C. Wright Mills (New York: Oxford University Press, 1946), p. 180.

criminal behavior and the nature of organized society's reactions to crime. These functions are implied by William Gamson's description of the perspectives from which power is viewed by partisans and authorities.[7] From the perspective of partisans in a community controversy, power refers to how the financial rewards, privileges, and social gratifications are distributed among the individuals and groups of the community. The inferior access of underprivileged segments of the population to these benefits is an explanation of crimes for economic gain and crimes against persons as symptoms of alienation from the values supported by the criminal law. From the perspective of the authorities, power is the ability of a society to mobilize and generate resources to attain its goals. The selection of certain kinds of deviance for the application of criminal sanctions and the administration of the criminal justice system generally reflect the objectives of the powerful groups striving to safeguard their own interests and values. Leadership in a democratic community thus becomes a matter of utilizing available resources in curbing crime for the sake of the social order, while concurrently finding some balance among competing interest groups in order to preserve community consensus.

Crime and sociocultural organization

The preceding brief inventory of sociological concepts places criminological studies within the context of the sociocultural organization affecting all human behavior. Richard Quinney makes this point in his insistence on the "social reality" of crime. Certain behaviors become criminal because they have been so defined by representatives of a politically organized society. They then become subject to punishments administered by agents of the state. As Quinney says, crime is *created* by the legal definitions making certain behaviors subject to the operations of the criminal justice system as a facet of the formal control structure of contemporary urban society. These definitions emerge out of the conflicts of interests among the segments of a heterogeneous society in which those with power shape public policy and the administration of justice. One consequence is that the criminal justice system has differential impact so that the probability of being defined as criminal varies among segments of society. Currents of public opinion also affect conceptions of the nature of the crime problem. In times of concern over threats to cherished values, groups with political power are likely to mobilize the criminal law and its enforcement in defense of their interests.[8]

[7] William A. Gamson, *Power and Discontent* (Homewood, Ill.: Dorsey Press, 1968), pp. 2–18.

[8] Richard Quinney, *The Social Reality of Crime* (Boston: Little, Brown & Co., 1970), pp. 14–23. Also see Dennis Chapman, *Sociology and the Stereotype of the Criminal* (London: Tavistock Publications, 1968), pp. 3–5.

TOLERANCE AND SOCIAL NORMS

Among the many kinds of deviants, "the criminal" is especially liable to be negatively evaluated. The wide spectrum of those technically qualified as violators of the criminal law encompasses a variety of images, however, as described by Jerry L. Simmons.[9] Probably the most widespread is the image of the criminal as a gross violator of the moral standards held sacred by the group making the evaluation; "the criminal" is identified with the murderer, rapist, or incorrigible thief. He also may be seen as "sick" from some hereditary taint, character weakness, physical fault, mental malfunctioning, or other form of "pathology" or viewed as "abnormal" in the sense of being somehow different from the usual or familiar kind of person. Perhaps he is only censured as a "boat-rocker" who interferes with the smooth functioning of society. The image of the criminal as a hero, wild and free of moral restraint, may even spark the envy of conventional citizens. Finally, he may be viewed as one who possesses the qualities of all human beings but who happened to break the law.

Attitudinal climate

The varying images of criminals suggest the complexity of the reactions in society to the range of behaviors that call for resort to methods of crime control. There are many gradations in the intensity and severity of these reactions. The great variations that occur in rejection or toleration suggest the need to pay careful attention to the sociocultural factors affecting the treatment the lawbreaker receives from the community at large and its authorized agents.

The complex interaction of sociocultural factors is suggested by Edwin Lemert's *tolerance quotient*.[10] The numerator in this quotient is a measure of the amount of disapproved conduct in a given community; theoretically, it reflects the actual incidence of crime in general or a specific form of crime. The denominator measures the degree of tolerance the people have for this behavior; it estimates the typical willingness of the community to withhold harsh reactions. This oversimplified statement focuses attention on two sets of factors: those affecting the level of criminal behavior and those affecting the attitudinal climate within which the behavior is evaluated by other people. Here our interest concentrates on the second set of factors.

Because the framers of criminal laws and their administrative agents

[9] Jerry L. Simmons, *Deviants* (Berkeley, Calif.: Glendessary Press, 1969), pp. 13–24.

[10] Edwin M. Lemert, *Social Pathology* (New York: McGraw-Hill Book Co., 1956), pp. 19, 57–58.

select certain deviant acts as targets for rigorous official action, the criminal justice system makes distinctions among law violators in its routine operations. To the extent that the criminal code and its enforcement are consistent with current public attitudes, the system reflects the relative importance the community attaches to a given norm compared with others. The crystalization of earlier mores into laws, however, tends to undermine a rational ordering of the severity of penal sanctions according to the contemporary social consequences of offenses. Laws against property crimes, for example, that were developed during the more personal age of agriculture are inappropriate in the contemporary urban setting in which property is more portable and entails intangible rights, and there are invisible powers to protect it.[11]

Police officers decry the public tolerance of law violations that undermines law enforcement. The actual behavior of individuals tends to be less conformist than would be indicated by their verbalized support of the official morality. Charles Warriner has hypothesized that this discrepancy is produced by the fear of citizens that community unity would be shattered if, for example, they openly announced their private use of whiskey contrary to a local prohibition law. Furthermore, the specialization of law enforcement has removed it from the direct experience of the citizen, except in the status of complainant or accused person. Bureaucratic processes and the delegation of responsibility to police agents have made crime control activities less personal and familiar to the citizen. Law enforcement becomes the job "they" get paid to do. Finally, vigorous law enforcement may have side effects, such as endangering privacy of the home or threatening civil rights, which tend to make tolerance preferable. Full-scale enforcement might also require revenues which would exceed the taxpayer's willingness to pay and engulf the courts and correctional institutions.[12]

Tolerance also is related to the qualities of some crimes that conceal them from detection. The aggressiveness inherent in the relatively simple techniques of assault, burglary, and robbery make them highly visible crimes. Fraud, embezzlement, and investment swindles, on the other hand, are masked because the behaviors exhibited in these crimes are similar to those of legitimate business. Embarrassment causes victims to be reluctant to report confidence games, extortion, and rape.

The images of "pathological criminals" or a "crime wave" have gripped the imaginations of a fearful public. Strenuous efforts to control crime have resulted, regardless of the small change that has taken place in the

---

[11] For further discussion, see Jerome Hall, *Theft, Law and Society* (Indianapolis, Ind.: Bobbs-Merrill Co., 1952); Hermann Mannheim, *Criminal Justice and Social Reconstruction* (New York: Oxford University Press, 1946), chap. 6.

[12] Charles K. Warriner, "The Nature and Functions of Official Morality," *American Journal of Sociology,* 64 (September 1958): 165–68.

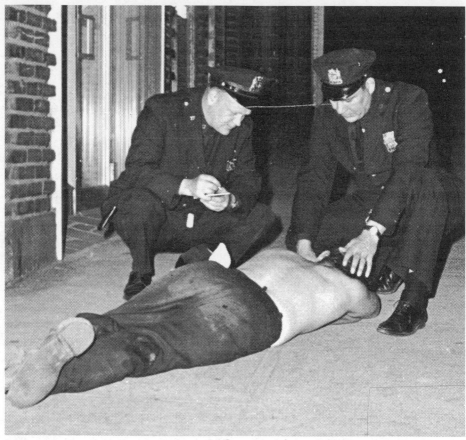

Figure 4–1. Social visibility and crimes against persons.

Crimes against persons have greater social visibility because the injury to the victim is obvious. Is this a victim of murder, a drunken derelict, or an injured accident victim? Whatever the decision, the incident is more likely to be included in police statistics than embezzlement, fraud, and similar crimes which are concealed within the conventional activities of daily life.

actual incidence of crimes. Under pressure to "do something" about "sexual psychopaths" and "habitual criminals," legislators have quickly enacted laws which have become dead letters when in practice they fail to correct the perceived problem.

Normality of crime

Images of "the dangerous criminal" exaggerate actual differences between lawbreakers and "respectable" people. In view of the great variety in human affairs and personalities, it is reasonable to conceive of a range of gradations between the extremes of conformity and nonconformity to social norms. Dennis Wrong has pointed out that, although man is essentially motivated by the desire to achieve a positive image of self by winning acceptance in the eyes of others, role norms do not shape man's behavior entirely. The social values to be supported through conformity to role expectations are challenged by the individual's desires for material and sensual satisfactions.[13] As a concession to the difficulty of always observing rules, Ruth Cavan notes, complete conformity to social norms by all persons is rarely demanded. Instead of reflecting categories of either sainthood or sin, most behavior falls somewhere between strong nonconformity and strong overconformity. Between the sexually aggressive antisocial person and the celibate are various degrees of sexual promiscuity or abstinence from socially approved sexual intercourse.[14]

Criminal behavior itself is normal, Émile Durkheim believes, in that in every society there are men who "draw upon themselves penal repression."[15] Because crimes are related to conditions of collective life, he sees them as a normal symptom of social morbidity. Only when crime rates exceed those usual in a given type of society does the patterning of criminality qualify as abnormality.

Durkheim believes a crimeless society to be a sociological impossibility because of the diversity of factors shaping human personality. Were absolute conformity to norms to be achieved, he fears society would lose the flexibility that comes with innovative violations of norms no longer consistent with current conditions. If the hypothetical society of saints were to emerge, the abhorrence previously directed against murder (now nonexistent) would be shifted against less serious offenses. The reaction against transgressors constitutes a force that strengthens the moral abhorrence of deviance, Durkheim believes.

[13] Dennis H. Wrong, "The Oversocialized Conception of Man in Modern Sociology," *American Sociological Review,* 26 (April 1961): 190–91.

[14] Ruth Shonle Cavan, "What Is Delinquency?" in Edward C. McDonagh and Jon E. Simpson (eds.), *Social Problems: Persistent Challenges* (New York: Holt, Rinehart & Winston, Inc., 1965), pp. 415–24.

[15] Émile Durkheim, *The Rules of Sociological Method,* trans. Sarah A. Solovay and John H. Mueller (Chicago: University of Chicago Press, 1938), pp. 67–71.

Contribution of the audience

The usual conception of the relationship between social norms and criminality, which sees the criminal act as shocking public conscience, emphasizes the lawbreaker's departure from the expectations supported by the criminal law. Reversing this relationship, Durkheim believes the public conscience makes certain behavior a criminal act because it reproves it.[16]

Kai T. Erikson defines *deviance* as conduct "which the people of a group consider so dangerous, or embarrassing or irritating that they bring special sanctions to bear against the persons who exhibit it."[17] To him, deviance is a property (trait or attribute) *conferred upon* that behavior by the people who come in direct or indirect contact with it. Rather than emphasizing the behavior of the person called a criminal, Erikson concentrates on the relationship between that behavior and the standards applied to a person occupying his status in the community. A social audience passes judgment on the deviant. A wide range of evaluations has been applied, for example, to what qualifies legally as theft; i.e., "borrowing" and "swiping" as well as "stealing." The evaluation of the audience determines which definition becomes socially relevant.

In Erving Goffman's terms, the criminal justice system confers on the criminal a *virtual social identity* that is discreditable and socially tainted, regardless of his *actual social identity* (his genuine characteristics). Through the sequence of arrest, jailing, conviction, and imprisonment, the administrative processing of the criminal justice system deprives the accused person of his reputation as a worthy person and places him in the social status of the criminal.[18] The actions taken in a series of *degradation ceremonies* express moral indignation publicly and treat the subject as though his personality and behavior could be completely described by the qualities "the criminal" is supposed to possess.[19] As an "enemy of society," or at least as some kind of social irritant, the accused individual is not seen as a fellow worker, a loving parent, or other type of reputable person, as he could be on the basis of behavior not involved in the criminal act per se.

Further, the accused person is called a criminal and treated as such even when he had no such self-image at the time of the given behavior.

[16] Émile Durkheim, *The Division of Labor in Society,* trans. George Simpson (Glencoe: Free Press, 1947), p. 81.

[17] Kai T. Erikson, *Wayward Puritans: A Study in the Sociology of Deviance* (New York: John Wiley & Sons, Inc., 1966), pp. 6–7.

[18] Erving Goffman, *Stigma: Notes on the Management of Spoiled Identity* (Englewood Cliffs, N.J.: Prentice-Hall, Inc., 1963), pp. 1–5.

[19] Harold Garfinkel, "Conditions of Successful Degradation Ceremonies," *American Journal of Sociology,* 61 (March 1956): 420–24.

For a variety of reasons, he may have broken the law without identifying himself with criminals. The shoplifter or embezzler frequently is surprised when treated as a thief. The differences between primary and secondary deviance have been noted by Edward Lemert. *Primary deviance* is disapproved conduct that does not enlist the self-identification of the transgressor with the deviant role. In *secondary deviance,* the person assumes deviant roles, but only after he has been assigned to a deviant status through the reaction of organized society to his transgression.[20] In reorganizing his attitudes toward himself, the accused person is pressed to accept a criminal status by the problems created by the way organized society reacts to him.

The concentration of certain characteristics among populations of places of penal confinement suggests that the criminal justice system applies screening criteria other than simple violations of criminal laws. A study of the characteristics of the persons sentenced to prison would reveal that they differ from those outside correctional institutions in ways that suggest a greater impact of criminal justice administration on the poor, minorities, homeless men, and other underprivileged groups. Further evidence of how the administrative process fails to be applied equally and constantly lies in the variations in arrest rates and size of prison populations among jurisdictions and over periods of time. A given form of crime draws punishments of various severity in the laws of the 50 states. Drives against gambling, drunkenness, and other kinds of deviance increase the numbers of persons processed, even though the incidence of actual crime has not changed significantly.

Paradoxically, the processes of the criminal justice system and the full force of public abhorrence, which are intended to control crime, can become means of defeating their own purposes when the identity of the accused person is fundamentally transformed to that of the genuine "enemy of society." Such unanticipated consequences illustrate the importance of finding a basis for crime causation in the social structure which, presumably, is being protected by the criminal justice system.

A KEY VARIABLE: SOCIOCULTURAL CONTEXT

A recurrent theme of this book is that criminal behavior is subject to the sociocultural organization of the total society, rather than being merely the individuated behavior of pathological beings.[21] As Part III will develop, criminal and noncriminal personalities are similar in that both are influenced by inherited gene structure and physical qualities, as well as by personality traits acquired through the unique social experi-

[20] Edwin M. Lemert, *Human Deviance, Social Problems, and Social Control* (Englewood Cliffs, N.J.: Prentice-Hall, Inc., 1967), p. 17.

[21] See especially Chapter 10.

ences of the individual.[22] Both are molded by the sociocultural organization toward some degree of conformity with the norms of their statuses
within the social system. The two kinds of personality differ in particular
roles and statuses, the responses of society to their types of behaviors,
and the significance to society of these behaviors.[23]

Other chapters in this section will carry forward the application of
sociological concepts to criminology. Social status is relevant in that variables such as age, sex, race, and socioeconomic level influence the likelihood of criminal behavior, the social form in which lawbreaking is undertaken, and the response of society to the offender.[24] Social institutions
operate within the realm of social control by performing functions designed to help the individual socialize his personality and satisfy personal
wants through conformity to the norms that have been set up to give order
to the social structure.[25] These institutions have traditionally sought the
prevention of crime through informal controls, but such controls have
been found wanting in the regulation of conduct within a culturally
heterogeneous, socially complex, and dynamic urban society. In the modern era, social institutions within the system of criminal justice have developed at a remarkable rate as a result of an increased reliance on formal
controls.

The operations of the components of the system of criminal justice
will be studied in Parts IV and V. The deficiencies of these operations
will be discussed, and possible remedies will be suggested. Part VI will
concentrate on reform, alternatives to imprisonment, and the restructuring of correctional agencies.

SUMMARY

The normative basis of society is relevant to both criminological research and practice, particularly within the sociocultural environment of
an urban society. Ideally, law observance is produced through socialization of personality, general acceptance of preferred norms as binding on
individual conduct, and common agreement on fundamental values.
These means of maintaining social order are taxed by an urban society
characterized by a complex social structure and a high rate of social
change. The criminal law and its implementing agents have been increasingly enlisted in efforts to bring formal control mechanisms to the support of the informal controls exercised by individual conscience. The
involvement of norms in this development is illustrated by changes in the
public tolerance of "crime" and by the consequences that result from the

[22] Chapter 9 will take up the various approaches that emphasize qualities of
the offender as an individual.

[23] The theoretical implications of these distinctions are the topic of Chapter 10.

[24] These matters are taken up in Chapter 5.

[25] These functions of certain institutions are considered in Chapter 6.

conception of deviants as "abnormal." Particularly noteworthy is one effect public outrage has in increasing the dimensions of the crime problem: The stigmatized casual offender is persuaded that he is a full-fledged criminal.

FOR ADDITIONAL READING

Chambliss, William J., and Liell, John T. "The Legal Process in the Community Setting." *Crime and Delinquency,* 12 (October 1966): 310–17.

Clark, Alexander L., and Gibbs, Jack P. "Social Control: A Reformulation." *Social Problems,* 12 (Spring 1965): 398–415.

Coser, James A. "Some Functions of Deviant Behavior and Normative Flexibility." *American Journal of Sociology,* 68 (September 1968): 172–81.

Harp, John, and Taietz, Philip. "Academic Integrity and Social Structure: A Study of Cheating among College Students." *Social Problems,* 13 (Spring 1966): 365–73.

Kitsuse, John I. "Social Reactions to Deviant Behavior: Problems of Theory and Method." *Social Problems,* 9 (Winter 1962): 247–57.

LaPiere, Richard T. *A Theory of Social Control.* New York: McGraw-Hill Book Co., 1956.

Linton, Ralph. *The Cultural Background of Personality.* New York: D. Appleton-Century, 1945.

Nadel, S. F. "Social Control and Self-Regulation." *Social Forces,* 31 (March 1953): 265–73.

Parsons, Talcott. "The Law and Social Control," In W. M. Evan (ed.), *Law and Society,* pp. 56–72. New York: Free Press of Glencoe, 1962.

Rooney, Elizabeth A., and Gibbons, Don C. "Social Reactions to 'Crimes Without Victims.' " *Social Problems,* 13 (Spring 1966): 400–410.

Scheff, Thomas J. (assisted by Daniel M. Culver). "The Societal Reaction to Deviance: Ascriptive Elements in the Psychiatric Screening of Mental Patients in a Midwestern State." *Social Problems,* 11 (Spring 1964): 401–13.

Schur, Edwin M. *Our Criminal Society: The Social and Legal Sources of Crime in America.* Englewood Cliffs, N.J.: Prentice-Hall, 1969.

Toby, Jackson. "Criminal Motivation: A Sociocultural Analysis." *British Journal of Criminology,* 2 (April 1962): 317–36.

Van Vechten, Courtland C. "The Tolerance Quotient as a Device for Defining Certain Social Concepts." *American Journal of Sociology,* 46 (1940): 35–44.

5

Social status and crime

The status of an individual, or his position in the social order in regard to certain attributes, can provide an explanation for the relation of criminal behavior to the sociocultural organization of society. Age, sex, socioeconomic, and racial statuses illustrate the effects of sociocultural organization on the likelihood of a given individual committing a crime, the most probable kind of offense in which he will engage, and the style of response organized society will make to his alleged transgressions.

The social positions occupied by a person are indexes of his power and access to rewards. Age, sex, and race are examples of *ascribed status* to the extent that they are derived from membership in a category regardless of the choice or effort of the individual. Socioeconomic status may be ascribed when the individual's material possessions (or lack of possessions) are treated as proof of his personal qualifications for the honors (or discreditable reputation) which go to those who are "successful" and are denied to the "failures." To the extent that socioeconomic status is produced by individual qualities and efforts, it is an example of *achieved status*. Achieved status is affected by the three ascribed statuses whenever the personal and social characteristics attributed to age, sex, and race influence the individual's behavior and life chances.

AGE STATUS AS A FACTOR

Age is a major status determinant from the perspectives of physiology, psychology, and sociology. Organic growth, maturation, and senescence affect mental and temperamental capacities, as well as the functioning of the body. Certain bodily and mental characteristics are generally common to persons of the same age but different in those of appreciably different ages. The most noteworthy physiological change is the maturation of sex functioning and secondary sex characteristics. Maximum physical efficiency appears to peak at age 25, then decline gradually into the sixties, when the rate of decline accelerates. Psychological tests suggest that learning ability grows rapidly through adolescence and then gradually declines.

Effects of cultural values

Age status systems exist in all societies, but they vary with particular cultural values. American society curiously diverges in its approach to youth. This age group has been protected by increasing the years of compulsory education, restricting early marriage, and extending parental support, even into early marriage. At the same time, increasing freedom from parental control has been granted. This divergence contributes to a lack of clear definitions of the rights and duties of youth and complicates decisions on life's vocation and the selection of a mate. During adolescence, sexual urges and aspirations for adult privileges are experienced before there are socially approved means of gratification.

"Normality" in the middle stages of life involves marriage, parenthood, "success" in gainful employment, demonstrated independence of decision and action, and conformity with norms associated with adult behavior.[1] The obligations of marriage and parenthood demand personal adjustments of those who approach them with the rarified expectations of the "cult of romance." The vigorous twenties and thirties find most American men conditioned to "get ahead" and achieve "success." Those who do not reach the top or fail to maintain a worthy pace in occupational competition face disillusionment in their forties and fifties.

Advanced age brings changes in status within the family and community. Employment is generally ended as a source of income and as a link to a place in the community. Narrowing of the social world lends new significance to family relationships at a time when advancing age may have lowered the individual's status within the family. Senility (a pathological condition) may aggravate conditions.

Crime rates and age

Crime rates vary with the age of the offender. American data show that individuals from ages 15 to 25 have the highest arrest rates,[2] but those younger than 15 are not covered by these reports. Norwegian police data indicate that the number of suspects increases strongly from the age of 5 and reaches maximum frequency at 13 or 14, after which the number

[1] Richard Dewey and W. J. Humber, *The Development of Human Behavior* (New York: Macmillan Co., 1951), pp. 314–16.

[2] See the current issue of the *Uniform Crime Reports,* prepared by the Federal Bureau of Investigation on the basis of data voluntarily submitted by law enforcement agencies.

decreases.[3] British statistics consistently show 13 or 14 to be the peak age for crimes against property, and the coincidence of the peak year with the last year of compulsory schooling, suggesting a relationship between status shifts and the incidence of crime, has been noted.[4] On leaving school, the individual can change his work situation at will, and increased financial resources allow a greater range of leisure pursuits. When the continuity and constancy of interaction with a specific group of peers are reduced, the individual is less vulnerable to delinquency-prone youth groups.

The aging process is related to repetition of crimes. Thorsten Sellin reviewed several European studies to cite evidence that the younger a person is when first convicted, the greater is the likelihood that he will be convicted again and that he will continue to commit crimes over a longer period.[5] In a study of 454 reformatory inmates over 10 years subsequent to parole, Sheldon and Eleanor Glueck found progressive decrease in the incidence of further offenses with increase of age up to age 36. After this age, the improvement in behavior declined markedly. They concluded that this improvement is "very probably a natural accompaniment of the 'settling down' process of growth or maturation" and speculated that the process of maturation ends largely by about the 36th year. Of all the factors they studied, they considered this process to be "the key to an understanding of the reasons for reformation."[6]

Differences in kinds of crime

The offenses of youth (less than 21 years) tend to be against property, while middle-aged adults (35–49 years) and senior adults (over 49 years) are especially prone to commit crimes suggesting personal disorganization. Young adults (21–34 years) are in a state of transition between these two patterns, with crimes of aggression against persons, crimes against property, and crimes of personal disorganization intermingled.

Youths lead in automobile theft, burglary, breaking-entering, and larceny-theft when age groups are compared according to crime rates. They also have a high proportion of arrests for possession of weapons and narcotic drugs.

Young adults have the greatest tendency toward prostitution and com-

[3] Knut Sveri, "Criminality and Age," *Acta Sociologica*, 5 (1961): 76–86.

[4] I. J. McKissack, "The Peak Age for Property Crimes," *British Journal of Criminology*, 7(April 1967): 184–94.

[5] Thorsten Sellin, "Recidivism and Maturation," *NPPA Journal*, 4 (July 1958): 241–50. For later review, see T. C. N. Gibbens and R. H. Ahrenfeldt, *Cultural Factors in Delinquency* (London: Tavistock Publications, 1966), pp. 40–44.

[6] Sheldon and Eleanor T. Glueck, *Juvenile Delinquents Grown Up* (New York: Commonwealth Fund, 1940), pp. 103–6, 200.

mercialized vice, use of narcotic drugs, criminal homicide, offenses against the family and children, forgery and counterfeiting, embezzlement and fraud, aggravated assault, other assaults, and gambling. They also rank high in burglary, breaking-entering, larceny-theft, drunkenness, and driving while intoxicated.

Middle-aged adults have the highest rate for drunkenness, gambling, and driving while intoxicated. They also rank high in embezzlement, fraud, offenses against the family and children, forgery, counterfeiting, and sex offenses other than rape.

Senior adults do not dominate in any of the offenses because of their relatively low incidence of crime. However, their share of arrests is high for drunkenness, vagrancy, gambling, and driving while intoxicated. Youths and young adults jointly dominate forcible rape, other sex offenses, robbery, stolen property, and possession of weapons.

Explanations for age differences

Generally, the more aggressive crimes and crimes against property are committed by younger offenders, while the more sophisticated crimes and crimes of dissipation are characteristic of older persons. The various ways in which these patterns are explained may be summarized under two general approaches.

One approach emphasizes the effect of advancing age in *reducing the likelihood* of attempting crime. Declining physical strength and retardation of physical movement make crime more risky, especially violent and aggressive crimes. Correctional treatment and the gaining of maturity decreases the proportion of persons in each succeeding age group that is prone to crime. The proportion of recidivists drops increasingly in succeeding age groups because they are more likely to be killed or to be imprisoned for relatively longer periods. The pressures toward crime affecting youth are lessened as advancing age reduces the discrepancy between social and economic needs and the means available for their gratification. The interest in religion awakened in some elderly persons may strengthen their resistance to criminality.

A second approach emphasizes the effect of age in *increasing the offender's ability to avoid detection*. Older criminals lack the recklessness and thirst for excitement likely to induce youths to undertake crimes that require vigorous action but are easier to detect. With time, a person is more likely to have an established place in society; he also has greater opportunities to commit crimes within his occupation which are more difficult to detect and prosecute. The youth is less likely to have the job responsibilities that offer the opportunity to embezzle. Antisocial behavior by persons at the extremes in the age continuum tends to elicit less drastic action by the police and the courts than that of persons in the late teens through the fifties. There may be more sympathy for the very young, and the elderly offender may be regarded as less of a threat to society because he has fewer years of life before him.

SEX STATUS AND CRIME

The sex of the individual affects the position he occupies in society and in various groups. Physiologically, sexual differences are related to the childbearing functions and variations in bodily development, but these differences are also subject to cultural norms. While women are supposed to be more delicate and emotional and less aggressive and self-reliant than men, we are witnessing the movement of women into occupations traditionally considered exclusively male, and the most prestigious male occupations today employ intuitive and social skills previously identified with feminine behavior.[7] In the family, the birth process and maternal responsibilities have made the mother's role predominant, but the father is becoming more active in the daily life of the urban family.[8] Genetic differences are not sufficient to explain the differences in set statuses, especially because they vary from one society to another and from one time to another in a society undergoing a high rate of change.

Sex status is of criminological interest because females have a lower probability of becoming subject to the attention of the criminal justice system. Females also differ from males in the kinds of crime they are likely to commit. In both respects, physiological and cultural factors are interrelated in the judgment that crime is more typically male behavior. Physical strength and pugnacity are emphasized in both maleness and crimes such as assault and violent homicide, for example, and, because aggression is assumed to be the male quality and passivity the female quality in sex relations, rape is a male crime.

Differences in crimes perpetrated

Female crimes usually are unique in type of victim and offender's methods. Otto Pollak found that in only infanticides and abandonment of children was there a definite preponderance of women offenders.[9] The victims of crime committed by women are likely to be drawn from those with whom they have the most frequent contact, such as family members and lovers; the female pickpocket is an exception.[10] In crimes against

[7] Charles Winick, "The Beige Epoch: Depolarization of Sex Roles in America," *Annals of American Academy of Political and Social Science,* 376 (March 1968): 19.

[8] Leonard Benson, *Fatherhood: A Sociological Perspective* (New York: Random House, 1968), pp. 37–73, 85–89.

[9] Otto Pollak, *The Criminality of Women* (Philadelphia: University of Pennsylvania Press, 1950), p. 92.

[10] Ibid., p. 13.

property, a woman is more likely to be an accessory than a full participant in robberies and burglaries. Women are likely to be receivers of goods stolen by their families rather than professional fences.

As compared with men, women on the average begin their crimes at an older age, and they tend to continue high crime rates into more advanced ages. Pollak has explained this pattern as the effects of the physiological crises undergone by older women and of the greater protection of girls than boys in the years of youth.[11] His first explanation draws on physiological factors related to age status, and his second is based on cultural implications of differences between the sexes in family expectations for adolescent roles.

The traditional dependent and passive role of females has limited their economic and occupational self-sufficiency. Edwin Schur suggests that this limitation protects them from the social pressures conducive to the offenses characteristic of males as economic providers who face occupational stresses and opportunities for crime. Prostitution and abortion, on the other hand, are examples of offenses related to the economic and sexual subordination of women. Women frequently play an accessory or instigator role in crimes perpetrated by males. Ironically, Schur notes, to the extent that modern woman is able to gain sexual equality she is likely to achieve also her full share of criminality, because cross-cultural data show greatest differences between the sexes in crime roles in countries where women are kept in a closely protected subordinate status.[12]

accomodation

Reasons for fewer female convictions

Some offenses are dominated by males to a greater extent than others, when measured by official crime statistics. Predominately male offenses include burglary and breaking-entering, automobile theft, robbery, weapons, and driving while intoxicated. While prostitution and commercialized vice are primary female offenses, men are behind the scenes as panders and managers. There is a relatively high proportion of women among persons arrested for embezzlement and fraud, forgery and counterfeiting, and larceny-theft, and for sex offenses other than rape, such as offenses against chastity, common decency, and morals. A study of juveniles reported that delinquency rates for males were higher than for females for all offenses, with the difference in frequency least marked for hit-and-run accidents and nonmarijuana drug activities.[13]

Female felons differ from their male counterparts in several respects. The crimes for which females are imprisoned are more likely to be seri-

[11] Ibid., p. 104.

[12] Edwin M. Schur, *Our Criminal Society* (Englewood Cliffs, N.J.: Prentice-Hall, Inc., 1969), p. 43.

[13] Michael J. Hindelang, "Age, Sex, and the Versatility of Delinquent Involvements," *Social Problems,* 18 (Spring 1971): 522–35.

ous offenses. Larceny, forgery, manslaughter, aggravated assault, and murder account for a larger share of female than male felon commitments to state prisons. Women offenders are also likely to receive shorter sentences. They are slightly older, more largely drawn from black populations, and less likely to be single in marital status.

These comparisons of male and female offenses reflect the operations of the system of criminal justice, not the relative probability that either sex will engage in law violations. The enactment and enforcement of criminal law assume that crime is a male behavior. Physiologically, assault and violent murder are considered to be expressive of male physical strength and pugnacity, and rape is deemed characteristic of male sexual aggression. Culturally, the male is seen as breadwinner; he is more likely to be prosecuted for nonsupport, than the wife or mother. The female is expected to be passive and dependent, and male chivalry calls for lenient treatment of most female offenders. Female transgressions are also more likely to be treated lightly because it is assumed that women behave irrationally. The male victim of a female offender risks ridicule if he reports the crime, and he may fear that her arrest will cause her to make unsubstantiated charges against him. Reporting the crime may bring clandestine sex behavior to light, or it may be inferred to the disadvantage of male victims.

The traditional association of women with the home, as a homemaker or domestic employee, gives them an advantage in concealing their crimes from official attention. Infanticide, abortion, blackmail, and sex offenses by women against their children are difficult to detect. Because of the difficulty of distinguishing the legitimate but absent-minded shopper from the shoplifter, stores are reluctant to prosecute for this crime, which is particularly prevalent among women. The relatively personal employer-employee relationship in domestic employment makes prosecution of household thieves unlikely.

The facts noted above that women receive shorter sentences than men and that a greater proportion of female felons imprisoned are committed for serious offenses are evidence that women offenders are treated with greater leniency. There is a reluctance to impose the stigmatization of arrest, conviction, and incarceration on women. In California, it has been found that the ratio of boy to girl offenders is lower for offenses that prompt less severe community reaction. The ratio of boys to girls was 9 to 1 for police arrests, 4 to 1 for referrals to probation departments, and 2 to 1 for dependency and neglect cases.[14]

Factors other than leniency are involved in differential crime rates for males and females. First, many of the offenses frequently committed by women are among those most likely to be underreported in criminal

[14] Joseph W. Eaton and Kenneth Polk, *Measuring Delinquency* (Pittsburgh: University of Pittsburgh Press, 1961), p. 19.

statistics: shoplifting of nonprofessional character, thefts by prostitutes, domestic thefts, abortions, infanticide, perjury, and disturbance of the peace.

Second, the female may be subjected to greater parental supervision so that she is less likely to be delinquent. Joseph Eaton and Kenneth Polk found differences among the three major ethnic groups of Los Angeles County in the relative frequency of female juveniles being referred for probation. The male rate was 3.7 times as great as the female rate for Anglo-whites, 4.4 times for blacks, and 6.2 times for Mexican-Americans. This suggests that the blacks and Mexican-Americans were more effective in controlling girls than boys.[15]

Third, the sex of the offender influences the kind of complainant who initiates the process of treating the case as a delinquency or crime. For example, one of the significant differences between boys and girls adjudged to be delinquent is that petitions relating to girls are most often made by the parent, usually the mother, and petitions relating to boys are most often made by law enforcement officials. Under these circumstances, the girl's case is more likely to be viewed as a symptom of family disorganization and less likely to elicit a punitive reaction.

SOCIOECONOMIC STATUS

The social class system operates as a ranking device that has great influence on the social experiences of the individual. Each person is assigned a status at birth based on the status of his family, his place of residence, his nativity, and his race. In an open class system such as ours, his status can be changed through personal achievement as evaluated on the basis of relative wealth, occupation, talent, formal education, or membership in groups with power. Attached to his class status are norms which he learns through socialization within his family and other intimate groups.

Deprivation and socialization

As a motivation for crime, poverty is a relative matter. The millionaire down to his last swimming pool may feel underprivileged, while another man deems himself successful if he is able to purchase a battered automobile. The crux of the concept of *relative deprivation* is that the given individual (or group) considers himself underprivileged when he compares his lot with some desired standard. The sense of deprivation is dependent on a comparison of the imagined situation of some other person or group serving as the basis for comparison.[16]

15 Ibid., pp. 19–21.
16 W. G. Runciman, *Relative Deprivation and Social Justice* (London: Routledge and Kegan Paul, 1966), p. 10.

The standard against which poverty is determined is subject to economic and cultural changes. Inflation of prices undermines the appropriateness of absolute income levels in fixing the poverty line. Material possessions are a badge of a "decent" standard of living under criteria which are periodically redefined culturally. Today a refrigerator is accepted as such a criterion, whereas an icebox or a pail suspended in a well was acceptable in earlier days. Recently, economic deprivation in terms of inferior access to decent housing or a good education has become associated with social injustice, intolerable for a democracy. Greater emphasis is being placed on society's responsibility for its members, and less on holding the poverty-stricken individual solely responsible for his circumstances.

Socioeconomic classes differ in child-training practices, values, conceptions of parental roles, and social sources of anxieties. These differences have sometimes been cited as evidence in support of the argument that variances in crime rates among the social classes are produced by differences in toilet training, occupational and educational expectations, attitudes toward physical aggression, respect for private property, or patterns in expenditure of income. Subcultural theories (to be considered in Chapter 10) argue that lower-class parents are more likely to employ physical punishment and middle-class parents psychological punishments based on withholding love and instilling a sense of shame. It has been suggested that when physical punishment is employed regularly, the punisher is more clearly defined as an external target for the child's aggression and as a behavior model for the physical expression of aggression.[17]

In summarizing studies over a 25-year period, Urie Bronfenbrenner noted that middle-class parents were consistently found to be more acceptant and equalitarian and working-class parents more oriented toward maintaining order and obedience through reliance on physical punishment. From about 1930 until the end of World War II, working-class mothers were more permissive in feeding, weaning, and toilet training. In the postwar period, however, middle-class mothers became the most permissive in these respects.[18] Bronfenbrenner attributed this change to the greater access of middle-class parents to publications and professional counsel on infant care and child rearing. In the same vein, Melvin Kohn believes middle-class parents are more likely to discuss their children's behavior with friends, neighbors, and teachers, but working-class parents are more likely to retain traditional methods because of lower educational

[17] Martin Gold, "Suicide, Homicide, and Socialization of Aggression," *American Journal of Sociology,* 63 (May 1958): 651–61.

[18] Urie Bronfenbrenner, "Socialization and Social Class through Time and Space," in Eleanor E. Maccoby, Theodore M. Newcomb, and Eugene L. Hartley (eds.), *Readings in Social Psychology,* 3d ed. (New York: Holt, Rinehart, & Winston, Inc., 1958), pp. 424–25.

attainments, more routinized job experiences, and the middle-class orientation of family experts.[19]

Studies have demonstrated that delinquent and criminal behaviors are not limited to the lower economic classes. In comparing the classes, Albert Cohen guessed that "conceivably" a greater proportion of the delinquencies of the working-class children, as compared to those of upper-class children, is not reported.[20] Walter Reckless's speculation that both the upper and lower classes have high risks of crime compared with the middle class is based on two assumptions. First, the upper classes are exposed to opportunities for evasions of taxes, misuse of professional knowledge and skills, and other examples of "white-collar crimes." Second, the middle-class subculture, to an important degree, insulates it against activities usually treated as crimes.[21]

Socioeconomic status and crime rates

Socioeconomic status affects the likelihood that a deviant will be included in official rates of delinquency and crime. In their study of "Yankee City," W. Lloyd Warner and Paul S. Lunt found that arrest rates decline consistently with increased social class status, and the lower classes undergo 90 percent of the arrests while composing only 57.8 percent of the population.[22] Cyril Burt found that poor or very poor families represented less than one third of the population of London but contributed over half the total volume of delinquency.[23]

Many studies have assumed that official statistics accurately reflect the extent and distribution of crimes among the social classes. Because of the distortions of arrest, judicial, and prison statistics, the conclusions are questionable. They describe the functioning of the system of criminal justice more accurately than the actual incidence of crime. The offenses of the lower classes are more subject to police scrutiny, and members of these classes have deficient resources for evading punishment when apprehended. Studies show infractions of the middle and upper classes are grossly underestimated by arrest rates.[24]

---

[19] Melvin L. Kohn, *Class and Conformity: A Study in Values* (Homewood, Ill.: Dorsey Press, 1969), pp. 5–7.

[20] Albert K. Cohen, *Delinquent Boys: The Culture of the Gang* (Glencoe, Ill.: Free Press, 1955), pp. 37–41.

[21] Walter C. Reckless, *The Crime Problem,* 4th ed. (New York: Appleton-Century-Crofts, 1967), pp. 109–12.

[22] W. Lloyd Warner and Paul S. Lunt, *The Social Life of a Modern Community* (New Haven, Conn.: Yale University Press, 1941), p. 376.

[23] Cyril Burt, *The Young Delinquent* (New York: D. Appleton Co., 1929), pp. 65–66.

[24] For example, see Robert Dentler and Lawrence J. Monroe, "Early Adolescent Theft," *American Sociological Review,* 26 (October 1961): 733–43; Martin

One study sought a more reliable answer than that provided by arrest statistics.[25] Samples of high school students were drawn in six western and midwestern cities ranging in size from 10,000 to 25,000. Father's occupation was utilized as an index of the socioeconomic level of the children. Four status groups were established: (1) unskilled and semi-skilled labor (e.g., migratory worker to restaurant cook); (2) skilled labor and craftsmen (e.g., housepainter to linotype operator); (3) white-collar and small business (e.g., newspaper columnist to owner-operator of a mine); and (4) professional and large business (e.g., interior decorator to U.S. Supreme Court justice). No significant difference was found in delinquent behavior of boys and girls in different socioeconomic strata.

The general applicability of the conclusions of this study were questioned by John P. Clark and Eugene P. Wenninger, for several reasons.[26] First, samples were drawn from communities ranging only from rural to small city. Second, these communities lacked sufficient concentration of persons in the extremely high and low classes. Third, the lower class of rural communities would be more likely to have low rates of misconduct. Therefore, Clark and Wenninger submitted a questionnaire that asked for self-reporting of crimes to public high school students (6th through 12th grades) in four communities chosen to represent four unique social class structures: rural farm, lower urban (heavily unskilled occupations), industrial city, and upper urban (heavily executive and professional). They reported that the incidence of most self-reported offenses became greater, especially the more serious offenses and those requiring more sophistication, as the comparison moved from rural farm to upper urban to industrial city and to lower urban.

Clark and Wenninger see several implications in their data. First, they suggest that illegal behavior in small communities or "status areas" of a large metropolis is related to the community-wide norms to which juveniles adhere regardless of their social classes. Apparently, the community's population must reach some size (they suggest 40,000) before social class becomes a significant factor in delinquencies. Second, it is possible that nuisance offenses are committed by all youngsters, but lower-class juveniles in large urban areas are likely to perpetrate serious offenses. Third, it appears that the social class that dominates a community largely determines the nature of the delinquency. Supposedly,

Gold, "Undetected Delinquent Behavior," *Journal of Research in Crime and Delinquency,* 3 (January 1966): 27–46; Albert J. Reiss, Jr., and Albert L. Rhodes, "The Distribution of Juvenile Delinquency in the Social Class Structure," *American Sociological Review,* 26 (October 1961): 730–32.

[25] F. Ivan Nye, James F. Short, Jr., and Virgil J. Olson, "Socioeconomic Status and Delinquent Behavior," *American Journal of Sociology,* 63 (January 1958): 381–89.

[26] John P. Clark and Eugene P. Wenninger, "Socio-Economic Class and Area as Correlates of Illegal Behavior among Juveniles," *American Sociological Review,* 27 (December 1962): 826–34.

lower-class boys living in a middle-class community are either not participants in the lower-class culture or are dominated culturally by the numerically predominant middle class. This interpretation would suggest that only a large metropolis could produce the large and relatively homogeneous areas conducive to development of a delinquent subculture among lower-class adolescents.

Socioeconomic status and delinquency areas

"Delinquency area" has been used to describe sections of the city assumed to produce delinquents because of physical deterioration, high proportion of population on welfare rolls, and high proportion of ethnic and racial minorities.[27] These factors work against the consistent cultural standards and the social life that are conducive to acceptance of middle-class norms supported by laws.[28] The problem of the slum, according to Herbert Gans, lies in the economic and social conditions that produce it, not in the symptom of obsolete housing which looms so large to middle-class observers.

Thus the risk of delinquency is affected by the range of residential choices available to a family. Inadequate housing has been described as a source of stress in that overcrowding and poor sanitation can undermine the family as an agency of social control. A study of the English town of Croydon found delinquency rates to be significantly greater for overcrowded homes.[29] Baltimore's census tract data also indicated high correlations between overcrowding, substandard housing, and delinquency, but physical and economic aspects of housing were not associated with delinquency when other factors were held constant, indicating that social factors of housing, rather than the economic level of the community, are related to delinquency.[30]

It is doubtful that bad housing in itself is a direct cause of distorted personality and antisocial behavior, but it does have less direct social effects. First, the immediate physical environment may affect the child's emotional security. Cramped living quarters are supposed to cause tensions and conflicts among family members, and the lack of privacy may cause the child to witness taboo behavior. Second, the lack of living space and the deteriorated appearance of the residence dissuade children from entertaining friends at home. This reduces the parents' knowledge of the

[27] Clifford R. Shaw and Henry D. McKay, *Juvenile Delinquency and Urban Areas* (Chicago: University of Chicago Press, 1942), pp. 435–36.

[28] Herbert J. Gans, *The Urban Villagers: Group and Class in the Life of Italian-Americans* (New York: Free Press, 1962), pp. 142–55.

[29] Terence Morris, *The Criminal Area* (London: Routledge and Kegan Paul, 1957), p. 169.

[30] Bernard Lander, *Towards an Understanding of Juvenile Delinquency* (New York: Columbia University Press, 1954), pp. 78–80.

child's activities outside the home, which become more frequent when the street becomes a refuge.[31] Third, the home usually reflects the physical nature of the immediate neighborhood. Inadequate housing, therefore, suggests a neighborhood environment adverse to the development of wholesome attitudes and values. Fourth, the disrepair of the home may be symptomatic of the irresponsible attitudes of the adult residents and family disorganization.

The relationship between socioeconomic status and crime operates within a social structure which systematically maintains the frustrations of poverty beyond lack of money alone. The services the contemporary community is supposed to provide citizens to help them cope with the personal problems which collectively constitute community issues are deficient in low-income neighborhoods. The curious lack of awareness of slum conditions among outsiders, except for policemen, vote-seeking politicians, and other occupational groups with a specific mission, has been noted.[32] Pessimism, passivity, and cynicism about organizations are responsible for the withdrawal of slum residents from outsiders, and alienation is a vehicle for keeping residents locked into the narrow world of the ghetto.[33] Poverty becomes a trap maintained by a social structure that sets criteria for admission to socioeconomic opportunity which the poor are unlikely to be able to meet: effective literacy, knowledge of testing techniques, ability to satisfy screening requirements for applicants for training jobs, or access to information on opportunities. A system of economic exploitation also feeds on the poor through consumer fraud, overpricing, and exorbitant rentals for substandard housing.[34]

There are inherent inequities related to socioeconomic status in the administration of criminal justice (see in Part IV). Law enforcement is brought to bear disproportionately on the lower classes because of the greater visibility of the kinds of offenses they are most likely to perpetrate. The divergence of their subcultural norms from those of the dominant classes is also a factor. Bail practices and the importance of representation by counsel work to the disadvantage of the economically underprivileged trial defendant.

The medical care system also is deficient in providing preventive care and outpatient services for the poor.[35] Socioeconomic status is an important variable in decreasing the probability that the individual will receive

[31] Alvin L. Schorr, "Housing the Poor," in Warren Bloomberg, Jr., and Henry J. Schmandt (eds.), *Urban Poverty: Its Social and Political Dimensions* (Beverly Hills, Calif.: Sage Publications, Inc., 1970), pp. 206–8.

[32] David R. Hunter, *The Slums: Challenge and Response* (New York: Free Press, 1964), pp. 33–34.

[33] Bonnie Bullough, "Alienation in the Ghetto," *American Journal of Sociology*, 72 (March 1967): 469–78.

[34] David Caplovitz, *The Poor Pay More* (New York: Free Press, 1968).

[35] John A. Ross, "Social Class and Medical Care," *Journal of Health and Human Behavior,* 3 (Spring 1962): 35–40.

treatment that will deter him from expressing his personal maladjustments in law violations. The lower the social class status of the mentally ill person, the less available is effective psychiatric care.[36] Not only is the lower-class person less willing to accept the middle-class orientation of the helping professions, but social agencies tend to prefer the nonpoor as clients for this reason.[37]

CRIME AMONG BLACKS

Crime among blacks may be studied as a topic in itself and as a part of the broader relationship between personal qualities and crime. For both the criminal and the black, integration into society rests on personal qualities and behavior, yet little opportunity is given either to demonstrate worthiness. Both "the Negro" and "the criminal" are victims of stereotypes—false images acquired when increased social distance weakens the capacity of members of two conflicting groups to perceive each other as unique personalities. These stereotypes stigmatize their targets, ignoring variations between individuals while they exaggerate negative qualities and underestimate positive ones. The hostilities of the victims of such stereotyping are aroused against the social values they are expected to support in order to qualify for full citizenship.

Quirks of statistics

A number of factors related to the inferior socioeconomic status of blacks complicate the determination of reliable facts on which to base comparison of the incidence of crimes by blacks. They also hinder interpretation of the significance of patterns in such incidence.

First, census and criminal statistics are based on the popular conception of race rather than on an anthropological differentiation. The popular approach classifies the individual as black if there is any degree of known black ancestry. On the basis of Melville J. Herskovits's estimates of the racial composition of the American population, almost 40 percent of the "black" offenders are at least half white.[38] If a person were defined as "black" only when his ancestry was at least half black, a large proportion of "black" crime would be transferred to other racial categories.

Second, crimes of blacks against whites are of more concern to local

[36] James T. McMahon, "The Working Class Psychiatric Patient: a Clinical View," in Frank Riessman, Jerome Cohen, and Arthur Pearl (eds.), *Mental Health of the Poor* (New York: Free Press, 1964), p. 284.

[37] Richard A. Cloward and Irwin Epstein, "Private Social Welfare's Disengagement from the Poor: The Case of Family Adjustment Agencies," in George A. Brager and Francis P. Purcell (eds.), *Community Action against Poverty* (New Haven, Conn.: College and University Press, 1967), pp. 40–63.

[38] Melville J. Herskovits, *The Anthropometry of the American Negro* (New York: Columbia University Press, 1930), p. 177.

officials than are crimes of blacks against blacks. In at least some areas, the former are treated with unusual severity and the latter with unusual leniency. These patterns may cancel each other out, but more probably, since the major share of crimes by blacks is against other black persons, the crime rates understate the situation.

Third, comparisons of white and black crime rates fail to take into account the differences between the populations in economic, educational, and other characteristics that influence exposure to risk of criminality.[39] For example, because of their higher death rates, blacks usually have a greater concentration in the younger age groups where arrest rates are higher.

Fourth, the higher prison commitment rates of blacks reflect in part inferior community facilities and specialized institutions for blacks with social problems that are not usually included within the scope of crime. The prison serves as a dumping ground when social problems previously ignored are recognized. Increased urbanism requires the community to take formal action to deal with the mentally defective, the sexually deviant, the alcoholic, the irresponsible parent, and the psychotic. When there are no institutions specializing in such problems and when informal procedures no longer suffice, the jail or prison may serve as an expedient, particularly among the socially and economically underprivileged.

Fifth, FBI statistics are weighted heavily by urban crime patterns of the North and West, exaggerating to some degree the incidence of black crime. The instabilities encouraged by the heavy black migration to these areas are given undue influence in national statistics. Similarly, the stability of the rural South works against recognition in FBI statistics of the lower crime rates among southern rural blacks.

Patterns of crime among blacks

Blacks are arrested and sent to prison in greater numbers than their share of the total population would indicate.[40] They are more likely to be arrested for every offense reported to the FBI, but the likelihood varies among the various offenses. This variance demonstrates that a simple biological explanation is insufficient to explain the higher crime rates among blacks.

When offenses are ranked in order of rate of incidence for each race, it is found that the two races bear strong resemblance in their tendencies toward certain crimes. Generally, whites have high rates for the same crimes in which blacks have high rates, and lower rates for those in which

[39] Edward Green, "Race, Social Status, and Criminal Arrest," *American Sociological Review*, 35 (June 1970): 476–90.

[40] Morris A. Forslund, "A Comparison of Negro and White Crime Rates," *Journal of Criminal Law, Criminology, and Police Science*, 61 (June 1970): 214–18.

blacks have lower rates. When offenses are compared on the basis of race, blacks rank perceptibly higher than whites in relative size of rates for gambling, aggravated assault, weapons, and robbery. Whites rank perceptibly higher for automobile theft, driving while intoxicated, embezzlement and fraud, forgery and counterfeiting, and sex offenses other than rape. However, the rankings of the other offenses within each race are similar.

Generally, the difference between the races is greater for crimes against persons than for crimes against property. The ratio of black to white arrests for robbery is high, but this crime includes elements of aggression against persons. Since crimes against property show the lowest percentage of offenses cleared by arrest, this tendency has the result of including more black offenders in arrest statistics than white offenders.

The crimes of blacks against persons are directed largely against members of their own race. Of 108 admitted to North Carolina prisons for first degree murder between 1950 and 1960, 96 had been convicted of slaying another black.

In crimes against property, the arrest ratios show a relative underrepresentation of blacks among automobile thefts, embezzlers, and forgers. This reflects the dominance by whites of white-collar jobs offering opportunities for embezzlement and forgery. William Wattenberg and James Balistrieri have offered as one explanation for the relatively smaller importance of automobile theft among blacks the point that white delinquents are more likely to define the automobile as a prestige symbol among peer groups.[41]

Causes of crime among blacks

Are crimes among blacks symptoms of something inherent in the black individual or reflections of something he experiences in a special way or to an unusual degree? Are they a product of his race or his environment?

As a biological concept, race is a plastic and relative term. Migration and other contacts between peoples have eliminated pure races and complicated the study of physical anthropology. In fact, Herskovits has described the American black as a new racial type.[42] A case can be made that race is more myth than scientific fact,[43] but color nevertheless causes the black to be treated as a separate social entity.

To prove that black criminal behavior is caused directly by the biology

[41] William F. Wattenberg and James Balistrieri, "Automobile Theft: A 'Favored Group' Delinquency," *American Journal of Sociology,* 57 (May 1952): 575–79.

[42] Melville J. Herskovits, *The American Negro* (New York: Alfred A. Knopf, Inc., 1928), pp. 9 and 33.

[43] M. F. Ashley-Montagu, *Man's Most Dangerous Myth: The Fallacy of Race* 4th ed. (Cleveland: World Publishing Co., 1964).

of race, it would be necessary to establish certain facts. First, blacks would have to be shown to be of a single personality type. They are not. Second, the effects of environmental circumstances and differential operation of the system of justice would have to be canceled out. Third, it would be necessary to rule out the influence of minority status itself on behavior. The black may become criminal because he is denied full opportunity and citizenship on the basis of biological criteria, not because he embodies such criteria. Fourth, it would be necessary to prove that other races would not behave the same as blacks if they were placed in the same circumstances. Fifth, behavior among blacks often is judged according to white middle-class norms of thrift, ambition, abstinence, and sexual behavior. Since lack of social acceptability is not the equivalent of criminality, it would be necessary to rule out the influence of differential morality.

Finally, if the relationship between blacks and crime were a simple biological one, it would be necessary for race to change as differences in the definition of crime arise over time and space. Racial changes, however, are accomplished through mutation and amalgamation, processes which are relatively slow.

Certain factors in the black's environment have an effect on his likelihood of becoming a crime statistic.

"Black culture."   The cultural hypothesis contends that crimes among blacks stem from unique personality traits produced by traditions brought from Africa and nurtured in slavery. It is assumed that unique patterns of thought have been handed down through the generations to make blacks more emotional, less provident, and more inclined toward violence and unrestrained sexual behavior. In fact, however, slavery stripped the American black of his African heritage.[44] The recent efforts of blacks to gain the socioeconomic privileges esteemed in American culture are evidence of their acceptance of it.

Low socioeconomic status.   Gunnar Myrdal sees crime among blacks as the result of inferior socioeconomic status.[45] He reports that upper and middle classes among blacks are at least as law-abiding as their white counterparts. Race, however, is a factor in determining socioeconomic status. The burden of discrimination and the effects of poverty combine to create conditions that enhance the possibility of a black turning to crime because of a discrepancy between his aspirations and his resources for attaining them. In 1947 average family income was $2,801 for nonwhites and $5,478 for whites. In 1970 the respective averages were

[44] E. Franklin Frazier, *The Negro Family in the United States* (Chicago: University of Chicago Press, 1932), chaps. i and ii.

[45] Gunnar Myrdal, *An American Dilemma* (New York: Harper & Bros., 1944), p. 979.

$6,516 and $10,236. Although the discrepancy has been reduced, nonwhites continue to lag to a marked degree in access to financial resources.[46]

Migration and urban disorganization.   Since World War II, American blacks have shaken loose from rural localism in the South to migrate to cities and to the North and West.[47] The American black migrant has faced a specific problem of assimilation because, in the historical context of racism, his physical characteristics mark him as a social stranger. The adjustment to urban areas of the North and West is also a special challenge to the black migrant because the southern rural racial caste system handles informally many of the vices prevalent in lower-class black groups. The black committing a minor offense in the city must adjust to a formal police reaction to his transgression.

The present-day lack of moral consensus has a greater impact on deteriorated areas where inferior economic means force migrants into substandard housing. Environmental factors of such areas encourage personal tendencies toward crime. These influences are not limited to black persons, but racial discrimination increases the likelihood that the black migrant will be thrust into such areas.

Family disorganization and poverty.   Family disorganization probably has figured more largely in crimes of blacks than of whites. Among blacks, it has stemmed from slavery and its influences on the contemporary racial caste system, from the effects of the southern plantation and sharecropper economy, from the instability deriving from emancipation and migration, and from the low average socioeconomic status of the black.

Under slavery the mother was the pivot of the black family. The father's role was rather casual and easily interrupted. The survival of the matriarchal family is shown by the larger proportion of families with a female head among blacks than among whites. However, the matriarchal family is not characteristic of all blacks. In fact, a variety of family types exists. The small patriarchal family in which the father assumes economic responsibility and authority is found particularly among middle-class blacks. The extended family, encompassing four generations, exists among many families in the rural South. Upper- and middle-class blacks have accepted the equalitarian family.

The effect of family disorganization on black crime rates appears to be the same as on those of whites. The uniqueness lies in the greater impact of socioeconomic influences, past and present, on black family life. Increased geographical mobility has exerted new pressures on family

[46] U.S. Bureau of the Census, *The Social and Economic Status of Negroes in the United States,* 1971 Special Studies, Current Population Reports, Series P–23, No. 42, July 1972, Table 17.

[47] Ibid., p. 1.

stability and has exposed black families disproportionately to the disorganizing effects of defective community life.

SUMMARY

Although age, sex, and race are physical characteristics, their relationship to crime is largely sociocultural. They can be measures of an individual's position in the social order, or his status. Together with socioeconomic status, they affect social relationships within the setting of a society.

The status categories are criminal behavior determinants because they affect the likelihood that an individual will engage in crime and, if he does, the kind of crime he is most likely to perpetrate. They also affect the nature of society's response to crime. By focusing on each of the four status categories, this chapter has demonstrated how the patterns of the relationship of status to crime affect both criminals and noncriminals in a sociocultural system.

FOR ADDITIONAL READING

Bullock, Henry Allen. "Significance of the Racial Factor in the Length of Prison Sentences." *Journal of Criminal Law, Criminology, and Police Science,* 52 (November–December 1961): 411–17.

Carr-Saunders, A. M., Mannheim, Hermann, and Rhodes, E. C. *Young Offenders.* New York: Macmillan Co., 1944.

Chambliss, William J., and Nagasawa, Richard H. "On the Validity of Official Statistics—A Comparative Study of White, Black, and Japanese High School Boys." *Journal of Research in Crime and Delinquency,* 6 (January 1969): 71–77.

East, W. Norwood. "Crime, Senescence, and Senility." *Journal of Mental Hygiene,* 90 (October 1944): 835–50.

Epstein, Cynthia F. *Woman's Place.* Berkeley: University of California Press, 1970.

Fishman, Leo (ed.). *Poverty Amid Affluence.* New Haven: Yale University Press, 1966.

Friedan, Betty. *The Feminine Mystique.* New York: Dell Publishing Co., 1963.

Harrington, Michael. *The Other America.* Baltimore: Penguin Books, 1963.

Lens, Sidney. *Poverty: America's Enduring Paradox.* New York: Thomas Y. Crowell Co., 1969.

McDonald, Thomas D. "Correlates of Civil Rights Activity and Negro Intra-Racial Violence." Ph.D. dissertation, Southern Illinois University, Carbondale, Ill., 1972.

Moberg, David O. "Old Age and Crime." *Journal of Criminal Law, Criminology, and Police Science,* 43 (March–April 1953): 764–76.

Schultz, Leroy G. "Why the Negro Carries Weapons." *Journal of Criminal Law, Criminology, and Police Science,* 53 (December 1962): 476–83.

Tregar, Harvey. "Reluctance of the Social Agency." *Federal Probation,* 29 (March 1965): 23–28.

West, D. J. *The Young Offender.* Baltimore: Penguin Books, 1967.

Willie, Charles V. "The Relative Contribution of Family Status and Economic Status to Juvenile Delinquency." *Social Problems,* 14 (Winter 1967): 326–35.

Wolfgang, Marvin E. *Crime and Race.* New York: Institute of Human Relations Press, 1964.

6

Social institutions
and crime

Criminology, particularly its correctional aspects, fits within the context of the study of social control. The enforcement of enacted laws and the imposition of legal penalties are a phase of a process in which norms are seen as means of maintaining order and regularity in human relationships.

The two preceding chapters illustrated how criminological issues are involved in the sociocultural organization of society at large by demonstrating the relationships between norms, status, and sociocultural issues. This chapter moves up the ladder of abstraction to examine the involvement of criminal behavior and crime control in the operation of social institutions, a framework within which social norms affect behavior.

Norms become institutional when they are supported by an effective consensus of society and backed by severe penalties against violators. Institutional norms are related to each other in definite patterns which sociologists call "social institutions." Each such institution can be viewed as a complex of norms centering around relatively distinct values and regulating the modes of meeting important recurrent situations.[1]

Somewhat as a seismograph measures and records earthquakes and tremors, the functioning of social institutions gives out signals about the community's success in preventing and controlling crime and delinquency. Edgar May cites the public welfare department as a measuring device that records the tremors of a faulty school system, the closing of a factory, the layoffs caused by automation, and the distinctions made because of the social status of the individual.[2] The institutions included in the criminal justice system also record such tremors: Police blotters and court records reflect the application of criminal law by social institutions of formal control to individual deviations from the norms that criminal statutes and ordinances are designed to safeguard.

[1] Robin M. Williams, Jr., *American Society: A Sociological Interpretation,* 3d ed. (New York: Alfred A. Knopf, Inc., 1970), pp. 37–38.

[2] Edgar May, *The Wasted Americans* (New York: New American Library, 1964), p. 188.

Compared with the institutions of criminal justice, the social institutions of the family, school, church, and mass communications are less obviously related to the control of crime and delinquency. Nevertheless, they also provide signals about the community's success in preventing and controlling deviance, and their functions are fundamental to the study of crime causation.

EFFECTS OF FAMILY RELATIONSHIPS

Every individual is simultaneously a member of a family system and of a social class system. The family's functions are procreation and socialization, while the class system serves as a ranking device.[3] The relationships between the two systems have important implications for the personality development of the child and, consequently, for the study of crime. First, the status of the family in the social structure affects the child's experiences and problems in relationships outside the family. Second, the family serves as a screen between the child and the extrafamily environment. Family experiences shape the way the child perceives and evaluates the world and help determine his capacity to deal with situations.[4] Third, through the family the child is introduced to his culture and gains competence in living within its normative restrictions. The family is expected to inculcate respect for the social conventions. Fourth, family life is supposed to gratify the child's need to be wanted, to have his accomplishments recognized, and to attain a secure place in the world.

Crucial position of the family

As a social institution, the American family has undergone fundamental changes. Economic, educational, protective, and recreational functions have been supplemented, and in some ways supplanted, by other institutions. Whereas the earlier farm family produced much of the goods and services it consumed, the contemporary family as an economic unit can be viewed largely in terms of expending income acquired by the work activities of its members outside the home. The school and the state have assumed many functions in preparing the young for adulthood and in protecting family members from enemies, disease, and want. Commercialized and public recreational programs operate outside direct family control. Urban incentives for birth control, changing sex mores, and new courtship patterns have fundamentally altered the place of the family in regulating sexual behavior.

[3] August B. Hollingshead, "Class Differences in Family Stability," in Herman D. Stein and Richard A. Cloward (eds.), *Social Perspectives in Behavior* (Glencoe, Ill.: Free Press, 1958).

[4] Albert K. Cohen, *Delinquent Boys: The Culture of the Gang* (Glencoe, Ill.: Free Press, 1955), p. 77.

The family is in a particularly strategic position to serve as an instrument for adapting to new conditions because it has the functions of socializing its members for adult roles and mediating between its members and the changing demands of other social institutions. Clark Vincent finds these interdependent functions to be especially important because the family typically adjusts itself to the demands of other institutions. An example of the revision of family norms is the switch from the economic and religious arguments that a high birth rate is congenial to general social interests to the viewpoint that a low birth rate is economically and morally superior. The family also tends to serve a primary adaptive role because it lacks organizational spokesmen such as are found in business, educational, religious, and governmental affairs, and its resistance to change is therefore reduced.[5]

Proposed solutions to social problems such as crime and delinquency usually either indict the failures of the family or would have the family assume the major burden of the social impact of the proposals. Urban renewal forces the lower-income family to move and thus lose its cultural setting. In lieu of custodial institutions, families are urged to take a more direct part in caring for the aged, the mentally ill, and the convicted offender. Vincent notes a pattern in this kind of recognition of the importance of the family in which the marital relationship—the most persistent element in family life—plays second fiddle to the interests of individual members in roles of primary interest to particular reform groups. The mental illness or criminality of the inmate of a custodial institution, the alcoholism or drug abuse of the family member, or the ennui of the factory worker are the chief concern. Vincent calls for greater concentration on strengthening "marital health" itself rather than simply assuming its existence, as is done in proposals of criminological reformers that the family's participation in delinquency prevention programs be increased or that it assume caretaker functions in probation and parole.

Family relations and deviance

Delinquency frequently is attributed to a lack of agreement on values or a confusion of values among family members. Family anomie, as evidenced by ineffective integration of the family with the outside community and insufficient norms for the regulation of intrafamily relationships, is believed to undermine the effectiveness of the family in forestalling juvenile delinquency. Lester Jaffe reports that in his group of research subjects, high value confusion scores were significantly associated with family difficulties such as marital conflict, crowded homes, marginal income, irregular employment of father, and serious illness.

---

[5] Clark E. Vincent, "Mental Health and the Family," *Journal of Marriage and the Family,* 29 (February 1967): 18–39.

These difficulties also were associated with high scores in delinquency proneness.[6]

While the parent may be a direct agent in turning the child toward delinquency by teaching or praising antisocial behavior, it is more likely that he will have a less direct influence. Hurt in his own experiences, the parent may express hostility against schools, churches, places of employment, and other community institutions. Children of such parents are stimulated to strike back at the world, to mistrust others, and to evade rules. If the child finds his parents are not trustworthy, he may lose the ability to trust any person of primary importance to him. The parent may create a poor model for moral behavior by boasting of a "smart deal." Children may be denied satisfaction of their material, physical, and emotional needs because of parental neglect. At the other extreme, the parent may set the level of expectation too high for the child's capacity and exert excessive pressures for conformity.

Believing that delinquency is associated with a general withdrawal from family life and an indifference to family expectations, Peter Venezia developed a test for measuring the amount of knowledge the individual has of the members of his family. Respondents were asked where their parents met, what their brothers do in their free time, and the street address of the father's job. When the test was applied to juvenile delinquents, it was found they had significantly less family information than nondelinquents used as a control group.[7]

Data of the Cambridge-Somerville Youth Study were used in findings that sons of criminals had a significantly higher incidence of criminality than did sons of noncriminals. However, sons of criminals who had rejected them had a significantly higher rate of criminality than did sons who enjoyed warm or passive relationships with their criminal fathers. The adage "like father, like son" is only part of the story. It cannot be assumed that criminals' sons become criminals as a result of an affectionate bond with their fathers. It is more likely that rejection by the father creates aggressive tendencies channeled into crime because the father serves as a criminal model.[8]

Studying adults sentenced initially sometime after marriage, researchers have provided evidence that family conflicts are also related to adult criminality, although juvenile delinquency is more frequently cited as a product of family conflict. Four groups of adult crimes related to family conflicts were differentiated. One group consists of criminality located entirely within the family circle: incest, murder of spouse, nonsupport,

[6] Lester D. Jaffe, "Delinquency Proneness and Family Anomie," *Journal of Criminal Law, Criminology and Police Science,* 54 (June 1963): 146–54.

[7] Peter S. Venezia, "Delinquency as a Function of Intrafamily Relationships," *Journal of Research in Crime and Delinquency,* 5 (July 1968): 148–73.

[8] Joan and William McCord, "The Effects of Parental Role Model on Criminality," *Journal of Social Issues,* 14 (1958): 66–75.

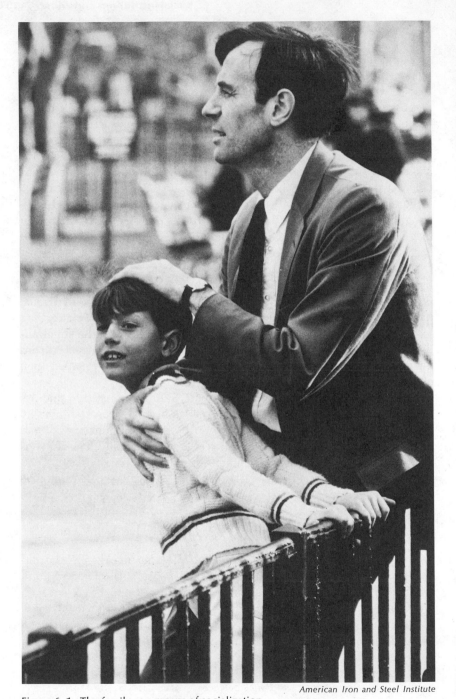

Figure 6–1. The family as a means of socialization.
The family serves as the primary agency for socialization vital to delinquency prevention. The affectionate bond of father and son is a component in family relationships which helps determine the course of personality development.

assault, and abusive behavior. Another group is characterized by acting-out criminal behavior within the home which spills over into check forgery, drunken driving, and similar offenses in the community. A third group encompasses criminal behavior entirely outside the family, but the offenses are symptomatic of family conflicts or problems. The fourth consists of offenses related to stable marriages in which feelings of inadequacy in individuals culminate in excessive stress that produces criminal acts outside the home.[9]

Broken homes

Virtually all studies of delinquents or adult criminals report a high incidence of broken homes. When death, desertion, divorce, or long separation cause the absence of one or both parents, the child is supposedly subjected to economic handicaps, loss of affectional relationships, and inadequate socialization. The relationship between broken homes and delinquency, however, is more complicated than is ordinarily assumed.

The child accused of minor infractions is more likely to be referred to the court if there is evidence of inadequate control because of a broken home, while the father's promise to make restitution is more likely to bring release of the child from the unbroken home.[10] Parents or neighbors may make complaints to the police with less provocation when children from broken homes are involved. It may be that single parents are more likely to go to the police when children defy them. It has been reported that ungovernability, as a broad category, is characteristic of delinquents from broken homes and that boys from broken homes more frequently openly defy parents.[11]

Compared to the higher-income family, the economically marginal family suffers more severely from the loss of the breadwinner. Since income is related to status, the marginal family is also more likely to experience a loss in prestige. Furthermore, the one-parent family with low income faces difficulties in providing an adequate environment for meeting emotional and socialization needs. Living in impoverished and disorganized areas of the city, the child of such a family lacks opportunity and incentive to participate in the activities of character-building institutions, and he is more vulnerable to the influences which divert spontaneous play groups into delinquency.

Simply reporting the proportion of delinquencies among children from

[9] Bruno M. Cormier et al., "Family Conflicts and Criminal Behavior," *Canadian Journal of Corrections*, 3 (January 1961): 18–37.

[10] Philip M. Smith, "Broken Homes and Juvenile Delinquency," *Sociology and Social Research*, 39 (May–June 1955): 309.

[11] F. Ivan Nye, *Family Relationships and Delinquent Behavior* (New York: John Wiley & Sons, Inc., 1958), pp. 42–45.

broken homes does not test the question whether such homes have greater potentiality for producing delinquents. Studies indicate that broken and unbroken homes do not differ significantly in this regard.[12] The effect of the broken home lies in its impact on the particular child. Although separation from parents erodes some of the child's confidence in relationships with others, Gordon Trasler found the quality of the child's environment before and after the event to be more crucial in determining the child's psychological disturbance than the fact of separation from his parents.[13] A study of juvenile probationers indicated that boys in intact but emotionally adverse homes were significantly more disturbed than those from broken but not adverse homes.[14] Information on family income of children referred to courts was used to determine that the proportion of children from broken families and the seriousness of offense decline with greater family income, indicating that income level is more important than family composition in affecting referral for delinquency.[15]

Are parents to blame?

The past hundred years have brought a gradual reduction in the absolute authority of parents over their children. Paradoxically, the failure of some parents to live up to the expectations of their increasingly difficult role continues to draw imputations of personal, psychological, or moral inadequacies. While the moral stigmatization of being jobless has been eased in recognition of the fact that impersonal economic factors affect employment, a similar recognition of the great forces impinging on family life has not been extended to parents.[16]

Factors beyond the control of parents may weaken their capacity to meet the child's needs and to help solve the problems he encounters outside the home. Increased employment away from home has deprived the family of much of its control over its immediate environment. More frequent contacts outside the home and local neighborhood have reduced family control over conduct.

It is doubtful that the "woodshed for parents" approach will reduce

[12] Richard S. Sterne, *Delinquent Conduct and Broken Homes* (New Haven, Conn.: College & University Press, 1964); Nye, *Family Relationships and Delinquent Behavior.*

[13] Gordon Trasler, *In Place of Parents: A Study of Foster Care* (London: Routledge & Kegan Paul, 1960), p. 230. Also see Lee Burchinal, "Characteristics of Adolescents from Unbroken, Broken, and Reconstituted Families," *Journal of Marriage and the Family,* 26 (February 1964): 44–51.

[14] D. H. Stott, "Family Situations Conducive to Behavior Disturbance in Delinquents," *Social Work,* 10 (April 1965): 14–17.

[15] Roland J. Chilton and Gerald E. Markle, "Family Disruption, Delinquent Conduct and the Effect of Subclassification," *American Sociological Review,* 37 (February 1972): 93–99.

[16] V. George, *Foster Care: Theory and Practice* (London: Routledge & Kegan Paul, 1970) p. 219.

the incidence of delinquency. Automatic infliction of punishment on parents of delinquents risks making them scapegoats for community failure to provide services for treatment of the fundamental causes of delinquency. Parents may be motivated to increase pressure on children when in fact such pressure itself was a factor in the delinquency. Children may regard punished parents as martyrs, thus strengthening their adverse influence. When parents lack the motivation and knowledge to meet their responsibilities, there is a need for more subtle and continued efforts than coercion. However, legal authority can be applied fruitfully in carefully selected cases as a means of gaining parents' participation in long-term treatment.[17]

Increased employment among mothers has been cited as a major factor in delinquency, due largely to a belief that normal socialization and personality development are blocked by the mother's absence from the home during the day. Elizabeth Herzog questions this view, citing cultures where "nannies" and other mother substitutes have been used without impairing the healthy personality development of the children. She notes that some women are better mothers if their mothering activities are only part time. The effects of daily separation from the mother depend on the prevalence of this pattern in the local community, the quality of the provisions made for child care, and the mother's attitude toward the child.[18] Eleanor Maccoby suggests that the mother's sporadic employment and her child's delinquency are interrelated because both stem from the same family characteristics, such as lack of family self-respect or affection, emotionally disturbed husbands, or poor work habits of husbands. Maccoby believes that if the working mother arranges adequate care for her child in her absence, the child is no more likely to be delinquent than is the adequately supervised child of a nonworking mother.[19]

FORMAL EDUCATION AND CAUSES OF CRIME

Of the extrafamily agencies, the school has the closest contact with children over the longest period of time. Because education has assumed the largest share of the responsibility of inculcating a sense of civic responsibility, it is a means of social control.

With the emphasis for "success" in society based on technical competence gained through formal and specialized training, the school plays a major role in determining who will rise in class status and who will not.

[17] Helen L. Witmer (ed.), *Parents and Delinquency* (Washington, D.C.: Department of Health, Education, and Welfare, 1954), pp. 15–24.

[18] Elizabeth Herzog, *Children of Working Mothers* (Washington, D.C.: Department of Health, Education, and Welfare, 1960), pp. 18–20.

[19] Eleanor E. Maccoby, "Children and Working Mothers," *The Child,* 5 (May–June 1958): 84.

It is a gateway to opportunity for those able to survive its academic and personality testing. The school also can restrict upward mobility when its curriculum is irrelevant to the adult experiences its pupils will have and when graduates are eligible only for "blind alley" jobs.

The school and delinquency

Major educational changes are crucial if effective prevention and reduction of delinquency are to be achieved. While changes also are necessary in other social institutions, evidence strongly suggests that delinquencies do result at least in part from negative or adverse school experiences and fundamental defects within the educational system, especially in its impact on lower income youth. Walter Schafer and Kenneth Polk have made an inventory of education's defects: (1) the accumulation of pupil tensions from the conflict between high value placed on educational achievement and the middle-class standards imposed on pupils conditioned to lower-class values, (2) the reinforcement of a feeling among some pupils that school experience is fundamentally irrelevant to later life, (3) insufficient opportunity in schools for children to gain a sense of commitment to community values which their families and neighborhood do not develop, and (4) the school's participation in the rejection of "troublemakers" by the community at large, setting the stage for delinquency.[20]

Delinquents generally are retarded in their studies and are apt to find school a continuing irritation and threat to their sense of worth.[21] It should not be assumed that all dropouts are delinquency prone or that they are a homogeneous group lacking aptitudes. However, analysis of dropouts reveals the strong etiological similarity to delinquency: low socioeconomic status of the pupil's family, low intelligence of many adolescents leaving schools, lack of motivation and related poor school performance, emotional instability and personality defects, ineffective adjustment of instruction and subjects to pupil needs, lack of participation in extracurricular activities, disinterest in subjects, grade retardation, unsympathetic attitudes of parents to education, broken homes, feeling of not "belonging" in the classroom, vague academic or vocational plans, and truancy.[22]

[20] Walter E. Schafer and Kenneth Polk, "Delinquency and the Schools," in President's Commission on Law Enforcement and Administration of Justice, *Task Force Report: Juvenile Delinquency and Youth Crime* (Washington, D.C.: U.S. Government Printing Office, 1967), pp. 223–34.

[21] Bruce Barlow, "Delinquency and School Failure," *Federal Probation,* 25 (June 1961): 15–17.

[22] William C. Kvaraceus, *Juvenile Delinquency* (Washington, D.C.: National Education Association, 1958), p. 17; George C. Brook, "High School Drop-Outs and Corrective Measures," *Federal Probation,* 23 (September 1959): 33.

Identification of personality problems

Even before truancy signals maladjustment, the school is in a position to identify children with problems and channel them toward the community programs designed to provide services that can prevent later frustrations and deviant behavior. There are estimates that a fifth of school populations is disturbed enough to require guidance, and about a tenth needs clinical treatment.[23]

In school the child is initiated into the world outside the family and is exposed to the necessity of conforming to other rules than those of his family. His later experiences with authority are colored by his experiences in the school. The teacher has the problem of molding a variety of youngsters into a group pursuing systematically the set of tasks determined for the particular school grade. The imposition of arbitrary rules too often transforms the classroom into a setting characterized by monotony, regimentation, and authoritarianism.

Because he has the most frequent one-to-one contacts with the child, the classroom teacher can recognize the maladjusted child and assist him in cultivating good social relationships. Recognition of the individual qualities of the pupil is essential, especially when the child brings hostilities and tensions to school. Opportunities for achievement must be geared to the child, if he is not to feel threatened or guilty. While general policies, standardization of techniques, and routine procedures promote effective organization for large schools, when used indiscriminately they handicap the classroom teacher's efforts to tailor his methods to the particular child.

School as a treatment resource

Because the school's interest in the development of the child is generally recognized, it has unique advantages for treatment aimed at prevention of delinquency. When a social worker is identified with a school, the parents are more likely to accept treatment services without fear that the child will be stigmatized. The skilled and understanding teacher can use the discipline and privileges of the school setting to stimulate and support the child in working out his problems. The teacher can offer treatment workers valuable information on the child's behavior and probable treatment needs. The school's social, recreational, medical, and remedial activities can be used to meet the individual needs of the child.[24]

The possibilities of the school as a treatment center are suggested by

[23] Robert M. MacIver, *The Prevention and Control of Delinquency* (New York: Atherton Press, 1967), p. 105.

[24] Sybil A. Stone, Elsa Castendyck, and Harold B. Hanson, *Children in the Community* (Washington, D.C.: U.S. Children's Bureau, 1948), pp. 91–92.

projects in two communities, Quincy, Illinois, and New York City. In Quincy, the approach was to revise the school program as a means of meeting the needs of maladjusted children more adequately. Two ninth-grade experimental classrooms were established. Sixty eighth graders were chosen as being below average in ability and school performance. Most of the children were school discipline problems, and 41 percent had police or court records. The group was divided randomly into three groups of equal size. The control group continued regular classes. Each of the other two groups spent half to three quarters of their day with a teacher chosen because of her interest in and sympathy for the problem child. Every effort was made to make their learning a pleasant experience, and they were not pushed to learn. Generally, the special program appeared to influence the interests, attitudes, and aggressive behavior of the children more than their academic achievements or personality patterns. The delinquency rate of the experimental groups declined more than a third, while the rate more than tripled for the control group.[25]

The project in New York City was based on broadening the function of the school within the community by extending the length of the school day and increasing the involvement of parents in school and community affairs.[26] The schools were in areas of a low socioeconomic level where children have limited cultural backgrounds and where the school is apt to be the only institution trying to meet their needs. Each of the six grades of a school had an extra teacher who worked with small groups of children and provided a recreation program of dramatics, dancing, painting, carpentry, and similar activities. Committees of parents and other interested individuals solicited volunteer helpers for the school and publicized the program. The project had several objectives. Because the size of classes was reduced, the regular teacher was able to give more individual attention to pupils. Education and recreation were made a single comprehensive experience, so that the group teacher was able to experience the child as a whole personality. A psychiatric social worker provided assistance during the day. Through alliance of teacher and social worker, the school reached out to assist disturbed children who might not be reached by traditional casework services.

Social class and the school

Children from different social classes react to school in different ways. Pupils in lower-class neighborhoods frequently regard it with indifference.

---

[25] Paul Hoover Bowman, "Effects of a Revised School Program on Potential Delinquents," *Annals of the American Academy of Political and Social Science,* 322 (March 1959): 60–61.

[26] Adele Franklin, "The All-Day Neighborhood Schools," *Annals of the American Academy of Political and Social Science,* 322 (March 1959): 62–68.

The emphasis in schools on middle-class values further reduces the identification of the lower-class child with the activities of formal education. Stephen Abrahamson has reported "overwhelming evidence" that middle-class pupils are more likely than lower-class pupils to receive high grades.[27] A study of marks in English provided evidence of a significant negative correlation with juvenile court records and serious delinquencies. It was not clear whether higher grades were conferred because of the advantage of middle-class conditioning in preparing children for school or whether there was an unconscious discrimination in conferring marks.[28]

Why should middle-class standards enter into evaluation of pupils? Albert Cohen suggests these reasons: The teacher is hired by the school system, which is dominated by middle-class people, to indoctrinate the children in middle-class aspirations, character, skills, and manners. The teacher himself is almost certain to be a middle-class person, and his career rests on middle-class criteria. The teacher is likely to favor "well-behaved" pupils over those who are "lazy" or boisterous.[29] Since the teacher is likely to prefer to instruct pupils sharing his class orientation, the school in the lower-class neighborhood tends to draw less than its share of competent teachers.

Another study indicates that school vandalism tends to be highest when teacher morale is low and there is a minimum of contacts between teachers and parents. Vandalism is also greatest at schools in areas with low socioeconomic status and high community instability.[30] This suggests that teacher morale, family identification with the school, and quality of community life are related to delinquency.

Assuming that delinquency rates are inflated by socially underprivileged ghetto youth, a research project followed 13- and 14-year-old educationally and socially maladjusted youths through their 18th and 19th years. Although most of these probable "losers" in adult life wanted to be part of the group, the researchers report, they did not know how to measure up to the school's expectations, and they met formidable obstacles in facing the problems of trying to grow up. Lack of appropriate male role models worked against opportunities to be worthy men. Frequent change of residence and parental indifference to schooling complicated the boys' adjustment to school. The ghetto neighborhood exposed them to a high risk of getting into "trouble" and delinquency and to a

[27] Stephen Abrahamson, "Our Status System and Scholastic Rewards," *Journal of Educational Sociology,* 25 (April 1952): 441–50.

[28] A. Lewis Rhodes and Albert J. Reiss, Jr., "Apathy, Truancy and Delinquency as Adaptations to School Failure," *Social Forces,* 48 (September 1969); 20–21.

[29] Cohen, *Delinquent Boys,* pp. 113–14.

[30] Nathan Goldman, *A Socio-Psychological Study of School Vandalism* (Syracuse, N.Y.: Syracuse University Research Institute, 1959), pp. 20–24 and 107–8.

sense of alienation from the larger society. The boys were encouraged to believe that luck or the power of alien people had more to do with their fate than their capacity to control their environment rationally.[31]

ORGANIZED RELIGION AND CRIME

For many, the teachings of the church offer the best guide to enduring meanings of human life, aspiration, suffering, and death. The believer gains personal and social security. The self-control practiced by adherents and the application of sanctions against deviants have enabled organized religion to contribute to societal cohesion, especially in times of crisis. The churches' primary contribution is their universal belief in the dignity and worth of the individual person.[32] In addition, the humanitarianism of those who are religiously motivated often has eased the impact of economic want and social deprivation.

Religion and deviance

The effectiveness of religion as an answer to crime and delinquency has been blunted by the imperialism of religious groups who identify "morality" with conformity to their own standards and self-interests; by the substitution of membership in a particular denomination for profound personal religious belief; and by the value conflicts and intergroup tensions characteristic of the heterogeneous cultures of urban societies. Joseph Fitzpatrick, S.J., sees religious belief as a profoundly personal experience that can lead to identification of the ultimate purpose of life with the Divine. This belief can be expressed in a self-disciplined, self-denying search for personal and social perfection.[33] Such a search can be a means of social control when the norms associated with religious belief are consistent with the social order and with the socialization of personality to accommodate the needs of that order.

Religious belief can be the means of strengthening ingroup solidarity by mobilizing self-satisfying individual efforts for the general welfare. It lends itself to both informal and formal controls based on humanitarian and other ideals. On the other hand, in a society characterized by tensions between groups and conflicting cultural orientations, the moral force of

[31] Winston M. Abstrom and Robert J. Havighurst, *400 Losers: Delinquent Boys in High School* (San Francisco: Jossey-Bass, Inc., 1971), pp. 221–22.

[32] Robert and Muriel Webb, "How the Churches Can Help in the Prevention and Treatment of Juvenile Delinquency," *Federal Probation,* 21 (December 1957): 22.

[33] Joseph P. Fitzpatrick, S.J., "The Role of Religion in Programs for the Prevention and Correction of Crime and Delinquency," in President's Commission on Law Enforcement and Administration of Justice, *Task Force Report: Juvenile Delinquency and Youth Crime* (Washington, D.C.: U.S. Government Printing Office, 1967), pp. 317–22.

Curtis and Davis, Architects (Frank Lotz Miller)

Figure 6–2. A modern setting for spiritual experience.

Modern architectural design is employed to express the power of religious belief to tie the individual to society. Such a symbol is the chapel at the Fox Lake Correctional Institution in Wisconsin.

religion may be employed to impose the self-interests of the dominant segment of society upon other groups. American history includes the examples of witchcraft trials, the appeals of white supremacists to the Gospel, and the use of theology to regulate recreational and work activities in ways congenial to the vested interests of employers.

Religious denomination or membership in a church are simple indexes that are easy to use in the administration of any policy that requires distinctions among individuals on the basis of religious belief. They also are obvious standards in research into the effects of religious distinctions on the behavior of individuals or the activities of programs. Because religious affiliation and church membership, in and of themselves, are not reliable measures of religion as a personal experience, however, these indexes are subject to moral imperialism and to the error of mistaking overt behavior for sincere inner convictions. Much of the research on the relationship between religion and delinquency makes this error,[34] and declining church attendance is often cited by social critics who attribute "rising crime and immorality" to an erosion of religiosity.[35]

Even when the persistence of the society gives evidence of widespread consensus, urban societies are subject to religious tensions and conflicts because of the complexity of their structure and the heterogeneous subcultures within them. Migration and differential birth rates may upset the balance among groups of differing religious affiliations. Conflicts among the social classes and economic interest groups are likely to be colored by differences in religious perspectives on drinking, sexual behavior, access to economic opportunity, education, and similar matters which can become public issues. These conflicts increase the probability that religion will be used for the protection of class position or special socioeconomic interests.

Implications for crime control

Most of the studies on the relationship between religion and social deviance assume that religious affiliation or church attendance measures inner religious conviction. Generally, therefore, they indicate that religiosity lacks strong effects, positively or negatively, on delinquency and crime.[36] One study suggests that religious behavior is not a unified character trait to be related directly and simply to delinquency and that religious belief can be regarded as completely distinct from the practice of "deceit" in situations of daily life.[37]

[34] Ibid., pp. 317–18; Hermann Mannheim, *Comparative Criminology* (Boston: Houghton Mifflin Co., 1965), pp. 570–71.

[35] Travis Hirschi and Rodney Stark, "Hellfire and Delinquency," *Social Problems,* 17 (Fall 1969): 202–3.

[36] Fitzpatrick, "Role of Religion," pp. 317–18.

[37] Hugh Hartshorne and Mark A. May, *Studies in the Nature of Character,* Vol. 1, *Studies in Deceit* (New York: The Macmillan Co., 1928).

Nevertheless, the employment of religion as a factor in crime control has tended to emphasize exhortation and denunciation as though proclamation of "the Word" would divert youth from delinquency and return the fallen to the path of righteousness. Some judges have transmitted records of defendants to clergymen or have required church attendance as a condition of probation. Prisons have required church attendance and have identified it as evidence of character change, although the trend in correctional institutions is away from such a policy. Mandatory church attendance, in fact, can be considered an infringement of religious liberty because it involves lending official authority to pressures toward routinized religious conformity.[38] The advisability of applying exhortation and denunciation has been questioned when previous moral sanctions failed to produce inner conviction in an individual; intensification of such pressures is unlikely to bring meaningful conformity in such cases.[39]

The organized church overlooks its potential as a community force for the prevention of delinquency when the pastor is concerned with the immediate personal problems of church members to the exclusion of far-reaching community issues. The movement of churches from deteriorated urban areas as they follow the bulk of their congregations to the suburbs has left those behind without church support. When the activities of a church are irrelevant to both individuals' problems and community issues, alienation is increased as a possible source of antisocial behavior.

Fitzpatrick cites examples of churches that have utilized the principles of psychological intervention and community organization in coordinated community programs of delinquency prevention and correction. He believes that a sense of religious identification can play a significant role, in conjunction with the strength and solidarity of the racial or ethnic community, in developing and reinforcing a sense of identity. In such a setting, religious identification can be a means of helping the individual recognize that others care about him. These are ways in which religious programs can contribute to the prevention and correction of social deviation.[40]

Religion and penological history

The idea of prisoner rehabilitation has roots in religion. The idea of reformation has been traced to Hosea, who conceived of God's wrath against unfaithful Israel as punishment to purify and redeem, rather than

[38] Don J. Hager, "Religion, Delinquency and Society," *Social Work,* 14 (July 1957): 16–21.

[39] Richard V. McCann, "The Self-Image and Delinquency: Some Implications for Religion," *Federal Probation,* 20 (September 1956): 23.

[40] Fitzpatrick, "Role of Religion," pp. 323–30.

destroy, her.[41] Before the scientific method was generally recognized, religious faith in universal salvation was sufficient to give popular justification to the idea that criminals are not incorrigible.

The Quakers accorded America a prominent place in penological history with their development of the Pennsylvania system in the late 18th and early 19th centuries, which relied heavily on solitary confinement as a means of moral regeneration (see Chapter 16). Throughout the history of American and English prisons, the influence of Quakers has been strong, particularly in relation to their numbers. This is explained in part by their own persecution in England prior to emigrating to America, when thousands were thrust into jails. Their leader, George Fox, wrote judges from his filthy cell to protest jail conditions and the execution of minor offenders. William Penn was a prisoner in the Tower of London. Elizabeth Fry worked in Newgate prison from 1813 until her death in 1845 to establish a school, religious services, and an industrial program and give moral support to prisoners.[42]

The core of Puritanism was an intense zeal for salvation, both one's own and the community's. Some of this zeal was directed to the challenge of vested injustice. One religious justification for reforming criminals was that neglect and bad usage by the community made it in part responsible for the sins of its "children." By espousing the "social gospel," clergymen pricked the popular conscience and used the teachings of Jesus to further humanitarian enterprises.[43] Beginning around 1800, Gospel revivals stimulated lower socioeconomic groups to express in religious terms the equalitarian ideals of the American Revolution.[44] With equal ardor, however, religion was employed to inhibit change and to establish conservative control to counteract the ferment of the 19th century. Laymen and clergy alike saw the inculcation of Protestant morality as a means of restoring stability, sobriety, and safety. These contrasting uses of religion have left their mark in the use of moral judgments by both humanitarians and conservatives in arguments over such issues as capital punishment, objectives of prison discipline, and the conceptions of the offender.

Morality by persuasion and by compulsion became a major characteristic of American life in the 19th century, when ardent believers in Protestant theology formed societies, subsidized Gospel preachers, circulated Bibles, and issued tracts against war, liquor, and slavery. Initially, the benevolent societies emphasized persuasion. Religious arguments were

[41] John L. Gillen, *Criminology and Penology* (New York: D. Appleton-Century, 1945), p. 221.

[42] Henry Van Etten, "Prisons and Prisoners," in John Kavanaugh (ed.), *The Quaker Approach* (New York: G. P. Putnam's Sons, 1953).

[43] Arthur M. Schlesinger, *The American as Reformer* (Cambridge, Mass.: Harvard University Press, 1951), pp. 12–14.

[44] Gunnar Myrdal, *An American Dilemma* (New York: Harper & Bros., 1944), pp. 10–11.

supplemented by horror stories of the evils of slavery and drink. Workers were urged to advance their own economic interests by keeping the Sabbath, paying their debts, and being obedient and faithful employees.[45]

The failure of moral persuasion brought political action by 1840 to push national and state governments to compel morality. The force of the law was directed against gambling, drinking, sexual irregularity, family nonsupport, and other "immoral" behaviors. These efforts produced the "revolving door" jail, to which alcoholic offenders are sentenced repetitively, and encouraged the naïve belief that humanitarian sentiments were sufficient to ensure penal reform and efficient prison administration.

Religious interest in criminals, however, has been the impetus for programs of prisoner rehabilitation. Emphasis on charitable tolerance, education, and the conversion of sinners has stimulated interest in rehabilitation. Genuine religious conversion can be analogous to the changes in attitudes and values sought in secular terms by rehabilitation programs. Membership in a church congregation affords a sense of belonging, a means of acquiring the status of an accepted person, and a follow-up device through which the released prisoner can be integrated into the community.[46]

Religious spirit has stimulated individuals and groups to become concerned about the welfare of prisoners, in the face of general indifference. Their efforts have ranged from religious exhortation to case work. The Philadelphia Society for the Relief of Distressed Prisoners gathered food and clothing for jail inmates before the American Revolution.[47] The Quakers have a long record of service. Since 1885 the Salvation Army has worked in correctional institutions and provided services for the released prisoner and the inmate's family.[48] Volunteers of America, founded by Maud Booth after an 1896 visit to Sing Sing penitentiary, sponsors prison visitation, preparole investigation, job placement, and other services.[49]

MASS COMMUNICATION MEDIA

The word "communication" carries the meaning of the establishment of a common understanding among beings. In this sense, the institutions of mass communication are crucial to the social interactions which con-

[45] Clifford S. Griffin, *Their Brother's Keepers* (New Brunswick, N.J.: Rutgers University Press, 1961), pp. x–xiv and 104–9.

[46] The prison chaplain's role is discussed in Chapter 20, pp. 504–5.

[47] Harry Elmer Barnes and Negley K. Teeters, *New Horizons in Criminology,* 3d ed. (Englewood Cliffs, N.J.: Prentice-Hall, Inc., 1959), pp. 548–59.

[48] J. Stanley Sheppard, "Religion and Crime," in Vernon C. Branham and Samuel B. Kutash (eds.), *Encyclopedia of Criminology* (New York: Philosophical Library, Inc., 1949).

[49] John F. McMahon, "The Work of the Volunteers of America in the Field of Correction," *American Journal of Correction,* 25 (May–June 1963): 24–29.

vert a heterogeneous collection of human beings into a society. Complex normative systems characterize the organized activities of these institutions, which employ the technologies of printing and electronics.

The significance of mass media

Newspapers and periodicals, motion pictures, and radio and television programming comprise the social institutions of mass communication. "Mass" is the linkage between these media and the urban society they serve. Impersonal messages are transmitted by a complex organization of vocational specialists and received almost instantaneously by a large, relatively anonymous and heterogeneous audience.[50] A large number of specialists develop and transmit the messages within the structure of a bureaucratic organization that is expensive to create and maintain. The high cost of employing such media makes it advisable to assemble the largest possible audience from the array of groups in a heterogeneous society differentiated according to age, sex, occupation, and other variables. The larger the audience, the lower the per unit cost of producing the issue of the newspaper or particular television program. Both high costs and complexity of operations tend to orient these institutions to their economic self-interests. Such an orientation can dominate actual management practices and run counter to the disinterested public service that the ideals of democracy would foster in agencies of mass communication.

The pervasiveness of mass communications can be suggested by certain statistics on American television. With 96 percent of homes having one or more television sets, the programming is watched for at least two hours a day by most adults and children. Frequent viewing begins at about age 3, remains high until about 12, declines during the teen years, increases in the middle adult years, and rises again in later ages.[51] Consciously or unconsciously, the mass media disseminate information that is crucial to coordination of the complex urban social system and to the functioning of a democratic political order.

The pervasiveness of mass communications inevitably links it with the widespread social problem of delinquency and crime. Curiously, most attention has been concentrated on the possibility that the mass media will increase the numbers of criminals by fostering social deviance and undermining authority. Both those who fear the effects of mass media and those who extol their usefulness in extending the cultural horizons of man see them as acting powerfully and directly to stimulate predictable

[50] See, for example, Charles R. Wright, *Mass Communication: A Sociological Perspective* (New York: Random House, Inc., 1959), pp. 13–16.

[51] Surgeon General's Scientific Advisory Committee on Television and Social Behavior, *Television and Growing Up: The Impact of Televised Violence* (Washington, D.C.: U.S. Government Printing Office, 1972), pp. 2–4.

reactions from an atomistic mass of consumers.[52] This view overstates the power of mass media and underestimates the influence of both the consumer's preexisting attitudes and the environment within which the message is received.

Those who are suspicious of the effects of mass media raise three major questions about their relationship to crime:

1. Do the mass media encourage the development of attitudes and behavioral tendencies favorable to law violations?
2. Do the mass media teach the techniques of crime and delinquency?
3. Do the mass media erode the strength of moral values which stand against the spread of crime?

These questions share the idea that the function of mass media should be to support the established order and to forestall deviation from its norms. In the assessment that follows, the view is taken that the mass media are not all-powerful, and their function should be in the realm of public education within the limits of the normative systems of the society they serve.

In recognition of the role the mass media can play in society, governmental regulation of the cinema in Europe has been characterized in recent years by concern for the preservation of common values and moral principles, greater consciousness of the influence of films on young people, and acceptance of the principle that rules must be applied with great flexibility in judging a given work on its merits. As educational considerations for youth have superseded heavy-handed, arbitrary censorship for the protection of society at large, cinema regulatory board membership in European countries has been changed to include teachers and cinema professionals.[53]

Stimulation of criminal behavior?

In considering whether the mass media encourage the development of attitudes and behavioral tendencies favorable to law violations, critics cite the conditioning of viewers by scenes of violence or sexual eroticism and the possibility they will try to imitate such scenes. In addition to possible traumatic effects, such scenes are abhorred on grounds that they may release latent aggressive tendencies. Repeated presentation of criminal offenses is seen as a powerful form of insidious inculcation which distorts the sense of right and wrong, especially when the transgressor is portrayed

[52] Elihu Katz and Paul Lazarsfeld, *Personal Influence* (Glencoe, Ill.: Free Press, 1955), p. 16.

[53] H. Michard, "The Cinema and the Protection of Youth," in *The Cinema and the Protection of Youth* (Strasbourg, France: European Committee on Crime Problems, Council of Europe, 1958), pp. 54–59.

in a way likely to arouse the viewer's sympathy or admiration.[54] Mass media are charged with encouraging the role of thrill-seeking spectator rather than responsible and active participant in community affairs.

A more reasonable assessment would be that although the power of the mass media is not as direct and overwhelming as these criticisms imply, it is the responsibility of the managers of mass communications to avoid supplementing or strengthening the themes of violence and eroticism that are present in American culture. The brevity of mass media messages means that only some of the multitudinous elements making up human experience can be abstracted. When the experience that is packaged and disseminated is of an antisocial nature, there is the potentiality that the impression will be conveyed that atypical behavior is usual and antisocial values are descriptive of all American culture. Crime-provoking messages are more likely when the economic necessity to attract large audiences in order to meet high production costs motivates managers to rely on themes of violence or eroticism.

A governmental commission studied the effects on viewers of violent television programs. Its report concluded that aggressive behavior can be stimulated among unstable persons under some circumstances, but the evidence is too complex and incomplete for sweeping generalizations. Emphasizing the need to recognize the operation of factors other than the mass media message alone, the commission continues:

We have noted in the studies at hand a modest association between viewing of violence and aggression among at least some children, and we have noted some data which are consonant with the interpretation that viewing produces the aggression; this evidence is not conclusive, however, and some of the data are also consonant with other interpretations. . . . The evidence (or more accurately, the difficulty of finding evidence) suggests that the effect is small compared with many other possible causes, such as parental attitudes or knowledge of and experience with the real violence of our society. The sheer amount of television violence may be unimportant compared with such subtle matters as what the medium says about it: is it approved or disapproved, committed by sympathetic or unsympathetic characters, shown to be effective or not, punished or unpunished?[55]

A course in crime?

Do the mass media teach the techniques of crime and delinquency? They are occasionally blamed for instructing individuals in specific crime techniques, thus encouraging them to rob a bank, burglarize a house, or skyjack an airplane. A 1966 television drama centered on the placement

[54] Ibid., pp. 40–41.
[55] Surgeon General's Scientific Advisory Committee, *Television and Growing Up*, pp. 6–8.

of a bomb on a transcontinental airliner; within 24 hours the airlines had received five hoax phone calls.[56]

Mass media have the potentials of providing incidental learning because consumers depend upon them as a source of information and entertainment. William Catton, Jr., has suggested that criminal behavior may coincide with events portrayed by mass media because the individual had the expectation or hope that such an event would be portrayed.[57] The mass media thereby endow the behavior with a certain prestige in the mind of the deviant, as well as conferring prestige by focusing public attention on him if he does commit the crime. Catton points out that certain impulses have been inactive in such persons. When they discover that someone has acted according to a similar impulse, they are encouraged to do so also.

The influence of mass media is more likely to be in the reinforcement of attitudes already present in the individual or in his immediate environment, rather than through fundamental change in attitudes brought about by the media alone. The individual brings his predispositions to the viewing situation, and the significance of the message is screened by the social conditions within which he is exposed, by his predetermined perception of the message, and by his retention of the impressions he derives. The norms of his immediate group shape his screening of the message within the contours of his unique personality. The maximum effect of a given message comes with the recurrence of a theme upon successive presentations, the capacity of the message to evoke primarily emotional reactions, its relevance to the individual's needs and interests, his readiness to learn, and the set of values he applies for evaluating the message.[58]

Undermining of values?

The mass media have been charged with affecting moral attitudes toward crime in various ways. They have been accused of undermining respect for law and order and interfering with efficient criminal justice administration when criminals are portrayed as heroes or victims of persecution and policemen are presented as bunglers and brutes. Premature news stories may prevent the apprehension of culprits. Sensational reports may distort mundane facts for the sake of making a "better" story,[59] may

[56] Albert Engvall Siegal, "The Effects of Media Violence on Social Learning," in David L. Lange, Robert K. Baker, and Sandra J. Ball (eds.), *Mass Media and Violence* (Washington, D.C.: U.S. Government Printing Office, November 1969), pp. 271–72.

[57] William R. Catton, Jr., "Mass Media as Activators of Latent Tendencies," ibid., pp. 304–5.

[58] J. D. Halloran, "The Influence of Films on Individuals and Groups," in *Cinema and Protection of Youth,* pp. 112–14.

[59] Terry Ann Knopf, "Media Myths on Violence," *New Society,* 424 (November 12, 1970): 856–59.

influence public opinion, and may deny the arrested person a fair, objective trial. Themes of "easy money" and widespread perpetration of crimes could encourage frustrated, suggestible individuals to try their hand at lawbreaking. Frederick Wertham has been prominent among those who believe that provocative "comic" books furnish excuses for an abnormal interest in sex, aggression, cruelty, and deceit.[60]

The critics, Jack Lyle believes, confuse manifestations of conditions and problems with the conditions and problems themselves. As institutions of society, the media reflect how the members of society choose to use them. In a democratic society, citizens are expected to be tolerant of opposing points of view. The media inevitably interpret the events they report to some degree, reflecting the perceptions and social values of the individuals and groups that frame the message. The expectation that the mass media will present only "good" messages raises the question: Who is to make the decisions as to what is "good" and in what directions society should move?[61]

SUMMARY

The criminologist's interest in social institutions is linked to his concern with how the behaviors of individuals and groups can be controlled to make them contributory to social order. By centering attention on the normative framework, this chapter sought to give meaning to the relationships between crime and the family, school, church, and mass media as spheres of human activities. Thus the chapter has served to emphasize the viewpoint that criminal behavior is a part of the total constellation of all human behaviors.

FOR ADDITIONAL READING

Cipes, Robert M. "Controlling Crime News: Sense or Censorship?" *Atlantic Monthly,* 220 (August 1967): 47–53.

Elder, Glen H., Jr. "Family Structure and Educational Attainment: A Cross-National Analysis." *American Sociological Review,* 30 (February 1965): 81–96.

Fooner, Michael. "Money and Economic Factors in Crime and Delinquency." *Criminology,* 8 (February 1971): 311–32.

Gagnon, John H., and Simon, William. "Pornography—Raging Menace or Paper Tiger?" *Trans-action,* 4 (July–August 1967): 41–48.

Grygier, Tadeusz, G.; Chesley, Joan; and Tuters, Elizabeth Wilson. "Parental Deprivation: A Study of Delinquent Children." *British Journal of Criminology,* 9 (July 1969): 209–53.

[60] Frederick Wertham, *Seduction of the Innocent* (New York: Rinehart & Co., 1954).

[61] Jack Lyle, "Contemporary Functions of the Mass Media," in Lange, Baker, and Ball, *Mass Media and Violence,* pp. 191–92.

Halloran, J. D. *The Effects of Mass Communication.* Leicester, England: Leicester University Press, 1971.

Heiss, Jerold. "On the Transmission of Marital Instability in Black Families." *American Sociological Review,* 37 (February 1972): 82–92.

Jaffe, Lester D. "Delinquency Proneness and Family Anomie." *Journal of Criminal Law, Criminology and Police Science,* 54 (June 1963): 146–54.

Khleif, B. B. "Teachers as Predictors of Juvenile Delinquency and Psychiatric Disturbance." *Social Problems,* 11 (Winter 1964): 270–82.

Little, Alan. " 'Parental Deprivation, Separation and Crime': A Test on Adolescent Recidivists." *British Journal of Criminology,* 5 (October 1965): 419–30.

MacDougall, Curtis D. *The Press and Its Problems.* Dubuque, Iowa: William C. Brown Co., Publishers, 1965.

Mannino, F. V. "Family Factors Related to School Persistence." *Journal of Educational Sociology,* 35 (January 1962): 193–202.

Marx, Gary T. "Religion: Opiate or Inspiration of Civil Rights Militancy among Negroes." *American Sociological Review,* 32 (February 1967): 64–72.

Miller, Marshall E. "The Place of Religion in the Lives of Juvenile Offenders." *Federal Probation,* 29 (March 1965): 50–53.

Rich, John Martin. "How Social Class Values Affect Teacher-Pupil Relations." *Journal of Educational Sociology,* 33 (May 1960): 355–59.

Rudwick, Elliott M. "Race Labeling and the Press." *Journal of Negro Education,* 31 (Spring 1962): 177–81.

Sugarman, B. N. "Social Class and Values as Related to Achievement and Conduct in School." *Sociological Review,* 14 (1966): 287–301.

7

Criminal behavior systems

One of the most fascinating aspects of criminal behavior is that it is socially patterned. The police term *modus operandi* refers to the styles of crime perpetration that characterize certain recidivists. Beyond the practical utility of this insight for the apprehension of criminals, *modus operandi* suggests that certain factors are operating to lend regularity and predictability to criminal behavior.

Some time ago, August B. Hollingshead defined the characteristics of a *behavior system,* a concept that will be employed in this chapter to categorize regularities among classes of criminal behavior. Behavior systems are most perceptible as vocational specialties in contemporary American society, although racial and cultural minorities also qualify as examples. Each behavior system is characterized by an identifiable complex of common cultural values, techniques, and behavior patterns, as well as a specialized language. Novices are not accepted as colleagues until they have acquired a specialized body of knowledge and appropriate behavior patterns, and controls are applied to the recruitment of members, their relations with one another, and their relations with nonmembers.[1]

In applying the concept of behavior system to crime, this chapter further documents the involvement of criminal behavior within the sociocultural organization of society and demonstrates the differences among classes of crime that qualify them as criminal behavior systems. Crimes of professional criminals qualify for this distinction to the greatest degree, whereas the violent personal crimes of murder and rape are least likely to do so. White-collar crime qualifies as a behavior system, but an important issue is whether or not this category actually should be included within the context of criminal behavior.

[1] August B. Hollingshead, "Behavior Systems as a Field for Research," *American Sociological Research,* 4 (December 1939): 816–17.

SOCIETY AND PATTERNS OF CRIME

Criminals are more like law-abiding persons in being subject to the sociocultural influences of society than is recognized in the stereotype of the criminal as a totally pathological being. The nature of the sociocultural organization influences the choice of particular behaviors to be defined as criminal. Certain behaviors are regarded as so harmful socially that they are penalized as crimes. The particular set of cultural values affords the setting within which the political evaluation is made that certain acts threaten group survival. For example, new interests to be protected by law were created in the Industrial Revolution by the rise of the factory system, increased complexity of business organizations, and growing impersonality in trade relations.[2]

Settings favorable to lawbreaking

The characteristics of a sociocultural organization may afford a setting favorable to the incidence of certain kinds of crime. American culture has a special proclivity for violence, and puritanical mores add to sexual frustrations.[3] As abstract symbols of wealth and impersonality in urban society, paper money, stocks, and bonds promote economic exchange, but they also invite depersonalization of social relationships. The general public finds it easier to excuse property crimes when the large size of the organization victimized depersonalizes it. In a test of whether individuals, when forced to choose, would be more likely to approve of stealing from large-scale, impersonal organizations than from small-scale, personal ones, nearly all respondents disapproved of stealing, but the intensity of disapproval varied with the size of the organization involved. The rationalizations offered were that large business was supposed to be impersonal, powerful, ruthless, exploitative, and bureaucratically wasteful. Many expressed a "Robin Hood" philosophy. Rationalizations for stealing from government were that it was so big and wealthy it could afford the loss, and it was bureaucratically inefficient, at any rate. Some argued that government belongs to the people and that stealing from "themselves" is less criminal.[4]

[2] Albert Morris, "Changing Concepts of Crime," in Vernon C. Burnham and Samuel B. Kutash (eds.), Encyclopedia of Criminology (New York: Philosophical Library, Inc., 1949), pp. 48–50.

[3] For example, see, in Annals of American Academy of Political and Social Science, Vol. 391 (September 1970), Allen D. Grimshaw, "Interpreting Collective Violence: An Argument for the Importance of Social Structure," pp. 9–20; and Hugh Davis Graham, "The Paradox of American Violence: A Historical Appraisal," pp. 74–82.

[4] Erwin O. Smigel, "Public Attitudes toward Stealing as Related to Size of Victim Organization," in Erwin O. Smigel and H. Laurence Ross (eds.), Crimes against Bureaucracy (New York: Van Nostrand Reinhold Co., 1970), pp. 15–28.

Many crimes are related to what C. Wright Mills terms "structural immorality."[5] Between fully reputable businessmen and those who perpetrate clear-cut crimes against property falls a heterogeneous group which Frank Gibney has loosely labeled "operators." The "sharper" swindles the buying or investing public by exploiting once-legitimate businesses. The "taker" accepts bribes and kickbacks in business or politics. The "fixer" makes his way by peddling influence, jobs, and money to gain a percentage of the profits of others. White-collar criminals also would be included among the operators.[6] The confidence game thrives when the total culture encourages connivance among respectable people in making high profits by exploiting others. The racketeer exists because the corruption he symbolizes persists in the fabric of the larger community.[7] He provides stability to illicit businesses, such as prostitution and gambling, which are patronized by noncriminals. Car clouting (stealing from parked automobiles) and car stripping (removing accessories and parts) are successful professional crimes only when automobile dealers and garages buy secondhand items without question when offered low prices.[8]

The criminal and the victim

The cultural system and social organization produce a group of victims to which criminals are attracted and adjust their techniques. As David Maurer puts it, career criminals follow the "eddies of humanity like sharks playing in a school of herring."[9] The haunts of pickpockets are places that accommodate large human aggregations. Confidence men operate at winter resorts and other places where people of means are susceptible to quickly cultivated acquaintanceships. Professional shoplifters have more favorable opportunities with self-service stores, especially if they are overcrowded and inexperienced personnel are hired for holiday rushes. In a study of bad-check writing as a crime in Nebraska, it was found that the businesses most likely to be affected were engaged in relatively small transactions and dealt with many strangers as customers. Victims of this offense have difficulty in dealing with it because one type

[5] C. Wright Mills, *The Power Elite* (New York: Oxford University Press, Inc., 1956), pp. 343–44.

[6] Frank Gibney, *The Operators* (New York: Harper & Bros., 1960), pp. 14–16.

[7] For a summary of the participation of syndicated crime in American municipal politics, see Virgil M. Peterson, *Barbarians in Our Midst* (Boston: Little, Brown & Co., 1952), chap. 14.

[8] For an interesting description of the participation of small businessmen in systematic use of arson, see the story of Sam Sapphire in Robert Rice, *The Business of Crime* (London: Victor Gollancz, Ltd., 1956).

[9] David W. Maurer, *Whiz Mob: A Correlation of the Technical Argot of Pickpockets and Their Behavior Patterns* (Gainesville, Fla.: American Dialect Society, November 1955), p. 23.

gure 7–1. Criminal investigation in action.

keeping with the concept of a criminal behavior system, safe burglary reflects qualities
the society that is being victimized. For example, urban society emphasizes money as a
eans of economic exchange and as a social value. The portability of much urban property
nds itself to property crime. The safe burglar gears his crime to locations where loot
concentrated. On the other hand, crime detection benefits from other characteristics
an urban society, such as technological advances and applied science.

of habitual bad-check writer is the quasi-responsible person who is careless with bookkeeping and must be pressed to make his checks good.[10]

In many criminal deeds there is a mutuality that cannot be accounted for by the usual conception of evildoer versus passive evil-sufferer.[11] The victim has qualities (such as sexual attractiveness or gullibility) or material possessions that attract the criminal. Beyond this creation of the possibility of a crime, the victim may also precipitate it by motivating, unconsciously or consciously, the criminal to single him out as a target.[12] The victim may be so gullible that he invites the attention of the swindler as an "easy mark." His gullibility may be a personal quality or reflect his status as a social stranger inexperienced in the situation within which the swindler operates. Maurer points out that a confidence man prospers only because of the fundamental dishonesty of his victim.[13] Other crimes also may be planned to minimize the possibility that the victim will appeal to the police. Store thieves are protected when managers fear offending legitimate customers. A crime may be concealed by the victim for fear his own offenses will be revealed—the hijacked cargo is illicit, or the listing of the safe's contents will reveal that the victim has been filing false income tax reports.

Practices in legitimate society frequently can be turned to criminal behavior. The mechanic has skills for entering a locked automobile. The accountant has skills necessary for embezzlement and fraud. The confidence game draws on the same manipulative skills and "front" used in salesmanship.

Defensive tactics

The career criminal adapts to the larger sociocultural organization to avoid detection and imprisonment. Risk is minimized by criminal techniques and knowledge of the environment within which the criminal operates. The professional avoids crimes against persons, especially violent ones which aggravate strong official reactions. Professional thieves acquaint themselves with the patrol schedules of police to time their crimes. The skilled professional also takes into account the behavior of his victim and the qualities of the crime location. Burglars adjust to the safeguards of the intended victim and the qualities of the place of theft, keeping up with changes in doors, windows, locks, and alarms. Techniques have

[10] Frederick K. Beutel, *Some Potentialities of Experimental Jurisprudence as a New Branch of Social Science* (Lincoln: University of Nebraska Press, 1957), p. 345.

[11] Hans Von Hentig, *The Criminal and His Victim* (New Haven, Conn.: Yale University Press, 1948), pp. 383–84.

[12] Stephen Schafer, *The Victim and His Criminal* (New York: Random House, Inc., 1968), pp. 79–80.

[13] David W. Maurer, *The Big Con* (New York: Pocket Books, Inc., 1949), p. 2.

changed with the decline in exterior fire escapes, warded locks vulnerable to skeleton keys, and dumbwaiters.[14] The favorite hours for crime vary according to the probability the place will be unoccupied—commercial places at night and residences in the day-time. Because the white-collar criminal's offenses are embedded within the activities of his legitimate business, he is protected by the intricacies of his occupational specialty and his reputable status.

The risk of crime is related to the degree of tolerance with which the particular kind of offense is regarded. High-visibility crimes are more likely to attract official reaction and punishment because of their violence, obvious breaks in the daily routine, the physical appearance or behavior of the offender which mark him as a law violator, or the dissimilarity of criminal techniques from those employed in legitimate activities.

Professional criminals protect themselves through knowledge of the subterranean workings of the system of justice. The "fix" is an illicit system that favors those accused who are able to gain the assistance of persons of influence or those wise in the workings of judicial procedure. Maurer asserts that the criminal culture cannot operate continuously and professionally without the connivance of a minority of corrupt officials.[15] The "fix" has several forms: bribery of the arresting officer or other official, employment of an influential person who specializes in fixes for professional criminals, or paying off the victim.[16] The career criminal's defense system also includes careful planning of crimes to minimize disturbance of routine patterns of life at the place of crime, a well-developed "grapevine," linkages to officials, and setting aside a cash reserve ("fall dough") to be used to win freedom in case of arrest.

OCCUPATION AND CRIMINAL BEHAVIOR

An occupation has been defined as any type of activity to which a number of persons devote themselves regularly for pay. In the course of specialized training and continuous association, the occupational group develops a subculture of its own and a body of social relations peculiar to and common to its members. If an occupation is a set of repeated and somewhat standardized activities, certain attitudes toward life develop out of the concentration on particular values and objects in the course of the thinking and doing associated with the activities.[17]

[14] Susan Black, "A Reporter at Large: Burglary, I," *The New Yorker,* 39 (December 7, 1963): 79.

[15] Maurer, *Whiz Mob,* p. 129.

[16] Edwin H. Sutherland (ed.), *The Professional Thief* (Chicago: University of Chicago Press, 1958), chap. 4.

[17] Emory S. Bogardus, *Sociology,* 3d ed. (New York: Macmillan Co., 1950), pp. 164, 168.

Occupational concepts

The stereotyped images of the army officer, pastor, physician, professional athlete, and other occupational specialists exaggerate the attitudes and life orientations produced by their personal qualifications and training. This chapter will employ some concepts which capture more meaningfully the insights reflected in the occupational stereotypes. These concepts will be useful in analyzing the differences between general categories of criminal behavior and their interdependence with the sociocultural organization of society.

The term "career" connotes a relatively orderly sequence in a person's life, with passage from one status to another. An occupational career is the succession of related jobs filled in an orderly series. The career provides a broad framework of incentives which motivate the aspirant to move through the sequence of statuses.[18] The medical student undertakes the drawn-out and arduous sequence of statuses from premedical student, medical student, intern, and novice physician to fullfledged physician. He is motivated by the medical career as a system of organized incentives which provide financial compensation, rights, privileges, membership in a colleague group of high prestige, and a sense of dedicated and indispensable service to mankind. The subjective side of a career has been described by Everett C. Hughes as the moving perspective in which the person sees his life as a whole and interprets the meaning of his various attributes and actions and the things that happen to him.[19]

The professional acquires a fund of theoretical knowledge through prolonged, intensive study.[20] His specialized knowledge and a body of theory enable him to deal with specific concrete events in a systematic fashion. The professional has authority over others on the basis of theoretical knowledge of which laymen are comparatively ignorant. This status of expert in a particular field of knowledge also entails obligations, as expressed in codes of professional ethics. The professional is granted privileges and powers by the total society, including control over admission into the profession. He operates through a network of formal and informal groups that generate a subculture consisting of values and norms to which the neophyte must adjust if he is to be accepted as a colleague. Closely related is the career concept whereby the neophyte is expected to conceive of his work as a "calling," a life devoted to "good works." Recognized professionals include physicians, attorneys, professors, and scientists.

[18] Robert Dubin, *The World of Work* (Englewood Cliffs, N.J.: Prentice-Hall, Inc., 1958), pp. 276–78.

[19] Everett C. Hughes, "Institutional Office and the Person," *American Journal of Sociology*, 43 (November 1937): 409–10.

[20] Ernest Greenwood, "Attributes of a Profession," in Sigmund Nosow and William H. Form (eds.), *Man, Work and Society* (New York: Basic Books, Inc., 1962): pp. 206–17.

The occupational subcultures affect personality and behavior because its specialists are exposed to a distinctive code of folkways and mores and because the work is patterned by the nature of the occupational activity. The social world of the physician is characterized by sick people, the hospital environment, irregular hours, emergencies, and the battle against disease and death. The life of the railroader is characterized by frequent changes of residence and extreme dependence on the clock.[21] The economic structure of the restaurant and relationships with customers have an effect on the social world of the waitress.[22]

A given occupation also dominates relationships away from the job. The specialist's occupation is an engrossing part of his life, coloring his choice of identification groups and largely determining his status in the community. The job provides income which affects his standard of living, choice of place of residence, and the groups from which friends may be chosen. It takes up certain portions of his day, influencing the time of his recreational and other off-the-job associations. It puts him in association with certain kinds of people as work partners or users of his services.

Assumption of occupational status involves selection from among candidates, training in occupational skills and attitudes, and acceptance as a colleague. A number of questions related to occupational status are relevant to the adoption of criminal behavior. What are the functions of family, school, recreational activities, communication media, chance associations with particular individuals, and many other focal centers of social interaction in determining the selection of an occupation? In what ways do particular experiences accelerate interest in an occupation, and in what ways do they serve as barriers? How are these selective factors affected by social class, race, sex, age, and ethnic minority status? How is the learning process controlled to regulate the flow of recruits to protect the interests of those already in the occupation? What is the nature of the occupational subculture transmitted to neophytes in the course of learning occupational skills? What is the orientation of the subculture to the more inclusive culture of the society? How do the functions of the occupation in the society color the values emphasized by the occupational subculture?

Crime as an occupational subculture

The concept of occupation is useful for differentiating criminal behaviors according to the degree of commitment to criminal values and the degree to which a given form of crime qualifies as a career.

[21] William F. Cottrell, *The Railroader* (Stanford, Calif.: Stanford University Press, 1940).

[22] William Foote Whyte, "When Workers and Customers Meet," in William Foote Whyte (ed.), *Industry and Society* (New York: McGraw-Hill Book Co., 1946).

As a term, "commitment" refers to the consistency with which a person follows a line of behavior because he has accepted the requirements of a certain group. He is intensively committed to criminality when his feelings about himself and his behavior reflect the criminal group's attitudes toward him.[23] When an individual is strongly committed to a criminal culture, the consistency of his crime-oriented behavior is difficult to redirect through rehabilitative programs. To "go straight" would cause him to appear "dishonest" in the sense that he would have to cut himself off from his previous criminal associates and deny his previous beliefs, such as "only suckers work."

A normative system is termed "legitimate," according to Max Weber, when the individual regards the rules in his social relationships as binding on his conduct and imitates the actors serving as models for these rules. Disobedience would be abhorrent to his sense of duty.[24] Usually, "legitimate" refers to compliance with the law and "illegitimate" to criminal activities. Richard A. Cloward and Lloyd E. Ohlin substitute a broader usage in analyzing the behavior of delinquents who have withdrawn their attribution of legitimacy from certain of the norms maintained by law-abiding groups and have given it instead to patterns of conduct defined as illegitimate by police and courts. The norms of the delinquent subculture require the practice of theft, street warfare, and perhaps use of drugs. The fully indoctrinated member of the conflict gang attributes legitimacy to these norms in that he perceives of these rules as ones he *must* follow. Conversely, the competing official norms are illegitimate in that they are not binding on his conduct.[25]

When committed to a criminal culture, the offender orients his life around the values of that culture and identifies himself with criminal groups. They become his reference groups. Identification with similar criminals is promoted by sharing common occupational activities and argot, common threats of apprehension and imprisonment, and the common experience of rejection by the larger society. The offender becomes a member of an ingroup which stands in opposition to the society of "square Johns" to be outwitted and victimized. He rates himself according to the criteria of these groups and his status within them. His knowledge of crime and his skill in its techniques are determining factors in fixing his status. Consequently, crime becomes his way of life and the basis of his life organization.

In the development of a criminal career, criminal knowledge, techniques, and attitudes are acquired systematically and progressively. Prone-

[23] Howard S. Becker, *Outsiders: Studies in the Sociology of Deviance* (New York: Free Press, 1963), pp. 27–28.

[24] Max Weber, *The Theory of Social and Economic Organization,* trans. A. M. Henderson and Talcott Parsons (New York: Oxford University Press, Inc., 1947), pp. 124–25.

[25] Richard A. Cloward and Lloyd E. Ohlin, *Delinquency and Opportunity* (Glencoe, Ill.: Free Press, 1955), pp. 16–20.

ness to crime is not sufficient to explain systematic criminality. The novice must have access to "illegitimate opportunity," to the learning of sophisticated techniques, and to organized means of disposing of loot and safeguarding himself against apprehension and imprisonment.

PROFESSIONAL CRIMINALS

Professional criminals regard crime as a full-time occupation and are committed to a criminal value system. Walter Reckless distinguishes between "professional criminal careers" and "ordinary criminal careers." *Professional career criminals,* he says, are more developed in skills and techniques in perpetration of crimes and avoidance of detection and apprehension. Professional career criminals hold themselves aloof from "ordinary career" criminals, whom they regard as "amateurs." *Ordinary career criminals* display much less skill and dexterity and are more likely to use force, whereas the professional regards violence and use of weapons as a lack of resourcefulness.[26]

No criminal group meets the criteria of a profession to the degree sufficient to merit inclusion under a precise definition. Nevertheless, some criminals are differentiated from others in qualities which are captured by the term "professional." These qualities are discussed in the subsections that follow.

Development of skills

Professional criminals require techniques and social skills at a level of relatively intensive development. Because these special skills are required, professional criminals usually limit themselves to one form of crime. In crimes requiring teams, they are likely to specialize in one role. This characteristic has enabled police to develop *modus operandi* files listing criminals by type of crime and style of operation. The criminal is not regarded as professional until he is proficient in a specialty with particular techniques.

Manual skill is important to pickpockets, especially the "hook" who extracts the wallet. He chooses the victim ("mark") and usually falls in behind him. He communicates with the "stall" by sign, signal, or an argot term to indicate how the task is to be done. Depending on the location of the wallet, the stall will use his entire body, including hands and feet, to maneuver and hold the mark so that the wallet can be extracted while the operation is concealed from onlookers.[27]

Professional criminals are distinguished from less systematic criminals in some kinds of offenses by the development of mechanical devices. The

[26] Walter C. Reckless, *The Crime Problem,* 4th ed. (New York: Appleton-Century-Crofts, 1967), pp. 279–80.

[27] Maurer, *Whiz Mob,* chap. 5.

shoplifter, for example, may use the "booster box" wrapped to suggest it is prepared for mailing. A trapdoor in the box opens to receive stolen items. The "booster coat" has a loosened lining to allow items to be dropped to the billowy bottom. The coat may be rigged with hooks to hold concealed items. Other devices are "booster aprons," baggy bloomers, and false-bottom baby buggies.

All rackets demand ability to manipulate people. The thief depends on his approach, "front," wits, and frequently his talking ability.[28] The mark must be distracted from his wallet. The confidence man needs manipulative ability, especially in the "big con" when the mark is put on the "send" to obtain money after being told of a way to make a large profit.[29] The "roper" locates the mark and brings him to the "inside man" at the "store." The inside man presents himself, perhaps, as a prosperous financier with secret information on stocks. The store may be a fake broker's office or a fake betting parlor. The confidence men present themselves as prosperous, charming, and reputable businessmen who know some way to make easy money. Keen psychological insights are employed to charm the mark, excite his cupidity, and "cool him off" so he will not create a public stir after being fleeced. Clever staging of events is necessary to inspire faith on short acquaintance.[30]

Such manipulation by the professional criminal is dissimilar to that of legitimate occupations. First, the social relationships between victim and criminal operate under two systems of rules—the rules derived from a criminal culture to which the criminal commits himself and of which the victim is unaware, and those the victim is led to believe are operating. The swindler represents himself as a financier or in some other status while offering the victim the false hope of excessive profits.

Second, the mock social situation is created to achieve the relatively immediate goals of the criminal. The false situation has no further significance to the criminal once the immediate goal has been achieved. In contrast, the high-pressure salesman, for example, may strain ethical standards in making a sale, but his obligations are extended into the future through guarantees of product performance and the importance of reputation in assuring the continuity of business operations.

Third, the deception of the victim is based on the criminal's role performance as judged by the victim. But, like the stage actor, the criminal temporarily assumes a status which is not his own without committing himself to the rules. He is playing a game.

The professional must have "larceny sense" or "grift know," an ability to deal with unusual situations in the best possible manner because that is

---

[28] Sutherland, *Professional Thief,* p. 3.

[29] Maurer, *Big Con,* p. 289.

[30] For details on the operation of various confidence games, see John C. R. MacDonald, *Crime Is a Business* (Stanford, Calif.: Stanford University Press, 1939).

due to his personal resourcefulness. He must be able to think fast in order to exploit unusual factors in a particular situation. The experienced thief spots something "phoney" when a "touch" looks too easy.[31]

Regulation of recruitment

Professional criminals regulate the admission of recruits through control of learning opportunities. Recruitment involves the individual's more or less conscious choice of some form of crime as his major income-producing activity, and, concurrently, his admission to the learning opportunities through which he acquires the necessary knowledge and skills. In accepting the occupation, the novice assumes the status of a criminal within the social structure of the community and the status of his criminal specialty in the prestige ranking system of professional criminals. In both aspects, his relationships with other persons and his typical social experiences are affected by the criminal status he occupies.

The individual's interest in becoming a professional criminal is not sufficient for admission as a novice, Julian Roebuck and Ronald Johnson note in their discussion of the "jack-of-all-trades" criminal type. These offenders typically do not specialize in particular kinds of crime, choice of place to loot, or sort of property taken. The crimes usually are not planned. When there is a plan, the crime is carried out regardless of unexpected difficulties, such as change in the watchman's habitual routine of patrol. The offender has knowledge of criminal activities, has criminal associates, and organizes his life around crime. Nevertheless, he is not admitted to professional criminal groups because of clumsiness, lack of self-discipline, frequent arrests and incarcerations, or inability to settle down into one type of crime. He therefore lacks opportunity for intimate association with more proficient criminals.[32]

The novice thief first cuts himself off from the legitimate world and begins to hang around places frequented by thieves. Eventually he may be given a minor role in a theft requiring little skill. He is expected to have a fundamental knowledge, but his partners guide him when necessary. If he does well he may be given more important duties as he gains skill through "on-the-job" training.[33]

Most pickpockets, Maurer declares, are born into a family living within a criminal culture which cultivates criminal skills and is hostile toward the dominant culture.[34] In addition to the mode of recruitment in which a professional notices a boy with "possibilities" and gives him a chance to prove himself with initially easy tasks, professional thieves may recruit

[31] Sutherland, *Professional Thief*, pp. 32–33.

[32] Julian Roebuck and Ronald Johnson, "The Jack-of-All-Trades Offender," *Crime and Delinquency,* 8 (April 1962): 178–79.

[33] Sutherland, *Professional Thief*, p. 23.

[34] Maurer, *Whiz Mob*, pp. 156–61.

partners from experienced thieves without any particular recruiting system. Sometime and somehow, however, each thief had to learn the techniques before he gained admission as a colleague. Initial contacts are made through associations in jail, efforts by amateur thieves to dispose of loot, inclusion of an "inside" employee in a particular theft, or in the course of legitimate occupational duties, such as those of hotel clerks and bellboys, taxi drivers, and waiters, likely to place employees in contact with criminals. Most professional thieves initially had legitimate employment. Amateur thieves reared in slums usually lack the social abilities and "front" required of professional thieves.[35]

Subculture and self-image

Professional criminals have an occupational culture and a conception of self as criminal. The nonprofessional criminal may break the law repeatedly, but he retains the basic attitudes and morals of the dominant culture, feeling shame and guilt when found out. Professionals worry about violations of the criminal value system and stigmatization by the dominant culture, but they have no more sense of guilt concerning their victims, as Maurer puts it, than a fox taking chickens from a farmer.[36]

This divorce from the dominant culture is fundamental to the professional criminal. He has a conception of himself as a criminal. Crime is his means of livelihood and his way of life. He is isolated from the larger society by its stigmatization, its threat to his safety, and his commitment to the criminal culture. The professional rationalizes by describing criminal justice as hypocritical, devious, slow-moving, favoring special groups, and either corrupt or inconsistent in administration.[37] The suspicion of the dominant culture of "square Johns" runs deep. Maurer tells of a pickpocket who was troubled by his son's desire to become a Cub Scout. The father "knew" that the Scouts make "stool pigeons out of all those kids."[38]

The development of the professional criminal has similarities to the acquisition of an occupational personality by any young adult whose image of himself may be related to the position of engineer, physician, or army officer. Development of interest and acquisition of skill are inherent in the situation of the novice interacting with the experienced criminal. In the course of learning specialized skills, the novice is subjected to the narrowing of his field of interest to certain tasks. In his informal relations with persons of similar interest, he acquires the criminal ideology.

The normative yardstick used by professionals to measure one another

[35] Sutherland, *Professional Thief,* pp. 21–23.

[36] Maurer, *Whiz Mob,* pp. 16–17.

[37] Jack Black, "A Burglar Looks at Laws and Codes,"*Harper's Magazine,* 160 (February 1930): 312–13.

[38] Maurer, *Whiz Mob,* pp. 153–54.

has been described above. Pickpockets and burglars consider death an appropriate penalty for holding out loot on partners. Among the risks of the "trade" are loss of a good "score" (criminal profit) or being sent to prison for a crime of which one is innocent. Friends must help one another in time of trouble. To preserve the loyalty of his associates, the professional must demonstrate equal loyalty by not informing on them. Pickpocket mobs use the formula "in with the pinches, in with the pokes." If one pickpocket is entitled to the profits, he is obligated to put up a share of the "fall dough" to pay the arrested thief's way out of trouble directly related to picking pockets.[39]

Writing of his life as a criminal and prisoner, Victor Nelson mourns the effect on the "criminal code" of the loss of exclusiveness in the criminal population. In the old days when a criminal was shunned by all respectable people, he was forced into a criminal group and, for his own survival, had to abide by the moral principles of that group. Now, says Nelson, laws are broken by nearly everyone, and the sharp dividing line between criminals and honest men has broken down.[40]

The existence of the criminal culture is best illustrated by its argot, which dates back to at least 16th-century England.[41] This persistence attests to the transmission of an occupational subculture only dimly recognized by members of the dominant society. Ordinarily, the specialized language is not spoken in public, to prevent attracting attention that might interfere with crimes. Professionals will judge the trustworthiness of a stranger by his grasp of the argot.[42] The terms are useful for communicating information vital to conducting criminal activities, thereby reflecting the techniques and recurrent experiences of a criminal specialty.

ROBBERY: VIOLENCE AND ECONOMIC GAIN

Robbery is a peculiar crime in several respects. It combines elements of violence and an income-producing activity, although most forms of economic crime avoid violence as an excessive risk. Second, as a corollary of the first point, robbery threatens both the personal security and property of citizens. Weapons may be employed in robberies for four reasons: to prop up the self-confidence of the criminal, to intimidate the victim without intention of using the weapon, to employ the weapon if thought necessary to handle the victim, and to ensure escape. All of these reasons raise the possibility of violence to varying degrees, but not all

[39] Ibid., pp. 184–85.
[40] Victor F. Nelson, *Prison Days and Nights* (Garden City, N.Y.: Garden City Publishing Co., 1933), pp. 118–19.
[41] Maurer, *Whiz Mob,* p. 52.
[42] Sutherland, *Professional Thief,* p. 20.

robbers are armed.[43] Third, robbers differ in their degree of qualification as professional criminals, as described above.

Most robbers are of three major types, according to John Conklin. The *professional robber* carefully plans his robbery, executes the crime with a group of accomplices, is committed firmly to robbery as an economic endeavor, and uses his gains to support a hedonistic life style.[44] The *opportunist robber* lacks a long-term commitment to robbery and engages in that crime, between other forms of theft such as larceny and shoplifting, only when a likely target appears. Robbery is more of an opportunity for extra money than a form of livelihood. Opportunism tends to direct him toward elderly women with purses, drunks, and cab drivers, making the vulnerability of the targets more important than the amount of loot available. The *addict robber,* driven by a need for funds to support his habit, rarely plans the crime for substantial loot or high probability of evading apprehension.

A study of 25 convicted armed robbers found them to differ from other professional criminals in that their organization is more of a loose confederation of individuals than a long-term group structure utilizing "fall dough" and the "fix" as defensive measures. The rapid accumulation of money is the predominant goal of armed robbers, rather than the etiquette of relationships among colleagues or outsiders. Therefore the organization of robbers is more in the nature of a partnership than a persistent set of leadership and specialized roles.[45]

Amateur thieves

Businesses and industries suffer substantial losses from thefts perpetrated by persons who conceive of themselves essentially as honest citizens. Such offenders are not subjected to the admission procedures of professional thieves and do not necessarily develop criminal techniques intensively. Employee pilfering is a serious drain on the financial resources of business and industrial enterprises, yet it persists because of work-group norms which create ambivalent attitudes about who really owns property at the plant, store, or office.[46]

Such amateur thefts, including white-collar crimes, take a heavy toll in the form of economic losses and the undermining of the moral state of the community—a toll far in excess of that imposed by the professional

[43] John E. Conklin, *Robbery and the Criminal Justice System* (Philadelphia: J. B. Lippincott Co., 1972), pp. 108–12.

[44] Ibid., pp. 63–75.

[45] Werner J. Eisenstadter, "The Social Organization of Armed Robbery," *Social Problems,* 17 (Summer 1969): 64–83.

[46] Donald N. M. Horning, "Blue-Collar Theft: Conceptions of Property Attitudes toward Pilfering, and Work Group Norms in a Modern Industrial Plant," in Smigel and Ross, *Crimes against Bureaucracy,* pp. 46–64.

thief.[47] Some 70 to 80 percent of inventory shrinkage is probably attributable to employee theft and shoplifting.[48]

Professional thieves compose only a small fraction of all shoplifters. A study of arrested chronic shoplifters found that the offender was most likely to be female. In 90 percent of the cases, she identified herself with respectable society and lacked criminal associations. Nevertheless, she usually had special devices and techniques for systematic theft; it was unlikely she was a neurotic with an uncontrollable urge to take some pretty bauble. Although technically a "first offender" without a prior arrest record, the amateur shoplifter usually had been systematically involved in such thefts.[49]

SYNDICATED CRIME

Syndicated crime refers to the perversion of the organizational scheme of legitimate business to provide illicit "services," such as prostitution, gambling, liquor, or "protection." The illicit business is steady in that its operations involve recurrent transactions, whereas burglaries and robberies are planned and perpetrated as a chain of autonomous operations. Syndicated crime is a business in daily operation for profit-making purposes.[50] Its salaried staff engages in a series of interrelated transactions through an established network of contacts. The dimensions and complexity of the illicit operations require a division of labor in business staff. Accountants and legal counsel are employed for their skills, and capital and other skilled personnel are employed in substantial quantities in large-scale, interstate operations that usually involve more than one kind of product or service. The operations are on several vertical levels, such as supplier, manufacturer, wholesaler, and retailer. The members of the organization frequently do not know the identity of one another.

Organized crime differs from reputable business in that its directors are cynical and antisocial. Naked force, threats of violence, and protection from criminal prosecution are necessary to assure long-term, systematic operation. The syndicate offers illegal goods and services. High profits provide means to corrupt susceptible officials, infiltrate legitimate businesses, and win cooperation of some members of legitimate society.

[47] Norman Jaspan and Hillel Black, "$4,000,000 a Day," in Gresham M. Sykes and Thomas E. Drabek (eds.), *Law and the Lawless* (New York: Random House, Inc., 1969), p. 265.

[48] President's Commission on Law Enforcement and Administration of Justice, *The Challenge of Crime in a Free Society* (Washington, D.C.: U.S. Government Printing Office, 1967), pp. 42–43.

[49] Mary Owen Cameron, *The Booster and the Snitch* (New York: Free Press of Glencoe, 1964), pp. 58–60.

[50] See discussion of similarity with legitimate economic institutions, Chapter 8, p. 201.

Origin of syndicated crime

The usual belief is that Prohibition brought forth syndicated crime, but the organizational techniques have been traced to the wars between labor and management in the World War I years, when some employers hired early-day hoodlum gangs against strikers. Some labor unions also hired thugs in the 1920s.[51] Louis Adamic suggests that the employment of gunmen and sluggers in industrial disputes was brief and sporadic and that in the intervals between strikes and lockouts, they started enterprises which evolved into syndicates. Criminals, first employed to meet emergencies, would propose that they give the union "steady protection" at a fixed rate. Refused, they would turn to violence and union election rigging to get their own people in control. When the law did not provide security, union leaders on occasion turned to racketeers for protection from other gangsters.[52]

Big-city racketeering may have arisen because it was found useful in enforcing mores not yet absorbed into legality.[53] A racketeer sells an illicit form of policing. In a time of cutthroat competition among small businesses, his bombings maintain discipline through intimidation. The racketeer provides price control, regularity of services, and, to a small degree, quality control in meeting the demands for illicit services such as prostitution and gambling. He is a businessman in enforcing contracts, financing operations, and making the other arrangements for services. The racketeer is lawless in the nature of his business and the policing techniques he employs, but violence occurs only when his system of maintaining order breaks down.

Similar to a pattern in the development of American industry, a large number of small, fragmented criminal enterprises were consolidated into a larger organization, or syndicate, as a means of increasing profits. In one view, regarded as questionable by some students of crime syndicates, this movement toward consolidation benefited from the importation of the traditions of the Mafia by immigrants from Sicily. Daniel P. Moynihan believes that this view exaggerates the contribution audacity and the peasant habit of group loyalty could make to a complex development.[54] The cultural environment and the techniques for the development of such monopolies already were present in the American milieu. Further, it appears that only a portion of American criminal syndicates can be identi-

[51] Burton B. Turkus and Sid Feder, *Murder, Inc.* (New York: Bantam Books, Inc., 1960), pp. 290–91.

[52] Louis Adamic, "Racketeers and Organized Labor in Chicago," *Harper's Magazine,* 161 (September 1930): 415.

[53] R. L. Duffus, "The Function of the Racketeer," *New Republic,* 58 (March 27, 1929): 166–68.

[54] Daniel P. Moynihan, "The Private Government of Crime," *Reporter,* 25 (July 6, 1961): 15.

fied with Mafia traditions.[55] In Chicago, the southern Italians, especially those from Sicily, arrived in the years before 1900 and 1914. The timing of their arrival produced children who, at maturity, faced new educational requirements for job qualification, greater barriers to legitimate job opportunities from a less fluid social structure, and opposition from earlier immigrants from northern Italy. Prohibition gave them their opportunity in organized crime. By 1930 American-Italians represented only 31 percent of Chicago's organized crime leadership.[56]

Another key question is whether the following description of the nature and structure of the Cosa Nostra is descriptive of crime syndicates in general or merely an impressionistic interpretation of practices in a portion of organized crime. Unquestionably, criminals do enter into cooperative activities at varying levels of organizational structure. Nevertheless, the evidence presented at congressional hearings and by law enforcement personnel fails to demonstrate that a single "commission" dominates a nationwide crime syndicate or that unquestioned obedience of members is achieved by the ruling authority.[57]

Burton Turkus and Sid Feder have advanced the idea that a loose national alliance emerged in 1934. The rivalries among the gangs would not permit a single czar of national crime, but a central control based on cooperation would be the means of arbitrating intergang disputes without the heavy costs of warfare in money and blood. A board of governors would set intergang policy over a confederation of illicit business groups bound together by a common interest in safe and profitable operations. Each boss would be unmolested in his own territory, and killings there would require his permission unless they were ordered by the policy board. Political connections and protective devices would be pooled. This plan was to become the basis of establishing a degree of "law and order" among the systematically lawless.[58]

Nature of criminal syndicates

The President's Crime Commission reported syndicates in all sections of the country. Police departments reported organized crime in 80 percent of the cities over one million population, in 20 percent of the cities with a population between a quarter million and a million, and half of the cities between 100,000 and 250,000. Other information indicated this estimate was conservative. Further, small cities have been the prey of local racke-

[55] *Organized Crime and Illicit Traffic in Narcotics,* Part I U.S. Senate Permanent Subcommittee on Investigations, 88th Cong., 1st sess., September–October 1963 (Washington, D.C.: U.S. Government Printing Office, 1963), p. 263.

[56] Humbert S. Nelli, "Italians and Crime in Chicago: The Formative Years, 1890–1920," *American Journal of Sociology,* 74 (January 1969): 388–90.

[57] Gordon Hawkins, "God and the Mafia,"*Public Interest,* 14 (Winter 1969): 24–51.

[58] Turkus and Feder, *Murder, Inc.,* pp. 82–84.

teers, sometimes affiliated with criminals in nearby large cities.[59] The Federal Bureau of Investigation contends that 24 criminal cartels operate in large cities with frequent intercommunication in a loose confederation. Cosa Nostra ("Our Thing"), which has been called the largest organization, is the model for the description below.

Because force is a key element in welding individual members into a criminal organization, it is understandable that some of the syndicates present a militaristic structure.[60] At the top is a commission *(friemeson)* which serves as a kangaroo court to settle disputes and inflict punishments. Each "family" has a boss, an underboss, lieutenants, and at the bottom the "soldiers" or "button men." Disputes are settled with each family through a *consigio,* a lower-level kangaroo court. Each family has 450 members, more or less. The family is not necessarily descriptive of any kinship or emotional relationship. Rather it is a secret organization loosely bound by a common interest in illicit economic gain.[61]

The hierarchy of statuses is symbolized by acts of deference in address, tone of voice, and general demeanor. Position in the organizational hierarchy is emphasized, but seniority in age is a factor. A basic norm is that permission must be obtained from the family to enter an illegal enterprise, to commit a crime, or even to borrow from a usurer.[62] Disciplining is done within a family, ranging from demotion and loss of income to murder, usually by a fellow family member.

Organized crime prefers enterprises which have a large turnover and in which government will encounter difficulties in accounting and control. High profits are assured by establishment of monopolies through persuasion, intimidation, violence, and murder. Alliances with law enforcement officials protect the syndicate members and result in the harassment of criminal competitors. Gambling is the most lucrative of the rackets. Narcotics, usurious loans (shylocking), commercialized prostitution, and labor-management racketeering also provide high income.

Racketeers have infiltrated approximately 50 areas of business enterprise, including advertising, amusement industry, appliances, automobile industry, baking, ballrooms, bowling alleys, banking (shylocking), basketball, boxing, cigarette distribution, coal, communication facilities, construction, drugstore, drug companies, electrical equipment, florists, food, football, garment industry, gasoline stations, garages, hotels, insurance, jukeboxes and coin vending, laundry and dry cleaning, liquor, loan and bonding business, Nevada gambling houses, news services, oil industry,

[59] President's Commission on Law Enforcement and Administration of Justice, *Task Force Report: Organized Crime* (Washington, D.C.: U.S. Government Printing Office, 1967), p. 5.

[60] Ralph Salerno and John S. Tompkins, *The Crime Confederation,* (Garden City, N.Y.: Doubleday & Co., Inc., 1969), pp. 113–16.

[61] *Organized Crime and Illicit Traffic,* pp. 80–83. Also see Francis Ianni, *A Family Business* (New York: Russell Sage Foundation, 1972).

[62] *Organized Crime and Illicit Traffic,* p. 69.

racing and racetracks, radio stations, real estate, restaurants, scrap business, shipping, surplus sales, tailoring, theaters, and transportation.[63]

A distinction can be made between simon-pure rackets and collusive agreements, according to Gordon Hostettler and Thomas Beesley. *Simon-pure rackets* are opportunistic exploitations by individuals of circumstances promising illicit profits. *Collusive agreements* are conspiracies to exploit the structure of otherwise legitimate business and/or labor union organizations. The cleaning and dyeing industry in Chicago illustrates the collusive agreement. Customers leave garments at small shops to be transported to large cleaning and dyeing plants. The industry is organized under a masters' cleaners and dyers association. Two labor unions dominate the industry: the truck drivers who pick up garments and the cleaning plant workers. When racketeers control the association and the two unions, they are able to impose their will upon small shop owners and plant owners through strikes or refusal to pick up garments. Sterner measures are destruction of owners' property and customers' garments.[64]

Bankruptcy frauds,[65] arson plots to obtain insurance settlements, and stock frauds have also been employed. Legitimate businesses are useful as fronts for illicit transactions. Coin-vending machines are a good base for gambling operations because they cover the transportation of slot machines and the gathering of money from bookies under the guise of "service." Narcotics may be concealed in shipments of legitimate goods.[66]

Difficulties in rooting out syndicates

Municipal corruption, the latent benefits of illicit businesses, insulation tactics, and splintered law enforcement partially explain the difficulty of eliminating crime syndicates. John A. Gardiner notes the benefits of gambling. Taking bets has enabled small, outmoded stores to survive technological changes. An alternative ladder of social mobility is provided for those lacking the prerequisites for success in the legitimate world. Landlords benefit from high rents for bookie parlors. Private clubs and charitable organizations frequently depend on gambling as a source of revenue.[67]

Top syndicate leaders have learned to avoid direct involvement in

[63] *Third Interim Report,* U.S. Senate Special Committee to Investigate Organized Crime in Interstate Commerce, U.S. Senate Report No. 305, 83d Cong., 1st sess. (Washington, D.C.: U.S. Government Printing Office, 1951), p. 171.

[64] Gordon L. Hostettler and Thomas Q. Beesley, *It's A Racket* (Chicago: Les Quin Books, 1929), pp. 29–36.

[65] Nathaniel E. Kossack, " 'Scam'—The Planned Bankruptcy Racket," *New York Certified Public Accountant,* 35 (June 1965): 417–23.

[66] Gerald L. Goettel, "Why the Crime Syndicate Can't Be Touched," *Harper's Magazine,* 221 (November 1960): p. 38.

[67] John A. Gardiner, *The Politics of Corruption: Organized Crime in an American City* (New York: Russell Sage Foundation, 1970), pp. 79–86.

crimes. Their contacts with subordinates are through "buffers," a sort of administrative assistant. Written correspondence is avoided in favor of telephones to avoid creation of evidence. A "sit-down," a face-to-face conference of top leaders, is employed rarely to settle intergroup disputes. The boss divorces himself from direct financial transactions by employing the "money mover," a trusted aide who invests money through a chain of intermediaries. Contacts among members are segmental.[68]

The racketeer, aware that high living and public notoriety attract unwelcome notice, wears the gray flannel suit of the organization man of business. His personal conduct is free of obvious misdeeds, although his early career is marked by violent crimes. Syndicate leaders have learned to use the techniques of modern public relations to create the appearance of legitimacy and to cultivate important public officials. Among the techniques are substantial charitable and political contributions, ownership of legitimate enterprises, and memberships in religious, fraternal, and civic organizations.[69]

The code of secrecy imposed on subordinates protects the bosses and their activities from the attention of outsiders. Anyone willing to testify is difficult to keep alive. Other kinds of witnesses also are difficult to obtain because they are likely to be coconspirators. Organized rackets, such as gambling and narcotics, make the victim a party to the offense. In antitrust actions the businessman has joined the conspiracy out of fear or the quest for profits to be gained through criminally imposed monopolies.[70]

American courts and law enforcement agencies are splintered among jurisdictions in keeping with the historic emphasis on local government as a check against political authoritarianism. Police investigation and court action are in separate agencies, which are further divided into federal, state, and local levels. The overwhelming proportion of actions against criminals is by nonfederal agencies. The investigative, intelligence, and other law enforcement functions of the federal government are spread among a host of agencies, each with strictly limited authority.

Strategies for resolving the problem

The sporadic public concern over syndicated crime generally has been based on conceptions of crime as an individualistic phenomenon. "Throw the rascals out" is the usual prescription for the ailment. The political

---

[68] *Organized Crime and Illicit Traffic*, pp. 66–83.

[69] *Legislation Relating to Organized Crime: Hearings before Subcommittee No. 5 of the Committee on the Judiciary*, U.S. House Committee on the Judiciary, 87th Cong., 1st sess., May, 1961, Serial No. 16 (Washington, D.C.: U.S. Government Printing Office, 1961), p. 106.

[70] Ibid., pp. 104–5.

solution proposed is the installation of energetic and incorruptible public
officials, what Moynihan calls the "new broom" fallacy.[71] This course of
action ignores the underlying social system of organized crime, which
persists in spite of the turnover of membership. Changes in political power
fail to modify the system of organized crime to any extent. New reform
leaders are seldom prepared to deal with the illicit system after the election is won.

One method employed against syndicated crime is traditional police
action against the "small fry" to increase the overhead costs of syndicates.
The lower-level employees (bookies, still operators, narcotics importers,
officials who accept "fixes," and so on) are arrested and imprisoned. The
bosses are obligated to aid the families of imprisoned employees and to
provide legal services. These costs reduce profits. Recruitment is deterred
by failure of protective devices.[72] The usual regulations of business practices also are employed, such as prosecution for tax evasion. Successful
prosecution of racketeers is made difficult because most statutes are directed against the operation of racketeering, not its organization. For
example, the organizers of the numbers racket usually are untouched by
statutes as long as they avoid direct contact with the distribution and payoff of numbers.[73]

Another approach would be to legalize gambling, a key source of syndicate profits. Judge John M. Murtagh questions a moral distinction between the legality of a bet at a racetrack and the illegality of street-corner
betting. This double morality diverts police from dealing with traditional
crimes and involves some of them in corruption.[74] Earl Johnson, Jr., objects to legalization because he believes the criminal organizations would
merely transfer their activities to new areas. He advocates raising the level
of penalties against organized crime. Because syndicated crime is not
deterred by penalties at a level effective for other types of criminals, he
would make punishable by several years in prison those offenses now usually punishable only by fine or short-term imprisonment. Anticrime legislation would distinguish between criminal organizations and individual
offenders, even though the same law is involved. Penalties could be increased when the criminal organization exceeds a certain number of
members and a certain scale of operations, as measured by gross income.
For example, when the number of bets accepted daily exceeds a certain
number, the accused would be convicted of a felony. Johnson also urges
compulsory reports to the police, granting of immunity from prosecution

[71] Moynihan, "Private Government of Crime," pp. 14–16.

[72] Edwyn Silberling, "The Federal Attack on Organized Crime," *Crime and
Delinquency,* 8 (October 1962): 367.

[73] George Edwards, "Sentencing the Racketeer," *Crime and Delinquency,* 9
(October 1963): 391–97.

[74] John M. Murtagh, "Gambling and Police Corruption," *Atlantic Monthly,*
206 (November 1960): 52–53.

to witnesses involved in syndicated crimes, and legalization of wiretapping as enforcement techniques.[75]

The recommendations of the President's Crime Commission for combatting syndicated crime are summarized in Figure 7–2.

Figure 7–2. Recommendations for control of syndicated crime

Recommendations of the President's Commission on
Law Enforcement and Administration of Justice for the
control of syndicated crime.

Action by States and Municipalities

In states where organized crime exists, the attorney general should form a special unit to gather information and assist in prosecution.
Major police departments should establish special intelligence units.
States should develop investigation commissions.
Under stringent safeguards, electronic surveillance should be legalized.
Enforcement officials should regularly brief leaders at all levels of government concerning organized crime activities.

Grand juries

Grand juries should be impaneled annually in each jurisdiction subjected to syndicate activities.
The prosecutor should have sufficient fulltime manpower for investigative activities.
Immunity against later criminal prosecution should be extended to witnesses.
Requirements for proof of perjury should be eased to assure truthful testimony.
Residential facilities should be available, to protect witnesses.

Role of the Federal Government

A centralized, computerized intelligence unit should be created.
Research in crime syndicate organization and activities should be supported.
The Department of Justice should expand technical assistance to local jurisdictions.
A permanent joint congressional committee should be created to promote legislation and to place the prestige of the Congress behind the drive on organized crime.

Enforcement Techniques

Extended prison terms should be given persons convicted of felonies perpetrated as supervisors or managers of illegal businesses.
Federal and state departments of justice should regulate businesses infiltrated by syndicates.
Private business associations should be encouraged to discover and prevent illegal business practices by syndicates.

Adapted from: President's Commission on Law Enforcement and Administration of Justice, *The Challenge of Crime in a Free Society* (Washington, D.C.: U.S. Government Printing Office, 1967), pp. 200–209.

[75] Earl Johnson, Jr., "Organized Crime: Challenge to the American Legal System," Part III, *Journal of Criminal Law, Criminology and Police Science*, 54 (June 1963): 143.

MURDER: PATTERNS OF PASSION

The act of murder has a quality of absolute finality that is relatively unusual among crimes. Although the crime usually takes only a moment or two, the consequences for the victim cannot be undone. The murder is the climax of preceding events which must be probed for explanation. In a culture placing a high premium on the sanctity of human life, the killing of another man is the ultimate renunciation of behavior norms and the supreme protest against one's lot in a social situation.

Homicide is usually understood to mean the killing of one man by a human agency, with suicide excluded. Criminal homicide occurs only under circumstances which make it punishable by law. The executioner does not commit criminal homicide because he is carrying out a duty imposed by a court acting under law. Similarly, a soldier or a policeman killing another man in the course of performing his duty is not involved in criminal homicide.

Criminal homicide is divided into two major categories: (1) murder and nonnegligent manslaughter, and (2) manslaughter by negligence. Our interest here is in murder, which is the unlawful killing of one human being by another, with malice aforethought. First degree murder is committed with premeditated malice aforethought. Second degree murder is without premeditation. Manslaughter is unlawful killing without malice. Voluntary manslaughter involves unlawful intention to produce injury but under mitigating circumstances, such as extreme provocation or mutual combat. Manslaughter by negligence refers to the negligent doing or omission of lawful acts under circumstances dangerous to life.

What came before the incident?

The dyadic interaction between slayer and victim culminates in a murder which, when it is an unlawful killing, represents a tearing of the fabric of normal social relationships. Although the actual killing is the climax of a series of social interactions, the social and psychological significance of the event lies outside of the brief time span of the criminal action per se. The likelihood that an individual will resort to violence is influenced by cultural factors and his status within a social system. The sociocultural organization affects the "choice" of victim, the method of perpetrating the crime, the kind of events likely to trigger homicide, and the societal response to the crime.

Most murders are the outcome of either a long-standing quarrel or a dispute arising out of a more immediate situation. In this respect, murder is usually an act of passion.[76] Murder committed with another crime also

---

[76] This does not suggest that systematic and repetitive use of murder is unknown. Earlier, this chapter noted deliberate use of murder in syndicated crime. The Thugs of India regarded murder as a hereditary profession—see James L.

can involve emotions such as fear of detection, hostility, and passion aroused in rape. Even though murder is generally a crime of passion, it can be considered to be patterned socially and culturally because both frequency and form of perpetration are associated with the sociocultural organization of which the murderer (and usually the victim as well) is a member. Thus even those crimes that appear to the casual observer to be the most individualistic in motivation, like murder, are subject to the influences of culture and social interaction.

As individuals, murderers may qualify through other behaviors as participants in criminal behavior systems such as professional crime, but as murderers they generally do not follow a criminal career. Murderers are less likely to be committed to a criminal culture, to demonstrate progressive acquisition of criminal techniques, and to identify themselves with other criminals.

Violence and social status

Homicide is a product of a social situation and of a confrontation between particular personalities in extreme conflict. The likelihood of violence of such events varies with the nature of the sociocultural organization and the person's status within that organization.

Cultural influence on the perpetration of homicide is suggested by the patterning of kinds of weapons employed. In a study of homicide among African tribes, Paul Bohannan noted that emphasis on cutting and striking instruments was to be expected because of the rarity of firearms, but two of the tribes differed from the others in a preference for stabbing over striking and beating.[77] In his Philadelphia study, Marvin Wolfgang found shooting employed in a third of the homicides, but the races differed in resort to beating or stabbing. Stabbings were almost three times more prevalent among black victims than were beatings. The relationship was the exact reverse for white victims.[78] The tradition of carrying weapons suggests a subculture of violence requiring the ready availability of weapons for self-defense, which may spell the difference between aggravated assault and homicide.

Crimes of violence are more likely when the subculture favors such reactions in quarrels. Wolfgang suggests the existence of a "subculture of violence" among lower-class males of both white and black races. A

Sleeman, *Thug, or a Million Murders* (London: Sampson Low, Marston & Co., Ltd., 1933). Renaissance Florence incorporated poisoning and assassination in a system of acquiring and maintaining political power—see Marvin E. Wolfgang, "Political Crimes and Punishments in Renaissance Florence," *Journal of Criminal Law, Criminology, and Police Science*, 44 (January–February 1954): 555–81.

[77] Paul Bohannan (ed.), *African Homicide and Suicide* (Princeton, N.J.: Princeton University Press, 1950), pp. 247–48.

[78] Marvin E. Wolfgang, *Patterns in Criminal Homicide* (Philadelphia: University of Pennsylvania Press, 1958), pp. 83–86.

jostle, a slightly derogatory remark, or the appearance of a weapon in the hands of an adversary stimulate differential reactions by members of the several social classes. The upper-middle and upper social classes, says Wolfgang, would regard as trivial the social and personal stimuli which evoke combat among members of the lower class.[79] The lower-class male is expected to demonstrate courage and defend his status through quick resort to physical combat.[80]

A negative relation between homicide and status is theorized by Andrew Henry and James Short, Jr., who see a positive relationship between homicide and the strength of the "relational system"—the degree of involvement in social relationships with other persons. They assume that the relational system of the married person or ruralite is stronger, on the average, than is the relational system of the unmarried or urbanite. The strength of external restraint to which the individual's behavior is subjected is considered to vary positively with the strength of the relational system. A person in lower positions in the status hierarchy is required to conform to the demands and expectations of persons of higher status "merely by virtue of his low status." Therefore, the person in the lower position is supposed to have a deeper involvement in the relational system.[81]

Arthur Wood places greater emphasis on the subjective definition of social conditions as limiting behavior in ways so stressful and frustrating that higher rates of homicide results. He assumes that homicide is more frequent among persons alienated, demoralized, and showing reactions of hostility. But Wood suggests that such personalities are more prevalent in status systems where those in low-status positions find that even their modicum of status is being questioned. When the lowly status is not questioned, fatalistic and submissive attitudes are more likely to deter as a means of protest.[82] Henry and Short see low status per se as making the individual vulnerable to externally imposed social restraints. Wood says the individual must define external restraint as undesirable before social conditions related to low status become factors in higher homicide rates.

Wood is on firmer footing than Henry and Short because he opens the way for analysis of the differential relationship of low status and homicide in varying social circumstances. The individual is more likely to experience emotional stress and frustration when he is exposed to a social system based on achieved rather than ascribed status. When he is taught

[79] Ibid., pp. 188–89.

[80] For a description of several types of violence over 60 years in a southern Illinois county, see Paul M. Angle, *Bloody Williamson* (New York: Alfred A. Knopf, Inc., 1966).

[81] Andrew F. Henry and James F. Short, Jr., *Suicide and Homicide* (Glencoe, Ill.: Free Press, 1948), pp. 16–17.

[82] Arthur L. Wood, "A Socio-Cultural Analysis of Murder, Suicide, and Economic Crime in Ceylon," *American Sociological Review,* 26 (October 1961): 744–53.

that social position and material rewards are distributed on the basis of individual achievement, the individual is more likely to consider intolerable the uncertainties of his lowly position and the discrepances between his accomplishments and his aspirations. Insecure personalities may be the product of differential child-rearing practices among the social classes, but Wood believes low-status position becomes a factor in homicide when lowly status is correlated with conceptions of social egalitarianism or when the lowly status is threatened by social changes, such as loss of land by peasants. Persons of higher status avoid violence because they have less direct and more effective ways of expressing aggression. Furthermore, their status level is sufficiently high that violence can bring loss of status.

Another aspect of the status and homicide relationship is the "choice" of victim. The crime may be the culmination of a series of social interactions within an institutional setting (family, place of employment, recreational establishment, and so on), with the fatal conflict emerging from relationships of slayer and victim within the institutional status system. A study of 172 murders in Denmark revealed that 57 percent of the victims were members of the slayer's family, 30.8 percent were acquaintances, and 12.2 percent were strangers.[83] Among homicides in Central India, it was found that kinsmen constituted 48.6 percent of the victims and close associates (neighbors, friends, sweethearts, or co-workers), 42.4 percent. In 94.5 percent of the cases, the offender and victim were of the same religion. The same caste was involved in 83.7 percent of the crimes.[84]

Pressure from the sociocultural organization

The degree of social pressure exerted on individuals by the sociocultural organization is a factor in homicide. Émile Durkheim suggested that in most nations where homicide is very common, a sort of immunity against suicide is conferred. Whereas suicides and many forms of crime tend to decline in time of war, homicides increase. Suicide is more characteristic of urban areas, but homicide rates are especially high among offenses in rural areas. Furthermore family life moderates suicide but stimulates homicide. Consequently, Durkheim saw suicide and homicide as having different relationships with the sociocultural organization.[85] Durkheim's typology of suicides will be adopted here as a conceptual framework for considering the relationship between homicide and the nature of the sociocultural organization.

[83] Kaare Svalastoga, "Homicide and Social Contact in Denmark," *American Journal of Sociology,* 62 (July 1956): 40.

[84] Edwin D. Driver, "Interaction and Criminal Homicide in India," *Social Forces,* 40 (December 1961): 153–58.

[85] Émile Durkheim, *Suicide,* trans. John A. Spaulding and George Simpson (Glencoe, Ill.: Free Press, 1951), pp. 338–59.

Anomic homicide reflects the lack of institutional control over the slayer induced by the breakdown of social norms or a failure to integrate him within the legitimate social structure. Homicide, therefore, would be a product of insufficient social pressures to bind the slayer to the rules associated with his status within the society's institutional framework. Bohannan suggests as examples the killer who is at odds with his society and homicides by members of "extrasocietal" institutions such as criminal syndicates and terrorist movements, which arise when the recognized and approved institutions are inadequate for the purposes of certain groups.[86]

Altruistic homicide results from the demands and expectations of customs in a well-integrated society. The culture itself may enjoin homicide under two sets of circumstances. First, the taking of life in specified situations endangering the security of the community is included under the official duties of the soldier, policeman, and executioner. Killings by officials reached mass proportions under the Nazi regime in Germany, when millions were sent to the gas chambers in the name of "promoting racial purity" and achieving "national destiny."

Second, value conflicts open the way for claims of individuals not in any official status that their acts advance the welfare of society or otherwise serve higher purposes. In "mercy deaths" life is taken from a suffering person as a means of ending his great pain. Evidencing value conflicts, the killer demonstrates his compliance with one set of norms (humanitarianism) by violating another (sanctity of human life). Bohannan cites the custom among Mediterranean and Arab peoples who in the past required men to kill their unchaste sisters.[87] In employing the "unwritten-law defense," the man who kills his wife's paramour or daughter's seducer does not defy the legal process. He gambles that public sympathies and mores in support of his deed will release him from punishment as a criminal. In this sense, the defense is an attempt to exploit a discrepancy between the mores and the formal law by creating a conflict between the sanctity of human life and the sanctity of the home as social values. In fact, the mores may press the individual toward murder in that the cuckold faces ridicule if the paramour goes unpunished.[88]

Egoistic homicide is a product of the relatively weak integration of individuals or subgroups within the social structure and, consequently, a weak commitment to the social institutions. In anomic homicide, emphasis is placed on the failure of the given society to exert control over the behavior of certain individuals or subgroups. Egoistic homicide differs in that the emphasis is placed on the degree of variation in behaviors permitted individual members, assuming that the society succeeds in achieving the degree of control sought.

[86] Bohannan, *African Homicide and Suicide,* pp. 12–13.

[87] Ibid., p. 13.

[88] Rupert B. Vance and Waller Wynne, Jr., "Folk Rationalizations in the 'Unwritten Law,'" *American Journal of Sociology,* 39 (January 1934): 483–92.

Bohannan points out that egoistic homicide is associated with societies which are "loosely structured"[89] so that a considerable variation of individual behaviors is permitted. Although cultures usually prohibit homicide, the broader range of individual behaviors permitted would enhance the possibility of homicides being employed as a means of resolving conflicts. In a closely structured society, rights and duties are strictly enforced, and a high degree of conformity to group norms is demanded. The strong integration of individuals within social groups would inhibit violent reactions against other persons, including homicide, as a means of resolving tensions, frustrations, and conflicts.

A study of suicide, homicide, and the social structure in Ceylon noted a relationship between homicide rates and the degree of adherence to behavioral norms demanded in a culture. The lowland Sinhalese, who have had the longest and most intensive contact with Europeans and represent the most loosely structured section of Ceylonese society, had the highest homicide rate. The Tamils are a Hindu people who share India's rigid caste system and emphasis on strict conformity to traditional practices. The homicide rate of the Tamils was about half that of the Sinhalese. Homicide rates were highest in those provinces where the Sinhalese compose the greatest share of the population. The rates were lowest when the Sinhalese are less than 60 percent of the province's population, but their suicide rates were higher. Thus the study found that the suicide rate will vary *directly,* and the homicide rate *inversely,* with the degree to which a society is closely structured.[90]

SEX OFFENSES

The legislatures of the states have enacted complex sets of statutes restricting almost every variety of noncoital sex. Because the laws differ greatly in their definitions and in the degrees of punishment imposed, legal regulation of sex behavior is a crazy quilt inspired largely by a driving interest to suppress deviant sexual behavior that is deemed destructive of the moral fiber of society. Legal controls also are intended to maintain the right of the individual to be protected from sexual coercion, the right of the child to be safeguarded from sexual exploitation, and the right of the community to be insulated from offensive public displays of sexual behavior.[91] These purposes have been cited as justification for resort to the criminal law to deal with homosexuality, one of the two sex offenses

[89] Bohannan, *African Homicide and Suicide,* p. 13.

[90] Jacqueline H. Straus and Murray A. Straus, "Suicide, Homicide, and Social Structure in Ceylon," *American Journal of Sociology,* 58 (March 1953): 466–69.

[91] Jon J. Gallo et al., "The Consenting Adult Homosexual and the Law: An Empirical Study of Enforcement and Administration in Los Angeles County," *U.C.L.A. Law Review,* 13 (March 1966): 657, 793.

to be discussed here. They apply as well to rape, the other one, in which protection against physical aggression also figures.

Pathology versus individualistic treatment

Although sex offenses vary in the specific behavior prohibited and in their concern with heterosexual or homosexual relations, all are creatures of laws enacted in an attempt to publicly enforce standards of private morality. When the criminal law is called on to enforce moral standards, any objective or reliable study of sexual deviants officially labeled "criminals" is obstructed. Such study is further complicated by the fractionation of criminal law among jurisdictions that has produced a variety of legal norms and various means for their administration and has resulted in a heterogeneous collection of crime statistics. Efforts to enforce private morality through techniques of crime control have given tangible evidence of the shortcomings of a blanket definition of entire classes of moral offenders as pathological beings. Under some laws, those so classified include married couples engaging in extramarital and "abnormal" sexual intercourse, adults engaging in consensual homosexuality, child molesters, prostitutes, and rapists. Another deficiency of legal norms is that they fail to take the psychological and sociological essence of the prohibited behavior into account.

Consenting adult homosexuality

The failure to distinguish between homosexuality as a condition and homosexual behavior complicates attempts at legalized suppression and the compiling of statistics on numbers of homosexuals. Michael Schofield believes homosexuality to be a condition characterized by a psychosexual propensity toward other persons of the same sex. The behavior of people who have this condition but control their urges cannot be characterized as homosexual. Out of curiosity or in exceptional situations, such as being confined in a one-sex establishment, other individuals will engage temporarily in homosexual practices without a commitment to the subcultural values associated with persistent homosexual behavior.[92] The person giving expression to this condition is likely to have a stable emotional attachment to a particular member of the same sex which is conducive to the privacy that will protect him from official recognition of the homosexual relationship. Therefore, genuine homosexuals are underrepresented in the group exposed to official actions designed to suppress homosexual behavior.

[92] Michael Schofield, *Sociological Aspects of Homosexuality* (Boston: Little, Brown & Co., 1965), pp. 147–48.

The identification of homosexuals is complicated by myths which are contrary to the findings of research. Feminine mannerisms, vocal inflections, and way of dress fail to distinguish homosexuals from nonhomosexuals because the two groups are similar within the range of psychological characteristics, and homosexuals are too varied to constitute a clinical identity.[93] Although the individual identified publicly as a homosexual is commonly viewed as suffering from a pathology that precedes his homosexual behavior, homosexuals have been found to have a capacity for dealing effectively with the problems of everyday life.[94] The Wolfenden Report in Great Britain pointed out that a single specific cause for homosexuality has not been determined.[95] Another myth is that homosexuals are likely to molest children, an offense which draws particular public horror, but Schofield finds the child molester distinctive from the homosexual who is involved in consensual relations with other adults. The child molester has more pronounced heterosexual interests, less promiscuity, less tendency to mix with homosexuals, and greater feelings of shame and guilt.[96]

The resort to the criminal law to suppress homosexual relations between consenting adults involves the system of criminal justice in the application of coercion to tasks that are unlikely to be achieved. Sexual behavior is a particularly private aspect of interpersonal relationships because of the strong mores involved, the great impact of sexuality as a stimulant of behavior, and the complexity of psychosexual development. The criminal justice system itself risks loss of prestige when public attitudes toward the prohibited behavior exist in great variety.[97] The Wolfenden Committee defined the function of the criminal law as "to preserve public order and decency, to protect the citizen from what is offensive or injurious, and to provide sufficient safeguards against exploitation and corruption of others." It denied that the law's function is to intervene in the private lives of citizens, to enforce any particular pattern of conduct, or to attempt to cover all fields of behavior.[98]

Members of overt homosexual groups are bound together by values

---

[93] Evelyn Hooker, "The Adjustment of the Overt Male Homosexual," *Journal of Projective Techniques,* 21 (March 1958): 18–31; Marcel T. Saghir et al., "Homosexuality: III. Psychiatric Disorders and Disability in the Male Homosexual," *American Journal of Psychiatry,* 126 (February 1970): 1079–86.

[94] William Simon and John H. Gagnon, "Homosexuality: The Formulation of a Sociological Perspective," *Journal of Health and Social Behavior,* 8 (September 1967): 180–81.

[95] *The Wolfenden Report; Report of the Committee on Homosexual Offenses and Prostitution* (New York: Stein and Day Publishers, 1963), pp. 31–33.

[96] Schofield, *Sociological Aspects of Homosexuality,* pp. 149–54. Also see John H. Gagnon, "Female Child Victims of Sex Offenders," *Social Problems,* 13 (Fall 1965): 176–92.

[97] For discussion of legitimacy of police authority, see Chapter 13, pp. 338–39.

[98] *The Wolfenden Report,* pp. 23–24.

supporting homosexuality and by a common defense against public stigmatization. This group cohesion works against the success of treatment strategies intended to divorce the active homosexual from homosexual groups and affiliation with their subcultural values. By stimulating a sense of common defense, suppressive measures by agents of criminal justice, paradoxically, aggravate the difficulties of treatment efforts.

In response to the increasing candor in public discussion of sex issues, overt homosexuals have developed a number of *homophile organizations,* some of which have made the rights of homosexuals a public issue.[99] The *homosexual community* is made up of a variety of groups which bind their members through common interests, acceptance of one another, reassurances that homosexuality is normal, and a common defense against enemies.[100] Through defensive tactics that exploit public places that are easily recognized but concealed from observation (such as restrooms), homosexuals are able to make sexual encounters with strangers without social commitment beyond the immediate situation.[101] Support for these activities is provided by segments of the nonhomosexual community in "gay bars," beaches, and restaurants catering to homosexuals and providing places for congregation.

Rape and social patterns

Although recognizing that rape is an expression of intrapsychic conflicts related to psychosexual development, Memachem Amir drew on his data to conclude that perpetration of this crime is socially and culturally patterned. His data consist of all cases of forcible rape reported to Philadelphia police for the years 1958–60. Blacks exceeded whites fourfold among both victims and offenders in absolute numbers, as well as in terms of their proportion to the general population. Computed on the basis of their respective numbers in the total Philadelphia population classified according to age and sex, black women were 12 times more likely to be raped than white women, and black men were 12 times more likely than white men to be in police files as rapists. Forcible rape occurred significantly more often between blacks than between whites. The age group of 15 to 19 had the highest rates among offenders and victims, and both groups generally were unmarried. Ninety percent of the offenders of both races were drawn from the lower part of the occupational

99 Edward Sagarin, *Odd Man In: Societies of Deviants in America* (Chicago: Quadrangle Books, Inc., 1969), pp. 81–83, 89–95.

100 Simon and Gagnon, "Homosexuality," pp. 182–83; Maurice Leznoff and William A. Westley, "The Homosexual Community," *Social Problems,* 3 (April 1956): 260–63; Evelyn Hooker, "The Homosexual Community," in James O. Palmer and Michael J. Goldstein (eds.), *Perspectives in Psychopathology* (New York: Oxford University Press, 1966), pp. 357–61.

101 Laud Humphreys, *Tearoom Trade: Impersonal Sex in Public Places* (Chicago: Aldine Publishing Co., 1970), pp. 2–3, 152–54.

scale. The incidents were planned 71 percent of the time, and 48 percent of the rape victims were at least prior acquaintances of the offender.[102]

Because of these patterns of differential distribution in Philadelphia's population, Amir believes the motives for rape are realities, or "social facts," as Durkheim uses the term, that arise from status and situational factors related to the lower-class subculture, especially among blacks, and are learned and maintained primarily in peer groups by adolescents and young adults. He found that since half the victims were at least acquaintances of their assailants, both were likely to be members of the same subculture. Adolescent and young males drew his chief attention because rape represents male aggression. Amir explained this aggression as an offshoot of the violence attributed to the lower-class subculture. Such a culture places less constraint against the idea of rape and more readily accepts the justifications advanced by the offender to explain the act. The sex aspect of the crime reflects elements of the lower-class black subculture: lack of a positive male role model within the family, the pattern of male dominance outside the family circle, early sexual experience, and male use of sexual exploitation of women to achieve prestige and status among peers.[103]

WHITE-COLLAR CRIME

Edwin H. Sutherland defines a *white-collar crime* as a crime committed by a person of respectability and high social status in the course of his occupation. He excludes crimes not part of occupational procedures, such as murder, adultery, and intoxication. Among white-collar crimes, Sutherland lists restraint of trade, misrepresentation in advertising, infringement of patents, "unfair labor practices," rebates, financial fraud, and violations of trust. He cites white-collar crimes of the medical profession: illegal sales of alcohol and narcotics, abortion, illegal services to criminals, fraudulent reports in accident cases, fraud in income tax returns, unnecessary treatment and surgical operations, fake specialists, and fee-splitting.[104]

Gilbert Geis notes that studies on white-collar crime include three distinct types of activity which differ according to the social class status of the offender and whether he commits his transgression as a single individual or in compact with other offenders: (1) individuals as individuals (for example, doctors or lawyers), (2) employees of corporations or

[102] Memachem Amir, *Patterns in Forcible Rape* (Chicago: University of Chicago Press, 1971), pp. 337–45.

[103] Ibid., pp. 319–31.

[104] Edwin H. Sutherland, *White Collar Crime* (New York: Holt, Rinehart & Winston, Inc., 1961), pp. 9, 12, 18.

businesses (such as embezzlers), and (3) policymaking officials for a firm (for example, in antitrust cases).[105]

Avoidance of judicial reaction

The violator's occupational role in legitimate society is seen as crucial by Donald Newman because other criteria are not universal. *Most* of the laws violated are not part of the criminal code because the bulk of white-collar legislation regulates business and professional activities and administrative procedures. *Most* of the white-collar violators have high social status in legitimate society, but, Newman points out, the farmer may water the milk and the television repairman may make unnecessary repairs.[106]

The white-collar criminal is not prosecuted as frequently as the usual criminal. Where there is prosecution, he is more likely to be handled by administrative agencies: the Internal Revenue Service, National Labor Relations Board, Food and Drug Administration, or Federal Trade Commission.

Why this emphasis on administrative rather than judicial agencies? Sutherland offers three explanations: the status of the businessman, the trend away from punishment, and the relatively unorganized resentment of the public against white-collar crimes.[107] The prestige of businessmen causes legislators and administrators of criminal justice to fear antagonizing them.[108] However, the major factor seems to be reluctance to conceive of these reputable people as criminals. Apparently the overall trend away from punishments in criminal justice has been more pronounced for white-collar crimes because it is difficult to unify public sentiments against crimes without a highly visible loss such as theft of an automobile. The comparative lack of publicity for white-collar offenses tends to forestall public resentment.

[105] Gilbert Geis (ed.), *White-Collar Crime* (New York: Atherton Press, Inc., 1968), p. 16.

[106] Donald J. Newman, "White Collar Crime," *Law and Contemporary Problems,* 23 (Autumn 1958): 737.

[107] Sutherland, *White Collar Crime,* p. 46.

[108] Marshall Clinard points out that criminal proceedings constituted less than 6 percent of all World War II OPA cases where sanction actions were taken. He offers explanations: The complexity of case preparation was an unusual burden on the Justice Department. The potential number of cases would have clogged federal courts already overwhelmed. The states were reluctant to approve prosecution because of unfamiliarity with, or lack of sympathy for, OPA regulations. Although convictions were secured in 93 percent of the cases prosecuted, comparatively light sentences were imposed because of lack of criminal record of offenders and lenient attitude of the courts. Many OPA prosecution attorneys feared use of the criminal sanction would cost them the loss of potential clients after the war. See Clinard, *The Black Market* (New York: Rinehart & Co., Inc., 1952), pp. 238–45.

Is white-collar crime a crime?

When, as in white-collar crimes, administrative decisions are used as the basis for defining nonconformists as criminals, the way is open for a particular administrator to brand as crimes any behavior he abhors. The moral values of the administrator would thus be substituted for what Paul Tappan regards as the "clarity and precision" of the legalistic definition of crime.[109] The same agency directs investigations, conducts hearings on cases, and administers punishment. Because formal criminal procedures are often absent, it is argued, the defendants lack the usual legal safeguards unless the findings are appealed to conventional courts. The assumption is that a specific, previously stated definition of certain behavior as criminal is a unique safeguard of court procedures against whimsical and arbitrary punishments.

In response to these criticisms, Sutherland agrees that an act is not a crime unless it is punishable by the state, but he points out that insistence on conviction in court is an administrative distinction too restricted in defining the criminal population. He includes white-collar offenses among crimes because they have been legally described as socially harmful and because legal penalities have been attached. The fact that an unlawful act is *punishable,* says Sutherland, is more important than whether it *is* punished.[110] He insists that the actual difference in presumption of innocence is not great when procedures of criminal courts and administrative agencies are compared. Rather, he believes, the differences in procedures were designed to protect the offender from the stigma of criminal prosecution.[111] Furthermore, as Newman points out, white-collar crimes, as well as traditional offenses, are adaptations of the principles of theft, fraud, and the like to modern socioeconomic institutions.[112]

Some sociologists object to inclusion of white-collar offenses among crimes on grounds that neither the offenders nor the mores define the prohibited conduct as criminal. George Vold sees a paradox in the labeling of reputable persons as criminals because he believes high status to be conferred by the community on the basis of demonstrated qualities and competence gained through sustained, substantial effort. Because the community defines both "high status" and the criminal law, the logic of white-collar crime is questionable, he contends; the concept assumes that the same community which confers high status on certain individuals also would stigmatize some of the same individuals as criminals.[113] Ernest W.

[109] Paul W. Tappan, "Who Is the Criminal?" *American Sociological Review,* 12 (February 1947): 99–100.

[110] Sutherland, *White Collar Crime,* pp. 30–31, 35.

[111] Ibid., pp. 40–43.

[112] Newman, "White Collar Crime," p. 743.

[113] George B. Vold, *Theoretical Criminology* (New York: Oxford University Press, Inc., 1958), pp. 253–55.

Burgess argues that the definition of criminals should be limited to persons who conceive of themselves as criminals and are so conceived by society. When, for example, Office of Price Administration regulations were suddenly thrust upon businessmen, transactions previously regarded as legal were made illegal. Without supporting mores, the public would not stigmatize business misconduct at the level applied to conventional crimes. In fact, Burgess argues, large sections of the population participated in black-market purchases, although Frank Hartung cites evidence that both violators and the public regarded OPA violations as criminal and that OPA controls included statutes dating back as far as 1906.[114] Reports of governmental agencies have been cited to demonstrate that white-collar offenses were not uncommon before the rise of wartime black markets.[115] Clinard believes only a small percentage of American consumers participated with full knowledge and volition in the black market.

Sutherland notes that white-collar offenders frequently resemble professional thieves in their repeated violations of the law, the customary absence of stigmatization by occupational colleagues, their expressions of contempt for government and its personnel, the deliberateness with which the offenses are perpetrated, and the organized manner of perpetration. When engaging in white-collar violations, corporations resemble professional criminals in that rationality is employed in the careful choice of a method of perpetration to minimize the danger of detection and identification, the probability of protest from victims, and the chances that proof of guilt will be obvious. Further, money and social prestige are used to "fix" any case involving prosecution.[116]

White-collar crime and the sociocultural organization

The inclusion of white-collar violations within the study of criminology is consistent with the view that the same sociocultural processes that produce lawful behavior also produce criminality. Offenders convicted of conventional crimes are drawn disproportionately from the lower social classes. When offenses more characteristic of the middle and upper classes are included among crimes, the possibility of class bias is reduced in criminological research and the administration of criminal law.

Strong competition in private enterprises accelerates diffusion of sharp practices which have brought high profits. Some white-collar offenses represent "normal" business procedures which are passed on as part of the occupational subculture. The ideology of "business is business" blurs the

[114] Frank E. Hartung, "White Collar Offenses in the Wholesale Meat Industry in Detroit," in Geis (ed.), *White-Collar Crime*, pp. 169–72, including comment by Ernest W. Burgess.

[115] Sutherland, *White Collar Crime*, pp. 17–40, 56–62, 95–122, 128–42, 152–213; Clinard, *The Black Market*, p. 94.

[116] Sutherland, *White Collar Crime*, pp. 218–20, 230–32.

distinction between honesty and criminality. When recruited into a business activity, the young man may be urged by superiors and colleagues to employ unethical or illegal tactics. The unethical but "successful" businessman is protected from public censure by his status in a social structure based on a culture which extols the values of "free enterprise." The rapid pace of social change and the technical complexity of business affairs have aggravated social disorganization, which is favorable to unethical business practices.[117]

White-collar violations frequently demonstrate patterns of interrelated behavior within a social structure. When the wartime violations of OPA regulations in the Detroit wholesale meat industry were studied, it was found that it was the established businessman who was the black-marketeer. Rather than involving a single isolated violation, however, the offenses formed a chain involving a number of businessmen. The price violation at any stage was passed on by businessmen at later stages of the processor-wholesaler-retailer-consumer chain, at the expense of the ultimate consumer. The wholesaler could not violate regulations unless other businessmen were willing to pay prices in violation of OPA regulations and to pass on illegal prices to those later in the chain.[118]

The high selectivity of offenses by white-collar criminals suggests the integration of the offenses within the sociocultural organization of society. Such offenses are possible because the criminal has a status within the socioeconomic structure of society which offers opportunities for them. The attainment of such a status indicates a degree of conformity to the norms of legitimate society which regulate the selection from among candidates of those who will fill positions that offer opportunities for white-collar crimes.

In his study of imprisoned trust violators, Donald Cressey found that a "nonshareable problem" contributed to the crime. The offender encountered some difficulty which had to be kept secret and private (heavy betting losses, an illicit love affair, and so on) according to the offender's own definition of his situation. Because money contributes to the solution of most of these problems, the troubled individual may have turned to trust violations to secure it. Personality traits may explain why the individual becomes involved in such a problem and why he defines it as one to be kept secret. But, says Cressey, possession of certain personality traits does not explain violations of financial trust. The offender must have contact with an ideology affording a rationalization which enables him to conceive of himself as being released from the obligations of a trusted person because of his nonshareable problem. The definition of a particular problem as nonshareable also reflects a social class ideology.

[117] Ibid., chap. 14.
[118] Hartung, "White Collar Offenses," pp. 166–68.

A person in a lower-class status is less likely to be condemned by his peers for an illicit love affair or gambling.[119]

The social structure of the occupation contributes to white-collar crime when alternative behaviors are possible within an occupational role organization. When an occupation is experiencing the impact of rapid change, social strain may result from divergent role expectations, especially when the occupation is marginal between business and professional activities. Chiropody, optometry, osteopathy, and pharmacy are examples of occupations dealing directly with clients in social situations pregnant with possible clashes between profit-making motivations and professional regard for the ethics of public service. The pharmacist role, for example, includes both merchandising aspects oriented to monetary gain and professional linkages to medicine through the compounding and dispensing of prescriptions. This marginal occupational status of the pharmacist invites variance among individuals in their definition of appropriate behaviors along a continuum ranging from high professional ethics to unstinting quest for business profits. Such individuals may transgress the boundary between questionable practices and law violations to become white-collar criminals.[120]

Implications of white-collar offenses

The more general implications of white-collar crime to criminology lie in its organized forms within the sociocultural organization of society. Criminality in high places is a major threat to the stability of society and the moral order. Marshall Clinard points out that wartime black-market crimes set an example of disobedience to the law by presumably reputable businessmen that was far more flagrant than in the case of most robberies, burglaries, or larcenies. Of every 5 business concerns, 1 was subjected to some kind of OPA action, and serious sanctions were applied to about 1 out of every 15 of the three million business concerns. The OPA estimated the black market in retail food alone varied from 3 to 5 percent of the nation's food budget of $27 billion.[121]

A major threat is posed by the integration of many forms of white-collar crime within the structure of legitimate business. Many single white-collar offenses begin a progressive chain of offenses through the manufacturing-wholesaling-retailing levels of trade, to increase the total

[119] Donald R. Cressey, *Other People's Money* (Glencoe, Ill.: Free Press, 1953), pp. 34–35, 143–46.

[120] In a study of prescription violators, Earl R. Quinney found professional-oriented pharmacists to abstain from violations. Pharmacists strongly oriented toward business were disproportionately represented among violators. See Quinney, "Occupational Structure and Criminal Behavior: Retail Pharmacists," *Social Problems,* 2 (Fall 1963): 179–85.

[121] Clinard, *The Black Market,* p. 243, 29–37.

financial cost to the consumer.[122] This is a threat because it undermines public confidence in legitimate business and presses honest businessmen to adopt similar practices in order to survive.

White-collar crimes, and the hesitation that is characteristic of efforts to punish such violators, are useful barometers of changes in the structure of society. Criminal law reflects the values of dominant groups which are able to protect their social and economic interests through legislation as an expression of their political power. When new groups are in political ascendancy, there is the possibility that new legal definitions of crimes may be created, such as the gradual change in Norwegian social structure brought about by the rise of the labor movement to political power and the decline of the business group. New legal crimes of the white-collar type have resulted from the translation of labor's political power into economic terms. However, the resistance of businessmen to this trend has retarded implementation of these laws.[123]

SUMMARY

Criminal behavior systems differ in the degree of the various offenders' commitments to a criminal culture, self-identification with other criminals, and progressive acquisition of criminal techniques. The professional criminal demonstrates these qualities to the highest degree, and the murderer, generally, to the least. Criminal behavior is subject to the socio-cultural organization of society and cannot be classified merely as individuated behavior by pathological beings. By setting patterns of crime in relationship to the structuring of social life, criminal behavior systems have the promise of lending deeper significance to efforts to deal with crime and criminals.

FOR ADDITIONAL READING

Anderson, Robert T. "From Mafia to Cosa Nostra." *American Journal of Sociology,* 53 (November 1965): 302–10.

Clinard, Marshall B., and Quinney, Richard (eds.), *Criminal Behavior Systems: A Typology.* New York: Holt, Rinehart & Winston, 1967.

Edwards, L. J. "Compensation to Victims of Crimes of Violence." *Federal Probation,* 30 (June 1966): 3–10.

Ferdinand, Theodore N. *Typologies of Delinquency.* New York: Random House, 1966.

Fooner, Michael. "Victim-Induced Criminality." *Science,* 153 (September 2, 1966): 1080–83.

[122] Hartung, "White Collar Offenses," pp. 166–67.

[123] Vilhelm Aubert, "White Collar Crime and Social Structure," *American Journal of Sociology,* 58 (November 1952): 269.

Gastil, Raymond G. "Homicide and a Regional Culture of Violence." *American Sociological Review,* 36 (June 1971): 412–27.

Gebhard, Paul H.; Gagnon, John H.; Pomeroy, Wardell B.; and Christenson, Cornelia V. *Sex Offenders: An Analysis of Types.* New York: Harper & Row, Publishers, 1965.

Huffman, Arthur V. "The Behavior Patterns of Criminals." *Journal of Social Therapy,* 8 (1962): 15–33.

Lunden, Walter A.; Saterlee, J. L.; and Connell, L. D. "Shoplifting among College Students." *College Store Journal,* 32, Sec. 2 (February–March 1967): 69–78.

Mays, John Barron. *Crime and the Social Structure.* London: Faber & Faber, 1963.

McClintock, Frederick H. *Crimes of Violence.* New York: St. Martin's Press, 1963.

———— and Gibson, Evelyn. *Robbery in London.* London: Macmillan & Co., 1961.

Megargee, Edwin I. "Assault with Intent to Kill." *Trans-action,* 2 (September–October 1965): 27–51.

Mendelsohn, B. "The Origin of the Doctrine of Victimology." *Excerpta Criminologica,* 3 (May–June 1963): 239–44.

Messick, Hans. *The Silent Syndicate.* New York: Macmillan Co., 1967.

Roebuck, Julian. *Criminal Typology.* Springfield, Ill.: Charles C Thomas, Publisher, 1967.

Rubin, Gerald D. "Employees as Offenders." *Journal of Research in Crime and Delinquency,* 6 (January 1969): 17–33.

Scarr, Harry A. *Patterns of Burglary.* Washington, D.C.: National Institute of Law Enforcement and Criminal Justice, U.S. Department of Justice, February 1972.

Shover, Neal. "Structures and Careers in Burglary," *Journal of Criminal Law, Criminology, and Police Science,* 63 (December 1972): 540–49.

Turner, Wallace. *Gambler's Money: The New Force in American Life.* Boston: Houghton Mifflin Co., 1965.

Tyler, Gus. *Organized Crime in America.* Ann Arbor: University of Michigan Press, 1962.

West, Donald J. *Murder Followed by Suicide.* Cambridge, Mass.: Harvard University Press, 1966.

Part III

Explanations for criminal behavior

Theories are intellectual tools for grasping the essential meaning concealed in a mass of apparently unrelated details. Such a meaning should enable us to move beyond sheer speculation, based on only what is visible to the casual observer, to a progressive discovery of the more profound meanings of criminal behavior. Many disciplines are involved in this search for truth; some researchers concentrate primarily on the individual criminal, while others center on the environment within which criminal behavior occurs. In the course of reviewing and evaluating various kinds of theories, Part III will investigate the thinking of many of those who have struggled with the elusiveness of crime as personal and social behavior.

$$8$$

Foundations of
theory and practice

The intellectual and cultural frames of reference characteristic of a given time have shaped the explanations advanced for criminal behavior, as well as societal reactions to criminals. These explanations and modes of response have become part of the heritage that has a profound influence on contemporary thought and practice. This chapter will review a portion of this heritage and provide a topical framework for the presentation of individualistic and environmental theories in the next two chapters.

THE CLASSICAL SCHOOL

The historical roots of punitive measures, which are still dominant in corrections and the system of criminal justice, may be traced to efforts to remedy the incredible corruption, arbitrariness, and cruelty of the criminal law in 18th-century Europe. In France, Montesquieu cited defects in the criminal laws of his time, arguing that the severity of punishment should be balanced with the gravity of the offense, and Voltaire mobilized public opinion in support of reform. Major credit for demonstrating what the faults were and what the remedies should be, however, is generally given to the Italian Cesare Beccaria (1738–1794).[1]

Beccaria and Bentham

In *An Essay on Crime and Punishment,* Beccaria protested the cruelty of punishments and the irregularity of proceedings in the courts of his day:

Surely, the groans of the weak, sacrificed to the cruel ignorance and indolence of the powerful, the barbarous torments lavished, and multiplied with useless severity, for crimes either not proved, or in their nature impossible, the filth and horrors of a prison, increased by the most cruel tormentor of the miser-

[1] M. T. Maestro, *Voltaire and Beccaria as Reformers of the Criminal Law* (New York: Columbia University Press, 1942), pp. 49–50.

169

able, uncertainty, ought to have aroused the attention of those whose business is to direct the opinion of mankind.[2]

In framing a program of reform, Beccaria depended heavily on the social contract theory. This theory contends that men originally were without government but created the state through a "social contract" by which they surrendered some of their "natural liberties" in return for the security that government could provide against antisocial acts.[3] Although it was necessary for individuals to give up part of their liberty for the sake of protection for the social collectivity, Beccaria felt they would want to surrender the smallest portions possible. The aggregate of these small portions "forms the right of punishing; all that extends beyond this, is abuse, not justice."[4]

On this basis, Beccaria argued that "the authority for making penal laws can reside only with the legislator, who represents the whole society united by the social contract." The judge, therefore, would not be allowed to inflict any punishment not ordained by law. The penalties imposed would be according to a scale determined by the degree of danger the given crime poses for society. With an exact and universal scale of crimes and punishment, men would know what the penalty would be for a certain antisocial act. The purpose of punishment would be to prevent the criminal from doing further injury to society and to prevent other persons from committing similar crimes. This requires setting penalties that would "make the strongest and most lasting impressions on the minds of others, with the least torment to the body of the criminal." The preventive effect would be maximized by prompt and certain punishment.[5]

In urging that the goal of punishment should be to deter a given crime, Beccaria was following the utilitarian concepts of free will and hedonism put forth by Jeremy Bentham (1748–1832). The Utilitarians assumed that man exercises free will in directing his behavior to seek pleasure and avoid pain, and the moral responsibility of the offender was taken for granted. Under "the principle of greatest felicity," the pursuit of maximum happiness was seen as the only "right and proper and universally desirable" purpose of human action. Accordingly, a *felicity calculus* was introduced to mete out punishment to counterbalance the pleasure produced by crime. The level of punishment would never be less than "what is sufficient to outweigh the profit of the offence,"—"profit" including any advantage, not merely pecuniary profit. The greater the mischief of

[2] Cesare Beccaria, *An Essay on Crime and Punishment* (Philadelphia: Philip H. Nicklin, 1819), p. xiii.

[3] Beccaria was following ideas of his day expressed by social contract theorists: Thomas Hobbes, John Locke, Montesquieu (Charles de Secondat, Baron de Montesquieu), Francois Marie Arouet Voltaire, and Jean Jacques Rousseau.

[4] Beccaria, op. cit., p. 18.

[5] Ibid., pp. 20, 28–30, 33–34, 47, 74–75, 93–96.

the offense, the greater would be the expense imposed through punishment. When two offenses were in prospect, the offender would be induced to select the one drawing the lesser punishment. The degree of punishment would never exceed that necessary to bring about conformity with the rules. If the offense showed the offender was a recidivist, or if the administration of punishment lacked certainty and promptness after perpetration of the offense, the magnitude of the punishment would be increased.[6]

The intimate contact between philosophers and rulers of many Continental European states gave remarkable force to Beccaria's views. Voltaire particularly gave them enthusiastic support. Frederick the Great stimulated revision of Prussian criminal law. Gustavus III of Sweden abolished the use of torture in 1772 and reduced the infliction of the death penalty. Joseph II of Austria abolished capital punishment in 1787 for all crimes except high treason and murder. The Criminal Code of Tuscany of 1786 attempted to protect individual rights, abolished capital punishment, and made the readaptation of offenders to normal life the major purpose of punishment. The French Penal Code of 1791 reduced the number of capital offenses from 115 to 32, restricted the decision-making authority of judges, and sought to moderate and graduate punishments and to achieve criminal reformation through labor.[7]

The neoclassical school

In the practical application of classical theory, the ignoring of individual differences and the assumption of untrammeled free will resulted in injustices. Gradually, therefore, the concept of limited responsibility crept in. The revised French code of 1819, for example, retained the essential principles of the classical school, but the system of defined and invariable punishments was modified. The judge was given a measure of discretion in varying punishments within minimum and maximum limitations fixed by law.[8]

Classical theory was founded on ideas abstracted from the concrete reality of the events they were supposed to describe. The ideals of the theory were difficult, if not impossible, to apply uniformly in the realities encountered in the administration of justice. Because every person was considered equally free and therefore equally responsible for his acts, classical theory denied the judge the opportunity to recognize extenuating

[6] Jeremy Bentham, *An Introduction to the Principles of Morals and Legislation,* edited by J. H. Burns and H. L. A. Hart (London: Athlone Press, University of London, 1970), pp. 11, 165–70.

[7] Leon Radzinowicz, *A History of English Law and Its Administration from 1950,* Vol. I (New York: Macmillan Co., 1948), pp. 286–95.

[8] John L. Gillin, *Criminology and Penology,* 3d ed. (New York: D. Appleton-Century, 1945), p. 231.

circumstances. Neoclassical theory, although also committed to the concept of responsibility under free will, provided some mitigation of the injustices inherent in classical theory. Judges were to be given sentencing discretion within maximum and minimum limits. Extenuating circumstances in the criminal, as distinct from circumstantial details of the offense situation, were to be recognized in the imposition of penalties. Minors were to be considered incapable of crime because they had not reached the age of responsibility. Persons insane or mentally defective at the time of the offense were not to be held responsible.

The introduction of the idea of limited responsibility ran counter to the concept of freedom of the will, which neoclassical theory supported. Thus the theory was involved in the practical difficulties of applying abstract distinctions between who should be held responsible and who should not. In practice, judges and juries tend to make decisions on the supposed menace of the crime to society—a concept of social responsibility for crime—regardless of the question of the offender's responsibility as determined by free will. Rather than relying on abstract principles, juries are likely to make their decisions on the basis of the circumstances in each case.[9]

Uniform standards of judgment continue to be an elusive goal for criminal justice because of the inconsistencies produced by the neoclassical support of free will, while recognizing the need for individualization of punishment. On one hand, punishment is supposed to be imposed uniformly and severely for the sake of safeguarding the community against the menace of crime. On the other, judges and correctional workers are expected to upset the uniformity and to provide for leniency in recognition of individual differences among offenders.[10]

CRITIQUE OF THE PUNITIVE APPROACH OF THE CLASSICAL SCHOOL

In endeavoring to achieve equality before the law and to limit the corruptive effects of arbitrary power in the courts, classical theory emphasized the crime rather than the qualities of the offender and relied on the administration of a predetermined, rational scale of punishments. Although the neoclassical school gave a greater degree of recognition to individual differences among offenders, approximations of the classical principles have formed the basis for penal punishment as the core of our system of criminal justice. In actual practice, how have these applications of felicity calculus worked out?

9 Ibid., p. 233.
10 See Donald R. Cressey, "Sources of Resistance to the Use of Offenders and Ex-Offenders in the Correctional Process," in *Offenders as a Correctional Manpower Resource* (Washington, D.C.: Joint Commission on Correctional Manpower and Training, 1968), pp. 32–33.

Rationales for penal punishment

The central argument advanced for penal punishment is that of *deterrence:* offenses of criminals and potential lawbreakers will be forestalled by the fear that pain will be inflicted in the future. Physical punishment has been described as a means of impressing on the public consciousness the unsuitability and disrepute of the forbidden act, thereby gradually and indirectly reeducating the public in terms of right and wrong.[11]

Punishment also is defended under the arguments of retribution and incapacitation. *Retribution* involves the official and deliberate infliction of pain and hardship in a measure designed to counterbalance the pain and hardship the lawbreaker has inflicted on society and/or himself. Initially, retribution served the state's purpose in limiting clan feuds and victims' retaliation against the transgressor.[12] Philosophers have debated the reasons for this transfer to government of the victim's desire to strike back at the offender. Heinrich Oppenheimer lists three theories: (1) in the theological view, retaliation fulfills a religious mission to punish the criminal; (2) in the aesthetic view, punishment resolves the social discord created by the offense and reestablishes a sense of harmony through requital; and (3) in the expiatory view, guilt must be washed away through suffering.[13] Ledger Wood advances a fourth explanation, a "utilitarian theory," in which punishment is considered to be a means of achieving beneficial and social consequences through application of a specific form and degree of punishment that is deemed most appropriate after careful individualized study of the offender. In this fashion, the offender is moved by punishment toward conformity with the social norms. Wood's "utilitarian" punishment differs from therapeutic use of authority in that he assumes some degree of punishment is always appropriate.[14]

Pessimism about the corrigibility of the prisoner and the outcome of any form of treatment characterizes the argument of *incapacitation:* at least, the incarceration of the criminal will deny him the opportunity for crimes while he is in prison. Incapacitation implies social selection because certain categories of persons are withdrawn from the community in hopes of reducing criminality. In this respect, the prison resembles a "pest house" employed to rid the community of disease.

From a genetic point of view, prolonged imprisonment denies certain individuals temporarily the opportunity to contribute to procreation. In

[11] Gustav Aschaffenburg, *Crime and Its Repression* (Boston: Little, Brown & Co., 1913), p. 259.

[12] Max Grünhut, *Penal Reform* (London: Oxford University Press, 1948), p. 3.

[13] Heinrich Oppenheimer, *The Rationale of Punishment* (London: University of London Press, 1913), pp. 182–83.

[14] Ledger Wood, "Responsibility and Punishment," *Journal of Criminal Law and Criminology,* 28 (January–February 1938): 635.

earlier periods the extreme deprivations of prison life could shorten the lives of inmates, thus modifying the composition of the nation's population to that extent. The effect of such genetic selection depends on the traits of those groups in the community most likely to be imprisoned. Because of the differential impact of criminal penalties among the social classes, those imprisoned were most likely to represent the socially and economically underprivileged.

Incapacitation is a remnant of what Oppenheimer called the "theory of disablement," whereby the offender was deprived of the power of doing future mischief through death, expulsion, calling down the wrath of some deity, mutilation, or branding. The mutilation would deprive the thief of his hands and the sex offender of his sex organs. To brand the offender would make him recognizable as a criminal. Long-term imprisonment would release the offender as an old man, too broken in spirit and body to be of further danger.[15] Changes in public sentiments have deprived the "theory of disablement" of support.

Unanticipated consequences of punishment

Indiscriminate and arbitrary punishment tends to cause character to deteriorate. The offender is a constellation of many personal qualities and attitudes. The decision to punish rests on assessments of the offender which emphasize those aspects of his behavior and personality regarded as most reprehensible. The more favorable characteristics are largely ignored. The decision to punish usually is made on the basis of criteria offering little opportunity to recognize the shades between "all good" and "all bad."

One of the purposes of deterrence is to increase the offender's future respect for the law, but punishment for its own sake may result in the undermining of his self-respect or move him toward confirmed criminality. When fear is learned within the context of a new situation, trial-and-error behavior is stimulated, but too strong a threat can have adverse results: inattentiveness to the lesson which is supposed to be learned, aggression against the threatener, and resort to various psychological strategems as defensive avoidance.[16]

Punishment may teach the offender to be more cautious "next time" and motivate him to develop more sophisticated techniques for evading detection. In rejecting his rejecters, he may appear as a heroic symbol to other offenders and even occasionally as a martyr to the general public. This casts the official representatives of law and order in the role of persecutor.

Punishment has failed to alleviate the problem of crime, in spite of the

[15] Oppenheimer, *The Rationale of Punishment,* pp. 255–56.

[16] Carl I. Hovland, Irving L. Janis, and Harold H. Kelley, *Communication and Persuasion* (New Haven, Conn.: Yale University Press, 1953), pp. 84–89.

infliction of the most severe penalties over centuries. Adultery and rape have been punished by castration. Punishment in medieval Europe and Colonial America included cutting off ears and hands, branding thieves, and piercing the tongues of liars with hot irons. Offenders were placed in stocks and pillories to inflict personal humiliation and public disgrace.[17] Deliberate policies of severe punishment swelled the ranks of criminals and jeopardized public support of the system of justice. Since the common people were often more merciful than the judges and the lawmakers, they frequently perjured themselves when serving on juries. When the death penalty was authorized for thefts of property of value in excess of 39 shillings, English juries frequently would return verdicts of guilt for theft of property worth 39 shillings when the actual value was as much as a thousand pounds.[18]

Effects of punishment on offender behavior

Whether or not the experience of being punished will have a significant effect on the future behavior of a particular offender depends on the interpretation he gives the experience. Punishment is most likely to be effective in modifying behavior when two factors are present: first, the punisher is of equivalent social rank or is a comrade of the person punished; second, comrades accept the punishment as just, and the peers of the person punished do not support him against the punisher. When the punisher and the person punished express conflicting social norms, punishment is effective to the extent that it permits communication of the social norms the punitive experience is supposed to inculcate. Punishment per se obstructs such communication, requiring the punisher to assume that the person punished will use the same perspective in evaluating the punishment experience. The offender is isolated from the very groups which would educate him in the norms he is expected to accept.

The punitive reaction assumes that all criminals differ markedly from noncriminals; yet some convicted offenders differ only in their behavior in a single criminal incident. When all are subjected to the punitive reaction, the offender not committed to criminal values is pushed away from the noncriminal groups to which he had been committed before undergoing punishment. Physical isolation of the offender from the noncriminal world symbolizes and deepens his social-psychological isolation from that world. As Laurence Sears puts it, when social isolation is carried too far, "it defeats its own purpose, for it cuts the nerve of effort."[19]

---

[17] Harry Elmer Barnes, "Shall We Get Tough or Be Sensible in Facing the Increase of Crime?" *Federal Probation,* 23 (June 1959): 31–32.

[18] Leo Page, *Crime and the Community* (London: Faber and Faber, Ltd., 1937), pp. 53–54.

[19] Laurence Sears, *Responsibility: Its Development through Punishment and Reward* (New York: Columbia University Press, 1939), p. 135.

In prescribing a degree of punishment for an offender, the judge must impute to him a certain state of mind that is meaningful in the light of the offender's own traits, the elements of his situation, and the overall value system within which those traits and elements operate.[20] When the judge and the offender have undergone the same pattern of personality conditioning within an equivalent socioeconomic environment, this difficult assignment may be accomplished. But when these circumstances do not exist, the imputation of certain motives to the offender becomes hazardous.

Effective use of punishment is limited to two possibilities. First, its sanctions would be applied only after a careful individualized study of the subject. This transfers the issue to the therapeutic use of authority. Second, its sanctions would be applied in a standardized manner according to criteria only indirectly related to the personality of the subject. An example would be the contemporary practice of fixing sentence on the basis of the seriousness with which legislators have regarded the crime, not on the basis of variation among human beings.

The negativism of punishment

Punishment warns against committing crimes, but it offers no counsel concerning the nature of proper behavior. It offers no solutions to the personal and social problems to be overcome as a prerequisite to the abandonment of criminal behavior. A crime may be symptomatic of the blocking of the offender's personal goals. Instead of altering these goals or improving the capacity to attain them through socially approved techniques, indiscriminate punishment may increase the blockage of goal attainment. Punishment as a reaction to delinquency and crime tends to reduce, if not eliminate, the possibility of effective treatment. When relying on punitive techniques, the agency tends to consider its work done once the punishment has been administered.[21]

The punitive ideology centers on the immediate situation, ignoring the serious difficulties the reformed offender will encounter in seeking a place for himself in the outside world after undergoing punishment. The punitive experience, in and of itself, does not change attitudes from antisocial to social. The stigmatization of undergoing punishment clings to the offender as he seeks employment and social acceptance, although presumably his punitive experiences have qualified him for readmission to society as a "cleansed" *former* criminal. Punishment per se offers him no

[20] Howard Becker, "Interpretative Sociology and Constructive Typology," in Georges Gurvitch and Wilbert E. Moore (eds.), *Twentieth Century Sociology* (New York: Philosophical Library, Inc., 1945), p. 75.

[21] Justine Wise Polier, "The Woodshed Is No Answer," *Federal Probation,* 20 (September 1956): 5.

counseling or material assistance in his role of lost lamb returned to the fold. In fact, his punitive experiences may aggravate his hostilities and his urge to improve his criminal skills, thereby extending the degree of the threat he poses.

Deterrent effects

In the application of punishment, it is usually assumed that an increase in severity of penalty will increase deterrent effect. A fundamental defect of this approach has been the failure to determine whether a milder alternative might not produce better results. There is a lack of reliable information for making intelligent distinctions between two sets of conditions —those under which penal sanctions do deter prohibited behavior and those under which they produce undesirable side effects.[22]

The use of punishment for deterrence must avoid the overseverity of application which arouses public sympathy for the offender. This means the range of severity among punishments is restricted by the level of brutality acceptable in the contemporary culture. The decline in the use of capital punishment culminating in the Supreme Court's decision prohibiting it and the mitigation of the severity of conditions of imprisonment since the early 1900s reflect the effects of humanitarianism in reducing support for such punishments. As Arthur Koestler terms it, the "minimum effective punishment" has been lowered.[23] If a punishment is regarded as excessive according to contemporary mores, the terror of its threat is lost through declining use. Once a public has had time to adjust to a lower level of severity of punishment, a milder penalty might have as much deterrent effect as a harsh penalty formerly had. The deterrent function of punishment has the least effect on those populations most likely to contribute to the work of courts and prisons, because members of such populations experience deprivations routinely in daily life.

It is impossible to fashion a practical legal "slide rule" which will determine the exact degrees of retribution appropriate for a list of crimes ranging from handkerchief theft to murder. This impossibility is demonstrated by the wide divergence in sentences imposed by courts within a single state. The concept of paying one's "debt" for a particular crime with a particular punishment enables the offender to believe that this payment frees him to run up a new "account."[24] Furthermore, many

[22] Norval Morris and Frank Zimring, "Deterrence and Corrections," *Annals of American Academy of Political and Social Science,* 381 (January 1969): 137–46. Also see W. Craig Biddle, "A Legislative Study of the Effectiveness of Criminal Penalties," *Crime and Delinquency,* 15 (July 1969): 354–58.

[23] Arthur Koestler, *Reflections on Hanging* (New York: Macmillan Co., 1957), p. 36.

[24] Austin MacCormick, "The Prison's Role in Crime Prevention," *Journal of Criminal Law and Criminology,* 41 (May–June 1950): 40.

criminals are of the type that cannot be deterred: insane, mentally defective, and persons under the situational stress of passion. Neoclassical theory attempted to meet this difficulty.

Punishment is a tool to be used sparingly in the education of the public in law observance. This educational purpose requires that the decision to employ punishment and the choice of the specific penalty be fitted to social and cultural circumstances.[25] A given penalty may have the desired effect under the values of one culture but fail when applied within the context of different values in another society. The qualities of the particular population (such as social class, race, sex, and degree of criminality) to which the penalty is to be applied must be considered. The degree of deterrence varies with the chances of keeping the particular type of crime secret and, consequently, avoiding social reprobation. A respectable bookkeeper would fear the social shame and economic ruin more than the penal punishment itself if he were apprehended as an embezzler. The bootlegger or smuggler would regard the prison sentence as an occupational risk. The target population must be aware that the legal norm exists and that nonconformity involves risk of punishment.

In final analysis, certainty and promptitude of punishment are the most important factors in achieving deterrence. Both these characteristics of the administration of penalties are products of the factors considered above.

THE POSITIVE SCHOOL

The positive school of criminology, which sought to apply the scientific method to the study of criminological phenomenon, had its genesis in the work of three late 19th-century Italians, Cesare Lombroso (1836–1909), Enrico Ferri (1856–1928), and Raffaele Garofalo (1852–1934). Educated for medicine and specializing in psychiatry, Lombroso became interested in the anthropological study of criminals. As an army doctor, he noticed that offender-soldiers differed from disciplined troops by the greater prevalence (and indecency) of tattoos. He is chiefly identified today with his contention that the criminal bears the physical traits of the "primitive savage"—the so-called "born criminal." Ferri, a student of mathematics and criminal law, sympathized with Lombroso's biological theory of crime causation, but he was the most modern of the three positivists in his analysis of crime as the product of geographical, anthropological, and economic forces. Garofalo was a magistrate, senator, professor of criminal law, and prolific writer. He differed from his

---

[25] John C. Ball, "The Deterrence Concept in Criminology and Law," *Journal of Criminal Law, Criminology, and Police Science* 46 (September–October 1955): 347–54.

colleagues by placing greater emphasis on judicial reform and the psychological anomalies of the criminal.[26]

Atavism and physical types

While performing a post mortem examination of a famous brigand of extraordinary agility and cynicism, Lombroso found a distinct depression on the interior of the lower back part of the skull where the spine protrudes into the normal human skull. He had found this same characteristic in "inferior" animals, and the discovery was a revelation that caused him to envisage the criminal as an atavistic being who was presumed to possess the "ferocious instincts" of "primitive" humanity. Whereas direct heredity preserves the stability of the species, *atavism* (a biological "throwback") is characterized by the reappearance of traits of remote ancestors. In the belief that the criminal bears the traits of the "primitive savage," Lombroso cited such atavistic anatomic traits as: narrowness of the forehead, exaggerated development of frontal sinuses and cranial vault, disproportionate development of the cheekbones, abnormal projection of the jaw, eye defects and peculiarities, large ears or ears resembling those of the chimpanzee, fleshy or protruding lips, abundance of wrinkles, and too many fingers. He endeavored to support his anatomic evidence by citing assumptions that earlier societies and savage tribes tolerated behavior now defined as criminal.[27]

His later writings referred to relationships between criminals and two other groups with pathological conditions—the "morally insane" and epileptics. Because many anomalies he had found in criminals could not be explained by atavism, he searched for some pathological agent which arrested the development of certain organs, particularly the development of nerve centers, during the fetal stage of an individual. He came to believe this agent was associated with epilepsy and therefore added the idea of degeneration to atavism.[28]

Lombroso described three general types of criminals. *Born criminals,* constituting about one third of all offenders, are the products of atavism. *Insane criminals,* exhibiting degeneracy similar to epileptics, include "hysterical persons," alcoholics, dipsomaniacs, pyromaniacs, kleptomaniacs, and the "temporarily insane." *Criminaloids,* who are drawn into crime by environmental factors or situational opportunities, differ from "born criminals" in degree, not in kind. The physical stigma are less

[26] George B. Vold, *Theoretical Criminology* (New York: Oxford University Press, 1958), pp. 28–38.

[27] Constancio Bernaldo de Quiros, *Modern Theories of Criminality,* trans. Alfonso de Salvio (Boston: Little, Brown & Co., 1911), pp. 13–15.

[28] Marvin E. Wolfgang, "Cesare Lombroso," in Hermann Mannheim (ed.), *Pioneers in Criminology* (Chicago: Quadrangle Books, 1960), pp. 187–88.

marked, but, Lombroso said, when criminaloids have a long sojourn in prison, they "can no longer be distinguished from born criminals except by the slighter character of their physical marks of criminality." In later editions of his work he referred to two additional types. *Criminals by passion,* differing markedly from born criminals, exhibit more "harmonious lines of body, beauty of soul, and nervous and emotional sensitiveness." Nevertheless, they resemble epileptics in "their tendency to excesses, impulsiveness, suddenness in their outbreaks, and frequent amnesia." *Occasional criminals* ("or better, pseudo-criminals") do not seek opportunities for crimes but fall into the meshes of crime "for very insignificant reasons."[29]

Although recognizing the influence of social and environmental factors on crime causation, Lombroso never brought himself to include among criminals offenders who did not exhibit organic, mental, or physical characteristics that could explain their criminal behavior.[30] Lombroso's unilateral theory of atavism has become a discarded myth.

Certainly, anthropology makes its contribution to criminology, and biological factors are most germane. As Chapter 9 will discuss, there were later efforts to revive physical types as *the* answer to the riddle of criminal behavior, but they also suffered from faulty premises, questionable methodology, and overly ambitious reliance on a single explanation.

The contributions of the positive school, however, were not limited to Lombroso's theory of atavism. Other contributions, suggested by the term "positive," make it an essential topic in a review of the development of criminological theory.

The scientific method and criminology

Auguste Comte (1798–1857), the father of positivism and the person who gave sociology its name, argued that the expansion of human knowledge required the application of the scientific ("positive") method of observation, experimentation, and comparison. The Lombrosians were identified as the positive school because they advocated reliance on the scientific method to explain criminological phenomenon and substituted the investigation of facts for inquiry about ultimate origins or causes. Departing from the speculative approach of the classical school, the positive school proposed to establish fundamental principles for criminology similar to the laws of nature that were being uncovered by natural science.

The classical school saw lawbreaking as rational behavior by persons endowed with free will and believed such behavior could be channeled into support of the interests of society through the establishment of a

---

[29] Cesare Lombroso, *Crime: Its Causes and Remedies* (Boston: Little, Brown & Co., 1918), pp. 365–76.

[30] Thorsten Sellin, "A New Phase of Criminal Anthropology in Italy," *Annals of American Academy of Political and Social Science,* 125 (May 1926): 235–36.

system of rewards and punishments. In opposition, the positive school argued that behavior is determined by biology or social circumstance, and each type of man has an ingrained proclivity to virtue or vice. Effective crime control measures could be implemented only after identification of the types of men and the social forces producing them.[31] The clash was between the metaphysical conception of free will, to be controlled by enacted law, and determinism—the doctrine that every event is the inevitable result of antecedent conditions.

Ferri described the positive school as a new phase in the evolution of criminal science, bringing life to the narrow field of abstract legal technicality through the discovery of facts. He saw this new phase as essential in meeting the crime problem:

The impotence of punishment to repress crimes, in spite of the prodigality of effort and expense that it has entailed—the ever increasing number of habitual criminals—the dangerous and sometimes absurd contrast between the facts of psychiatry and the mystic theories of the moral responsibility of man—the arrested development or exaggeration in the forms of procedure—the introduction into this superannuated procedure of new institutions which do not fuse with it—all this, and still other reasons, demanded and still demand a scientific and legislative remedy.[32]

Ferri criticized metaphysical philosophy for producing absolute opposition between incompatible conclusions "sprung from the logical fantasy of thinkers." Positive philosophy, he said, engenders only partial differences of personal interpretation and builds on indestructible conclusions based on verified experimentation.[33]

In place of the concept of moral responsibility, Ferri offered the theory of social accountability. The person does not exist only as an individual but rather as an element of a society. Without law, it is impossible for men to live together. Legally and socially, the individual has rights and duties because there are relationships among men. On the basis of these assumptions, Ferri argued, the individual is socially accountable (or responsible) for his actions, which have effects that rebound from society upon the individual himself. Society cannot be denied the right of self-preservation, irrespective of the moral responsibility of the individual, Ferri decided.[34]

Previous to the work of Lombroso and his followers, criminology had been dominated by the classical school, with its "endless theoretical arguments" and sterile efforts to fix the penalty which was supposed to "fit

[31] Albert K. Cohen, *Deviance and Control* (Englewood Cliffs, N.J.: Prentice-Hall, Inc., 1966), p. 49.

[32] Enrico Ferri, *Criminal Sociology,* trans. Joseph I. Kelly and John Lisle (Boston: Little, Brown & Co., 1917), p. 8.

[33] Ibid., pp. 9–10.

[34] Ibid., pp. 360–63.

the crime," according to Hermann Mannheim. It is to Lombroso's lasting credit "that he saved criminal science from the shackles of merely academic abstractions and fertilized it with the rich treasures of the natural science."[35] However, it is an exaggeration to identify the total development of scientific criminology with this one school, because Lombroso had predecessors. Alfred Lindesmith and Yale Levin describe as "particularly ironical" the assumption that "the notoriously slipshod methods" of Lombroso should be the basis of the claim that he established criminological science. They see his contribution, rather, as the establishment of criminal anthropology.[36] The most balanced assessment appears to be that the merit of the positive school was its confrontation of the speculative approach of the classical school with the investigative techniques of the scientific method.

Emphasis on the individual offender

Medicine made progress when it switched from the treatment of diseases as abstract entities to the treatment of specific patients and their particular conditions and characteristics. Similarly, the Lombrosians moved away from the study of crimes as abstract entities—homicide, robbery, and forgery as juridical abstractions. Instead, crimes were to be analyzed as natural and social acts of human beings in a search for "the natural causes of the phenomenon of social pathology which we call crime" and remedies which "may repress it within certain bounds."[37] Prevention of crime was emphasized in the positivists' proposal to use scientific methods in a detailed classification of criminals according to type and in the development of measures designed to curb offenders according to the degree of danger they posed for society.[38] Analyses of individual criminals were to provide scientific means of achieving the protection of society which was the key objective of the Lombrosians.

The positive school placed new emphasis on the relationship between the offender as an individual and the treatment he would receive in endeavors to reduce the impact of crime on society. This orientation was a fundamental change from the classical school's concentration on the crime as a legal entity and its belief that penalties should largely be fixed regardless of the characteristics of the individual offender and the social conditions under which the criminal act occurred. In directing attention to the question of why certain individuals became criminal, the Lom-

[35] Hermann Mannheim, *Group Problems in Crime and Punishment* (London: Routledge and Kegan Paul, 1955), pp. 70–71.

[36] Alfred Lindesmith and Yale Levin, "The Lombrosian Myth in Criminology," *American Journal of Sociology,* 42 (March 1937): 664.

[37] Ferri, *Criminal Sociology,* pp. 11–12, 18–19.

[38] Hermann Mannheim, "Introduction," in Mannheim, *Pioneers in Criminology,* p. 16.

brosians participated in the development of one of two general streams of criminological thought—what we shall call "individualistic theories." The other stream—which we call "environmental theories"—involved analysis of the existence and distribution of crime in society.

The Lombrosians gave secondary importance to environmental factors. Although Lombroso devoted increasing attention to such factors as climate, rainfall, density of population, and economic conditions, he saw them as operating through the expression of physical criminal tendencies. Ferri found biological explanations insufficient and incomplete, but he believed "criminal neuroses" (distinct from atavism or degeneracy but biological in origin) caused criminal behavior when they were favored by conditions in the natural and social environments.[39] Garofalo regarded Lombroso's criminal anthropology as lacking convincing proof but nevertheless regarded the regressive characteristics of criminals as obvious and saw their source in a moral anomaly based on hereditary transmission of criminal propensities.[40]

Scientific methods, the positivists proposed, should be employed for the classification of criminals according to the individual, physical, and social characteristics of criminality. On the basis of criteria established by research, appropriate measures would be taken to deal with the offender according to the degree of danger he posed for the society. Ferri recommended three kinds of measures. First, imprisonment for an indeterminant period should be imposed when justified by the harm inflicted and by the determinative motive and anthropological characteristics of the offender. Second, reparation of the harm suffered by crime victims in lieu of imprisonment would be appropriate when the criminal act is not serious and the offender not dangerous. Third, the action taken against the convicted offender would be based on his "physiopsychological qualities" rather than on the nature of his misdeed or a uniform penalty. The classification systems of anthropological criminologists would be the means of relating treatment to the causes of the offender's criminality. The principles employed in evaluation of offenders would provide for easy and practical prison administration in spite of the difficulties of obtaining competent treatment personnel.[41]

In basing correctional treatment on evaluation of individual offenders according to criteria developed from analysis of patterns found among criminals, the positivists had a hand in the establishment of a practice common to American prisons. Paradoxically, they also contributed to an emphasis on custodial supervision and doubts that inmates can be changed. These contributions are products of the positivists' emphasis on the protection of society from criminals and the pessimism derived from

[39] Ferri, *Criminal Sociology,* pp. 111–15.

[40] Raffaele Garofalo, *Criminology* (Boston: Little, Brown & Co., 1914), pp. 74, 92–95.

[41] Ferri, *Criminal Sociology,* pp. 502–18.

the concept of the born criminal. These views of the Lombrosians stood in contrast to their sharp criticisms of the repressive prisons of their day and their advocacy of alternatives to imprisonment, such as probation. "It would be a mistake, however," Lombroso wrote, "to imagine that the measures which have been shown to be effective with other criminals could be successfully applied to born criminals; for these are, for the most part, refractory to all treatment, even to the most affectionate care begun at the very cradle."[42] For acts shocking the moral sense of society, Garofalo urged elimination of criminals through death because imprisonment for life raised the possibility of escape or pardon.[43]

Lombroso: A paradoxical figure

In the development of criminology, Lombroso is a paradox. Some scholars date the beginning of modern criminology with the work of the positive school of which he was the leader; but, as Thorsten Sellin notes, he was not a social scientist and not even the founder of modern biological investigation of criminological causes. Lombroso's ideas proved so challenging, however, that they succeeded "in driving hundreds of fellow students to search for the truth."[44] The introduction of the scientific methods of research has been credited to the positive school, but Lombroso's work is replete with faulty philosophical deductions, questionable methods of measurement, the absence of adequate control groups, the use of questionable data, and the free use of speculation in interpretations based on meager data.[45] Lombroso and his colleagues are credited with stimulating interest in the study of the criminal rather than concern with philosophical abstractions; yet Lombroso is strongly identified with his concept of the "born criminal" as a biological "throwback"—a concept which essentially ignores the wide variation in characteristics among offenders.

Several explanations may be offered for these paradoxes. The first is based on the two opposed tendencies in philosophy that can be identified in the "positivistic organicism" of Comte. In providing the first theoretical construction of sociology as a new discipline, Comte emphasized *positivism,* which rejects all assumptions and ideas exceeding the limits of scientific techniques in investigation and rests its interpretations exclusively on experience. However, he also imposed the assumptions of organicism, in violation of the emphasis in positivism on verifying components of a system. *Organicism* holds that the relationships among parts of society can be compared to those among the organs of a living body,

[42] Lombroso, *Crime,* p. 432.

[43] Garofalo, *Criminology,* pp. 219–21.

[44] Thorsten Sellin, "The Lombrosian Myth in Criminology," *American Journal of Sociology,* 42 (May 1937): 897–99.

[45] Wolfgang, "Cesare Lombroso," pp .193–207.

and that therefore the organization of society, rather than its components, is responsible for its life. In committing the study of society to investigation of various possible assumptions about the nature of phenomena, organicism opposes the view of positivism that verification of scientific methods is the sole basis for explaining phenomena. The Comtean synthesis of positivism and organicism was accepted in spite of its inconsistency, Don Martindale believes, because the intellectual and social currents of Comte's time, characterized by the conservative reaction to the social disequilibrium of the French Revolution, required some intellectual accommodation of the scientific method with the conservative conception of society as being superior to its parts. Comte's synthesis fitted a need peculiar to his time, in spite of the inherent inconsistency of his position.[46]

Lombroso's position was similarly useful in appearing to combine scientific methods with an explanation for criminality that would be congenial to conservative groups in the power structure of society. He located the source of criminality, essentially, in the abnormality of individuals, with only incidental attention to the social structure. The positive school emphasized the wisdom of the scientific expert in deciding what kinds of human beings will commit crime and in prescribing appropriate treatment. Because this service was supposed to be performed without the consent of the person diagnosed as a criminal, the positive school was especially vulnerable to totalitarian patterns of government. An example of such vulnerability was Ferri's participation in the drafting of a penal code in Mussolini's regime.[47]

The second explanation for the paradox of Lombroso's position is the point that the longevity of the work of any thinker rests on the historian's interpretation of his work within the intellectual patterns of his age. In this sense, as Hermann Mannheim notes, certain ideas and theories seemed to have been "in the air," only waiting for Lombroso to take them up.[48] To interpret Lombroso's writing solely in the light of subsequent developments exaggerates his faults; undoubtedly, the positivists did not foresee the full consequences of their views. Furthermore, there were individual differences within the positive school, and the similarities between positivists and the nonpositivists are often overlooked.

Third, in emphasizing the physical features of individuals, positive theory was consistent with the popular folklore derived from the earlier pseudosciences of physiognomy and phrenology.[49] The biological concepts were congenial to Darwinism, which had had a profound effect on the development of natural sciences. The linkage of positivism with a

[46] Don Martindale, *The Nature and Types of Sociological Theory* (Boston: Houghton Mifflin Co., 1960), pp. 52–53, 62–63.

[47] Vold, *Theoretical Criminology*, pp. 35–36.

[48] Mannheim, "Introduction," pp. 4–6, 17, 23–29.

[49] Bernaldo de Quiros, *Modern Theories of Criminality*, pp. 2–4.

physical-type explanation accommodated both popular folklore and the emphasis on the natural sciences in the intellectual climate of Lombroso's day.

IDEOLOGICAL HERITAGE AND CRIMINOLOGICAL PRACTICE

As products of their respective ages, the classical and positive schools endeavored to reform the workings of criminal justice. Their ideas have become part of the heritage shaping the activities of contemporary criminological practitioners.

Contradictions and contemporary ideologies

One of the sources of the inconsistencies and administrative problems that plague police departments, courts, and correctional agencies has been identified as the preservation in the system of criminal justice of irreconcilable perspectives derived from the classical and positive schools.[50] In keeping with the rationalism of the classical school, criminal acts and law violations are today supposed to be deterred by "swift, certain, and severe" punishment. Primary concern is directed toward the crime as a legal entity. The positive school has contributed to the policy of severe punishment by emphasizing social protection as an objective and raising the image of the incorrigible "born criminal." From the positive school's emphasis on the individual offender and the scientific method also comes the claim of the criminal justice system that it recognizes individual differences among offenders in sentencing and correctional practices. The treatment of the offender is said to be based on scientific analysis of his characteristics and the social conditions affecting his criminal behavior. The ultimate objective is said to be the restoration of the offender to a useful and satisfactory life through correction of his individual deficiencies and elimination of the sources of criminal behavior in his relationships with the social environment. Such practices as indeterminate sentences, probation, clinical analyses of offenders, and prison classification procedures are directly traceable to the positive school.

The inherent contradictions of the two theories are preserved and expressed in criminological practice in the various ideologies that have been developed in attempts to make sense out of work with offenders. As a system for organizing beliefs, an ideology provides its adherents with an intellectual orientation. Because the adherents accept a particular set of beliefs, they are provided with justifications for their behavior and expla-

---

[50] See Mabel A. Elliot, *Conflicting Penal Theories in Statutory Criminal Law* (Chicago: University of Chicago Press, 1931); Richard Quinney, *The Problem of Crime* (New York: Dodd, Mead and Company, 1970), pp. 21–27; Nathaniel Cantor, "Conflicts in Penal Theory and Practice," *Journal of Criminal Law and Criminology,* 26 (September–October 1935): 330–50.

nations for the events in which they are engaged. A criminological ideology gives the practitioner reassurance that his work is important and his methods are efficient.

The beliefs incorporated in the ideologies of criminological workers are adapted from the "practical wisdom" of folklores inherited from the ideas of past criminological theorists, whether or not the ideas are still valid and germane. They also are products of the "practical wisdom" of earlier generations of practitioners who have provided the learning content to which contemporary workers are socialized in the course of their apprenticeship. The call for professionalization of practice that has been heard in recent decades presumably encourages the introduction of new beliefs more consistent with the discoveries of criminological science. This objective implies that the narrowing of divergencies between criminological practice and relevant theories would lend direction and effectiveness to the system of criminal justice.

Ideologies of contemporary practitioners may be differentiated grossly according to the tendency to evaluate criminal behavior as conscious defiance of rules (the free-will view of the classical school) or as evidence of the effect of forces external to the offender (the determinism of the positive school). On the basis of this distinction, Clarice Stoll postulates that adherents of the free-will view will prefer to restrict and castigate deviants, and their opponents will treat deviants without reproach. The presence of both types of preference in the criminal justice system produces contradictions among classes of personnel in the goals they see for criminological work and in their typical interactions with offenders. Stoll suggests these contradictions are more likely when two conditions are present: the ideologies of the various sets of personnel are in conflict, and the system incorporating the categories of personnel lacks established means of resolving the contradictions.[51] Both these conditions are present in the system of criminal justice.

Among police, judicial, and correctional personnel, a wide range of beliefs exists. To simplify, there are three general categories of criminological ideologies: punitive, therapeutic, and preventive. In practice, these categories are not necessarily mutually exclusive.

Punitive ideology

Associating the offender with unmitigated evil, incorrigibility, and intractable hostility to "good" society, the punitive ideology focuses attention on the threat his behavior poses to his victim and to society. The major objective is protection of society. The orientation is toward the past in that the offender is judged largely in terms of what he did rather than in terms of his capacity for improved behavior in the future. The

---

[51] Clarice S. Stoll, "Images of Man and Social Control," *Social Forces,* 47 (December 1968): 121–22.

techniques employed center around the infliction of pain and restrictions upon the offender through coercion. Hans von Hentig sees punishment as "organized hurt" for the offender. Just as pain is supposed to ·cause avoidance actions in everyday life, the punitive ideology deliberately creates an artificial danger so that the offender's senses will be directed to change his behavior.[52]

The conception that crime is caused simply by "bad" criminals is central to the "hard line" approach to crime control—an extreme position held by some advocates of the punitive ideology. Fred Inbau and Frank Carrington believe "certain liberal social scientists" claim they can explain the motivations of the criminal but can do little to protect the innocent against the mugger or armed robber. The "hard line" prescription is massive citizen support for the policeman "when he is doing his job properly," drastic curtailment of the "contrived rights" of criminal suspects which only "protect the guilty without any compensating benefits," and public accountability for sentencing practices which release "a potentially dangerous felon" into the community.[53] In opposition to the "hard line" approach, Daniel Skoler cites the incredible financial costs of coercive prison confinement. He recommends concentration on the *capacity* of lawbreakers for lawful behavior, the development of their motivation and resources for strengthening this capacity, increasing the relevance of this capacity to their lives as community members, and making crime control programs part of the community as a social system.[54]

Therapeutic ideology

The central objective of the therapeutic ideology is modification of the relationship between the offender's personality as a criminal and his behavioral capacities on one hand and his social environment on the other. Oriented largely to the immediate future, various strategies of intervention are employed to bring changes either in the individual offender or in his relationships with his environment, with the ultimate aim of improving his conformity with approved norms.

The emphasis on the qualities and treatment needs of the offender frequently conflicts with a hard-line demand for social protection and the arbitrary setting of penalties according to the presumed seriousness of the given crime. Adherents of the punitive ideology sometimes claim that their efforts to impose "discipline" upon offenders can qualify as "ther-

[52] Hans von Hentig, *Punishment: Its Origin, Purpose and Psychology* (London: William Hodge, 1937), pp. 1–2.

[53] Fred E. Inbau and Frank G. Carrington, "The Case for the So-Called 'Hard Line' Approach to Crime," *Annals of American Academy of Political and Social Science,* 397 (September 1971): 19–27.

[54] Daniel L. Skoler, "There's More to Crime Control than the 'Get Tough' Approach," *Annals of American Academy of Political and Social Science,* 397 (September 1971): 28–39; our earlier analysis of punishment is also relevant.

Figure 8–1. Symbol of social protection as prison's duty.

Symbolic of the punitive ideology, the guard tower emphasizes concern of prison officials over the possible threat some convicted criminals pose to the community outside prison walls. Safekeeping is the legal responsibility of correctional institutions, but only a minority of prisoners requires this degree of custody.

apy." Such sterile claims, however, should not be confused with three notions of therapeutic ideology noted by Marc Ancel as having a long history of advocating something more than punishment for its own sake. First, there has been concern for the protection of society beyond the use of punishment simply as a means by which the offender can atone for his crime. Second, there has been a desire to ameliorate the criminality of the individual—perhaps his reeducation—over and above the infliction of a penalty to make him an example to other persons or to restore the social balance upset by the crime. Third, humanitarianism traditionally respects the person to whom none but a humane treatment can be applied. Plato made a distinction between incorrigibles and criminals who can be cured. The penal law of ancient China invoked the idea of repentance. Muslim law provided measures of reeducation for children, and judges were bound to consider the crime situation and the personality in a number of offenses.[55]

Adherents of the therapeutic ideology differ in their relative emphasis on two images of their clients. The image of the *destitute offender* emphasizes his vulnerability to socioeconomic or psychological forces external to himself and beyond his management. Strategies of intervention would increase his capacities to cope with his environment through such measures as vocational training, medical care, strengthening his capacity to understand his problems, and fitting him for more effective role performance in his social system. Social reform may also be involved in efforts to correct defects of the social system which deny him social and economic opportunity. The image of the *maladjusted offender* imputes some kind of abnormality or malfunctioning in the individual offender which separates him from the usual run of people. This emphasis on the offender as an individual per se draws on psychiatric and psychological principles.

Preventive ideology

The preventive ideology is characterized by three themes. The idea of prevention implies first that something evil, unpleasant or destructive will develop in the future. Second, some kind of deliberate action can either forestall this undesirable development or mitigate its effects. This theme conveys some measure of optimism that problems are manageable and that human ingenuity will provide the means of overcoming them. Third, the orientation is toward the immediate or distant future rather than the past—although the histories of individuals or social institutions are considered pertinent to the expectation that undesirable events are both probable and can be forestalled.

[55] Marc Ancel, *Social Defence: A Modern Approach to Criminal Problems* (New York: Schocken Books, 1966), pp. 28–30.

There is considerable overlap between the preventive ideology and the other two ideologies. The preventive ideology, however, also has been associated with social reform. *Punitive prevention,* depending on the classical school's contention that the threat of the pains of penalties will deter crime, involves preventive patrol by police and making an example of apprehended offenders. However, prevention is identified predominantly with the therapeutic ideology through measures such as vocational training (development of job skills is supposed to make crime unnecessary) and mental health care (alleviation of mental disturbances is supposed to forestall antisocial behavior). Because criminal behavior and the response to it involve the social structure, crime prevention also may involve efforts to reform social institutions as a means of alleviating conditions conducive to crime. Crime prevention is discussed more fully in Chapter 22.

PRELIMINARY REVIEW OF THEORIES

Precisely defined, "theory" refers to a reasoned set of propositions, derived from and supported by verified evidence, that explains the occurrence of a general class of events. Scientific methods are applied to the gathering of relevant facts and their objective analysis to produce reliable conclusions. Doctrines, on the other hand, rely primarily on the faith of adherents in particular beliefs. In this century, scientific study has taken several approaches to the development of theories, as distinguished from doctrines.

Multiple-factor and monocausal theories

Because of the diversity of relevant factors, some criminologists have adopted a multiple-factor explanation for criminal behavior. They abstain from dogmatic defense of any particular theory. Their tolerance of many ideas is congenial to the withholding of judgment that characterizes science, and it is refreshing as contrasted to the passion of advocates of a pet theory who lack the support of objective evidence. However, the tolerance of the multiple-factor approach obstructs the discovery of reliable principles when congeniality becomes an end in itself.

Other theorists have offered hypotheses based on the belief that a single set of factors is solely responsible for criminal behavior. Monocausal explanations have the virtue of enabling the researcher to mobilize the concepts and principles of the discipline with which he is most familiar. His conclusions may be a substantial contribution to criminology when placed within the context of the findings of other researchers drawn from other disciplines. Our conception of theoretical criminology as a collection of sciences is congenial to this idea of a partnership among specialists who share a common interest in criminological issues. Monocausal explanations, however, suffer substantial defects when advanced as *the* answer to the riddle of crime. In the past, these explanations have not survived because the complexity of criminal etiology defies simplistic explanations.

Probabilistic approach

Modern criminological theories have taken a different direction in trying to make sense out of the chaos of diverse discrete events. They are less ambitious in trying to capture all the elements influencing behavior. Instead, they concentrate on certain variables among all those that are associated with deviant behavior. Thus criminology is advanced as a total scientific effort through an accumulation of specialized studies.

The modern theories assume that relationships stem from such a variety of factors that a given outcome can be predicted only as likely rather than as inevitable. Clarence Schrag notes that theorists following this approach do not see criminal responses as the inevitable product of any single aspect of the environment, or physical characteristic, or personality trait, or social situation, or any other observable entity. They believe no one set of variables inevitably produces crime and see varying probabilities among individuals and social groups that a particular set of causal factors will have this result.[56]

David Matza describes this change in perspective as a movement from the "hard determinism" of the positive school to a "soft determinism." The positivists conceived of man as being fundamentally constrained by causes, similar to the operation of physical laws on chemical particles. Soft determinism maintains the principle of universal causality but denies that men are completely or uniformly subject to forces external to their own motivations. Individuals differ in their power to defy the constraints of environment forces, but none is a complete slave to impersonal forces. Soft determinism recognizes that human beings differ from chemical particles and that scientific inquiry must acknowledge that human beings, as dynamic participants in events, are capable of exercising their own initiative.[57]

In the next two chapters, our review will group criminological theories broadly as individualistic and environmental. The categorization of criminological theories into individualistic and environmental approaches is

---

[56] Clarence Schrag, *Crime and Justice: American Style* (Rockville, Md.: Center for Studies of Crime and Delinquency, National Institute of Mental Health, 1971), p. 81.

[57] David Matza, *Delinquency and Drift* (New York: John Wiley & Sons, Inc., 1964), pp. 5–12.

consistent with the history of criminological schools of thought summarized earlier in this chapter.

Individualistic theories

Some behavioral scientists think man is by nature autonomous, and group restrictions are artificially imposed. He submits to the rules and restrictions of organized groups, but this submission is supposed to be an artificial aspect of his personality. Under this conception, the sources of criminality are sought in the characteristics of the individual offender. These individualistic approaches will be reviewed in Chapter 9.

Individual-oriented approaches emphasize the development of the personality. The environment and experiences of early years are assumed to create *predisposing factors* which make some individuals vulnerable to *precipitating factors* in the contemporary environment of the offender. Crime may be explained as the result of genetic defects, emotional imbalance, psychiatric disorder, asocial drives, ego-superego conflict, or faulty socialization and education. The environment of the individual usually is recognized as a part of the etiology of crime, but the focus of attention is on the individual or the immediate family.

Biological or genetic explanations assume that the criminal is structurally different from the noncriminal. "Feeblemindedness" theories see how the criminal as lacking sufficient mental capacity to know the difference between right and wrong, to foresee the consequences of misbehavior, or to avoid being induced into crime by others. The maturing of the disciplines of psychology and psychiatry has strengthened interest in the individual offender and in the latent significance of his behavior as a symptom. He may be suffering from a psychological defect or disorder, he may be unable to sublimate his "primitive," antisocial impulses, or he may be expressing symbolically some unconscious urge resulting from an early traumatic experience. Psychological approaches are similar in that all hold crime to be the result of some individual maladjustment, and treatment is directed primarily toward the individual.

Environmental theories

Generally, environmental theories emphasize the influences external to the individual which play a part in the etiology of criminal behavior. Together, these theories involve every relationship between man and the aggregate of external conditions and influences affecting him as an organism and as a social creature. Environmental correlates of crime such as human geography and economic relationships (to be considered in the following sections) have influenced the development of theories in various disciplines. The influence of the physical environment is expressed through climate, availability and kind of natural resources, topography, and similar factors. Economic circumstances affect the probability and character of criminal behavior.[58]

Environmental theories in criminology see the shaping and expression of human behavior in terms of processes in the social environment that impinge on the individual and forces that operate within his organism. Thereby, the influences of group behavior are injected into the search for both the causes of crime and a means of coping with deviant behavior.

Sociology treats crime as interrelated with the social and cultural systems of the total society. From this perspective, the individual, whether criminal or noncriminal, is involved in social interactions within groups which influence his attitudes, his orientation toward his live experiences, and even his conception of himself. Criminals are regarded as being subject to the sociocultural organization of the society upon which they prey.[59] Group affiliations play a part in the causation of delinquency and crime because they influence the individual's personality development, affect his opportunities for fulfilling his social and economic aspirations in legitimate ways, and affect the chances that he will commit a particular kind of crime—burglary or embezzlement, for example. Sociological (or environmental) theories are presented in Chapter 10.

HUMAN GEOGRAPHY AS AN ENVIRONMENT

The regions of the United States differ in their rates of total crime and in the relative incidence of the various offenses as reported by law enforcement agencies. These differences are symptoms of the complex relationships between human behavior and the physical environment. Geographers, historians, economists, and sociologists have pointed out the relationships existing between the natural environment of a habitat and the social environment created by its inhabitants. The natural environment is composed of flora, fauna, climate, soil, minerals, water, landscape character, and geographical location. In the process of adjustment to the natural environment, the inhabitants of a region develop a social consensus based on common beliefs, customs, institutions, dialect, and history.

Relationships of geography and culture

Regional differences influence all human behavior, including criminal behavior. We have already noted that crimes are sociocultural phenomena in that criminal laws reflect the character and interests of those groups in

---

[58] Economic opportunity is a crucial aspect of social class status. See Chapter 5, pp. 89–95.

[59] Chapter 7 presented evidence in support of this view.

a society that are most influential in shaping legislation. Regions differ in the distribution of their populations according to various characteristics: age, sex, race, degree of urban versus rural residence, occupation, residential mobility, socioeconomic status, and educational attainment. These demographic characteristics influence both the likelihood of an individual being regarded as a criminal and the type of crime he is likely to perpetrate.

The relationships between criminal behavior and the physical environment are screened by cultural factors which rule out any simple and direct influence of geographical factors alone.[60] Geographical environment permits, but does not dictate, the patterns of human activities. The natural vegetation, soils, and land configuration influence the existence and characteristics of agriculture, herding, forestry, and fishing as technologies. Location of mineral and fuel resources affects industrialization and population patterns. Geographical and technological factors influence the major trade routes and consequently the location and size of urban centers. Nevertheless, anthropologists have found a variety of technologies in a single type of natural environment, as well as a certain technology practiced in a variety of natural environments. With his progress in technological efficiency, man has been able to overcome qualities of a specific environment which once prevented the development of certain forms of industry and commerce or restricted the growth and concentration of populations. Consequently, there is a trend toward the reduction of differences among regions in customs and demographic characteristics. This in turn influences the quantity and quality of crimes. The expansion of industry, commerce, and mass communication has reduced the importance of geography in differentiating regions from one another according to occupation, product specialization, and population qualities related to industrialization and urbanization. Previously, geographical isolation encouraged regions to develop distinctive customs and mores. These distinctions also are disappearing, but less rapidly.[61]

Evidence of interaction

Crimes known to the police, which are reported annually by the Federal Bureau of Investigation, indicate that New England has the lowest rates for homicide, robbery, and aggravated assault. The East South Central and West North census divisions have the lowest rates for automobile theft and larceny. The homicide rates are highest in the South Atlantic and East South Central divisions; the latter division has the highest

[60] For fuller discussion, see William F. Ogburn and Meyer F. Nimkoff, *A Handbook of Sociology*. 4th ed. (London: Routledge and Kegan Paul, 1960), pp. 71–82.

[61] Herbert J. Gans, "Diversity Is Not Dead," *New Republic*, 144 (April 3, 1961): 11.

rate for aggravated assault. The East North Central, Middle Atlantic, and Pacific divisions lead to robbery. The Pacific division is highest in larceny and automobile theft.

The usefulness of these summary statements is limited by the fluctuation of states within a given division; in fact, Richard Quinney found the states themselves to be too broad a geographical area for effective capture of the relationships between offense rates and qualities of the population structure. He correlated FBI data with population variables which are related indirectly to qualities of the physical environment: percent of the population employed in manufacturing, occupational diversity, and percentage of males in white-collar occupations—each differentiated by rural or urban residence. The correlation coefficients were not universally statistically significant, but the various classes of crime varied. As the percentage of population employed in manufacturing increased, larceny, robbery, and automobile theft rates declined. Forcible rape had a similar relationship with manufacturing employment, but the decline of the crime rate was less marked; changes in the relationship were slight in the case of aggravated assault and murder. Increasing occupational diversity had little effect upon crime in urban areas, with the exception of burglary; the effect was significant for all offenses in rural areas and especially marked for crimes against persons. As the proportion of white-collar males became greater, urban rates for automobile theft and larceny increased strongly but other offenses were less affected; in urban areas, rates for aggravated assault and murder declined, burglary rates increased, and rates for other offenses changed little.[62]

The interaction of geography, history, and culture has been cited in various ways in studies of the particular identification of the southern states with the violence that is characteristic of the United States. The geographical features of many southern states originally lent themselves to the plantation economy and the slavery system which, in turn, contributed to social class differences and, until recently, a unique concentration of blacks. The South continued as a geographical frontier longer than the North, which was subjected both to more continuous settlement through immigration and to the forces of urbanization. Raymond Gastil points out that the street duel and stealthy, nighttime mob murders were common in southern history. To measure the relationship between state homicide rates and southern characteristics, he developed an "index of southernness" based essentially on the inclusion of persons with southern backgrounds in the population of a given state. Gastil concluded there is a significant relationship between murder rates and residence in the South.[63]

[62] Richard Quinney, "Structural Characteristics, Population Areas, and Crime Rates in the United States," *Journal of Criminal Law, Criminology and Police Science,* 57 (March 1966): 45–52.

[63] Raymond D. Gastil, "Homicide and a Regional Culture of Violence," *American Sociological Review,* 36 (June 1971): 412–27.

Crime by the calendar and clock

Earlier criminological literature offers many studies of the relationship between the seasons and crime. Several 19th-century studies cited statistical evidence from Italy, France, and Germany that violent crimes against persons increased in the summer months and those against property increased in the winter. Warmer temperatures were supposed to heighten emotion, stimulate activity, and otherwise directly affect the physical mechanism. The more abundant food supply and lessened need for heavy clothing in summer months were believed to reduce the motivation for crimes against property.[64]

Seasonal variations in criminality have also been seen as the result of changes in the length of days and in temperature. These changes might, for example, directly promote or inhibit temptation toward criminal attacks against persons. Property crimes might be influenced indirectly in that seasonal conditions of temperature and light affect the difficulty of earning a living. Georg von Mayr contended that some crimes are "impure" in that they combine elements of crimes against persons and of crimes against property. Therefore, robbery and similar crimes would blunt the differential effect of seasonal changes,[65] when crimes against property as a category are compared with crimes against persons as a category.

Joseph Cohen has found the monthly trend of aggravated assault to rise from a low in January, reach the annual average early in May, attain a peak in midsummer, and decline gradually and continuously through November. The Christmas holiday gives a slight increase to December. In general, he finds murders to be more frequent in the summer than in the winter, but there are marked variations in peak and low months from year to year and from area to area. For robbery, the peak month is December, with a consistent decline to July and a subsequent rise through November. Burglary, breaking-entering, and larceny-theft and automobile theft rates are less regular in pattern than robbery rates over the years. Crimes against persons, on the whole, tend to increase in the summer, while property crimes predominate in the winter.[66]

One would expect forcible rape and aggravated assault to have their greatest frequency during the summer months when there are increased opportunities for contacts outside the immediate circle of family and work associates. In addition to the summer peak, murder is likely to have a high incidence during holidays, which can create incidents or aggravate personal crises into violence. Property crimes are high in the colder

[64] Joseph Cohen, "The Geography of Crime," *Annals of American Academy of Political and Social Science,* 217 (September 1941): 30.

[65] Cited by Gerhard J. Falk, "The Influence of the Seasons on the Crime Rate," *Journal of Criminal Law and Criminology,* 43 (July–August 1952): 204–7.

[66] Cohen, "Geography of Crime," pp. 32–34.

months when the number of hours of darkness is greater and there is increased economic pressure on persons with slender resources. Because of the variety of offenses included in this category, larceny-theft tends to fluctuate less over the months. Although pocketpicking and shoplifting are distributed through the seasons rather consistently, pocketpicking has a greater concentration in the warm months.

Generally, police department reports show the daily incidence of serious crime is highest during the hours from 8 P.M. to midnight when muggers, rapists, holdup men, automobile thieves, and burglars are active under the cover of darkness. Families are together, parties are underway, and people congregate in taverns with the possibility that quarrels will precipitate assault or murder.

The distribution of crimes over the hours of the day is associated with the presence of the victim on the scene of the crime and the absence of bystanders when these factors are essential to perpetration of the crime. Thefts from motor vehicles and dwellings are more characteristic of the daylight hours than are thefts from business establishments. Motor vehicles and residences are more likely to be untended during these hours, while business establishments are most likely to be populated. Thefts from persons on the street are simpler to perpetrate when darkness conceals the crime. Homicides are likely to stem from quarrels at any time.

ECONOMIC RELATIONSHIPS AND CRIME

Economic activities are essential in every society to supply life's necessities, comforts, and luxuries. In preliterate societies production for use rather than for sale integrated economic activities within the structure of family life, religion, politics, and general social relations.[67] America's "business civilization" has significantly separated the contemporary economic system from other areas of life.

Economic activities are of fundamental importance to the study of criminal behavior. Mannheim has pointed out that if traffic offenses are omitted, the administration of criminal justice all over the world must devote probably three quarters of its time and energy to "economic crimes."[68] The frustration of aspirations for material success and the desire for material gratifications are important stimuli to crime. Modern industrialism and machine technology have reduced the control that the individual, the family, and the local community have over material means for gratification. Machine technology has been criticized for stultifying creativity and aborting purposiveness. Money valuation provides a common measure for ordinarily noneconomic values that permits them to

[67] Robin M. Williams, Jr., *American Society: A Sociological Interpretation*, 3d. ed. (New York: Alfred A. Knopf, 1970), p. 166.

[68] Hermann Mannheim, *Criminal Justice and Social Reconstruction* (New York: John Wiley & Sons, Inc., 1958), p. 82.

work freely in the social system. Dollars become the measuring rod for prestige, maintenance of the debtor's honor, works of art, and other phenomena not usually associated with the "pecuniary realm." Moral, aesthetic, and pecuniary values are all part of a general value system. The pecuniary values lend social efficiency to the individual and group transactions which express and implement moral and aesthetic values. Money supports both the church and the brothel. Consequently, Charles Cooley believes elimination of pecuniary values is not the path to social reform. When commercialism dominates unduly, his solution would be reform of the total value system, not elimination of the money valuation which provides a universal medium for diverse persons to cooperate in supporting "higher values."[69]

Since economic institutions are founded on the principle that "goods" are scarce, fraud, embezzlement, theft, and robbery become shortcuts to acquisition of the means for need gratification. The impersonality of social relationships within an elaborate economic structure insulates many individuals against pangs of conscience. The occupational structure of an economy affects the nature of crimes and the distribution of opportunities to commit certain crimes. Cattle theft is more likely in a herding technology, embezzlement in a business economy.

An example of economic determinism

When economic ends and economic institutions are considered to be *the* explanation for human behavior, the result is *economic determinism.* This extreme and one-sided view considers criminals to be creatures of economic institutions. In an example of this approach, William A. Bonger (1876–1940), a Dutch scholar with socialist convictions, saw crime as largely the product of capitalism.

Observing that crime was rare among simpler peoples where peaceableness, hospitality, kindness, and other symptoms of altruism prevailed, Bonger asked why some members of these peaceable societies are capable of crime, regardless of race and climate.[70] The cause, he felt, must be in the social environment. In applying this general idea to contemporary urban-industrial society, he proceeded to force every aspect of environment to fit his particular monocausal view. He held that capitalism determines the nature of the social environment within which men interact in an urban-industrial society. Man has a capacity both for selfish and altruistic conduct. Capitalism, Bonger contended, stimulates the selfish side of man. Instead of producing goods for personal consumption, individuals strive to create a surplus to be exchanged for a profit. This results

---

[69] Charles H. Cooley, "The Sphere of Pecuniary Valuation," *American Journal of Sociology,* 19 (November 1913): 188–203.

[70] William A. Bonger, *Criminality and Economic Conditions,* trans. Henry P. Horton (Boston: Little, Brown & Co., 1916), pp. 381–92.

in intense competition between buyers and sellers, between sellers of the same or similar commodities, and between capital and labor. Consequently, men work for themselves, not to satisfy the wants of others.[71]

The assumption that capitalism breeds selfishness and social irresponsibility is the core of Bonger's environmental explanation for crime. Crime is seen as the legacy of capitalism because selfishness and social irresponsibility are said to cause unemployment, illiteracy, forced delay of marriage, and other environmental factors favorable to crime. For example, rape supposedly is caused by "the economic condition which prevents some individuals from marrying at the natural age, the inferior social position of women, alcoholism, and above all the sexual demoralization and lack of civilization in the lowest strata of society."[72]

Another conception of economic influences

In setting up economic factors as *the* cause of crime, Bonger ignored the tangle of interrelationships among social, cultural, economic, political, religious, and other sets of factors. He assumed that poverty is the basic explanation of crime. However, economic factors operate in conjunction with other factors (age status, for instance) to affect social deviation, rather than in the direct and simple manner assumed by economic determinists such as Bonger. Economic fluctuations probably have diverse effects on various groups within the total population as differentiated by age, occupation, quality of family relationship, cultural standards, commitment to criminal values, and similar variables. Since insecurities may stem from sources other than simple economic deprivation, the raising of standards of living for all citizens does not promise the elimination of crime. Instead, a multidimensional attack on sociological, psychological, and economic sources of insecurity appears to be in order.

The complex interrelationships between economic and social factors in the rise of delinquency are illustrated in a study comparing delinquent rates of central-city and suburban juveniles by family income and unemployment status. The number of delinquent acts was seen as dependent on the number of delinquent opportunities created by the economic and social characteristics of the environment and on the variation among individuals in tendencies to commit delinquent acts. With the rather gross data of this study, Belton Fleisher strove to relate a measure of delinquency to family income, the male civilian unemployment rate, the number of separated or divorced females over age 14, the proportion of population over age 5 living in a different community five years previously, and the proportion of the population that is nonwhite. His statistical analysis indicated that a 10 percent increase in family income would re-

[71] Ibid., p. 405.
[72] Ibid., p. 620.

duce the number of separated or divorced women sufficiently to decrease delinquency rates by between 15 and 20 percent in highly delinquent areas. A reduction by half of unemployment rates in high unemployment areas would raise average income by as much as 5 percent and, through the income effect, decrease the delinquency rate by 10 percent.[73]

The operation of economic principles in both legitimate and criminal organizations is illustrated by an analysis of organized crime in the United States by Thomas Schelling which suggests reasons for the difficulty in coping with this kind of crime. Similar to large-scale legitimate enterprises, crime syndicates must exceed a minimal size to meet the costs of equipment and specialized personnel, can increase prices when they control the market and the demand is great, and must assume costs which are external to the operations when many enterprises have access to the market. Examples of such costs to syndicates would be the interruption of regular operations by violence, anticrime legislation, shortage of goods, or police interference. The underworld learned that tax laws could be evaded by concealing extortion in the provision of services (wire service for bookies, installation of pinball machines, distribution of beer, and so on), with the "retailer" passing the higher cost on to the customer. Schelling cites two paradoxes in criminal enterprise. First, the legal prohibition of certain goods and services operates to create a monopoly for organized crime similar to the protection a tariff gives to some legitimate enterprises. Second, organized crime has an advantage for the community over individuated crime in that it motivates criminals to minimize violence.[74]

Some patterned relationships

Adult crimes against property, such as theft, burglary, and robbery, appear to increase in periods of economic depression and unemployment. This pattern is most definite for property crimes involving violence. Property crimes without violence demonstrate less consistent and definite trends. A study of the juvenile statistics of England and Wales reported a slight tendency for larcenies and crimes to increase in depression and decrease in prosperity. Property offenses with violence evidenced a definite increase with depression and decrease with prosperity.[75]

Daniel Glasner and Kent Rice endeavored to test two hypotheses frequently used in studies of the relationship between crime and economic conditions:

[73] Belton M. Fleisher, "The Effect of Income on Delinquency," *American Economic Review,* 56 (March 1966): 118–37.

[74] Thomas C. Schelling, "Economics and Criminal Enterprise," *Public Interest,* No. 7 (Spring 1967): 61–78; also see Chapter 7 above, pp. 141–45.

[75] Dorothy S. Thomas, *Social Aspects of the Business Cycle* (New York: Alfred A. Knopf, Inc., 1927), pp. 138–39.

1. The frequency of crimes committed by juveniles varies inversely with unemployment rates.
2. The frequency of property crimes committed by adults varies directly with unemployment rates.

Glaser and Rice believe that the opposing effects described by the hypotheses would explain failures of earlier studies to find marked relationships between crime and economic conditions. They used two kinds of data: FBI *Uniform Crime Reports* on arrests of property offenders for the years 1932 to 1950, and arrests of males grouped by age for the years 1930 to 56 as reported by the police of Boston, Cincinnati, and Chicago for property theft, crimes against persons, and misdemeanors.[76]

According to Glaser and Rice, the FBI data verify the first hypothesis. The municipal evidence is less clear-cut. Only the Boston data differentiate ages younger than 20 years. For property crimes only, the 10 to 17 age group (as a group by itself) conforms to the pattern described by the first hypothesis, although the correlation was not statistically significant. However, the 18 to 20 age group follows the adult pattern. For crimes against persons and misdemeanors, both the 10 to 17 and 18 to 20 age groups conform to the first hypothesis, but again without a statistically significant correlation.

The FBI data verify the second hypothesis for ages 19 through 34, but an unexpected inverse relationship is revealed between crime and unemployment for adults 35 and over. The municipal data support the second hypothesis without the unexpected twist for the older adults. Glaser and Rise offer two explanations for the unexpected relationship in national data. First, older persons are unable to adjust to increased economic means in times of prosperity and become personally disorganized. Arrests of "personal disorganization" misdemeanants are related negatively to unemployment for older age groups. It may be that senior citizens are needed more by their adult children during depressions, so that they derive a higher sense of personal worth. The parental function of older adults would be eroded by the self-sufficiency of adult offspring in prosperity.

The second explanation involves statistical methodology. An age-specific rate is the number of arrests of persons of a given age divided by the total number of inhabitants of the particular community of that age. *Uniform Crime Reports* reflect a wide fluctuation year by year in the composition of the police departments sending arrest data to the FBI. Therefore, the population from which the offenders were selected differs each year in terms of the particular cities from which they were drawn. Unable to compute age-specific rates from the national data, Glaser and

[76] Daniel Glaser and Kent Rice, "Crime, Age and Employment," *American Sociological Review*, 24 (October 1959): 679–86. The following data and conclusions are also from this source.

Rice made a methodological adjustment by studying the shifts in the proportion of total arrests contributed by each of the specific age groups. Consequently, a marked increase in arrests of the middle-age groups would produce, as artifacts, negative relationships for the other age groups. Because the unexpected relationship between arrests and unemployment for the older adults did not occur in the municipal data, Glaser and Rice speculated that the deviation of the older adults from the hypothesized pattern stems from the lack of appropriate national data for precise analysis.

SUMMARY

To provide historical background and orientation for the review of criminological theories that follows in the next two chapters, this chapter presented the ideas of the classical and positive schools of thought which set the stage for modern scientific analysis. From these roots also have developed fundamental ideological contradictions which have troubled the contemporary system of criminal justice. Three ideologies characterizing criminological practice, punitive, therapeutic, and preventive, were delineated.

As a format for the following presentation of theories, two general categories were defined: individualistic and environmental theories. The nature and complexity of environmental factors were illustrated with a discussion of the criminological implications of human geography and economic relationships.

FOR ADDITIONAL READING

Andenaes, Johannes. "Does Punishment Deter Crime?" *Criminal Law Quarterly,* 11 (November 1968) : 76–93.

Appel, James B., and Peterson, Neil J. "What's Wrong with Punishment?" *Journal of Criminal Law, Criminology and Police Science,* 56 (December 1965): 450–53.

Bittner, Egon, and Platt, Anthony M. "The Meaning of Punishment." *Issues in Criminology,* 2 (Spring 1966): 79–99.

Brearley, H. D. *Homicide in the United States,* chap. 9. Chapel Hill: University of North Carolina Press, 1932.

Chambliss, William J. "Types of Deviance and the Effectiveness of Legal Sanctions." *Wisconsin Law Review,* 1967 (Summer 1967), 703–19.

Chang, Dae H. "Environmental Influences on Criminal Activity in Korea." *Criminology,* 10 (November 1972): 338–52.

Cormier, Bruno M.; Kennedy, Miriam; and Sendbuehler, M. "Cell Breakage and Gate Fever: A Study of Two Syndromes Found in the Deprivation of Liberty." *British Journal of Criminology,* 7 (July 1967): 317–24.

Fleischer, Belton M. *The Economics of Delinquency.* Chicago: Quadrangle Books, 1966.

Gerber, Rudolph J., and McAnany, Patrick D. (eds.). *Contemporary Punishment: Views, Explanations, and Justifications.* Notre Dame, Ind.: University of Notre Dame Press, 1972.

Grupp, Stanley E. (ed.). *Positive School of Criminology.* Pittsburgh: University of Pittsburgh Press, 1968.

Honderick, Ted. *Punishment: The Supposed Justifications.* London: Hutchinson, 1969.

Jeffery, Clarence Ray. "The Historical Development of Criminology." In Hermann Mannheim (ed.), *Pioneers in Criminology.* Chicago: Quadrangle Books, 1966.

Kaplan, Sidney J. "The Geography of Crime." In Joseph S. Roucek (ed.), *Sociology of Crime,* pp. 160–92. New York: Philosophical Library, 1961.

Lejins, Peter P. "Hereditary Endowment, Environmental Influences and Criminality." In Herbert A. Bloch (ed.), *Crime in America,* pp. 315–29. New York: Philosophical Library, 1961.

Manfred, Curry. "The Relationship of Weather Conditions, Facial Characteristics and Crime." *Journal of Criminal Law and Criminology,* 39 (July–August 1948): 253–61.

Schafer, Stephan. *Theories in Criminology.* New York: Random House, 1969.

Tarde, Gabriel. *Penal Philosophy.* Trans. Rapelje Howell. Montclair, N.J.: Patterson Smith, 1968.

Walker, Nigel. *Crime and Punishment in Britain,* chap. 6. Edinburgh, Scotland: Edinburgh University Press, 1968.

9

Theories concentrating on the individual offender

Like all human beings, the criminal is formed by the factors shaping his personality. In addition to the genetic endowment of his heredity, these include the features of his physique, his psychological capacities, and the emotional adjustments he makes to the tensions of life. The diversity of these factors has attracted the attention of criminological researchers drawn from a wide range of sciences: anthropology, biology, law, psychiatry, psychology, and sociology.

These fields share an interest in the influence of group factors on criminal behavior, but many of their studies have concentrated on the behavior of criminals apart from group influences. This chapter will focus on those explanations of criminal behavior that view offenders as individuals per se. Because the proponents of each of these theories frequently advanced monocausal explanations, each approach will be studied as a candidate for the one single answer to the riddle of crime. Some of these theories continue to be expressed in the folklore of many laymen and a few criminological workers. In addition to challenging the irrationality of this folklore, our analysis is intended to provide background on the biological or psychological factors which are crucial to the study of criminal behavior as the product of many influences.

BIOLOGICAL FACTORS

Biological explanations assume that individuals vary in behavior because their biological structures differ, and criminals and noncriminals are categorically distinct in this respect. The explanations summarized below attribute criminality to some internal force beyond the control of the lawbreaker. This assumption has profound implications for a system of criminal justice founded on the principles of moral responsibility which sees punishment as a means of deterring crime. If these explanations are accepted by courts, evidence that the defendant has a biological anomaly would diminish his responsibility for a given crime and would lead to decisions reducing his guilt and punishment. On the other hand, the assumption raises the specter of a pathological creature driven inexorably to the perpetration of loathsome or fearsome crimes. Contrary to the legal rights or actual behavior of the individual classified as such a "monster," the aroused fears of the public call for his enforced detention as a means of protecting the community.

Physiognomy: An early example

An early example of biological explanations for criminality was based on physiognomy, the art of discovering character by observation and measurement of outward appearance, especially the face. Johan Caspar Lavater (1741–1801), a Swiss theologian, regarded lack of a beard in men, the "shifty" eye, and the "weak" chin as clues to unfavorable traits. Similarly, phrenology, as popularized by Franz Joseph Gall (1758–1828), assumed that the exterior of the skull conforms to the shape of the brain, that the various faculties are localized in different parts of the brain, and that, consequently, the "bumps" on the skull show the relative development of such faculties as congeniality, friendliness, self-esteem, firmness, sexual passion, love of offspring, and so on.[1] "Bumps" showing high development of sexual passion, combativeness, secretiveness, and similar "lower propensities" were supposed to reveal criminal tendencies.

An American doctor, Charles Caldwell (1772–1853) carried the doctrine further, suggesting that uncontrolled animal propensities would propel the individual to specific crimes. Unless checked by higher faculties, the faculty of destructiveness would lead to murder, combativeness to assault and murder, secretiveness to treason and fraud, and so on.[2] The rise of scientific neurology refuted this notion by demonstrating that the mind is not divided into separate "faculties."

Premises of biological views

The belief in the biological inheritance of crime is based on one of two assumptions. The first is that the criminal act itself is inherited. Under this view, there must be some direct connection between the biological structure and the behavior which is assumed to be inherited.[3] Differences in human behaviors are supposed to be determined by genetic characteristics in ways distinguishing criminals from noncriminals.

[1] Arthur E. Fink, *Causes of Crime: Biological Theories in the United States, 1800–1915* (Philadelphia: University of Pennsylvania Press, 1938), pp. 2–3.

[2] George B. Vold, *Theoretical Criminology* (New York: Oxford University Press, 1958), pp. 45–47.

[3] Marshall B. Clinard, *Sociology of Deviant Behavior,* 3d ed. (New York: Holt, Rinehart, & Winston, Inc., 1968), pp. 56–57.

In conflict with this view, behavior is defined as criminal according to sociocultural criteria. Criminal behavior is defined differently from time to time and from jurisdiction to jurisdiction because the definitions themselves are sociocultural phenomena. Criminal behavior is only a fraction of total nonconforming behavior. The "direct connection" between biological structure and "inherited" criminal behavior would have to be capable of amazing flexibility if these variations over time and space in definitions of crime were to be explained on the biological basis. Ashley-Montagu points out that mind is created through social organization of previously unorganized nervous tissue; behavior is the expression of that nervous tissue according to the cultural pattern of that social organization.[4] It is appropriate to say that biology provides the cellular elements from which the cultural organization creates mind, including crime as part of the variety of resultant behaviors.

Under the second general assumption, the inheritance of crime is viewed as a propensity, tendency, or mental predisposition which is part of the physical endowment. Considering the lack of knowledge of the complicated interrelationships between biology and environment, it is not surprising that the scholars of the late 19th century generally believed that certain biological family stocks would produce feeblemindedness, degeneracy, poverty, and crime. Studies like those of the Jukes and the Kallikaks reflected this intellectual atmosphere.[5]

Physical types

Theories relating criminality to physical types contend that biological structure is of first importance in determining behavior and that certain physical qualities mark the criminal. Sometimes these theories include an additional idea that criminal behavior is evidence of atavism, a reversion to a more primitive stage in the biological evolution of man. Cesare Lombroso is predominantly identified with the concept of atavism as an adaptation of Charles Darwin's theory of the evolutionary development of plants and animals. Although Lombroso gave increasing recognition of environmental factors in his explanation of criminal behavior, he continued to insist that the "born criminal" is a major physical type. His views were discussed earlier.[6]

Physical-type theory, as a form of determinism, was given a rigorous test early in this century and evaluated as inadequate. Employing carefully designed statistical methodology in an eight-year study, Charles

---

[4] M. F. Ashley-Montagu, "The Biologist Looks at Crime," *Annals of the American Academy of Political and Social Science*, 217 (September 1941): 47–48.

[5] Richard L. Dugdale, *The Jukes: A Study in Crime, Pauperism and Heredity*, 4th ed. (New York: G. P. Putnam's Sons, 1942); Henry H. Goddard, *The Kallikak Family* (New York: Macmillan Co., 1912).

[6] See Chapter 8, pp. 179–80.

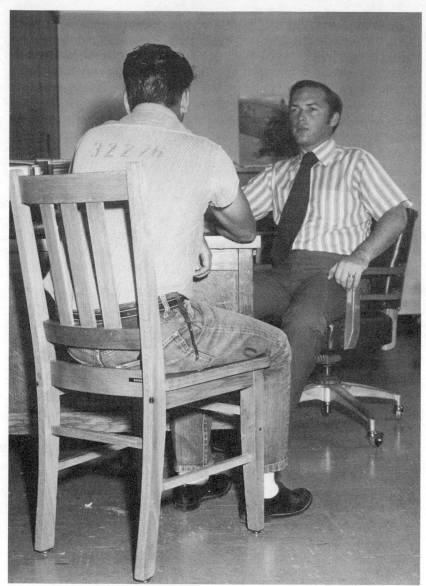

Figure 9–1. Treatment on a one-to-one basis.

The individual-oriented approaches offer the key advantage of staff-inmate contacts on a personal basis in which the particular problems of the individual are the central concern.

Goring compared measurements of about 37 specific physical characteristics of some 3,000 English recidivist prisoners with similar measurements of university students, hospital patients, and members of the British
army. He found no unusual anomalies to differentiate the prisoners and
failed to find significant differences among different kinds of criminals.
Goring concluded: "In fact, both with regard to measurements and the
presence of physical anomalies in criminals, our statistics present a startling conformity with similar statistics of the law-abiding classes. . . . Our
inevitable conclusion must be that there is no such thing as a physical
criminal type."[7]

Anthropologist Earnest A. Hooton has attempted to rescue the physical-type idea from the grave Goring dug. Based on a study of 13,873 male
criminals in 10 states and a civilian group of 3,023, Hooton's conclusions
were that "Criminals are organically inferior. Crime is the resultant of the
impact of environment upon low grade human organisms." To eliminate
crime, the physically, mentally, and morally unfit must be exterminated
or segregated completely in a "socially aseptic environment."[8]

The following morphological characteristics are among those Hooton
claimed to be more common among criminals than among civilians: low
and sloping foreheads, thin lips, compressed jaw angles, straight hair,
thin beards and body hair, thick head hair, red-brown hair, blue-gray and
mixed eyes, nasal bridges and tips varying to both extremes of breadth
and narrowness, protruding and small ears, tattooing, long thin necks,
and sloping shoulders.[9] He asserted that tall, thin men tend to be murderers and robbers, undersized men tend to be thieves and burglars, and
short, heavy men are prone to assaultive and sex crimes. Hooton, as Vold
points out, ignored the fact that more than half of his prisoners had served
previous terms and a very large proportion of these previous sentences
had been for crimes different from the offense of the current term.[10]

Sheldon's "constitutional psychiatry"

Ernest Kretschmer, a professor of psychiatry in Germany, has sought
to relate body type and certain mental illnesses. William H. Sheldon, a
medically trained psychologist, goes beyond Kretschmer, Lombroso, and
Hooton in methodology and complexity of theory. Sheldon views psychoanalysis as beginning with conscious reactions to probe the "unconscious." He equates "unconscious" and the body because he sees the body

[7] Charles Goring, *The English Convict: A Statistical Study* (London: His Majesty's Stationery Office, 1913), p. 173.

[8] Earnest A. Hooton, *The American Criminal: An Anthropological Study*
(Cambridge, Mass.: Harvard University Press, 1939), Vol. I, p. 309.

[9] Earnest H. Hooton, *Crime and Man* (Cambridge, Mass.: Harvard University
Press, 1939), p. 301.

[10] Vold, *Theoretical Criminology*, p. 62.

as the tangible record of the established habits that "for the most part are transmitted in the parental germinal cells." Because as a "constitutional psychologist" he employs anthropometric measurement and profile photographs of his subjects, Sheldon argues that he is "completely objective," while the psychoanalyst must approach human motivation through "devious and subjective verbalization."[11]

Sheldon applied his methods to delineate three body types. In simple terms, these somatotypes are *endomorph* (round, soft, fat bodies, with short tapering limbs and small bones); *mesomorphic* (muscular, large trunk, heavy chest, large wrists and hands, and heavy bones); and *ectomorphic* (lean and delicate body, droopy shoulders, small face, and delicate bones). Temperament also has three types: *viscerotonia* (relaxed, comfort-loving, greedy for affection and approval, slow in reaction, even in emotions, tolerant, and so on); *somatotonia* (assertive, adventure-loving, psychologically callous, energetic, compulsive, ruthless, and so on); and *cerebrotonia* (tight in posture, physiologically overresponsive, emotionally restrained, unpredictable in attitude, mentally overintense, and so on).

Sheldon differs from his predecessors in that he does not use these types as distinct entities. Persons are ranked along a subject scale of 1 to 7 in terms of their possession of all three components in varying proportions. When the classification of a specific body is changed, it demonstrates an error in the judgment of the person making the rating, not a change in the body, according to Sheldon.[12] Through statistical correlation, he has attempted to associate temperamental patterns with each of the body types. The typical endomorph corresponds to the viscerotonic, the ectomorph to the cerebrotonic, and the mesomorph to the somatotonic.

For his study of delinquency, Sheldon selected 200 boys aged 15 to 21 that had been referred to a rehabilitation home for problem boys. The 200 were selected from 400 because more complete information was available about them. He established an "Index of Delinquency," or "Index of Disappointingness," as a quantitative summary of a person's shortcomings in IQ insufficiency, psychiatric problems, and residual delinquency. Psychiatric problems include psychoses, psychoneuroses, cerebrophobic delinquency (alcoholism, drug addiction), and gynandrophrenic delinquency (homosexuality and "stubborn perverseness" about "responsibility"). Residual delinquency includes those who "persist in mischief" without being "excusable" on psychiatric grounds or on grounds of insufficiency; this appears to be the legally defined delinquency which he rejects elsewhere.[13]

---

[11] William H. Sheldon, *Varieties of Delinquent Youth* (New York: Harper & Bros., 1949), pp. 4–5.

[12] Ibid., p. 36.

[13] Ibid., pp. 105–7.

Sheldon found the delinquents to be predominately mesomorphic, with moderate endomorphy and slight ectomorphy. Sixteen delinquents were classified as "residual criminals" and as markedly mesomorphic. The entire group was mildly psychoneurotic. The psychotics and "residual criminals" tended to be diagnosed as manic-depressives.

Sheldon and Eleanor Glueck applied the somatotype system to 500 boys "persistently" delinquent matched with 500 "true nondelinquents" in Boston public schools in terms of age, general intelligence, ethnicoracial derivation, and slum residence. However, because they considered that there was no proof that the somatotype is permanent and immutable, they did not employ Sheldon's rating technique. Instead their somatotype classification was made directly through inspection of photographs of their subjects.[14] They associated type of physique with 67 individual traits and 42 family conditions. They agreed with Sheldon that mesomorphs apparently have a higher delinquency potential than other body types because of their greater tendency toward aggressive traits (physical strength, energy, insensitivity, tendency to express tensions and frustrations), together with relative freedom from feelings of inadequacy, emotional instability, and so on.[15]

Evaluation of physical-type theories

Instead of attempting proof, physical-type studies have taken for granted the "degeneracy" of criminals. Hooton concluded that criminals are organically inferior. To prove this, his research should have demonstrated that certain physical characteristics are inferior; for example, that blue-gray eyes are less efficient for vision or are at a lower rung on the evolutionary ladder. Then, if he had demonstrated that such eyes are more prevalent among criminals than among noncriminals, he would have had a case. Apparently, he believes it sufficient to say that blue-gray eyes are more prevalent among the prisoners he studied than among those subjects he deemed representative of noncriminals. The facts of his own study do not dissuade him from the prestudy conviction that biological inferiority is characteristic of criminals. Therefore, any characteristic linked to criminals becomes "inferior." Sheldon made the same assumption.

The studies have been criticized for inadequate sampling and their misuse of control groups. Ideally, the offenders studied should represent all criminals, and the subjects in the control groups should represent all noncriminals. Thereby, differences found between the two samples would be applicable to the respective populations they were supposed to represent. In using prisoners to represent criminals, Hooton ignored the effects of the differential selection of prisoners from the total body of offenders

---

[14] Sheldon and Eleanor Glueck, *Physique and Delinquency* (New York: Harper & Bros., 1956), pp.286–87.

[15] Ibid., p. 219.

that the system of criminal justice makes according to factors extraneous to criminal behavior.[16] Hooton's control group was too small and included firemen and militiamen who had been accepted for these occupations after passing a physical examination, thus exaggerating physical differences btween offenders and nonoffenders.

The methodology in analysis was also questionable. The scoring of delinquents by Sheldon was subjective and unreliable. The scaling was inconsistent logically and unlikely to be duplicated by other investigators.[17] Hooton's sample included persons from various states, occupational groups, and age groups. Within these groups, there were differences as great as, or greater than, those between criminals and noncriminals. The statistical differences between his criminal and control groups are insignificant. The authors reach opposite conclusions concerning which physical type is "inferior." Hooton sees the criminal as an inadequately developed, runty fellow, while Sheldon chooses the husky, athletic type.[18]

Neither author used his data to establish evidence concerning the inheritance of criminality. They did not rule out the possibility that diet and other environmental factors influence the state of physical development. Interpretation of body build is complicated by factors such as age, sex, race, amount of physical activity, and personality. Knowledge of physical development suggests that the poor physique of many prisoners is the result of growth failure caused by insufficient nourishment, lack of exercise, and even psychic factors. These ingredients requisite to growth must be available at the proper time in the sequence of growth stages.[19]

Physiological characteristics, screened through cultural standards defining their relationship with prestige and social acceptance, have influence on behavior, but not in the direct relationship with criminality hypothesized by physical-type theorists. Psychiatrists have noted that a person with a physical abnormality may compensate by strenuous legitimate activities, rationalize his situation, retreat into psychoses, or turn to anti-social behavior. In the latter instance, physical stigmata are translated into psychological deformity to cause crime. Where the cause of anti-social behavior is a disfigurement, the actual physical defect usually is minor. Medical care or surgical reconstruction is only preliminary to the treatment of the psychological effects of the physical abnormality.[20]

[16] Chapter 5 discussed the differential impact of race and social class.

[17] Albert Cohen, Alfred Lindesmith, and Karl Schuessler, *The Sutherland Papers* (Bloomington: Indiana University Press, 1963), pp. 282–83.

[18] Clinard, *Sociology of Deviant Behavior*, p. 174.

[19] Richard M. Snodgrasse, "Crime and the Constitution Human: A Survey," *Journal of Criminal Law, Criminology and Police Science*, 42 (May–June 1951): 18–52.

[20] Ralph S. Banay, "Physical Disfigurement as a Factor in Delinquency and Crime," *Federal Probation*, 7 (January–March 1943): 20–24.

Identical-twin studies

One approach toward separating the influence of heredity from that of environment has been the study of identical (born of a single fertilized ovum) and fraternal (born of separate ova) twins. Only the identical twins would be genetically alike. Ashley-Montagu summarized German and American studies in which one or both of a twin pair were criminal. Of 104 one-egg pairs, both twins were criminal in 70 pairs (67.3 percent), and only one twin was criminal in 34 pairs. Of the 112 two-egg pairs, both twins were criminal in 37 pairs (33.0 percent), and only one twin was criminal in 75 pairs. Those twins who were genetically alike had the greater tendency to be alike in criminal behavior.[21]

Does this prove that criminality is inherited? Subsequent criticisms have pointed out the fundamental oversimplification of these studies; ignoring the complex interactions between the two sets of factors, they assumed the issue was heredity *or* environment, whereas they should have tested the interactions under the assumption of heredity *and* environment.[22] Ashley-Montagu noted that twin studies ignored environmental factors. Because they are identical in appearance, the one-egg twins are more likely to be close companions and therefore to encounter together the procriminal influences in their environment. The difficulty of determining reliably whether a pair is derived from one egg has also been cited.[23] L. S. Penrose saw relatively little significance in learning that two persons with identical heredities have the same defects because this has no bearing on what happens to persons with different heredities when they are exposed to the same social circumstances.[24]

The extra Y chromosome

In 1965 a prostitute in Paris was brutally strangled. In 1967 a widow was stabbed to death in Sydney, Australia. In 1968 a woman was savagely beaten to death in Queens, New York. In all three cases the accused murderers were tall in stature and were classified as having the XYY chromosomal structure. These cases have focused public attention on the criminological implications of a technique, developed in 1956, of determining the numbers of chromosomes as a new method of relating biolog-

21 Ashley-Montagu, "The Biologist Looks at Crime," pp. 53–54.

22 For example, see review of this issue in Clinard, *Sociology of Deviant Behavior,* pp. 56–59.

23 See Hermann Mannheim, *Comparative Criminology* (Boston: Houghton Mifflin Co., 1965), pp. 231–35.

24 L. S. Penrose, "Genetics and the Criminal," *British Journal of Delinquency,* 6 (July 1955): 22–23.

ical heredity to criminal behavior. A voluminous research literature on the XYY chromosome has developed recently.[25]

Chromosomes contain the genetic material transmitting hereditary messages from generation to generation through combination in 23 pairs of the chromosomes contained in female ovum and male sperm cells. In the male pair determining the sex of the infant, the larger X chromosome normally will produce a female infant, and the smaller Y chromosome will produce a male infant. If this process fails to operate effectively, the infant may be born with either too few or too many chromosomes. Among these possibilities is the XYY abnormality in which the person is usually found to be outwardly male but sterile and to have some breast enlargement and some degree of mental retardation.[26]

Many recent genetic studies have found chromosomal deviations among mental patients, retarded persons, homosexuals, and criminals. The size of groups studied has been small, and the XYY syndrome has varied from 0.66 to 8.8 percent of the sample. Among criminals the prevalence of the syndrome has exceeded that of the general population at a statistically significant level. Higher rates of violent crimes were found to be prevalent among these individuals.[27] Studies are inconsistent in finding distinctive physiological characteristics among persons with the XYY syndrome, other than unusual tallness. Even the factor of greater physical stature has been questioned by discovery of some chromosomally normal siblings as tall as their XYY brothers. Differences in intelligence and various personality dimensions have not been established. Research studies provide evidence that XYY males are not predictably aggressive and, as a group, appear somewhat less aggressive than the comparable XY group.[28]

Eugenics

Eugenics deals with improvement of the inborn qualities of the races. If one believes that criminality is inherited biologically, a program of eugenics would appear to be logical. Arthur Fink has summarized three approaches found in the literature of sterilization.[29] The *punitive* approach assumes that the criminal would be subject to retributive punishment by asexualization. Protection of society by reduction of criminal

[25] See Richard G. Fox, "The Extra Y Chromosome and Deviant Behavior: A Bibliography," Centre of Criminology, University of Toronto, Toronto, Ont., September 1970 (mimeo.).

[26] Richard G. Fox, "The XYY Offender: A Modern Myth?" *Journal of Criminal Law, Criminology and Police Science*, 62 (March 1971): 61.

[27] Menachem Amir and Yitzchak Berman, "Chromosomal Deviation and Crime," *Federal Probation*, 34 (June 1970): 57–58.

[28] Theodore R. Sarbin and Jeffrey E. Miller, "Demonism Revisited: The XYY Chromosomal Anomaly," *Issues in Criminology*, 5 (Summer 1970): 195–207.

[29] Fink, *Causes of Crime*, p. 188.

virility is a secondary purpose. The *therapeutic* approach assumes that sterilization would benefit certain individuals, especially those with mental disorders. The *eugenic* approach seeks to prevent crime by cutting off the criminal strain. One study[30] found 0.7 percent convicted criminals, 1.2 percent insane, and 0.7 percent mentally defective among the 8,000 parents of adolescent offenders. If it can be assumed that the parents were not counted more than once if they were both convicted criminals and either insane or mentally defective, Penrose estimates that even after a century of an exhaustive sterilization program, 90 percent of the population would remain unaffected.[31]

Endocrinology

Recognition of the effects of ductless gland secretion on behavior excited speculation concerning a biochemical explanation for criminality. The pituitary regulates growth. The thyroid regulates the rate of bodily metabolism. The adrenals secrete hormones to make extra energy available in an emergency. The gonads determine sex drive and development of secondary sex characteristics. Endocrine dysfunction creates physical pathology and affects behavior.

Some have sought to explain all criminal behavior on this basis.[32] Louis Berman saw crime as a "perversion of the instinctive drives dependent upon a deficiency and imbalance of the endocrine glands."[33] On the basis of a study of 498 delinquent girls among his cases, Leizer Grimberg, a neuropsychiatrist, concluded that delinquency is the result of a defective endocrine system. He classified practically all the girls as either physically overdeveloped or underdeveloped for their age and pointed out that almost all demonstrated endocrine dysfunctioning. He saw delinquency as a result of environmental factors operating upon this organic inferiority.[34]

Conclusive evaluation of the relationship between glandular imbalance or dysfunction and criminality awaits further research. However, it appears that glandular dysfunction is a precipitating factor rather than a primary agent.[35] A simple glandular determinism ignores motivational

[30] W. Norwood East, P. Stocks, and H. T. P. Young, *The Adolescent Criminal* (London: J. & A. Churchill, 1942).

[31] Penrose, "Genetics and the Criminal," p. 24.

[32] Max G. Schlapp and E. H. Smith, *The New Criminology* (New York: Boni and Liveright, 1929).

[33] Louis Berman, "Crime and the Endocrine Glands," *American Journal of Psychiatry,* 12 (September 1932): 226.

[34] Leizer E. Grimberg, *Emotion and Delinquency* (New York: Brentano's, 1928), pp. 109–12.

[35] William C. Young, *Glandular Physiology and Therapy,* 5th ed. (Philadelphia: J. B. Lippincott Co., 1954), p. 517.

and emotional factors which may affect the endocrine system.[36] Physiological defense mechanisms operate to safeguard the organism against stress. Therefore, glandular difficulties may be a response to a social-psychological situation. Furthermore, endocrine dysfunction and metabolic derangement do not necessarily result in deviant behavior.[37]

MENTAL DEFICIENCY

In early times mentally deficient persons were lumped with the insane. In 1838, Jean E. D. Esquirol (1772–1840), a French alienist, and Isaac Ray (1807–1881), an American, were the first to distinguish between the mentally deranged (those whose mental faculties had developed before the onset of their functional abnormality) and the mentally deficient (those who never developed their mental faculties.)[38]

Views on linkage to crime

Efforts to link mental deficiency and crime took several forms. The term "moral insanity" coupled imbecility with moral perversion, which was supposed to cause the individual of "degenerate stock" to act without relation to the accepted moral values.[39] Another view, influenced by Lombroso, assumed that the imbecile shared the born criminal's anatomical, physiological, and psychical degeneracy. In still another view, mental deficiency alone was considered the direct cause of deviant behavior.

The development of psychometric tests brought a wave of attempts to prove the relationship between crime and mental deficiency. Henry Goddard contended that at least half of all criminals are mentally defective.[40] Goring believed defective intelligence to be a major cause of all types of crime, except for some kinds of fraud.[41] In 1931, however, E. H. Sutherland reported 359 American studies that contained test results for 175,000 offenders. These studies seldom supported Goddard's conclusion.[42] After surveying research on the subject, Mary Woodward concluded that low intelligence plays little or no part in delinquency.[43]

[36] Richard R. Korn and Lloyd W. McCorkle, *Criminology and Penology* (New York: Henry Holt & Co., Inc., 1959), p. 209.

[37] Young, *Glandular Physiology and Therapy*, p. 517.

[38] Fink, *Causes of Crime*, p. 211.

[39] Henry H. Goddard, *Feeblemindedness: Its Cause and Consequences* (New York: Macmillan Co., 1923), p. 213.

[40] Ibid., p. 575.

[41] Goring, *The English Convict*, p. 260.

[42] Cohen, Lindesmith, and Schuessler, *The Sutherland Papers*, p. 308.

[43] Mary Woodward, "The Role of Low Intelligence in Delinquency," *British Journal of Delinquency*, 5 (April 1955): 300.

Evaluation of mental deficiency as a cause of crime

It is difficult to determine the influence of intelligence on the inter-action of criminality and the stresses created by socioeconomic factors. First, the growth curve in learning ability reaches its peak somewhere between the 14th and 16th years, then declines sharply. A given mental age will produce a different IQ score according to the adult year level chosen as the standard.[44] Second, testing assumes the individual's growth prior to testing is a reliable basis for predicting future mental growth, but changes in learning opportunity may accelerate or slow the learning rate.[45] Third, mental deficiency is usually discussed as a neurological proposition requiring evidence of a biological nature, but the evidence offered involves behavior which is not limited to biological data.[46] General intelligence is affected by the individual's cultural background. Fur-ther, offenders are drawn disproportionately from the ill-educated, ethnic and racial minorities, and low socioeconomic status groups. The result-ant cultural differences between the offender and the nonoffender groups distort the test results as measures of "native" general intelligence.[47]

It has been suggested that the lack of institutions for mental defectives caused a heavier concentration of this group in earlier prisons. The shaved heads and ungainly uniforms exaggerated their abnormality. Reactions to harsh discipline were reflected in such prisoners' facial expressions.[48]

The inability of a mentally deficient person to make adequate social adjustments is crucial to the crimes he may commit, not mental deficiency per se. Persons at all mental levels may become criminal. The degree of intelligence may affect the manner of committing offenses and success in evading detection or punishment, but the motivation for crimes cannot be attributed solely to low intelligence. In fact, mental deficiency may re-duce criminality by insulating the individual from frustrations or by in-terfering with his participation with others in offenses.

PSYCHOLOGICAL STUDIES

Contemporary psychological theory has been described as "far from uniform" and consisting of several independent groups.[49] Psychiatry, in-

---

[44] Harry M. Shulman, "Intelligence and Delinquency," *Journal of Criminal Law and Criminology,* 41 (March–April 1951): 763–81.

[45] Ibid.

[46] Frank E. Hartung, "A Critique of the Sociological Approach to Crime and Corrections," *Law and Contemporary Problems,* 23 (August 1958): 718.

[47] Kenneth Eells, *et al., Intelligence and Cultural Differences* (Chicago: University of Chicago Press, 1951), p. 68.

[48] W. Norwood East, "Physical Factors and Criminal Behavior," *Journal of Clinical Psychopathology,* 8 (July 1946): 15.

[49] Benjamin B. Wolman, *Contemporary Theories and Systems in Psychology* (New York: Harper & Bros., 1960), p. 3.

cluding psychoanalysis, is diverse in itself. Related fields have studied problems relevant to criminology in measurement of individual differences, testing of intelligence, evaluation of personality factors, investigation of physiological factors, and consideration of social-psychological influences on personality.

Learning and reinforcement

Psychological theories of conditioning and social learning are especially relevant to the etiology and correction of delinquency. The frequency, consistency, and intensity of a given stimulus influence the probability of a certain response in a repeated situation. If the organism's response to a particular situation is followed by a reinforcing stimulus, the response will be strengthened on future occasions when the organism is again in that situation or a similar one.[50] Psychologists have developed principles for study of the etiology of behavior in the presence of positive and negative reinforcements administered by agents external to the individual to elicit a given response.

Appropriate for the correction of crime and delinquency are the procedures grouped under the general term *behavior modification*. "Modeling" refers to the acquisition of response patterns by observing the performance of persons serving as models. "Aversive control" involves the use of punishing stimuli to inhibit undesirable behavior or facilitate the appearance of more appropriate behavior. "Extinction" of delinquent behavior may be sought by eliminating the rewards ordinarily producing the behavior. "Desensitization through counterconditioning" operates, through the elimination of fear and anxiety aroused by certain stimuli, to decrease the delinquent behavior associated with efforts to deal with the emotion-arousing situation.[51]

Behavioral modification techniques have an advantage because they are amenable to application by nonprofessional staff under appropriate training and supervision.[52] One research project offered delinquents the job of talking into tape recorders on any subject they desired. The objective was to develop dependability and promptness in attendance through the "natural" behavior of staff as models, avoidance of punishment, rewards (bonuses over regular pay, verbal praise, food, cigarettes) tailored to the qualities of the individual, and personal freedom. Three years after

[50] Arthur W. Staats, *Learning, Language and Cognition* (New York: Holt, Rinehart & Winston, Inc., 1968), p. 58.

[51] Simplified adaptation of sophisticated analysis by Albert Bandura in his *Principles of Behavior Modification* (New York: Holt, Rinehart & Winston, Inc., 1969).

[52] Ralph Wetzel, "Use of Behavioral Techniques in a Case of Compulsive Stealing," *Journal of Consulting Psychology,* 30 (October 1966): 367–74.

termination of employment, follow-up indicated a significant decrease in arrests and penal incarceration.[53]

Psychoanalytic explanations of behavior

Within the general field of psychiatry, psychoanalytic writers have been strongly influenced by Sigmund Freud, who held that the explanation for all behavior could be found in the unconscious, or the world of inner feelings. The unconscious becomes the scene of mental conflict when there are incompatible elements in the personality. The *id* is largely unconscious in operation, and is the source of basic biological drives present at birth. The *ego* is the conscious personality which represents the growth of attitudes, habits, and ideas through contact with the material and social world. Arising out of relations of the id and the ego, the *superego* reflects the mores of the groups shaping the individual's social experience.

Although aware that there are developmental factors in the personality apart from constitutional influences, Freud saw personality as based on biological drives that arise from sources of constant stimulation within the body and make demands upon the mind. In this respect, Freud appears to resemble the physical-type theorists, but he saw instincts as capable of modification according to the direction in which mental energy is channeled. Two such forms of modification are changes in the objects to which the biological drive is attached and the process of sublimation, through which the biological drive serves social purposes. Always emphasizing the individual, Freud saw the infant as asocial (neither social nor antisocial), with his first feelings directed toward himself. The prototype of any social relationship is seen as object love, which at first expresses a love-hate relationship in a "cannibalistic" swallowing of objects. With a growing consideration of the love object, the child learns, in a new feeling of "tenderness," to be concerned about its survival in order to preserve it. Thus the normal adult becomes capable of having consideration for other persons.[54]

Freud saw toilet training as the first interference with the child's "primitive instinctual drives" and his first experience in the crime-punishment relationship. Since the child's first interest in the outside world is directed toward members of the immediate family, psychological management of relationships with father, mother, and other siblings becomes the central

[53] Ralph Schwitzgebel and D. A. Kolb, "Inducing Behavior Changes in Adolescent Delinquents," *Behavior Research and Therapy,* 1 (March 1964): 297–304. Also see Irwin G. Sarason, "Verbal Learning, Modeling, and Juvenile Delinquency," *American Psychologist,* 23 (April 1968): 254–66.

[54] Franz Alexander and Hugo Staub, *The Criminal, the Judge and the Public* (Glencoe, Ill.: Free Press, 1956), pp. 30–35.

problem in development of the adult person. In keeping with Freud's conception of the infant as asocial, Franz Alexander and Hugo Staub saw the differentiation between criminal and noncriminal personalities as the consequence of the outcome of two stages in personality development. In the first, or "oral-sadistic phase" of development, the drive of the newborn child is to dominate, as expressed in the "cannibalistic possession of the mother's breast." From the age of about four to puberty, the "normal" individual becomes different from the criminal in that he partly represses "his genuine instinctual drives" and partly transforms them into "socially acceptable strivings." Crime then is largely a result of a "defect in the bringing up" rather than a "congenital defect."[55] Alexander and Staub contend that how the child overcomes conflicts in relationships with members of his family determines whether his behavior becomes criminal.

Psychoanalysis holds that contradictory and irrational behavior is made clear once the latent conflicts within the unconscious are brought to the surface. To cure the psychiatric disorder, it is necessary to discover the unconscious experiences and motivations of which the irrational act is but a symptom. In rambling expression of thoughts, through discussing dreams and through slips of the tongue, the patient is supposed to open "windows to the unconscious" by revealing ideas ordinarily not present in his conscious thoughts.

Types of mental disorders

Of the general classes of mental disorders, psychoses and psychoneuroses are of chief interest here. Psychoses include schizophrenia, manic-depressive disorders, and paranoia. In psychoses, the patient manifests severe decompression (exaggerated and deviant defensive patterns), marked distortion of reality, and loss of contact with reality. The schizophrenic has a strong tendency to retreat from reality. Through delusions and hallucinations, he is likely to exhibit marked disturbances in thought processes. The manic-depressive shows extreme fluctuations in mood, with related disturbances in thought and behavior. Paranoid disorders involve delusions of persecution and/or grandeur, but the patient otherwise maintains a relatively intact personality structure—a fact that may complicate recognition of his mental illness.

Psychoneurotics (also called neurotics) are unhappy, anxious individuals who do not exhibit the gross falsification of external reality and loss of contact with reality found among psychotics. They do not require hospitalization, but they feel basically inadequate, exhibit anxiety, are painfully aware of themselves, and lack insights into the causes of the difficulties in maintaining satisfying relationships with others.

Fully developed neuroses have been found to be relatively rare as

[55] Ibid., pp. 30–31.

factors in delinquency: neuroses entail the suppression of psychological impulse, rather than the acting out of such impulses which characterizes crime. The crimes of the neurotic are symbolic, or related to unconscious need to be punished, displaced aggression, and various compulsions. Psychoneuroses most frequently involved in crime are amnesia as a type of conversion and kleptomania and pyromania as compulsions.[56]

Psychoses may originate from either psychological stresses or organic brain pathology. Psychotics with schizophrenic disorders show a strong tendency to withdraw from reality, with emotional "blunting" and disharmony and marked disturbances in thought processes. Delusions and hallucinations are common. In paranoid disorders, the patient has delusions, usually of persecution and/or grandeur, but his personality structure is intact otherwise. The manic-depressive reactions and psychotic depressive reactions involve extreme fluctuations in mood and disturbances in thought and behavior.

Although some psychotic patients may commit violent crimes, the majority are apathetic. When he does break the law, the schizophrenic, for example, is more likely to commit technical violations symptomatic of his inability to cope with his problems.[57]

Likewise, few criminals are definitely psychotic. The best estimate is 1½ to 2 percent. The schizophrenic is the most common among psychotic offenders. His lack of social inhibitions may free him to commit any type of crime—murder, rape, embezzlement, swindling, or forgery.[58] The maniac-depressive patient is more likely to commit crimes during melancholia rather than in intense excitement. Because of his intense concern over what he considers to be an impending social disaster, he may kill those dear to him to save them from misery. Although the manic may commit serious assault on anyone interfering with him, he is easily distracted from his purpose, and his violence is ill-directed. The crimes of the paranoiac are usually the direct outcome of the patient's delusions and are in retaliation for the "relentless persecution" he perceives.

Variations in psychiatric views

The view that criminality is simply a form of neurosis is not universal among psychiatrists. For example, Manfred Guttsmacher believes that "normal criminals" comprise 70 to 80 percent of all criminals. He defines these as criminals who have identified with asocial elements in society. In

56 Lawson G. Lowrey, "Delinquent and Criminal Personality," in J. McV. Hunt (ed.), *Personality and the Behavior Disorders* (New York: Ronald Press Co., 1944), pp. 809–10.

57 Angus MacNiven, "Psychoses and Criminal Responsibility," in R. N. Craig *et al., Mental Abnormality and Crime* (London: Macmillan & Co., Ltd., 1944), pp. 14–32.

58 David Abrahamson, *Who Are the Guilty?* (New York: Grove Press, Inc., 1952), pp. 164–70.

addition, there is a small group of "accidental or occasional criminals" who have essentially healthy superegos but succumb to a particular set of circumstances.[59]

An alternative psychiatric explanation relates the criminality of especially passive and dependent persons to their vulnerability to changes in the structure of society which undermine their socioeconomic position.[60] The similarity of this explanation to the anomie theory suggests some convergence of psychiatric and sociological interpretations.[61] Along this line, psychiatry has shown concern for preventive and therapeutic services organized around the model of *community psychiatry,* which recognizes mental illness as a socially defined condition and endeavors to supplement patient-oriented treatment with services operating within the community as a social system.[62]

The usual conception of mental illness conforms to the *disease model,* which assumes that each condition is marked by a unique set of observable symptoms reflecting the effects of some pernicious agent: physical, chemical, intrapsychic, genetic, interpersonal, or social. A malign process within the organism is supposed to persist over time to deprive the patient of control of his behavior. The disease model is difficult to apply in the diagnosis of mental illness, which lacks the clear-cut symptoms of organic pathology and does not develop in a sequence of progressive states as do many physical illnesses.[63]

A *psychosocial model* of mental illnesses has been suggested as superior to the disease model. Thomas Szasz has been prominent among psychiatrists objecting to the arbitrary equating of mental illness with organic disease, on grounds that mental illness connotes a deviation from the social expectations derived from a sociocultural system. The likelihood that the behavior of an individual will be evaluated as mental illness depends in part on whether it seriously upsets the familiar routines of the groups of which he is a member in daily life—family, work groups, recreational groups, and so on. The chance of being labeled as a mental case

[59] Manfred S. Guttmacher, "The Psychiatric Approach to Crime and Correction," in Richard W. Nice (ed.), *Criminal Psychology* (New York: Philosophical Library, Inc., 1962), p. 118.

[60] David Feldman, "Psychoanalysis and Crime," in Bernard Rosenberg, Israel Gerver, and F. William Howton (eds.), *Mass Society in Crisis* (New York: Macmillan Co., 1964), p. 56.

[61] See Chapter 10, pp. 242–46, for discussion of anomie theory.

[62] Leonard J. Duhl and Robert L. Leopold (eds.), *Mental Health and Urban Social Policy* (San Francisco: Jossey-Bass, Inc., Publishers, 1968), pp. xii–xiii, 3–4.

[63] Merlin Taber *et al.,* "Disease Ideology and Mental Health Research," *Social Problems,* 16 (Winter 1969): 349–57. Also see David Mechanic, *Mental Health and Social Policy* (Englewood Cliffs, N.J.: Prentice-Hall, Inc., 1969), pp. 18–20; and Jules V. Coleman, "Social Factors Influencing the Development and Containment of Psychiatric Symptoms," in Thomas J. Scheff (ed.), *Mental Illness and Social Processes* (New York: Harper & Row, 1967), pp. 158–67.

is magnified when the deviant behavior is interpreted by others (family members, neighbors, officials in relevant positions of authority, and so on) as constituting a threat to the security and general welfare of the community.[64] This interpretation provides an example of the convergence of the social problems of mental illness and crime.

The appearance of community psychiatry and the fuller recognition of social factors in the etiology of mental illness suggest the possibility of greater effectiveness in the use of psychiatry in preventing delinquency and crime and correcting criminal behavior. Through a marriage of social and behavioral sciences, community psychiatry constitutes a movement that goes beyond the individual patient's psychiatric problems to include his family and work setting and the larger community environment in a broad mental health program. The movement suggests greater balance against what Marshall Clinard regards as psychiatry's overemphasis on a rigid character structure produced by childhood experiences in the family in the early years of personality development. In consequence, the influence of later experiences, peer-group activities and values, and the host of sources of mental conflicts outside early childhood within the family circle has been underestimated.[65]

Evaluation: Crime as psychopathy

When psychopathology has been extended beyond clear-cut mental illness to attempt to explain all criminal behavior, it has drawn sharp and telling criticism. In considering the applications of psychoanalytic principles to the study of rape, for example, Menachem Amir cites the failure to distinguish between acts of rape stemming from a neurosis directly related to psychosexual maladjustment and acts symptomatic of a social context which affords explanations beyond sexual pathology. Why, he asks, is forcible rape chosen as a solution to problems of interpersonal relations by a disproportionate number of persons in certain age, ethnic, or class positions within the social structure? He argues that the clinical approach that emphasizes mental processes fails to account for differential distribution and patterns of crime among groups making up the community's population.[66]

Psychiatric research has been sharply criticized for a lack of precision and consistency in diagnostic categories and for inadequate research

---

[64] Thomas S. Szasz, "The Myth of Mental Illness," in Stephan P. Spitzer and Norman K. Denzin (eds.), *The Mental Patient: Studies in the Sociology of Deviance* (New York: McGraw-Hill Book Co., 1968), pp. 22–26. Also see discussion of labeling theory in the next chapter, pp. 258–64.

[65] Clinard, *Sociology of Deviant Behavior*, pp. 186–87.

[66] Menachem Amir, *Patterns of Forcible Rape* (Chicago: University of Chicago Press, 1971), pp. 289–99, 319.

methodology. Gordon Trasler cites the vague use of such terms as "aggressiveness," "negativism," and "disturbed behavior."[67] Michael Hakeem drew up a long list of behavior types and personality traits regarded as symptoms of "predelinquency" in a community mental health demonstration project: bashfulness, crying, daydreaming, eating disturbance, obscenity, stubbornness, underactivity, and untidiness. Research has failed to reduce these personality traits and behaviors to measurable units.[68] In large measure these defects in research stem from exclusive concentration on mental, chemical, and organic factors within the patient; because inner mental life is not subject to direct observation, collection of psychoanalytic material is time-consuming, unlikely to produce a sufficient number of cases for reliable research findings, and vulnerable to varying interpretations among researchers forced into speculation beyond the sphere of verifiable opinion. The psychosocial model lends itself to more effective research derived from fuller use of control groups and more meaningful diagnostic categories.

In a study of 1,110 white juvenile probationers, Alfred Reiss, Jr., correlated aspects of the environment with three personality types based on psychiatric diagnoses.[69] His study is useful in making an important point: personality traits offer significant clues to behavior only when examined within their social context. Both personality traits and social context influence the possibility of delinquent adjustments to problems of life.

According to Reiss, the *relatively integrated type* came from homes well integrated into the community life although located in residential areas with high delinquency rates. Among the types, these probationers had been the least likely to participate in boys' gangs and had demonstrated the highest level of school achievement and postgraduation job success. Reiss predicted that these delinquents were the most likely to become noncriminal adults.

The second group had *weak ego controls* and demonstrated either low self-esteem or high aggression and hostility. They were described as very insecure and most likely to be lone offenders. Their homes were usually outside the high-delinquency areas but had more frequent marital discord and nonconventional ideas. If these boys were still in school, they were the most likely to have low grades. If out of school, they had the poorest employment records. They did not participate as often in peer groups and were most likely to be lone offenders. Their problems reflected parental anxieties and conflicts.

Those with *defective superegos,* the third of Reiss's personality types,

---

[67] Gordon Trasler, *The Explanation of Criminality* (London: Routledge & Kegan Paul, Ltd., 1962), pp. 33–34.

[68] Michael Hakeem, "A Critique of the Psychiatric Approach to Prevention of Juvenile Delinquency," *Social Problems,* 5 (Winter 1957–58): 198–201.

[69] Alfred J. Reiss, Jr., "Social Correlates of Psychological Types of Delinquency," *American Sociological Review,* 17 (December 1952): 710–18.

had not internalized the mores of the larger community and experienced no sense of guilt. They were most likely to come from families including other delinquents and residing in slums. Frequently they were members of gangs. Their delinquencies were approved by their peer groups, reducing mental conflict. Usually they had been raised in broken homes without effective control over children, within an atmosphere of moral uncertainty and marital conflict.

Assessing 113 studies of personality differences between criminals and noncriminals, Karl Schuessler and Donald Cressey offered several general criticisms. The results of the tests failed to establish the personality components of criminal behavior. Frequently, test results supported the view that criminals and noncriminals have similar distributions of personality traits. Because of this overlap in distributions, they considered it "practically impossible" to predict individual delinquency from an individual test score. The test results did not distinguish between personality traits caused by criminal experiences and criminal experience caused by personality traits.[70] Hermann Mannheim properly cautions, however, that these conclusions do not imply the final impossibility of distinguishing the personalities of delinquents and nondelinquents; rather, Schuessler and Cressey demonstrated the inadequacies of the studies they surveyed. For example, the later development of the Minnesota Multiphasic Personality Inventory (MMPI) has brought some advances, not universally acclaimed but widely regarded as useful.[71]

A more recent review was made of 94 studies in the 1950–65 period on personality characteristics of criminals. The MMPI results were called impressive but far from conclusive. Even statistically significant differences for a study group did not prove delinquency to be a product of deviant personality. Failure to control other variables such as social class status and the continued elusiveness of the precise meaning of "personality" placed important limitations on the interpretation of results. Often the differences *within* delinquent and nondelinquent populations exceeded differences *between* the two groups. The studies failed to determine whether criminal behavior is a product of a certain personality trait or the trait was developed during the criminal career.[72]

Citing the improvement of tests since the time of the Schuessler-Cressey critique, Herbert Quay is optimistic about the possibility of consistent and systematic demonstration of differences in personality between subgroups *within* the total delinquent group. Because delinquents are not psychologically homogeneous, he has recommended concentration on differences

[70] Karl F. Schuessler and Donald R. Cressey, "Personality Characteristics of Criminals," *American Journal of Sociology*, 55 (March 1950): 476–84.

[71] Mannheim, *Comparative Criminology*, pp. 287–89.

[72] Gordon P. Waldo and Simon Dinitz, "Personality Attributes of the Criminal: An Analysis of Research Studies, 1950–65," *Journal of Research in Crime and Delinquency*, 4 (July 1967): 185–201.

among delinquents rather than less promising efforts to study *the* "delinquent."[73]

SUMMARY

This chapter was concerned with theories oriented toward the offender as an individual, essentially free of group influences. The nature and functioning of the human body and the level of intelligence, attitudes, personality traits, and psychiatric variables of individuals are important to the study of criminal behavior. When employed as a simple and monocausal explanation for all crimes, however, each of the theories based on these factors has serious weaknesses. Furthermore, as a class they fail to bear on the issues involved in organizing an effective and systematic response to the problem of crime.

FOR ADDITIONAL READING

Baker, Brian C. "XYY Chromosome Syndrome and the Law." *Criminologica,* 7 (February 1970): 2–35.

Berkowitz, Leonard. *Aggression: A Social Psychological Analysis,* chap. 11. New York: McGraw-Hill Book Co., 1962.

Craft, Michael. *Psychopathic Disorders.* London: Pergamon Press, 1966.

Dreher, Robert H. "Origin, Development and Present Status of Insanity as a Defense to Criminal Responsibility in the Common Law." *Journal of History of Behavioral Sciences,* 3 (January 1967): 47–57.

Eckland, Bruce K. "Genetics and Sociology: A Reconsideration." *American Sociological Review,* 32 (April 1967): 173–94.

Eysenck, H. J. *Crime and Personality.* Boston: Houghton Mifflin Co., 1964.

Geiger, Sara G. "Organic Factors in Delinquency," *Journal of Social Therapy,* 6 (1960): 224–37.

Hartung, Frank E. *Crime, Law and Society,* chaps. 6 and 7. Detroit: Wayne State University Press, 1965.

Hood, Ernest B. "Behavioral Implications for the Human XYY Genotype." *Science,* 179 (January 12, 1973): 139–50.

Lejins, Peter P. "Hereditary Endowment, Environmental Influences and Criminality." In Herbert A. Bloch (ed.), *Crime in America* pp. 315–28. New York: Philosophical Library, Inc., 1961.

Lindner, Robert M. *Stone Walls and Men.* New York: Odyssey Press, Inc., 1946.

Megaree, Edwin I. "Undercontrolled and Overcontrolled Personality Types in Extreme Antisocial Aggression." *Psychological Monographs,* 80 (1966): 1–29.

[73] Herbert C. Quay, "Personality and Delinquency," in Herbert C. Quay (ed.), *Juvenile Delinquency: Research and Theory* (Princeton, N.J.: D. Van Nostrand Company, 1965), pp. 139, 166.

Nielsen, Johannes. "The XYY Syndrome in a Mental Hospital: Genetically Determined Criminality." *British Journal of Criminology*, 8 (April 1968): 186–203.

Rosanoff, Aaron J., et al. "Criminality and Delinquency in Twins." *Journal of Criminal Law and Criminology*, 24 (January–February 1934): 923–34.

Rosenhan, D. L. "On Being Sane in Insane Places," *Science*, 179 (January 1973): 250–58.

Schafer, Stephen. *Theories in Criminology*, chaps. 8 and 9. New York: Random House, 1969.

Tappan, Paul W. *Crime, Justice and Correction*, pp. 83–188. New York: McGraw-Hill Book Co., 1960.

Toch, Hans. *Violent Men: An Inquiry into the Psychology of Violence*. Chicago: Aldine Publishing Co., 1969.

Walker, Nigel. *Crime and Punishment in Britain*, chaps. 3, 4, and 5. Edinburgh, Scotland: Edinburgh University Press, 1968.

Williams, Glanville L. *The Mental Element in Crime*. London: Oxford University Press, 1965.

Winick, Charles. "A Primer of Psychological Theories Holding Implications for Legal Work." *American Behavioral Scientist*, 7 (December 1963): 45–47.

10

Sociological study
of crime and criminals

Sociological studies, which deal with the sociocultural environment, emphasize the situation within which the offender breaks the law. These theories hold that the social system within which individuals interact affects the probability that they will offend and the nature of the offenses they are likely to perpetrate. This chapter presents the various sociological theories and considers their relevance to criminology as environmental approaches emphasizing human interaction within groups.

SOCIAL DISORGANIZATION THEORIES

A society is considered "disorganized" when the unity of the group declines because the institutionalized patterns of behavior are no longer effective and social controls over individual behavior break down. Azmy Ibrahim prefers the expression "disorganization *in* society" because it directs attention to the effects of conflicts among the socially organized groups composing society.[1] The idea that society itself is disorganized cannot be reconciled with the fact that organization is the essence of society. Ernest Burgess indicates the relativity of the idea of disorganization by referring to the stages of organization, disorganization, and reorganization that society repetitively passes through. In the organization stage, some groups become restive and protest the conditions they consider unsatisfactory in the contemporary social order, while upholders of the status quo strive to maintain it. Various remedial or reform measures are undertaken during the disorganization stage, and some new order appears in the reorganization stage.[2]

[1] Azmy Ishak Ibrahim, "Disorganization in Society, But Not Social Disorganization," *American Sociologist,* 3 (February 1968): 47–48.
[2] Ernest W. Burgess, "Social Problems and Social Processes," in Arnold M. Rose (ed.), *Human Behavior and Social Processes* (Boston: Houghton Mifflin Co., 1962), pp. 385–86.

Disorganization theory falls under the "control" theories which hold that deviance, rather than conformity, harmony, and social order, is typical in social relationships. Deficiencies in the social system loom large in the explanations these theorists advance for crime and delinquency for a number of reasons, as pointed out by Clarence Schrag. First, when the social organization is weak, an amoral individual soon learns that norm violations may be more efficient than conformity in attaining his goals. Second, the members of groups may be exposed to normative guidelines which are too vague for effective role performance, regardless of the individual's desire to conform. Discrepancies between avowed prescriptive norms and actual behavior disturb patterns of social cooperation, especially when the social system promotes these discrepancies. Third, organized groups may conflict with each other because of opposing goals. Later chapters will study the inconsistency of goals assigned to the police and correctional institutions. Police agencies are expected to curb aggressive criminals with stern measures and yet provide a variety of social services. Prisons are called on concurrently to protect the community from "dangerous criminals" and to correct the psychological and social defects of "underprivileged persons." Fourth, delinquency and crime aggravate social disorganization in that, by definition of certain behaviors as criminal, the social and economic costs of crime place an especially heavy burden on society.[3]

Urbanism and disorganization

Social change and some of the qualities characteristic of urban society are associated with social disorganization. *Social change* refers to modification of the social environment, upsetting the previous balance of group relationships. This modification can result from a variety of sources: exhaustion of local mineral resources, increasing birth or migration rates, discovery of new technologies for converting natural resources for human consumption, and so on. The contemporary social system may be subjected to strains because of changes in norms transmitted by families to future generations, revision of population characteristics by the in-migration of new racial or ethnic groups, scarcities of goods which strain traditional relationships among groups, and shifts in the community power structure.[4]

Nonurban societies are less vulnerable to social disorganization because they are held together by *similarities among group members*. So-

---

[3] Clarence Schrag, *Crime and Justice: American Style* (Rockville, Md.: Center for Studies of Crime and Delinquency, National Institute of Mental Health, 1971), pp. 95, 105.

[4] Wilbert E. Moore, "A Reconsideration of Theories of Change," *American Sociological Review*, 25 (December 1960): 810–18.

ciologists have considered this form of cohesion under several terms: *"gemeinschaft,"*[5] "mechanical solidarity,"[6] or "sacred society."[7] Through strong identification with one another, the members of such a group develop a sense of mutuality. The other fellow's fate is bound up with one's own through close contacts over a long period of time. The small size of these groups favors intimacy in interpersonal relations. The homogeneity of group customs and traits of members lends uniformity to behavior. There is relatively little change over time in the circumstances of life. Most of the group members engage in similar kinds of work and perform similar roles in recurrent social activities. The group is isolated from dissimilar groups. Few strangers appear to challenge customs and beliefs. There is an aversion to change which lends a sacred quality to traditional ways.[8]

Urban societies tend to be organized on a basis of *differences among group members* which complement one another. This type of relationship has been termed *"gesellschaft,"*[9] "organic solidarity,"[10] or "secular society."[11] The mutual dependence of many kinds of roles holds the group together. Relationships between persons tend to be restricted to a specific segment of social life and to be relatively impersonal. Traditions have an effect on individual behavior, so that it is motivated by self-interest and frequently determined through conscious weighing of ends and means. Resistance to change is at a minimum, and the group has easy contact with other groups likely to expose it to unfamiliar ideas and beliefs. In fact, even the native sons of such a group are comparative strangers.

Among the characteristics of urbanism as a way of life are heterogeneity of cultural norms and behavior patterns, functional specialization, population mobility, and impersonality in interpersonal relations. Heterogeneity undermines the social consensus which supports informal social controls through the socialization of personality, long-term social intimacy, and a common cultural heritage.

The increased use of money for purchasing services and greater mobility have freed the individual of much of his dependence upon intimate group ties for the necessities of life. The individual may be cut off from the intimate groups which formerly provided his social and material needs while maintaining a form of control over his behavior. The restau-

[5] Ferdinand Töennies, *Fundamental Concepts of Sociology,* trans. Charles P. Loomis (New York: American Book Co., 1940), pp. 21–22.

[6] Émile Durkheim, *The Division of Labor,* trans. George Simpson (Glencoe, Ill.: Free Press, 1947), p. 109.

[7] Howard Becker, *Man in Reciprocity* (New York: Frederick A. Praeger, Inc., 1956), pp. 191–93.

[8] Ibid., p. 137.

[9] Töennies, *Fundamental Concepts of Sociology,* p. 23.

[10] Durkheim, *Division of Labor,* p. 131.

[11] Becker, *Man in Reciprocity,* pp. 193–95.

SPRING 3100 *magazine, New York City Police Department*

Figure 10–1. Law enforcement and urban society.

Urban life presents an environment favorable to the development of deviance. In the hustle and confusion of urban crowds, social intimacy and the effectiveness of informal controls are decreased. As symbols of the greater reliance on formal controls, two auxiliary policemen patrol a busy street in New York City.

rant and laundry provide meals and a clean shirt for a fee without exerting the controls imposed by the family. The money economy also places
pressures on the individual which can lead to lawbreaking when the importance attached to materialistic rewards overemphasizes money and
makes it an end in itself.

Mobility among a people promotes individuation by increasing the
turnover of group membership. Urban life is marked by a high degree of
spatial mobility—frequent changes in residence, daily movements to and
from work, and a search for amusement. Since integration of the individual within a social group implies a reasonable period of membership
in the group, high spatial mobility weakens identification and affiliation
with stable groups. The urbanite selectively identifies himself with relatively small clusters of like-minded persons, holding others at arm's
length through manners which, while polite, are mechanical and basically
indifferent. Impersonality supports the democracy of being judged on the
basis of individual accomplishment, but it also enables the criminal to
evade apprehension and provides him opportunities for preying on
strangers.

Disorganization from the group perspective

Most frequently, social disorganization is envisaged as group breakdown; that is, when the orderly processes of social interaction and effective functioning of a group break down, there is social disorganization.[12]
Numerous interrelated factors, as discussed above, are seen as disrupting
the relationships of individuals within groups and of groups with one
another.

Charles Cooley conceived of social institutions as emerging out of
commonly felt needs. The institutional organization would be efficient
when individual needs and institutional forms were complementary in
character. In his view, disorganization occurs as the result of "formal-
ism" in institutions, whereby the individual no longer is motivated from
within to maintain "harmony between human nature and its instrument."[13] As products of past experience and contrivance, social institutions tend to be oriented more toward former circumstances than those
of the present. Their longevity is promoted by loyalty, pride, and sentiment even when according to Joyce Hertzler, they no longer serve their
intended purposes and become "crystalized depositories of archaic attitudes, beliefs, codes, habits, and social procedures."[14]

[12] Mabel A. Elliott and Francis E. Merrill, *Social Disorganization,* 4th ed. (New
York: Harper & Bros., 1961), p. 23.

[13] Charles Horton Cooley, *Social Organization* (New York: Charles Scribner's
Sons, 1909), p. 347.

[14] Joyce O. Hertzler, *Society in Action* (New York: Dryden Press, 1954), p.
297.

The classic application of the group-breakdown approach was the work of William Thomas and Florian Znaniecki, who studied Polish-Americans—described by Herbert Blumer as being at that time "perhaps the most disorganized of all the immigrant groups" in the United States.[15] The authors presented two questions: How, with the help of existing social organization and culture, are "desirable mental and moral characteristics" produced in individuals? How, with the help of the existing mental and moral characteristics of individuals, is a "desirable" type of social organization and culture produced? They considered two kinds of data to be essential: the objective cultural elements of social life (which they called "social values") and the subjective characteristics of the members of the social group ("attitudes").[16]

A foodstuff, a coin, a piece of poetry, a university, or a scientific theory are values in that they have meanings to members of some social group and, therefore, become the target of social activity. Poetry acquires significance in social interaction when particular scribbles arouse sentimental and intellectual reactions. The significance of natural objects, therefore, is a product of the conditioning of individuals within a culture. Attitude, the individual counterpart of the social value, refers to the internalization of values as the basis for the individual's participation in group life.

A norm is binding on the members of the group because it is a value in that it has a meaning to the members. As part of culture, the rules form harmonious systems known as social institutions. The totality of institutions found in a social group constitutes the social organization of the group. Because these values are rules, the attitudes they are supposed to elicit from group members necessarily are opposed by other attitudes held by at least some of the members. If the desired attitudes were not opposed, the support of rules would not be necessary. The rules serve the purpose of deterring the expression of the opposing attitudes in overt behavior. Therefore, values and attitudes become concepts for the study of social control. The power of rules in influencing human life stems from the member's consciousness that they represent attitudes of his group and his realization of the social consequences he will suffer if he follows or breaks the rules.[17]

Thomas and Znaniecki see personality development as interaction between the group and the individual. The individual strives to satisfy his needs inside a situation marked by the social demands exerted by the group. They conceive of character as the set of organized and fixed

[15] Herbert Blumer, *Critiques of Research in the Social Sciences*, Bulletin 44, Social Science Research Council (New York, 1939), p. 104.

[16] William I. Thomas and Florian Znaniecki, *The Polish Peasant in Europe and America*, 2 vols. (New York: Alfred A. Knopf, Inc., 1927), pp. 20–21.

[17] Ibid., pp. 31–33.

groups of attitudes developed by social influences. Temperament is defined as the fundamental, original group of attitudes of the individual which exist independently of any social influence. Whereas temperament is seen as impulsive and "natural," character is more conscious and intellectual. The social rules function to bring the temperamental attitudes into a structure of character attitudes constituting the life organization of the individual.[18]

These authors are especially concerned about the effect on life organization when the individual is subjected to new social demands because of change in the sociocultural environment. Stability of society is maintained by uniformity of behavior in keeping with uniform, consciously followed rules. The life organization assumes schemes of social situations experienced by the individual. For a social conformist living in a stable society, a few narrow schemes are sufficient to lead him through situations which are forever defined the same way. Even when he encounters unexpected situations, the familiar schemes may be adaptable. But what if the individual finds that the old rules are no longer successful in meeting unexpected situations?[19]

Thomas and Znaniecki defined social disorganization as a decrease of the influence of existing social rules upon individual members of the group. All societies experience some disorganization because some individuals break rules, but in stable societies social sanctions and reorganization reinforce the decaying organization. If these measures are insufficient, social disorganization becomes more prevalent. Social disorganization is explained in terms of the rise of new attitudes which cause the rules to be interpreted differently. The rules no longer give the individual a life organization scheme that enables him to cope with unfamiliar social situations. No longer does he suppress attitudes which are in opposition to those supporting group solidarity.[20]

Herbert Blumer considers the Thomas and Znaniecki study a sociological classic. The authors tried to lay a basis in scientific social research and scientific theory. By centering on the influence of change on an entire society, the study did provide a conceptual framework for analysis of the behavior patterns of groups and individuals. However, as Blumer demonstrates, the concepts were defined obscurely. Although the study was based methodologically on personal documents (letters, diaries, and so on), the conclusions and concepts were products of the researcher's intellectual grasp of the phenomena and of their previous ideas, rather than emerging out of the documents.[21]

[18] Ibid., p. 1844.
[19] Ibid., pp. 1852–55.
[20] Ibid., p. 1128.
[21] Blumer, *Critiques of Research*, pp. 69–82.

Disorganization from the cultural perspective

Social disorganization may also be viewed as the product of *cultural conflict*. Under the impact of rapid or sudden change, wide chasms may appear between old and new values, between indigenous and imported values, and between traditional and deliberately imposed values. Sources of change include immigration, war, development of new forms of communication, and new industries. From this perspective, social disorganization has been characterized by change-induced cleavages within the value system of a previously integrated society, the coexistence within a society of independent systems of norms, or the diffusion of the allegiance of society's members among many segmental groups.[22]

Thorsten Sellin has suggested that criminologists extend their study beyond crime and criminals to the conflicts of conduct norms that confront people when more or less divergent rules of conduct govern specific life situations. The individual is identified with a number of social groups, each of which has conduct norms applicable to situations created by its activities. As a member of a family which is the transmitting agency for the norms of groups from which the parents came, he possesses all of the family's norms pertaining to conduct in routine life situations. However, he is also a member of a play group, a work group, a political group, a religious group, and other groups. From these he acquires norms which may sustain, weaken, or even contradict those he has incorporated in his personality. The more complex the culture, the greater is the chance that the norms of the various groups will conflict.[23]

Others view disorganization as related to the culture as a whole. Why does the United States have a high crime rate compared to that of other nations? Donald Taft sees American culture as dynamic, complex, materialistic, and competitive and believes the crime rate to be basically attributable to the *criminogenic culture*. Admiration is directed toward those who are "successful" in a competitive struggle, yet others are placed in situations where they fall short of "success." There are gulfs between precept and practice. Although democratic values are espoused, in practice individual virtues are ranked according to races, classes, nationalities, or cliques. Thus the processes of criminal justice are made to appear to be additional evidence of discrimination and exploitation. The behavior of large minorities fails to follow the Puritanical sex codes that are still given lip service. While the social institutions become involved in the climate of competition, exploitation, and efforts to obtain something for

---

[22] Louis Wirth, "Ideological Aspects of Social Organization," *American Sociological Review,* 5 (August 1940): 474.

[23] Thorsten Sellin, *Cultural Conflict and Crime* (New York: Social Science Research Council, 1938), p. 130.

nothing and schools and communication media emphasize competitive rather than socializing activities, the scope of the law forbids satisfactions that are in wide demand.[24]

Contemporary crime has also been seen as rooted in the frontier past. Much of our unwillingness to accept the restraint of law has sprung from the cultural heritage of revolt against oppressive, restraining laws and the lawlessness of men of the frontier. Mabel Elliott believes that the "relative simplicity of the Elizabethan colonial period" failed to provide a firm foundation for the economic, political, and social structures of dynamic urban industrialism. With the closing of the period which created the myth of equal and unlimited opportunity, many "men of brains and enterprise" could reach great fortunes "only by despoiling the gains of others."[25]

Under the concept of cultural lag, another theory assumes that some aspects of culture change more rapidly than others. Because the various aspects are interrelated, the uneven rate of change among them disturbs the equilibrium of the whole. The cultural-lag approach advances the idea that some aspects will be ahead while others are behind; the specific assumption is that inventions in the material sphere of culture stimulate change at a pace unequaled in the overall culture of a society. Mechanical invention is seen as setting the pace by its impact on society's institutions, customs, and philosophies.[26] For example, factory technology has produced automobiles, which have contributed to spatial mobility.

The hypothesis of cultural lag has been criticized for complicating objective determination of the direction of the lag and the manner of correcting it. Lewis Mumford argues that change in a direction opposite to that set by the machine may be necessary to forestall human deterioration. It may be that machine technology (increased capacity to kill in war) is the laggard, while nonmaterial culture (a deeper sense of humanitarianism and concern for the underprivileged peoples of the world) is the pacesetter.[27] There are two sets of variables of major importance in the study of cultural lag: the instruments of change and the cultural resistance to them. Change may be resisted by vested interests, by traditional hostility to the new, by habit, by fear, or by reverence for the past. Abbott Herman suggests that the cultural-lag advocates have unduly emphasized the first set of variables. He calls for careful inquiry into the

---

[24] Donald R. Taft and Ralph W. England, Jr., *Criminology*, 4th ed. (New York: Macmillan Co., 1964), pp. 277–78.

[25] Mabel A. Elliott, *Crime in Modern Society* (New York: Harper & Bros., 1952), p. 273.

[26] William F. Ogburn and Meyer F. Nimkoff, *Sociology*, 3d ed. (Boston: Houghton Mifflin Co., 1958), p. 711.

[27] Lewis Mumford, *Technics and Civilization* (New York: Harcourt, Brace & Co., 1934), pp. 316–17.

involvement of social values in both the creation of change and the resistance to it.[28]

Evaluation of social disorganization theories

The strength of the social disorganization theories is their original objective: to explore the social processes leading to problems. Crime, family difficulties, unemployment, and so on are treated not as disparate problems but as coming from common sources. Crime prevention and treatment are part of a general attack on all problems. Unfortunately, social disorganization theories most often have been used as "window dressing," to be dropped when analysis of the fundamental facts of social problems is undertaken.[29]

The approach has been criticized for lack of objectivity. The very word "disorganization" implies disapproval and the abnormality of an unfortunate temporary condition. Change, however, is always with us and is not necessarily on the debit side of society's ledger. Some theorists identify order with an unchanging agreement among members of society, whereas the dynamic conditions of urban life call for continuous accommodation among the cultural norms if consensus is to be maintained.

Descriptions of earlier folk societies exaggerate their simplicity of social structure, their insulation from forces of change, the universality of compliance among members, and their cultural homogeneity. The disorganization of contemporary societies also is frequently exaggerated because, in qualifying as societies, they demonstrate social order regardless of the impact of urban conditions. Contemporary circumstances have neither freed individuals of cultural control nor altered the fundamental nature of political life.[30] The criticisms of contemporary life appear excessive. One might wonder whether there is anyone at all who is not regarded as a truant from a psychiatrist's couch, alcoholic ward, or prison cell.

Similarly, the social disorganization approach has overlooked the degree of social organization existing in "deteriorated" and "delinquency" areas whose populations are said to be too heterogeneous, economically depressed, and mobile to have any real stake in the neighborhood or larger community. The existence of cultural diversity is not tantamount to encouragement of delinquency. Albert Cohen questions whether any ethnic or racial group condones stealing, vandalism, and the general neg-

[28] Abbott P. Herman, *An Approach to Social Problems* (Boston: Ginn & Co., 1949), pp. 32–33.

[29] Richard C. Fuller, "The Problem of Teaching Social Problems," *American Journal of Sociology,* 44 (November 1938): 417.

[30] Richard T. LaPiere, *A Theory of Social Control* (New York: McGraw-Hill Book Co., 1960), pp. 19–24.

ativism of what he defines as a delinquent subculture. Some ethnic groups may tolerate certain kinds of group delinquency, but there is a general agreement on the essential "wrongness" of these activities, except under special circumstances.[31] In fact, the deviants themselves and the deviant behaviors usually are patterned rather than reflections of a normless void. Social control has not diminished in the heterogeneous urban society. Instead, the very differences among individuals and groups have formed a different basis for social solidarity.[32]

CULTURAL TRANSMISSION AND LEARNING: THE THEORY OF DIFFERENTIAL ASSOCIATION

The study of culture is relevant also to criminology in terms of the relationship between cultural transmission and learning. Our examination of criminal behavior systems has demonstrated the patterning of criminal behavior. These patterns can be explained as the outgrowth of a cultural heritage passed down through the generations or developed by exchange of knowledge between individuals in the present. Thus learning is a process for the advancement of criminal conduct as well as prosocial attitudes.

Elements of Sutherland's theory

The theory of differential association advanced by Edwin H. Sutherland views criminal behavior, like all social behavior, as learned rather than inherited. Sutherland presented this theory in final form in the 1947 edition of his textbook, in a statement of nine propositions. He believes this learning takes place through interaction with other persons; the sharing of understandings and a feeling of social intimacy within groups involves the process of communication among beings. Most of the learning takes place within intimate personal groups. The content of learning criminal behavior includes techniques of committing the crime and such psychological elements as the specific direction of motives, drives, rationalizations (reasons given), and attitudes. The principle of *differential association* states that a person becomes delinquent when he encounters an excess of definitions favorable to lawbreaking over those unfavorable to it. These definitions operate with varying frequency, duration, and intensity. All the typical learning mechanisms are involved in the learning that results from association with criminal and anticriminal patterns. Because both criminal and noncriminal behaviors are expressions of general needs and values, criminal behavior alone cannot be explained on

[31] Albert Cohen, *Delinquent Boys: The Culture of the Gang* (Glencoe, Ill.: Free Press, 1955), p. 34.

[32] Frank E. Hartung, "A Critique of the Sociological Approach to Crime and Corrections," *Law and Contemporary Problems,* 23 (Autumn 1958): 721.

the basis of those needs and values. Both criminals and noncriminals seek money and happiness; it is insufficient to explain crime as a quest for money or personal gratification.[33]

The genius of Sutherland should be assessed against the prevailing views at the time his theory emerged. Individualistic theories (the subject of Chapter 9) and diffusive multiple-factor "theories" were dominant; his criticisms of these speculations gave him prominence when sociology's chief contribution to criminology was as a critic of the research of other disciplines. In advancing his theory of differential association, Sutherland moved beyond reaction to the theories of others to propose an alternative theory cast in a sociological mold. He became convinced that, although the individual's tendencies toward or against criminal behavior are products of his personal history, they are expressed in a reaction to the immediate situation as he defines it. His theory is genetic in that it concerns the processes that operated in the earlier history of individuals, but he also assumes that the situation in which the crime occurs will be defined in terms of the tendencies they have acquired to date.

While Sutherland spoke of *definitions* favorable or unfavorable to crime, the number of exposures to procriminal patterns is the crucial variable, not the number of criminals with whom one comes into contact, as Cohen has pointed out.[34] The exposures also can involve interaction with respectable conformists as well as criminals. Furthermore, the effect of exposure varies according to frequency, duration, and intensity, to rule out any arbitrary relationship between criminal contacts and development of deviant behavior.

The postulate on which the theory is based, Sutherland wrote, is "that crime is rooted in the social organization and is an expression of the social organization." Some groups are organized for criminal behavior; others are organized against it. In that sense, the community's crime rates express differential group organization.[35]

Sutherland saw differential association as a statement of cultural conflict from the point of view of the person committing crime. The "excess of definitions," then, represents the effects on the person's definition of the crime-inducing situation as a consequence of his greater exposure to norms favorable to crime than to norms opposing it. Thereby he has an answer to the question: Once initiated, why doesn't criminal behavior increase indefinitely until everyone is a criminal? His reply: The increased effectiveness of criminal organization arouses other groups to initiate increasingly effective anticrime organization. The crime rate increases as a

[33] Adapted from Edwin H. Sutherland, *Principles of Criminology,* 4th ed. (Philadelphia: J. B. Lippincott Co., 1947), pp. 6–7.

[34] Albert K. Cohen, *Deviance and Control* (Englewood Cliffs, N.J.: Prentice-Hall, Inc., 1966), pp. 95–96.

[35] Edwin H. Sutherland, "A Statement of the Theory," in Albert Cohen, Alfred Lindesmith, and Karl Schuessler (eds.), *The Sutherland Papers* (Bloomington: Indiana University Press, 1956), p. 11.

result of this differential group organization because the higher rates reflect greater effort against the criminals. Differential association explains the earlier increase in crimes because of fuller opportunities to learn criminal ways and attitudes. Differential group organization explains the eventual slackening of this acceleration and the reversal of crime trends.[36]

Differential association and learning theories

In terms of the learning mechanisms involved and the needs and values expressed, differential association regards the process of becoming a criminal as the same as that for all personality development. The specific techniques of crimes may be learned through association with criminals, but many criminal techniques are also employed in legitimate activities. Something must be acquired in addition to criminal techniques; the criminal must learn plausible explanations and socially acceptable reasons for his criminal acts. These are in terms of definitions he has acquired through his association with criminals and his acceptance of their orientation to society.

By placing crime causation within the province of learning, Sutherland rejected physiological and other distinct factors as the explanation for criminal behavior. Concurrently, he opened the way for probing of the complex questions: What motivates the learner to initiate the process? What shapes the selection of a particular response? What are the cues that elicit the particular response? What are the rewards that transform random or chance behavior into habitual and recurrent behavior? He has been criticized for underestimating the complexity of learning and for failing to account for the origin of the criminality which would have to exist before it can be learned.[37]

By stressing interaction in a process of communication, he turned the search for causes toward social psychology, which is concerned with norms and culture. He undermined the popular views that criminal and noncriminal behaviors are sharply distinct and that the former is purely pathological. However, his references to definitions "favorable" and "unfavorable" to violation of the law did not identify with sufficient precision and clarity what factors he saw as involved in causation or how these factors were interrelated.

Evaluation of differential association theory

Evaluation of the theory of differential association has been complicated by the imprecision of terms used in the original statement and the

[36] Edwin H. Sutherland, "Development of the Theory," in Cohen, Lindesmith, and Schuessler, *The Sutherland Papers*, pp. 20–22.

[37] Clarence Ray Jeffery, "An Integrated Theory of Crime and Criminal Behavior," *Journal of Criminal Law, Criminology and Police Science*, 49 (March–April

removal by death of the author, who was most equipped to interpret meanings. It is difficult to differentiate between Sutherland's ideas and those advanced by his interpreters, especially when the standards being applied stem from the development of research methods that followed framing of the theory. When Melvin DeFleur and Richard Quinney developed a model of the theory stated in operational language designed for computer use, they found Sutherland's verbal terms "primitive." They concluded that his statement was at such a high level of abstraction and the relationships between variables were so vague that it is impossible to test the theory with empirical data.[38]

Recognizing the relevance of the theory to learning, Clarence Jeffery attempted to put differential association in the "modern dress" of operant conditioning, which sees crime as a product of stimuli (environmental conditions) strengthened by subsequent reinforcing stimuli released by earlier responses and eliminated through negative reinforcement (punishment). (Operant conditioning deals with the problem of the persistence of behavior and does not explain the appearance of the behavior.) Jeffery's theory of "differential reinforcement" states: The reinforcing quality of different stimuli differ for different actors, depending on the conditioning history of each. Some individuals have been reinforced for criminal behavior; others have not. Some individuals have been punished for criminal behavior; others have not. An individual is not necessarily reinforced and/or punished after a criminal act, but even intermittent reinforcement will maintain a criminal or noncriminal pattern. In short, operant behavior is maintained by its consequences.[39]

Attempts to apply Sutherland's theory to noncareer property offenders have indicated that it is unsatisfactory for explaining these types of crime. Check forgers, for example, do not seem to have had criminal antecedents or early criminal associations.[40] When Donald Cressey interviewed criminal violators of financial trust at three prisons about their acquisition of criminal techniques and rationalizations, respondents were unable to trace the source of their justification that they were "borrowing" funds.

1959): 537–38; Cressey reviews the major criticisms of the theory in Edwin H. Sutherland and Donald R. Cressey, *Criminology,* 8th ed. (Philadelphia: J. B. Lippincott Co., 1970), pp. 78–91.

[38] Melvin L. DeFleur and Richard Quinney, "A Reformulation of Sutherland's Association Theory and a Strategy for Empirical Verification," *Journal of Research in Crime and Delinquency,* 3 (January 1966): 1–22. Also see, in the same issue, Donald R. Cressey, "The Language of Set Theory and Differential Association," pp. 22–26.

[39] Clarence Ray Jeffery, "Criminal Behavior and Learning Theory," *Journal of Criminal Law, Criminology and Police Science,* 56 (September 1965): 294–300; for a more precise statement in the same direction, see Robert L. Burgess and Ronald L. Akers, "A Differential Association-Reinforcement Theory of Criminal Behavior," *Social Problems,* 14 (Fall 1966): 128–47.

[40] Edwin M. Lemert, "The Behavior of the Systematic Check Forger," *Social Problems,* 6 (Fall 1958): 141–49.

Cressey contends that differential association cannot be tested empirically according to the mathematical terms implied by Sutherland. To determine the excess of definitions favorable to violations of law, it is necessary to list all the prior associations of violators with criminals and noncriminals. Since such observations cannot be made, Cressey recommends that the theory be modified to center attention on the presence or absence of a specific, learned vocabulary to determine whether a person is criminal or noncriminal.[41]

Clarence Schrag points out that the theory fails to account for the conflicting social situations it assumes. The theory also implies that all individuals are conformists to the norms of their particular groups and that groups are similar in their capacity to command the allegiance of members, the solidarity of each group depending on the nature of contacts between members and nonmembers. Therefore, Schrag argues, social disorganization, not the deviant behavior of individuals, is the source of criminality. A serious omission of differential association theory is its failure to account for intergroup conflict and social disorganization.[42]

ANOMIE AND CRIME: THE MEANS-END THEORY

Norms which are supposedly bench marks for conforming behavior can have the effect of directing at least some individuals toward criminal behavior. In advancing this seemingly paradoxical idea, Robert Merton summarizes a *means-ends theory:* "Social structures exert a definite pressure upon certain persons in the society to engage in non-conformist rather than conformist conduct."[43] He notes the possibility that crime and delinquency may result from a contradiction between ends in the form of cultural values and the means the social structure provides for achieving them. In support of the central theme of this book, the etiology of crime is placed within the sociocultural organization of society.

The culture holds out certain legitimate objectives, or ends, for members of society. For example, Americans are enjoined to strive for occupational "success." The schools, radio, newspapers, and television emphasize that all individuals have a moral right to be "successful" men, regardless of social origin. Social institutions are supposed to provide means of attaining this objective. Training, for example, opens the door to occupations conferring prestige and material rewards.

---

[41] Donald R. Cressey, "Application and Verification of the Differential Association Theory," *Journal of Criminal Law, Criminology and Police Science,* 43 (May–June 1952): 43–52.

[42] Schrag, *Crime and Justice,* p. 51.

[43] Robert K. Merton, *Social Theory and Social Structure* (Glencoe, Ill.: Free Press, 1949), pp. 125–26.

Two interpretations: Anomy and anomie

Émile Durkheim applied the term "anomy" to the deregulation by cultural norms of individuals when a social crisis or abrupt social change undermines the society's normative system. As a sociocultural creature, man has appetites beyond those having a fairly specific basis in his organic constitution, such as hunger and sex. Therefore, Durkheim says, man's desires surpass the means at his command for their gratification. Unless his desires are limited by some source external to him, man will experience great restlessness. The norms of his society operate as such a limitation. When the controls of the moral order are removed, the restlessness is released to make the individuals intolerant of all limitations they may encounter. "All the advantages of social influence are lost so far as they are concerned; their moral education has to be recommenced."[44]

The abrupt growth of power and wealth has such an effect, Durkheim believes, because the traditional ways of distributing rewards and privileges are upset by the greater scale of social resources. The previous limits on human aspirations are lifted for some people who previously were curbed by the moral order. The abrupt growth of power and wealth in society strains the patterns of relationships that had been operating. Securing power and wealth deceives men into believing that they depend only on themselves and produces the state of "anomy," in which the previously operating norms no longer regulate their behavior. A new system of moral limitations is required, but the rise of a new public conscience, appropriate to the new social conditions, takes time, according to Durkheim.[45]

Merton gave a new twist to Durkheim's concept by substituting the social structure for the innate desires of individual men as the causal factor in deviance. Merton's central hypothesis is that criminal and other aberrant behavior can be regarded as a symptom of dissociation between culturally prescribed aspirations and socially structured avenues for realizing these aspirations. *Anomie,* in Merton's terms, is a breakdown in the cultural structure as the consequence of this acute disjuncture. A fundamental discrepancy is created because there are major differences in the availability of opportunities for "success" among members at various levels of social class, ethnic, and racial status. There is a greater difference among individuals in their relative access to *means* for attaining material "success" than in their exposure to material "success" as a universal *end* for human aspiration. Presumably, there would be a greater

---

[44] Emile Durkheim, *Suicide: A Study in Sociology,* trans. John A. Spaulding and George Simpson (Glencoe, Ill.: Free Press, 1951), pp. 246–52.

[45] Ibid., p. 253.

pressure of discontent among those who experience the greatest discrepancy. It is supposed that these individuals would be more likely to become social deviants, thus producing differential crime rates among social classes, ethnic groups, and "racial" categories.

Mertin makes two distinctions. First, to the majority of Americans, the social institutions convey the cultural message of the availability of opportunity which stresses the importance of qualifying and striving for socioeconomic rewards, especially in material possessions. Second, a social structure is supposed to lend reality to the promises of culture. A discrepancy rises between culturally induced aspiration and the realities of the operation of the social structure. The gap is produced by differences between groups in chances to realize these aspirations; some are deprived either through lack of qualifications or because legitimate avenues for socioeconomic opportunity are not equally accessible. Poverty and racial discrimination, as deepseated sources of criminal behavior, are examples of strains between the cultural and social systems. Human society is a reality because a large proportion of the people conform to both cultural goals and institutional means.[46]

Four deviant adaptations

In reference to the strains between cultured and social systems, Merton delineates four types of deviant behavior.[47]

Innovation. The individual assimilates the cultural goal but does not equally internalize the institutional norms governing the means for its attainment. Adaptation to cultural goals is positive and to institutionalized means is negative. For example, crime syndicates accept many of the norms of bureaucratic organization, and the swindler accepts the norms of "sharp" businessmen. In both instances, the emphasis on material success is shared with legitimate businessmen, but the means that are adopted for gaining this cultural goal are prohibited by criminal law. Merton cites the tendency of both eminently "successful" and "unsuccessful" men to attribute their fate to "luck."[48] Since this implies little relation between worth and consequences, the cynicism suggested by the innovation response is encouraged. In a society with heavy emphasis on pecuniary success, there is likely to be this sort of imbalance unless provision is made for socialization of personalities in ethics of social responsibility.

Ritualism. Lofty goals of great pecuniary success and rapid social mobility are scaled down or abandoned to bring them to a level where they can be satisfied within the limitations of institutional norms. Adap-

---

[46] Merton, *Social Theory and Social Structure,* pp. 128, 162.

[47] Ibid., pp. 134–36.

[48] Ibid., pp. 138–39.

tation to cultural goals is negative and to institutionalized means is positive. This adaptation is one of "playing safe" and "not sticking one's neck out." Individuals are more likely to be zealously conformist bureaucrats than criminals. However, prison files include histories of conformists who dramatically reversed themselves to engage in illicit behavior.

Retreatism. Both the cultural goals and the institutional means are rejected by individuals who retreat from the society of which they are supposed to be members. This group includes psychotics, outcasts, vagabonds, drunkards, drug addicts, "hippies," and similar "aliens" in their own land. In one way or another they have abandoned the quest for the goals characteristic of their culture and thus have become subject to criminal laws that endeavor to control moral behavior.

Rebellion. Because of alienation from cultural goals, both goals and institutional means are rejected, but with the intention of modifying the social structure. Aggressive crimes and property offenses may express alienation from both legitimate social means and cultural ends.

Evaluation of anomie theory

The theory of anomie has been applauded as a plausible and sociologically sophisticated explanation for adult theft, especially professional theft. However, doubt has been expressed concerning its applicability as an explanation for all delinquency and crime. Extensive criminal behavior in the affluent middle and upper classes, F. Ivan Nye argues, runs counter to the premise of the theory.[49] Marshall Clinard wonders why, if this theory holds, many economically deprived people do not resort to crime.[50] A crucial issue is whether this explanation would be appropriate for explaining crime in a society which does not have the dynamic and heterogeneous characteristics of contemporary American culture.

Edwin Lemert believes that Merton's distinction between the cultural system and the social structure is too rigid to capture the behaviors of individuals because it assumes the culture to be more integrated and its priority of values more descriptive of the feelings and perceptions of individual group members than is in fact the case. Instead Lemert sees the individual as subject to the competing claims of various groups in the complex array of interactions within a pluralistic society.[51] The anomie theory has been criticized by Clinard for envisaging atomistic individuals selecting adaptations to the social system without recognition of the im-

[49] F. Ivan Nye, *Family Relationships and Delinquent Behavior* (New York: John Wiley & Sons, Inc., 1958), p. 2.

[50] Marshall B. Clinard, "Criminological Research," in Robert K. Merton, Leonard Broom, and Leonard S. Cottrell, Jr. (eds.), *Sociology Today* (New York: Basic Books, Inc., Publishers, 1959), p. 514.

[51] Edwin M. Lemert, "Social Structure, Social Control, and Deviation," in Marshall B. Clinard (ed.), *Anomie and Deviant Behavior: A Discussion and Critique* (New York: Free Press, 1964), pp. 60, 68.

portance of interactions within groups as influences on their behavior. The deviant act is seen as an abrupt switch from conformity to deviance, rather than a gradual process extending through a series of social interactions.[52] Finally, citing the great influence of peer group norms on delinquent gang members, James F. Short, Jr., argues that the social structure should include both local community norms and those operating *within* peer groups.[53]

Differential illegitimate opportunity

Merton's failure to recognize the existence of an illegitimate opportunity structure accompanying the legitimate opportunity structure has been remedied by Richard Cloward and Lloyd Ohlin.[54] Their view is consistent with the well-established generalization that delinquency areas are socially patterned. William F. Whyte found the fundamental problem of an urban slum to be the failure of its social organization to mesh with the structure of the community around it. The slum resident has to choose between two opportunity structures: the world of business and politics dominated by upper-class people and the world of rackets and politics based on local patterns.[55] A typology of delinquency areas proposed by Solomon Kobrin would be differentiated on a range of degrees of integration with conventional and/or criminal value systems. When the two worlds are integrated, crime syndicate leaders maintain memberships in churches, fraternal societies, political parties, and other local community institutions, and conventional people tolerate organized crime. This stable position of racket enterprise works against violent crime and provides career opportunities in crime for slum youth. In areas where the two value systems are not integrated, adult criminality is neither systematic nor organized, and juvenile crime is controlled by neither the conventional nor a criminal social order. Delinquencies assume a more violent character, and an illicit opportunity structure is less apparent.[56]

Applying the concepts of career and occupational training discussed earlier in relation to criminal behavior, Cloward and Ohlin point out how the availability of illegitimate means of achieving cultural goals influences crime.[57] If the slum youth decides he cannot "make it legitimately," not all illegitimate means will be equally available to him be-

[52] Marshall B. Clinard, "The Theoretical Implications of Anomie and Deviant Behavior," in ibid., pp. 55–56.

[53] James F. Short, Jr., "Gang Delinquency and Anomie," in ibid., p. 116.

[54] Richard A. Cloward and Lloyd E. Ohlin, *Delinquency and Opportunity: A Theory of Delinquent Gangs* (New York: Free Press of Glencoe, 1960).

[55] William Foote Whyte, *Street Corner Society,* enlarged ed. (Chicago: University of Chicago Press, 1955), pp. 272–74.

[56] Solomon Kobrin, "The Conflict of Values in Delinquency Areas," *American Sociological Review,* 16 (October 1951): 657–59.

[57] See Chapter 7, pp. 132–35.

cause he must gain access to learning situations. Thus in the deviant subcultures discussed below, only a portion of slum youth has access to illegitimate opportunity.

Delinquent subculture. This category of deviant subculture requires certain forms of delinquent activity in performing the dominant subcultural roles.[58] Social class lines act as barriers preventing slum youth from experiencing personally the success models of the society at large. The successful criminal is likely to be a hero to the slum youth. Street gangs provide a form of age grading whereby boys "graduate" into older age gangs in successive stages of learning and performing deviant roles. Through contacts with criminals, dealers in stolen goods, police, politicians, and bail bondsmen, the adolescent learns the skills and folklore of the illegitimate world. Since the impulsive, unpredictable individual has no place in the business of crime, the aspirant for stable criminal status is pressed to discipline himself within an illicit organization.[59]

Conflict subculture. When conventional and deviant values are not integrated, the slum cannot provide access to either legitimate opportunities or stable criminal careers. Adult criminals lack organization to protect themselves against police. If systematic learning of criminal techniques is unavailable, adolescents are denied illegitimate channels to success goals and their frustrations are increased. Illicit groups do not afford the controls which limit the violence of delinquent gangs in the integrated slum.[60]

Retreatist subculture. The retreatist is a "double failure," unable to achieve success goals through legitimate or illegitimate means. He becomes detached from the social structure and retreats from the world. These individuated persons can be considered as participants in a subculture, however, because a web of associations is necessary, for example, in learning the techniques for using drugs and obtaining a steady supply.[61]

Although empirical findings are not conclusive, research shows communities with high delinquency rates have a diversity of gang types, lack a high degree of cultural consistency among gangs, and show more versatility in gang goals and activities than the Cloward-Ohlin theory suggests.[62]

DEVIANT SUBCULTURES AND DELINQUENCY

In a complex society a multitude of ethnic, regional, and occupational groups differ from one another in language, clothing, etiquette, beliefs,

[58] Cloward and Ohlin, *Delinquency and Opportunity,* p. 7.

[59] Ibid., pp. 161–71.

[60] Ibid., pp. 171–78.

[61] Ibid., pp. 178–86.

[62] Schrag, *Crime and Justice,* p. 71.

and life styles. This cultural differentiation may be viewed as marking off relatively distinct subcultures, within each of which people share values that are not characteristic of the society as a whole. Subcultures differ in their persistence, but a vital element is the transmission of norms through generations of members. The particular norms associated with deviation must be passed on through learning in a relatively uniform manner. Subcultures also differ in origin. Among the sources of development are migration of a group into a new cultural environment, social or physical segregation of a group from the larger society, and occupational specialization within a group.

The deviant subculture should be considered as distinct from other subcultures the particular deviants may also share. Imprecise use of the concept results in its application to a broader population of deviants than is justified. For example, juvenile delinquents may also be included within a lower-class subculture, a minority-group subculture, or an adolescent subculture. When this distinction is ignored, the delinquent subculture may be extrapolated to include elements of other subcultures. Then the delinquent subculture is presented as though it exclusively encompasses behavior which also is found among youths of a particular environment who are not necessarily delinquent. In effect, delinquent subculture is applied to a broader range of behaviors than actually is subject to the concept. Many juvenile gang behaviors are not delinquent, and many delinquencies are not subcultural in origin.

Delinquency as a repudiation of middle-class norms

Cohen believes children learn to become delinquents by becoming members of groups in which delinquent conduct is the accepted practice. He sees a "delinquent subculture" as persisting most conspiciously in slum areas through transmission of beliefs, values, and knowledge in a succession of juvenile groups.[63]

The middle class tends to emphasize certain standards, especially for the male: high personal aspiration, self-reliance, academic achievement, postponement and subordination of immediate satisfactions and self-indulgence, rational thought and planning, cultivation of courtesy and personality, control of physical aggression, "wholesome" and "constructive" recreation, and respect for property rights. The working-class child is likely to experience a watered-down version of these standards in family contacts and is less likely to make the middle-class norms his own. The background of working-class youths equips them poorly for school and for movement up the social class ladder. Consequently, they are apt to find themselves consistently at the bottom of social prestige rankings and suffering repeated blows to their self-esteem. For these common prob-

[63] Cohen, *Delinquent Boys*, p. 13.

lems of adjustment, youths so situated in the social structure may accept one of three subcultural solutions, Cohen believes.[64]

The working-class boy may adopt the *college-boy* route of upward mobility. To obtain a college education, he must conform to the middle-class norms of academic achievement, but, equally important, he must practice thrift to pay for his education, while corner-boy groups place value on sharing money with friends. Thus the college boy sets himself apart from the activities of his peers.

The working-class boy may also employ the *stable corner-boy response*. Although he does not permanently surrender hopes for upward mobility, he also does not rupture his relations with working-class adults. Unlike the boy who exhibits the delinquent response, he does not incur the active hostility of middle-class persons and therefore keeps open the way to the opportunities these people control.[65]

The *delinquent response* is the explicit and wholesale repudiation of middle-class standards and the adoption of their antithesis. The "stable corner-boy response" temporizes with middle-class morality, but the delinquent subculture does not.[66] Cohen suggests that the boy taking the "delinquent solution" has internalized middle-class norms sufficiently to be ambivalent toward his own corner-boy behavior. Because the boy is subjected to anxieties by both low self-esteem and status deprivations, he accepts the delinquent subculture.[67] David Bordua interprets this explanation as saying that a little internalization is a dangerous thing.[68] Lower-class socialization has failed to equip the boys to meet the criteria of the middle-class measuring rod, although they have partially accepted these criteria. Merger of self-derogation and status deprivation is supposed to explain the irrationality of gang delinquency.

Cohen describes the "delinquent subculture" as nonutilitarian, malicious, and negativistic. It is *nonutilitarian* in the sense that stealing does not serve any economic purpose and takes on some qualities of a sport. But why should this particular kind of sport be chosen by these boys? The choice reflects *malice,* which emphasizes enjoyment of the discomfiture of others and a delight in defiance of taboos. There is enjoyment in terrorizing "good" children and in flouting the authority of teachers. The delinquent subculture is *negativistic* in that the norms of the larger culture are turned upside down. Whatever is wrong according to the larger culture becomes right in the delinquent subculture *because* it is wrong by the norms of the larger culture.[69] Cohen believes most delinquency would

[64] Ibid., pp. 88–91, 95–97.

[65] Ibid., pp. 128–29.

[66] Ibid., pp. 129–30.

[67] Ibid., pp. 125–28.

[68] David J. Bordua, *Sociological Theories and Their Implications for Juvenile Delinquency* (Washington, D.C.: U.S. Children's Bureau, 1960), p. 10.

[69] Cohen, *Delinquent Boys,* pp. 25–28.

not occur without the legitimatization given to deviance by the delinquency subculture. A reference group assures support to the individual in his deviant behavior.[70]

Critique of middle-class repudiation theory

Doubt has been expressed that the relationship between gang delinquency and class conflict is as complete and universal as Cohen suggests. Gresham Sykes and David Matza contend that a gang member rationalizes his deviant behavior through the "techniques of neutralization" rather than by rejecting middle-class standards. The deviant may deny responsibilty for his behavior under the argument that unloving parents, evil companions, or slum conditions propelled him helplessly, in spite of his claimed allegiance to the dominant norms. He may deny that his illegal acts are wrong in terms of injuring anyone. Actual injury may be justified on grounds that the victim deserved it because he is the wrongdoer, and the delinquent is some kind of socially motivated hero. The deviant may question the motives of those who condemn him in order to shift attention from his own transgressions. Finally, he may claim he was motivated by a "higher loyalty" to family or friends.[71]

The theme of rejection leads Milton Yinger to refer to the deviant subculture as a contraculture. Out of frustration, anxiety and resentment, the basis of the deviant group's values becomes conflict, and the dominant culture is seen as repressing the public's tendencies to accept the norms of the contraculture. In this case, the deviant culture is only partially distinct.[72] Similarly, contraculture has been described as only one example of *derivative subcultures* spun off from the main culture.[73]

When Lois DeFleur found no evidence of a reaction subculture in the Cohen model among delinquents of Corboda, Argentina, she concluded that the class structure of the given society must be taken into account. In Argentina delinquency is concentrated at the bottom of this class structure, but the poor are deprived of contact with the major social institutions of society. Therefore, DeFleur says, there is an absence of a reaction subculture in Cohen's terms.[74] Clinard believes lower-class delinquency gangs serve simple needs in addition to permitting expressions of protest against middle-class values. These needs are adventure; excitement; pro-

[70] Ibid., p. 135.

[71] Gresham Sykes and David Matza, "Techniques of Neutralization: A Theory of Delinquency," *American Sociological Review*, 22 (December 1957): 664–70.

[72] Milton Yinger, "Contraculture and Subculture," *American Sociological Review*, 25 (October 1960): 625–35.

[73] Jack L. Roach and Orville R. Gursslin, "An Evaluation of the Concept 'Culture of Poverty,'" *Social Forces*, 45 (March 1967): 383–92.

[74] Lois B. DeFleur, "Alternative Strategies for the Development of Delinquency Theories Applicable to Other Cultures," *Social Problems*, 17 (Summer 1969): 30–39.

tection against other gangs; racial, ethnic, and religious identification; and dislike for the police. The protest is more likely to be against older adults who restrict adolescent participation in society, rather than against the middle class as a whole.[75]

In a study of junior and senior high school pupils, Albert J. Reiss, Jr., and Albert Rhodes reported that the more the lower-class boy was in the minority in school and in his residential area, the less likely he was to become delinquent. This outcome conflicts with the implication of Cohen's theory that lower-class delinquency rates would be higher in areas where competition with middle-class boys is greatest. They explain that for any status group, the largest proportion of delinquents came from those areas in which that social class was the most universal among the residents. Among all social classes the risk of delinquency was greatest in the lower-class residential areas and in the areas with high rates of delinquency. Peer-oriented delinquency appears to be the most common form of delinquency for both the lower and middle classes, but the delinquent subculture appears to be limited to the lower classes, as Cohen claims.[76]

Delinquency as a product of lower-class culture

In another view, the values and social structural forms of delinquency are seen as existing in their own right, rather than representing reactions against middle-class culture. Walter Miller believes lower-class communities have long-established traditions and are becoming larger in population and increasingly distinctive as a cultural system.[77] The days of the "melting pot" and frequent movement up the class status ladder have vanished, to be replaced by a relatively homogeneous and stabilized native, white, lower-class culture.[78]

Miller describes six "focal concerns" of the lower-class culture. Concern over "trouble" means avoidance of complications with official authorities or agencies of middle-class society. "Toughness" (physical prowess, "masculinity," and bravery) is probably related to the rearing of a large proportion of lower-class males in predominately female households. "Smartness" is conceptualized as capacity to outwit or dupe others and to avoid being outwitted, through minimum physical effort and maximum mental agility. The routine of lower-class life places a premium on "excitement," to be sought through alcohol, sexual adventure, and gam-

[75] Clinard, "Criminological Research," p. 515.

[76] Albert J. Reiss, Jr., and Albert Lewis Rhodes, "The Distribution of Juvenile Delinquency in the Social Class Structure," *American Sociological Review,* 26 (October 1961): 724, 729.

[77] Walter B. Miller, "Lower Class Culture as a Generating Milieu of Gang Delinquency," *Journal of Social Issues,* 14 (1958): 5–6.

[78] Walter B. Miller, "Implications of Urban Lower Class Culture for Social Work," *Social Service Review,* 33 (September 1959): 225.

bling. The concern over "fate" centers around the belief that life is ruled by a set of forces beyond the control of the individual. A person is "lucky" or "jinxed." "Autonomy" is overtly valued, as expressed in such phrases as: "No one's gonna push me around! I don't need nobody to take care of me!"[79]

The lower-class cultural system poses special problems for male psychological maturation, Miller explains. Family instability favors the "one-sex peer unit" rather than the two-parent family unit. The street-corner group is seen as the adolescent variant of the one-sex peer unit. In the absence of a male or his steady economic support, the "female-based household" fails to provide clear-cut masculine role identification models for juvenile rehearsal of behavior. The male adolescent street-corner group serves this function in support of the focal concerns of the lower-class culture.[80]

In Miller's view, the adolescent street-corner group attracts its members through the desire to belong and to acquire status. To achieve these goals, the adolescent must demonstrate a knowledge of, and an adherence to, the standards of these groups, which are those of the lower class. The gang fight, the automobile theft, and assault on others violate the law, but they are motivated to achieve ends which are valued in the lower classes. The gangs' objective is to achieve these ends with a minimum investment of energy. Therefore, the rebellion and rejection of middle-class values in such delinquency are only the manifestations of a deep-seated motivation.[81]

Critique of the lower-class culture view

Miller also describes a "law-abiding" lower class composed of "conventional" households. Their children are more likely to aspire seriously to upward class mobility through education. If these people also are to be considered carriers of "lower-class culture" in Miller's terms, he may be describing only one segment of the lower class in which the absence of the father interferes with the family's functioning as a channel of socialization.[82]

Grave doubts have been expressed concerning the theory that problems of masculinity generate delinquency, which both Cohen and Miller support. Cloward and Ohlin point out that the masculine-identity crisis may be expressed in forms that are not transgressions of legal norms. They call attention to a fundamental disagreement concerning the distribution of female-centered households which are supposed to generate the

[79] Miller, "Lower Class Culture as a Generating Milieu," pp. 6–13.
[80] Ibid., pp. 14–15.
[81] Ibid., pp. 7–19.
[82] Bordua, *Sociological Theories and Their Implications,* p. 11.

crisis.[83] Cohen considers these households to be most characteristic of the middle classes.[84] Talcott Parsons finds them in both the middle and lower classes.[85] Miller sees a considerable proportion of lower-class males reared in predominantly female households.[86] Bordua points out that only the black has a history of a female-dominated household among the low-status groups of society.[87] Cloward and Ohlin criticize Miller for failing to account for the origin of delinquent norms, for defining "delinquent gangs" so broadly that his theory cannot account for delinquent behavior, and for exaggerating the cultural independence of the lower and middle classes.[88]

ROLE-SELF THEORY

The development of the sense of self and the function of roles in linking individuals and society are important social- psychological aspects of criminal etiology and correction. The earlier discussion of criminal behavior systems suggested this linkage. In the next chapter, social-psychological principles are utilized in the description of group therapies as strategies for treatment of offenders. Labeling theories, discussed in the next section, relate the concept of self-image to the concept of ascribed status to focus attention on the unanticipated consequences of people-processing systems that thrust individuals into stigmatized deviant roles.

Identification and the development of self-concepts

George Mead explains that the self is developed through social experience whereby the person learns to respond to himself from the particular standpoint of individual members of the social group to which he belongs or the generalized standpoint of the group as a whole. The child learns to act toward himself from the viewpoint of the whole group, not from the perspective of one particular individual. In groups individuals interact with one another through simultaneous performance of a set of reciprocal roles. Mead compares the playing of a set of roles to a game. To participate in games the child must learn the "rules," that is, he must learn what is expected of him as a participant and also what is expected of all the other players. He takes to the total game situation not only the

[83] Cloward and Ohlin, *Delinquency and Opportunity,* p. 162.

[84] Cohen, *Delinquent Culture,* p. 162.

[85] Talcott Parsons, *Essays in Sociological Theory,* rev. ed. (Glencoe, Ill.: Free Press, 1954), p. 162.

[86] Miller, "Lower Class Culture as a Generating Milieu," p. 9.

[87] David J. Bordua, "Delinquency Subcultures: Sociological Interpretations of Gang Delinquency," *Annals of the American Academy of Political and Social Science,* 338 (November 1961): 130–31.

[88] Cloward and Ohlin, *Delinquency and Opportunity,* pp. 69–76.

attitude of each player toward himself and his expected role but also the attitude of each player on the team. The attitudes of the total team are integrated to form a "generalized other," which Mead defines as "the attitude of the whole community." By taking over the attitude of the generalized other, the individual becomes subject to the control of the community, because in this way the community becomes a determining factor in the individual's thinking.[89]

Identification has been seen as a factor missing in this analysis. If 18 strangers choose sides to play baseball on the spur of the moment, their knowledge of the rules of baseball will enable each to play his particular position. To this point, role is a sort of empty bottle of behavior, and formal relations are without motive or incentive. But make this a World Series game. The roles and rules are the same, but there is a great difference in that the "empty bottle" of formal role relationships has acquired content. This content, according to Nelson Foote, is *identity*. One learns many more roles than he ever plays overtly, and he limits his real behavior to a selected few that he knows and defines as *his own*. If he is to exhibit definiteness and force (motivation) in behavior, he must know which role is his in each situation by knowing *who* he is. Foote uses *identification* to mean appropriation of and commitment to a particular identity or series of identities.[90]

In the psychiatric interpretation of "rationalization," the individual who advances plausible or socially conforming reasons for his conduct may thereby conceal his true reasons, which could be socially unacceptable. In contrast, the social-psychological interpretation employs "rationalization" in the sense of motivation, a process through which the individual participant in group life defines a situation calling for performance of a particular act. The words used by the participant are linguistic constructs for organizing actions to constitute patterns in group life and the history of the individual. The justifications advanced by lawbreakers (their "vocabulary of motives") have been learned socioculturally;[91] they are not individually invented and expressive only of some immediate, short-term manipulation of the truth of the actor's evaluation of his social world.[92] In Foote's terms, "identification" connotes the individual's acceptance of role norms (including those of a role in a delinquent group) as bearing on how he should behave in certain situations.

The self may be viewed as an organization of behavior imposed upon

[89] George Herbert Mead, *Mind, Self and Society* (Chicago: University of Chicago Press, 1944), pp. 136–38 and 144–45.

[90] Nelson N. Foote, "Identification as the Basis for a Theory of Motivation," *American Sociological Review*, 16 (February 1951): 16–17.

[91] Here is a linkage with Sutherland's emphasis on the "principle of differential association" in learning of criminal techniques and attitudes.

[92] Frank E. Hartung, *Crime, Law and Society* (Detroit: Wayne State University Press, 1965), pp. 63–64.

the individual by societal expectations. The self changes with time through the course of a life, but a thread of continuity is contributed by the constancy of personal identity. "Keeping a good name" symbolizes the identification of experiences by the individual as his own and his acceptance of responsibility for actions identified as his own.[93]

Differential identification

Sutherland's theory of differential association, discussed above, has been criticized for appearing to regard "association" in the sense of "contact." This implies that Sutherland believed that a person must come in physical proximity with criminals as a prerequisite to becoming criminal. There is reason to doubt that this was Sutherland's belief, however.[94] His theory has also been criticized for not explaining lone crimes for which the source of learning is not apparent.

Daniel Glaser advances the hypothesis of *differential identification:* "A person pursues criminal behavior to the extent that he identifies himself with real or imaginary persons from whose perspective his criminal behavior seems acceptable." Glaser reconceptualizes Sutherland's theory to place greater emphasis on the social interaction in which the individual selects persons with whom he identifies and who serve as models for his behavior. Included is the individual's interaction with himself in rationalizing his conduct. Most individuals are believed to identify themselves with both criminal and noncriminal persons in the course of their lives. They may have direct experience in delinquency groups. They may identify with criminal roles presented in fiction, movies, television, or the press. They may react against anticriminal groups.[95] Thereby, Glaser opens the way for reference-group theory.

The association of individuals in particular membership groups does not account for all influences on their behavior. The individual may turn to crime because he identifies with reference groups far from his immediate social world. He may even identify with groups which conform to his expectations only in his imagination. In a world of dynamic relationships and transitory social contacts, identifications may change more rapidly than the less flexible associations would suggest. Consequently, Glaser deems differential identification to be a more useful concept because it does not insist that a major portion of criminality is learned through participation in criminal groups.

Any factor is relevant to differential identification to the extent that it affects individual A's choice of individual B to serve as individual A's

[93] Alfred R. Lindesmith and Anselm L. Strauss, *Social Psychology,* rev. ed. (New York: Holt, Rinehart & Winston, Inc., 1956), pp. 46–47.

[94] Hartung, "Critique of the Sociological Approach," p. 731.

[95] Daniel Glaser, "Criminality Theories and Behavior Images," *American Journal of Sociology,* 61 (March 1956): 440.

perspective in evaluation of individual A's behavior. Such factors include economic conditions, prior frustrations, learned moral creeds, group relationships, and all other features of the individual's life.

Reference-group theory

Reference-group theory centers attention on all groups to which individuals are oriented. One definition of the term "reference group" is "that group whose perspective constitutes the frame of reference of the actor without necessarily being the group in which he aspires for acceptance."[96] Ralph Turner points out that except for emphasizing that the individual may derive his values from groups of which he is not a member, this definition is part of role theory. He suggests that the reference group under this interpretation is an "identification group" in that the individual takes the role of a member while adopting the member's standpoint as his own.[97]

With the cultural diversity of urban society, modern man finds himself in different roles in relation to diverse groups which frequently demand that he make contradictory adjustments. Muzafer Sherif considers the values and norms of a person's reference groups to be the "major anchorages" in which his experience of self-identity is organized.[98]

Theodore Newcomb points out that individuals go through changes in membership groups, especially in a complex society. With changing age, occupation, or marital status, they become eligible for new membership groups, especially in a complex society. The likelihood of an individual becoming dissatisfied with membership in a particular group is increased in a dynamic society with differences among groups in privileges and opportunities. Consequently, the strength of a membership group as a point of reference for a particular person will decrease when the degree of satisfaction it can provide for his personal needs lessens.[99]

Since an individual's reference groups are not necessarily his membership groups, his search for self-identity involves at least four possible relationships between the two kinds of groups. First, a person's membership groups serve as reference groups in that he has learned to use the norms shared by the members. The family into which one is born is the primary example. Second, a person's membership groups of the past may remain his reference groups of the present, supplying the explanation for

[96] Tamotsu Shibutani, "Reference Groups as Perspectives," *American Journal of Sociology,* 60 (May 1955): 562–63.

[97] Ralph H. Turner, "Role Taking, Role Standpoint, and Reference Group Behavior," *American Journal of Sociology,* 61 (January 1956): 237–38.

[98] Muzafer Sherif, "The Concept of Reference Groups in Human Relations," in Muzafer Sherif and M. O. Wilson (eds.), *Group Relations at the Crossroads* (New York: Harper & Bros., 1953), pp. 205–7.

[99] Theodore M. Newcomb, *Social Psychology* (New York: Dryden Press, 1950), p. 226.

current behavior that is not appropriate to the norms and values of present membership groups. Third, a person may aspire to join a group because it possesses the values and norms to which he is already committed. His reference group existed before he acquired a particular membership group. Fourth, a person may aspire to membership in a group to whose values and norms he is indoctrinated so that he makes it a reference group. An example would be the nondelinquent slum boy who joins a delinquent street gang for the sake of congenial relationships with a peer group.

Newcomb distinguishes between positive reference groups, in which a person is motivated to be accepted and treated as a member, and negative reference groups, in which he does not seek membership or to which he stands in opposition.[100] This point has usefulness for criminology, as Newcomb points out. First, a negative reference group may be a major source of motivation. A prime example in criminology is the isolation of the prison inmate who, in the course of rejecting his rejecters, may join a procriminal reference group. Second, membership may serve as both positive and negative reference groups for the same persons. Newcomb says the American adolescent may share most of his family's attitudes, but he may be hostile toward those that concern his choice of friends or his behavior in the role of son. This ambivalence opens the door to restoration of offenders to the ranks of law-abiding groups. Negative reference groups of delinquent gangs (prosocial groups of the larger community) also serve as positive reference groups for at least some gang members. Third, a positive reference group may immunize the individual against the pressures of a negative reference group. Fourth, anticriminal groups may continue to motivate some criminals even after they have become negative reference groups from these criminals' point of view.[101]

Insulation against criminal values

The idea of self-concept is relevant to reference-group research. A study by Walter Reckless, and Simon Dinitz, with Barbara Kay, reversed the usual question to ask why some boys remain nondelinquent in areas high in delinquency and concluded that the insulation against delinquency exists in the boy's image of himself as "good." Conversely, the potentially delinquent boy expects to be taken to juvenile court or jail. The methodology involved the nominations by sixth-grade teachers of boys in white, high-delinquency areas of Columbus, Ohio, as being headed either for contact with the police and courts or unlikely to become delinquents. The names of nominated boys and their families were subsequently screened through police and juvenile court files for previous contact. The nomi-

[100] Ibid., p. 226.
[101] Ibid., p. 227.

nees and their mothers were interviewed to obtain background character-istics and information on attitudes concerning self-images. Delinquency vulnerability and social responsibility scales of the Gough California Inventory were administered to the boys.[102]

Reckless and Dinitz, with Frank Scarpitti, assume that a "good" self-concept represents a favorable internalization of presumably favorable life experiences. They consider this "good" self-concept to be "undoubt-edly a product of favorable socialization" which veers boys away from delinquency.[103] Nondelinquent attitudes and meanings are accumulated through interaction within a cohesive and harmonious family situation and a circle of friends who are virtually free of police or court contacts. However, the collaborators in the study considered a "socially appropri-ate" concept of self and others to be the basic component in steering boys away from delinquency. The source of the concept of self and others was traced to primary group relationships. "Insulated" boys seemed to have defined themselves as "good" boys and to have been thought of as "good" by their parents and teachers. Conversely, potentially delinquent boys seemed to have defined themselves and to have been defined in the oppo-site manner. It was suggested that this self-concept, as an insulation against delinquency, is both reflected in and a reflection of the definition of significant others in the lives of nondelinquents.[104]

LABELING APPROACH

Particularly appropriate to the study of the criminal justice system are the contributions of theorists lumped together as adherents of the "label-ing school." These theorists are chiefly concerned with the criminaliza-tion process by which the system, which is composed of the agents of a segment of the community, seeks out violators of the criminal law and considers them qualified for the status of criminal.

Power and conflict

Traditionally, the criminal law has been conceived of as an extension of a general agreement among members of the community that certain norms are particularly crucial to the interests of all citizens and that it is appropriate to bring the authority of the state to bear against the violators of these norms. The labeling school differs by conceiving of the criminal

[102] Walter C. Reckless, Simon Dinitz, and Barbara Kay, "The Self Component in Potential Delinquency and Potential Nondelinquency," *American Sociological Review,* 22 (October 1957): 566–67.

[103] Simon Dinitz, Frank R. Scarpitti, and Walter C. Reckless, "Delinquency Vulnerability: A Cross Group and Longitudinal Analysis," *American Sociological Review,* 27 (August 1962): 157.

[104] Reckless, Dinitz, and Kay, "The Self Component in Potential Delinquency," pp. 566–69.

justice system as an expression of the differential distribution of power among the groups composing the community. The bonds of society are seen as deriving from conflict among these interest groups rather than from a fundamental consensus among members.[105]

Richard Quinney believes persons and behavior become criminal because they are so defined by the agents of politically organized society who are responsible for formulating and administering criminal law. He holds that crime is created through this formulation and application of criminal definitions. Because crime is the product of a judgment external to the actor and therefore not inherent in his behavior, the fluctuations in arrest and conviction rates are more symptomatic of the formulation and administration of criminal law than of criminal behaviors themselves. Furthermore, Quinney says, these criminal definitions describe behaviors which conflict with the interests of those groups in the society or community who possess power to shape public policy. The greater the conflict of interests between segments of the society, the greater the probability that criminal definitions will be employed by the powerful groups to safeguard their interests.[106]

A statute is normally interpreted as an expression of the correspondence of its legal norms with the more pervasive social norms of society. Except for a few deviants, virtually everyone in the community is supposed to regard the statute's officially announced norm as some addition to the stock of social norms binding on his daily conduct. More realistically, Austin Turk believes, the announcement of legal norms is increasingly the product of conflict among groups with differing social norms, and an increasing share of legal norms fail to correspond one to one with social norms. The degree of conformity to legal norms varies with the "social clout" that the norm announcers are seen as possessing by the various categories of citizens. Legal norms become binding on conduct more because deference to authority is established than because they are accepted within the larger body of social norms.[107]

Deviance as assigned status

Labeling theorists see deviance as a property conferred upon behavior that is judged by an audience to be so dangerous, embarrassing, or irritating that special sanctions should be brought to bear against those who exhibit it.[108] Deviance is conceived of as a social process through which

[105] Chapter 4, pp. 71–73, discusses power, differentiates order and conflict theories, and anticipates other matters brought up here.

[106] Richard Quinney, *The Social Reality of Crime* (Boston: Little, Brown & Co., 1970), pp. 15–20.

[107] Austin T. Turk, "Conflict and Criminality," *American Sociological Review*, 31 (June 1966): 345–46.

[108] Kai T. Erikson, *Wayward Puritans: A Study in the Sociology of Deviance* (New York: John Wiley & Sons, Inc., 1966), pp. 6–7.

an audience interprets behavior as defiant, defines persons exhibiting it as a kind of deviant, and responds to them in an appropriate manner.[109] The individual subjected to this social process is *assigned* a deviant status whereby he is exposed to the experiences the social audience and their agents consider appropriate for the occupant of that status.

Edwin Schur believes *process* to be the key theme; emphasis is placed on the constant change in the conditions under which the individual first engages in deviance and his deviant career develops. A deviant career will show a series of tentative relationships with other persons, moving sometimes toward firmer commitment to deviant norms and sometimes toward affiliation with legitimate groups. This series of tentative and backtracking behaviors occurs within the environment of a social structure which also is undergoing change.[110] This dynamic interpretation stands in contrast to the more static view of order theorists who treat the sociocultural milieu largely as though it consists of a relatively unchanging set of variables to which the deviant exhibits "maladjustment." Cohen refers to the "assumption of discontinuity," which describes deviant behavior as leaping abruptly from conformity to deviance without recognition of the processes of progressive involvement in deviancy and disinvolvement in the dominant social order.[111]

In distinguishing between the personality of the actor and the act which stimulated the assignment of the deviant status, labeling theorists cite the possibility that societal responses may change a casual rulebreaker into a confirmed criminal.[112] Lemert's distinction between primary and secondary deviance was noted in Chapter 4. In *primary deviance,* which arises from a wide variety of causes, the self-identification of the rule-breaker with the assigned deviant status is not necessarily enlisted. In *secondary deviance,* he assumes the deviant role *after* he has been assigned the deviant status. He shifts his allegiance from legitimate to illegitimate norms because of the disapproving, degradational, and isolating reaction of society to his behavior.[113] The imputation of certain character qualities in secondary deviance, regardless of an individual's genuine qualities, builds something new into his psyche. This development is attributed by labeling theorists especially to the screening process of the criminal justice system.

Within a changing and culturally heterogeneous society, the definition

[109] John T. Kitsuse, "Societal Reaction to Deviant Behavior: Problems of Theory and Method," *Social Problems,* 9 (Winter 1969): 248.

[110] Edwin M. Schur, "Reactions to Deviance: A Critical Assessment," *American Journal of Sociology,* 75 (November 1969): 310–11.

[111] Albert K. Cohen, "The Sociology of the Deviant Act: Anomie Theory and Beyond," *American Sociological Review,* 30 (February 1965): 8–9.

[112] Howard S. Becker, *Outsiders: Studies in the Sociology of Deviance* (New York: Free Press, 1963), pp. 41–58.

[113] Edwin M. Lemert, *Human Deviance, Social Problems, and Social Control* (Englewood Cliffs, N.J.: Prentice Hall, Inc., 1967), p. 17.

of persons and behavior as criminal may become the tool of what Howard Becker calls *moral entrepreneurs,* who employ political power to create new sets of legal norms as means of molding behavior in a model they prefer. Moral crusades against vice, for example, produce legal norms institutionalized into law enforcement actions against the use of alcohol or marijuana.

When new enforcement agencies are established or additional enforcement tasks are given to existing agencies, the personnel are given a stake in the preservation of these legal norms for the sake of continuing their careers. This includes a self-interest in providing evidence which appears to demonstrate that serious deviance exists. The agencies are also likely to seek additional resources for enforcement, arguing that they cannot otherwise eliminate the prohibited behavior. Programs of enforcement are framed without knowledge of the realities of subsequent enforcement, including the personalities of those who will carry out enforcement tasks. Within the realities of law enforcement, police practices may diverge from original expectations of the framers of the law because universal and unequivocal enforcement is beyond the resources made available to the agency. One effect is that the enforcers select only a portion of all law violators as the prime target of enforcement work. Through such selective enforcement, the police, whether or not this is the intention, create a particular group of deviants in that the characteristics of this group are a product of differential enforcement.[114]

Evaluation of labeling theory

One of the assets of labeling theories is that they reveal the costs of extending criminal law to efforts to control behavior in areas where the system of criminal justice is ill-suited. The *criminalization of deviance,* as Edwin Schur calls it, produces unenforceable laws in matters such as abortion, homosexuality, and drug abuse because they involve the willing exchange of socially disapproved but widely demanded goods and services.[115] Law enforcement pays a price when the moral message of the law is contradicted by a total absence of enforcement, the growth of cynicism among policemen, or discriminatory prosecution on grounds unrelated to the evil the law is supposed to eliminate.[116]

Although criminal laws vary among societies and are subject to arbitrary administration, Jack Gibbs believes social norms have similar characteristics. Inevitably some acts will be considered criminal simply because they are proscribed. He finds the basic conception of deviant be-

114 Becker, *Outsiders,* pp. 146–63.

115 Edwin M. Schur, *Crime without Victims: Deviant Behavior and Public Policy* (Englewood Cliffs, N.J.: Prentice-Hall, Inc., 1965), pp. 5–8.

116 Sanford H. Kadish, "The Crisis of Overcriminalization," *Annals of American Academy of Political and Social Science,* 374 (November 1967): p. 160.

havior to be excessively relativistic in making the societal reaction, which is highly variable among groups, the criteria for the identification of deviants. Furthermore, he finds the word "theory" to be premature in describing a collection of fundamentally inconsistent statements among a number of scholars. Gibbs contends three questions are not answered adequately: Why does the incidence of a particular act vary from one population to the next? Why do some persons commit the act while others do not? Why is the act considered deviant and/or criminal in some societies and not in others?[117]

The search for answers to these and similar questions entails study of the social system within which both deviance and reactions to deviance occur. Labeling theorists, Rodolfo Alvarez points out, see two variables as separate: the rule-breaking of A and the formal reactions it elicits from B. They appear to be outraged that some persons are given greater latitude than others to break rules. Labeling theorists tend to see this differential evaluation as illustrating the dominance of the weak by groups holding political power. The short-term effectiveness of naked force, however, necessitates a search for a basis for a stable accommodation in which the subordinate group will accept the leadership of the dominant group. This accommodation involves the subordinate group's evaluation of the rule-breaking behavior of one of its members. In a situation lacking clear normative guidelines, the guilt of the rule-breaker is not established, and there is a possibility that he will receive positive as well as negative evaluations. The youth officially defined as a delinquent may be regarded as a hero by the reference group most influential in determining his own self-image. Whether written or unwritten, rules lack specificity and, therefore, require interpretation in each situation.[118]

In Alvarez's view, to say that the imposition of formal sanctions (imprisonment, for example) "creates" deviancy implies that a negative evaluation of the rule-breaker by the other participants in his groups is inevitable. Questioning this "inevitability," he hypothesizes that the nature of the group's informal evaluation of the presumed rule-breaker is influenced by the status he occupies within the group and whether or not the group is achieving its goals. In terms appropriate for criminology, the reactions to the deviant are products of the workings of the social system, rather than a simple degradation of the rule-breaker through punishment imposed by formal control agencies such as the police, courts, and prisons.

Alvarez carried out an experiment with students to measure the effect

<hr/>

[117] Jack P. Gibbs, "Conceptions of Deviant Behavior: The Old and the New," *Pacific Sociological Review,* 9 (Spring 1966): 9–14. Also see Richard H. Ward, "The Labeling Theory: A Critical Analysis," *Criminology,* 9 (August–November 1971): 282–83.

[118] Rodolfo Alvarez, "Informal Reactions to Deviance in Simulated Work Organizations: A Laboratory Experiment," *American Sociological Review,* 33 (December 1968): 895–915.

of the application of penalties when the hierarchial status of respondents, feelings of collective success or failure among work groups, and the nature of the sanctions applied all differed. Deviants in the higher status received more esteem than those in the lower one, but findings were complicated by whether or not the work group was successful in task performance. For similar acts of deviance, the higher status person lost less esteem in successful groups than in unsuccessful groups. Demotion had greater impact than promotion, but effects were complicated by operation of the other variables.

Bernard Thorsell and Lloyd Klemke claim that labeling theorists have concentrated on the negative effects of labeling and have virtually ignored the positive effects that result when the technique is applied under certain conditions. They argue that future deviance is likely to be terminated if labeling is at the primary rather than secondary level and is carried out confidentially, applied by some significant other person or ingroup, easily removable when the deviance ceases, favorable rather than derogatory, and associated with efforts to reintegrate the deviant into the community.[119] Their criticisms appear to underestimate the peculiar force of officially implemented stigmatization that is incidental to criminal justice duties, but their reference to the style of administration has validity. As Alvarez indicates, the definition of deviance operates within complex situations in which the consequences for the deviant are largely shaped by those who formulate and administer sanction systems.

When labeling theory is applied to mental illness, Walter Gove finds the case to be overstated in two respects: authorities are employing a fairly rigorous (if largely informal) screening process, and a substantial majority of those hospitalized are suffering from serious disturbances. Although hospitalization may have debilitating effects on patients, it is also associated with restitutive processes, such as strengthening the family's capacity to receive the returned patient constructively.[120] David Mechanic finds merit in the labeling approach but rejects as absurd any notion that certain patterns of behavior will disappear simply because the labeling process is withheld.[121]

In a study of police contacts with juveniles, it was found that officers had limited information on which to base initial disposition. For nearly all minor violators and some serious delinquents, the youths' resemblance to visible characteristics of disreputable groups and their demeanor toward officers affected the decision.[122] Nevertheless, the labeling of youths

[119] Bernard A. Thorsell and Lloyd W. Klemke, "The Labeling Process: Reinforcement and Deterrent?" *Law and Society Review,* 6 (February 1972): 393–403.

[120] Walter R. Gove, "Societal Reaction as an Explanation of Mental Illness," *American Sociological Review,* 35 (October 1970): 873–84.

[121] David Mechanic, *Mental Health and Social Policy* (Englewood Cliffs, N.J.: Prentice-Hall, Inc., 1969), 47–48.

[122] Irving Piliavin and Scott Briar, "Police Encounters with Juveniles," *American Journal of Sociology,* 70 (September 1964): 206–14.

as deviants operates in a more complex way than simply indiscriminate use of police authority, as noted in results of a study by Donald Black and Albert J. Reiss, Jr. Citizens directly initiated most of the encounters with police, and complainants largely determined arrest decisions. For black juveniles, black complainants were likely to be involved in the most severe decisions. The bulk of encounters pertained to minor offenses, and the probability of arrest was low regardless of degree of seriousness.[123]

Judith Lorber suggests that the deviant's own participation in the labeling process has been overlooked. He may invite labeling by conveying an impression that he hopes will lead his audience to impose a certain label on him. She cites individuals who exploit feigned or actual illness to gain the side benefits of sympathy, avoidance of work, or unearned monetary benefits.[124]

SUMMARY

Judging by the past three chapters, the criminological theorist may think he knows the secret of influencing behavior, but he wins few friends. Our summary of selected theories documents the crucial role of intellectual criticism in the development of valid and reliable explanations. The alternate presentation and refutation of ideas is likely to spread confusion among those who anticipate final and simple answers to complex questions. The analysis of criminological theories, however, recognizes that criminal behavior has varied sources, as does all human behavior, and consequently is not amenable to a single approach. Criticism is a means of determining the limits within which a given approach is fruitful. It reveals the shortcomings of proposed solutions and raises new questions.

Social disorganization theories treat specific problems (crime, alcoholism, unemployment, and so on) as having common causes, but these theories are weakened when their advocates treat the effects of change as uniformly evil. Sutherland explains criminality as a product of learned behavior in the course of social interaction, refuting a common view that offenders are biologically and psychologically abnormal. Merton's means-end theory points to the importance of discrepancies between the legitimate cultural and social systems. Cloward and Ohlin go beyond this to reemphasize the existence of illegitimate cultural and social systems.

As examples of subculture theorists, Cohen and Miller emphasize social class in distinguishing the major patterns among underprivileged youth seeking a place in society. Self-role theories focus attention on the

[123] Donald J. Black and Albert J. Reiss, Jr., "Police Control of Juveniles," *American Sociological Review,* 35 (February 1970): 63–77.

[124] Judith Lorber, "Deviance as Performance: The Case of Illness," *Social Problems,* 14 (Winter 1967): 302–10.

involvement of criminal behavior within the context of personality development and behavior in the sociocultural environment. Grounded in concepts of power and conflict, labeling theories have given new force to criticisms of the operation of the criminal justice system and to recognition of the sociocultural setting of criminal behavior.

FOR ADDITIONAL READING

Arnold, David O. *The Sociology of Subcultures.* Berkeley, Calif.: Glendessary Press, 1970.

Cicourel, Aaron V. *The Social Organization of Juvenile Justice.* New York: John Wiley & Sons, 1968.

Downes, David M. *The Delinquent Solution: A Study in Subcultural Theory.* New York: Free Press, 1966.

Dubin, Robert. "Deviant Behavior and Social Structure: Continuities in Social Theory." *American Sociological Review,* 24 (April 1959): 147–64.

Empey, LaMar T. "Delinquency Subcultures: Theory and Recent Research." *Journal of Research in Crime and Delinquency,* 4 (January 1967): 32–42.

Gold, Martin. *Status Forces in Delinquent Boys.* Ann Arbor: Institute for Social Research, University of Michigan, 1963.

Guenther, Anthony, (ed.). *Criminal Behavior and Social Systems: Contributions of American Sociology.* Chicago: Rand McNally & Co., 1970.

Hepburn, John R. "Subcultures, Violence, and the Subculture of Violence: An Old Rut or a New Road?" *Criminology,* 9 (May 1971): 87–98.

Kituse, John I., and Dietrick, David C. "Delinquent Boys: A Critique." *American Sociological Review,* 24 (April 1959): 208–24.

Lerman, Paul. "Argot, Symbolic Deviance and Subcultural Delinquency." *American Sociological Review,* 32 (April 1967): 209–24.

Martindale, Don. "Social Disorganization: The Conflict of Normative and Empirical Approaches." In Howard P. Becker and Alvin Boskoff (eds.), *Modern Sociological Theory in Continuity and Change,* pp. 340–67. New York: Dryden Press, 1959.

Matza, David. *Delinquency and Drift.* New York: John Wiley & Sons, 1965.

Powell, Elwin H. "Crime as a Function of Anomie." *Journal of Criminal Law, Criminology and Police Science,* 57 (June 1966): 161–71.

Schur, Edwin M. *Labeling Deviant Behavior: Its Sociological Significance.* New York: Harper & Row, 1971.

Short, James F., Jr. (ed.). *Gang Delinquency and Delinquent Subcultures.* New York: Harper & Row, 1968.

Spergel, Irving. *Racketville, Slumtown, Haulburg: An Exploratory Study of Delinquent Subcultures.* Chicago: University of Chicago Press, 1964.

Turk, Austin T. *Criminality and Legal Order.* Chicago: Rand McNally & Co., 1969.

Voss, Harwin L. "Differential Association and Reported Delinquent Behavior: A Replication." *Social Problems,* 12 (Summer 1964): 78–85.

Wertman, Carl, and Piliavin, Irving. "Gang Members and the Police." In David J. Bordua (ed.), *The Police: Six Sociological Essays*, pp. 56–98. New York: John Wiley & Sons, 1967.

Wolfgang, Marvin E., and Ferracuti, Franco. *The Subculture of Violence: Toward an Integrated Theory in Criminology*. New York: Barnes & Noble, 1967.

Theories and
applied criminology

Social reform and intervention, the two general strategies for coping with the crime problem, are based to varying degrees on theories such as the ones we have reviewed. In its particular way, each type of theory constitutes an intellectual pathway along which descriptions of crime and reactions to it can proceed, through selective and penetrating observation, to understanding. They are also the vehicles for mobilizing basic postulates to explain what otherwise would appear to be only random events. The understanding of criminological issues which such theories foster permits the criminal justice establishment to achieve the purposes and responsibilities it serves for society.

Criminological theories frequently are grouped according to where they see the causes of crime as being primarily placed. *Biogenic theories* concentrate on the organism in analyses of the individual's genetic heritage or body chemistry or the behavioral propensities of human beings. Also concentrating on the individual, *psychogenic theories* focus on perceptions of the environment and the emotional responses which are associated with learning. The strengthening of behavioral tendencies through rewards and the process of modeling, or the acquisition of behavior by observing the performance of other persons, are also taken into consideration. *Sociogenic theories* place primary emphasis on sociocultural phenomenon: the systems of social norms, including legal norms; the arrangement of groups in social structures; the effects of demographic characterstics such as age, race, and occupation; the distribution of socioeconomic opportunities, and so on.

STRATEGIES OF SOCIAL REFORM AND INTERVENTION

Criminological theories are applicable to each of the three broad approaches to the crime problem: crime prevention, crime control, and treatment. Crime prevention (the topic of Chapter 22) includes a wide range of activities intended to forestall future crimes. Crime control entails the efforts of the components of the system of criminal justice to suppress crime through the tactics of surveillance, apprehension, and punishment. This is prominent in our analysis of police departments, courts, and correctional agencies, as well as the criminal justice system as a whole. Treatment, as defined broadly below and developed in Chapter 20, covers a wide range of strategies for intervention focusing on behavior as a means of reducing the incidence of law violations. The three broad approaches utilize the strategies of social reform or intervention.

Theories and social reform

Social reform, the subject of Chapter 25, may be defined as a change in the institutional patterns of society that is deliberately sought as a means of reducing the divergence between actual social conditions and the cultural ideals and goals they are intended to achieve. Whereas revolution would uproot the social system and substitute some new set of premises as a basis for social order, reform accepts contemporary premises and focuses on failures to implement the actions that would make them a reality in serving human needs. For example, reform directs efforts toward strengthening the family and school as instruments for socializing personality or seeks modification of the nature of the labor force as a means of broadening access to economic opportunity. In such instances, reform is predicated upon a continued faith in the family, the school, and private enterprise as key elements in the institutional framework for achieving social and personal goals.

The application of social reform to the difficulties raised by crime implies that crime can be fitted to the concept of *societal problem* in at least two respects. First, crime is seen as a *public issue* which, as C. Wright Mills has said, "transcends the local environments of the individual and the range of his inner life."[1] The criminal offense possibly expresses the personal frustrations of the perpetrator and certainly adds to the "troubles" of his victim. Collectively, however, the personal aspects of crime add to the burden imposed on social relationships and the economy generally. Significantly, criminological issues transcend individual troubles because they involve the total social order of urban society that is supposed to fulfill the aspirations and supply the needs of its members. "Urban society" is stipulated because its complex technology and intricate social organization demand a particularly high level of coordination among units—a coordination that is placed in jeopardy by a high rate of crime. Conversely, certain types of crime stem from inadequate delivery of human services vital to meeting human needs in urban society—a failure related to insufficient coordination of delivery systems.

[1] C. Wright Mills, *The Sociological Imagination* (New York: Oxford University Press, 1959), pp. 8–9.

The periodic emergence of an alleged "law and order" crisis is explained in part by the relevance to other crucial public issues of criminal behavior and the official responses to crime. Such issues involves, among others, the safeguarding of civil rights; the stability of the family as it is related to the possibility of delinquent behavior; the adequacy of mental health care; the inequities of access to social and economic opportunity provided by the educational system; and the employment of the criminal law to deal with such forms of deviance as drug abuse and homosexuality. The interdependence of crime and other major public issues dictates the orientation of theoretical and applied criminologists to the organization and functions of the social structure.

The concept of crime as a societal problem is also implied because crime is involved with the units constituting the organization of society. The solutions employed to control or correct crime require societal efforts that go beyond the unguided social processes of individuals and personal groups. Effective prevention, control, and treatment require concerted action by society because, as Sarajane Heidt and Amitai Etzioni note, the problem's seeming intractability and even its existence lie in the failure of members of society to participate authentically in its solution. "Authentic" refers to the genuineness of the response of society to the claims of its members for service.[2] Social reform implies a belief that, through readjustment of the social structure, man is capable of alleviating social problems (such as crime) that arise through a discrepancy between such claims and the performance of units composing the social structure.

Sociogenic theories are most obviously applicable to social reform in that they are concerned with the relative efficiency of man-made organizations as sociocultural screens between man and his natural environment.[3] Disorganization theory, on one hand, calls for action against particular individuals or groups who fail to follow the normative guidelines that would produce a smoothly functioning society. On the other hand, it calls for reform of a social structure that has lost its relevance to human needs under the impact of rapid change, cultural conflict, and other forces weakening social cohesion. Differential association and self-role theories place the search for causes of crime in the learning processes of social organizations as they are related to norms that are either favorable or unfavorable to criminal behavior. The concepts of socially-structured strain under anomie theory and differentiated sets of cultural norms under subcultural theory suggest the relevance of investigating society itself for sources of criminality and means of alleviating the effects of crime. The labeling approach demonstrates how agents of crimi-

[2] Sarajane Heidt and Amitai Etzioni (eds.), *Societal Guidance: A New Approach to Social Problems* (New York: Thomas Y. Crowell Co., 1969), pp. 1–2.

[3] Chapter 8 reviewed the relevance of geography and economic factors to criminology.

nal justice can aggravate the dimensions of the crime problem. Although it probably underestimates the complexity of the processes through which deviance emerges and is officially recognized, this view does point out that the distribution of power in society must be considered for a valid interpretation of the social significance of applied criminology.

While psychogenic theories are especially relevant to strategies of intervention, they also have implications for social reform because the ultimate meaning of any improvement in the social structure is its impact on individuals. In this respect, social reform frequently entails the strengthening and expanding of systems for delivery of services such as mental health care, vocational counseling, and reorientation of deviant attitudes. When reform calls for restructuring of the community order, individual-oriented theories are relevant to problems of resocialization and adjustment to unfamiliar roles.

Biogenic theories have lost their legitimacy as monocausal explanations, although the XYY syndrome recently has attracted interest.[4] Biogenic factors, of course, are relevant as an aspect of personality development. It is conceivable, furthermore, that fuller understanding of the function of heredity in shaping behavior will make genetic engineering and differential use of birth control an aspect of social reform. Nevertheless, the current state of knowledge and crucial moral issues justify, at best, a minor and secondary place for biogenic factors in framing criminological policies.

Theories and intervention

The meanings of treatment, which will be explored later in this chapter, vary with the theoretical premises upon which a particular explanation for crime is based, but all share the conviction that intervention is necessary. *Intervention* involves the directing of some action toward the deviant, as an individual or as a member of groups, with the expectation of reducing the likelihood of future crimes. The method involves insertion of the interventive action between the supposed cause of crime and the effect of criminal behavior.

Individual-oriented treatment utilizes a series of one-to-one relationships, such as between pupil and teacher or clinical psychologist and patient. In correctional institutions and the delinquency prevention program, the clinical methods of medicine are utilized to diagnose, prescribe, and provide treatment for a series of individual clients. It is believed that psychogenic theories can provide a solution to the crime problem by creating a larger supply of services and eliminating the failures of the current service delivery system.

Sociogenic theories concentrate on the factors external to the client

[4] See Chapter 9, pp. 213–14.

which contribute to the rise and persistence of criminality, largely because of discrepancies between the offender's needs and the satisfactions provided by his environment. In addition to striving to increase the capacity of clients for effective participation in community life, delinquency prevention and criminal correction programs based on these theories would reduce any discrepancy between the clients' behavior and the norms regarded as essential to community order. For example, the Cloward-Ohlin theory of differential opportunity was influential in the Mobilization for Youth program begun in 1962 in New York City. This program was directed against the effects of poverty that are expressed in juvenile delinquency. The bulk of the effort was designed to change the structure of economic opportunity through job training, work projects for unemployed youth, and improvement of slum schools. Heavy emphasis was placed on the tailoring of vocational training to the needs and psychologies of underprivileged groups.[5]

Individual-oriented psychological intervention

The application of psychological principles varies widely. One important distinction is between group-oriented therapies and psychotherapy, the latter defined as being oriented to the individual patient even though therapeutic intervention may occur in groups. *Psychotherapy* relies primarily on the healer's ability to mobilize healing forces in the sufferer.

Psychotherapeutic approaches differ in theories and methods as to the task of the therapist, the task of the client, and the type of relationship created. The therapist is assigned roles which range from great ambiguity to clear structure, from warmth to relative aloofness from client, and from great activity to passivity in relationships. Therapies differ in directing the client toward either remembering past events or finding solutions of present problems. Some approaches emphasize expression of feelings (catharsis); others stress the gaining of insight into problems. Supportive methods give the patient assistance through such techniques as persuasion, suggestion, relaxation, and reassurance. Reconstructive methods try to affect a permanent reorganization in the patient's personality structure.[6]

The predelinquent or offender is expected to come to the treatment site in the community or correctional institution prepared to accept the expert services of the treatment specialist, presumably because he recognizes his need for them. The client offers some preliminary statement of

---

[5] Peter Marris and Martin Rein, *Dilemmas of Social Reform* (New York: Atherton Press, 1967); George A. Brager and Francis Purcell (eds.), *Community Action against Poverty* (New Haven, Conn.: College & University Press, 1967).

[6] James L. McCary and Daniel E. Sheer (eds.), *Six Approaches to Psychotherapy* (New York: Dryden Press, 1955), pp. 2–3.

his problem—a self-diagnosis that is not necessarily accurate and always incomplete. From this beginning, the clinician strives to assemble reliable and complete facts through interviews and various tests. From his diagnosis of the problem, the clinician, in consultation with other experts, frames a treatment plan most likely to overcome the client's problem. After the plan has been implemented, the clinician checks periodically on the effects of the prescribed treatment regimen. Perhaps the original diagnosis is found to be inaccurate, or unrecognized factors are revealed. The client may not be conforming to the regimen. Perhaps he has made sufficient progress in overcoming the problem that the plan should be revised accordingly.

Group-treatment approach

Theories based on the group approach see criminality as a property of groups. The persistence of criminality is regarded as not solely the result of the individual's own personality structure but also dependent on his affiliation with groups expressing criminal behaviors, attitudes, beliefs, and values. As we have seen, human personality is acquired through social relationships based on the values of the given society. Similarly, the group shapes the characteristics of its members to an important degree: their aggressive or cooperative qualities, aspirations, beliefs, prejudices, moral concepts, and the objects of their love or hate. Criminality is favored when the individual obtains his satisfactions by participating in groups which structure behavior that leads to criminality through their rules, customs, and rituals.

Since the development of criminality involves interaction with groups, intervention has been undertaken to change criminal behaviors into prosocial behavior through the pressures exerted by groups on their members. Dorwin Cartwright suggests this intervention may be undertaken from two points of view. When the group is a *medium of change,* the objective is to enlist in support of the preferred behavior the group norms and the individual member's need for group support in relationships personally satisfying to him. The goal is to convert a deviant into a nondeviant by making him a member of a prosocial group. The strategy requires a strong sense of belonging to the group among members, the capacity of the group to attract the loyalty of members, the relevance of the group's norms and values to its members, the prestige of the member in the eyes of other members, and the capacity of the group to penalize the deviant member in ways significant to him.

When the group is a *target of change,* Cartwright says, the source of deviance is the group's norms, style of leadership, emotional atmosphere, or criteria for rating members according to prestige. The objective is to change the culture of a deviant group and to win its adherence to prosocial norms. Somehow the group members are to be persuaded that the

Figure 11–1. Group interaction and identification.

Through free discussion of topics seen as crucial by the participants, convicted offenders are exposed to the influence process known as "internalization." The objective is to gain the individual's acceptance of preferred norms as relevant to the solution of his own problems.

present nature of the deviant group is contrary to their own interests and thus they should press for change. Free discussion and universal access to relevant information is favorable to the conversion of dissatisfactions into means for strengthening group unity on some new basis. Changes in the nature of a group are associated with changes in its relationships with other groups in its particular social universe. For example, changes in a prison inmate group are associated with the prison employee group, which makes it personally worthwhile for inmates to accept norms congenial to treatment objectives.[7]

Four types of group therapy are commonly used in treatment of offenders: repressive-inspirational, didactic, analytical, and guided group interaction.[8] Under the repressive-inspirational technique the therapist presents a variety of auditory stimuli such as music, reading of news, or debates by members as the basis for social experiences. It is a combination of an evangelistic meeting and commercial salesmanship in which the participants are urged to suppress antisocial thoughts and find an inspiration in activities such as work and religion.

In didactic groups the therapist assumes major responsibility for the group's functioning. He needs the training and experience of a "master educator" to identify and modify the factors involved in the patient's maladjustment. The therapist may use authoritarian methods or employ more passive techniques requiring the patient to regulate his exposure to reeducation. This is determined by the therapist on the basis of the individual's potentialities for self-direction.[9]

The analytical approach applies psychoanalytic theories in small, face-to-face groups under a group leader in a supportive emotional atmosphere that encourages free interaction. The purpose is to achieve mutual examination of the member's relationships with other persons important in his life. The patient is encouraged to indulge in uninhibited conversation. The therapist forgoes his sheltered position and exposes himself to the role of participant-observer. In the analytical approach, attempts are made to bring to the conscious awareness of the patient the repressed experiences that lie at the root of his behavioral difficulties. Transference is an important technique whereby the patient acts out his neurotic feelings and attitudes by relating to the therapist as a new parent figure. The therapist, through careful timing in his use of the intuitive material presented by the patient, assists him to make connections between past and present events and to work out his problems.[10]

[7] Dorwin Cartwright, "Achieving Change in People: Some Applications of Group Dynamics Theory," Lawrence E. Hartrigg (ed.), *Prison within Society: A Reader in Penology* (Garden City, N.Y.: Doubleday Anchor, 1969), pp. 282–87.

[8] Lloyd W. McCorkle, "Group Therapy in the Treatment of Offenders," *Federal Probation,* 16 (December 1952): 22.

[9] Frederick Thorne, "Directive and Personality Counseling," in McCary and Sheer, *Six Approaches to Psychotherapy,* pp. 236–40.

[10] Daniel E. Sheer, "Summary," in ibid., pp. 351–52.

Guided group interaction is a modification of analytical psychotherapy. Offenders freely discuss their problems in a friendly, supportive group atmosphere under a leader. A mutual give-and-take discussion is encouraged by an easy, informal atmosphere in which the members are equals and the leader adopts a permissive but noncondoning role. The control of the members evolves out of the group discussion and participation. The development of the group climate depends heavily on the leader's skill and ease in handling the offenders' reactions to him. He is expected to weave the free-flowing discussion into a pattern that is meaningful and purposeful to the participants, but he must avoid violating group democracy.

PARAMETERS OF TREATMENT

Treatment is ordinarily conceived of as a highly personalized one-to-one relationship between a well-trained professional and his client. The personal dimension is of primary importance, as indicated by the analysis below of "treatment as reciprocity." Nevertheless, equivalent attention should be devoted to the location in which the outcome of this interaction will operate—the community to which the client will return and which provides the conditions to which he is supposed to become adjusted.

Treatment as management

At the highest level of abstraction, *treatment* refers to any organized and deliberate intervention regardless of the particular image held of man's nature or the control strategy employed. This broad definition would include the selective imposition of punishment to forestall future misconduct without any intention of modifying the deviant's psychology, although this is usually regarded as an element in "treatment." In this sense, punishment as a means of achieving compliance will be included in the analysis of major organized treatment programs.

The management of correctional programs through the imposition of some rationale upon their activities to lend order to their responses to the criminal can result in such actions as systematically applied coercion. Traditionally, management has been identified primarily with the restraint of criminal clients and the administration of bureaucratic methods for the sake of organizational order. This overlooks two elements of systematic treatment. First, because every aspect of the immediate environment has impact on the client, the management of every phase of the organization's activities can have a programmed influence on his behavior and affect his interpretation of the experiences he is undergoing. Second, treatment outcome depends greatly on spontaneous relationships among offenders and between offenders and staff—a spontaneity likely to be stifled by the routines of bureaucratic administration and suppressive policies.

Treatment as management entails the organization of all agency activities and decisions to mobilize spontaneous relationships systematically in support of efforts to change offenders in the preferred direction.[11] Management of spontaneous relationships calls for a high level of flexibility and ingenuity in administration. Intensive intervention and internalization place particularly strong demands on the competence of therapists, because the ambition of the objective and the probable difficulties that will be raised are related to the client's particular degree of maladjustment. Both intervention and, to a lesser degree, the effects of social reform on the environment to which the client will return, test the capacities of the therapist and his colleagues to provide supporting services, as suggested by the concepts of treatment as reciprocity and treatment as process.

Treatment as reciprocity

Treatment of the criminal usually is equated with the quest for internalized control which will enable the criminal to change his personality, beliefs, or motivations so that he refrains voluntarily from criminal acts.[12] *Treatment as reciprocity* refers to the development of a mutuality of obligations and respect between client and staff member through which the client is persuaded to accept as his own the objectives of the programmed activities. The definition implies solicitude and demonstrated regard for the client.

Solicitude is a sense of thoughtfulness for another's welfare out of humanitarian concern for his long-term interests and recognition that his participation in treatment is essential to its success. The client is usually subject to the authority of the therapist because his specialized competence is presumed to be essential to the client's own long-term interests. But, in the criminological setting, the therapist also represents the coercive power of the criminal law, a source of authority that frequently complicates his expression of solicitude and his ability to gain the client's voluntary participation.

Custody, as a concept, is rather ambivalent in its relation to solicitude. In one sense of custody, attention is concentrated on the restrictions deemed essential to safeguard the community against the threat the offender supposedly poses. In another sense, custody imposes on officials the responsibility of providing food, shelter, medical care, and other basic

[11] For relevant examples, see Elliot Studt, Sheldon L. Messinger, and Thomas P. Wilson, *C-Unit: Search for Community in Prison* (New York: Russell Sage Foundation, 1968), pp. 139, 163–64, 172–85.

[12] Seymour L. Halleck, *Psychiatry and the Dilemmas of Crime* (New York: Harper and Row, 1967), p. 233.

needs that the involuntary inmate is unable to obtain for himself. Only in the second sense does custody convey a theme of solicitude, but even here the concern expresses duty more than humanitarianism. This ambivalence suggests the barriers raised against individualized responses to inmates when management is dominated by the goal of custodial safekeeping. Humanitarian concern is exhibited by some custodians, but even the tight-lipped solicitude characteristic of the second version of custody provides an inferior opportunity for gaining the full-fledged participation of the client in the treatment processes.

Closely related to solicitude is *demonstrated regard for the client.* Our way of "treating" the other fellow conveys a particular impression of our image of him. The way he "treats" the client will communicate what the therapist thinks of his worth as a human being. If the client regards the counseling or other service as crucial to his own interests, the special competence of the staff member is an important means of gaining the client's full cooperation. Demonstrated regard is an essential element in this competence. Evidence of solicitude is germane to the gaining of rapport which can encourage the client to discipline his own behavior and thus serve the interests of custodial safekeeping in the long run. In this sense, demonstrated regard is a vehicle for substituting the informal controls of conscience and duty for the formal controls of physical restrictions and surveillance. If correctional programs are to have any long-term impact on offender behavior, this substitution is a valuable payoff for the program that conveys a sense of regard for the client.

Treatment as process

Treatment as reciprocity deals with the dynamics of social interaction between the staff member and his client. This one-to-one relationship and the staff member's capacity to gain an effective relationship with the client are important aspects of all rehabilitation efforts.

Treatment as process adds another dimension to the analysis—the guidance of staff-client relationships through tentative, backtracking behaviors to produce the client's adherence to preferred norms as the eventual outcome. "Tentative, backtracking behaviors" refers to the irregularity of the course of the client's responses to the treatment regimen, which departs from the image of continuous progress through predetermined stages of "adjustment."

This departure tests the skills and knowledge of the treatment staff in handling variations among clients in rate and course of "progress." Clients' perceptions of the meaning of the experiences they undergo also vary. The outcome of such treatment depends ultimately upon the development of a sense of mutuality between staff member and client (treatment as reciprocity), which requires recognition of the unique qualities of each client. The emphasis on individualized treatment calls for well-trained personnel with caseloads that will allow them to give personal attention to clients. Management policies must permit individualized decision making, and the client should be given a part in determining his personal destiny. Evaluation of criminological practices reveals serious deficits in the provision of these essential conditions.[13]

Another aspect of treatment as process is insufficiently recognized—the technique is necessarily related to the larger social environment within which treatment outcome will be tested for long-term effect. "Tentative, backtracking behaviors" call for great patience from the treatment staff. The justification for this patience and the quest for reciprocity with the client lies in the reasonable expectation that criminal behavior will no longer be in prospect when the client rejoins the community. Thus the treatment environment should be relevant to the later community environment in terms of norms and typical problem situations. Furthermore, the methods of influence employed should produce appropriate subsequent behavior. Three effective strategies of intervention rely on the three methods of influencing behavior defined by Herbert Kelman: compliance, identification, and internalization.[14]

COMPLIANCE AND INTERVENTION

Compliance refers to the adoption of an induced behavior by the deviant as a means of gaining rewards or avoiding punishments, rather than adoption based on acceptance of the norms supporting the preferred behavior. Through manipulation of rewards and punishments, coercion is applied by a control system that is external to the individual deviant, following policies intended to promote law and order without requiring acquisition of an inner conviction by the deviant that compliance is intrinsically desirable.[15]

The restraint model

To a significant degree, the criminal justice system reacts against criminals under the assumption that the administration of penalties, in and of itself, will forestall further transgressions. The supposedly blanketing effects of generalized punishments are relied on, rather than fitting the penalty to the specific offender. Deterrence is supposed to result automatically from some uniformly applied coercive force. Some argue that

[13] For evidence of the deficiencies of "social work" personnel in prisons, see Elmer H. Johnson, "The Present Level of Social Work in Prisons," *Crime and Delinquency,* 9 (July 1963): 290–96.

[14] Herbert C. Kelman, "Compliance, Identification, and Internalization: Three Processes of Attitude Change," *Journal of Conflict Resolution,* 2 (April 1958): 53.

[15] Ibid.

"treatment" includes any restraint of the criminal, whether exile, incarceration, or physical or chemical restraint.[16]

The classical school emphasized the swift and certain imposition of punishments against the criminal *act* as distinguished from the qualities of the actor. It also called for fitting the severity of the punishment to the ranking of a given criminal act along a continuum of differing degrees of impact on society's interests. The routine administration of criminal justice tends to blur the latter condition and to produce a system relying predominately on restraint alone.[17] The early Pennsylvania prison system placed faith in the deterrent effect of solitary confinement. The early Auburn prison system assumed conformity would be the consequence of compulsory silence in congregate situations, isolation of felons from one another during nonworking hours, stern punishments uniformly imposed, and rigorous surveillance.[18]

In corrections, the *restraint model* of organizations accepts the offenders as they are when they arrive from courts and tries to make their stay in prison as comfortable as possible to staff and inmates. The emphasis is on running a prison with minimum disturbance—"keep the lid on." Coercion alone is relied on. Inmates "do their time" and "treatment," to all intents and purposes, is simply a means of relieving tensions which hold potential for upsetting the "quiet joint," according to Vincent O'Leary and David Duffee.[19]

In applying the restraint model to corrections, O'Leary and Duffee note the tendency to demand conformity to agency norms as a safeguard against public criticism of the agency or disturbance of agency routines (the prison as a "quiet joint," for example). In this instance, restraint serves the instrumental goals of the agency rather than acting as a means of safeguarding the outside community.[20] Associated with this use of coercive power are a number of public and moral issues identified with the inconsistency of totalitarian practices in a democracy, the suppression of individual deviance for the sake of administrative convenience, and the aggravation of deviance by excessive retaliation against law violators who are not personally committed to criminal values.[21]

---

[16] Halleck, *Psychiatry and the Dilemmas of Crime,* p. 233.

[17] See discussion of the crime-control model, Chapter 12, p. 302.

[18] See Chapter 16, pp. 405–8.

[19] Vincent O'Leary and David Duffee, "Correctional Policy: A Classification of Goals Designed for Change," *Crime and Delinquency,* 17 (October 1971): 381–82.

[20] Ibid.

[21] For examples, see discussion of police authority and democracy, Chapter 13; the implications of plea bargaining, Chapter 14; bail practices, Chapter 15; and the effects of penal confinement, Chapter 19. The adverse consequences of suppression for the policing of morals are suggested in Chapter 1, pp. 21–23, and Chapter 2, pp. 36–38.

The rectification model

The official position of criminal justice administrators often departs from the restraint model, even though punishment may be advocated as the primary strategy for dealing with criminals. The restraint model makes no claims beyond the general effects of the administration of punitive policies, but administrators are likely to argue that punishment is a means of changing offenders in ways useful to the outside community. Declining public support for punishment per se on humanitarian grounds has pressed administrators to justify penal policies based on compliance as a method of influencing behavior.

In the *rectification model,* agencies seek to manage punitive experiences of convicted offenders to encourage them to comply with community norms. In this way they can both avoid future punishments and elicit reactions from officials that are favorable to their immediate self-interests. In relying on compliance as a method of influencing offender behavior, the rectification model implies a resolve to change behavior that is lacking in the restraint model. The two models are similar in their faith in the supposedly blanketing effects of a rigid and conforming regime. Regulatory supervision and "firm but fair" administration take precedent over activities usually associated with treatment: vocational training, psychological intervention, moral instruction, and so on. The authoritarian demand that offenders comply with the community's preferred norms is regarded as sufficient.[22]

Management and conditioning

In lieu of the rather primitive theory of the rectification model, behavior modification has appeared in recent years as an approach that seeks compliance through principles of psychological conditioning and systematic management of the environment. Behavior modification deals with overt behavior and the measurement of observable events in the deviant's environment. Thus it deemphasizes reciprocity and process as aspects of treatment interaction and emphasizes management of the structure within which interaction occurs. In operant conditioning, a reward is given the client when he produces the required behavior once or several times. The control of rewards is known as contingency management.

Other techniques, grouped under the term "classical conditioning," include aversion suppression and electronic monitoring. Aversion suppression employs electric shock or an emetic to induce vomiting under conditions which press the deviant to identify unpleasant sensations with use of alcohol or drugs or homosexual behavior. In electronic monitoring,

[22] To avoid confusion with the term "social reform," we substitute "rectification" for the "reform model" used by O'Leary and Duffee in "Correctional Policy," pp. 379–80.

a small device is strapped to the wrist of the parolee or other individual under supervision. The device reports his location to a central station, possibly indicates physiological processes (for example, penile erection of sex deviates), and transmits an electric shock to inhibit prohibited behavior.[23]

In the CASE project (Contingencies Applicable to Special Education) at the National Training School for Boys, Washington, D.C., young inmates were awarded points, conditional on completing a test with at least 90 percent of the answers correct, for a range of academic courses. The points (a reward equivalent to wages as an incentive) were means of "renting" a private student office, paying admission to a recreation lounge, purchasing goods at a "store," or investing in further courses for additional rewards. Contingency management was involved in that the gaining of rewards sought by the individual was dependent upon his participation in the reduction of his educational deficits. The project directors reported that initial success was reinforcing, as demonstrated by growing interest in schooling.[24]

The Robert F. Kennedy Federal Youth Center, Morgantown, West Virginia, is a minimum-security facility which evaluates youths at admission according to behavioral characteristics, maturity level, and psychological orientation. They are assigned to quarters designed to be appropriate to treatment needs and control requirements. Specific individual goals for each inmate are established in education, work, and cottage living. Points are awarded as in the CASE project, and greater privileges are granted with achievement.[25]

At Draper Correctional Center, Elmore, Alabama, teaching machines are the basis for an education program in which the inmates agree to complete a given amount of study per week. Satisfactory performance earns the inmate a work break and other opportunities for self-selected free-time activities contingent upon overall progress.[26]

Behavior modification techniques have also been applied to juvenile probationers. A truant and rebellious girl was influenced by the granting of home telephone privileges, contingent upon school attendance. A young boy habitually played with matches; he was motivated to abandon this practice by placing a star on a chart for every day and granting him

[23] Ralph K. Schwitzgebel, *Development and Legal Regulation of Coercive Behavior: Modification Techniques with Offenders* (Chevy Chase, Md.: National Institute of Mental Health, 1971), pp. 5–21.

[24] Harold L. Cohen, James Filipczak, and John Bis, "A Study of Contingencies Applicable to Special Education: Case I," in Roger Ulrich, Thomas Stachnik, and John Mabry (eds.), *Control of Human Behavior,* Vol. II (Glenview, Ill.: Scott, Foresman & Co., 1970), pp. 51–69.

[25] Ray Gerard, "Institutional Innovations in Juvenile Corrections," *Federal Probation,* 34 (December 1970): 37–44.

[26] Carl B. Clements and John M. McKee, "Programmed Instruction for Institutionalized Offenders: Contingency Management and Performance Contracts," *Psychological Reports,* 22 (June 1968): 957–64.

a 25-cent reward for each week he abstained from it, and by praise from his father.[27]

The basing of behavior modification in conditioning theory promises to lend discretion and a sense of purpose to the administration of punishment. The reliance on compliance is similar to that in the rectification model, but grounding in conditioning theory adds the factor of recognition of individual differences among clients to the management of a system of punishments and rewards. On the other hand, behavior modification conveys a theme of "hard determinism" which, as in the case of the positive school, insists that men are universally subject to forces external to their own motivations. This position casts the scientist in the role of the unchallengeable expert authorized to determine the destiny of his clients, regardless of their legal rights or personal wishes. The attraction of behavior modification to many criminological workers may be explained partially by the emphasis on compliance for the sake of social protection, another central principle of the positivists.[28] Finally, behavioral modification proposes management of the agency environment for therapeutic purposes, but its tendency toward hard determinism fails to recognize the importance of the spontaneous relationships that are crucial in the definition of treatment as management.

IDENTIFICATION AND INTERNALIZATION: THE REHABILITATION MODEL

In crime prevention and corrections, the most prevalent form for organizing treatment is the *rehabilitation model,* based on the clinical approach and the application of psychogenic theories by treatment professionals.[29] The focus is on the client as an individual and the treatment requirements of a specific case. Generalized principles are considered useful only to the degree that they are applicable to the particular case at hand.[30]

Following the style of the medical clinician, this model is based on the assumption that crime resembles disease in that some malign process within the organism persists over time to deprive the "sick" offender of control over his behavior. The goal of treatment is to overcome the pernicious agent—physical, chemical, intrapsychic, genetic, interpersonal, or social—which is believed to be associated with this malign process.

[27] Gaylord L. Thorne, Ronald G. Tharp, and Ralph J. Wetzel, "Behavior Modification Techniques: New Tools for Probation Officers," *Federal Probation,* 31 (June 1967): 21–27.

[28] See Chapter 8, pp. 186–87.

[29] O'Leary and Duffee, "Correctional Policy," pp. 380–81.

[30] The "idiographic thesis" takes the emphasis on the individual to the extreme, contending that scientific classification of personality is impossible because each personality is unlike any other. See Gordon Trasler, *The Explanation of Criminality* (London: Routledge & Kegan Paul, 1962), p. 24.

Each of several categories of behavioral maladjustment is seen as distinguishable from other categories because of its unique set of symptoms.[31] Although medical disabilities are recognized, psychological distress usually is considered the primary source of personal deficits in educational attainment, stable employment, management of interpersonal relationships, and other qualities of an effective and satisfying life. Academic education, religious counseling, vocational training, and social casework are among the services mobilized, but they are regarded as essentially ancillary to psychological intervention.

Limited intervention and identification

The rehabilitation model usually undertakes limited intervention in the sense of attempting to develop the latent capacities the offender brings with him to the treatment program. Vocational training, academic education, and counseling are means of orienting him toward roles identified with the interests of legitimate society. Psychological intervention may be limited to remedial efforts rather than seeking profound changes of personality. The limited objectives are usually dictated by the relatively short time available for treatment in the light of short sentences, even when the staff claims to be implementing deep therapy.

Limited intervention under the rehabilitation model relies primarily on the development of a sense of trust of the client in the staff member. In this sense, identification is the primary method of influencing the deviant toward change. *Identification* involves the adoption by the deviant of the desired behavior because it produces a satisfying relationship with another person or group. When the behavior is grounded in a social relationship crucial to the deviant, he presumably will be motivated to conform to the expectations associated with that relationship.[32] Identification differs from compliance in its demand for reciprocity—the sense of mutuality between therapist and his client which is the basis of a satisfying relationship. Identification also calls for what we defined earlier as "treatment as management." The spontaneous relationships between staff members and clients provide opportunities for the development of the spirit of mutuality from which, presumably, the deviant will be motivated to accept the norms supported by the influence agent.

Intensive intervention and internalization

Under the rehabilitation model, individual-oriented intervention also may be undertaken with the objective of achieving profound personality change in offenders who are evaluated as suffering from serious psycho-

[31] Adapted from Merlin Taber *et al.,* "Disease Ideology and Mental Health Research," *Social Problems,* 16 (Winter 1969): 349–57.
[32] Kelman, "Compliance, Identification, and Internalization," p. 53.

logical disturbances. The approach may be individual depth psychotherapy of the patient's personal maladjustment as rooted in early life experiences. The skillful analysis of a well-trained therapist is required because the patient only dimly understands his difficulties. The site of the rehabilitation model is a community psychiatric clinic or a prison resembling a mental hospital. The client also may be viewed as being so vocationally and socially inept that a major resocialization effort must be undertaken. The approach may be an elaborate educational program designed to resocialize the personality into a middle-class form, along with the development of relevant vocational skills.

In addition to the intensity of change undertaken, this version of the rehabilitation model differs from the first version in the method of influencing attitude change. *Internalization* depends on the client's acceptance of the preferred norms as relevant to the solutions of his life problems and as congruent with his values and needs. Kelman emphasizes that the satisfaction derived from internalization is due to the content of the new behavior as distinguished from the key importance in identification of the desired relationship with another person or group, regardless of content.[33] The offender is supposed to be motivated in the desired direction because he recognizes previously unseen opportunities and judges the influence agent to be trustworthy and expert in matters that are important to him personally. Compared with identification, internalization involves more ambitious goals in changing long-term behavior because the offender must accept the preferred norms as binding on his conduct.

THE REINTEGRATION MODEL: ORIENTATION TOWARD COMMUNITY

All approaches to treatment claim to prepare the offender for effective citizenship. The theme is least characteristic of the restraint model, which relies on coercion to maintain the external appearance of an orderly regimen, with only incidental attention to the offender as a product to be eventually returned to the community. The rectification model, relying on compliance as a method of changing behavior, makes a clear claim that authoritarian management of the offender's experiences within a given program will result in his conformity to community norms. The contingency management of behavior modification is a more sophisticated effort in the same direction that holds greater potential because it is grounded in conditioning principles which could be relevant to the client's subsequent experiences. The rehabilitation model, the most prevalent among the established models of correctional agencies, makes the strongest claim that it can produce clients prepared for community reentry if

[33] Ibid., p. 53.

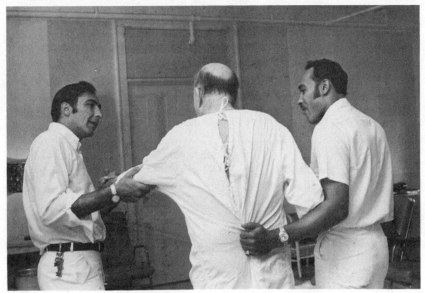

Office of Economic Opportunity (Stuart A. Oring)

Figure 11–2. The reintegration model in action.

As a method of influencing change, internalization depends on the capacity of offenders to respond to opportunities for responsibility within socially approved norms. The existence of this capacity has been demonstrated, for example, by a cooperative project between Norfolk Prison and Medford State Hospital near Framingham, Mass., funded by the Office of Economic Opportunity. The project director had spent 18 years in prison before earning a master's in psychology, and the assistant director had served 40 years as a prison inmate. The 10 prisoners working in the wards as psychiatric aides-in-training in the photograph above provided a resource for increasing the personal attention given patients, while they were being trained vocationally.

the adverse influences of custodial practices and penal confinement can be counteracted.

Emergence of a new model

One of the significant recent developments has been the emergence of the *reintegration model* as an independent organizational type for corrections. Whereas the models described above view the problems of the offender's reentry into the community as a secondary—sometimes only incidental—concern, the reintegration model focuses primarily on the preparation of the offender for performance of the roles and assumption of the obligations that will permit him to participate in community life in ways that are personally satisfying and socially acceptable.

O'Leary and Duffee see this model as being oriented concurrently in two directions.[34] First, using the internalization method of influencing behavior, the staff strives to provide experiences in which offender-clients test acceptable alternatives among behaviors. The motivation for new behaviors among offender-clients is supposed to emerge in a climate in which they share with staff the control of the program; that is, the participation of clients in the decision-making processes is authentic. Errors in the management of the program are revealed by failures of clients and staff to establish goals mutually in keeping with internalization's emphasis on the acceptance of new norms by clients.

Second, changes are sought within the institutional framework of the correctional agency and the outside community. The recognition of the need for changes in institutional patterns inserts elements of social reform in the intervention strategy and opens to change correctional systems that previously were largely isolated from influences of the outside community. Further, the change is sought in those community patterns that stigmatize the former offender and limit his access to the opportunities for which his acceptance of community norms and his newly acquired skills have made him eligible.[35]

This reintegration model is emergent, rather than an accomplished reality; contemporary practices suggest only a movement in that direction. American prison systems have expanded work-release programs to a remarkable degree. Increased interest is being expressed in offender participation in roles usually limited to staff, but implementation of the idea is rare.[36] Probation and parole practices provide a role for the community worker specializing in intervention for clients in the community's system of human services.[37] Nevertheless, the present status of community-based

---

[34] O'Leary and Duffee, "Correctional Policy," pp. 382–83.

[35] See discussion of the "rehabilitation bargain," Chapter 24, pp. 589–90.

[36] See Chapter 21, p. 535.

[37] See Chapter 23, pp. 568–69.

corrections is not described by the reintegration model. It is more aptly portrayed as an adaptation of the rehabilitation model, undertaking limited intervention and relying on identification as the method of influencing behavior.

Theory and reintegration

The reintegration model represents the breakdown of the myth that the response to the convicted offender can be divorced from the community environment within which the offense occurred and to which the convicted offender is highly likely to return. The paramount importance to criminology of the community will be developed in Part VI. The reintegration model emphasizes the interdependence of intervention and social reform, but the rehabilitation model implies a growing awareness of the importance of the community as a concept if the offender is to become subject to the informal controls that largely regulate the behavior of noncriminals.

Proposals for reform of the traditional prison include full-fledged collaboration of staff and inmates, new institutions to provide interchange between inmates and the outside community, and interdependence of institutional and community-based programs. As an ultimate goal, the reintegration model also implies that criminal justice is one aspect of the community's system of human services, rather than an autonomous system relying exclusively on suppression and punishment under the compliance method of influencing behavior. Preventive and therapeutic functions, we shall see, are implied in the public servant and preventive roles of the policeman[38] and the court's use of probation and treatment of juveniles.[39]

Sociogenic theories, presented earlier as relevant to social reform, become relevant to intervention under the reintegration model. Such social forces as community norms, differential experiences of the social classes, subcultural differences, and the impact of technological change on job opportunity affect the probability of restoring the convicted offender to the status and role of full participant in community life. As a method of influencing his behavior, internalization calls for his recognition of personal opportunities that will become available if he accepts the preferred norms as his own—that is, if he becomes subject to informal controls.

The establishment of this goal implies that criminal justice has a practical interest in the community variables examined as aspects of sociogenic theories. For example, anomie theory points to the discrepancy created when individuals are socialized to seek "success" as defined by

---

[38] See Chapter 13, pp. 333–36.
[39] See Chapter 14, pp. 367–70.

cultural values but find their access to social and economic opportunity blocked by the social structure. John Galliher believes vocational training in prisons is of little value in opening legitimate opportunity to offenders unless they also are instructed in techniques of social manipulation that will help them overcome prejudices against hiring former prisoners and provide the skills necessary in jobs, such as sales, that require such techniques.[40] Offenders frequently have demonstrated appropriate skills in manipulating victims of confidence games and other kinds of property crime.[41] Through instruction and counseling, the illegal manipulators could learn legitimate applications for their skills, and other offenders could learn the middle-class use of work meanings, gain a means of projecting a favorable image to middle-class gatekeepers to opportunity, and otherwise present "the front" which is as important as technical knowledge in job performance.

Whereas compliance insists on complete conformity to preferred norms, internalization recognizes greater variability among clients in their stance toward these norms. For example, instruction in social manipulation could result in the offender gaining greater competence in illegal activities. Advocates of internalization regard compliance as rather inefficient in producing lasting adherence to legitimate norms after the offender is no longer in custody. They believe it would be more realistic in the long run to recognize the importance of granting the client greater freedom in interpreting norms according to his own values and interests.

In this vein, Irving Rosow argues that the most promising target for change-inducing pressure, among deviants requiring such pressure, is the "chameleon"—the individual who is competent, skillful, and active in meeting behavioral expectations but who is not committed to the values upon which his current behavior is based.[42] The challenge raised by internalization as a method of influence is to move beyond the superficial and temporary adaptation of the chameleon to his immediate situation and gain his lasting commitment to the preferred norms because he comes to recognize them as useful to him in the long term.

SUMMARY

In one sense, this chapter has been transitional between previous analyses and the chapters to follow. Scientific concepts and theories are useful for understanding the patterns of criminal behavior. The remainder of the book is devoted to prevention, control, and treatment as sets of

[40] John F. Galliher, "Training in Social Manipulation as a Rehabilitative Technique," *Crime and Delinquency,* 17 (October 1971): 431–36.

[41] The similarities between legitimate and criminal behavior systems have been noted; see Chapter 7, pp. 134–39.

[42] Irving Rosow, "Forms and Functions of Adult Socialization," *Social Forces,* 44 (September 1965): 35–45.

strategies designed to deal with the crime problem. Theories provide intellectual frameworks for lending order to an otherwise confusing array of events which confront those who would employ any of these strategies through either social reform or intervention. After considering treatment as management, as reciprocity, and as process, three methods of influencing behavior—compliance, identification, and internalization—were examined. These methods were applied selectively to alternative models for organizing intervention: restraint, rectification, rehabilitation, and reintegration.

FOR ADDITIONAL READING

Baumgold, John. "Developing Sensitivity behind Bars." *Sociological Inquiry,* 41 (Spring 1971): 211–16.

Biderman, Albert D., and Zimmer, Herbert (eds.). *The Manipulation of Human Behavior.* New York: John Wiley & Sons, 1961.

Buchler, R. E.; Patterson, G. R.; and Furniss, J. M. "The Reinforcement of Behavior in Institutional Settings." *Behavior Research and Therapy,* 4 (August 1966): 157–67.

Gibbons, Don C. *Changing the Lawbreaker.* Englewood Cliffs, N.J.: Prentice-Hall, 1965.

Glasser, William. *Reality Therapy: A New Approach to Psychiatry.* New York: Harper & Row, 1965.

Johnson, Elmer H. "A Basic Error: Dealing with Inmates as though They Were Abnormal." *Federal Probation,* 35 (March 1971): 39–44.

————— "The Professional in Correction: Status and Prospects." *Social Forces,* 40 (December 1961): 168–76.

Kahn, Alfred J. "From Delinquency Treatment to Community Development." In Paul F. Lazarsfeld, William M. Sewell, and Harold L. Wilensky (eds.), *The Uses of Sociology,* pp. 477–505. New York: Basic Books, 1967.

Konopka, Gisela. *Social Group Work: A Helping Process.* Englewood Cliffs, N.J.: Prentice-Hall, 1963.

Meyer, Henry J.; Borgatta, Edgar F.; and Jones, Wyatt C. *Girls at Vocational High.* New York: Russell Sage Foundation, 1965.

Middendorf, Wolf. *The Effectiveness of Punishment.* South Hackensack, N.J.: Fred B. Rothman & Co., 1968.

Nastir, Michael; Dezzani, D.; and Silbert, Mimi. "Atascadero: Ramifications of a Maximum Security Treatment Institution." *Issues in Criminology,* 2 (Spring 1966): 29–46.

Nelson, Elmer K., Jr. *Developing Correctional Administrators.* Washington, D.C.: Joint Commission on Correctional Manpower and Training, 1969.

Phillips, Elery L. "Achievement Place: Token Reinforcement Procedures in a Home-Style Rehabilitation Setting for 'Pre-Delinquent' Boys," in Roger Ulrick, Thomas Stacknik, and John Mabry (eds.), *Control of Human Behavior,* Vol. I, pp. 70–80. Glenview, Ill.: Scott, Foresman & Co., 1970.

Roberts, Albert R. *Sourcebook on Prison Education.* Springfield, Ill.: Charles C Thomas, 1971.

Sarason, Irwin G. "Verbal Learning, Modeling, and Juvenile Delinquency," *American Psychologist,* 23 (April 1968): 254–66.

Sarri, Rosemary C., and Vinter, Robert D. "Group Treatment Strategies in Juvenile Correctional Programs." *Crime and Delinquency,* 11 (October 1965): 326–40.

Schwitzgebel, Ralph. *Streetcorner Research: An Experimental Approach to the Juvenile Delinquent.* Cambridge, Mass.: Harvard University Press, 1965.

Uehling, Harold F. "Group Therapy Turns Repression into Expression for Prison Inmates." *Federal Probation,* 26 (March 1962): 43–49.

Zimberoff, Steven J. "Behavior Modification with Delinquents." *Correctional Psychologist,* 3 (September–October 1968): 11–25.

Part IV

The system of criminal justice

The system of criminal justice has three interdependent major components—police, courts, and corrections. Each has its own tasks. The policeman initiates the process of criminal justice through apprehension and arrest. His discretion in arrest decisions has a vital effect on the efficiency of the overall system because he mans the input gateway. The quality of the evidence he gathers determines to an important degree whether the court can do its part. Discretion also operates through the prosecutor, who determines whether the case should go to trial and strongly influences the quality of justice. In turn, the courts determine the kinds of persons who will be subject to the correctional apparatus. This part of the book studies the operation of the system short of commitment of the convicted criminal to correctional programs.

Administration of criminal justice

The manner in which a particular society deals with criminals is a useful index of its fundamental values. History records such practices as tortures, sadistic forms of execution, and deliberate cruelties in prisons. By modern standards, the peoples of earlier days appear to have been barbarians in this respect. Within the context of the customs and values of their societies, however, their practices were "natural" and even desirable to most of the people. Our own ways of handling offenders someday may appear to be naïve, inhumane, and uncivilized.

Contemporary practices have their roots in the past, but many have taken on new meaning. For example, imprisonment increasingly supports the therapeutic ideology, whereas earlier applications tended to support punishment as an end in itself. Another general pattern is change in the relative use of the various modes of official response to crime; imprisonment, probation, and parole are employed to a greater degree today than in earlier eras, whereas capital punishment has been inflicted less often, if at all.

INSTITUTIONALIZED RESPONSES TO CRIME

The responses to criminal behavior operate at institutional and subinstitutional levels. As individuals and members of groups, the "average" citizen reacts to the criminal rather sporadically at the subinstitutional level. There are patterns to these responses, but they are not included within the institutional framework of organized and systematic responses. General public interest in the operations of criminal justice and correction is likely to be aroused only under special circumstances as, for example, when crime is particularly notorious. On occasion a criminal may become a folk "hero" if he appears to be clever or a victim of some form of persecution. The inadequacy of institutionalized responses could be demonstrated dramatically by a case of apparently gross injustice.

This chapter concerns itself with the institutional level, on which societal responses are implemented by officials who occupy status positions within the structure developed specifically to deal with criminal behavior. These officials include functionaries in law enforcement, agencies, courts, probation and parole departments, and correctional establishments. They implement the general modes of societal response to criminal behavior: banishment, fines and reparations, corporal punishments, forms of leniency, imprisonment, and capital punishment. Subsequent chapters will treat the activities of these functionaries in more detail.

Criminal justice in the community structure

Criminal justice often is justified on the grounds that it contributes to the social order of the community and the well-being of its citizens. In the community, men relate to one another in work, religion, education of children, recreation, buying and selling of goods and services, maintenance of roads and sewer systems, and provision of safeguards against fire, disease, and crime. These are community activities in that individuals enter into relationships with one another in an organized fashion to carry them out. The community functions as a social system to the extent that it contains both the structures for maintaining social organization and a workable consensus which binds its residents together through the sharing of collective sentiments and common interests.

As part of the structure of the community, the police, courts, and correctional agencies have a place in the overall organization of government that ought to enable them to contribute to the social order through interrelationships with other social institutions, such as the family, school, business enterprises, and social service agencies. Achievement of this purpose, however, is difficult in the face of the far-reaching changes underway in contemporary cities. The rise of an urban-industrial society has had revolutionary effects on the work of criminal justice. Both the greater size and heterogeneity of the urban population and the increased rate of mobility have made the work more difficult. At the same time, there has been an expansion of duties in areas other than the suppression of crimes. Increasingly complex and varied activities have aggravated the problems of organizational weaknesses. As governmental agencies, the vehicles of criminal justice are vulnerable to the weaknesses of local government. Consequently they are often characterized by duplication of activities, fragmentation of effort, inadequate personnel and services due to insufficient local tax revenues, and vulnerability to control by municipal machine politicians.

In recent years, a movement initiated at the federal level has sought means of remedying the chaos and fiscal starvation that beset local criminal justice. The traditional emphasis on local control of criminal justice has been increasingly questioned since the 1960s, when the Supreme Court initiated a sweeping reexamination of law enforcement throughout the nation. Crime and violence have become a national political issue. The Johnson administration initiated legislation in 1967 for massive federal aid to state and local criminal justice, and the Department of Justice has become the focal point of attempts to develop a national criminal justice policy through either legislative standards or financial assistance programs.[1]

The concept of a criminal justice system

The word "system" implies a regular, orderly method of action. In general, the criminal justice *system* is composed of the police, courts, and correctional agencies. Within each of these three major components, personnel of many kinds carry out the responsibilities assigned to each worker within the total scheme. An overall system exists to the extent that each task event contributes to the functions of all personnel in producing the desired outcome. Whether or not an arrest is made is the first of a series of decisions by these personnel that determines how far the apprehended suspect proceeds through the criminal justice system. The decisions may lead to release without prosecution or to choices between pretrial detention versus release on bail; conviction versus acquittal; probation versus imprisonment; or parole from prison versus confinement until termination of sentence.

From the perspectives of those caught up in the machinery of justice, the system is likely to be seen as a collection of impersonal forces administered by distant, inhuman functionaries. "They" make decisions determining whether the offender is to be "shipped out" to unfamiliar and perhaps frightening places where he will be expected to "shape up" to others' standards.

This system is elusive of any clear-cut definition but has been described as a loose federation of offices and agencies through which officials of various professional identities work. The relationships are amorphous because the segments of the system are structurally independent, there is no common agreement on specific objectives and means of achieving them, and the apparatus has been developed historically as a blend of outmoded traditions and recently emergent values. The system can only partially be a product of deliberate consideration of goals and means of implementation because the community at large lacks agreement on how the agencies should control crime. Conflicting goals also confound legislatures and appellate courts in their attempts to provide consistent, manageable purposes for the system. Disparities and inconsistencies are in-

---

[1] John T. Elliff, *Crime, Dissent, and the Attorney General: The Justice Department in the 1960's* (Beverly Hills, Calif.: Sage Publications, 1971), pp. 15–82.

evitable in light of the multiplicity of approaches to crime control and the range and divergence of behaviors defined as criminal.[2]

Some of the terms that have been used in analysis of components of the system do not clearly apply to the operations of the overall system of crime control.[3] The loose confederation of agencies, each with its own sets of affiliations with other organizations and occupational roles, lacks the unitary nature suggested by the term "organization." The term "bureaucracy" suggests the routine, standardized, impersonal handling of a large volume of "cases" but does not encompass all the factors creating inconsistencies in the operation of criminal justice. Under public pressure to terminate quickly some "law and order crisis," legislators may impose impossible tasks on agencies. As members of the community at large, criminal justice personnel may share the false beliefs about "criminals" which undermine orderly administration.

Recognizing that this apparatus is neither monolithic nor internally consistent in design and operations, the President's Crime Commission defined any criminal justice system as the apparatus society uses to enforce the standards of conduct necessary to protect individuals and the community.

It operates by apprehending, prosecuting, convicting, and sentencing those members of the community who violate the basic rules of group existence. The action taken against lawbreakers is designed to serve three purposes beyond the immediate punitive one. It removes dangerous people from the community; it deters others from criminal behavior; and it gives society an opportunity to attempt to transform lawbreakers into law-abiding citizens. What most significantly distinguishes the system of one country from that of another is the extent and the form of the protections it offers individuals in the process of determining guilt and imposing punishment. Our system of justice deliberately sacrifices much in efficiency and even in effectiveness in order to preserve local autonomy and to protect the individual.[4]

Albert Blumstein implies that this imprecise conception of system could lend itself to techniques of analysis useful for reform if attention is directed to the job the agencies are expected to perform. Because government decisions have become very complex, methods of system analysis have been developed for quantitative comparisons of the costs and effects of alternative decisions. If numbers can be made meaningful in terms of the social value implications of criminal justice issues, Blumstein argues, the effectiveness of criminal justice can be advanced through

[2] Frank J. Remington et al., Criminal Justice Administration: Material and Cases (Indianapolis, Ind.: Bobbs-Merrill Co., 1969), pp. 8–10.

[3] Ibid., pp. 6–8.

[4] President's Commission on Law Enforcement and Administration of Justice, The Challenge of Crime in a Free Society (Washington, D.C.: U.S. Government Printing Office, 1967), p. 7.

reliable answers to such questions as: Do higher arrest rates produce improved crime control through correction of antisocial attitudes? Does nonbail release reduce the courts' workload? Does free legal counsel to defendants affect the workload of correctional agencies?[5]

Stages in administration

In idealized and simplified form, the sequence of procedures applied to persons processed by the criminal justice system is as outlined below.[6] As later chapters will document, actual practices depart from this routine sufficiently to arouse demands for reform of criminal justice administration.

As Figure 12–1 indicates, only a portion of the total number of crimes perpetrated is processed by the police as gatekeepers to the system. Law enforcement officers undertake investigation of cases originated by complaint of a crime victim or their own observation of a crime. The first official action is arrest. The statutes ordinarily require the officer to take the arrested person promptly to a magistrate (in practice, the next morning in most cases). Quality of evidence is supposed to determine the police decision whether or not to prosecute. In many jurisdictions, the evidence is taken to the prosecutor, who decides the question and what the charge will be.

If prosecution has been decided upon, the prisoner goes before a magistrate to be informed of the charge against him, his right to obtain an attorney, the conditions under which he may be released, and the choice he may make to waive a preliminary examination that will determine whether the evidence justifies holding him for trial. If the suspect is held for further action, the prosecutor will file a formal accusation (an information), or a grand jury will consider the evidence and return a formal accusation (indictment). Then the defendant appears before the court to plead. If he pleads guilty, the judge is supposed to make certain that the plea is truthful and has been made voluntarily. If the plea is not guilty, the defendant is supposed to have a choice between a jury trial or one before only the judge.

If the trial results in conviction, the judge sets a time for sentencing. The usual choices are between fine, probation, or imprisonment. In probation the convicted person is returned to the community with the super-

---

[5] Albert Blumstein, "Systems Analysis and the Criminal Justice System," *Annals of American Academy of Political and Social Science*, 374 (November 1967): 93–95.

[6] This subsection was adapted from Remington *et al., Criminal Justice Administration* pp. 50–52, and Vernon C. Branham and Samuel B. Kutash (eds.), *Encyclopedia of Criminology* (New York: Philosophical Library, 1949), pp. 188, 420–22.

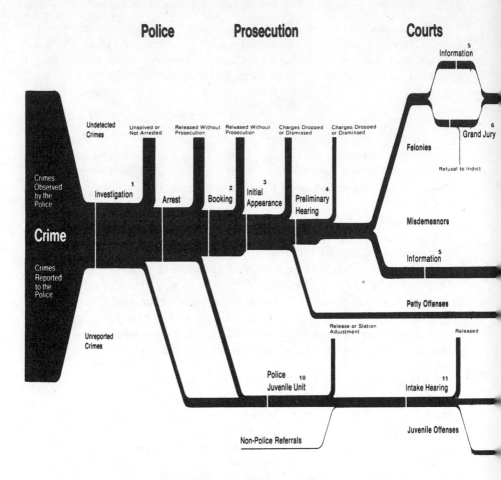

Police   Prosecution   Courts

Figure 12–1. A general view of the criminal justice system.

Note: This chart presents a simple but comprehensive view of the movement of cases through the criminal justice system. Procedures in individual jurisdictions may vary from the pattern shown here. The differing weights of line indicate the relative volumes of cases disposed of at various points in the system, but this is only suggestive since there are no nationwide data of this sort.

[1] May continue until trial.

[2] Administrative record of arrest. First step at which temporary release on bail may be available.

[3] Before magistrate, commissioner, or justice of peace. Formal notice of charge, advice of rights. Bail set. Summary trials for petty offenses usually conducted here without further processing.

[4] Preliminary testing of evidence against defendant. Charge may be reduced. No separate preliminary hearing for misdemeanors in some systems.

[5] Charge filed by prosecutor on basis of information submitted by police or citizens. Alternative to grand jury indictment; often used in felonies, almost always in misdemeanors.

Corrections

Charge Dismissed   Acquitted

Probation

7
Arraignment   Trial   Sentencing   Revocation
                                                                    Penitentiary   Out
                                                                                        of
               Guilty Pleas   System

                                                                              Parole

                                                                      Revocation

        8
Reduction of Charge   Appeal   **9**
                                                Habeas
                                                Corpus

Charge Dismissed   Acquitted   Probation

7
Arraignment   Trial   Sentencing   Revocation
                                                                                        Out
               Guilty Pleas   of
                                            Fine   Jail   System

                                                    Nonpayment

                        Released

                                    Probation

            Adjudicatory Hearing   Revocation
                                                        Juvenile Institution   Out
                                                                                        of
        12   System
Nonadjudicatory
Disposition   Parole

                                                    Revocation

6 Reviews whether government evidence sufficient to justify trial. Some states have no grand jury system; others seldom use it.

7 Appearance for plea; defendant elects trial by judge or jury (if available); counsel for indigent usually appointed here in felonies, often not at all in other cases.

8 Charge may be reduced at any time prior to trial in return for plea of guilty or for other reasons.

9 Challenge on constitutional grounds to legality of detention. May be sought at any point in process.

10 Police often hold informal hearings, dismiss or adjust many cases without further processing.

11 Probation officer decides desirability of further court action.

12 Welfare agency, social services, counseling, medical care, etc., for cases where adjudicatory handling not needed.

Source: The President's Commission on Law Enforcement and Administration of Justice, *The Challenge of Crime in a Free Society* (Washington, D.C.: U.S. Government Printing Office, 1967), pp. 8–9.

vision of a probation officer and under specified conditions. This decision
sometimes is preceded by an investigation by the probation officer into
the individual's background and social situation (presentence investigation).

If sentenced, the offender goes to a correctional institution for a term
determined by the judge within statutory limits for the given offense. Misdemeanors draw a sentence of less than a year and usually are served in
a facility operated by local government. Felonies, considered more serious crimes, usually draw longer sentences served in state or federal institutions. The length of confinement may be shortened through "good-
time" awards granted by prison authorities, commutations of sentence
and paroles administered by a parole board; and amnesty and pardon by
the chief executive of the state or the federal government. *"Good-time"*
awards reduce time served on the basis of approved conduct or work performance. *Commutation* of sentence reduces the original sentence. *Parole*
constitutes release into the community with supervision by a parole officer and under certain conditions after the prisoner has served a portion
of his prison sentence. A *pardon* excuses the offender from the penalty
on the grounds that it was too severe or his guilt is in doubt. *Amnesty* is
a blanket pardon granted to a group of persons rather than particular
individuals.

ISSUES RELATED TO "EFFICIENCY"

The current system probably works at an unprecedented level of coordination among and within its various components. Yet there is an
image of inefficiency because the level of expectation applied to law enforcement has risen in urban society. The increased flexibility of society
brought about by urbanization and industrialization has meant a decline
in social integration through custom, neighborliness, and long-term association, at the same time that the growth of tightly woven economic and
political systems has contributed to an unprecedented demand for public
order.

Among the formal control agencies which have evolved to maintain
order, law enforcement has developed as an organization devoted to managing the behavior of persons who are clients of police agencies, either
as offenders or as those the laws are designed to protect. The police are
supposed to assure that a set of rules will prevail so that the citizenry does
not have to respond personally to an attack on person or property. Individual retaliation is forestalled by law enforcement which, according to
the ideals of criminal justice, protects the violator as well as his victim.[7]

[7] See Albert J. Reiss, Jr., and David J. Bordua, "Environment and Organization: A Perspective on the Police," in David J. Bordua (ed.), *The Police: Six Sociological Essays* (New York: John Wiley & Sons, Inc., 1967), pp. 25–29.

Conflicts and organizational defects

Careful \examination of the criminal justice systems refutes any perception of a single, highly coordinated, efficient system moving confidentially and vigorously toward clearly delineated, common goals. Conflicts and strains exist among the police, courts, and correctional agencies as each pursues its specialized purposes. Each component processes the law violator without full awareness of the problems and activities of the others. Members of one component are likely to hold reservations about the support received from those in other components. Even within a component, tensions exist: "hard-line" versus "community-oriented" policemen, "hanging" versus "treatment-oriented" judges, treatment versus custodial staffs in correctional institutions, and prison versus parole personnel.

The administrative apparatus of criminal justice suffers from serious organizational defects which will be documented in later chapters. Some law enforcement agencies have utilized personnel inefficiently, tolerated inadequate performance, or provided erratic leadership. The organization of courts has been described as archaic and wasteful, as demonstrated by clogged calendars, excessive delay, and concurrent jurisdictions. Correctional agencies are burdened with obsolete facilities and excessive orientation to safekeeping in staffing and organizational ideology. All parts of the system demonstrate a resistance to the changes that are required by contemporary conditions.

No matter how efficient the agencies may be, their personnel will encounter evidence of dissatisfaction with their work. The law and its implementation will lag behind public expectations on how it should be employed. There will be disagreements among various interest groups about the objectives and functions of criminal law. People are particularly impatient when the force of the law is directed toward them.

Our own traditions impose inconsistent expectations on our Anglo-American legal system.[8] The roots of our common law are derived from an individualism which is inappropriate in an age of large-scale organizations. The irony of white-collar crime is that petty offenders are prosecuted while the social crimes of great organizations receive little attention. The traditional emphasis on crimes against persons that colors the criminal law lends persistence to this paradox. Individualism also is expressed in our reliance on the adversary system in which trials become a kind of combat between the prosecution and defense, and the poverty of defendants undermines equality before the courts. Nevertheless, the passing of a law is seen as the shortcut to social reform, without the necessity of changing individual behavior or the social structure.

[8] Roscoe Pound, "The Causes of Popular Dissatisfaction with the Administration of Criminal Justice," *Crime and Delinquency,* 10 (October, 1964): 355–71.

One consequence is that heavier work loads are placed on the administrative apparatus of criminal justice agencies. The criminal law is pressed into the enforcement of morals, so that personnel of law enforcement bodies, courts, and correctional agencies are burdened with a large volume of persons accused of excessive drinking, drug abuse, sexual misconduct, and so on. The jails and prisons are clogged with people caught up in efforts to apply criminal punishments for personal disorganization behavior of such a magnitude that it has been defined as constituting a social problem.

Designed inefficiency

Any demand for greater efficiency in the administration of criminal justice should be balanced against the prospect of the cold, inhuman, and unloving efficiency that could result from universal application of abstract legal rules. Beyond the effects of internal contradictions in this system, William Seagle points to the "painstaking deliberation" with which a democracy designs inefficiency into such administration to safeguard the democratic rights of the individual.[9] To illustrate this designed inefficiency, Herbert Packer describes two competing models in the operation of criminal justice: crime control versus due process.[10]

Emphasizing repression of criminal behavior, the *crime-control model* is dedicated to efficiency of law enforcement as a safeguard for public order. Success requires a high rate of apprehension and conviction. Since the police and court establishments have insufficient resources for the volume of apprehended offenders, speedy processing is sought through informal and standardized procedures. A presumption of guilt enables the overall system to operate much like an assembly-line conveyer belt, with the cases processed at a series of stations. These stations represent prearrest investigation, arrest, postarrest investigation, preparation for trial, trial or entry of plea, conviction or acquittal, and disposition of the convicted offender. The presumption of guilt is stronger as the defendant moves farther along the sequence of stations. Routine procedures are the means for efficient handling.

The *due-process model* presumes innocence until proof of guilt. This model resembles an obstacle course, with impediments set up against the further progress of the defendant through criminal justice processing. The reliability of fact-finding is recurrently challenged by errors of witnesses, coerced confessions, and other possible distortions. Guilt is determined in procedurally regular fashion according to legal rules which must be

[9] William Seagle, *Law: The Science of Inefficiency* (New York: Macmillan Co., 1952), pp. 1–5.

[10] Herbert L. Packer, *The Limits of the Criminal Sanction* (Stanford, Calif.: Stanford University Press, 1968), pp. 154–73.

satisfied apart from the question whether the defendant actually behaved as the charge alleges.

In carrying out their work, the functionaries of the criminal justice system implement various strategies utilizing authority. The remainder of this chapter will consider several of these modes of official response to behavior prohibited by criminal law. Later chapters will consider more specifically the application of such strategies to the work of law enforcement, courts, or correctional agencies.

BANISHMENT

In earlier days outlawry was often a form of capital punishment because banishment of an offender by his own people deprived him of tribal protection against enemies. Even in the Middle Ages expulsion from one city could end in hanging in another.[11] Banishment continues today in several forms. A family may bar from its circle the relative who has transgressed. The court may order the offender to leave the community in order to separate hostile parties and prevent the continuation of a dispute or feud.

A remnant of earlier banishment is the application of what Caleb Foote has called "vagrancy-type" law on the basis of his study of Philadelphia magistrates' courts.[12] He includes vagrancy, common drunkenness, and disorderly conduct under "vagrancy-type" law. Vagrancy-law enforcement is intended to keep the "bums" out of the city, control "suspicious" persons, and "clean up" the city by getting rid of "undesirable" persons. Common law defines a vagrant as an idle person who is without visible means of support and who, although able to work, refuses to do so. "Common drunkenness" implies a fixed habit of drunkenness. "Disorderly conduct" usually involves boisterous and unseemly noise that annoys peaceful residents near a public place.

Almost 40 percent of the total nontraffic arrests in the United States are for public drunkenness, and public drunkenness statutes usually include "loud and boisterous," "disorderly," or "vagrancy" labels. This element of law enforcement, which constitutes a heavy burden for criminal justice, is primarily directed against skid-row derelict men in a "revolving door" style of repeated arrests and releases. Studying the patterns of these arrests in Chicago and New York City, Raymond Nimmer found they were intended to either be of service to "helpless derelicts" or to remove "unsightly derelicts," to varying degrees according to jurisdictions and police rationales. Intoxication itself is not the key cause of such

[11] Hans Von Hentig, *Punishment: Its Origin, Purpose and Psychology* (London: William Hodge, 1937), p. 18.

[12] Caleb Foote, "Vagrancy-Type Law and Its Administration," *University of Pennsylvania Law Review,* 104 (March 1956): 603–50.

arrests; the immediate community's tolerance of the skid-row habitué's presence largely determines the level of police activity. Nimmer recommends that such arrests and prosecutions simply be eliminated.[13]

Underprivileged groups often are the targets of strategies applied by an interesting combination of aesthetes, moralists, and politicians to uphold vagrancy-type law. Under this general heading is the use of criminal process to gain the advantage of procedural simplicity in dealing with noncriminal problems. A mentally ill person is sent to a correctional institution "for treatment." Criminal process is used against an aged person who constitutes a difficult problem for a family or welfare agency. A family quarrel or landlord-boarder dispute is settled as a "disturbance of the peace" case.

Foote reports that the prosecution of vagrancy-type cases he studied deprived defendants of the most elementary requirements of a fair hearing.[14] The chief factor appears to have been the desire for rapid disposition of cases because of the heavy work load imposed on the courts. Defendants rarely were informed of the charge against them until the "trial" was completed. There was no pretense of proving through competent evidence guilt for the crime charged. Defendants were uncounseled and unaided. No records were kept. Appeal was rare. Most of the magistrates lacked legal training, and the courts had no treatment resources or constructive welfare facilities.

FINES AND REPARATIONS

Legislatures and courts have moved toward increased use of fines as the favored technique for enforcing public controls on traffic, employment, manufacture and distribution of goods, insurance, and similar matters. Fines are most likely to be imposed for embezzlement, fraud, larceny, lottery and other gambling violations, loitering, and disorderly conduct. They are the usual alternative to short prison sentences and are more likely to be prevalent in prosperity when the convicted offender more often has economic means.

Providing he has the means to pay, the fine permits the convicted person to choose what personal gratification he will sacrifice so he can replace the money he has lost. Charles Miller suggests that the fine is more likely to deter further offenses if material gain was the purpose of the crime—a gain converted into a loss through the fine.[15]

The use of a short prison term for persons unable to pay fines raises the question of favorable treatment of the well-to-do. Max Grünhut be-

[13] Raymond T. Nimmer, *Two Million Unnecessary Arrests* (Chicago: American Bar Foundation, 1971).

[14] Foote, "Vagrancy-Type Law."

[15] Charles H. Miller, "The Fine: Price Tag or Rehabilitative Force," *NPPA Journal*, 2 (October 1965): 379.

lieves this penalization of the poor could be corrected if fines are assessed according to the offender's resources rather than the gravity of the offense, or installment payments are permitted.[16]

Restitution

The idea of restitution developed during the Middle Ages, although sporadic references to it can be found as far back as ancient Greece.[17] Vengeful retaliation through blood feuds was replaced in Germanic common law by a system that combined punishment of the offender with monetary satisfactions for the injured party. The compensation varied according to the crime and the age, rank, sex, and prestige of the injured party. During the Middle Ages authorities gradually infringed upon the rights of the injured parties, and the offender's property went to the feudal barons and ecclesiastical powers. The victim became forgotten.

While punishment of crime is the concern of the state, the damage of the crime to the victim is regarded almost as a private matter. Most of the traditional crimes involve injury of one individual by another, but the state prohibits the victim from taking the law into his own hands to exact punishment. Although these crimes upset the balance between criminal and victim as well as between criminal and society, the state's concern is limited largely to restoring the latter balance, and the victim is referred to civil law.[18]

In *spiritual restitution,* a concept conceived by Stephen Schafer, the victim is compensated for his injury by the emotional satisfactions gained through the evil visited upon the wrongdoer.[19] Punishment is supposed to satisfy feelings of revenge against the offender, but this rationalization usually centers on the vicarious experience of the general public which projects itself into the victim's situation.[20] Spiritual restitution resembles punishment in that a source external to the offender strives to reestablish social and psychological equilibrium. The victim's satisfaction is incidental to meeting the supposed public demand for vengeance as a safeguard against lynch law.

Creative restitution, as conceived by Albert Eglash, is without punitive implications and has the objective of directing the offender toward social responsibility and other constructive attitudes by making amends to those

[16] Max Grünhut, *Penal Reform* (Oxford, England: Clarendon Press, 1948), p. 6.

[17] Stephen Schafer, *Restitution to Victims of Crimes* (Chicago: Quadrangle Books, Inc., 1960), pp. 3–8.

[18] Ibid., pp. 117–19.

[19] Ibid., p. 120.

[20] Nathaniel F. Cantor, *Crime and Society* (New York: Henry Holt & Co., Inc., 1939), pp. 393–94.

he has injured by his crime.[21] Whereas suffering is the key characteristic of punishment, creative restitution emphasizes constructive effort by the offender to make the crime situation better than he found it. His reparative act is related directly to the offense: the juvenile offender not only repairs the rural mailbox he tore down but paints it as well. It is argued that creative restitution reconciles the offender and the victim and motivates the offender to work for the correction of others, whereas punishment erects psychological barriers to rehabilitation.[22]

Spontaneous restitution is conceived of by Barbara Dockar-Drysdale as a mechanism of the rehabilitative process wherein the offender makes atonement for destructive and hostile behavior stemming from emotional maladjustment.[23] The atonement does not necessarily have any equivalence to the damage inflicted. The girl who steals money from an institutional staff member may polish all the furniture in the victim's room. Spontaneous restitution appears to serve as a bridge between the overt expression of inner emotional stresses and the removal of inner compulsions toward other delinquent behavior. This requires a permissive environment—one that frees the offender to choose his own means of restitution in keeping with his own needs. Dockar-Drysdale criticizes enforced restitution on the grounds that it utilizes means of restitution that are artificial to the offender and blocks the natural process by which the offender directs hostile feelings into constructive channels appropriate to his unique needs. Spontaneous retribution is more likely to relate directly to the hostile feelings and transform them into feelings of guilt and zeal for making restitution.

CORPORAL PUNISHMENTS

The popular acceptance of humanitarianism has dissipated faith in the efficacy of mutilation, branding, and flogging in halting the spread of crime. As recently as 1939, a survey by the Attorney General reported that 26 prisons were employing such corporal punishments as the lash, ball and chain, shackling, cold baths, and gagging. Negley Teeters's 1952 inquiry into prison practices found that only one of 58 prisons responding to his questionnaire acknowledged the use of flogging, and no other corporal punishments were reported.[24]

---

[21] Albert Eglash, "Creative Restitution, Some Suggestions for Prison Rehabilitation Programs," *American Journal of Correction,* 20 (November–December 1958): 20.

[22] Albert Eglash and Ernest Papanek, "Creative Restitution: A Corrective Technique and a Theory," *Journal of Individual Psychology,* 15 (November 1959): 226–30.

[23] Barbara Dockar-Drysdale, "Some Aspects of Damage and Restitution," *British Journal of Delinquency,* 4 (July 1953): 4–13.

[24] Negley K. Teeters, "A Limited Survey of Some Prison Practices and Policies," *Prison World,* 14 (May–June 1952): 5 f.

The retribution, retaliation, deterrent, and expiation arguments of the punitive ideology are most frequently advanced for corporal punishment. The presumed benefits to children of whipping are cited. "My father gave us plenty of whippings," the advocate may aver. "We didn't appreciate it then, but it certainly gave us self-discipline and good character." This oversimplification assumes that pain on the backside also makes a deep impression on the brain and that this impression is constructive from a social point of view. Even if this debatable assertion were accepted, does it support flogging for criminals? Robert Caldwell denies that the two situations are identical.[25] In one case, the idealized whipping is administered within the emotional context of the family by someone the child loves and respects. His behavior after the punishment is subject to supervision. For the criminal, flogging is formal, impersonal, and cold-blooded, administered by someone not involved personally in the offense situation. The emotional relationship between the punisher and the person punished that is present in the home situation is lacking in flogging criminals. The degrees of pain involved are not equivalent. Observers are more likely to sympathize with the person being flogged, erasing the "lesson" to be learned.

Evidence has been offered to refute the deterrent argument. In his evaluation of Delaware's whipping post, "Red Hannah," Caldwell assesses the subsequent behavior of 211 prisoners flogged in New Castle County for the years 1928, 1932, 1936, and 1940, and of 516 who legally could have been whipped but were not. Of those whipped, 66.8 percent were convicted again of some crime before 1943, and 52.1 percent were convicted of a major crime before 1943. For the unwhipped the equivalent percentages were 52.3 and 33.5 respectively.[26] In similar research the British Home Office compared the subsequent records of 440 sentenced for robbery with violence in the 1921–30 period with 142 sentenced to corporal punishment. Of those flogged 55 percent were subsequently convicted of a serious crime, compared to 43.9 percent of those not flogged.[27]

FORMS OF LENIENCY

Through its agents, society selects certain forms of deviance to be treated officially as crimes. Among deviants who thereby could be classified as criminals, some are not prosecuted officially and some are treated more leniently than the literal interpretation of the law would require. The population of law violators always is greater than that of those sub-

---

[25] Robert G. Caldwell, *Red Hannah—Delaware's Whipping Post* (Philadelphia: University of Pennsylvania Press, 1947), p. 88.

[26] Ibid., p. 78.

[27] Gordon Rose, *The Struggle for Penal Reform* (London: Stevens & Sons, 1961), p. 210.

jected to official actions. In this sense, leniency refers to the reduction or withholding of punishment of offenders, exclusive of those presumably innocent of crime.

Because "leniency" as a term has emotional undertones, the various conceptions held by those who practice, advocate, or censure it must be distinguished. Meanings attached to leniency may be grouped in two categories. The first suggests softening or relaxing of standards, thereby reducing the efficiency of some organized effort. The second suggests mildness and lack of severity, thereby reducing arbitrariness in imposition of punishment without regard for ultimate consequences. It is in the latter meaning that leniency is a legitimate societal reaction to crime.

Rehabilitative leniency

Rehabilitative leniency grants the offender some reduction in punishment, after careful study of the offender and his situation, on the reasonable expectation that he has the capacity and inclination to modify his future behavior and attitudes to bring himself into conformity with standards of good citizenship. Examples would be the granting of probation in lieu of imprisonment, reduction in the length of sentence through executive commutation, or approval of parole as a means of reducing the time spent in prison. In each instance, we assume that the decision maker was persuaded, primarily by evidence, that the reduction in penalties would promote the offender's future prosocial behavior.

Administrative leniency

Administrative leniency is the withholding of punishments in whole or in part because the results will advance the interests of society in general, of a particular agency, or of its functionaries. Full enforcement would extend the operating costs of the agency beyond the resources granted it and could involve the agency in unusual administrative detail. If it is possible to do so without risk of scandal or breakdown in agency efficiency, the burden of detail will be avoided through administrative "blindness." Full enforcement also may threaten other values through ricochet effect: all-out prosecution of the embezzler may eliminate the possibility of recovering the savings of widows and orphans.

Irrational leniency

Irrational leniency is the unsystematic and sentimental granting of exceptions in the bestowing of rewards or the withholding of punishment. Motivations for such leniency include sympathy for the underdog, personal political advantage, and friendship. The offender may abase himself before the sentencing judge, express tearful contrition, and vow improved future behavior. Without objective and complete investigation of the offender's personality and behavior, the judge may extend leniency out of sympathy in cases where accurate diagnosis would indicate sterner action. Some governors have extended pardons en masse at Christmas time or at time of leaving office, without proper investigation of the cases. Irrational leniency is encouraged by similarity between the offender and the decision maker in terms of social class, religious affiliation, occupation, and statuses. However, the major cause is the lack of objective and sound criteria in employing administrative discretion. Platitudes such as "He is entitled to a second chance" arouse humanitarian sentiments without examining probable future behavior.

Application of leniency

Leniency is applied in all three forms in the many decision-making procedures found within the system of criminal justice. Full enforcement of the law would require resources beyond the level granted to any agency. Accordingly, the number of persons processed through the system will be less than the number of candidates that would be eligible if the principles under which the agencies claim to operate were uniformly applied.

Inevitably, some proportion of the eligible candidates will benefit from irrational leniency in the form of arrests not made, cases dropped by the prosecutor, probation or suspended sentences given by the judge, or awards by prison or parole officials to reduce the length of confinement. By placing the decision maker in the role of a charitable dispenser of rewards, irrational leniency provides him with emotional satisfaction while not necessarily serving the interests of the community. Reduction in the volume of cases and agency operating costs both promotes the use of administrative leniency and is its principal benefit.

Rehabilitative leniency is the preferred form when the system has the goal of curbing crime through remedying the personality defects of the offenders and the circumstances of his environment that are conducive to further criminality. It assumes individualized and objective study of the factors involved, and the emphasis is on producing outcomes congenial to the ultimate interests of the community rather than the secondary benefits granted the decision maker.

IMPRISONMENT

Imprisonment as a form of punishment is a comparatively recent idea. When the court resorts to imprisonment, its only explicit purpose is the deprivation of liberty. If it has other purposes in mind, these usually are not communicated to prison officials in specific terms. Furthermore, the authority and responsibility of the judge do not extend into the situation the convicted offender will encounter. His keepers may be subject to statutory regulation of the manner in which they treat the inmate, but the specifics of the regime and of the forms of treatment imposed upon the inmate are determined by the prison administration in accordance with prison policies.

Correctional institutions will be discussed in subsequent chapters. Here discussion will be restricted to the subject of prison sentences. Most sentences are longer in the United States than in most other countries. Few men are sent to prison for more than five years in any Western European country.

Results of long sentences

One inevitable result of long sentences is that, by increasing the average stay in prison, they add to the size of prison populations. Excessively long sentences contribute to prison discontent and hostility, even desperation and hopelessness. This aggravates the already difficult tasks of the warden, possibly leading to riots and escape attempts. The possibility of discrepancies in length of sentences for similar crimes is increased, encouraging a conception among certain prisoners that they are victims of injustice. The loss of a sense of purpose by inmates negates rehabilitative efforts. The prisoner dependent upon commutation and parole is subjected to the tensions created by the uncertainty of his release date.

Reduction of average length of sentences has been opposed. Fears have been expressed that public safety would be endangered by subversion of the protective function of the prison. The reliance on this function assumes that all long-term prisoners are more dangerous than short-termers, although examination of prisoner case histories and behavior in prison does not support this assumption. Wardens generally agree that only a small minority of their inmates can be considered dangerous. In fact, most lifers are amenable prisoners and exceptional candidates for parole because their crimes usually reflect an absence of commitment to criminal values.

The hidden issue is whether any arbitrary policy can be as effective as one that relates length of sentence to the characteristics of the offender. The punitive ideology supports the arbitrary policy and the use of standardized sentences determined by the presumed threat of a given offense to society and its values. The policy of relating the sentence to the offender's characteristics reflects the therapeutic ideology, which emphasizes the progress of the specific inmate in meeting treatment objectives. So that long-term inmates are not released only when they reach senility or feel bitterness over loss of the fruitful years, under this policy parole would be used to release them at the point in their prison career when the probability of prosocial behavior is at a maximum.

The fear that earlier release of long-termers would result in a crime

St. Louis Post-Dispatch *(Robert LaRouche)*

Figure 12–2. Night in a prison cellblock.

If long-term imprisonment is justified as a protection of society against dangerous criminals, the keeper must maintain vigilance in the cellblock against the behavioral effects of the pains of confinement.

wave has been denied by Sol Rubin.[28] He cites occasions when large groups of long-term prisoners were released suddenly, before correctional authorities expected them to be. Examples are the release of prisoners as a result of court decisions, the World War II release of prisoners for enlistment or war work, and the releases at various times through political corruption. In these instances mass crime did not occur. Rubin would limit all terms to a maximum of five years or, as an alternative, depending upon the offenses, would favor setting two maximum limits, such as four and seven years. If the judge prefers a longer term, he would request an appellate court to increase the penalty. This procedure would restrict long sentences to extraordinary cases.

Indeterminate sentences

The Michigan state legislature enacted the first indeterminate-sentence law in 1869, but it was limited to women.[29] The *definite sentence* specifies a certain number of years. The *indefinite sentence* sets a fixed maximum and usually a fixed minimum of, say, from three to five years. The *indeterminate sentence* indicates neither minimum nor maximum limits.[30] The idealized form is open-ended; that is, the offender is released from the correctional institution, in a manner similar to medical practice, only when the institutional phase of his treatment has been completed.

Because of the complexity of human behavior, the difficulty of diagnosis, and the uncertainty in prediction of treatment results, the open-ended form would delay decision on release until the offender has been studied and treated over a longer period of time than that available to the sentencing court. This transfers the decision from the judge to the correctional agency under the therapeutic principle that the length of sentence served should be determined in accordance with the offender's capacity to meet the obligations of the free community, rather than on the basis of any punitive purpose. The indeterminate sentence is supposed to facilitate parole and protection of society through differentiation of habitual criminals from offenders more likely to be rehabilitated.

The major criticism of this practice is that indeterminate-sentence laws are passed by legislators who predict that offenders will merit a shorter sentence than judges would set under the definite-sentence law. Critics contend that the legislators are in no better position than the judges to predict the future behavior of a specific offender. However, the crucial factor is the matter of facilitation of parole, in that indeterminate

[28] Sol Rubin, "Long Prison Terms and the Form of Sentence," *NPPA Journal,* 2 (October 1956): 339–40.

[29] Zebulon R. Brockway, "Beginnings of Prison Reform in America," *Charities,* 13 (February 4, 1905): 437–44.

[30] Paul W. Tappan, *Crime, Justice and Correction* (New York: McGraw-Hill Book Co., 1960), p. 430.

sentence gives the parole authorities fuller opportunity to parole an inmate earlier. Rubin believes that these criticisms have no real merit because the parole board has discretion to release the prisoner whether the sentence is definite or indeterminate.[31] Critics also contend that the indeterminate sentence encourages hypocrisy among prisoners, is inefficient because prison and parole officials are unqualified for appropriate decision making, and lacks adequate, if any, criteria for determining release time in a responsible manner.[32] They believe the officials would be unable to distinguish between the prison-wise but incorrigible prisoner and the worthy candidate for release because some inmates would pretend to hold approved attitudes.

It has been suggested that the open-ended sentence is appropriate only for psychotic and feebleminded offenders requiring medical treatment and long-term custody.[33] The version most frequently used is a compromise which fixes minimum and maximum terms and leaves the time of release to be determined by a parole or prison board. Although this is referred to as an "indeterminate sentence" in practice, to all intents and purposes it is the "indefinite sentence." This version divides the authority between the sentencing court and the parole or prison board, paying heed to the tradition that the court has superior experience and opportunity for determining the appropriate sentence. At the same time, limited discretion is afforded correctional officials to recognize the success of treatment by shortening the period of confinement.

Debate over the open-ended sentence assumes that either the sentencing court or the correctional agency possesses the resources needed for efficient determination of the proper period of confinement. In practice both the court and the prison usually fall short. The open-ended sentence is of practical usefulness to the extent that its administrators are skillful in determining the crucial factors behind the criminality of the specific inmate, have been able to apply appropriate treatment methods, and can employ valid criteria which are capable of regularized administration. Too frequently, these qualifications are found in neither courts nor prisons.

Nevertheless, if we accept the states' description of the type of sentencing employed, the Federal Bureau of Prisons data indicate that indeterminate sentences result in longer periods behind bars than definite sentences when averages for all sentences of each type are computed. For first releases in 1960, the average number of months served was 29.5 and 27.2 months, respectively. This is consistent with the argument that indeterminate sentences offer greater social protection and assurance of

[31] Sol Rubin, "The Indeterminant Sentence: Success or Failure?" *Focus,* 28 (March 1949): 47.

[32] Nathaniel F. Cantor, "A Disposition Tribunal," *Proceedings of American Prison Association, 1937,* pp. 26–27.

[33] Paul W. Tappan, "Sentences for Sex Criminals," *Journal of Criminal Law, Criminology, and Police Science,* 42 (September–October 1951): 332.

improved behavior by holding the inmate until his treatment has been completed. This evaluation is supported in that the shorter original sentences are less characteristic of the indeterminate sentences than of the definite sentences. For original terms of five years or more including life, the indeterminate-sentence group spent a shorter average period behind bars. Of all prisoners released from indeterminate sentences, 33 percent had been given original terms of six months to five years, compared with 70.4 percent of the definite-sentence group. The dominance of the short-termers among the latter prisoners explains the lower average period of incarceration for the definite sentences; it is among the shorter-term prisoners that the delay of release for further treatment would be more likely.[34]

CAPITAL PUNISHMENT

The death penalty arouses much interest and controversy, despite the recent rarity of its infliction in the United States. Compared to the amount of concern devoted to the recipients of such sentences, the attention given to the many other prisoners in federal and state correctional institutions is negligible. The last execution in the United States took place June 2, 1967, in Colorado.[35]

In June 1972 the U.S. Supreme Court introduced a major barrier to continued use of the death penalty by reversing the sentences in three cases. By a 5-4 decision, the Court ruled that capital punishment as administered in the United States is "cruel and unusual" punishment in violation of the English Amendment. In support of the majority opinion, Justice Brennan stated:

In sum, the punishment is inconsistent with all four principles: Death is an unusually severe and degrading punishment; there is a strong probability that it is inflicted arbitrarily; its rejection by contemporary society is virtually total; and there is no reason to believe that it serves any penal purpose more effectively than the less severe punishment of imprisonment. The function of these principles is to enable the court to determine whether a punishment comports with human dignity. Death quite simply does not.[36]

Prior to this decision, efforts to abolish the death penalty usually produced a public issue; since 1950, at least half of the state legislatures have studied bills designed for this purpose. At this writing, many legislatures are debating proposals advanced by advocates of capital punish-

[34] *Prisoners Released from State and Federal Institutions, 1960* (Washington, D.C.: Federal Bureau of Prisons, April 1963), pp. 71–73.

[35] *National Prisoner Statistics: Capital Punishment, 1930–1970* (Washington, D.C.: Federal Bureau of Prisons, August 1971), p. 4.

[36] *Furman* v. *Georgia*, 225 Ga. 253, 167 S.E. 2d 628 (1969); *Jackson* v. *Georgia*, 225 Ga. 790, 171 S.E. 2d 501 (1969); *Branch* v. *Texas*, 447 S.W. 2d 932 (Tex. Ct. Crim. App. 1969); *Cert. granted*, 403 U.S. 932 (1971).

ment which, they hope, will counter the effect of the Court's decision. Their efforts add a new dimension to earlier debates which had modestly increased the number of abolition states in the 1960s. Delaware abolished the capital penalty in 1958, but it was restored in 1961 by a one-vote margin in the legislature. Nine states have abolished the penalty: Michigan (until 1963 the only capital crime was treason), 1846; Wisconsin, 1853; Maine, 1887; Minnesota, 1911; Oregon, 1964; Iowa and West Virginia, 1965, and Alaska and Hawaii, who had abolished it as territories and continued to abstain after gaining statehood. In addition, four other states have abolished capital punishment except for murder by a life prisoner and/or murder of a police officer on duty: Rhode Island (1852), North Dakota (1915), New York (1965), and Vermont (1965).

Since 1930, 10 other states have used the death penalty sparingly: New Hampshire and South Dakota (1), Idaho (3), Vermont and Nebraska (4), Montana (6), Wyoming (7), New Mexico (8), Delaware (12), and Utah (13). Since the same date the U.S. Army and Air Force have carried out 160 executions—148 during the war years of 1942–50; three each year in 1954, 1955, and 1957; and one each in 1958, 1959, and 1961. The Navy has executed no one since 1849.[37]

For the death penalty

Even if capital punishment ceases to be part of the law, the arguments over its merits will continue. Defenders center much of their case on the supposedly deterrent effect of capital punishment. They contend that its repeal would unleash criminals now restrained by their fear of the executioner. It is assumed that capital offenders are beyond hope of rehabilitation and that execution is less costly to the taxpayer than the other alternative, long imprisonment. When told that executions violate the sanctity of human life, they retort that when the murderer has shown that he respects this sanctity, the death chamber can be abolished.

Moreover, they see capital punishment as essential to the administration of criminal law. With abolishment of the supreme penalty, the vicious criminal would be less inhibited in his resort to violence against the policeman. For his own protection, the policeman would be compelled to retaliate. Therefore, the argument concludes, a spiral of increased hostility would bring more deaths of policemen in the line of duty. Substitution of life imprisonment would raise the probability that the serious offender would be released after a prison term to prey again on society. Other defenders of capital punishment criticize the use of life imprisonment on humanitarian grounds, pronouncing it inhumane to

[37] Ibid.; *National Prison Statistics: Executions, 1930–1965* (Washington, D.C.: Federal Bureau of Prisons, June 1966), p. 6.

substitute the cruelty of long years behind bars for the quick punishment of death.[38] Furthermore, they argue, life imprisonment imposes on the prison guard the ordeal of maintaining anxious watch over the lifer without hope. Then too, the advocates of retention of the death penalty warn that its repeal might result in a return to lynch law and, possibly, bring about a collapse of moral values because of the loss of the execution as a symbol of the fate of the monstrous transgressor. Major support for retention has come from law enforcement officials, judges, and district attorneys. Opposition has come from humanitarian organizations, clergymen, and social scientists.

Against the death penalty

Opponents deny the deterrent value of the death chair. They say man cannot conceive of his own death because he cannot knowingly anticipate the cessation of all experience.[39] Capital offenses tend to be committed under impulse, rather than after the calculated planning of the professional criminal. A large share of capital offenders had not been previously convicted of a crime.[40] First degree murder represents only a portion of criminal homicides, which themselves amount to less than 1 percent of total crimes. Since first degree murder is the major capital crime, capital punishment has little relationship to the total crime problem.

When Thorsten Sellin grouped states according to similar social and economic characteristics, he was unable to distinguish states that had abolished the penalty from others using it. Because the trends of homicide rates of comparable states were similar regardless of the use or nonuse of the death penalty, he concluded that executions have no discernible effect on homicide rates. Using reports from several American and European states which either tried abolition for a time or permanently abolished the death penalty, Sellin found generally no effects on the capital crime rates. He also found no significant differences when he compared rates of policemen killed in abolition states with those for capital punishment states.[41]

Opponents of the death penalty further contend that the use of death row interferes with efficient administration of justice; without the death sentence, the jury is more likely to convict. Because taking of life is a

[38] Jacques Barzun, "In Favor of Capital Punishment," in James A. McCafferty (ed.), *Capital Punishment* (Chicago: Aldine-Atherton, 1972), pp. 97–100.

[39] George Devereux, "Motivation and Control of Crime," *Journal of Psychopathy,* 3 (April 1942): 562–63.

[40] Elmer H. Johnson, "Selective Factors in Capital Punishment," *Social Forces,* 36 (December 1957): 168–69.

[41] Thorsten Sellin, *The Death Penalty* (Philadelphia: American Law Institute, 1959), pp. 34–57.

serious matter, long court procedures increase the costs of administering justice and aggravate court congestion. It has been estimated that the Caryl Chessman case in California cost the state more than half a million dollars.[42]

Capital punishment is also criticized on the grounds that it results in injustice. Many executed persons have been mentally unsound, although pronounced legally sane. Those executed tend to be disproportionately drawn from the poor and the ignorant. The innocent may be convicted under this penalty, which is irrevocable once it has been imposed; cases have been documented of convictions for crimes not committed.[43] It is contended that cases involving capital crimes are exceptionally subject to such errors because of pressures for haste in disposition and irresponsible methods in the apprehension and prosecution of suspects. In rebuttal, advocates of retention of the death penalty declare that penal laws distinguish between crimes in terms of their threat to the fundamental values of society and provide safeguards against misuse of the death penalty. They cite the long period of confinement in death row as evidence of the legal precautions taken against injustice.

Opponents of the penalty contend that the state is placed in the position of violating basic values of an enlightened society, especially humanitarian values. Abolitionists call capital punishment a grim anachronism from an earlier day when human life was held in low esteem, knowledge of human psychology was less adequate, and the spirit of revenge dominated criminal law. They describe execution as cold-blooded murder by the state, even though few capital crimes are committed so deliberately. The offender is subjected to an organized ritual of awaiting his death, although he did not impose this ordeal upon his victim. They see irony in the safeguarding of the health and continued life of the offender until the moment of execution, and even greater irony in the assignment of the duty which symbolizes the acme of the punitive ideology to prison officials committed to the treatment-therapeutic ideology. The heavy psychological burden of this duty falls upon officials who have no function in the earlier determination of guilt and sentencing.

It is argued that the administration of the death penalty is inconsistent with the principles upon which it is supposed to be based. The principle of deterrence would indicate that the execution should be given maximum public display, but it has become a private affair. To be effective,

---

[42] *Report of Joint Legislative Committee on Capital Punishment* (Harrisburg: General Assembly of Pennsylvania, June 1961), p. 12.

[43] Jerome and Barbara Frank, *Not Guilty* (Garden City, N.Y.: Doubleday & Co., Inc., 1957); Edwin M. Borchard and E. R. Lutz, *Convicting the Innocent* (Garden City, N.Y.: Garden City Publishing Co., 1934); Otto Pollak, "The Errors of Justice," *Annals of the American Academy of Political and Social Science*, 284 (November 1952): 115–23; Arthur Koestler, *Reflections on Hanging* (New York: Macmillan Co., 1957); Erle Stanley Gardner, *Court of Last Resort* (New York: William Morrow & Co., Inc., 1952).

punishment should be swift and certain, but two major trends have been an increased delay after sentencing and a decline in the number of impositions of the death penalty. In the 1960s and early 1970s, the increasing accumulation of men in death rows aggravated the stresses of confinement while awaiting this final fate and the administrative problems of managing a substantial group of people kept in idleness under these stresses.

SUMMARY

Society reacts to criminals through the institutional structure manned by officials who carry out their duties in law enforcement, courts, and corrections. These functionaries implement the general modes of societal response to criminal behavior: banishment, fines and reparations, corporal punishments, forms of leniency, imprisonment, and capital punishment. Attention, however, was concentrated on the nature of the rather disorderly system of criminal justice and the conflicts inherent in it.

FOR ADDITIONAL READING

Bedau, Hugo Adam (ed.). *The Death Penalty in America: An Anthology.* Rev. ed. Garden City, N.Y.: Anchor Books, Doubleday & Co., 1964.

Bertel, David J. "Selected Problems of Public Compensation to Victims of Crime." *Issues in Criminology,* 3 (Spring 1968): 217–31.

Blumstein, Albert, and Larsen, Richard C. "A Systems Approach to the Study of Crime and Criminal Justice." In Philip M. Morse (ed.), *Operations Research for Public Systems,* pp. 159–80. Cambridge, Mass.: M.I.T. Press, 1967.

Bresler, Fenton. *Reprieve: A Study of a System.* London, England: George G. Harrap & Co., 1965.

Burdman, Milton. "The Conflict Between Freedom and Order." *Crime and Delinquency,* 15 (July 1969): 371–76.

Chambliss, William J. "A Sociological Analysis of the Law of Vagrancy." *Social Problems,* 12 (Summer 1964): 67–77.

DiSalle, Michael V. *The Power of Life or Death.* New York: Random House, 1965.

Jacob, Bruce R. "Reparation or Restitution by the Criminal Offender to His Victim: Applicability of an Ancient Concept in the Modern Correctional Process." *Journal of Criminal Law, Criminology and Police Science,* 61 (June 1970): 152–67.

Lynch, Brent T. "Exile within the United States." *Crime and Delinquency,* 11 (January 1965): 22–29.

Reckless, Walter C. "The Use of the Death Penalty: A Factual Statement." In James A. McCafferty (ed.), *Capital Punishment.* Chicago: Aldine-Atherton, 1972.

Schwartz, Richard D., and Skolnick, Jerome H. (eds.). *Society and the Legal Order: Cases and Materials in the Sociology of Law.* New York: Basic Books, 1970.

Sigurdson, Herbert A.; Carter, Robert M.; and McEachern, A. W. "Methodological Impediments to Comprehensive Criminal Justice Planning." *Criminology,* 9 (August–November 1971): 248–67.

Swanson, Alan H. "Sexual Psychopath Statues: Summary and Analysis." *Journal of Criminal Law, Criminology, and Police Science,* 51 (July–August 1960): 215–35.

Ullrich, W. "What Does Life Imprisonment Mean?" *International Criminal Police Review,* 187 (April 1965): 97–106.

13

The police

As a law enforcement officer, my fundamental duty is to serve mankind; to safeguard lives and property; to protect the innocent against deception, the weak against oppression or intimidation, and the peaceful against violence and disorder; and to respect the constitutional rights of all men to liberty, equality and justice.

These words from the *Law Enforcement Code of Ethics* suggest the public image of law enforcement preferred by police officials. Such ideals challenge the capacities of individual policemen and their leaders to meet responsibilities vital to the interests of citizens and the community. Both citizens and policemen behave largely within organizational structures. This chapter will consider certain problems related to the achievement of these ideals within the structure of police agencies and the structure of the community as a whole.

POLICE AUTHORITY AND DEMOCRACY

In establishing the basis for our democratic institutions, the Constitution gave to the individual certain guarantees against arbitrary and authoritarian government. The original text provided for protection against being held for a crime without cause (writ of habeas corpus), being punished for an act that was not illegal when performed (ex post facto law), being singled out for punishment by an act of Congress (bill of attainder), or being convicted of treason except for specified offenses and by procedures spelled out in the Constitution. These protections were supplemented by the Bill of Rights, which prohibited "unreasonable searches and seizures" of persons, houses, papers, and effects; guaranteed "due process of law" with respect to life, liberty, and property; guaranteed the rights of the accused, including trial by jury and the right to counsel; and prohibited excessive bail or fines and cruel and unusual punishments.

The Constitutional guarantees are pertinent to police work because they imply a distrust of potential police behavior. Further, the manner in which police authority is exercised determines in large measure whether or not these guarantees emerge as realities.

Making democracy a reality

The law enforcement agency must recognize that the social equilibrium of a democratic community rests on discretion in the use of its authority. Two major distinctions between totalitarian and democratic societies are the legal limitations on police power and the sharp differentiation between police and judicial functions. It is fundamental to a democracy that arrest not be tantamount to conviction. In everyday activities, the legal safeguards affect means of suppressing criminals through arrest, use of force, and search and seizure of evidence.

In general, a police officer may arrest with or without a warrant if a crime is committed in his presence or if he has reasonable grounds for believing the suspect to be guilty of a felony. He may question a person engaged in suspicious activity in order to obtain a satisfactory explanation for conduct or a sufficient basis for a lawful arrest. The large number of arrests for "suspicion" and "disorderly conduct" suggest that police practices often depart from these criteria. The law restricts the use of force to that degree necessary to bring the arrested person within the officer's custody and control. If lawful arrest is resisted, the officer may use only such force as is reasonably necessary to overcome the resistance, unless the person arrested is charged with a felony dangerous to life.[1] Under the Fourth Amendment, search may be made under a warrant describing the place or persons to be searched and the things to be seized. Courts have permitted search incidental to a lawful arrest where the object of the search is a movable vehicle or when the accused has consented to the search.[2] However, legal ambiguities and divergencies in court interpretation place the policeman in a difficult position in this respect.

In a series of recent decisions, the U.S. Supreme Court has set guidelines concerning illegal police practices and procedural consequences. *Mapp* v. *Ohio* (1961) found that evidence obtained during an illegal search and seizure was inadmissible in both state and federal courts. *Escobedo* v. *Illinois* (1964) ruled that the suspect has a constitutional right to counsel *when arrested* and that he must be advised of his right to remain silent. The *McNabb-Mallory* rule (1953 and 1957) bars use of confessions made during illegal detention in federal cases, including failure to bring the suspect to a magistrate promptly. *Miranda* v. *Arizona* (1966) held that statements obtained as a result of police interrogation

[1] Roy C. Hall, Jr., *The Law of Arrest,* 2d ed. (Chapel Hill: University of North Carolina Press, 1961), p. 93.

[2] Richard C. Donnelly, "Police Authority and Practices," *Annals of the American Academy of Political and Social Science,* 339 (January 1962): 97.

of a suspect in custody are inadmissible at trial unless counsel has been made available to him or he has waived his right to it.

Some police executives vigorously protest such restrictions on arrest procedures as "hamstringing" the collection of evidence and apprehension of criminals. Because most arrests are made at a critical moment, O. W. Wilson contends that police should be authorized to question persons on the basis of a reasonable suspicion that a crime is contemplated and should be authorized to search a person suspected of possessing a dangerous weapon.[3] Wilson also defends the practice of holding an arrested person for at least 24 hours (excluding days when the court is not in session) before bringing him before a magistrate. He believes courts punish society when police overzealousness becomes the grounds on which guilty persons are freed. Presumably, the self-discipline of the police and the limits of public tolerance of police behavior should be sufficient to safeguard democratic rights. Lawrence Tiffany doubts that the police higher echelon has control over the day-to-day decisions of the patrolman or that courts have any capacity to control the conditions which lead to patrol malpractice.[4] Monrad Paulsen disagrees and defends the exclusion of illegally acquired evidence as the most practical way to curb possible police invasions of civic rights.[5]

The provision of legal counsel immediately upon arrest is intended to prevent the use of violence and coercion (the "third degree") to extract a confession. While agreeing that such tactics should be prohibited, Fred Inbau calls for continued use of psychological trickery in interrogation to obtain incriminating evidence from the guilty. Immediate provision of legal counsel would deny the privacy which Inbau regards as essential to such interrogation tactics.[6] Bernard Weisberg retorts that such secrecy is productive of police abuses which undermine public confidence.[7]

Distrust of governmental control

Thomas Jefferson has been identified with a political philosophy which proposed that, in a democracy, the "least government" is the "best gov-

---

[3] O. W. Wilson, "Police Arrest Privileges in a Free Society: A Plea for Modernization," in Claude R. Sowle (ed.), *Police Power and Individual Freedom* (Chicago: Aldine Publishing Co., 1962), pp. 24–51.

[4] Lawrence P. Tiffany, "The Fourth Amendment and Police-Citizen Confrontations," *Journal of Criminal Law, Criminology and Police Science,* 60 (December 1969): 442–54.

[5] Monrad G. Paulsen, "The Exclusionary Rule and Misconduct by the Police," in Sowle, *Police Power and Individual Freedom,* p. 97.

[6] Fred E. Inbau, "Police Interrogation: A Practical Necessity," in ibid., pp. 1–52.

[7] Bernard Weisberg, "Police Interrogation of Arrested Persons: A Skeptical View," in ibid., pp. 179–80.

ernment," decentralization of power is to be preferred over strong centralized government, and authority should be vested in the legislative branch to a greater degree than in the executive branch. The settlers of the American frontier also contributed to such traditions as high regard for the individual, popular participation in government, and localization of government as a means of keeping it, particularly responsive to the wishes of the individual citizen. The tendency was to see absolute liberty as equivalent to an absence of government.

Under the federal system of governmental structure established by the Constitution, police power was withheld from the national government and reserved to the states. The fragmentation of police power is an expression of the distrust of centralized government, especially in an area that is so fertile for the growth of executive tyranny.

The social institutions related to law enforcement have their origin in the freeman's participation in police work. The contemporary organizations responsible for law enforcement originated in the Anglo-Saxon period in England, when every able-bodied freeman was obligated to be a member of one of the groups of 10 men which together comprised the collective security system for the local community. When "hue and cry" was raised against a criminal, every man in earshot was required to join in the pursuit. Even with the growth of cities in England, the common citizen was expected to perform police functions. This largely voluntary system broke down when faced by powerful 18th-century gangsters, and England first distinguished between the legal powers of police officers and lay citizens in 1827, with the creation of the forerunner of modern police departments. Lay police forces have also existed in the United States, especially during the California Gold Rush, when popular tribunals and vigilance committees involved the entire community in dealing with crime waves.[8]

With the increased complexities of law enforcement in large urban areas, the informal organization of law enforcement became grossly inadequate. Because law enforcement traditionally has been regarded as a local matter in the United States, mid-19th-century efforts to cope with the manifold unprecedented problems of law enforcement were of great variety. The generally haphazard modifications have left a legacy of administrative confusion and overlapping responsibilities. The continuation of inefficiently small police units is encouraged by popular suspicion of centralized government. Agencies report to autonomous local governments. There is no fundamental coordination of activities, and functions overlap considerably. Originally, the sheriff or constable was the enforcement agent, but these officials have ceased to be a major factor out-

[8] Jerome Hall, "Police and Law in a Democratic Society," *Indiana Law Journal,* 28 (Winter 1953): 135–38.

side a few rural areas.[9] The development of rapid transportation and the movement of urban culture into rural areas have created circumstances revealing the inadequacies of sheriffs in training and equipment.

DILEMMAS OF LAW ENFORCEMENT

The difficulties of law enforcement stem from the functions served by the police in the legal system and the necessity of accommodating that system to the features of a particular community. In the legal system the primary police purpose is to deal with the criminal in action, through routine patrol, detection of crime, accumulation of evidence, and recovery of stolen property. As a component of the criminal justice system and keepers of the gateway to the judiciary and correctional systems, the police are involved in the procedural aspects of legal power. Because they are so involved, they must observe the canons of legality while facing dilemmas of making legally sound decisions, exercising internal or external control, serving conflicting purposes, and evaluating effectiveness.

Decision making

The individual patrolman is expected to make legally sound, intelligent decisions congenial to the maintenance of community order. His performance of duties is complicated by what Jerome Skolnick calls the basic dilemma of law enforcement in a democracy: a conflict between the patrolman's exercise of judgment and the pressure of police bureaucracies on subordinates to obey the rules designed to maintain the unity of the police organization.[10]

The policeman's decision as to whether or not to arrest a suspect is complicated by serious issues.[11] The discretion he must exercise is fraught with ambiguities when the intent of the criminal justice system is to recognize individual characteristics of the offender but the officer lacks either objective means or sufficient time to determine those characteristics or their relative importance. The granting of immunity to informants hinders the consistent administration of justice. The officer frequently lacks clear guidance on the quality of evidence appropriate for an arrest that will result in subsequent conviction.

The question whether the judiciary should be made a part of the arrest decision has two sides. One view is that most arrests should be made on a

[9] Virgil W. Peterson, "Issues and Problems in Metropolitan Area Police Scandals," *Journal of Criminal Law, Criminology and Police Science,* 48 (July–August 1957): 129.

[10] Jerome H. Skolnick, *Justice without Trial* (New York: John Wiley and Sons, Inc., 1966), p. 232.

[11] Wayne R. La Fave, *Arrest: The Decision to Take a Suspect into Custody* (Boston: Little, Brown & Co., 1965), pp. 492–507; Sowle, *Police Power and Individual Freedom.*

warrant obtained from a judicial officer to assure that the evidence is sufficient. A contrary argument is that such a procedure would overburden
the court, and the realities of the situation would result in routine administration. Finally, since the courts affect the ultimate significance of an
arrest by subsequently excluding evidence on grounds that it was seized
as an incident of an illegal arrest, there is a question whether such rulings
motivate police to conform to legal requirements or cause them to employ arrests for harassment and other purposes than conviction.

There are also thorny legal issues concerning the quality of investigation after the suspect is in custody. Is it desirable to allow enforcement
officers to convict him on the basis of information he provides, or is the
risk of "third degree" methods sufficient to prohibit in-custody interrogation? The issue of early access to counsel in the police station involves
weighing the possibility of impeding the investigation against the defendant's particular need of a lawyer at that time.

Defining clientele

As a social control agency, law enforcement serves the community as a
whole. It is difficult to delineate its clientele as a specific population, however. Offenders may be defined as clients receiving services to their ultimate advantage if the arrest culminates in therapy that enhances their
capacity to achieve personal goals in prosocial ways. If the consequences
are solely punitive, however, the clientele consists of the citizens who are
being protected against criminals. Since the laws being enforced reflect
the operation of the power structure in setting the priorities among values
to be protected, there are differences in the degree of protection given the
various socioeconomic groups in the community. To say that all citizens
are equals as clients for law enforcement is to ignore the realities of social
stratification. Definition of the clientele in these terms is a complex
methodological problem.

In another sense, the clientele consists of the other agencies included
in the system of criminal justice. The police administer the intake of persons referred to courts, probation, prisons, parole, and community-based
corrections. As one of the few public agencies operating around the clock,
the police also attract a clientele requiring services of a humanitarian and
therapeutic nature. These clients who confront the police in noncriminal
situations, are not assimilated into the conception of the police as enforcers of the criminal law.

Police departments are organized primarily to carry out a reactive
rather than a proactive strategy.[12] The *reactive strategy* relies on the citizen complainant to originate information on crimes. The *proactive*

[12] Albert J. Reiss, Jr., and David J. Bordua, "Environment and Organization:
A Perspective on the Police," in David J. Bordua (ed.), *The Police: Six Sociological Essays* (New York: John Wiley & Sons, Inc., 1967), p. 40.

strategy depends on the police to originate information through tactics such as surveillance and undercover work. The inquisitorial role of the latter strategy tends to create public attitudes which see law enforcement as the sole business of the police and a rather sordid affair. Reliance on the reactive strategy disregards the fact that a citizen is unlikely to report a crime in which he is not the victim. Thus police clientele afford a distorted sample of the universe of offenders.

Internal versus external control

Like all organizations, police agencies are confronted with the possibility of transgressions by individual members of the department. The deviations may be violations of regulations, improper behavior that does not violate departmental policy, or clearly illegal behavior. The President's Crime Commission lists illegal police behavior as improper political influences, nonenforcement of laws (especially those related to organized crime), "fixing" of traffic tickets, minor thefts, and occasional thefts.[13]

Police agencies seek to police their own functionaries by either internal or external control. *Internal control* refers to the imposition by the police agency of administrative controls to prevent misconduct of its personnel or in reaction to it. The President's Crime Commission says the agency must go beyond the mere announcement of policies in ambivalent compliance with court decisions or reluctant response to citizen complaints. The inherent difficulties of monitoring the behavior of officers dispersed throughout a large area calls for the will to conform to ethical standards on the part of both supervisory and field personnel.[14] Formalized regulations are unlikely to cover all the contingencies that can arise in the heterogeneous events spontaneously encountered by patrolmen.

Police transgressions and scandals are consequences of a cultural environment that goes beyond the behavior of the individual officer. So-called "good citizens" contribute to a general moral erosion by offering bribes, supporting the custom of "handouts" of merchandise to officers, and demanding that "undesirable" elements in the community receive vigorous police reactions. Inadequate police salaries play an obvious part, but insufficient budgets have other less tangible effects. Departments affected by scandals have usually suffered from a lack of competent

[13] For amplification of points made in this section, see President's Commission on Law Enforcement, *Task Force Report: The Police* (Washington, D.C.: U.S. Government Printing Office, 1967), chaps. 2, 6, and 7.

[14] See Herman Goldstein, "Administrative Problems in Controlling the Exercise of Police Authority," *Journal of Criminal Law, Criminology and Police Science,* 58 (June 1967): 160–72; Robert L. Derbyshire, "The Social Control Role of the Police in Changing Urban Communities," *Excerpta Criminologica,* 6 (May–June 1966): 315–21.

supervisory personnel who could have hindered commission of crimes by policemen by spot checking their activities. These departments also were found to have antiquated equipment, inadequate administration, and low standards for recruiting policemen.[15] Such conditions favor the persistence of an occupational subculture which presses officers to tolerate the transgressions of their colleagues or to consider the transgressions as "normal" behavior.

External control emanates from sources outside the police agency, such as the executives of local government, the district attorney, or the judiciary. Control by city councils and mayors raises the possibility of involvement in politics. Elected officials rarely use their power to review police behavior that draws citizen complaints. Public discussion of issues and policies would mitigate the secrecy which promotes improper political influence. The district attorney's interest in police operations is limited to cases likely to involve prosecution. Control by the judiciary tends to be haphazard and dependent on the personal values of the individual judge and many forms of police misconduct are not violations of the criminal law.

Vehicles have also been set up for civilian review of charges of police transgressions. *Citizen advisory committees* involve members of the community in policy making, but in some cases the function is advisory only, and police agencies are not bound by the recommendations. If an officer is guilty of misconduct, civil damages are legally available, but this course of action is restricted by legal expenses and the difficulty of establishing proof.

Civilian review boards, created to investigate and determine the validity of citizen complaints, have stimulated hot debate. They have operated in Washington, D.C., Philadelphia, Rochester, and New York City. After a heated campaign in New York City, the civilian board was replaced by one composed of civilian police employees. The boards have been accused of bureaucratic sloth, obscure procedures, and inadequate investigation. However, studies of the work of such boards have indicated that police morale is not preceptibly impaired, tensions over law enforcement have been alleviated, and complainants generally have been favorably impressed.

The *ombudsman* is an official with the duty to receive citizens' complaints and authority to obtain the appropriate information from governmental agencies to determine the merits of the complaints. In Sweden, where the office has existed since 1809, the ombudsman has the power

---

[15] Virgil W. Peterson, "The Chicago Police Scandals," *Atlantic Monthly,* 206 (October 1960): 62–64; Mort Stern, "What Makes a Policeman Go Wrong?" *Journal of Criminal Law, Criminology and Police Science,* 53 (March 1962): 100; Quinn Tamm, "Rebuilding a Scandal-Torn Police Force," *Police Chief,* 29 (February 1962): 35.

to order prosecution, but public reprimand or criticism usually is sufficient. The extension of this concept to American government is another
possibility for external control.[16]

Determining success

Law enforcement agencies exist because there is a discrepancy between the behavior of some persons and the ideal behavior visualized by
the framers of laws. When law is observed, law enforcement is unnecessary. Law enforcement may be seen as something to be regretted—an
expression of our incapacity to arrange our own affairs.[17] Law enforcement agencies seek to eliminate nonobservance and achieve a state of
human "perfection" in which the effectiveness of conscience and other
informal controls will end the need for formal laws. Thus these agencies
are trying to put themselves out of business.

This view complicates the reliability of criteria to be used in evaluating
police effectiveness. Generally, police success is rated according to data
on police activities: crime rates, arrests, crimes cleared by arrest, value
of solen property recovered. Another criteria could be the solution of a
particular crime problem that has incited public outrage. A rising arrest
rate may indicate police effectiveness in the short term, but ultimately it
is a symptom of declining law observance. Attitudes toward law observance stem from the community's culture; they are not solely a product
of police actions.

The policeman is encouraged to see himself primarily as a guardian of
public order. When his success is measured by such factors as crimes
cleared by conviction, he is placed in a quandry by court lectures on
techniques of interrogation, status of confession, and the use of force.
Dismissal of charges against arrested suspects affects police morale when
they believe their authority on the street and their task performance have
been undermined.

Reliance on criteria such as crimes cleared by arrest raises another
crucial issue: Is it in the public interest that a police bureaucracy be created so that every offender is known and equally subjected to its administration?[18] Assume that police agencies are successful in increasing their
enforcement effectiveness through improvements in management and
utilization of personnel. Assume also that progress in computer and surveillance technology can be exploited to increase the capacity of the

[16] Timothy D. Naegele, "Civilian Complaints against the Police in Los Angeles," *Issues in Criminology,* 3 (Summer 1967): 7–34.

[17] Karl N. Llewellyn, "Law Observance versus Law Enforcement," *Proceedings
of the National Conference of Social Work, 1928,* pp. 127–38.

[18] Jerome H. Skolnick and J. Richard Woodworth, "Bureaucracy, Information,
and Social Control: A Study of a Morals Detail," in Bordua, *The Police,* pp. 99–
136.

police to be aware of law violations regardless of citizen complaints. In light of the use of criminal law to regulate moral behavior, it must be considered whether police efficiency as measured by arrests is congenial with the long-term interests of a democratic society.

Conflicting purposes

Although the primary police purpose is to deal with criminals in action, most daily transactions are related to such secondary purposes as crime prevention and a wide variety of regulatory functions not concerned directly with criminals. Crime prevention on the manifest level is consistent with the primary purpose in that it involves the deterrent effects of regular patrol and relative certainty of apprehension. In the latent level it moves outside law enforcement to promote law observance. Educational campaigns are conducted and cooperation with other community agencies is encouraged in programs designed to forestall the development of criminal careers. Police regulatory functions include direction of automobile traffic, enforcement of sanitation and licensing regulations, control of crowds, action against obscene literature, civilian defense, and disaster duty. These secondary functions make the policeman the representative of government in matters not involving actual criminal behavior and thrust him into the roles of public servant and peace-keeper.

POLICE ROLES IN RELATIONS WITH THE PUBLIC

Police service is the sum of a host of one-to-one relationships between an officer and another person under a variety of circumstances. The officer is tested intellectually, emotionally, ethically, and physically to a degree equaled in other vocations only by those drawing much greater economic and social rewards. Unpredictable events must be evaluated quickly and intelligently. Officers must have the social and psychological skills necessary to effectively manage interactions with citizens.[19] Emotional maturity is required in the use of authority under circumstances which arouse hostilities and other emotions among participants. Because he encounters many persons with deficient ethics, the policeman must have strong moral fiber.

Paradoxically, the most severe test of the dedicated officer frequently is imposed by the very order he is expected to maintain. An agent of formal control in society, the policeman himself is subject to informal and formal controls that press him to conform with role norms intended to fit him into a social scheme. He experiences role conflict when he does not receive clear or consistent guidelines on what a "good policeman"

---

[19] James R. Hudson, "Police-Citizen Encounters that Lead to Citizen Complaint," *Social Problems,* 18 (Fall 1970): 179–84.

should do. Then, in spite of the best of intentions, the officer finds his role performance to be unsatisfactory because of failures of the social structure within which he functions.[20]

Guardian of society

The primary function of the police emphasizes the *guardian-of-society* role wherein the state's authority is used legitimately to protect citizens against criminals. Coercion, discretion, strained relations with the public, restrictions on self-interest, occupational tensions, and secrecy are often components of this role.

Force is not restricted to governmental affairs. Individuals fight one another. Parents spank their children. Violence occurs in labor-management disputes. Vigilantes seize "undesirable" persons. These are unusual occurrences, however, whereas the police officer has the occupational prerogative to employ force whenever required.

Certain occupations emphasize the necessity of practitioners to use discretion in applying the authority conferred on them. Physicians, psychiatrists, judges, military officers, and even college professors make decisions in matters of grave importance to individuals under their control. They occupy status positions in social systems which grant them authority related to the achievement of the objectives of the systems. Their occupational training is supposed to yield the specialized knowledge and occupational ethics essential to the proper use of authority. It is possible that individuals in such status positions will exploit this authority to enhance their own prestige, to advance personal economic ends, or to persecute individuals under their control.

Similarly, the policeman's authority is necessary to the function of law enforcement within the social system of the community,[21] but this authority also can be perverted.[22] Therefore, responsible police management recognizes the importance of careful selection of recruits and training of policemen to avoid producing a "bully with a badge."

Authority associated with the guardian-of-society role is likely to isolate the policeman from many of the citizens he is called on to protect. Public attitudes do not universally present a united front against criminals, nor does the public always actively support the apprehension of criminals. It is difficult at times to distinguish noncriminals from criminals in moral philosophy. Some laws to be enforced do not receive the support of a universal moral consensus.

[20] Elmer H. Johnson, "Police: An Analysis of Role Conflict," *Police,* 14 (January–February 1970): 47–52.

[21] The police uniform itself symbolizes this authority to both the wearer and the perceiver; see Nathan Joseph and Nicholas Alex, "The Uniform: A Sociological Perspective," *American Journal of Sociology,* 77 (January 1972): 719–30.

[22] William A. Westley, "Violence and the Police," *Social Forces,* 34 (March 1956): 354–57.

These factors, along with the affinity of a common job experience, result in self-identifications favorable to the creation of colleague groups among policemen. Acceptance into the fraternity of badge wearers is one answer to the effects of attitudes which invest the police occupation with some of the qualities of a minority group.[23] Police morale is highly susceptible to public attitudes. A study of police attitudes after departmental reform found sergeants who had favorable opinions regarding increased departmental efficiency were low in morale because they believed citizen respect and cooperation had not increased accordingly. Those officers who did not think well of the department were not affected by their perception of citizen attitudes.[24]

The policeman's actions are subject to close scrutiny and criticism because his obligations are defined by the police agency as being as sacred and direct as those of a wartime soldier. He is expected to demonstrate loyalty and organizational discipline, live an exemplary private life, and be available for duty at all hours. These restrictions on the officer's self-interest should be interpreted in the context of other factors: the growing size and complexity of police bureaucracies, the greater emphasis on administrative control to increase efficiency, and the mounting pressure on patrolmen from pressure groups involved in racial and other community controversies.

These developments add to the role conflicts of the policeman who sees himself as the guardian of society and help explain the establishment of police unionism. Hervey Juris found a third of all cities of over 50,000 population were engaged in a collective bargaining relationship with their police employee organizations in 1968. Critics oppose police unionism as a movement designed only to protect the self-interests of police employees. They argue that the movement undermines community safety by strikes and hinders the improvement of police effectiveness through recruiting better personnel and rewarding the most capable policemen with job promotion. There is also fear that police unionism favors the politicization of employees through participation in legislative and party politics, to the detriment of the overall police organization.[25]

All occupations have their secrets, withheld from those not admitted to occupational colleagueship. So do the police. Restrictions on expression of self-interest, occupational tensions, threats to job tenure, and limited economic opportunities are common experiences of the officer. Group identity requires winning acceptance as a member of the inner group and thereby gaining access to the secrets of the occupation, acquired through informal contacts with colleagues. These relationships

23 Stern, "What Makes a Policeman Go Wrong?" p. 99.

24 James Q. Wilson, "Police Morale, Reform, and Citizen Respect," in Bordua, *The Police*, p. 155.

25 Hervey A. Juris, "The Implications of Police Unionism," *Law and Society Review*, 6 (November 1971): 231–45.

give emotional support against the uncertainties of interactions between the patrolman and the police hierarchy and the pressures that come from outside the police organization. This colleagual loyalty can have the effect of protecting the law-violating, unethical officer.[26]

Paradoxically, the guardian-of-society role provides a veil of occupational secrecy to conceal police practices from the public being protected. Secrecy is employed to gain and maintain a psychological advantage over the suspect. In the battle of wits with the suspect, the detective places a mantle of secrecy about the clues he obtains, regardless of the civil rights identified with American democracy. In this way he can, perhaps, snarl the suspect in inconsistent statements. To preserve their communications network regarding criminal activities, police protect from other criminals and their own colleagues the petty offenders who supply information. Such covert police affiliations with "enemies of society" can come under public suspicion.

Peace-keeper

Charged with preserving order in the community, the policeman as *peace-keeper* is required to perform a variety of tasks, from enforcing traffic regulations, through settling of a family dispute disturbing a neighborhood, to dealing with a large-scale riot. He must find a balance between individual rights and public interests or between behavioral problems and threats to the community safety.

Michael Banton distinguishes between the ordinary patrolman and specialists such as detectives, traffic officers, and members of vice and fraud squads. The contacts of these specialists tend to be of an inquisitory character, chiefly with offenders or persons with information about offenses. Patrolmen interact with all sorts of people. Most of their contacts center on assisting citizens rather than apprehending offenders. In his research contacts with patrolmen, Banton was struck by the high proportion of instances in which the power to arrest was not invoked. Officers in these instances were operating within the informal control context of community mores rather than as officials exercising authority as officeholders.[27]

Instrument of the law

Through regulations not directly concerned with crime, the policeman frequently becomes a third party in disputes. His arrest decisions may fix

[26] Ellwyn R. Stoddard, "The Informal 'Code' of Police Deviancy: A Group Approach to 'Blue-Coat Crime,'" *Journal of Criminal Law, Criminology and Police Science*, 59 (June 1968): 201–13.

[27] Michael Banton, *The Policeman and the Community* (New York: Basic Books, Inc., 1964), pp. 6–7.

liability in civil cases or extend the stigma of crime to such incidents as automobile accidents, labor disputes, and racial strife. He is an agent of the law as a means of settling disputes and accommodating conflicting interests. His task is to preserve the basic orderliness which makes possible the host of social transactions forming the social life of the community.

In times of rapid social change in a democracy, this role is complicated because the policeman is not the framer of laws and maker of mores. In a period of civil strife, he is called on to "do something" although there are conflicting instructions from the many segments of the power structure. The leaders at the top of the structure may seek to employ police authority to resist the accommodative process whereby a new equilibrium can be reached. At best, police coercion is only one phase of the total process of reorganizing community relationships to meet new circumstances. The difficulties for police in applying the law objectively are illustrated by the disturbances associated with the civil rights movement.

Public servant

The officer is cast as a humanitarian when he performs duties as a *public servant* in finding lost children, recovering drowned bodies, referring individuals for emergency health services, mediating family dissention, providing ambulance services, and so on. The preponderance of such services is illustrated by a study showing only 16 percent of all telephone calls received by Detroit police in 1968 were related to predatory crime.[28]

The involvement of police in such services is attributable in large measure to the failure of other community agencies to provide round-the-clock service over an entire city. The police fill an institutional vacuum because they deal with problems of the poor and ignorant that other social agencies are not anxious to serve. Because community services are not organized to afford an effective functional division of labor among the agencies to provide specialized emergency services, the police must do so, although more qualified agencies do not recognize their work as legitimate.[29]

Whether the police should be involved in community service is debated. One view is that the guardian-of-society role is primary, the public-servant role impedes genuine police work. Then too, at least some of the service functions can be handled better by more specialized agencies. On the other hand, the public-servant role is the most effective means of gaining the public confidence essential to guardian-of-society functions.

[28] Thomas E. Bercal, "Calls for Police Assistance," *American Behavioral Scientist,* 13 (July–August 1970): 682.

[29] Elaine Cumming, Ian Cumming, and Laura Edell, "Policeman as Philosopher, Guide and Friend," *Social Problems,* 12 (Winter 1965): 276–86.

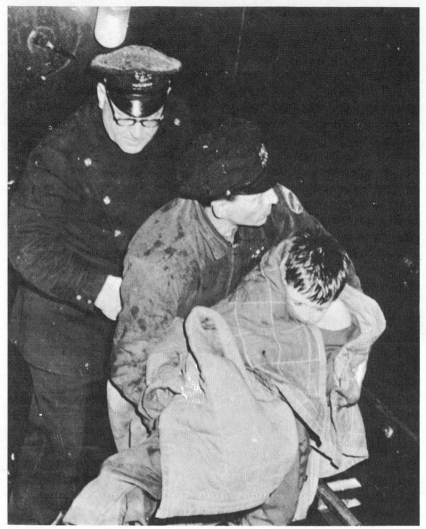

Figure 13–1. Expansion of police duties.

The emergency service squads of metropolitan police agencies are an example of the expansion of police duties outside the enforcement of criminal law. These squads handle emergencies involving machinery, gases, debris, poisons, and electricity and are responsible for rescuing people from elevators, shafts, excavations, and other unusual places.

Prevention of crime

As the first line of defense against crime, the policeman has early contact with offenders and potential delinquents. As a *preventer of crime* he is expected to use this opportunity to divert individuals from the path to crime.

One conception of preventive work by police emphasizes employment of the *suppression and control* methods of law enforcement activities. Routine patrol and inspection give special attention to places of commercialized recreation and uninhabited structures because of the opportunities they offer for the expression of delinquent tendencies. Investigation of unusual occurrences or crimes may reveal adult behavior contributing to juvenile delinquencies. Surveillance of known criminals, statistical analysis and mapping of crime locations, and maintenance of files on operational techniques of known criminals are other methods. Advocates of strict law enforcement tend to see direct methods as the key to crime prevention: better street lighting, additional locks on doors, and the punishment of persons who leave keys in parked automobiles.

Curfew laws are a police measure frequently used to curb juvenile crimes. The objective is to impress the parents with their responsibility to control the associations children are likely to make on the street at night. Critics of the curfew measure contend that the causes of crime are too diverse to justify the belief that late hours on the streets are a major factor. The effectiveness of suppression is questioned because the curfew does not change a delinquent's personal character or needs. Only a small proportion of children are delinquents, but those out at night for legitimate reasons are subject to police questioning. Recent decades have brought radical changes in the legitimate pattern of living for juveniles, so that normal activities are likely to be disrupted by the curfew. Further, delinquencies are as likely to occur before the curfew deadline as afterward, and the constitutionality of curfew laws has been questioned.

A *therapeutic conception of prevention* by police requires them to make discriminative use of the power of arrest to open the way for treatment of the fundamental causes of an offense. Recognition of significant cues to personal or social difficulties may transform a traumatic incident into an opportunity for crime prevention.

Both the policeman and the schoolteacher are in strategic positions to detect signs of incipient delinquency. Because of the social circumstances of their work, however, the function of "delinquency detection" is more congenial to the teacher's role than to that of the patrolman. Teachers are oriented toward individual differences and psychological controls. Their contacts with individuals and the general public cause teachers to identify themselves, and to be identified with, the therapeutic ideology. They are in relatively long-term contact with their "clients," who are primarily children. Their interest in children is unlikely to arouse suspicion. The primary function of the patrolman is to deter, detect, and apprehend criminals in action. Police contacts with individuals and the general public tend to be segmental, highly specialized, and authoritarian. Children compose only one segment of the population with whom the patrolman comes in contact in performing his tasks, and legal safeguards for the accused person tend to compress the length of time of such contacts.

The police face additional difficulties in therapeutic prevention. The statutes usually are vague or unsystematic in giving answers on police responsibility and authority in regard to juveniles. If a juvenile is a violator of criminal statutes, the police authority is clear. But the juvenile court laws also include situations which do not involve violation of the law. If the individual does not agree to cooperate, police authority is nebulous. If the individual is a child, the officer must decide whether he is sufficiently mature and sophisticated to give consent to waive legal safeguards against questioning or search without a legal basis for arrest.[30]

LAW ENFORCEMENT AND THE COMMUNITY

The processes of urbanization and industrialization have produced large aggregations of people dependent on one another for goods and services, but with only infrequent and transitory interpersonal contacts. The sentimental bonds among individuals and groups that produce a sense of community therefore must be supported by written codes and formal controls. In the face of fundamental changes in the community, law enforcement agencies must determine how their authority can be utilized to maintain order without jeopardizing the social consensus essential to the preservation of the community. If the power structure of a community had condoned the use of police to maintain a system of racial segregation, for example, the revolution in racial mores would find policemen called "brutes" for the behavior which previously gained them honor as protectors of community solidarity.[31] The style of law enforcement strongly marks the quality of life in a given community, but, conversely, the attitudinal climate of the community affects the quality of law enforcement.

Police and community attitudes

The familiar saying, "A community has the police force it deserves," is usually related to financial support. It can also refer, however, to the

---

[30] Richard A. Myren and Lynn D. Swanson, *Police Work with Children* (Washington, D.C.: U.S. Children's Bureau, 1962), pp. 26–33.

[31] Elmer H. Johnson, "A Sociological Interpretation of Police Reaction and Responsibility to Civil Disobedience," *Journal of Criminal Law, Criminology and Police Science,* 58 (September 1967): 405–9.

extent that the community mores support the legal norms. These mores are always applied to the traditional crimes of murder, rape, and theft, but the newer areas of regulation do not necessarily elicit their support. The police often encounter ambivalent attitudes toward them. Reckless driving is deplored when tragedy results, but risk-taking in automobiles may be deemed a praiseworthy demonstration of youthful exuberance, individualistic scorn of conventionality, or competitive attitudes toward driving skills and horsepower. In some circles, a traffic conviction is a prestige symbol.

Since law enforcement ideally is intended to create a state of universal law observance, the policeman's work is educational in the broad sense. Repression and control measures are part of the total system of criminal justice which holds the fundamental premise that punishment will deter crime. However, policemen are too few to maintain surveillance that is sufficiently intense and continuous to apprehend all law violators. Under the principle of deterrence, an arrest is intended to modify the attitudes of offenders and potential offenders who observe the consequences of law violation. Ultimately, it is hoped the attitudes of the total community would be made consistent with law observance.

As citizens themselves, policemen reflect the attitudes prevalent in their community. When police brutality and corruption exist, they may stem from the personal qualities of particular policemen, from the recurrent experiences of dealing with violent and corrupt persons, or from the functioning of the police agency as a social system. However, it is difficult for brutality and corruption to exist to any important degree over the long term unless there is support among major segments of the population for such deviation. Even extralegal police actions against such unpopular targets as "radicals" are unlikely to draw censure or disapproval from the substantial proportion of Americans that politically condones attitudes that lead to such actions.[32]

The police probably are best equipped to deal with the traditional crimes of murder, rape, and aggravated assault, but these are only a small part of total crimes. A high proportion of arrests involves consumption of alcohol and gambling. The definition of these moral transgressions as crimes reflects societal efforts to bring some deviants under social control by the use of law enforcement techniques associated with the suppression of crime. Meanwhile, other otherwise respectable people freely engage in the behavior prohibited by these laws. This discrepancy places the police in the position of enforcing laws against some persons while they are not obeyed by a substantial number of those they were intended to serve.

[32] William A. Gamson and James McEvoy, "Police Violence and Its Public Support," *Annals of American Academy of Political and Social Science,* 391 (September 1970): 97–110.

Legitimacy and public relations

"Public relations," generally agreed to be an important aspect of law enforcement, is interpreted in various ways. In one view, current practices are deemed proper and effective; once the public is "informed," police problems are supposed to vanish. This "ballyhoo" version of public relations casts the police in the paternalistic role of the father who "knows best." Another conception is based on the concept that effective policing requires an understanding of community problems from the perspectives of the many publics it is supposed to serve.[33] Recognizing the functions of the police in maintaining the community as a social system serving its members, this community conception of public relations assumes that some meaningful accommodation can be found among the dissimilar or conflicting interests involved in community controversies.

The pertinence of the latter conception is underlined when the police image is eroded by antagonism between police and citizens, as evidenced by community indifference toward police problems, charges of police brutality, or complaints of insufficient police protection. To a great extent, the police-community relations problem is a racial one.[34] A mounting loss of public confidence in police practices was reflected in Harlan Hahn's survey of attitudes of residents of a Detroit black ghetto. About 80 percent of the respondents expressed beliefs that policemen treated some groups better than others, were more interested in keeping things quiet than helping neighborhood people, and were themselves involved in thefts and arson during riots. Many respondents indicated they would not request police assistance in an automobile accident or robbery.[35]

Such reports of the deteriorated image of law enforcement strikes at the heart of the police monopoly over legitimate coercion in the community. "Legitimacy" refers to the acceptance by citizens of this use of power as proper because they believe the norms being enforced *should* be binding on their behavior. Ultimately, effective police use of coercion depends on what the mores of the community will support as proper. When the policeman moves beyond the limits of those mores, coercion only breeds further coercion. This cycle eventually reaches a point where generated resistance deprives police power of the legitimacy that justifies it. To prevent the appearance or continuance of this cycle, the community

[33] Elmer H. Johnson, "Interrelatedness of Law Enforcement Programs: A Fundamental Dimension," *Journal of Criminal Law, Criminology and Police Science,* 60 (December 1969): 514–15.

[34] Deborah Johnson and Robert J. Gregory, "Police-Community Relations in the United States," *Journal of Criminal Law, Criminology and Police Science,* 62 (March 1971): 96.

[35] Harlan Hahn, "Ghetto Assessments of Police Protection and Authority," *Law and Society Review,* 6 (November 1971): 183–94.

version of public relations assigns the police agency the responsibility of being aware, and responsive to, community mores. This calls for flexibility in the face of dynamic conditions in community life—a flexibility that is suppressed by the "ballyhoo" version of public relations.

The community version of public relations can involve citywide advisory councils, neighborhood advisory committees, youth discussion groups, or police-community relations storefronts as means of developing two-way communication between the police and the public. Some departments establish police-community relations divisions as separate operating units, thereby giving the patrolman on the street the impression that community relations is something someone else in authority does. Community relations, however, must be a part of daily police operations on the street. Data from a study of patrol contacts indicate that citizens were more appreciative of and satisfied with police action when the officers thoroughly investigated the disturbance or crime incident or demonstrated concern for the persons involved. The researchers concluded that community relations must be based on reliable and continuing assessment of the impact of police practices on citizens contacted by officers.[36] Then the specific means of promoting congenial relationships with antagonistic groups and the training of officers can be directed at the crux of the problem of deteriorating public confidence.

POLICE SCIENCE

Criminalistics has been defined as the application of the physical sciences to the investigation of crimes.[37] Chemistry, physics, biology, physical anthropology, medicine, and mathematics offer concepts and tools for uncovering and evaluating physical evidence. With personnel trained in criminalistics, police departments are able to exploit the value of evidence by applying such techniques as firearm and fingerprint identification, X-ray and ultraviolet examination, photography, hair and fiber identification, analysis of typewritten and handwritten documents, casting of footprints and tire marks, examination of bloodstains and crime tools, and tests for intoxication and toxicity. Statistics are applied to test the significance of measurements and the probability of a particular relationship occurring. Examples would be determining the probable error in an estimate of an automobile's speed on the basis of skid marks, or estimating the possibility of two vehicles having the same arrangement of four brands of tires.

[36] David J. Bordua and Larry L. Tifft, "Citizen Interviews, Organizational Feedback, and Police-Community Relations Decisions," *Law & Society Review,* 6 (November 1971): 155–94.

[37] Charles E. O'Hara and James W. Osterburg, *An Introduction to Criminalistics* (New York: Macmillan Co., 1959).

The polygraph

While the polygraph is popularly known as a "lie detector," it is really an emotion indicator. It records changes in the subject's blood pressure, pulse, and respiration. If the emotions of the subject affect these physiological activities, the device so indicates. However, the accuracy of the "lie detection" lies in the examiner's skills and perception in framing questions and in evaluating the subject's physiological responses. Accuracy may be affected by the nervousness of the subject because of the mere fact that he is suspected or because he has a sense of guilt from behavior unrelated to the crime; by physiological abnormalities such as diseases of the heart, mental abnormalities, and unobserved muscular movements; and by physiological or psychological conditions which inhibit the subject's responses.[38]

When proper safeguards are taken against the possibility of misinterpretation of emotional responses, examination by a competent polygraph examiner has advantages for law enforcement. Innocent persons are released sooner. Time, effort, and money are saved in investigation. The polygraph can determine the location of loot or weapons and can determine whether a claim of robbery losses has been inflated falsely. Deception can be ascertained with greater ease and certainty. The testing procedure has a psychological effect in inducing offenders to confess. The possible and actual use of the polygraph can prevent thefts from business.

Technological developments

Technology affords devices and techniques for dealing with law enforcement problems. The President's Crime Commission suggested possibilities for the use of technology to help police determine and apprehend criminals.[39] In many metropolitan departments, electronic computers process the enormous quantities of information associated with investigation, apprehension, and arrest. Communication centers hasten responses to calls for the police and systematize the allocation of personnel and equipment. Portable two-way radios increase the effectiveness of foot patrolmen. Nonlethal weapons enable the officer to subdue aggressive offenders without danger to bystanders. Innovative design could produce a police car with convenient radio controls, evidence-collecting equipment, devices to improve visibility, report-dictating equipment, and magnetometers to detect concealed weapons. If the time gap between the developments of physical science and their introduction into police prac-

[38] Fred E. Inbau, *Lie Detection and Criminal Interrogation* (Baltimore: Williams and Wilkins Co., 1948), p. 30.

[39] President's Commission on Law Enforcement and Administration of Justice, *Task Force Report: Science and Technology* (Washington, D.C.: U.S. Government Printing Office, 1967), chaps. 2 and 3.

Figure 13–2. Hub of Chicago Police communications.

The Chicago Police communications system controls over 1,800 vehicles covering 224 square miles and serves over 3.5 million people. The system utilizes 29 radio frequencies, 10 base transmitter locations with three satellite receiver stations, and 65 telephone trunk lines to receive emergency calls. There are three-abreast consoles and computer inquiry stations for each of the eight city zones. Above each console is an illuminated map showing the zone boundaries and numbers of all patrol car beats. Some consoles are citywide in coverage. One provides contact with all motor units. Two communicate with Detective, Youth, Task Force, and Headquarters units, and another with Traffic and Staff Services units.

tice were closed or shortened, crime laboratories would quickly become more efficient.

The effectiveness of surveillance can be strengthened through use of miniature microphones and recording equipment, wiretaps, closed-circuit television cameras, two-way mirrors, and parabolic microphones. An electronic system used to monitor the heart rate and geographical location of cardiac patients can be adapted to keep individuals, such as parolees, under surveillance.[40] Such a monitoring device would safeguard the community from chronic offenders without imprisonment, but on the other hand, it would invade privacy and threaten civil liberties by extending the range of surveillance.

PROBLEMS OF MANAGEMENT

Police organization is a conglomeration of overlapping agencies, especially in metropolitan centers. There were some 40,000 public law enforcement agencies on three levels of government, employing more than 371,000 men and women and costing over $2.5 billion, in 1965. Of the agencies 50 were federal, 200 state, 3,050 county, and 3,700 city, with most of the remainder distributed throughout boroughs, towns, and villages. All agencies were plagued at the time with serious manpower problems, perennial incapacity to maintain authorized strength, and personnel turnover.[41]

Organizational decentralization and fragmentation are carried to an extreme in the United States, a result of the disorder characteristic of the rapid growth of cities and the emphasis on localization of police power. The machinery of management and control of law enforcement agencies has been subjected to continual experiment and modification, with the result that a bewildering array of organizational schemes is to be found among American police departments. Police scandals stimulate experimentation with the organizational scheme, under the illusion that this is a cure-all for all human deficiencies.

Management deficiencies

The President's Crime Commission reported American law enforcement to be subject to serious management deficiencies:[42]

Many departments lack qualified leadership; there are no minimum standards of education and achievement for administrators and middle managers. Few departments offer training at this level. A 1964 study re-

[40] Ralph K. Schwitzgebel, "Issues in the Use of an Electronic Rehabilitation System with Chronic Recidivists," *Law & Society Review,* 3 (May 1969): 597–615.

[41] President's Commission on Law Enforcement, *Task Force Report: The Police,* pp. 7–11.

[42] Ibid., pp. 44–56.

vealed only 33.6 percent of America's police administrators had attended college, and of these only 9.2 percent possessed a degree.[43] The ladder to executive status usually is up through the ranks, with only chance opportunities to gain the prerequisite experience and knowledge.

Many departments are not organized according to well-established principles of management. Through unplanned evolution, many police forces are characterized by diffusion of authority, confused responsibility, lack of strong lines of direction and control, and improper grouping of functions.

Many departments resist change, fail to determine shortcomings of existing practice, and are reluctant to experiment with alternative methods of solving problems.

Many departments lack trained personnel in such fields as research and planning, law, business administration, and computer analysis. With the growth of police organizations, efficient management requires continual revision of plans and procedures, inspection to assure task performance and to root out corruption, and legal counsel.

Many departments fail to deploy and utilize personnel efficiently. Patrolmen are not distributed to be where crimes are most likely to occur. Supervision of personnel is frequently inadequate, providing opportunities for corruption. Traditionally, patrol and investigative forces have separate lines of command and tend to be isolated from one another. In addition, investigators are often divided into vice, robbery, burglary, fraud, homicide, and other squads which keep separate records and maintain separate operations. Foot patrol and two-man motor patrol, frequently used unnecessarily, waste manpower. Excessive and duplicate report writing diverts personnel from field duty.

Recruitment and retention

The intelligent employment of police authority depends ultimately on the qualifications of the individuals who deal directly with the diverse populations of urban society and the array of events that comprises law enforcement work. A recent Brookings Institution study revealed serious police manpower shortages resulting from decades of political neglect, public apathy, and police parochialism. Police agencies generally are understaffed and face serious difficulties in recruiting sufficient new personnel to fill job slots. A significant percentage of the men already on the force are unsuitable for modern law enforcement.[44] These deficiencies are more a matter of higher expectations for performance in light of the

[43] George W. O'Connor and Nelson A. Watson, *Juvenile Delinquency and Youth Crime: The Police Role* (Washington, D.C.: International Association of Chiefs of Police, 1964), p. 79.

[44] Charles B. Saunders, Jr., *Upgrading the American Police* (Washington, D.C.: Brookings Institution, 1970), p. 35.

increased demands urban conditions place on law enforcement than one of a deteriorating quality of policemen on the average.

The President's Crime Commission reported that in 1965 most departments fail to screen out incompetent candidates.[45] At that time, however, almost all large departments were below their authorized strength, and the proportion of candidates being accepted was declining. Many departments require moral fitness (determined by polygraph examination and a check of fingerprint records) and oral screening of appearance, speech, and judgment. Before application of such criteria, many candidates are found unqualified on the basis of age, height, physical condition, insufficient education (high school graduation is usually required), or insufficient length of residence in the area.

In addition to recruitment problems, the manpower dilemma stems from the loss of experienced personnel at an average rate of about 5 percent per year. Without sufficient recruitment, the average age of available personnel will increase disproportionately and eventually aggravate the personnel turnover problem.[46] Beyond the positive effects of screening out those officers found unsuitable, a high rate of turnover should call attention to the conditions that make for premature withdrawal from police service. John McNamara cites some of the qualities of the police bureaucracy and the environment of police work. Personnel are subjected to the discipline of a semimilitary organization; violators of departmental rules are subjected to deprivation of pay, vacation time, or job. These penalties rest on the assumption that task failures stem from willful disobedience or negligence rather than errors of judgment. Strict discipline imposed from above discourages the employment of the professional judgment necessary for intelligent decision making at the time of an incident. Thereby the officer is caught between the demands for flexibility and bureaucratic conformity in his work performance. Career advancement also poses uncertainties in that an adverse report in a personnel file can block promotion. The written examinations for promotion do not necessarily test the officer on the knowledge and skills actually required in the field.[47]

Although he usually starts his police career without cynicism, the rookie soon confronts the divergence between the ideal standards voiced in training and the conditions of patrol on the streets. Under the wing of veteran officers, the rookie is likely to be urged to be "tough." According to Arthur Niederhoffer, he is pressed to become cynical in two senses: cynicism toward people in general encouraged by the corrupt and defeated clients often encountered in police work, and cynicism toward

[45] President's Commission on Law Enforcement, *Task Force Report: The Police,* pp. 125–26.

[46] Ibid., p. 9.

[47] John H. McNamara, "Uncertainties in Police Work: The Relevance of Police Recruits' Backgrounds and Training," in Bordua, *The Police,* pp. 177–90.

the police system itself because its practices fail to meet the ideal. Degree of cynicism is associated with length of service (leveling off after 5 or 10 years) and level of job position. It is also affected by the greater expectation of promotion among college graduates as compared to those with less education, middle-class patrolmen as opposed to men from the working class, and members of the vice squad as compared with the youth division, for example.[48]

Centralization as a solution

A frequent suggestion for overcoming organizational problems is that police forces be centralized on a national or state basis. Critics of this proposal argue that such a force would be incompatible with a democratic society, which is largely dependent upon public self-policing even when a professional force is maintained. The centralization of the police would cut the ties of sentiment that unite local residents and policemen, substituting a large bureaucracy which would emphasize efficiency achieved through impersonal procedures developed in abstraction from the local sentiments supporting self-discipline. Some argue that such impersonal bureaucracy might lend the police to use by a political dictator.

Other organizational plans entail less drastic changes: centralization at the county level, contact agreements between small governmental units and larger ones, incorporation of several units into police districts, and joint utilization of specialized personnel, equipment, and facilities by two or more police bodies without consolidation.

The police departments of Metropolitan Toronto were unified in 1957. Virgil Peterson noted objections to the move, which centered around several fears: Local residents would lose close contact with police administration because local police have a superior appreciation of local problems. The concentration of all calls through one communication center would create delays because of "jamming." The various sections of the metropolitan area have special problems requiring local police. Local residents would lose pride in "their" police. Transfer of personnel to distant divisions would create hardships. Immediate unification would be too difficult and should be done by degrees—if at all.

Peterson also noted the arguments in favor of unification: Duplication of services would be eliminated. Adequate finances would be available for proper equipment and a more equitable wage schedule. Centralization would speed communication for rapid action. There would be a properly equipped crime laboratory, uniform traffic control, and specialized branches for such areas as morality, traffic, crime investigation, training school, prisoner transportation, and centralized offender records. Centralized purchasing would cut operating expenses. Surveillance of re-

[48] Arthur Niederhoffer, *Behind the Shield: The Police in Urban Society* (Garden City, N.Y.: Doubleday Anchor, 1967), pp. 43–107.

ceivers and disposers of stolen goods would be more efficient. Establishment of a single police commissioner post would promote impartial and uniform law enforcement free of local politics. The number of unsolved crimes was cited as evidence for the need for police reorganization.[49]

By 1966 The Metropolitan Board of Commissioners was able to report consolidation of small inefficient operations into larger groupings, consolidation of the telephone and radio communications, standardization of recruitment and training, a promotional system based on merit, development of specialized squads and a record system, introduction of scientific equipment, location of modern stations to replace outmoded and poorly located ones, and an increase in percentage of offenses cleared.[50]

The police service contract has been advocated as having advantages over compulsory consolidation: simplicity in application, economic feasibility, and political practicality.[51] Under this arrangement, the smaller police jurisdiction voluntarily enters into an agreement with a larger police agency to pay for specific services. If the contract is drafted properly, the locality gains the advantages of specialized police services without losing its authority.

Another compromise would be to retain local control but make the granting of state financial aid conditional on meeting certain manpower, equipment, and efficiency standards. The state could operate schools for improving and standardizing the training of local police. One objection is that this would be a barrier to needed consolidation because each local government would cling to its force as a source of revenue. Furthermore, it is argued, grants-in-aid present possibilities for patronage and pork-barrel politics.

SUMMARY

The sociologist is interested in police work as an occupation and as an institutional component operating within the context of the total community. Law enforcement cannot be effective unless it is fitted into the fabric of community life. On occasion, the policeman stakes his life on performance of his duties, but his most important responsibility in a democracy is to meet his official responsibilities without infringing on the "inalienable rights" of the individual. Police efficiency is hampered by the organizational confusion which has been part of the political heritage. An urban-industrial society has brought demands on police

[49] Peterson, "Issues and Problems in Metropolitan Area Police Scandals," pp. 133–34.

[50] Metropolitan Board of Commissioners of Police, *Annual Report, 1966,* (Toronto, 1967) and statement submitted to the Special Committee of the Metropolitan Council on Metropolitan Affairs (typed).

[51] Gordon Misner, "The Police Service Contract in California," *Journal of Criminal Law, Criminology and Police Science,* 52 (November–December 1961): 445.

agencies that call for reassessment of the place and function of law enforcement among the social institutions. In response, police work has expanded in the variety of services afforded the public and the degree of training and personnel skills required. Police work has become a career field with challenges and opportunities.

FOR ADDITIONAL READING

Bakal, Carl. "Do Gun Control Laws Really Work?" *Saturday Review,* 50 (April 22, 1967): 20–21 ff.

Balch, Robert A. "The Police Personality: Fact or Fiction?" *Journal of Criminal Law, Criminology and Police Science,* 63 (March 1972): 106–19.

Becker, Harold K. *Issues in Police Administration.* Metuchen, N.J.: Scarecrow Press, 1970.

Bittner, Egon. "Police Discretion in Emergency Apprehension of Mentally Ill Persons." *Social Problems,* 14 (Winter 1967): 278–92.

———. "The Police on Skid-Row: A Study of Peace Keeping." *American Sociological Review,* 32 (October 1967): 699–715.

Bordua, David J., and Reiss, Albert J. Jr. "Command, Control, and Charisma: Reflections on Police Bureaucracy." *American Journal of Sociology,* 72 (July 1966): 68–75.

Brandstatter, S. A. F., and Radlet, L. A. (eds.). *Police and Community Relations: A Sourcebook.* Beverly Hills, Calif.: Glencoe Press, 1968.

Chwast, Jacob. "Value Conflicts in Law Enforcement." *Crime and Delinquency,* 11 (April 1965): 151–61.

Clark, John P. "Isolation of the Police: A Comparison of the British and American Situations." *Journal of Criminal Law, Criminology and Police Science,* 56 (September 1965): 307–19.

Conot, Robert. *Rivers of Blood, Years of Darkness.* New York: Bantam Books, 1967.

Cramer, James. *The World's Police.* London: Cassell & Co., 1964.

Edwards, George. *The Police on the Urban Frontier.* New York: Institute on Human Relations Press, 1968.

Hahn, Harlan (ed.). *Police in Urban Society.* Beverly Hills, Calif.: Sage Publications, 1971.

Iannone, N. F. *Supervision of Police Personnel.* Englewood Cliffs, N.J.: Prentice-Hall, 1970.

Inbau, Fred E., and Reid, John E. *Criminal Interrogation and Confessions.* Baltimore: Williams and Wilkins Co., 1967.

Kephart, William M. *Racial Factors and Urban Law Enforcement.* Philadelphia: University of Pennsylvania Press, 1957.

Lane, Roger. *Policing the City.* Cambridge, Mass.: Harvard University Press, 1967.

Milner, Neal A. *The Court and Local Law Enforcement.* Beverly Hills, Calif.: Sage Publications, 1971.

Piliavin, Irving, and Blair, Scott. "Police Encounters with Juveniles." *American Journal of Sociology,* 70 (September 1964): 206–14.

Skolnick, Jerome H. *Justice without Trial.* New York: John Wiley & Sons, 1966.

Smith, Bruce. *Police Systems in the United States.* New York: Harper & Row, Publishers, 1960.

"A Symposium on the Supreme Court and the Police." *Journal of Criminal Law, Criminology and Police Science,* 57, No. 3 (September 1966) and No. 4 (December 1966).

Van Allen, Edward J. *Our Handcuffed Police.* Mineola, N.Y.: Reportorial Press, 1968.

Vega, William. "The Liberal Policeman: A Contradiction in Terms?" *Issues in Criminology,* 4 (Fall 1968): 15–33.

Westley, William A. *Violence and the Police.* Cambridge, Mass.: The M.I.T. Press, 1970.

Wilson, O. W. *Police Administration.* New York: McGraw-Hill Book Co., 1971.

The courts

As the intermediary between law enforcement and corrections, the courts make two crucial decisions in the criminal justice process: Is the person guilty of a crime? What should be done with the convicted offender? In such decision making the courts are charged with the responsibility of convicting the guilty while protecting the innocent under safeguards of the Constitution, legislative statutes, and procedural rules. The courts have the ultimate functions of redressing wrongs, convicting the guilty, protecting the innocent, and harmonizing the relations between institutions and individual members of society. They are hampered in carrying out these functions by incompatibility between the ideals of law and order. Law imposes rational restraints upon the rules and procedures utilized to achieve the ideal of conformity that the concept of order entails.[1]

An urban-industrial society increases the complexity of the social arrangements necessary to give order to contacts between men. In recent years there has been an unprecedented increase in the numbers of laws and regulations designed to control individual conduct and to govern interpersonal relationships. The greater volume of laws strongly tests the judiciary's ability to balance the pressures toward conformity for the sake of order with the legal restraints intended to protect the rights of the individual.

PROCESSES OF CRIMINAL JUSTICE

The administrative processes of criminal justice[2] are initiated by arrest, usually without a warrant and ordinarily within a short time after commission of the crime. In most jurisdictions the law requires that the police produce the arrested individual before a magistrate for a preliminary

[1] Jerome H. Skolnick, *Justice without Trial* (New York: John Wiley & Sons, Inc., 1967), p. 9.
[2] For more detailed description of procedures, see chapter 12 above and Paul W. Tappan, *Crime, Justice, and Correction* (New York: McGraw-Hill Book Co., 1960), chap. 12.

hearing without unreasonable delay. Usually this period is defined as within 24 hours. The purpose is to determine whether the evidence is sufficient to hold the accused for trial.

If the accused is charged with a misdemeanor, he can be heard by the lower court and released, fined, or sentenced. If he is charged with a felony, the magistrate may bind him over to the prosecutor. He may be brought to trial either through indictment by a grand jury or by information of the prosecutor. The latter instrument is prepared by the prosecutor without submission to the grand jury and serves the same function as an indictment.

Next the accused is arraigned in trial court. After reading of the charge against him, he is required to enter his plea. If he pleads not guilty, he may ask or waive a jury trial. A trial date is set and a time fixed within which defense counsel may make motions, including challenge of the formal charge.

If the trial results in conviction, time is provided to make motions for a new trial or for arrest of judgment because of defects appearing in the record. There may be an appeal to a higher court. There may also be a delay to permit preparation of a presentence investigation of the convicted offender's background and potentiality for prosocial behavior. The final action is sentencing.

Disposition without trial

Although the legal structure implies that criminal cases will be decided by court trial, most cases are disposed of either through a decision not to charge the suspect with a criminal offense or through a plea of guilty. The President's Crime Commission reported that in many communities between one third and one half of the cases begun by arrest are disposed of by some form of dismissal by police, prosecutor, or judge. When a decision to prosecute is made, in many courts as much as 90 percent of all convictions is obtained by guilty pleas negotiated in advance between the prosecutor and the defense counsel or the accused.[3]

Early dispositions without trial not only relieve overburdened courts; they have other advantages.[4] Their flexibility and informality are more adaptable to individualized, rapid handling of cases than the more rigid and time-consuming formal procedures. Innocent persons can be screened with fewer adverse consequences for them. Because there is less emphasis on culpability and less public pressure for imposition of punishment at the pretrial stages, early dispositions are more likely to recognize the needs of the offender. In some cases, prosecution would not serve a legiti-

[3] President's Commission on Law Enforcement and Administration of Justice, *Task Force Report: The Courts* (Washington, D.C.: U.S. Government Printing Office, 1967), p. 4.

[4] Ibid.

mate purpose even when the offender is technically guilty. Offenders can be referred to social agencies when treatment is more appropriate than prosecution.

The dangers of dispositions without trial lie in their lack of safeguards against injustice. The defendant is not protected when decisions are made without objective scrutiny or sufficient information. In the absence of clear policy guidelines, either undue leniency or coercion can result. Nontrial dispositions are too informal and invisible to hold the decision maker accountable. Another difficulty is that the offender is often dropped out of the criminal process without the assistance or treatment necessary to prevent recurrence.[5]

Discharge without prosecution

The police are responsible for the first stage of the process of criminal justice, in which they make the decision to arrest. For less serious offenses the police may ignore the situation, release the offender after arrest, or refer the case to a social agency. Effective decision making by police in these circumstances is handicapped by limited access to relevant background information, shortage of time and personnel, and ambiguities of legal guidelines. The question arises as to how much discretion should be granted the policeman. The advantages of nontrial dispositions support the delegation of some decision making to police, but such delegated discretion calls for clarity in guidelines and visibility of administration. The lack of these qualities in the criminal justice system can make equal justice under the law difficult to attain.[6]

The prosecutor is in the best position to make the decision whether to press charges because of his knowledge of possible charges, sentencing alternatives, strength of the evidence, and limitations on resources available for prosecution. To be effective he requires valid and reliable information on the case, the potentiality of the offender for positive behavioral change, and the availability of treatment facilities. A precharge conference between prosecutor and defense counsel can afford a responsible means of noncriminal disposition when guidelines are established. The President's Crime Commission suggested criteria for the use of such conferences: the seriousness of the crime in its impact on the public sense of security and justice, the relative importance of deterrence in the policy toward the particular offense, the unusual prevalence of social or psychological difficulties susceptible to the work of community agencies, the amenability of the offender to treatment, and the impact of criminal charges on persons other than the offender.[7]

[5] Ibid., p. 6.

[6] See Skolnick, *Justice without Trial*, chap. 4.

[7] President's Commission on Law Enforcement, *Task Force Report: The Courts,* pp. 5–8.

Negotiated pleas

The high percentage of cases disposed of by guilty plea are largely the product of *plea bargaining* between the prosecutor and the defense counsel. The bargaining seeks an agreement under which the accused pleads guilty in exchange for a reduced charge or the prosecutor's recommendation of a shorter sentence. The procedure circumvents the risk of the adversary system and reduces the courts' work load. However, the invisibility and informality of plea bargaining open the way for the operation of chance and corruption.

In a study of felons convicted in a district court, Donald Newman found 93.8 percent had entered a plea of guilty. Over a third originally had entered a not-guilty plea but had changed their plea short of a trial. More of those who changed pleas had defense attorneys and were experiencing their first convictions than those who pleaded guilty immediately. Over half (54.3 percent) of those who pleaded guilty immediately claimed that they had bargained for their sentence, and 84 percent of the immediate guilty pleas came from recidivists. The recidivists expressed fear that the judge would evaluate them harshly because of their previous records if they lost their trials, and the prosecutor, whose recommendation would influence the sentence, would be angered by a court struggle. Their previous experiences with the machinery of justice had made them aware of the bargaining techniques and had placed them on a first-name basis with some of the police and court officials responsible for such bargaining.[8]

Newman reports four types of informal conviction agreements: (1) the offender obtained a reduction of the charge alleged in the complaint; (2) leniency was obtained in sentencing, usually probation; (3) multiple charges were combined into a concurrent sentence; and (4) the prosecutor agreed not to press one or more of the charges.[9] The several functions of negotiated pleas are suggested by the roles played by the prosecutor. As an administrator, he strives to dispose of cases rapidly. As an advocate, his goal is to maximize the number of convictions. As a judicial decision maker, he may seek the "right" outcome in view of the defendant's social circumstances and the peculiar circumstances of the crime. As a legislator, he grants concessions because he considers the law too harsh.[10]

Another facet of administrative accommodation is the informal resolution of problems without resort to criminal prosecution. Through

[8] Donald J. Newman, "Pleading Guilty for Considerations: A Study of Bargaining Justice," *Journal of Criminal Law, Criminology and Police Science,* 46 (March–April 1956): 783–84.

[9] Ibid., p. 787.

[10] Albert W. Alschuler, "The Prosecutor's Role in Plea Bargaining," *University of Chicago Law Review,* 36 (Fall 1968): 52–53.

threats, advice, or sympathy, the prosecutor disposes of many cases in extralegal fashion. Certain cases are difficult to handle successfully through criminal proceedings. In petty thefts, complaining witnesses tend to drop the matter when restitution is made. The wife frequently forgives the husband who deserted her. The prosecutor may exert pressure to cause husbands to support their dependents, embezzlers to reimburse their victims, or certain sex offenders to marry plaintiffs.

THE "LAW EXPLOSION"

The courts have experienced what Harry Jones calls a "mid-century law explosion." Population growth has increased the volume of cases. The increasing complexity of society has brought additional demands on legal institutions. The stabilizing influence of family and neighborhood controls has declined as a result of urbanization and population mobility. Technological advances have added such misdemeanors as traffic offenses to the business of the courts.[11]

Court administration has failed to respond effectively to these challenges. A multiplicity of courts and concurrent jurisdictions confuse court organization. Unnecessary compartmentalization, the determination of cases on jurisdictional technicalities, inflexibility in the face of the changing nature of litigation, and costly duplication of clerical staffs characterize the courts as a component of the criminal justice system.

The chaos of lower courts

Although the lower courts are concerned with the less serious offenses, the significance of their work is far from petty. Whereas public attention is directed toward the more dramatic cases of the felony courts, the vast majority of criminal cases is handled by the lower courts. There the bulk of defendants receives its impressions of the system of criminal justice. In spite of their importance, these courts receive the least attention, suffering shortages of competent personnel. They especially lack opportunity for proper study of cases and are hobbled by archaic administration.

At this level there is the greatest probability of injustice for poor, ignorant, or helpless defendants. The volume of cases contributes to perfunctory procedures as the defendants are herded quickly through the court. In the majority of cases, brief, stereotyped consideration is given to the evidence before fines and court costs are assessed. Often the proceedings of such *assembly-line justice* are marked by the expression of moral platitudes by the judge intended to impose some "lesson" on the defendants. The cash register's bell announces contributions to meeting the costs of local government by those least able to pay them.

[11] Harry W. Jones (ed.), *The Courts, the Public and the Law Explosion* (Englewood Cliffs, N.J.: Prentice-Hall, Inc., 1965), pp. 2–3.

Delays in judicial procedure

The volume of cases often overtakes archaic administration. In many states 18 months is required to process a case from arrest through trial to final disposition. Delay exacts its costs in hasty disposition, postponement of correctional treatment, undermining of the principle of deterrence, and suspicion of the efficiency of justice.

Procedural dawdling results from human qualities, including the reluctance of the functionaries of the institutions of justice to respond to the forces of change. Since litigants may delay suits for personal advantage, the courts are not wholly to blame. However, managerial efficiency has been blocked by the tendency to operate courts for the benefit of judges and lawyers.[12] The fundamental cause is the difficulty in distinguishing between *unreasonable* delay and delay essential to the system of justice. Delay can permit time for proper preparation of the case. Facts must be ascertained, answers to charges prepared, motions addressed to the pleadings, and opportunity given for settlements without a trial.

Proposals for reform

One set of reform proposals would increase the business transacted in a trial day. Pretrial procedures and conferences between the trial judge and attorneys could determine the real points in a controversy. Trial briefs could present the crucial evidence. In nonjury cases, the judge could hear the closing arguments of counsel and decide the case on the basis of his pretrial study when the facts are clear in his mind.[13] The time-consuming battle of experts could be avoided by selecting physicians, psychiatrists, and other experts from a special panel. A master calendar could schedule trials to reduce time lost between completion of one case and beginning of another. By fuller use of administrative assistants, the judge could be freed of routine duties to concentrate on judicial functions.

A second set of proposals would increase the availability of judges by increasing the number of courts, filling court vacancies more promptly, and transferring cases from overworked courts to those with vacant calendars. The equivalent of a business board of directors for courts would systematize court administration.

The President's Crime Commission echoed repeated recommendations of reformers that the criminal courts be unified under a central administration and that the current lower courts be replaced by a smaller number of district or county courts of limited jurisdiction and manned by salaried, law-trained judges. The judicial manpower of lower courts and their physical facilities would be improved to cope with the volume of cases.

[12] Arthur T. Vanderbilt, *The Challenge of Law Reform* (Princeton, N.J.: Princeton University Press, 1955), p. 132.
[13] Ibid., pp. 79–80.

Prosecutors, probation officers, and defense counsel would be provided where not available or sufficient.[14] Courts with a heavy volume of cases could employ computers to maintain case histories, expedite statistical reporting, monitor cases to assure they move through court processing as rapidly as possible, prepare documents, and predict impending case scheduling problems.[15] With increasing visibility of the shortcomings of their trial courts, states are moving with "glacial speed," according to James Gazell, to establish court administrator's offices for better management, consolidate the trial-court system, abolish fee offices, alter the procedure for selecting judges, and establish a criminal justice office at the state level.[16]

THE ADVERSARY SYSTEM

Under the adversary system the two contending parties hold the initiative in trials. The theory is that each litigant is strongly interested in the case outcome and will exert maximum energy in discovering and presenting the merits of his case and the weaknesses of his adversary's case. As a consequence, the truth will be unfolded for the decision of an impartial tribunal. The adversary system places a premium on adequate legal representation. The right to counsel is essential to protection of civil rights and to justice because the defendant lacks the technical skills and knowledge necessary in conducting legal procedures.

The proceedings can take on the qualities of ancient trial by combat, wherein a champion represented each of the disputants to determine the issue through physical combat (rather than purely logical argument). The trial becomes a drama in which the jury must make its decisions on the basis of on-the-spot behavior of witnesses and attorneys. The judge becomes an umpire between two contending groups who may be seeking victory through oratorical skill, psychological trickery, or knowledge of legal technicalities.

In such a confrontation, the litigant without adequate counsel is at a great disadvantage. Three methods are employed most frequently to afford representation to indigent defendants charged with crime.[17] Under the assigned-counsel system, the judge assigns an attorney when the defendant appears at arraignment without counsel. There is no system of rotation, and inexperienced lawyers tend to be overrepresented in the attorneys chosen for such service. The system does not assure investigation

---

[14] President's Commission on Law Enforcement, *Task Force Report: The Courts,* Chap. 3.

[15] Norman A. Halloran, "Modernized Court Administration," in President's Commission on Law Enforcement, *Task Force Report: The Courts,* Appendix E.

[16] James A. Gazell, "State Trial Courts: The Increasing Visibility of a Quagmire in Criminal Justice," *Criminology,* 9 (February 1972): 379–400.

[17] Special Committee to Study Defender Systems, *Equal Justice for the Accused* (Garden City, N.Y.: Doubleday & Co., Inc., 1959), pp. 47–48, 66–67.

of the facts of the case and the entrance of counsel into the legal proceedings at a sufficiently early stage. Assigned attorneys have been known to persuade the accused to plead guilty to save effort, and to seek repeated continuances in order to obtain additional fees from the accused or his relatives.[18] Many capable attorneys avoid assignment because they regard criminal law practice as disreputable.

The voluntary-defender system is based on a private, nongovernmental law office which centralizes the function of defending indigents. The office may be affiliated with a civil legal aid society and is supported financially as a charitable organization. It may utilize salaried legal and investigative staff but may also be aided by volunteers from private law offices or local law schools. This approach has practical limitations because of the uncertainty of its financial support, possible resistance from the bar or bench, and the physical difficulties of covering all the courts in a metropolitan area.[19]

Under the public-defender system, a public official affords equal protection under the law, with staff and office facilities maintained by public funds. Because his income is not affected by outcome of the trial, the public defender has no reason to prolong the case unnecessarily. The decreased delay reduces the chance of hostility by defendants and their families toward the machinery of justice and reduces the cost of court operations. Defense is conducted by experienced attorneys less likely to employ unscrupulous methods to circumvent justice.

Critics of the public-defender system contend that it is expensive for the taxpayer and uses public funds to protect the public's enemies, that it places two public officials in conflict in court, that our legal system provides other safeguards for the defendant, and that innocent defendants will not avail themselves of his services. Further, the public defender may be a political hack subservient to the court, and he might be too zealous in defending notorious guilty defendants in hopes of building a personal reputation. Retorts to these criticisms cite the defects of the assigned-counsel system, the protection of the innocent as a legal duty, the lack otherwise of any choice of counsel for the indigent defendant, and the possible use of merit examinations for selecting public defenders and their staffs.

MAJOR ROLES IN THE COURTROOM

The courts must operate within the limits of the law and of their own traditions. This imparts a degree of uniformity to the behavior of the judge, prosecutor, defense attorney, and other key figures in the opera-

[18] David Mars, "Public Defenders," *Journal of Criminal Law, Criminology, and Police Science,* 46 (July–August 1955): 201.

[19] Philip J. Finnegan, "The Work of the Public Defender in Cook County," *Journal of Criminal Law and Criminology,* 26 (January–February 1936): 68–72.

tion of courts. The trial is a sociological drama with certain roles for participants. The training, experience, and personality of the individuals occupying these roles have major effects on what transpires.

The judge

The judge plays a key role in the administration of justice. The ideal judge is well versed in law and in the art of focusing the trial on the truth. He has the courage, independence, and honesty essential to preserving individual liberties. He remains patient in the face of procedural delays and the trivialities of court work. Ideal judges can make an inadequate system of substantive law achieve justice after a fashion, while inadequate judges will defeat the best system of law.[20] The trial judge has an imposing place in the system of justice. Expectations concerning his attitudes affect plea bargaining and arrest practices. His behavior on the bench shapes public conceptions of justice.

The judge plays four roles. He *umpires* jury trials to assure that procedural rules are followed by the contending parties. He implements rules and principles enunciated by appellate courts to keep procedures current. In this role, he is supervising the fact-finding process within the limitations necessary to assure protection of civil rights. He also serves as a *legal advisor* to the jurors. In nonjury trials, he also is the *verdict decision maker* concerning guilt. A defendant freed by a trial judge's decision to acquit, even in the face of strong evidence of guilt, may not be further prosecuted. Finally, as *sentence decision maker,* he determines the disposition of the convicted offender. The power of the trial judge is indicated by the inability of appellate courts in most jurisdictions to adjust a sentence if it is within statutory limits, no matter how harsh or lenient.

Historically, the independence of the judiciary of American states has deteriorated under the impact of powerful currents of liberal political thought and "practical politics."[21] The democratic revolution which began at the time of Andrew Jackson encouraged the application of the principles of rotation of office to judicial positions and extended the list of offices subject to popular election. The reaction against authority gave additional force to efforts to curb the power of judges. Because most judicial positions are secured through gubernatorial appointment, legislature's choice, or election, judges are usually dependent on political service at the state level for their positions. The broad use of political spoils in Jackson's administration opened an era in which those who performed a service to the successful political party are rewarded by appointment to political office. The extension of this system to judgeships opened career oppor-

20 Vanderbilt, *Challenge of Law Reform*, p. 12.
21 Stuart H. Perry, "Politics and Judicial Administration," *Annals of the American Academy of Political and Social Science,* 169 (September 1933): 84.

tunities to politically minded lawyers, whose profession gave them the public visibility and skills valued by political candidates. The result was the growing influence of practical politics on the courts.

Merit selection is a more rational procedure for selecting judges than popular election alone. The qualifications of prospective judges are screened by a nonpartisan committee, and the field is narrowed to a few legally trained and otherwise qualified nominees from which appointments or candidates for election are selected.[22]

The prosecutor

The prosecutor has great influence on the effectiveness of the machinery of justice. He determines whether or not a case will be prosecuted or a bargain will be made to permit the accused person to obtain a lighter penalty. His efficiency in organizing and presenting evidence influence the case outcome. Because of the power of the office, election of the officeholder may open the door to manipulation of justice for political interests and an excessive zeal for convictions to ensure reelection.

The prosecutor shares with the defense attorney certain professional roles.[23] As an *investigator* he collects and evaluates evidence. As an *adversary* he opposes another attorney in court. As an *examiner* he questions witnesses. As a *decision maker* he plans the legal strategy. As an *advisor* he counsels his client, interprets laws, and imparts information.

Obstacles to effective prosecution include the conception of the office as a part-time position, the aggravation of the work load by the duty to represent local government in civil as well as criminal cases, and the ability of prosecutors to practice law privately when not engaged in official duties. One consequence is a generally low level of salaries for prosecutors. Because the office is elective and sensitive to political pressures, prosecutors tend to be influenced by practical rather than enlightened attitudes toward operation of the system of justice. A high proportion of novice prosecutors lack prior experience in the criminal process, thus presenting a need for training programs.[24]

The defense attorney

The functions of this vital role are suggested by the synonyms for the term "lawyer." The "counsel" is defined in two ways. He is one who gives advice in legal matters; therefore, his legal training is vital. He also

[22] President's Commission on Law Enforcement, *Task Force Report: The Courts,* pp. 67–68.

[23] Israel Gerver, "The Social Psychology of Witness Behavior with Special Reference to Criminal Courts," *Journal of Social Issues,* 13, No. 2 (1957): 23.

[24] President's Commission on Law Enforcement, *Task Force Report: The Courts,* pp. 72–74.

is engaged to conduct a case in court; therefore, his contributions to his client rest on his skill and experience in handling characteristic patterns of courtroom interaction. The "advocate" pleads the cause of another, requiring skills in perceiving and organizing the crucial facts into a case and then communicating them effectively in court. The "barrister" is admitted to the circle authorized to plead at the bar in the superior courts of law, having been found qualified to be a member of the legal profession. Therefore, he is a colleague among lawyers and subject to the standards of his profession.

The attorney contributes to more rational decision making. Sanford Kadish asserts that in the common-law system it has been the lawyer's traditional role to participate in the evolution of legal principles by case-by-case adjudication that clarifies the governing principles.[25] In demanding supportable conclusions consistent with past decisions, the attorney plays a part in preventing arbitrary decisions. As a member of a professional group, the attorney is subjected to a structure of statutory law, court precedents, and bar association codes in his practice of law. These formal controls over professional conduct are supplemented by informal patterns which arise out of his spontaneous relationships with public officials, clients, and other lawyers.

Criminal and civil lawyers differ in patterns of informal behavior. Although both types participate in a wide variety of community and political organizations, criminal lawyers tend to dissociate themselves from civic, recreational, and religious groups dominated by businessmen. Criminal lawyers participate more frequently in charitable organizations, draw more friends from occupations with social statuses ranked lower than businessmen, and are more active in politics. Arthur Wood explains these differences as symptomatic of the contacts necessary to obtain clients. Civil lawyers are motivated to participate in civic and recreational clubs because their clients are drawn from the middle and upper classes, while criminal lawyers tend to serve lower-status clients. Their concern for the legal rights of indigent and accused persons appears to cause criminal lawyers to identify themselves with humanitarianism, charitable work, and political liberalism.[26]

Criminal lawyers are dependent on government agencies to interview the jailed client, to obtain information, to negotiate bail, to bargain for an informal settlement, and for other purposes. Although defense attorneys and officials are opponents, both tend to seek a basis for accommodation. His practice encourages the criminal lawyer to evade the formal norms of his profession.[27] If the novice lawyer lacks connections with an

[25] Sanford H. Kadish, "The Advocate and the Expert-Counsel in the Peno-Correctional Process," *Minnesota Law Review,* 45 (1961): 831.

[26] Arthur Lewis Wood, "Informal Relations in the Practice of Criminal Law," *American Journal of Sociology,* 62 (July 1959): 48–55.

[27] Ibid., pp. 50–54.

established legal firm, he faces difficulties in establishing his practice which may divert him into criminal law, at least during the difficult initial period of his career. To obtain referral of criminal cases, the beginner establishes informal ties with officials and likely clients. Moreover, since many of his clients are guilty of some crime and since his professional success would be jeopardized if he lost too many cases, the criminal attorney is pressed to use the informal evasions which come under the heading of bargaining justice. The risks to the attorney are reduced by substituting social skills in dealing with officials for professional technical skills.

The juror

The use of juries has been criticized in terms of their selection, possible susceptibility to corruption, and lack of qualification for duties. The technicalities of the selection of jurors slow trial proceedings, but there are other causes of delay, such as the failure of judges to use their authority to minimize them. It has been argued that the requirement for a unanimous verdict makes it possible to deadlock a jury by bribing or coercing a single juror. Another contention is that too many incompetent and overly emotional persons are selected. The answers to such criticisms are complicated by the motives of the defendant or his lawyer in deciding whether to waive a jury; leniency in sentencing is balanced against the chance of being found guilty at all. Harry Kalvern, Jr., and Hans Zeisel found that defendants were most likely to forego jury trials when the type of crime charged was one that juries were more likely to judge severely than judges would. The authors marvel at the accuracy with which lawyers can discern the regularities of net jury leniency.[28]

In considering what types of persons should be eligible for jury service, one view gives priority to capacity to carry out the assigned task of the jury. Another emphasizes the importance of representation on the jury of a cross section of the community, with no economic, racial, political, or geographical group systematically or intentionally excluded. W. S. Robinson cites evidence of an excess of professional and semiprofessional people, proprietors, managers, and officials and a deficit of the lower occupational and economic classes among persons nominated for grand jury service.[29]

The issue of representativeness versus competence gives point to research conducted by the University of Chicago and reported by Rita James.[30] Tape-recorded proceedings of trials were played to persons se-

[28] Harry L. Kalvern, Jr., and Hans Zeisel, *The American Jury* (Boston: Little, Brown & Co., 1966), pp. 28–30.

[29] W. S. Robinson, "Bias, Probability, and Trial by Jury," *American Sociological Review,* 15 (February 1950): 76–78.

[30] Rita M. James, "Status and Competence of Jurors," *American Journal of Sociology,* 64 (May 1959): 565–70.

lected at random from the jury pools. Deliberations of these "juries" based on the proceedings were transcribed for analysis.

Jurors' deliberations require rather rapid formation of behavior patterns because they are grouped without common previous experience. The foreman is selected by authority outside the group and establishes a leadership pattern which may not be fully accepted by the specific jury. The jurors' deliberations preliminary to reaching a unanimous verdict require participation which may include giving suggestions, affording orientation for assessing facts, contributing to the process of reaching agreements, and obstructing this process.

The selection of jurors is a crucial issue. The patterns of deliberation emphasize the desirability of certain personal characteristics in the juror. Because college-educated persons are likely to have superior experience with group discussion, it could be assumed they would spend more time on the court's instructions and take responsibility for maintaining orderly procedures. It could also be assumed that less well-educated jurors would participate more in terms of opinion and the citation of personal experiences.

These assumptions were borne out in the James study, which revealed that jurors spent at least half their time exchanging experiences and opinions related to the trial. About a quarter of the time was related to procedural matters, 15 percent to reviewing the facts of the case, and 8 percent to court instructions. Jurors with grade-school educations placed greater emphasis on the substantive categories (testimony, opinions, personal and daily life experiences) and less on procedures and instruction than jurors with high school or college education. The same study assessed the quality of participation in deliberations by asking questions concerning each verbal contribution: Is it accurate? Is it pertinent to the jury's problem? Does it facilitate progress toward agreement on the verdict? A high percentage of accurate and pertinent comments was found to come from jurors of all types. There was no significant difference between educational categories in pertinency of opinion or accuracy in recall of testimony. However, the grade-school jurors' interpretation of the instructions was significantly less accurate. The concern for facilitating discussion was significantly greater for the college-educated group. There was no significant difference between the educational groups in their ability either to influence other jurors or to be persuaded by them.[31]

The witness

Under the adversary system, the opposing parties bring in witnesses, examine them, and make objections. In the trial each party vouches for its witnesses and the opponent attacks their credibility. The judge func-

31 Ibid., pp. 565–70.

tions as an impartial arbitrator. This places the decision maker, whether judge or jury, in the difficult position of determining the truth on the basis of the witness's reaction to a hostile attempt to shake his testimony.[32]

The trial witness functions within one of two roles. Usually, he gives evidence of personal observation as spectator or auditor of events pertinent to trial issues. Or he may testify as an expert on facts which require specialized training and experience for sound evaluation.

The witness may be handicapped in the performance of his role if undue stress is placed upon him, if he is denied the opportunity to unveil the truth, or if he is otherwise prevented from contributing to meaningful proceedings. Stress comes from two sources: the parties directly involved in the trial and the general public. The examination and cross-examination are policed by the judge. Some control must be exercised to avoid the possibility of stimulating the jurors' sympathy by subjecting the witness to unreasonable attack. The public, represented at the trial by spectators and the press, may contribute to the social climate interfering with role performance by the witness.[33]

The ability of the witness to withstand stress may depend upon his personality and his occupational, racial, ethnic, class, and religious statuses in the community.[34] His personality may affect his capacity to give effective and accurate testimony. The status of the witness in the community has some relationship to the status of the defendant. Similarity, or great differences between the two statuses, can create stress. The status of the defendant and the nature of his crime may have special implications within the context of the community because status relationships involve community issues beyond the scope of the trial itself. Examples of such issues are labor-management disputes, interracial conflicts, and political controversies.

The expert witness is subjected to a special brand of pressure. His qualifications as an authority open him to attack when he undermines the adversary's case. The role he is assigned may arouse the antagonism often directed against intellectuals.

Obtaining witnesses can be a problem. They object to the inconvenience of waiting in court for the case to be called and possible loss of wages. Witnesses can be intimidated by criminal defendants and subjected to ridicule in cross-examination.

Unreliable evidence by witnesses may stem from dishonesty, incorrect but sincere testimony, or recantation of testimony. Incorrect but

[32] Jack B. Weinstein, "The Law's Attempt to Obtain Useful Testimony," *Journal of Social Issues,* 13, No. 2 (1957): 7.

[33] Rudolph E. Morris, "Witness Performance under Stress: A Sociological Approach," *Journal of Social Issues,* 13, No. 2 (1957): 17–18.

[34] Ibid., pp. 20–21.

sincere testimony can be produced by a host of psychological factors. Emotions, bias, and expectancy influence perception. Poor lighting, long distance, and short duration may have adverse effects on accuracy. Taking an oath has various meanings to individuals, but even those who regard an oath as sacred can provide misinformation. Methods of eliciting facts in court may also color testimony.[35]

The courts have shown reluctance to turn to the physical and behavioral sciences for assistance in assuring accuracy and reliability in testimony. This is one facet of the hesitation to accept blood tests, photomicrographic analysis of metal, chemical tests, and other contributions of the physical sciences. It was 1911 before an American tribunal permitted the use of fingerprints to identify persons.[36] In regard to evaluating testimony, however, the courts have reasons to be cautious about the use of instrumental, chemical, and psychological aids.[37] Because witnesses are not always unreliable, the problem is to determine whether the witness is reliable in the specific situation under consideration. Lie detectors do not rule out errors in observation. Drugs such as scopolamine, sodium amytal, and sodium pentothal have been used to reduce self-protective inhibitions. However, the "facts" elicited by their use may only reflect the suggestions of the interrogator.

To simplify their work load, civil lawyers often obtain information from witnesses in their own offices, with only opposing counsel present. There is growing pressure against the use of pretrial publicity, which can arouse the emotions of the jurors. Another trend is toward permitting more discretion in application of the rules of evidence, especially in trials before a judge, to allow more effective determination of pertinent facts.[38] This reduces the effectiveness of such elements of the adversary system as surprise and proprietorship of information or witnesses.

SENTENCING

In sentencing the convicted offender, the trial judge must weigh the future of the defendant against his own responsibility to the community. This is a stern test of wisdom, knowledge, and insight.

The judge must consider the standards provided by the statute which has been violated, the public attitude toward the law, and the probable

[35] D. S. Greer, "Anything But the Truth? The Reliability of Testimony in Criminal Trials," *British Journal of Criminology,* 11 (April 1971): 131–54. Also see Charles Korte, "Group Influences on Helpfulness of Accident Witnesses," *Law and Society Review,* 5 (August 1970): 7–19.

[36] Sheldon Glueck, *Crime and Justice* (Boston: Little, Brown & Co., 1936), pp. 91–92.

[37] Joseph F. Kubis, "Instrumental, Chemical and Psychological Aids in the Interrogation of Witnesses," *Journal of Social Issues,* 13, No. 2 (1957): 40–49.

[38] Weinstein, "Law's Attempt to Obtain Useful Testimony," pp. 7–8.

deterrent effects of various alternatives for disposing of the case. Penal codes grade penalties according to seriousness of crime, but their logical consistency is colored by social exigencies. The judge must use discretion in assessing the individual qualities of the case in terms of the circumstances of the crime, the offender's characteristics, and the community's sentiments. His objectivity is strained when a controversial case produces political or journalistic pressures or public hysteria.

Factors affecting objectivity

The body of legal precepts would seem to ensure an abstract, even-handed dispensation of justice. In practice, however, the judiciary is confronted with the difficulties of fitting abstract principles to the highly variable situations that emerge from the dynamics of daily life and the great variation among individual personalities. Discrepancies between precept and practice are inevitable to some degree in any situation, even those in which the most competent and ethical occupants of authoritative statuses must make decisions that are crucial in the lives of those they affect. All men are influenced by the store of knowledge and the motivations that have shaped their biographies within a social context. Criminal cases frequently represent a conflict of social groups, with the defendant likely to be a member of the lower middle or working class and the judges and prosecutors likely to be members of the upper and upper middle classes, which also are predominant among the framers of criminal laws.[39] Like the scientist, the judge must strive to detach himself from his biographical situation, the extraneous influences of transitory community attitudes, and the temptation to place administrative ease ahead of his ultimate goal—justice for the accused person.

Most criticisms of sentencing practices center on the undue influence of the particular personality of the judge and the fact that his legal training does not fit him to understand the social and psychological effects of rehabilitation secured through individualized diagnosis and treatment. It must be recognized, however, the sentencing judge operates within a role strongly influenced by an ethos of efficiency and maximum production. He is poorly equipped by his law-school education to cope with the routine details of managing the business of the lower courts and must be instructed by clerks and other functionaries. These courts require voluminous, visible, and complex judicial decision making that is affected by the realities of budget administration, working relationships with the district attorney in plea bargaining, and the need to balance various community expectations about sentences. The judge often seeks to diffuse the anxieties and responsibilities of the decision-making process by depend-

---

[39] Stuart S. Nagel, *The Legal Process from a Behavioral Perspective* (Homewood, Ill.: Dorsey Press, 1969), p. 235.

ing on district attorneys and other court personnel in deciding dubious cases in a "practical" manner that will maximize the prospects for rapid disposition of cases.[40]

Disparity among sentences

Sentencing practices in the United States are unique among the world's legal systems. Within the limits set by legislatures, maximum sentences in America probably are the highest in the world. Without being subjected to any review of his determination of sentence, a single judge can decide absolutely the minimum period of time a convicted prisoner must remain in prison.[41] The lack of review contributes to the disparity among sentences which is a major target of critics of courts.

Edward Green suggests that the sentencing problem involves two aspects: disparity among sentences under apparently equivalent crime situations, and the possibility of consistent sentencing that is excessively severe. His study of nonjury convictions showed the disparity between sentences to be at a minimum when the case was obviously one of either mild or extreme gravity. It was in the intermediate area of gravity that the sentence was most likely to reflect the individuality of the judge.[42]

To measure differences among the 88 U.S. district courts, the Administrative Office of the Courts developed a weighting methodology which differentiates between sentencing alternatives, from suspended sentence through probation to sentences of varying lengths, for eight offenses. With the national average used as a comparison, the courts were found to range from 42 percent above expectation for western Tennessee to 48 percent below for Alaska. Ten courts equaled the national average for sentence severity, 9 were at least 20 percent above, and 15 were at least 20 percent below expectation.[43]

The existence of sentence disparities reflects the problem of reconciling individualization and uniformity. Individualization requires dealing with the offender in terms of his personality, his experience, and the nature of his offense. Therefore, similarity in offense is only one aspect of the treatment problem. On the other hand, the goal of uniformity in sentencing is expressed as resentment over disparities in sentences for com-

[40] Alexander B. Smith and Abraham S. Blumberg, "The Problem of Objectivity in Judicial Decision-Making," *Social Forces*, 46 (September 1967): 96–105.

[41] B. J. George, Jr., "Comparative Sentencing Techniques," *Federal Probation*, 23 (March 1959): 30–31.

[42] Edward Green, *Judicial Attitudes in Sentencing* (New York: St. Martin's Press, 1961), p. 69.

[43] *Federal Offenders in the United States District Courts* (Washington, D.C.: Administrative Office of the U.S. Courts, 1967), pp. 23–27. For review of other similar studies, see Julian C. D'Esposito, Jr., "Sentencing Disparity: Causes and Cures," *Journal of Criminal Law, Criminology and Police Science*, 60 (June 1966): 183–85.

parable crime situations. Disparities justify the resentment of offenders, aggravate disciplinary problems in prison, and undermine rehabilitation programs when claims of individualized sentences conceal capricious or erratic sentencing decisions.

Sol Rubin contends that substitution of the concepts of "equality and consistency" for "uniformity" does much to eliminate this issue.[44] Uniformity is sacrificed for equality in the differential protection given women, children, and certain minority groups in the passing of sentences. Some of the apparent inconsistency of sentencing stems from the judges' efforts to individualize the imposition of penalties. In his study, Green found general differences in sentencing which appeared to favor females, youths, and whites as compared respectively to males, older offenders, and blacks. However, he contended, closer analysis revealed that these differences were reflections of the relationship between these biosocial factors and offenses, rather than expressions of prejudice by the sentencing judge. He cited lower recidivism and fewer serious crimes among the "favored" groups and contended that elimination of these complicating factors reduced differences in sentencing severity to a negligible level.[45]

Remedies for sentencing problems

Among the strategies for improving sentencing practices is the indeterminate sentence, which transfers the ultimate decision, within minimum and maximum terms determined by the court, to a correctional board. Theoretically, a prison or parole board will have the advantages of reliable and complete diagnosis at the prison reception center, evaluation of the subsequent behavior of the imprisoned offender, and information obtained through investigation of the community setting. The achievement of effective individualized decision making by the board depends on the expertise of the members and the diagnositic and treatment resources available to the correctional agencies. Unfortunately, these agencies usually fall far short of the quality this approach assumes.

Another general strategy focuses on improvement of sentencing practices of judges. Through training sessions and the distribution of sentencing guides, judges can be made more aware of the variations among sentencing practices and perhaps be persuaded to modify their own decisions to ensure more uniformity and consistency among decisions. Seminars are held at which judges review typical cases, make sentencing decisions, and then discuss their justifications when their decisions depart from the average decisions among participants. Prediction tables, based on actual outcomes of past sentencing decisions for offenders with simi-

---

[44] Sol Rubin, "Sentencing Goals: Real and Ideal," *Federal Probation,* 21 (June 1957): 51–52.

[45] Green, *Judicial Attitudes in Sentencing,* p. 63.

lar offenses and backgrounds, have been advocated as one way of mobilizing the resources of science to deal with the problem. However, such statistical data will constitute a meaningful resource for sentencing reform only if judges who use the technique will recognize that a defendant may have characteristics not captured by statistical averages and that the outcome of an indicated sentencing decision depends on the actual availability of the treatment resources assumed to exist by the prediction tables. Another method advocated for improving sentencing practices is fuller use of presentence investigations by probation officers to provide reliable diagnosis of the offender and his social situation. Such a diagnosis can increase the probability that the judge's choice between prison and probation will be sound.

The sentencing authority of courts has been restricted in some respects by legislative mandate. In all civilized systems, according to Nigel Walker, the sentencing authority of judges is controlled within general limits. Fears of the results of leniency usually prompt legislative provisions for mandatory stern sentences in offenses such as murder and treason. Conversely, imprisonment is prohibited for a host of trivial offenses and, usually, for young offenders. Appeals from sentences or, in some cases, requirements that a justification for the sentence be stated are other safeguards.[46] Legislatures have even provided a schedule of factors and conditions to be considered in determining the type and length of the penal treatment. Such an extreme action produces a mechanical and complicated process of judicial arithmetic that frustrates the goal of individualized treatment.

Finally, sentences could be reviewed by an appellate body. This would provide more time for weighing sentences of defendants pleading guilty and stand as a safeguard against the abuses produced by the passions of the moment or the personality of the trial judge. Critics point to the delays this procedure entails, the cumbersome nature of its administration, and the substitution of documents for more personal acquaintance with the facts and setting of the crime.

JUVENILE COURT

Originating as an enlightened reform of the 19th-century practice of handling juvenile offenders as though they were adult criminals, the juvenile court was conceived in what H. Warren Dunham calls the *social-agency image*.[47] The humanitarian reformers of the late 19th century thought the juvenile court would counteract the corrosive effects of urban

---

[46] Nigel Walker, *Sentencing in a Rational Society* (New York: Basic Books, 1971), pp. 149–57.

[47] H. Warren Dunham, "The Juvenile Court: Contradictory Orientations in Processing Offenders," *Law and Contemporary Problems,* 23 (Summer 1958): 508–27.

life; by strengthening the middle-class conceptions of the family, school, and church, it would serve as an instrument of delinquency prevention. They assumed a "natural" dependence of adolescents in creating a special court to impose sanctions on premature moves toward independence or youthful misconduct.[48] Adolescent crimes and other forms of misconduct would be subjected to a rational social discipline applied at a tender age. The juvenile court was designed to employ the behavioral sciences in a social-agency model that would fit justice to the goal of overcoming the emotional strains and maladjustments that prompt misconduct in the young.

Hopes for a social invention

The Illinois legislature created the first statewide court especially for children in 1899. The original Juvenile Court Act and amendments brought together under one jurisdiction cases of dependent, neglected, and delinquent children. The children were not to be treated as criminals but rather were to be dealt with in informal, nonpublic hearings designed to ease their anxieties and to indicate concern. They were to be detained apart from adults, and their records were to be held in confidence to prevent stigmatization. The emphasis was on investigation, diagnosis, and treatment—not on adjudication of guilt. Lawyers were to be replaced by psychologists, psychiatrists, and social workers. Adversary tactics were to give way to social service approaches, including probation. Although separate, independent juvenile courts are relatively few, every American jurisdiction has followed this lead in providing some sort of special procedures for juvenile delinquents. Decades after creation of the first juvenile court, however, the President's Crime Commission found significant gaps still existing between ideal and actual court structures, practices, and personnel.[49]

Examining the evidence provided by studies, legislative inquiries, and informed observers, the Commission concluded that the juvenile court has not fulfilled its original hopes. It attributed the failure to "the community's continuing unwillingness" to provide the personnel, facilities, and concern necessary to permit the juvenile courts "to realize their potential and prevent them from taking on some of the undesirable features typical of lower criminal courts in this country."[50]

Alex Elson sees another source of failure. An essential conceptual flaw in the juvenile court has been its departure from the adversary sys-

[48] Anthony M. Platt, *The Child Savers: The Invention of Delinquency* (Chicago: University of Chicago Press, 1966): 169.

[49] President's Commission on Law Enforcement and Administration of Justice, *Task Force Report: Juvenile Delinquency and Youth Crime* (Washington, D.C.: U.S. Government Printing Office, 1967), pp. 2–4.

[50] Ibid., p. 7.

tem of criminal justice. Optimistic espousal of the *parens patriae* doctrine, he says, imposed the state (an outside authority without capacity for parental love) on the family as an arbitrator and judge. When the restraining forces of the natural parent-child relationship are lost, the outcome of juvenile court cases is determined by the temperament, character, and goodwill of the judge and the availability of time and resources for proper court administration. Ignoring the rules and forms which safeguard the rights of defendants (due process of law), the early reformers thought the benevolence of the juvenile court would be sufficient protection. They failed to anticipate the great variety of both juvenile court practices and quality of performance. Elson argues that the contemporary problem is how to preserve the assets of the juvenile court while altering its procedures through recognition of due-process safeguards. These safeguards, he believes, need not interfere with such commendable aspects of juvenile court performance as informality of hearings, minimization of publicity, preservation of confidentiality, and evidence of friendly concern for the child.[51]

The *legal image* of the juvenile court places it within the overall court system.[52] The advocates of the social-agency approach have been placed in a vulnerable position by such realities of judicial proceedings as the heterogeneous collection of cases before juvenile courts, their widespread failure to provide comparatively better care for child offenders, and the mixed quality of these courts. Juvenile cases include violations of the criminal code, truancy, curfew violations, "ungovernability," adoption, termination of parental rights, neglect, and dependency. The President's Crime Commission recommends that the business of the juvenile court should be limited to acts considered crimes when committed by an adult.[53]

The quality of juvenile court judges and proceedings has not measured up to expectations in a number of ways. One study found that about half of the judges have not received undergraduate degrees, a fifth have not been to college, and a fifth are not members of the bar. Almost 75 percent devote less than a quarter of their time to juvenile and family matters. Judicial hearings often are no more than 15-minute interviews.[54] The promises of confidentiality of juvenile court records and nonpublic, informal hearings have both been violated. Primary reliance on arrest for instigating action and the operation of detention facilities have dissipated

[51] Alex Elson, "Juvenile Courts and Due Process," in Margaret K. Rosenheim (ed.), *Justice for the Child* (Glencoe, Ill.: Free Press, 1962), pp. 95–117.

[52] Dunham, "Juvenile Court," pp. 508–27.

[53] President's Commission on Law Enforcement and Administration of Justice, *The Challenge of Crime in a Free Society* (Washington, D.C.: U.S. Government Printing Office, 1967), p. 85.

[54] Shirley D. McCune and Daniel L. Skoler, "Juvenile Court Judges in the United States—Part I: A National Profile," *Crime and Delinquency,* 11 (April 1965): 121–31.

the noncriminal tone of such proceedings. Juvenile training schools usually have failed to overcome the deleterious effects of imprisonment. Psychiatric and psychological services are lacking or in short supply for diagnosis. Dispositional alternatives are limited; probation either does not
exist or provides minimal supervision. Juvenile institutions too frequently
provide custodial keeping with little resources for vocational training or
therapeutic care.

The Gault decision

In 1967 the Supreme Court ruled in *Gault* v. *United States* to extend
civil rights to youths before juvenile courts in four respects. A timely and
adequate *notice of charges* is required in any delinquency proceedings
that can lead to an order of commitment to an institution. The child and
parents must be notified of the *right to counsel* in such a proceeding. The
juvenile has the *privilege against self-incrimination* when he is threatened
with deprivation of liberty. He has the *right to confrontation and cross-
examination* of his accusers.[55]

The impact of this decision on the juvenile court has been described
as revolutionary. It has promised to change the nature of the court's proceedings from that of a friendly, informal conference based on social
work principles to legal adjudication dominated by lawyers. With its jurisdiction narrowed to criminal law violations by juveniles, the juvenile
court will no longer be able to deal with their behavioral or social problems outside the province of the criminal law. The decision strikes at the
parens patriae role of the juvenile court judge, which was based on the
absence of challenge to his arbitrary, but benevolent, authority. The
quantitative need for lawyers and the increased length of proceedings
called for are likely to aggravate the work load of already congested juvenile courts. Alternatives to congested courts are to increase the number
of personnel or to divert the less serious cases to nonjudicial community
agencies.[56]

SUMMARY

The increased reliance of an urban society upon formal controls has
placed great strains on the courts. This chapter reviewed the administrative processes of courts to determine some of the discrepancies between
precept and practice which have brought proposals for court reform.

Major roles in the sociological drama of the trial were discussed to

[55] Fred D. Fant. "Impact of the Gault Decision on Probation Practice in Juvenile Courts," *Federal Probation*, 33 (September 1966): 14–17.

[56] Orman W. Ketcham, "Guidelines from Gault: Revolutionary Requirements
and Reappraisal," *Virginia Law Review*, 53 (December 1967): 1700–11.

trace the sources of these problems in the social structure of the legal system. It was particularly brought out that sentencing tests the capacity of the decision maker for objectivity and insight. The juvenile court represents an effort to add therapeutic considerations to legal institutions grounded in punitive principles. The current crisis of the juvenile court testifies to the difficulties of implementing this worthy objective.

FOR ADDITIONAL READING

Allen, Francis A. *The Borderline of Criminal Justice: Essays in Law and Criminology.* Chicago: University of Chicago Press, 1964.

Aspell, William P. "Should People Distrust Lawyers?" *Saturday Review,* 38 (December 17, 1955): 7–8 ff.

Bazelon, David J. "Justice Stumbles over Science," *Trans-action,* 4 (July–August 1967): 8–17.

Beemsterboer, Matthew J. "The Juvenile Court—Benevolence in the Star Chamber." *Journal of Criminal Law, Criminology and Police Science,* 50 (January–February 1960): 464–75.

Bowman, Addison M. "Appeals from Juvenile Courts." *Crime and Delinquency,* 11 (January 1965): 63–77.

Carlin, Jerome E. *Lawyers' Ethics.* New York: Russell Sage Foundation, 1966.

Cipes, Robert M. "Crime, Confessions, and the Court." *Atlantic Monthly,* 218 (September 1966): 51–58.

Davis, F. J.; Foster, H. H., Jr.; Jeffery, C. R.; and Davis, E. E. *Society and the Law: New Meanings for an Old Profession.* New York: Free Press of Glencoe, 1962.

Emerson, Robert M. *Judging Delinquents: Context and Process in Juvenile Courts.* Chicago: Aldine Publishing Co., 1970.

Haward, L. R. C. "Some Psychological Aspects of Oral Evidence." *British Journal of Criminology,* 3 (April 1963): 342–60.

Hostetler, Zona Fairbanks. "Poverty and the Law." In Ben B. Seligman (ed.), *Poverty as a Public Issue,* pp. 177–230. New York: Free Press of Glencoe, 1965.

Jones, Harry W. "The Trial Judge—Role Analysis and Profile." In Harry W. Jones (ed.), *The Courts, the Public and the Law Explosion,* pp. 124–25. Englewood Cliffs, N.J.: Prentice-Hall, Inc., 1965.

Klonoski, James R., and Mendelsohn, Robert I. *The Politics of Local Justice.* Boston: Little, Brown & Co., 1970.

Lemert, Edwin M. *Social Action and Legal Change: Revolution within the Juvenile Court.* Chicago: Aldine Publishing Co., 1970.

Marshall, James, and Mansson, Helge. "Punitiveness, Recall, and the Police." *Journal of Research in Crime and Delinquency,* 3 (July 1966): 129–39.

Nagel, Stuart S. "The Tipped Scales of American Justice." *Trans-action,* 3 (May–June 1966): 3–9.

Redmount, Robert S. "The Psychological Basis of Evidence Practices: Memory," *Journal of Criminal Law, Criminology and Police Science,* 50 (September–October 1959) : 249–64.

Rumble, Wilfred E., Jr. *American Legal Realism: Skepticism, Reform, and the Judicial Process.* Ithaca, N.Y.: Cornell University Press, 1968.

Samuels, Gertrude. "Justice in the Courtroom—Can the Poor Get It?" *Saturday Review,* 49 (September 29, 1966) : 25 ff.

Schwartz, Richard D., and Miller, James C. "Legal Evolution and Societal Complexity." *American Journal of Sociology,* 70 (September 1964): pp. 159–69.

Skolnick, Jerome H. "Social Control in the Adversary System." *Journal of Conflict Resolution,* 11 (March 1967) : 52–70.

Trebach, Harold S. *The Rationing of Justice.* New Brunswick, N.J.: Rutgers University Press, 1964.

Winter, Ralph K., Sr. "The Jury and the Risk of Nonpersuasion." *Law and Society Review,* 5 (February 1971) : 335–44.

Zeisel, Hans; Kalvern, Harry, Jr.; and Buchholz, Bernard. *Delay in Court.* Boston: Little, Brown & Co., 1959.

15
Detention and jails

As the oldest of penal institutions, the jail occupies a key place in prison history. When it was simply a place of short-term confinement, the early prison was essentially another jail, and many of its evils can be traced to the persistence of traditions developed in jails. While conditions in prisons have undergone relative progress, however, those in jails have remained substandard.

The jail remains a particularly notorious problem because of its diverse functions within the criminal justice system and the heterogeneous inmate population it collects. In both respects, the jail differs from the prison. Prisons typically are operated by the state and federal governments, whereas the jails, as creatures of local government, are subject to the administrative fragmentation and the budgetary undernourishment characteristic of municipalities. Both the jail and the prison receive sentenced prisoners, but the jail specializes in convicted offenders highly likely to reflect problems of personal disorganization with which the jail is unprepared to cope. The jail also serves as a temporary way station for sentenced offenders awaiting transfer to prison and for untried defendants not released into the community while awaiting trial. The heterogeneity of population is further aggravated by the use of the jail as a temporary holding place for the insane, children, alcoholics, and other types of persons posing problems of a noncriminal nature.

DIMENSIONS OF THE JAIL PROBLEM

In the Middle Ages prisons were used to hold accused persons for trial and to coerce convicted offenders into paying forfeitures of property. The jail has been traced to the reign of Henry II of England (1154–89), and it may have existed earlier.[1] Early European gaols were towers, gate-houses, town-hall cellars, and dungeons operated by private keepers for a profit. Inmates were charged entrance and discharge fees and fees for

[1] Louis N. Robinson, *Penology in the United States* (Philadelphia: John C. Winston Co., 1923), p. 33.

putting on and taking off irons. Prisoners with money could obtain special rooms and food, as well as the services of the tap and brothel. The general condition was one of lechery, debauchery, moral corruption, and pestilence.[2]

In the American colonial period, persons of both sexes and of all ages were confined in cramped, primitive quarters lacking the most rudimentary facilities. Inmates were dependent on benevolence for food and clothing. Condemnation of jail conditions has been widespread since the 1700s, but while the jail has been frequently criticized, efforts at reform have been largely insufficient or ineffectual.

Census of local facilities

The parameters of the jail problem in the United States can be described in terms of a 1970 census of the nation's jails conducted by the Law Enforcement Assistance Administration and the U.S. Bureau of the Census.[3] This census found 4,037 locally administered jails with the authority to retain adult prisoners for 48 hours or longer. This figure does not include federal or state prisons or other correctional institutions; facilities exclusively for juveniles, drunk tanks, lockups, and others for holding persons less than two full days; or state-operated jails in Connecticut, Delaware, and Rhode Island.

On March 15, 1970, the jails covered by the survey held 153,063 adults and 7,800 juveniles. One in every 20 adults was a female. Fifty-two percent of those incarcerated had not been convicted, including two thirds of the juveniles. Another 5 percent of the adults had been convicted but were awaiting appeal, sentencing, or other further legal action.

Five percent of the jails contained more inmates than they were designed to hold. Overcrowding was especially characteristic of large-city facilities intended for more than 299 persons. The actual extent of overcrowding is underestimated, because within any given jail there may be severe overcrowding in a section for adult males, for example, but sufficient excess space in sections for females or juveniles to produce overall underutilization of space.

Of the 3,319 jails operated by counties or municipalities of 25,000 or greater population, 86 percent had no educational facilities, only half provided medical facilities, and 47 institutions (1.4 percent) were without operating flush toilets. In these facilities nearly 25,000 cells (more than 25 percent) were built more than 50 years ago, 12,000 more than 75 years ago, and 5,416 more than a century ago.

The nation's jails employed 28,911 persons on a full-time equivalent

[2] Lionel W. Fox, *The English Prison and Borstal System* (London: Routledge & Kegan Paul, Ltd., 1952), pp. 19–21.

[3] *National Jail Census 1970* (Washington, D.C.: Law Enforcement Assistance Administration, U.S. Department of Justice, February 1971).

basis and 5,676 part-time employees the day of the survey, and in the fiscal year 1969 operating costs were $324 million. Over 30 percent of the full-time employees were located in New York and California alone and 42 percent of the operating costs was expended in California, New York, and Pennsylvania.

The jails described above are part of the misdemeanant institutions, which also include some state prisons. The usual definition of a misdemeanor is an offense carrying a maximum sentence of no more than one year in a local jail rather than a state prison. A few state prison systems, however, receive offenders confined after convictions legally defined as misdemeanors and sentenced to terms of less than a year. The counting of misdemeanors is further obscured by variations in legal definitions, the reducing of felony charges to misdemeanors, confinement of some felons with short sentences in local jails in some jurisdictions, and the inadequacies of record keeping. The President's Crime Commission reports that 22 percent of the prisoners in state institutions in 1965 were misdemeanants.[4]

Although the exact number of misdemeanant prisoners is uncertain, they do constitute the largest share of the persons handled by the criminal justice system. Of the nearly two million commitments to all correctional facilities and programs in 1965, more than two thirds were misdemeanants. They comprised 93.5 percent of all persons arraigned in 1962 in 12 states covered by a study. The ratio of misdemeanants to felons varied widely, from 4 times as many misdemeanants to 30 times as many (in New Hampshire).[5]

Volume and heterogeneity

The jail is intended to serve as a place of detention for the untried and for prisoners serving short sentences. Jail populations are inflated by delays in trials, safekeeping of defendants who could not be trusted to appear for trial, and holding of convicted offenders. The situation is further aggravated when the jail is pressed into service as a correctional facility without provision for a specialized staff or facilities for diagnostic and treatment services.[6]

Like the lower courts (see Chapter 14), jails are clogged with misdemeanants. A high volume of vagrants and drunks is produced by the practice of relying on police suppression instead of preventive and thera-

[4] President's Commission on Law Enforcement and Administration of Justice, *Task Force Report: Corrections* (Washington, D.C.: U.S. Government Printing Office, 1967), footnote, p. 79.

[5] Lee Silverstein, *In Defense of the Poor* (Chicago: American Bar Foundation, 1965).

[6] Mark S. Richmond, "The Jail Blight," *Crime and Delinquency*, 11 (April 1965): 134.

peutic measures to deal with social and psychological problems. The jail is also pressed into service to temporarily hold the insane and children. Thus it serves as a catchall for holding many individuals with problems of a noncriminal nature.

The jails also must cope with a mixed collection of personalities and with the disparate functions that short-term confinement is supposed to serve. Their populations represent four major types: persons held for investigation and preliminary hearings, those held for trial, those serving a jail sentence, and a small group awaiting transfer to penal or mental institutions. Vagrants, drug addicts, youthful first offenders, degenerates, habitual criminals, runaway children, AWOL soldiers, traffic law violators, and family offenders are thrust upon the jailer, who has neither the means nor the time to separate them by meaningful diagnosis. Usually physical space and institutional design are inadequate for isolation of various kinds of prisoners from one another, even on the basis of the most superficial and preliminary screening of personality factors. Overcrowding frequently complicates classification by sex and age.

Social environment

In the jail the offender gains his first experiences with involuntary confinement—impressions which will color his opinion of the criminal justice systems and may influence his adjustment to it. The physical conditions, the high rate of inmate turnover, the great variety of types of inmates, and the sheer volume of inmates can make for a high degree of tension and frustration among persons experiencing jail for the first time.

The advanced age of a facility does not indicate it must be unsanitary or in disrepair. However, many old jails, and some of those of less age, do not meet minimum standards. For example, researchers have described one jail where the ceiling of a cell block was caving in and doors jammed. Rotting plaster could be dug with a spoon. Although the fire marshall and sheriff called it a terrible firetrap, the county board reportedly refused requests for renovation even though there was a surplus in the treasury.[7]

The conditions encountered in most jails are suggested by the recollections of a psychiatrist sent by a magistrate to examine a prisoner.[8] The psychiatrist was ushered into a narrow room provided with two chairs and a bathtub. Doors were at each end of the room. Because there was barely sufficient light to see the prisoner, the psychiatrist groped around for a button, and an alarm bell sounded. As he finally had estab-

[7] Hans N. Mattick and Ronald P. Sweet, *Illinois Jails: Challenge and Opportunity for the 1970's,* survey of Center for Studies in Criminal Justice, Law School, University of Chicago (Chicago: Illinois Law Enforcement Commission, 1970), p. 3.

[8] B. A. Boyd, "Our Jails and the Psychiatrist Examination and Treatment of the Disturbed Offender," *Canadian Journal of Corrections,* 6 (October 1964): 477–79.

lished rapport with the inmate, a row of prisoners carrying dinner trays filed through the room.

Detention for trial should not assume the guilt of the person charged with a crime. Nevertheless the untried prisoner who is jailed is subjected to psychological stress, physical inconvenience, and interruption of normal life, even if he is subsequently found innocent. Untried status also has disadvantages for a work and treatment program. As wards of the court, the untried prisoners cannot be put to work, even when frustrated by idleness. The untried must be given all possible liberty to confer with counsel, friends, and relatives. Thus two sets of policies are required in handling the untried and the convicted.

Prolonged pretrial detention complicates the achievement of the purposes of imprisonment. If deterrence through punishment is the goal, the delay reduces the association in the prisoner's mind of the punishment with the criminal act. If rehabilitation is sought, prolonged pretrial detention obstructs the gaining of the offender's willing participation in the therapeutic process.

Jail inmates have a set of mores to which novices are pressured to conform. In the "kangaroo court," a clique of inmates extorts money from newcomers and forces degrading tasks upon them. This is largely a thing of the past, but the fellowship of common incarceration can lead to informal education in criminal techniques, homosexuality, and other deviant practices. A related problem is the possibility that young inmates may be forced into homosexual relationships.[9] Overcrowding, lack of staff supervision, and lack of organized activities aggravate these situations.

The emotional atmosphere is one of waiting under conditions of heightened anxiety, especially for the person in jail for the first time. Contact with the outside world may be lacking or sharply restricted. Tension may cause the offender to withdraw into hostile passivity, perhaps even suicide.

REASONS FOR THE JAIL PROBLEM

The conditions described above elicit a variety of interpretations from those who demand that something be done about the jail problem. Nevertheless, jail reform is resisted, and by more deep-seated factors than lack of humanitarian concern alone.

Low level of public concern

A common response to the problem is to lay it at the door of an apathetic public unwilling to do anything about conditions which appear

9 See Alan J. Davis, "Sexual Assaults in the Philadelphia Prison System and Sheriff's Van," *Trans-action,* 6 (December 1968): 8–16.

obvious to the critic but are "invisible" even to those who frequently pass by deteriorated jails. Inasmuch as inmates are drawn disproportionately from the poor, the jail problem shares the problems of poverty. Michael Harrington notes the general invisibility of the poor. Their living conditions go unnoticed by affluent citizens who speed along throughways skirting the urban slums or along turnpikes avoiding the rutted roads of rural poverty.[10] Inmates also are the targets of stigmata attached to those seen as "enemies of society" and disdain expressed for "failures" and social outcasts.

The processes of local government also often support this general "invisibility." Local government is sensitive to pressures from many directions. It must struggle to find revenue for a host of governmental functions and services sought by opposing interests.[11] Accordingly, local government tends to be reluctant to undertake jail reform because it is "invisible" to most of the public. The bulk of the citizens is likely to oppose either higher tax rates or the reduction of other services as means of implementing jail reform. Less conscientious judges even ignore the conditions of the facilities to which they sentence convicted misdemeanants.[12]

Sociocultural matrix of the problem

The specifics of the jail problem direct attention to the jail as a physical entity, to the jailer and his staff, and to the pathologies personified among the inmates. However, these are only tangible signs of the underlying factors that complicate jail reform. Public apathy is involved, but this too is symptomatic of the grounding of the problem in the structure of community life.

The jail management problem involves all the parts of the criminal justice system—police, courts, prosecutors, defense attorneys, jails, probation services, and parole at the local level and the juvenile level.[13] The jail inherits the inadequacies of these interdependent facets of the overall system because, as we shall see in the next section of this chapter, the jail serves certain functions for the system. Most jails are inadequate in facilities, but the absence of systematic planning in the overall system is just as vital to the problem.

Related to this fundamental defect is the paradoxical situation stemming from the American tradition that crime and treatment of offenders

[10] Michael Harrington, *The Other America* (New York: Macmillan Co., 1962), pp. 3–5.

[11] Henry Burns, Jr., "The American Jail in Perspective," *Crime and Delinquency,* 17 (October 1971): 447.

[12] See Mattick and Sweet, *Illinois Jails,* pp. 298–300.

[13] Richard A. McGee, "Our Sick Jails," *Federal Probation,* 35 (March 1971): 4.

are a local problem, although the tax bases of cities and counties which must deal with this problem are deteriorating in comparison with those of state and national governments. Correctional services receive a low priority in obtaining available funds in the face of the mounting fiscal demands of health, welfare, transportation, and education.[14] As suggested by the great number of jailers who occupy the archaic status of sheriff, the jails suffer from the overfragmentation of local government. Such fragmentation often means that local tax resources are insufficient to meet the mounting demand for governmental services. The small size of many jails that is a reflection of this fragmentation inflates the costs of providing the various specialized services and facilities called for in progressive jails.

Jail administration

Intelligent, alert, and trained personnel are the foundation of the well-managed jail.[15] Some jails are flimsy firetraps and easy pickings for escapists. However, if management and supervision are inadequate, even the most substantial jail is subject to escape and offers perils to its inmates. Diet is inadequate when management is inept. Lack of organized activity reflects poor administration and creates stultifying idleness as a seedbed for corruption of inmates.

Law enforcement officials operate most jails, but many leaders urge their transfer to correctional control to free police to concentrate on their primary mission of apprehending offenders. Most jailers are sheriffs elected to office, and attention is seldom given to their penological competence.[16] Prisoners may be subjected to illegal practices, such as the "third degree," because the officers lack skills to solve crimes otherwise. Under the fee system, if the sheriff is able to run the jail at a cost less than the daily allowance per inmate, he usually is permitted to pocket the savings. Prisoners sometimes have been held illegally to collect the daily fees. The fee system stems from the practice in England of the 17th and 18th centuries of letting jails to the highest bidder as a profit-making enterprise.

THREE FUNCTIONAL DESCRIPTIONS

As one of the ways of summarizing the plight of the jails, this troubled social institution may be examined in relation to three labels frequently applied to them: catchall, revolving-door, and way station. Each

---

[14] Ibid., p. 7. Also see Chapter 25 below, pp. 629–31.

[15] Myrl Alexander, *Jail Administration* (Springfield, Ill.: Charles C Thomas, Publisher, 1957), p. 11.

[16] Roy Casey, "Keeping People Out of Jail," *Proceedings of American Prison Association, 1939*, pp. 453–56.

emphasizes a particular function this institution serves within the overall system of criminal justice. In each instance the persistence of highly undesirable conditions in jails may be attributed to an important degree to practices extending beyond the confines of the jail or its personnel. In this sense, the jail is censured for conditions produced by sources outside its control.

Catchall jail

The term "catchall" describes the use of the jail as a dumping ground for human problems not handled by other institutions or as a place to hold persons until transfer to a more appropriate setting can be arranged. Urbanization has required the community to take formal action in dealing with the mentally defective, the alcoholic, the irresponsible family head, and the psychotic. These individuals could be tolerated to a greater degree in rural days when they were experienced personally as relatives or neighbors and when lower rates of population density made their behavior less of an aggravation. Before specialized institutions can deal with these deviants, some formal action is necessary which is direct, simple, quick, and cheap. The jail, and perhaps the prison, appear to meet these requirements, especially when the deviant is aggressive, rebels against authority, or threatens life and property. The jail also serves as a dumping ground for individuals arrested as a means of holding them for a few hours or days without any police intention of prosecuting them.[17]

Revolving-door jail

The term "revolving-door" reflects the repetitive and futile use of short-term sentences in an attempt to solve personality and social problems through confinement alone. The offender is expected to learn his "lesson" through the presumed deterrent effect of incarceration.

Since most jails lack a treatment program, the pattern becomes one of a series of short sentences that have no effect on the individual's misconduct or its underlying causes. If a treatment program does exist, the short term offers insufficient time for its effective utilization. One North Carolina prisoner has served 147 short sentences. There have been cases of an offender serving 13 30-day sentences in one calendar year because "good time" rewards reduced each sentence to 22 days. One superintendent tells of an incident in which an offender failed to finish mowing a lawn at the jail on the Saturday ending his 30-day sentence and promised to finish it Monday. On Monday he was received on a new 30-day sentence for drunkenness.

[17] Egon Bittner, *The Functions of the Police in Modern Society* (Washington, D.C.: National Institute of Mental Health, Center for Studies of Crime and Delinquency, 1970), pp. 110–11.

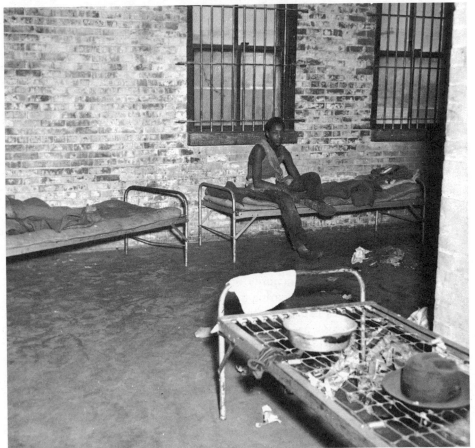

Figure 15–1. Three cots and one inmate.

The small jail with few inmates is more likely than larger local confinement facilities to lack adequate sanitation or programmed activities to break the monotony of waiting for something to happen.

Jailing of alcoholics is the most prominent example of the use of the revolving-door jail. Going to jail becomes a way of life for some alcoholics of lower socioeconomic status.[18] Because the alcoholic inmate makes up the bulk of the bookings and is likely to be jailed repeatedly, he constitutes a major burden on the jail. The inebriated offender presents several problems to the booking officer. Does the man's behavior indicate drunkenness, mild illness, or serious illness? Will he injure himself in the drunk tank? Will he need medication when he sobers up? Since he frequently presents a mixture of personal and social disabilities requiring simultaneous solution of many problems, should he be regarded as a hopeless prospect for the treatment resources that are available?

Jail as a way station

The usual jail serves as a "way station" for a large segment of its population, giving an air of impermanence and uncertainty to staff-inmate relationships which aborts officials' attempts to develop work or rehabilitation programs. The majority of the inmates are awaiting police investigation, a preliminary hearing before a magistrate, or trial. After conviction the inmates usually receive short sentences in the jail, too brief for systematic treatment, or are held awaiting transfer to a correctional institution. A sentence of more than a year generally requires commitment to a prison. Therefore, the effective work and treatment program must center around those prisoners receiving jail sentences of more than 30 days and less than a year. To have a sufficient number of longer-term misdemeanants, the jail must serve an area with a very large population.

JAILING AS TREATMENT

Although jail treatment is limited to short-term programs, it is possible that jails could be the beginning of constructive intervention to forestall further criminality. Admissions to prisons show that a large proportion of felons have histories of misdemeanors. Would it have been possible to forestall subsequent felonies if treatment programs had been initiated when earlier misdemeanors first brought the offenders to official attention? Before this objective could be reasonably achieved, many undesirable jail conditions would have to be remedied. Some jails have demonstrated that old structures can be modified, decent food provided, and a treatment program initiated that involves custodial officers.[19]

[18] Earl Rubington, "The 'Revolving Door' Game," *Crime and Delinquency,* 12 (October 1966): 332–38.

[19] For example, see John D. Case, "Modern Corrections in an Old County Jail," *American Journal of Correction,* 27 (January–February 1965): 4–6, 8–9; Lucile E. Blank, "Education in a Short-Term Institution," *American Journal of Correction,*

The jail could also advance treatment purposes through fuller recognition of its place within the field of corrections. Theoretically, jail staff could furnish valuable information for probation, prison, and parole workers who need accurate and complete information on the backgrounds and personalities of offenders placed in their charge. The stay in jail would be an opportunity in many instances to gather information on the offender's behavior and his ties to the local community. While these are the tasks of the probation officer who conducts presentence investigations for the court, not all offenders receive such investigations. The convicted felon frequently goes to prison with no such investigation having been conducted; if it was conducted, the information is unlikely to become available to prison authorities. In effect, it is proposed that the jail be given the mission and the necessary resources to become the gateway to the treatment aspects of the overall correctional system, as it is the gateway to the system's custodial features.

Jail as a condition of probation

Sentences to jail are most likely to be advocated by those who believe either that punishment has a deterrent effect or that short-term confinement has a rehabilitative effect. One example of the latter is the preference of a jail sentence over probation for those offenders the courts believe require closer security than probation provides. Even when probation is granted, some offenders have been confined in jail for the early portion of the probation period. The federal courts and five states (California, Iowa, Michigan, New Jersey, Illinois) have statutes permitting this procedure as one of the conditions of probation.[20]

Several defenses for this approach have been offered. Offenders of certain types (some mentally disturbed offenders, alcoholics undergoing "drying out," and narcotics users experiencing withdrawal) could be helped by personal contact during jail confinement. Others would be appropriate candidates on the basis of their attitudes, family and community relationships, previous criminal records, and psychological qualities. Probation is restrictive anyway, and the addition of temporary confinement would not be a fundamental change. Jail overcrowding would be relieved by earlier release on probation of offenders who were not immediately qualified for it. The treatment services of the jail would be extended through the work of probation officers, and the use of the jail would offer fuller protection to society against such offenders.

Against this approach, it is argued that the punitive aspects of con-

28 (November–December 1966): 21–23; Paula K. Drucker, "Short-Term Education in a Short-Term Penal Institution," *Crime and Delinquency,* 12 (January 1966): 58–69.

20 Sidney I. Dwoskin, "Jail as a Condition of Probation," *California Youth Authority,* 15 (1962): 10.

finement interfere with the attainment of the offender–probation officer rapport that is essential to the therapeutic process. Depersonalization and other aspects of confinement create attitudes in the offender impeding treatment, such as discouragement, apathy, and hostility. The jails are often overcrowded and lack the atmosphere and resources for treatment. Finally, it is argued that the skillful probation officer should not require the support of jail confinement.

"Short, sharp shock"

A typical reaction to exposure of the conditions in a given jail is that the inmates, as "undesirable" persons, deserve to be exposed to undesirable circumstances. This *post facto* rationalization can be further elaborated to argue that a punitive environment will forestall future misconduct and somehow build character. A variation is employed by advocates of a deliberately stern regime of short duration designed to instill in inmates the realization that further misconduct is not in their own interest. The intent of this policy is to employ sternness as a rehabilitative tool while avoiding the inhumanity of long-term exposure to filthy quarters and official brutality. Conditions in such programs are carefully controlled.

The "short, sharp shock" of short-term confinement of youthful offenders is utilized in Britain's experiment with detention centers. The Prison Act of 1952 authorized detention centers to administer a "short, sharp shock" to offenders, aged 14 to 21, who had not responded to treatment short of imprisonment but who were deemed by the court not to merit imprisonment. During a stay of three to six months, the young offenders were to be exposed to an austere regime of parades, drill, physical training, garden work, household duties, and evening classes. The emphasis was to be on achievement without tangible reward to maximize the shock of the experience over a period short enough to minimize the adverse effects of institutional life as a "school for crime."[21]

The success rate of the first two centers established was reported as "not impressive" in a 1962 report.[22] Of those released in 1959, 36.8 percent of the age group 17 to 21 and 13.8 percent of the age group 14 to 17 had offended again by 1960. The fault may lie in the selection of cases by the courts. Whereas the Home Secretary had suggested that the appropriate candidate would be "the well-developed undisciplined young rough who has hitherto come off best in his conflicts with authority and without having developed a bent for crime," 8 percent of the 1960 admissions had had previous institutional experience. A second possibility is that the three- to six-month period of confinement is too long for the

[21] "Magisterial Punishments—The Detention Centre," *Justice of Peace and Local Government Review,* 126 (September 8, 1962): 558–59.
[22] Ibid., p. 558.

"short, sharp shock" without risking the negative effects of confinement. A third possibility is that the deliberate use of punishment, even without brutality, is not effective for rehabilitation.

The detention centers of England were reoriented after an advisory council called attention in 1970 to the fact that the "short, sharp shock" was being interpreted as pure punitiveness. Imprecise expression of the aim and philosophy of the detention centers, the council said, provided ample scope for misinterpretation. Arguing that deprivation of the offender's liberty is sufficient punishment, the council called for constructive treatment, greater emphasis on the individual, and efforts to prepare the young offender for self-discipline in the free community.[23]

Along with a similar facility at North Sea Camp, the detention center at Holleslay Bay is an open facility described as a "fast-moving, disciplined environment, attempting training and first aid appropriate to the offender's needs."[24] Central themes are punctuality and swiftly moving scheduled activities; smart obedience to fair and constructive discipline; an attractive physical environment and a concerned social environment; training through vigorous work, education, and physical education; short-term "social first aid" through qualified counselors for diagnosis, and mobilization of after-care services for released inmates. The detainees receive sentences of either three or six months, but the period of stay usually is only two or four months because one third of the sentences is remitted. Thus the open detention centers have come to emphasize therapeutic measures within a short period of confinement while striving to minimize the purely punitive implications of "sharp shock."

DETENTION OF CHILDREN

The 1970 jail census reported 7,800 juveniles in jails on one day. Because of the rapid turnover of jail populations, it can be assumed that many times that number of juveniles are detained annually. The National Council on Crime and Delinquency estimates the figure as more than 100,000.[25] A recent survey of juvenile detention facilities produced an estimate that yearly admissions to such facilities total 488,800; there is an average daily population of 13,567. Over half of these homes were overcrowded at least some of the time.[26]

Sherwood Norman suggests two reasons why children are held in jails rather than juvenile detention homes. First, less than 10 percent of

[23] *Detention Centres: Report of the Advisory Council on the Penal System* (London: Her Majesty's Stationery Office, 1970), pp. 44–45.

[24] Information obtained during author's visit in spring of 1972.

[25] "Juvenile Detention," *Crime and Delinquency,* 13 (January 1967), p. 16.

[26] Nicholas A. Reuterman, Thomas R. Hughes, and Mary J. Love, "Juvenile Detention Facilities: Summary Report of a National Survey," *Criminology,* 9 (May 1971): 3–26.

the juvenile courts detain enough children to economically justify maintaining even the smallest detention home. Second, of those detention homes that have been built, most were badly designed or have insufficient staff and program to handle the aggressive delinquents who are turned over to jails.[27] However, the Children's Bureau doubts that more than a small proportion of jailed children require such secure facilities. Of the cases disposed by local authorities, 80 percent were allowed to remain in the community.[28]

Detention is used to hold children who require secure custody pending court disposition or while awaiting transfer to another court. It is also used for those awaiting transfer to an agency to which they have been committed by a court. The ideal detention home provides good physical care and secure custody; studies the child to provide a competent report to the court regarding his strengths, weaknesses, and needs; begins treatment by meeting the child's psychological needs; and provides access to caseworkers, preferably part of the detention home staff.[29]

In a study of detention homes in 11 counties by Helen Sumner, decisions to hold a child in a juvenile hall were found to be based on varied, sometimes contradictory, criteria. They also were often of dubious legality. The decision usually was made at a very brief hearing, with the information given the judge in a hurried and dreary manner. Case decisions were unlikely to be recorded as a means of assuring judicial accountability. Sumner concluded the differences in attitudes among the decision makers had more influence on variation among decisions than did differences among offenders.[30]

An earlier study by Gertrude Hengerer listed types of children likely to be referred to the court. First are those who are likely to run away or commit new offenses, even when under the supervision of a probation officer. This probability is indicated by the seriousness of their offenses and the intensity of the strain in their parental relationships. These few children require detention. Second, other children have the same characteristics, with the difference that they would avoid further difficulties if under intensive probationary supervision while awaiting court disposion. Probation without detention is advised. Third, there are children who require neither supervision nor detention because of the minor nature of their offenses and their personal problems. Fourth, some children require shelter care because of physical or moral danger in their home or

[27] Sherwood Norman, *Detention Practices* (New York: National Probation and Parole Association, 1960), p. 1.

[28] John J. Downey, "Why Children Are in Jail and How to Keep Them Out," *Children,* 17 (January–February 1970): 23.

[29] Gertrude M. Hengerer (ed.), *California Children in Detention and Shelter Care* (Sacramento: Temporary Child Care Study Committee, September 1954), p. 9.

[30] Helen Sumner, "Locking Them Up," *Crime and Delinquency,* 17 (April 1971): 168–79.

because of great strain in parent-child relationships. Detention is advised unless the child's sophistication would seriously endanger other children in the shelter.[31]

Because the detention facility may hold back children awaiting action by the court and those awaiting transfer to mental or correctional institutions, a problem is created which is aggravated when the child's length of stay is prolonged. The inexperienced child is exposed to seriously disturbed or more sophisticated peers who have been selected, on the basis of these qualities, for commitment to mental or correctional institutions. Hengerer's study found the average length of stay in detention facilities in 1951 was from 4 days in a small county to nearly 30 days in the state's most populous county. For individuals the time ranged from less than an hour to over a year. The long stays generally were caused by the insufficient capacity of correctional and mental institutions to receive youngsters, delays in clinical studies, difficulties in locating foster homes, and delay of juvenile court hearings.[32]

DETENTION OF THE INSANE

The detention of the insane in jails usually occurs when more suitable facilities are not considered to be available in an emergency. The abnormal behavior of other psychotics jailed as law violators can be evaluated as just "queerness" or the effects of drink. In a study of persons held in North Carolina county jails because of a mental disturbance, 21 percent were under the influence of alcohol at commitment.[33]

The North Carolina study found that a third of the mentally ill were in jail for a week or longer.[34] One was held for 52 days. Although it is asserted frequently that the jail is used only over weekends when access to mental hospitals is not possible, the least number of commitments was on Sunday and the second least on Saturday. When asked the specific reason for this use of the jail, county officials offered information on 75 of the 87 cases in which the patient was not under the influence of alcohol at commitment. Of these, 55 percent were described as violent, dangerous, or threatening assault. Seventeen percent of the cases involved warrants, court orders, allegations, or family requests that the patient be jailed. Twelve percent demonstrated uncontrollable, incoherent, or other severely abnormal behavior. The remaining cases were under observation or had escaped from a mental hospital.

Local officials offered various reasons for the jailing of mental patients. One was that if they were holding the patient in jail, they got quicker

---

[31] Hengerer, *California Children in Detention*, p. 4.

[32] Ibid., pp. 27–28.

[33] *Do They Belong in Jail?* (Raleigh: North Carolina Health Council, August 1958), p. 26.

[34] Ibid., pp. 27–29.

action on admittance from the state hospital. Hospital authorities retorted by pointing out the lack of waiting lists and the quick admission of qualified patients. The study committee objected to the use of local mistreatment of patients as an administrative weapon. Local jail officials also argued that the county could not afford the expense of keeping the emergency mental patient in a local hospital. This argument places governmental thrift ahead of humanitarian values. The opinion was also advanced that when a person is out of his mind, it doesn't make any difference where he is; so why not in jail? Psychiatrists, however, are not willing to predict how long a patient will remain in a dream world. Furthermore, without competent supervision and under the pressure of punitive confinement, the patient may injure himself.

BAIL PRACTICES

Certain aspects of the jail problem are directly related to bail practices. The denial of bail for the accused person awaiting trial adds to the jail population. It also increases the difficulty of handling unsentenced offenders together with sentenced prisoners.

Between the extremes of simple release or imprisonment of persons awaiting trial, the bond system represents a compromise solution to the problem of assuring the court that the accused will be present for trial. To back up their pledge, some accused are required to put up money in a sum set by the court. This guarantee can be provided by the accused, some other party, or a professional bondsman. Because money is involved, the penniless person is put at a disadvantage in this practice, contrary to the principles of equal justice, since jailing is the alternative.

Criticisms of current systems

Ronald Goldfarb, who calls the bail system a measure of the political and philosophical quality of American society, sees misuse of the system as a form of ransom. He charges that courts have misused bail by employing it for purposes other than guarantee of the defendant's appearance for trial. Bail has been used to punish, to teach the accused a lesson, to give expression to a personal view, to break "crime waves," and to deal with "subversives."[35]

Efforts to reform bail practices stem from several considerations.[36] Decrease in the number of defendants awaiting trial would reduce the numbers in jail and the rate of jail population turnover. Overcrowding and the pressure on frequently inadequate facilities would be relieved.

---

[35] Ronald Goldfarb, *Ransom: A Critique of the American Bail System* (New York: Harper & Row, Publishers, 1965), pp. 8–9, 46–82.

[36] Paul Wice and Rita James Simon, "Pretrial Release: A Survey of Alternative Practices," *Federal Probation,* 34 (December 1970): 60–61.

The professional bondsman would be eliminated or his influence on trial outcome curtailed. The cost of the jail to taxpayers would be minimized. Further, economic hardships of the defendant and his family are eased if he can continue income-producing activities while awaiting trial. He is also free to locate witnesses and otherwise act legitimately to strengthen his case.

National insurance companies are at the top of the bail bond business, according to Goldfarb, but local agents are the crux of the business because they can eliminate the risk in operations that produce $250 million a year in bonds. Since the courthouse agent must put up collateral to cover forfeitures of bond, the insurance company rarely suffers losses. Meager fiscal regulations have little effect on the agent, and his bond is rarely forfeited if the defendant absconds. Goldfarb says the bondsman performs few services except for tracing defendants when forfeiture is imminent. Furthermore, among bondsmen, there are too many unsavory characters and racketeers who sometimes have collusive arrangements with officials to promote their business.[37]

The professional bondsman, in effect, can determine whether the defendant will be held in jail pending trial. Although he is a private businessman, he has decisive influence at a crucial point in the administration of justice.[38] Because he is not a public official, there is no formal control over his decision whether to write a bail bond if the defendant cannot afford the premium or to refuse a bond if he has prejudices against the defendant.

Three bail systems

In addition to the traditional bail system, two efforts at reform have seen application in various jurisdictions. These are the reform system based on the Manhattan Bail Project of the Vera Foundation and the Illinois bail system.

Under the *traditional bail system,* the judge or magistrate is considered the sole determiner of whether the defendant will be released on his own recognizance prior to trial, be jailed in the interim, or be released on bail. However, the judge can diffuse responsibility for the decision by accepting the recommendation of the prosecutor, in a set of interactions described by Frederick Suffet. In the event of public protest, the prosecutor shares some of the judge's responsibility for releasing a "dangerous" person or an eventual absconder. By setting a money figure for bail the judge also can place some degree of responsibility for the defendant's arrival for trial on the professional bondsman, the defendant's family, or the defendant himself. Release on recognizance places entire responsi-

[37] Goldfarb, *Ransom,* pp. 95–115.
[38] Herbert Sturz, "An Alternative to the Bail System," *Federal Probation,* 26 (December 1962): 50–51.

bility on the defendant. The latter two practices, however, do not serve the judge as such against public outrage as does his acceptance of the recommendation of the prosecutor.[39]

In the *reform bail system,* the judge usually makes the final decision but employs some fact-finding system such as that developed by the Vera Foundation.[40] When an adult prisoner is brought into the detention facility, he is interviewed and his previous record and current charge are reviewed. If the information is verified, the judge receives a recommendation concerning worthiness of the defendant for release on his own recognizance. The recommendation is based on such factors as regularity in employment, favorable reports, and previous record. The approach assumes that the man with real roots in the community will find it difficult to disappear because Social Security numbers, driver's licenses, and income tax reports symbolize increased governmental knowledge of the individual's whereabouts. The crucial element, however, is that such criteria of the offender's stability in the community are reliable indications that he will appear for trial.

The *Illinois bail system* offers the defendant a unique alternative once the judge sets bail. Instead of going to a professional bondsman or otherwise raising the full amount of the bail, the defendant can execute a bond in the full amount of the bail and deposit with the court 10 percent of that amount. When he appears for trial, 90 percent of the deposit is refunded. Because the professional bondsman usually charges 10 percent of the total bond, the defendant saves money.

A survey of cities using one of these three bail bond systems found that the traditional method produced the lowest percentage of releases. However, it did not show significant advantages in a lower proportion of absconders as compared to defendants released on their own recognizance.[41]

Preventive detention

The controversy over pretrial detention versus bail was given additional fuel by the passage of the 1970 District of Columbia Crime bill, which authorized preventive detention of defendants charged with a "dangerous" crime, with obstructing justice, or with a "violent" crime. Defendants in the first two categories are automatically eligible for a detention hearing, but those charged with crimes of violence are to be screened to determine whether they had been convicted of a similar crime in the previous 10 years, had been certified as addicts, or were on re-

[39] Frederick Suffet, "Bail Setting: A Study of Courtroom Interaction," *Crime and Delinquency,* 12 (October 1966): 318–31.

[40] *Toward Justice for the Poor: The Manhattan Bail Project* (New York: Vera Foundation, 1964); Talbot Smith, "A New Approach to the Bail Practice," *Federal Probation,* 29 (March 1965): 3–6.

[41] Wice and Simon, "Pretrial Release," pp. 61–63.

lease for another crime of violence when arrested.[42] Such "poor risks" would not receive hearings but would be automatically detained.

The authorization of preventive detention in the District of Columbia raises serious constitutional questions related to the Eighth Amendment's prohibition of excessive bail. It also focuses attention on the use of bail for purposes other than assuring the defendant's presence at trial. Questions are raised as to whether future dangerous behavior can be predicted and, if so, whether the standards of such predictions can be administered in keeping with the principles of individualized justice.[43]

To test these questions, researchers studied pretrial crimes committed by defendants arrested in Boston during six months of 1968 to assess the number and seriousness of criminal offenses the District of Columbia legislation might have thwarted had it been in effect. Twenty-six variables, in addition to the six specified by the District of Columbia statute, were tested for their usefulness in predicting "dangerous" behavior. The data indicated that only 5.2 percent of the serious offenses could be predicted. Because this study covered a six-month period and the District of Columbia scheme limited preventive detention to 60 days, the latter was even less likely to be predictive. Of all persons arrested for violent or dangerous crimes in Boston in 1968, only 0.75 percent were at the time of arrest on bail while facing charges for an earlier crime perpetrated in the community. Thus the researchers concluded that preventive detention would have very little effect on rates of violent or dangerous crimes. Furthermore, administration of the law opened the way to even more flagrant expression of the invidious class and racial distinctions in present bail practices.[44]

JAIL REFORM EFFORTS

Persistent efforts have been made to overcome the jail problem in the United States. The National Sheriffs' Association and the National Jail Association have striven to carry out the principles of effective jail management. The National Council on Crime and Delinquency has provided construction designs and standards for detention facilities, conducted studies, offered consultation services, and sponsored training institutes. The Federal Bureau of Prisons employs inspectors to select jails acceptable for detention of federal prisoners. About 40 percent of the states set standards for jails; these efforts focus on construction and health standards without special concern for personnel, salaries, and programs. Nineteen states provide inspection, but only six subsidize improvements.

[42] Arthur R. Angel et al., "Preventive Detention: An Empirical Analysis," *Harvard Civil Rights—Civil Liberties Law Review,* 6 (March 1971): 303–4.

[43] Caleb Foote, "Preventive Detention—What Is the Issue?" *Prison Journal,* 50 (Autumn–Winter 1970): 4–5.

[44] Angel *et al.,* "Preventive Detentions," pp. 309–32, 369–70.

A growing number of conscientious, qualified, and determined jail and workhouse administrators are developing community support for reform and initiating pilot programs that demonstrate that correctional treatment can be successful.[45]

Suggested solutions

Probably the greatest need in overcoming the deficiencies of the majority of jails is to create general awareness at the local level that there is a serious problem. The details of reform have been well known for decades. Three specific steps are to remove the jail from politics, reduce the jail population, and provide employment and training.

Remove the jail from politics.   Placing the jails under a centralized agency would make it be possible to develop jails serving several governmental units. By providing economies on a per-inmate basis, these regional jails would support salary scales attracting trained career administrators and could offer treatment geared to short-term confinement. A basis would be provided for effective personnel training. The fee system could be replaced by tax-supported financing. Grants from the state or federal governments could subsidize some of the costs if certain personnel and operational standards were met.

Reduce the jail population.   One study estimated that the daily population of untried prisoners could be reduced by 43 percent through fuller use of personal recognizance in release procedures, admission to bail of cases involving burglary and robbery, and hastening of judicial administration to reduce the period of detention.[46] Greater use of fines, adjusted to the economic status of the defendant, has been advocated as an alternative to the jail. Greater use of probation has also been urged. The chronic alcoholic, the psychotic, the child, the ill, and the destitute should be removed to facilities more appropriate for their care and treatment. The National Council on Crime and Delinquency recommends that the local jail be used exclusively for persons awaiting trial and those sentenced to terms of less than 30 days.

Provide employment and treatment.   In some states and counties, farms and work camps provide constructive employment and treatment. Work release has vital advantages in providing paid employment to selected prisoners in the free community. The prisoner continues support of his dependents and has a job on release as a basis for reintegration into the community.[47] Fuller use of regional institutions, supported

[45] "Correction in the United States," *Crime and Delinquency,* 13 (January 1967): 148–50.

[46] *Plan for the House of Detention for Untried Adults in Philadelphia* (Philadelphia: Citizens' Committee to Support a House of Detention for Untried Adults, 1960), pp. 11–12.

[47] For discussion of work release, see Chapter 21.

by several local governments, or state-operated short-term institutions to provide such treatment or employment has been advocated.[48]

SUMMARY

The jail is the No. 1 problem among correctional institutions because it is locally administered, receives a heterogeneous population of inmates, and frequently serves as a short-term way station between freedom and long-term confinement. After reviewing the nature and causes of the various facets of the jail problem, efforts being made to cope with the inadequacies of the jails were indicated.

· It is easy to ignore progress in evaluating as difficult a problem as the jail. An appropriate closing note is the list of justifications offered by a student of jails for his contention that more improvements have been made in American jails since the middle 1940s than in all the preceding years of American history.[49] The "kangaroo court" has become a rarity (and then only through inmate subterfuge), although it was characteristic of most jails 30 years ago. The number of juveniles in jail has been reduced drastically. Personnel training has become available and is in increasing demand. Generally, three nourishing meals are served, and profiteering on food has declined. Standards of cleanliness have improved for most jails. How much remains to be done can be inferred by the limitations of these achievements.

FOR ADDITIONAL READING

Andry, R. G. *The Short-Term Prisoner*. London: Stevens & Sons, 1963.

Bases, Nan C., and McDonald, William F. *Preventive Detention in the District of Columbia: The First Ten Months*. Washington, D.C.: Georgetown Institute of Criminal Law Procedure, 1972.

Callahan, Joseph D. "New Programs at Chicago House of Correction." *American Journal of Correction*, 26 (May–June 1964): 6–8 ff.

Empey, LaMar. *Alternatives to Incarceration*. Washington, D.C.: U.S. Department of Health, Education, and Welfare, 1967.

Friedman, Sidney, and Esselstyn, T. Conway. "The Adjustment of Children of Jailed Inmates." *Federal Probation*, 29 (December 1965): 55–59.

Kirkpatrick, A. M. "Jails in Historical Perspective." *Canadian Journal of Corrections*, 6 (October 1964): 405–18.

Loth, David. "The Westchester Misdemeanant Survey." *Crime and Delinquency*, 13 (April 1967): 330–36.

---

[48] Roy Casey, "Catchall Jails," *Annals of the American Academy of Political and Social Science*, 293 (May 1954): 31.

[49] Myrl Alexander, "Jottings on Jails and Jailers," *Prison World*, 16 (July–August 1954): 14 ff.

McMillan, David. "Work Furlough for the Jailed Prisoner." *Federal Probation*, 29 (March 1965) : 33–34.

O'Connor, Gerald D. "The Impact of Initial Detention upon Male Delinquents." *Social Problems*, 18 (Fall 1970) : 194–99.

O'Rourke, Thomas P., and Salem, Richard G. "A Comparative Analysis of Pretrial Procedures." *Crime and Delinquency*, 14 (October 1968) : 367–73.

Rankin, A. "The Effect of Pre-Trial Detention." *New York University Law Review*, 39, No. 4 (1964) : 641–55.

Reichert, I. F., Jr. "Pretrial Release without Bail: Its Significance to Social and Psychiatric Workers." *American Journal of Orthopsychiatry*, 36, No. 2 (1966) : 206–7.

Robinson, Louis N. *Jails: Care and Treatment of Misdemeanant Prisoners in the United States.* Philadelphia: John C. Winston Co., 1944.

Rubin, Lillian. "The Racist Liberals—An Episode in a County Jail." *Transaction*, 5 (September 1968) : 39–44.

Sandhu, Harjit S. "The Impact of Short-Term Institutionalisation on Prison Inmates." *British Journal of Criminology*, 4 (July 1964) : 461–74.

Scudder, Kenyon J. "In Opposition to Probation with a Jail Sentence." *Federal Probation*, 23 (June 1959) : 12–17.

Smith, Talbot. "A New Approach to Bail Practice." *Federal Probation*, 29 (March 1965) : 3–6.

Sturz, Herbert. "The Manhattan Bail Project and Its Aftermath." *American Journal of Correction*, 27 (November–December 1965) : 14–17.

Part V
Confinement and correction

There are two types of correctional instruments—the various establishments for incarceration, and community-based programs employing diverse means of achieving correction, often through innovative strategies. Probation and parole are among the community-based programs to be considered in the final section of this book.

Correctional institutions are of great variety. In size, they range in inmate capacity from less than 50 in forestry camps to over 4,000 in monstrous prisons. In philosophy, they range from harsh punitiveness to advanced behavioral theories. In quality of program, they range from "human warehouses" to institutions well organized to uncover the latent causes of social deviation for individual offenders. The heterogeneity of institutions is a product of ideological conflicts drawn from diverse historical sources, fragmentation of administration among state and local governments, irregularity and inconsistency of public concern, and differences in the quality of administrative leadership.

As a social system and an organization, the prison is a worthy subject of study by the social scientists, particularly the criminologist. While in the future reliance on confinement as the primary societal response to criminality will probably be reduced, the correctional establishment will continue to be among those responses. Examination of contemporary prisons can assist in determining the proper functions and qualities of correctional institutions.

Historical roots of correctional practice

Penological history is one of organized cruelty, but it also encompasses the emergence of ideas which are progressive even by the standards of today. As prologue to the present and future, this history is relevant to an understanding of the doctrines and theories that underlie contemporary correctional practices, as well as to prediction of the probable future course of American corrections.

This chapter will document the history of many of the issues related to correctional institutions, the primary instrument for implementation of the penalties imposed by the system of criminal justice. Early penal reformers were often defeated in their efforts to cope with the discrepancies between the premises derived from the classical and positive schools.[1] Nevertheless, their efforts did produce practices and ideas which provide a basis for promising innovations advocated by contemporary reformers.

EARLY PENAL MEASURES

The Teutonic tribes of northwestern Europe at the beginning of the Christian era restrained vengeful retaliation against criminals by compelling victims to accept financial compensation. When, in Britain about the 12th century, the Crown took over the administration of justice, the compensations became an important source of revenue for English kings. Generally, imprisonment at that time had three purposes: detention awaiting trial, a means of exerting pressure for payment of fines, or temporary confinement before galley servitude. Torture became more prevalent after 1468 and capital punishments after 1688. Outlawry and mutilation were other early techniques of punishment.[2]

---

[1] The nature and significance of these discrepancies were discussed in Chapter 8, pp. 186–87.

[2] George Ives, *A History of Penal Methods* (London: Stanley Paul & Co., Ltd., 1944), pp. 2–18.

Medieval gaols and the hangman

In the Middle Ages the serf, servant, vagabond, lunatic, and petty offender were whipped. Public exhibition in the stocks was a serious penalty in the days when a man's reputation in his home village affected his life profoundly. With his neck and hands held between beams, the unhappy offender was the helpless target of missiles hurled by the crowd. Some punishments repaid the culprit in kind: the seller of short-weight loaves had bread tied around his neck. The dishonest fishmonger was forced to wear a necklace of stinking smelt, which must have been unpleasant even before modern commercials linked social status with odors. The village scold was gagged with a bridle of iron.[3]

Medieval cellars, gatehouses, and towers were pressed into service as detention facilities until punishment could be inflicted. Felons, misdemeanants, debtors, and the insane were thrust together without effort to segregate sexes or classes of prisoners. Sheriffs and local magistrates turned the maintenance of gaols and the treatment of inmates over to private keepers. Little effort was made to maintain order, and the gaols were dens of lechery, debauchery, moral corruption, and pestilence.[4] They were operated to make a profit by charging the inmates fees for admission and discharge, putting on and taking off chains, providing better quarters, and supplying meals, liquor, and women. With little significant change, these conditions became the heritage of American colonial jails which persisted into the 19th century.

The 17th century brought increased resort to the death penalty in England. By 1688, some 50 offenses were punishable by death, and by the end of the 18th century, capital statutes probably exceeded 200. Several factors explain this increase. First, the death penalty was relied on to control and deter criminals because the English suspected that a strong police force would encourage political dictatorship but crime and corruption were prevalent. Second, the English doubted that transportation (exiling cadres of convicted persons to colonies) or imprisonment could reduce crime. Lord Ellenborough in 1810 described the appalling horror of penal transportation as "a summer's excursion." The gaols were known as centers of corruption that were ineffective as instruments of punishment. Third, the doctrine, which relied on crude intimidation, appeared logical in terms of the faulty knowledge of crime causation and criminal psychology that existed at the time. Fourth, it was assumed that the function of government was to protect property rights and maintain public order; little recognition was given to the social evils experienced by the lower classes. Under these circumstances, a placid and uninter-

---

[3] Ibid., pp. 55–57.

[4] Lionel W. Fox, *The English Prison and Borstal System* (London: Routledge & Kegan Paul, Ltd., 1952), pp. 20–21.

Figure 16–1. Public ridicule as a punitive technique.

In the Middle Ages a major response to criminals was to shame them before fellow members of the community. With neck and hands held in the stocks, the offender was a helpless target for hurled missiles and public ridicule.

ested Parliament, with little debate or opposition, extended capital punishment to cover property crimes.[5]

Transportation of prisoners

The exploitation of the New World created a heavy demand for labor, and British gaols were emptied for shipments of laborers to Virginia and the West Indies. The rise of slave labor and the American Revolution ended this transportation temporarily, although British judges continued to impose sentences of 7, 14, or 21 years overseas. The gaols could not hold all those awaiting transportation to destinations that were no longer available. In 1776, the "temporary expediant" was to employ these prisoners for a year in cleansing the Thames or building Royal docks.[6] The prisoners were quartered in hulks anchored in the Thames until 1857 and at Gibraltar until 1875. These were floating typhus death traps and cesspools of moral contagion.[7] When Captain Cook's voyages attracted attention to Australia, transportation was resumed, thus aborting plans to construct two penitentiaries called for in the "Hard Labour" Act of 1779.

In 1787, the first fleet transporting prisoners to Australia carried 564 males and 192 females on an eight-month voyage to the present site of Sydney. The project was hampered by the rigors of an unsettled continent, corruption among the military guards, and famine. Subsequent voyages were handled by private contractors who were paid a per capita fee, inducing overloading of ships, starvation of prisoners, and other "hell-ship" conditions to maximize profits. When assigned to road, forestry, and quarry work, the chained convicts labored 10 hours a day. When settlers came in 1793, convicts were assigned to them. Generally, a lifer became eligible after eight years for a ticket of leave affording conditional release to the free community. Transportation to New South Wales was halted in 1840, and, until 1852, the islands off Australia became the new destination. The newer colony in western Australia received transported criminals until 1867.[8]

When Captain Alexander Maconochie began four years of command of a penal settlement at Norfolk Island in 1840, he advanced two fundamental beliefs: brutality and cruelty debase the person subjected to them and the society which tolerates them, and the treatment of the prisoner should be designed to fit him for return to society purged of criminal

[5] Leon Radzinowicz, *A History of English Criminal Law and Its Administration from 1750* (New York: Macmillan Co., 1948), Vol. I, pp. 23–25.

[6] William Branch-Johnson, *The English Prison Hulks* (London: Christopher Johnson, 1957), p. 3.

[7] Frederick H. Wines, *Punishment and Reformation* (New York: Thomas Y. Crowell Co., 1923), p. 187.

[8] Ives, *History of Penal Methods*, pp. 128–60.

tendencies. Maconochie proposed that the offender should be sentenced to perform a specified quantity of labor, instead of being sentenced for a period of time. The prisoner would have to earn a fixed number of "marks of commendation" by labor and good conduct to end his imprisonment. After an initial period of restraint, deprivation, and moral instruction to induce penitence, the prisoner would enter a second stage requiring him to earn marks to pay for his shelter, food, and clothing. By frugal living, industriousness, and examplary behavior, he could save his marks to meet the quota necessary for his release. Discipline would be maintained by fines expressed in marks and by withdrawal of privileges. This would avoid degrading punishments. When his tally of marks demonstrated his worthiness, the prisoner would be permitted to join with five or six other prisoners to form a work-task team. Because this segmentation of work parties required a guard force beyond the numbers available, trustworthy inmates would be used as foremen. The group as a whole would be held responsible for maintenance of conduct appropriate for earning marks.[9]

Maconochie faced problems in carrying out his proposals. More than half of the inmates were regarded as beyond reclamation because the penal colony had been used for prisoners who had committed second crimes after arrival in Australia; regulations and servility had been maintained by flogging, irons, and a diet of bread and water; quarters were inadequate, unsanitary, and overcrowded; and the guards were accustomed to compelling obedience through harshness and resented the innovations.

To restore dignity to the prisoners, flogging and use of chains was restricted to cases involving colony security. Through payment in marks, prisoners were permitted the means to have their families with them. Court proceedings were public, with prisoners of good conduct serving as jurors. Headstones were authorized for inmates' graves. Prisoners were employed as overseers with the hope of encouraging the development of responsibility.[10]

Maconochie was relieved of his command in 1844. Critics charged that the "wholesome and invigorating influence of a firm and resolute discipline" had disappeared without promised improvements in moral character. However, the major factor was increased expense of operations.[11]

AMERICAN CONTRIBUTIONS TO PRISON TRADITIONS

The development of the prison was a milestone. Previously, as we have seen, the crime problem was "solved" with the gallows, whipping post, mutilation, exile, fine, or transportation to penal colonies. Ancient Egypt

[9] John Vincent Barry, *Alexander Maconochie of Norfolk Island* (Melbourne, Australia: Oxford University Press, 1958), pp. 72–77.

[10] Ibid., pp. 79, 98–109; 112–18.

[11] Ibid., p. 147.

and Mesopotamia had prisons, but widespread use of long-term imprisonment as a punishment in itself did not emerge until the late 18th century,
with Philadelphia's Walnut Street Jail.

The elements of the prison as a social institution, however, can be
traced to earlier times. It is believed Filippo Franci established a correctional department in 1677 in his orphanage in Florence.[12] The Hospice
of Saint Michael in Rome, founded by Pope Clement XI, included correctional quarters for boys in 1704 and for women in 1735. It was
brought to the attention of the English after a 1778 visit by John Howard.
Thorsten Sellin points out that St. Michael's was not exclusively a correctional institution and not the first of its kind, but he credits it with an
important place in the development of the prison because of the unique
design of its cell blocks and the influence of Howard's writings.[13]

Sociocultural Implications

Americans became interested in the construction and support of prisons for criminals, asylums for the insane, almhouses for the poor, orphan
asylums for homeless children, and reformatories for delinquents in the
decades after 1820. David Rothman asks why Americans in the Jacksonian period turned in this direction, when previously the poor, homeless, and insane had been left to the care of families and neighbors and
the plight of criminals who were whipped, fined, placed in stocks, or
perhaps hung, had been largely ignored. In framing this question, Rothman is consistent with the fundamental premises of our book: first, that
penological developments are symptoms of the sociocultural patterns of
the society as a whole and, second, that the crime problem is intimately
related to other major social problems. He sees the emergence of institutions for various kinds of deviants as the product of demographic, economic, and intellectual developments which undermined the traditional
social control mechanisms that had been based on the family and neighborhood. The number and density of cities had greatly increased by 1830,
and the growth of manufacturing had accelerated. As a result, political
loyalties were being transferred from towns to state government, and
people were moving from one place to another and up and down the
social class ladder. With the colonial order falling apart, some new basis
had to be established for promoting social stability.[14]

Rothman believes the prison originally emerged as an institution because of a generally held conviction that criminality was produced by

[12] Fred E. Haynes, *American Prison System* (New York: McGraw-Hill Book
Co., 1939), p. 18.

[13] Thorsten Sellin, "The House of Correction in the Hospice of Saint Michael in
Rome," *Journal of Criminal Law and Criminology,* 20 (February 1930): 533–53.

[14] David J. Rothman, *The Discovery of the Asylum* (Boston: Little, Brown &
Co., 1971), pp. xiii–xiv, 57–58.

corruptions in the community that the family and church were failing to counteract. The penitentiary was supposed to remove the offender from temptations in the community and reform him through a consistent regimen. Because it was assumed that the prisoner is not inherently depraved, a well-administered and corruption-free institution could inculcate in him the discipline the faulty family and community life had failed to produce. Early prisons, however, had failed to cope with practical problems of prison administration, such as escapes, refractory prisoners, the unprecedented expenses of long-term care of inmates, the employment of undermotivated inmates in labor, and the corruptive influences of confinement. By 1820 it had become apparent that the prison had failed to qualify as a corruption-free environment, and the time was ripe for the development of prisons that would serve as correctional institutions.[15]

From this point, the Auburn and Pennsylvania prison systems emerged to attract international attention to what was then regarded as a remarkable American invention. The central principle was the isolation of the prisoner both from the general community and his fellow inmates. The basis was established for a penitentiary characterized by general uniformity, a precise organization of time and inmate movement about the prison, and a firmly set pattern of work. Because it was assumed that isolation and imposition of discipline would assure correction of the offender, wardens were encouraged to believe that safekeeping was their all-important task. Later disillusionment with the Auburn and Pennsylvania systems, in the middle of the 19th century, failed to arouse public interest. Rothman suggests the middle class tolerated the prison as a holding place because it was useful in controlling the lower classes and the unskilled immigrants who could be kept out of sight and mind as disturbers of peace and order. By 1860 the prisons were essentially custodial in quality, and the community increasingly utilized the prison to confine persons regarded as incorrigible criminals.[16]

In tracing this history in more detail, several points should become clear. The inadequacies of penal confinement as the primary reaction to crime have been long established, but the policy has persisted because it has served functions other than the rehabilitative effects envisioned by originators of the prison. Studying the outcomes of past reform efforts permits more informed evaluation of contemporary reform practices, many of which can be explained by ideas advanced a century or so ago. Because the prison is a social invention emerging only some 150 years ago, its persistence need not be assumed, certainly not in any particular form. History suggests that any penal reform, however, is a difficult enterprise which must take into account the sociocultural patterns of the society that criminological agencies are designed to serve.

15 Ibid., pp. 82–83, 90–93.
16 Ibid., pp. 94, 239–40, 245–46.

The Walnut Street Jail

In 1762, William Penn limited the death penalty in Pennsylvania to murder, called for fines and imprisonment as penalties for most offenses, and urged flogging as a milder penalty for adultery, arson, and rape. The Quakers placed Pennsylvania in the forefront of penological history by forming the Philadelphia Society for Alleviating the Miseries of Public Prisons in 1787. They transformed Philadelphia's Walnut Street Jail into the first American penitentiary.

Control of this pioneering prison was vested in an unpaid appointed board of inspectors. This set the pattern for prison management under the theory that voluntary service by citizens would be humane and efficient. Those convicted of more serious crimes were confined without labor in 16 solitary cells, each 6 feet wide by 8 feet long by 9 feet high, with an inner iron door, an outer wooden door, and blinds and wire on the single cell window to prevent passing of contraband. Prisoners were fed a coarse pudding of maize and molasses. For a primitive toilet, a large leaden pipe extended from each cell to the sewer. A stove in the corridor provided heat. Less hardened offenders were lodged together in eight rooms approximately 18 by 20 feet. Together they labored in a large stone structure at carpentry, joinery, weaving, shoemaking, tailoring, and nailmaking. Unskilled prisoners and vagrants beat hemp or picked moss and oakum. The women worked at spinning cotton yarn, carding wool, preparing flax and hemp, washing, and mending. Each male prisoner was credited with approximately the prevailing wage but was charged the cost of his maintenance, his trial, and his fine. If there was a balance against him at the expiration of his sentence, he was held until it was liquidated. If the balance was favorable to him, he received it. Untried prisoners could work if they desired. No irons or guard weapons were allowed. Except for female prisoners, silence was enforced in the shops and at meals, but low-tone conversation was permitted in the congregate night quarters before bedtime. Religious instruction and weekly services were offered.[17]

After a year the inspectors reported: "From the experiments already made, we have reason to congratulate our fellow-citizens on the happy reformation of the penal system. The prison is no longer a scene of debauchery, idleness and profanity; an epitome of human wretchedness; a seminary of crimes destructive to society; but a school of reformation and a place of public labor."[18] The success of the Philadelphia penitentiary lasted only for three or four years. The prison became so over-

[17] Orlando F. Lewis, *The Development of American Prisons and Prison Customs, 1776–1845* (Albany: Prison Association of New York, 1922), pp. 26–28.

[18] Francis C. Gray, *Prison Discipline in America* (London: John Murray Ltd., 1848), p. 22.

crowded that industrial activity became impossible. The length of the sentences and an increase in commitments brought the population to such numbers that the personal attention to prisoners possible in the early period could no longer be provided. City politicians replaced the Quakers originally on the board, and the Philadelphia Society became an organization of opposition.[19]

Solitary confinement as an issue: The Pennsylvania system

After 1800 the Quakers increasingly campaigned for solitary confinement without labor. They argued that this would permit solitary reflection as a means of achieving moral regeneration, would prevent criminal contagion, and would avoid identification of the ex-prisoner after his return to the community. The lack of labor would permit shortening the sentence because it would make the punishment more severe, they believed; isolation is a bitter experience for man, who is a social creature. The Quakers contended that the removal of such external stimuli as labor would be a punishment that would operate forcibly upon the mind. The Pennsylvania Law of 1818 called for a prison in Pittsburgh with separate cells for each prisoner, total deprivation of work, and enforced perpetual solitude. The theory of classification was abandoned, and each cell became a miniature prison in itself. Western Penitentiary at Pittsburgh was put into operation in 1827 with 190 individual cells, 7 by 9 feet each, forming a semicircle with a small yard in front of each cell. The construction was such that the cells were not soundproof and were too small to permit labor within them. By 1833 the board of managers recommended demolition of the prison because it was unsuitable for either solitary confinement or labor.[20]

Meanwhile, there was hot debate over Eastern Penitentiary, which was to open at Cherry Hill near Philadelphia in 1829. From its initiation in 1823, there had been two issues: first, solitary confinement versus the congregate system being developed at New York's Auburn Prison, and, second, solitary confinement without labor versus solitary confinement with labor. The latter issue was paramount. In 1827, a special commission of the legislature reported its opposition to separate confinement without labor on several grounds. Solitary confinement *with* labor was considered to be as effective in preventing communication between inmates and to be less expensive because the inmates would contribute to their support. It was also believed that labor assignments worked less havoc on mind and body and afforded a means of teaching honest trades.[21]

[19] Lewis, *Development of American Prisons,* pp. 39–40.
[20] Ibid., pp. 119–20.
[21] Ibid., p. 122.

However, solitary confinement without labor became the principle behind Eastern State Penitentiary, as the prototype of the Pennsylvania system. In imitation of earlier English jails, architect John Haviland perpetuated the traditions of medieval castles at the then staggering cost of $750,000. From a central rotunda, seven stone corridors branched out like wheel spokes, each corridor flanked by solitary cells 8 feet wide by 15 feet long and 12 feet high. A toilet and water spigot were in each cell. Heating was by hot air. Each cell on the lower floor had an individual walled exercise yard. Prisoners on the upper floor were allowed a second cell. All was enclosed by an imposing outer wall.[22]

The inmates were shut off completely from the outside world. Sole visitors to the prisoner were the board of managers, superintendent, physician, moral instructor, certain guards, and official visitors. On admission the prisoner entered his cell, usually not to emerge until the end of his sentence. For days he was alone except for the officer who brought his meals. The Bible was important to the prisoner because knowledge of it would prolong the infrequent visits of the moral instructor. Until 1840 the principal stimuli to good behavior was exposure to moral literature, and punishments ranging from reduced diet to straitjackets, gags, and throwing buckets of cold water on the offender.

Gustave de Beaumont and Alexis de Tocqueville, French students of early American prisons, commented favorably on the reformative effects of absolute solitude on prisoners:

Generally, their hearts are found ready to open themselves, and the facility of being moved renders them also fitter for reformation. They are particularly accessible to religious sentiments, and the remembrance of their family has an uncommon power over their minds. . . . Nothing distracts, in Philadelphia, the mind of the convicts from their meditations; and as they are always isolated, the presence of a person who comes to converse with them is the greatest benefit. . . . When we visited this penitentiary, one of the prisoners said to us: "It is with joy that I perceive the figure of the keepers, who visit my cell. This summer a cricket came into my yard; it looked like a companion. When a butterfly or any other animal happens to enter my cell, I never do it any harm."[23]

Development of the Auburn system

Thomas Eddy, a New York Quaker philanthropist, had been impressed with Walnut Street Jail in 1796. Influenced by Beccaria, Montesquieu, and Howard, he pressed successfully for reduction of the

---

[22] Blake McKelvey, *American Prisons* (Chicago: University of Chicago Press, 1936), p. 11.

[23] Gustave de Beaumont and Alexis de Tocqueville, *On the Penitentiary System in the United States and Its Application to France* (Carbondale, Ill.: Southern Illinois University Press, 1964), p. 83.

number of capital crimes and for the erection of prisons. He was the first warden of Newgate Prison opened near New York City in 1797. The 54 rooms of this prison measured 12 by 18 feet and could accommodate eight persons each. Eddy found this congregate lodging a major factor in its failure. As early as 1800, political appointments to the governing board supplanted Quakers bringing mismanagement and riots. Overcrowding aggravated moral contamination and created disorder. Mass pardons favored obedient prisoners over penitent, reformed criminals.[24] Eddy resigned in 1803.

The collapse of this prison was among the factors contributing to the rise of the concept of prison administration known as the Auburn system. In attempts to solve the problems created by congregate confinement at Newgate, a New York State Senate committee of 1822 called for shorter sentences and solitary confinement in enforced idleness on shortened rations. Another factor was the detailed report on prisons by the New York Society for Prevention of Pauperism in 1822, which called for solitary confinement of all prisoners, with labor in cells provided only for non-hardened criminals. Young and old, hardened and novice, criminals were to be isolated from one another under strict silence if separate cells were not available. Hard labor and moral instruction were viewed as the keys to prisoner reformation.[25]

Auburn Prison, which opened in New York in 1819, sought to develop a workable system of prison administration. William Brittin, a master carpenter, was warden and Elam Lynds, a hatter, principal keeper. The original plan was to use the Pennsylvania idea of solitary confinement, but the building contractor saved money by constructing inside cells, each 3½ feet wide by 7 feet long and 7 feet high.[26] Troubles like those at Newgate soon appeared at Auburn, and a three-grade system was proposed. The most incorrigible were to be placed in solitary cells without labor. In the second grade, more tractable inmates would be in solitary confinement with labor as a recreation. The best candidates for reformation would work in association during the day and be held in seclusion at night.[27] Eighty incorrigibles were placed in solitary cells without labor in December 1821, but by the end of 1823 the experiment was abandoned. Warden Gershom Powers described the results. A number of the prisoners had become insane. One lost an eye by beating his head against the wall. Another sprang through an open cell door and fell four galleries, an intervening stovepipe breaking his fall sufficiently to save his life. The health of many of the incorrigibles was seriously impaired, and hopes of achieving character reformation failed to be realized.[28] Twenty-six of

[24] Lewis, *Development of American Prisons*, pp. 43–57.

[25] Ibid., pp. 68, 84–85.

[26] McKelvey, *American Prisons*, p. 8.

[27] Lewis, *Development of American Prisons*, p. 80.

[28] Gray, *Prison Discipline in America*, pp. 39–40.

the prisoners were pardoned by the governor. Fourteen returned because of new crimes shortly after release.[29]

With the failure at Auburn of solitary confinement without labor, a compromise plan was adopted. Instead of permitting inmates to mingle, as is usual in prisons, in workrooms and large sleeping quarters, they were worked in association during the day to permit maximum industrial production but were separated absolutely at night. This was intended to minimize corruption of inmates by one another and to reduce opportunities for the hatching of inmate plots. It was thought that daytime physical proximity would not foster contamination and insurrection because interinmate communication would be suppressed by a rule of perpetual silence. Hard labor was deemed essential to reformation of character and to the economic solvency of the prison. Only congregate labor (men working as a team in association with one another) could be economically sound, it was argued.

Prisoners were separated absolutely from the outside world, and communication with friends and relatives was permitted only under exceptional circumstances. Hard and unremitting labor, perpetual silence; and unquestioning obedience were maintained by severe punishments. Warden Powers considered corporal punishment humane because of the short time required for its application and efficient because the inmate could return to work. Warden Elam Lynds believed that adult convicts were permanently and hopelessly incorrigible and that industrial efficiency was the supreme purpose of the prison.[30]

Competition between two systems

A bitter struggle emerged over the relative merits of the Pennsylvania and Auburn systems, fed largely by the militant zeal with which the Reverend Louis Dwight attacked the Pennsylvania system as though it were a religious heresy. His position as secretary of the Boston Prison Discipline Society gave him the opportunity to use its reports to gain a broad audience before which to espouse the Auburn system. These reports and his travels made him the best known American prison expert in the first half of the 19th century. He made a deep impression on prison traditions and methods. The acrimonious campaign conducted against the Pennsylvania system worked against objectivity in the collection of information and analysis of the relative merits of the two systems.

The arguments centered on relative reformative value, expenses of construction and operation, and effects on prisoners' minds and bodies. In their 1832 study, Beaumont and Tocqueville stated the belief that the solitary system would produce more honest citizens because it prevented

[29] Beaumont and Tocqueville, *Penitentiary System in the United States*, pp. 41–42.

[30] Lewis, *Development of American Prisons*, pp. 86–95.

contamination of treatable prisoners by incorrigibles. However, they thought congregate labor was superior in teaching obedience and industriousness.[31] They found that the Auburn prisoners were more severely treated in the physical sense, but the Philadelphia prisoners were more unhappy and exposed to greater health risks.[32] Years later, Orlando Lewis applied statistical data to determine that the Pennsylvania system was highly inferior in costs of construction and operation because of necessary differences in prison design and relative opportunities for factory methods of production.[33] He decided that the solitary system could not demonstrate superiority in capacity to reform prisoners, nor could it maintain lower rates of illness, mortality, and insanity. The economic advantages of the Auburn system explain its eventual triumph, Lewis believes.[34]

Emergence of the American penal system

By 1835 Americans had established the first genuine penal system in the world, although practices varied widely in the different states. Ten states were following the Auburn plan, and Ohio and Tennessee were constructing institutions similar to Auburn. Connecticut, which had used a copper mine at Simsbury as a penal institution in which prisoners were shackled with leg irons and chained collars during daylight work and slept on straw-covered platforms at the bottom of the mine shaft, replaced it by 1835 with Wethersfield, a model prison of the Auburn type under able Warden Moses Pilsbury. Pennsylvania and New Jersey had adopted the solitary system, which was not ended until after 1866, when Eastern Pennsylvania Penitentiary was forced by overcrowding to place two men in one cell. Maine was confining prisoners in underground pits at Thomaston which were not replaced by a conventional prison until 1845. Rhode Island had tiny cells in a wing of the Providence jail. Indiana and Illinois were maintaining makeshift jails. Georgia had built an inadequate congregate prison in 1817. Other states and territories were leaving the administration of justice to local authorities. Only Boston had a satisfactory institution for confining misdemeanants. Juvenile houses of reform had been established in New York, Philadelphia, and Boston. Otherwise, another decade would pass before Americans would follow the European example in creating separate juvenile institutions. Most states had substituted imprisonment for traditional corporal punishment as criminal codes were revised.[35]

[31] *Beaumont and Tocqueville, Penitentiary System in the United States,* pp. 57–58.
[32] Lewis, *Development of American Prisons,* p. 47.
[33] Ibid., p. 239.
[34] Ibid., pp. 250–51.
[35] McKelvey, *American Prisons,* pp. 16–21.

Prison overcrowding was the major problem in the decades immediately after the Civil War. There was increased humanitarian concern over poverty, insanity, and crime. State boards of charity were developed in Massachusetts, New York, Pennsylvania, Ohio, Illinois, Rhode Island, Michigan, Wisconsin, and North Carolina. This trend reflected demands for reform, increased economy, and centralized control. Results of the demands for reform were varied. Many prisons continued to be operated without change. However, some gains were achieved. Among them was greater tenure for many administrators, which helped them regard themselves as professional penologists. They tended to regard their Christianity, common sense, and practical prison experience as sufficient qualifications for expertness. They continued to accept earlier conceptions of the best tools for reforming criminals as being religion, industrial activity, and a rather unsophisticated faith in human kindness.[36]

Reformatories: An abortive experiment

The term "reformatory" usually refers to an institution for convicted youthful offenders. The object of such institutions is to achieve behavior change rather than to induce a penitential reaction. In the first attempt to establish reformatories in America, Zebulon Brockway was called to organize the Detroit House of Correction in 1861, with emphasis on the industrial program. His approach was strongly religious, but he surpassed the average pulpit reformer in his firm grasp of penological administration. He introduced wages for production above the quota, organized a Sunday school, and provided a chaplain and morning chapel services. A matron established an evening school for women. He made the first American application of the system of grading prisoners according to degree of reformation that had been employed by Maconochie and, as we shall see, by Walter Crofton in Ireland.[37]

Efforts of the New York Prison Association culminated in the opening of a reformatory on a farm outside Elmira in 1877. Brockway was assigned the superintendency and given the opportunity to implement a new conception of a correctional institution. Legislation provided indeterminate sentences, permitting the reformatory to release inmates on parole as soon as their reformation was assured. Commitments were limited to first-felony offenders, ages 16 to 31 years. Brockway quartered the inmates on the basis of three conduct grades. At entry the inmate was assigned an intermediate grade. The higher honor grade was earned after six months through good conduct and satisfactory performance in school and shop. Six months in honor grade made the inmate eligible for parole. Serious misconduct resulting in loss of marks dropped him to a lower

---

[36] Ibid., pp. 53–57.
[37] Ibid., p. 65.

grade and gave him the problem of earning promotion to become eligible
for parole.

Brockway hoped to create a school atmosphere conducive to self-
discipline by supporting the prestige of the honor grade through privileges
and housing accommodations. College professors headed divisions of
academic and moral education. Professors, public school principals, and
lawyers conducted classes in physical geography, natural science, geom-
etry, bookkeeping, human physiology, "sanitary science," Bible, ethics,
psychology, history, literature, and economics. Because some inmates
were not benefiting from this instruction, a course in terra-cotta modeling
was introduced for dullards. This led eventually to the establishment of
one of the pioneer trade schools, offering instruction in plumbing, tailor-
cutting, telegraphy, and printing. When efforts to restrict prison labor
were successful in 1888, Brockway was freed of the necessity that the institution pay its own way through industries and seized this opportunity
to extend the rehabilitative aspects of the program. He organized military
training, expanded the programs of calisthenic exercises, and operated
trade schools only in the morning so that inmates could work in the
afternoon.[38]

By 1901 reformatories also had been established at Ionia, Michigan;
Concord, Massachusetts; Huntingdon, Pennsylvania; St. Cloud, Minnesota; Buena Vista, Colorado; Pontiac, Illinois; Hutchinson, Kansas;
Mansfield, Ohio; Jeffersonville, Indiana; Green Bay, Wisconsin; and
Rahway, New Jersey. Although reformatories were opened later in other
states, the reformatory was on the decline by 1910. It represented an application to the crime problem of a general enthusiasm throughout society for public education as the answer to many problems of the time.
Indeterminate sentences and paroles pioneered by reformatories were
positive contributions to American penology. Traditional prisons were
influenced by features of the reformatory and adopted some of them.[39]
Nevertheless, certain characteristics of the reformatory doomed it to
become a junior prison, and it failed to justify the high hopes of its advocates. The failure to assign only those prisoners most likely to respond
to rehabilitation programs made the inmate culture a major obstacle.
The staffs were weighted heavily with "old guard" prison employees conditioned to the punitive ideology. Too few, overworked "instructors"
could not lessen the institution's traditionally heavy emphasis on industry
and custody.[40] Such a staff lacked the attitudes, aptitudes, and experience
necessary to make the grading system effective. The traditions of the repressive prison were also supported by the retention of the fortress archi-

[38] Ibid., pp. 109–13.

[39] Ibid., p. 159.

[40] Attorney General's Survey, *Prisons* (Washington, D.C.: U.S. Department of
Justice, 1939), Vol. V, pp. 23–25.

Figure 16–2. Traditional cellblock in early reformatory.

Elmira Reformatory, opened in New York in 1877, initiated the reformatory phase of the history of American prisons. This view of an Elmira cellblock shows how the physical design of the traditional prison was retained. However, under Zebulon Brockway, new conceptions of the correctional institution were introduced.

tecture characteristic of the maximum-security prison; recognition of the importance of physical surroundings did not come until later.

BRITISH CONTRIBUTIONS TO PRISON TRADITIONS

Although reform of the English criminal law came in the late 18th century, revision had been advocated by some statesmen, lawyers, and religious leaders as early as the 16th century. In England extensive revisions of the criminal code were made in the spirit of humanitarianism under the leadership of Jeremy Bentham (1748–1832), Samuel Romilly (1757–1818), James Mackintosh (1765–1832), Thomas Buxton (1786–1845), and Robert Peel (1788–1850). John Howard has been credited with sparking a general interest in the reformation of character as a major prison goal, although this purpose had been advocated earlier.[41] The humanitarian attack concentrated on the legal system itself and on capital punishment, but Howard devoted his life to prison reform after assuming the post of High Sheriff of Befordshire in 1773. He concentrated on inspection and criticism of horrible conditions in English and European prisons until he died in 1790 of the plague in the Ukraine. He called for sanitary and secure prisons, separations of the sexes, separate cells for sleeping, moral uplift through influence of prison chaplains, and useful work in properly equipped shops.[42]

Establishment of the British penal system

Romilly used pamphlets and debates in Parliament to campaign for reform of the criminal law and the penal system. Although his efforts in Parliament between 1808 and 1818 had little immediate effect, he did arouse public opinion. Numerous petitions for mitigation of criminal laws influenced the appointment by Parliament in 1819 of a "Committee of Inquiry into the Criminal Laws," in spite of the government's opposition. The investigation and concurrent debate prepared the public for subsequent reform. Bentham campaigned for penitentiaries offering useful labor. Effective action came during the 1821–27 tenure of Peel as Secretary of State for the Home Department. Capital statutes were reduced and consolidated; instead of 200, only 14 felonies were punishable by death. A statutory basis for an effective prison system was created. Standards of sanitation and humane treatment were introduced into local prisons. The severity of punishment of minor offenses was reduced. The administration of justice was overhauled, and the London Metropolitan Police was established in 1829 as a model for modern law enforcement agencies.[43]

---

[41] Wines, *Punishment and Reformation*, p. 123.
[42] Fox, *English Prison and Borstal System*, pp. 26–27.
[43] Ibid., pp. 33–34.

Millbank Prison had been built in 1812, but British prison construction really began with the end of transportation to penal colonies. The major contest was between the separate-confinement Pennsylvania plan and the congregate but silent Auburn system. The Pennsylvania system was introduced at Pentonville, which was built in 1842 and was the model for 54 new prisons, when William Crawford (1788–1847) returned to England with great admiration for the system after an inspection of American prisons. Until 1853 the prisoners at Pentonville wore masks in the corridors and during the exercise period, sat in separated pigeon-holes in chapel, and worked a crank in solitary cells to earn meals.[44] Under the Penal Servitude Act of 1857, which ended transportation, British felons were to serve a year of congregate labor and be given conditional release for the period of remission earned by hard work and good conduct.

More inmates and a centralized penal system

There were two major patterns in 19th-century English prison reform, according to Gordon Rose.[45] In the first half of the century, emphasis was placed on developing a suitable alternative to the filthy, corruption-ridden local prisons. Partially overlapping the first pattern in time was the second, in which the national government assumed greater responsibility in operating prisons as a place of long-term confinement. Before 1877 English prisons were under two forms of administrative authority, a set of institutions developed by the central government to take up the slack left by the declining use and abandonment of transportation, and an aggregate of local institutions under local authorities. However, beginning in 1840, the number of prisoners began to rise at an increasing rate. Although critics of the time blamed the increase on an easing of punishment as a deterrent to crime, Leo Page explains it as a result of economic distress, greater willingness of juries to convict when harsh penalties were not utilized, and the reduction of prisoner deaths from jail fever and the gallows.[46]

With the abandonment of transportation, Parliament in 1853 tried to reduce the population of overcrowded prisons by providing for the discharge at home, on tickets of leave, of prisoners under sentence of transportation. The ticket of leave was a form of release of prisoners before the completion of their sentences under conditions that they would abstain from crime and find legitimate employment. Such half measures, however, did not alleviate prison conditions. The Prisons Act of 1877

[44] Ives, *A History of Penal Methods,* pp. 182–86.

[45] Gordon Rose, *The Struggle for Penal Reform* (London: Stevens & Sons, 1961), pp. 1–2.

[46] Leo Page, *Crime and the Community* (London: Faber & Faber, Ltd., 1937), p. 56.

transferred ownership and control of all municipal prisons to the national government. Imprisonment had become the major penal tool, after playing a secondary role to the gallows and transportation to penal colonies. This did not signal the triumph of humanitarianism over repression, however. Rather, as Page assesses the English attitude toward crime in the latter half of the 19th century, there were inconstant trends which fluctuated between repression for the sake of deterrence and less harsh methods.[47]

The Irish system

Irish prisons, particularly, failed to produce the reformed prisoners that effective use of the tickets of leave required. Since punishment had failed to deter the hardened criminals in his charge, Sir Walter Crofton, as chairman of the board of directors of Irish prisons, resolved to train them "naturally" to a state of reformation that would justify public acceptance of the released prisoner. Flogging was abandoned, and the intention was to treat the inmates as "men," not as "convicts."

To achieve this objective, he introduced what became known as the Irish system. This system involved three stages. The first consisted of at least eight months in a cellular prison at Mountjoy, Dublin, under strong discipline. For the first four months, the prisoners were on a restricted diet and the only work permitted was picking oakum. Then the experienced shoemakers and tailors were put to work at their trades. There was no trade training at this prison, but one hour of schooling each day was provided, including orientation to the mark system and instruction on police efficiency in apprehending violators of tickets of leave. Violent prisoners and "idlers" were separated into groups. The violent prisoners were put in chains and fed a low diet.

At the second stage in the Irish system, if his conduct justified such action, the prisoner was transferred to Spike Island Prison to labor on fortifications. To progress through four conduct classes, he earned marks through orderly demeanor, effort in school, and industriousness at work. Modest wages were paid, graded according to conduct class.

In the third or intermediate stage, he was transferred to one of the small prison units with populations of less than 100, to work at projects such as land reclamation under a few unarmed guards. The working conditions were similar to those of free labor. These units served as filters between imprisonment and conditional release. The purpose was to demonstrate that the prisoner was being trusted and to show the public that he could be trusted. The advantages of moral rectitude and regular employment were emphasized in lectures to the inmates.[48] Releases

[47] Ibid., p. 61.

[48] Mary Carpenter, *Reformatory Prison Discipline as Developed by Sir Walter Crofton* (London: Longman, Green, Longman, 1872), pp. 2–25.

from prison under tickets of leave were conditioned on subsequent avoidance of further crimes, evil associations, and an "idle and dissolute" life. The moral instructor, J. P. Organ, sought jobs for inmates scheduled for release and supplemented police surveillance through bimonthly visits to the released prisoner's place of employment.[49]

Rose explains the success of Crofton and the Irish system as the result of the advantages of operating a small and compact system, which declined from a maximum of 3,933 inmates in 1854 to 1,575 in 1862. British reformers strongly advocated the Irish system, but their words were lost in the public clamor over a series of violent robberies in London and a general increase of crime in Great Britain in 1862. The Garrotters Act of 1863 imposed flogging for robbery with violence. Ticket-of-leave men were a special target of the newspapers' demand for action. The advocates of longer sentences and more severe prison policies were supported by the Royal Commission on Penal Servitude. At the same time there was a trend toward greater integration and tightening of penal treatment through centralization of administration.[50] In this way, the Irish system lost out.

LATER AMERICAN DEVELOPMENTS

Although perhaps not intentionally, the Auburn and Pennsylvania systems ushered into prisons "the filing system" form of administration, in which criminals are indexed and filed away until called for as though they are inert, lifeless objects. Assessing American prisons in 1921, Louis Robinson found some of them as deplorable as those of the 18th century.[51] In the years between the two world wars, American prison conditions were characterized by enforced idleness, untrained personnel, gross overcrowding, and other negations of the principles that had been enunciated earlier by penological reformers. Richard McGee describes the prisons of these times as crucibles of crime and degradation.[52]

The legacy of the past, according to the President's Crime Commission, is reflected in the grim and fortresslike prison architecture which arranges tiers of cells with a view to security, in the daily regimen of many such institutions, in the wide gulf between inmates and staff, and in the way groups of prisoners are marched about, from cells to dining room to shop. Although the architecture and routine of juvenile training schools are far less forbidding, they "too often emphasize in subtle ways that

[49] Ibid., p. 61.
[50] Rose, *Struggle for Penal Reform*, pp. 5–13.
[51] Louis N. Robinson, *Penology in the United States* (Philadelphia: John C. Winston Co., 1922), pp. 311–12.
[52] Richard A. McGee, "What's Past Is Prologue," *Annals of American Academy of Political and Social Science*, 381 (January 1969): 8.

restraint is their primary purpose and treatment a casual afterthought."[53]

Recent decades have produced some gains in corrections, however. Although levels of progress and degrees of persistence of the conditions of the past vary greatly among the states, the general pattern has been consistent upgrading of the standards of living for prisoners. American prisons have been noteworthy in their introduction of psychological diagnosis as a means of both lending direction to programmed activities and recognizing the individual qualities of inmates. Although application of these principles to classification procedures has sometimes been grossly deficient, their introduction signals recognition of the necessity of giving logical order to the prison as a social system.

The 1930s undermined the industrial model which had been looked to as the answer for prison reform. The high rate of general unemployment during the depression contributed to legislative prohibitions against the sale of prison-made goods on the open market. The resultant increase in idleness among prisoners, some experts hoped, would result in treatment programs to fill the vacuum, but in most states this hope was in vain. During these years, however, the Federal Bureau of Prisons and a few states developed the foundation of an improved prison system, with libraries, schools, visiting privileges, work programs, suitable housing, culinary facilities, and trained personnel.[54]

As the following chapters will document, correctional institutions lack such elements of a well-organized system as sufficient resources or coordination of services. There are, however, trends toward specialization, diversification, centralization, and alternatives to confinement.[55] Some states provide special facilities for drug addicts, alcoholics, sex offenders, and the mentally ill. Modern institutions provide a reasonably diverse range of academic and vocational training, casework, medical care, group counseling, and industrial employment.

At varying rates, prisons have improved staff competence through the recruitment of professionals and training programs for personnel. The autonomy of a single prison has become rare with a trend toward centralization of prisons into state systems. Concurrently with efforts to give greater thrust to treatment programs there has been some effort to reform the traditionally custodial environment of the prison. Increasing emphasis is being placed on alternatives to confinement: probation and parole,

[53] President's Commission on Law Enforcement and Administration of Justice, *The Challenge of Crime in a Free Society* (Washington, D.C.: U.S. Government Printing Office, 1967), p. 163.

[54] Negley K. Teeters, "State of Prisons in the United States, 1870–1970," *Federal Probation,* 33 (December 1969): 22.

[55] Clarence Schrag, "The Correctional System: Problems and Prospects," *Annals of American Academy of Political and Social Science,* 381 (January 1969): 19–20.

prerelease and work-release centers, halfway houses, and community treatment centers.

SUMMARY

The history of corrections points up the comparative recentness of the development of the prison as an institution. Previous modes of dealing with offenders indicate the possibilities of fuller utilization of alternatives to imprisonment or of revamping methods of employing the correctional institution. In tracing the contributions of pioneers to the ideas characteristic of contemporary corrections, we have gained a basis for understanding the functions and practices of contemporary agencies.

FOR ADDITIONAL READINGS

Babington, Anthony. *The English Bastille: A History of Newgate Gaol and Prison Conditions in Britain, 1188–1902*. London: MacDonald & Co., 1971.

Barry, John Vincent. *The Life and Death of John Price*. New York: Cambridge University Press, 1965.

DeFord, Miriam Allen. *Stone Walls: Prisons from Fetters to Furloughs*. Philadelphia: Chilton Book Co., 1962.

Lejins, Peter P. "Ideas Which Have Moved Corrections." In *Proceedings of American Correctional Association, 1970*, pp. 308–22.

Lewis, W. David. *From Newgate to Dannemora*. New York: Cornell University Press, 1965.

McGrath, W. T. (ed.). *Crime and Its Treatment in Canada*. New York: St. Martin's Press, 1965.

Playfair, Giles. *The Punitive Obsession: The Unvarnished History of the English Prison System*. London: Victor Gollancz, Ltd., 1971.

Powers, Edwin. *Crime and Punishment in Early Massachusetts, 1620–1692*. Boston: Beacon Press, 1966.

Pugh, Ralph B. *Imprisonment in Medieval England*. Cambridge, England: Cambridge University Press, 1968.

Putney, Snell, and Putney, Gladys J. "Origins of the Reformatory." *Journal of Criminal Law, Criminology and Police Science*, 53 (December 1962): 437–45.

Sellin, Thorsten. "A Look at Prison History," *Federal Probation*, 31 (September 1967): 18–23.

17

The prison as a formal organization

The correctional agency is a formal organization in that it is a product of man's deliberate effort to mobilize the skills and coordinate the activities of individuals for the accomplishment of official goals. It is an organizational scheme for promoting employee conformity to official expectations and for advancing the purposes of the agency.

Organization management in correctional institutions characteristically operates through the system of administration known as bureaucracy. This chapter will examine the effects of bureaucratic techniques on the prison as a formal organization.

BUREAUCRACY IN PRISONS

The correctional institution is a people-changing agency like the monastery, mental hospital, school, youth camp, and military base. These organizations are unique in that they work with human "material," and the methods employed must respect its human quality. Efforts to change individuals must recognize that humans are capable of modifying consequences by their reactions to the methods used. The variability of human conduct implies a continual strain between the uniqueness of the individual and the organizational drive to standardize behavior for the sake of "efficiency."[1]

Formal organization is a scheme for coordinating the activities of diverse specialists by drawing jurisdictional lines as a means of determining their specific responsibilities and authority within a set of interrelated activities. Codes of written rules and procedures systematize their activities, and written documents record and transmit the information vital to these activities. Each specialist is able to routinize his tasks within the

[1] David Street, Robert D. Vinter, and Charles Perrow, *Organization for Treatment* (New York: Free Press of Glencoe, 1966), pp. 4–6.

total complex of tasks. By standardizing tasks, the specialist is able to exploit repetitive operations in applying a technique or service to a larger number of units within a given length of time. Bureaucracy describes the method employed to put into operation the goals of the formal organization.

In the popular conception, the bureaucrat is tied up in red tape and is officious, smugly incompetent, and blind to individual differences. This emphasis on the negative side of bureaucracy obscures its value in meeting problems created by the increasing complexity of organization management. Max Weber has pointed to the advantages of a trained bureaucracy: precision, speed, unambiguity, knowledge of the files, continuity, discretion, unity, strict subordination, easing of friction, and reduction of material and personnel costs.[2] Properly employed, bureaucracy can be a useful administrative tool for meeting prison problems.

Formal organization in prisons

Primarily, the prison exists as a formal organization because the activities within its walls are patterned. The persistence of inmate culture regardless of place and time is evidence that systems of action are shared by inmates from prison to prison and from time to time. Chapter 11 described patterns of inmate behavior.

In addition to inmate patterns, there are also uniformities in the behaviors of keepers. Inherent in the formal organization of the prison are systems of ideas, roles, and statuses as resources for implementing meaningful social interaction. The behavior of individuals, giving flesh and blood to the organization, is systematized by social norms all are expected to follow. Each member is pressed to abide by the rules associated with his status in the organization. The norms compose a set because they express a system of ideas (ideology) which lends significance to the work of the members as individuals or as a collectivity.[3]

In this sense, the formal organization exists because the prison is an example of a social institution in which spontaneous or experimental behavior of the past has become regularized and passed down through generations of prison employees in the form of cultural norms. The novice employee is taught these ideas and rules much as a child is socialized by his parents. The norms of the prison culture become vehicles for regularizing employee behavior to the extent they are incorporated into the employees' personalities. The prison culture has been shaped by the functions assigned the prison as an agency of social control. The norms of the prison culture reflect the goals assigned the agency.

[2] Hans H. Gerth and C. Wright Mills (trans. and eds.), *From Max Weber: Essays in Sociology* (New York: Oxford University Press, Inc., 1946), p. 214.

[3] For discussion of the functions of ideologies, see Chapter 8.

Two kinds of authority

The prison organization disciplines the acts of individuals to fit them into a meaningful whole and to give authority to those occupying order-giving positions in the status system of the prison bureaucracy. Individuals submit to discipline, Talcott Parsons believes, because there are two sources of authority: technical competence, and the incumbency of a legally defined office.[4]

Technical competence calls for obedience because the person of superior formal status has specialized knowledge or experience that is necessary to achieve the ultimate purposes of the organization. The subordinate would presumably obey voluntarily because his own interests require the status holder's services. The authority of the correctional worker in a particular status in the organization is derived from his possession of the specialized knowledge, skills, and experience required. By demonstrating technical competence, the worker can gain acceptance by inmates of his authority. For example, if the vocational teacher has the technical competence to prepare inmates for jobs they hope to obtain after release from prison, he is in an advantageous position to gain their willing compliance with the rules of the educational endeavor.

Authority derived from *encumbency of a legally defined office* inheres in the possession of a "job slot" in the formal organization. Decision makers have authority over subordinates because they occupy official positions to which the authority is legally attached. Orders must be obeyed because the "boss" issues them, and the consent of the subordinate is of secondary importance. Because this form of authority is based on imposition of rules and on obedience for its own sake, it lends itself to what has been called a *punishment-centered bureaucracy,* to be discussed below.[5]

Assets and weaknesses of formal organization

Ideally, formal organization promotes managerial efficiency. By scaling the economic and psychic rewards granted the status holder, the organizational scheme can recognize differences in the importance of tasks, in their difficulty, and in the amount of training they require. Ambitious staff members are motivated to qualify themselves through training and to accept the risks of decision making as the price for gaining economic and psychic rewards.[6]

[4] A. M. Henderson and Talcott Parsons, *Max Weber: The Theory of Social and Economic Organization* (New York: Oxford University Press, Inc., 1947), pp. 58–59.

[5] Alvin W. Gouldner, *Patterns of Industrial Bureaucracy* (Glencoe, Ill.: Free Press, 1954), p. 24.

[6] Chester I. Barnard, "Functions and Pathology of Status Systems in Formal Or-

Limitation of the amount of discretion permitted employees at the lower levels of the status hierarchy allows the formal organization to recruit employees with less skill, personal aptitude, experience, and specialized training than would be necessary in decision-making situations. Among the human interactions within an organization, there are recurrent situations which lend themselves to standardized handling. Theoretically, it would be wasteful of talent to burden certain staff members with routine matters that can be isolated and turned over to employees at the lower status levels. By narrowing the number of jobs requiring special qualifications, a rational scheme for manning the prison promotes effective use of the available reservoir of talent.

In dealing with masses of persons, bureaucracy is an efficient tool because of the objectivity with which its code of calculable rules or standards for evaluating clients is applied without regard for personal sympathy or special favor. Attention is concentrated on the common characteristics of a group of events or persons prejudged as pertinent to the objectives sought. This placing of persons into categories permits recurrent and routine administration, avoiding the time-consuming necessity to issue special instructions for each situation.

Carried to an extreme, however, this depersonalization can aggravate the social debasement of the inmate. Probably the major defect of formal organization as applied to prisons is that it is too readily adaptable to a social system based on coercion, due to its emphasis on routinization of behavior. The individualization of treatment is obstructed when inmates are diagnosed at the prison's reception center according to limited, stereotyped categories, and their case histories present a series of glib generalized phrases telling little about the lives they are supposed to describe. Administration is swift, but the individual qualities of the subjects of that administration are lost in the process. Similarly, spontaneity of staff-inmate relationships is lost, to the detriment of treatment purposes when relationships are restricted to the jurisdiction of formal roles. The confidence of the client is vital to winning his participation in the therapeutic process. The personal qualities of both therapist and client defy efforts to standardize interaction within the narrow range provided by formal roles.

Why study formal organization?

The formal organization is a potential tool for penal reform because its rational basis facilitates change through the reformulation of policies, the alteration of authority and communication arrangements, and the introduction of new philosophies and kinds of personnel. We say "poten-

ganizations," in William Foote Whyte (ed.), *Industry and Society* (New York: McGraw-Hill Book Co., 1946), pp. 53–59.

tial" because formal organization also can maintain the conditions that should be changed.

The study of formal organization focuses attention on the prison itself as a phenomenon distinct from both employees and prisoners. The significance of the theoretical distinction between organizational structure and the individuals affected by it is that certain actions and consequences are enjoined independently of the personality of the persons involved.[7] The personality and personal aspirations of the persons so involved do contribute to the spontaneity and unpredictability of the human factor in the equation of social relationships. However, the deliberately created organizational scheme shapes the behavioral patterns and thought processes that operate within the prison. To praise or blame specific individuals solely for events within the walls would be an oversimplification.

Informal groups emerge largely because of efforts by individuals to fulfill personal wishes in spite of the limitations imposed by formal organization. Spontaneous groups among inmates are the inverse image of the formal organization, broadly speaking. A similar phenomenon is found among employees. Some identify with one another on the basis of friendships and common interests. Others resent one another. Cliques form because of bonds of congeniality derived from common interests in sports, religion, fraternal organizations, identification with a residential area, and a host of other shared experiences outside the job sphere. These emotional linkages cause the occupants of job slots to form personal alliances which color staff interrelationships. The interactions may subvert management objectives, but this is not necessarily the case. In fact, spontaneous behavior may remedy the defects of the formal scheme and enable it to work in spite of its limitations.

The formal structure shapes informal groups emerging among employees and inmates. Employees, who are selected from job applicants in terms of skills, aptitudes, education, and previous experience according to the criteria of the formal organization, select members of their own congeniality groups. A similar screening process operates for inmate groups through assignments to particular prisons, sleeping quarters, and work details.

THE PUNISHMENT-CENTERED BUREAUCRACY

The maximum-security prison is designed to maintain almost total control over inmates through concentration of power in the hands of a

---

[7] Phillip Selznick, "Foundations of the Theory of Organization," *American Sociological Review*, 13 (February 1948): 28. Also see Rudolf H. Moos, "The Assessment of the Social Climates of Correctional Institutions," *Journal of Research in Crime and Delinquency*, 5 (July 1968): 174–88; and Stephen G. Lubeck and LaMar T. Empey, "Mediatory vs Total Institution: The Case of the Runaway," *Social Problems* 16 (Fall 1968): 242–60.

ruling officialdom, a detailed set of regulations, routinization of behavior, and constant surveillance.[8] These are the characteristics of the punitive-centered bureaucracy—a form of organization which is likely to rely on the authority derived from encumbency of a legally defined office and is supported by the punitive ideology. The reliance on coercion and the pains of confinement means that inmates are unlikely to conform to official rules through a sense of duty or self-identification with the goals of the prison. Thus the central problem of the punishment-centered bureaucracy is to maintain order without the benefit of a personal commitment of a large share of the prison population to the goals of the prison's official organization.

Techniques of inmate control

Custodial prisons use a number of techniques to prevent or suppress inmate violations of official rules that have been designed to maintain order within the institution. For the majority of prisoners, good food, relief of tensions through counseling, and the activity of work and recreation forestall frustration. The monotonous routine of prison life and the apparently irresistible force of official authority encourage passive compliance. Self-control by inmates can also be motivated by the identification of some inmates with the values held by officials, fear of official reprisals, or the desire to retain or gain personal advantages in work or housing assignments. A minority among the prisoners is always willing to pass to officials inmates' secrets that are useful in maintaining control.

Probably the most promising preventive strategy is a just and constructive administration of punishments. When a correctional officer writes an excessive number of disciplinary reports, there is a possibility that he is using his official authority as a prop for his own sense of inadequacy. To avoid such situations, candidates for custodial positions should receive psychological screening. An inmate's violation of rules may signal underlying sources of frustration that call for therapy rather than arbitrary punishment. Ideally, a disciplinary committee would inform the inmate of the charge against him, hear his side of the story fully and without hostility, and tailor the decision to the objective of preventing future misconduct.[9]

In the punishment-centered bureaucracy, custodial reactions to major rule violations can be categorized as active control techniques involving isolation of the transgressor from more compliant inmates and the withdrawal of privileges. To increase surveillance or to break up an inmate

[8] Gresham M. Sykes, *Society of Captives* (Princeton, N.J.: Princeton University Press, 1958), pp. xiv–xv.

[9] Richard W. Nice, "The Adjustment Committee: Adversary or Adjunct to Treatment?" *American Journal of Correction,* 22 (November–December 1960): 26–30.

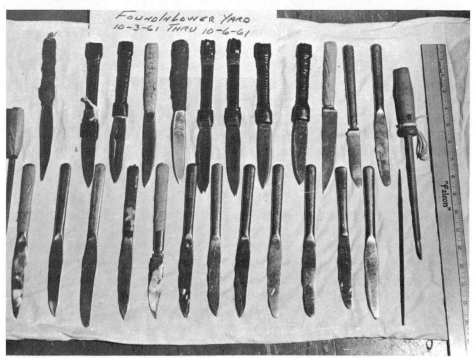

Figure 17–1. Display of improvised knives.

The necessity of control techniques in a maximum-security prison is indicated by this display of improvised knives taken from inmates in a three-day period.

clique, the deviant may be transferred to another prison specializing in a sterner level of custody. Another measure is the isolation of the transgressor in his own cell or in special punitive segregation quarters. Punishments also include demotion in conduct grade and loss of "good-time" rewards. Conduct grade suggests the trustworthiness of the inmate and determine the kind of work assignment for which he is eligible, as measured by opportunity for freedom in task initiative and provision for physical mobility without guarding. Inmates can be granted reduction of time served through "good time" rewards for acceptable conduct. Punishment reports can also delay release from prison on parole.

Surveillance techniques include periodic counts to make certain all inmates are present and the "shakedown" of inmates and their living quarters through such search techniques as running hands over the inmate's body, emptying pockets, and opening bundles. Such inspections also have the objective of finding contraband items such as drugs and escape equipment. Irregularly timed counts and shakedowns upset inmate conspiracies, as does periodic rotation of work and housing assignments. Officials also may encourage inmates to avoid alliances with their peers. When prisoners "do their own time" voluntarily, the creation of inmate cliques is discouraged.

Limitations on coercion

Although the prison bureaucracy has a degree of power unparalleled among American social institutions, the warden is limited in what he can do with and for inmates by the values of groups outside the prison.[10] Sympathies for the "helpless captive" clash with fears of the "ruthless criminal." The prison's functional relationships with other agencies are also checks on its authoritarianism. The parole board has access to prison records and inmates. Mental hospitals frequently treat disturbed inmates. Grand juries periodically inspect prisons. Courts receive prisoners' appeals on sentences and writs concerning penal treatment. A sharp discrepancy between public beliefs and his own actions is likely to embroil the official in public controversy.[11]

The "defects of total power" have been indicated by Gresham Sykes. As the sole control device, coercion requires surveillance and detailed instruction made possible only by constant alertness on the part of a relatively large number of custodial officers. Violent retaliation is ineffective in dealing with subtle forms of inmate opposition over the long term.

[10] Donald R. Cressey and Witold Knassowski, "Inmate Organization in American Prisons and Soviet Labor Camps," *Social Problems,* 5 (Winter 1957–58): 217.

[11] For discussion of the trend toward increased judicial supervision of prison disciplinary decisions, see Daniel J. Gallington, "Prison Disciplinary Decisions," *Journal of Criminal Law, Criminology and Police Science,* 60 (January 1969): 152–64.

Because the guard force on duty at any particular time is small compared to the inmate population, the custodial staff is insufficient for continual warfare. Confinement reduces the difference between punishment status and the usual lot of the prisoner. Punishment may even make a hero of the resistant prisoner. The automatic allocation of privileges has erased much of the relation between inmate compliance and the gaining of rewards. On his arrival in prison, the inmate is granted, with no effort on his part, privileges of visiting, recreation, receiving and sending mail, and reduction of sentence through "good time" rewards.[12]

Another drain on the strength of coercion is the personal feelings of custodial or correctional officers. Daily interaction between officers and inmates leads to the corruption of authority. The officer's duties frequently require him to be both a policeman and a work foreman; to create work motivation, he must reduce the aloofness appropriate to the policing function. He must personally apply abstract rules formulated for purposes he does not always understand, and he is the immediate target for the hostilities these rules may excite among inmates. As an employee at the lowest level of the status hierarchy, the correctional officer may have his own reasons for resenting bureaucratic organization which give him a sense of common interests with inmates. Face-to-face contact lessens any tendency to regard prisoners as uniformly evil or deserving of arbitrary punishments. Since his superiors tend to rank his efficiency on his ability to handle inmates, the guard is vulnerable in inmate maneuvers between complete compliance and overt rebellion.

Alliances with inmates

In the face of these defects of total power, the custodial prison maintains stability through accommodations with the inmate social system. Desired jobs, extra food, relaxation of rules, and other privileges are granted inmates who "cooperate," without abandoning their overt commitment to inmate groups. "Cooperation" can mean abstinence from violence or advocacy of a policy of "getting along." Through information and goods gained through association with guards, the "cooperative" inmate leader is able to maintain influence over prisoners. Inmate leaders do not "rock the boat" because the status quo gives them privileges and power. When these inmate-staff coalitions are destroyed by changes in inmate power structure or changes in prison staff, this delicate balance is upset.[13]

The customary inmate ban on any association with officials, which acts as a safeguard against the surveillance of officers, also maintains the monopoly of inmate leaders over communication between officials and

[12] Sykes, *Society of Captives,* pp. 48–58.
[13] Sykes, *Society of Captives,* pp. 125–26.

prisoners. Although the accommodation of certain prisoners indicates the guard's tacit recognitio.. of the inmate social system, his choice of inmates as receivers of covert rewards gives him the status of king maker among qualified inmates.[14]

The high priority given social protection as a prison goal creates a suspicion of all inmates which supports the custodian's dominance of the formal channels of communication within the authoritarian prison. Not only does the custodial officer have the most frequent, constant contact with prisoners, but inmates' complaints and requests flow through the security staff, which accordingly plays a crucial role in determining the results of inmate requests for interviews with officials, assignment to treatment programs, or transfer to other cell blocks or work tasks. For inmates, the correction of grievances and the solution of a multitude of personal problems rest largely with the custodial staff.[15]

BUREAUCRACY BASED ON COMPETENCE

The movement toward the rehabilitation model (see Chapter 11) depends on the application of technical competence as the basis of authority within the formal organization of the prison. If the inmate regards the services offered as germane to his own needs, the competent correctional specialist can gain his voluntary participation in the processes that will lead to the achievement of correctional purposes. A technically competent worker has the knowledge and decision-making skill appropriate to his job functions. He applies these skills in formulating individualized reactions to inmate behavior and problems, rather than the standardized responses characteristic of the punishment-centered bureaucracy.

An occupational system

Prison occupations may be categorized as professional, technical careerist, and semiskilled.[16] Technical competence ideally is called for in all three categories, to varying degrees.

Through prolonged and intensive study, the *professional* acquires a fund of theoretical knowledge he can apply to achieve systematic handling of a range of events. The professional's characteristic independence of thought is a safeguard against ossified procedures that can hinder

[14] Richard A. Cloward, "Social Control in the Prison," in Richard A. Cloward *et al., Theoretical Studies in Social Organization of the Prison* (New York: Social Science Research Council, 1960), pp. 42–45.

[15] Richard H. McCleery, "The Governmental Process and Informal Social Control," in Donald R. Cressy (ed.), *The Prison,* (New York: Holt, Rinehart & Winston, Inc., 1960), pp. 161–62.

[16] See Elmer H. Johnson, "Occupational System of Criminology: Its Environment and Problems," *Annales, Internationales de Criminologies,* No. 2 (1964), pp. 82–83.

individualized responses to clients. To balance conformity to organizational norms and initiative in decision making, the professional is disciplined in his sphere of competence largely by his occupational ethic.

In the term *technical careerist,* two concepts are combined to describe personnel competent in specific spheres through job experience and/or formal education. "Technical" refers to knowledge and skills essential to capable performance of vital tasks of at least intermediate difficulty. "Career" connotes a relatively orderly sequence of passage through a series of related jobs, with incentives motivating the aspirant to move through the sequence of novice, aide, and other intermediate statuses. The terminal status of a technical careerist is usually as a functionary in middle management. Everett Hughes has noted that commitment to a career is an orientation the individual can use to interpret his own qualities and the events affecting him.[17] In the course of his occupational experiences, the careerist in corrections becomes committed to an organizational ideology and identifies his personal interests with those of the prison. Whereas the professional identifies himself with fellow specialists regardless of workplace, the careerist is dedicated to the particular organization within which he works. His dedication to the agency makes him a particular asset in maintaining organizational stability.

The *semiskilled worker* accepts a job with the agency for the sake of income but does not commit himself to a correctional career. His low occupational specialization and training relegate him to the lowest statuses of the organization. He is a ready recruit for a "home guard" dedicated to protecting the immediate work group, even at the expense of the interests of the total organization. Since he has the most frequent contact with inmates, he can block the introduction or revision of procedures. The opposition may be that of the *traditionalizer* who is dedicated to outmoded practices he regards as based on sacred wisdom or that of the *utilizer,* who regards his work indifferently as a series of short-run tasks with no conception of their underlying significance.[18]

In a prison organization based on technical competence, the professionals would be the elite among executives, therapeutic and diagnostic specialists, and managers. They would be role models, agents of change, and interpreters of the theoretical foundation of correctional practice. Occupying positions in the middle level of the prison's status hierarchy, technical careerists would receive advanced training in the agency or a relevant undergraduate college education. In-service training and selection of recruits would be designed to improve the competence of the

---

[17] Everett C. Hughes, *Men and Their Work* (Glencoe, Ill.: Free Press, 1958), p. 63.

[18] Adapted from Robert W. Habenstein and Edwin A. Christ, *Professionalizer, Traditionalizer, and Utilizer* (Columbia: University of Missouri Press, 1955), pp. 42–43.

semiskilled workers, including correctional officers. Some would be moved toward the orientation of technical careerists.

Problems of manpower

Manpower deficiencies are a central problem in attempts to achieve correctional reform through technical competence. Table 17–1, which

TABLE 17–1

Employees in correctional institutions, 1965

Type of institution	Average daily population or totals	Number of employees by function		
		Custody	Service	Education, counseling
Absolute Numbers				
Juvenile	62,773	14,612	11,454	5,621
Adult	362,900	48,572	18,768	3,721
Percentages				
Juvenile	100.0	46.1	36.2	17.7
Adult	100.0	68.4	26.4	5.2
Ratio: Inmates per Employee				
Juvenile	1.98	4.30	5.48	11.17
Adult	5.11	7.47	19.34	97.53

Source: Adapted from President's Commission on Law Enforcement and Administration of Justice, *Task Force Report: Corrections* (Washington, D.C.: U.S. Government Printing Office, 1967), Table 2, p. 51.

samples the facts of available manpower, supports several conclusions. One is that juvenile institutions generally have ratios of fewer inmates per employee, especially among personnel assigned to tasks of education and counseling. However, even for juvenile institutions the tasks of safe-keeping and maintenance of institutional services absorb the bulk of available staff. The data in Table 17–1 actually underestimate the personnel problem because qualified full-time psychologists, psychiatrists, and teachers are concentrated in relatively few states, in excess of their proportionate share of total inmates. For example, eastern states with 23.7 percent of the adult prisoners have 32.6 percent of the teachers working in American prisons, compared with 18.1 percent working in southern states holding 27.7 percent of the prisoners.[19] The available treatment employees are distributed unevenly among correctional institutions. An undetermined but substantial proportion of inmates do not have access to personnel specializing in treatment.

[19] President's Commission on Law Enforcement and Administration of Justice, *Task Force Report: Corrections* (Washington, D.C.: U.S. Government Printing Office, 1967), p. 180.

Furthermore, the data do not indicate the level of formal training and other qualifications required in dealing with personality problems. One study did probe the level of training of "social workers." Of the 48 state prison systems, 18 reported no social workers, and 30 reported a total of 443 social workers on their staffs. Of these 30 systems, only 14 had any masters of social work. Only 29 percent of the 443 "social workers" were reported specifically to have college degrees.[20]

In-service training

While the importance of preservice training in developing professionals cannot be challenged, in-service training of present staff holds promise as the major device for increasing the supply of competent personnel during the current transition in correctional practices away from the restraint and rectification models and toward the rehabilitation and reintegration models.

In-service training can facilitate communication between management and personnel, among staff members, and between the agency and experts in allied fields. Theoreticians and experts from outside agencies can introduce new ideas and offer frames of reference to give significance to the discrete events of correctional practice. Prison employees are concerned with concrete applications of these ideas.

To stabilize the social system of the prison on the basis of a new status hierarchy and new roles, the staff first would be oriented to the proposed organizational structure and its functional relationships. Changes in the agency status-role system can upset familiar relationships and create anxiety among the "older hands." The shock of change can be reduced by stressing the benefits that can accrue to the workers themselves and demonstrating how familiar principles are incorporated into new ideas. Misinformation, a frequent source of anxiety, can be corrected. Dissatisfaction with the conditions to be corrected is an important resource in eliciting the support of informal groups. The flow of information up the chain of authority can be an effective means of securing modification of policies and procedures.

Sensitivity, the capacity to respond to stimulation, is a quality essential to treatment, whether defined as reciprocity or process (see Chapter 11). If the prison is to be a treatment institution, all personnel should have this capacity. Through in-service training, technical careerists and semiskilled workers can be encouraged to recognize two important aspects of sensitivity. The offender must be sensitized in his orientation to his social universe because his personality is an important ingredient in people work, and the worker must view the situation as the offender sees

[20] Elmer H. Johnson, "The Present Level of Social Work in Prisons," *Crime and Delinquency,* 9 (July 1963): 291.

it, if he is to move the offender from one form of conduct to another. Sensitivity training can help the prison employee to see himself as an actor in a social system which encompasses interactions of staff and offenders within the structure of correctional programs.

SUMMARY

The formal organization of a prison is intended to serve as a framework within which officials achieve assigned goals by regularizing the relationships among staff members. As a formal organization, the prison shares with other institutions the advantages and disadvantages of bureaucratic techniques for managing large groups of persons subject to its control. In this sense, the prison functions in ways only partially controlled by its administrators. Correctional institutions vary in the nature of their formal organization and the degree of formality characterizing the relationships among the human beings involved. The quality of staff competence also varies, limiting the effectiveness of some prisons regardless of the skill with which a "blueprint" scheme was developed. The complexity of prison operations and the necessity to coordinate specialized activities, however, have made bureaucracy a universal characteristic of prison administration.

FOR ADDITIONAL READING

Berk, Bernard B. "Organizational Goals and Inmate Organization." *American Journal of Sociology,* 71 (March 1966): 522–34.

Blau, Peter M., and Scott, W. Richard. *Formal Organizations.* San Francisco: Chandler Publishing Co., 1962.

Burns, Henry, Jr. "A Miniature Totalitarian State Maximum Security Prison." *Canadian Journal of Corrections,* 11 (July 1969): 153–64.

Craddick, Ray A. "A Note on the Dilemma of Custodial Officers in Counsellor Training." *Canadian Journal of Corrections,* 12 (April 1970): 117–19.

Etzioni, Amitai. *A Comparative Analysis of Complex Organizations.* New York: Free Press of Glencoe, 1961.

Johnson, Elmer H. "In-Service Training: A Key to Correctional Progress." *Criminologica,* 4 (November 1966): 16–26.

Julian, Joseph. "Compliance Patterns and Communication Blocks in Complex Organizations." *American Sociological Review,* 31 (June 1966): 382–89.

Litwak, Edward. "Models of Bureaucracy Which Permit Conflict." *American Journal of Sociology,* 67 (September 1961): 177–84.

Mouledous, Joseph C. "Organizational Goals and Structural Change: A Study of the Organization of a Prison System." *Social Forces,* 41 (March 1963): 283–90.

Targets for In-Service Training. Washington, D.C.: Joint Commission on Correctional Manpower and Training, 1967.

18

Operations of the prison's
formal organization

The operations of correctional institutions can be compared to a three-legged stool, the legs of which are custody, industry, and treatment. A one-legged stool is a precarious seat, and two legs are not much better. The three aspects are interdependent in their contributions to the total organization and to the operations of one another.

The justification of custody lies largely in the legal obligations of the warden to maintain safekeeping and the community's concern for its own security. Growing awareness of the social and psychological roots of criminal behavior and increased doubts about the efficacy of penological policies that emphasize safekeeping for its own sake have challenged the overwhelming priority previously placed on custody. Correctional executives dare not overlook custodial responsibilities, but the means employed are increasingly emphasizing a partnership with treatment programs.

A primary justification for prison industrial programs has been reduction of the taxpayers' burden. These programs draw objections, however, from free industry and organized labor, who dislike competition from prison-made goods. With public opinion ambivalent, advocates of prison industries are turning to justifications tied to either custodial or therapeutic purposes.

In continuing the study of the formal organization of correctional facilities, this chapter will investigate the diversity of such organizations in terms of factors that affect their operations. The possibilities of integrating either custodial or industrial programs with treatment objectives will be evaluated, but consideration of treatment programs will be delayed until Chapter 20, following analysis of the effects of confinement on inmates.

DIVERSITY AMONG PRISON ORGANIZATIONS

American correctional institutions vary widely in the nature of their formal organization. They differ in ultimate goals; the size, number, location, and design of physical plants; the size and quality of staffs and inmate populations; the quality of industrial and treatment programs; the philosophy of chief administrators; and their place in the organizational scheme of the state government.

Alternatives in organizational design

There are diverse schemes for fitting prisons into the overall structure of state government. These include providing an independent state prison department including both adult and juvenile institutions, having each prison report to a board or directly to the governor as a separate entity, and merging institutions with parole and probation agencies. Institutions, paroles, and probation, have been placed in a division of the department of public welfare; corrections in a department of institutions; and prisons and mental hospitals in a department of mental health and correction. A department of corrections with an independent youth authority has also been organized.[1]

Correctional agencies were initially decentralized when state responsibility in this area was limited to prisons. Because usually there was only one state prison and the scope of prison activities was narrow, authority could be concentrated in a board at the facility. When there were several prisons, each board reported directly to the governor. Such local boards are relatively inefficient because their members serve on a part-time basis and have insufficient correctional knowledge, and no provision is made for the coordination essential to a statewide system.[2] Expansion of correctional services through the addition of parole activities and specialized institutions such as reformatories and women's prisons has meant such boards must assume responsibility for a wider range of services.

The diversity of current schemes is a product of the singular histories of each state. Sometimes a particular reform group or a strong correctional administrator has left a mark. In some instances, the usefulness of penological patronage has hampered efficiency. Public inattention to the correctional institution and the false belief that no special competence is required for prison management have slowed the introduction of modern management principles. Furthermore, when habituated to independence in administration, middle managers tend to resist centralized control. This power struggle is characteristic of prison systems which have emerged out of a loose confederation of local prison camps or of systems which must impose control over previously autonomous units.

A number of issues have been raised in relation to the place of correctional institutions in the structure of state government. One is whether

[1] For a categorization of states according to organizational scheme, see Garrett Heyns, "Patterns of Corrections," *Crime and Delinquency,* 13 (July, 1967): 421–31.
[2] Ibid., p. 428.

correctional institutions should be allied with other kinds of institutions or there should be an autonomous department of correction. Autonomy is urged as a means of promoting staff morale through the sharing of a specific mission and the problems characteristic of the prison. Common traditions and organizational history may unify staff, but there remains the question of what constitutes an effective division of labor among governmental institutions. A main objection to merger of correctional institutions with mental hospitals or welfare agencies is that the special functions of penal institutions would be subordinated. Industrial programs have an accepted place in prisons but have all but vanished from mental hospitals. Prison officials support the therapeutic ideology in varying degrees, but some of them see the increasing emphasis on open institutions as unrealistic in the case of aggressive prisoners.

On the other hand, merger of correctional institutions within a larger, more inclusive organization simplifies the structure of state government. This scheme is more economical for smaller state governments because many services are common to all institutions. Merger with hospitals and welfare agencies favors the acceptance of the therapeutic ideology in correctional institutions and expedites recruitment of prison treatment personnel. Prisons are more likely to gain additional resources from their legislatures if their interests are presented together with those of other agencies that may be in greater public favor. The transfer of prisoners from one agency to another for specialized treatment would be simplified.

Another question is whether probation and/or parole should be integrated with correctional institutions. This would promote coordination of programs to make the correctional career of the offender a consistent experience. The trend toward community-based corrections assumes that parole is a continuation of the correctional process begun in an institution. Duplication of specialized services such as record keeping, staff training, and research could be avoided. On the other hand, integration of community programs with correctional institutions increases the possibility that prison authorities would use parole as a device to motivate compliance with prison rules, to alleviate prison overcrowding, or to reward manipulation-prone prisoners. Inclusion of probation in such a program raises a special issue because the granting of probation is a function of the court, but supervision is not consistent with the court's other functions. This is an argument for consolidation of probation supervision with a state correctional agency.

A third issue involves the management of juvenile correctional services by the same department handling adult corrections. Opponents of such a scheme contend juvenile offenders require a different treatment philosophy and kind of staff and that association with adult offenders has a deleterious effect on young offenders and on public attitudes toward juveniles. A favorable public image has given juvenile correctional agencies an advantage in gaining support.[3] On the other hand, since many juveniles pose the same problems as adult offenders, they pass into adult institutions, and some of the duplication of supporting services could be avoided by a consolidation of the two programs.

Size of inmate population

Organizational necessities are affected by the size of the offender population, which in turn is influenced by the size of the state's population. In 1970, the number of adult prisoners ranged from 226 in Vermont to 25,833 in California. The populations of state juvenile institutions ranged from 62 in Hawaii to 5,134 in California.[4]

Generally, the smaller populations are concentrated in the New England and Mountain states and the larger populations in the Middle Atlantic and East North Central sections. The kinds of offenders eligible for commitment to prisons will affect the size of the prison population in a given state. Approximately half of the states include misdemeanants in the prison population, but even in these states the proportion and type of misdemeanants so handled varies. Some state prisons accept only misdemeanants with longer sentences. Others take only female misdemeanants. To a lesser degree, prison populations vary according to the minimum age set legally for admission to prison.

The size of the prisoner population necessarily affects managerial efficiency. Unless there is a sufficient number of inmates of a specified type, there are not enough appropriate candidates for a specific kind of facility or treatment program to supply a constant flow of subjects, as is necessary for efficient use of staff and other resources. Examples of special facilities are first-offender units, youthful offender units, mental hygenic clinics or hospitals, trade training facilities, reception centers, and women's prisons. When these special groups are limited in number, the alternatives are to accept high per capita costs for the sake of individualization of treatment or to create heterogeneous populations of a size sufficient for economical operations, thus risking contamination of rehabilitatable offenders and forcing inmates into inappropriate treatment programs.

Every prison requires a minimum custodial and management staff regardless of prisoner population size. There must be a warden, guards, administrative personnel, and industrial and farming supervisors in sufficient number to perform minimum functions, some on a 24-hour basis. When the prison unit is small, the high per capita costs of minimum staffing become a barrier to the extension of rehabilitation programs. One

---

[3] Heyns, "Patterns of Correction," p. 430; Maurice A. Harmon, "Unraveling Administrative Organization of State Juvenile Services," *Crime and Delinquency*, 13 (July 1967): 436–37.

[4] Data from *Directory of Correctional Institutions and Agencies* (College Park, Md.: American Correctional Association, 1971).

Figure 18–1. Small prison units for highway maintenance.

The small prison is characteristic of some of the southern prison systems employing prisoners for highway maintenance. This 100-man field unit in North Carolina has a dormitory-type cellblock in the foreground. To the right of the cellblock is the canteen-hobby shop. The mess hall and clothes house are to the rear. To the left center is the segregation unit for punishment. Two guard towers permit surveillance of the wire fence, which is lighted at night.

possible strategy is to increase the average size of prison units and divert the savings on per capita costs into treatment programs. However, custodial and treatment objectives are complicated when the prisoner population rises above 200. The individuality of the inmate is lost in the population mass, and the problem of inmate control is complicated. A small increase in program quality calling for individualized attention requires relatively large expenditures. The scope of industrial operations in large penal institutions excites opposition to such programs from sources outside the prison.

Small, specialized units

Small correctional institutions have been established in a number of states—California, New York, Ohio, Michigan, Massachusetts, Maryland, Washington, and Wisconsin—although most of their prison units are large. Smaller units are used for forestry and farming operations or are designed to serve specialized functions. Such units as women's prisons, reception centers, and first-offender units are examples of the latter. The use of prisoners for highway maintenance has also resulted in an inmate population fragmented into small units in North Carolina, Florida, Alabama, Virginia, and Georgia.

The placement of inmates in work camps outside walled prisons has major advantages. It provides useful and instructive work for inmates in an environment favorable to mental as well as physical health, largely because the regimentation and monotony that are so marked in the maximum-custody prison are lacking. The camps make possible the separation of prisoners of various types, thus reducing the possibility of contamination of attitudes. The problem of prison overcrowding is relieved at a low cost, since the expense of constructing and manning the walled prison can be avoided. The work in forests and farms is valuable to the state in improving natural resources at low cost. The problem of prison idleness is relieved when meaningful employment is provided.[5]

The operation of a small unit can be more expensive, however, because a lower prisoner-staff ratio ideally is called for. Small population size in and of itself does not guarantee a genuine treatment program, and provision should be made for counseling, training, and other treatment services that will profit from greater staff-inmate intimacy.

Physical conditions of prisons

Of the 142 state prisons with more than 400 inmates in 1970, 37 percent had been opened before 1900 and 58 percent before 1925.[6] An old

[5] Seymour J. Gilman, "Correctional Camps Present an Answer—Michigan," *American Journal of Correction,* 17 (May–June 1955): 6–8.

[6] Data from *Directory of Correctional Institutions and Agencies.*

prison may have been remodeled or expanded, but the original construction will reflect the early conception of the prison as a fortress. Designed for a smaller population than they now hold and built before contemporary techniques of sanitation and ventilation were developed, these old prisons obstruct contemporary penological objectives. Exterior walls and cellblock design impede expansion for new industrial and treatment facilities or to accommodate increasing inmate populations. While it was found in 1970 that only 35 of the 142 major prisons had an average inmate population greater than "normal capacity," prison overcrowding is underestimated by this statistic because the fluctuation of population over the year is not considered.

Promising developments are reflected in some of the new prisons and in the expansion of some established institutions, as summarized by Norman Johnston. In an era of increasing prisoner populations and changes in penal philosophy, the high expense of constructing walls has contributed to a deemphasis on security. A uniquely prison style of architecture has tended to disappear as efforts have been made to ameliorate prison harshness and stress has been placed on normal living. Architectural techniques utilized to achieve these results have included the use of louver-type windows, preformed masonry screens, and informal arrangements of buildings on a "campus." Reduction in the massiveness of construction, more liberal use of glass, and bold use of bright colors have also been noted.[7]

CUSTODY AS AN ADJUNCT TO TREATMENT

The emphasis on suppression as the most important dimension of custodial duties is being questioned increasingly. A higher degree of experimentation with organizational schemes in which correctional or custodial officers will participate directly in the treatment process can be expected. Because the custodial officer has the most frequent contact with inmates, he has greater impact on them than any other functionary. Glaser's study of federal prisoners found inmates selected correctional officers most frequently as either most liked or most disliked among all prison personnel.[8] A second trend will be greater involvement of the inmates themselves in prison management for the sake of internal order.

The officer's role and characteristics

Alert and attitudinally flexible correctional officers are vital to the accomplishment of prison goals. Through frequent face-to-face contacts,

---

[7] Norman Johnston, "The Changing Face of Correctional Architecture," *Prison Journal,* 41 (Spring 1961): 14–20.

[8] Daniel Glaser, *The Effectiveness of a Prison and Parole System* (Indianapolis, Ind.: Bobbs-Merrill Co., Inc., 1964), pp. 133–35.

the officer's behavior strongly influences the evaluations placed by inmates on prison experiences. The officer's observation of his charges can provide information of great value to treatment specialists.

The role of a correctional officer depends on the orientation of the prison. When custody is the only factor, the "good jail man" takes a group of prisoners out and brings all of them back; he has a forceful personality and is courageous in dangerous situations. In an industrial program, the *correctional officer–work supervisor,* when there is such a hybrid role, must be informed in trades and capable of motivating workers. He must maintain production and security concurrently. When rehabilitation of prisoners is given high priority, the *supervisor* is expected to maintain security with minimum coercion and greater reliance on understanding of the factors shaping behavior.

There is also great interest in creating a *correctional officer–counselor* role, which requires active participation of correctional officers in the treatment process. This subprofessional role demands a reasonable degree of training in behavioral science to develop the insights and skills necessary to maintain the treatment process. The objective is to utilize the daily incidents of officer-inmate relations as opportunities to initiate and support treatment. When more sophisticated therapy is indicated, the officer would know when and how to initiate referral to treatment professionals with whom he is placed in direct communication by the role structure.

Generally, the position of correctional officer has a low prestige ranking among occupations. In one study, a sample of respondents ranked the correctional officer 16th, on the average, among 20 occupations, including teacher, salesclerk, policeman, soldier, farmer, carpenter, truck driver, printer's helper, and service station attendant.[9] Their low status appears to be due to the stereotyped image of the "convicts" they control and the poor opinion of prisons held by a substantial portion of the public. Such a low prestige ranking is inconsistent with the potential contribution of the correctional officer to the prison.

The quality of a custodial force depends on the kinds of persons who are recruited for and remain in correctional careers. A study of custodial officers in a southern maximum-security prison found that few persons with education beyond high school apply for custodial jobs. When recruits leaving the service were compared with those who stayed, there were no differences in educational, marital status, or previous military experience. However, of those who stayed, a disproportionate number were in the age group 36 through 45 years.[10]

Another study administered four ability, interest, and personality tests

[9] William C. Smith, "Some Selective Factors in the Retention of Prison Guards," Master's thesis, North Carolina State University at Raleigh, 1963, pp. 38–39.
[10] Ibid., pp. 70–72.

to a sample of 100 correctional officers. The scores were compared for officers with extremely "good" or "poor" performance ratings. The "good" officers were found to have a better verbal ability, higher social service interests, and lower clerical and computational interests. They were more self-confident, less critical and intolerant of others, more dominant in face-to-face situations, less subject to mood swings and worry, more likely to complete important social objectives, and more varied in pattern of interests.[11]

The possibilities for protection plus treatment

Although corrections generally has moved toward stressing rehabilitation as a goal, the public will not overlook failures to protect society from threats to its sense of security.

The correctional institution cannot have entrance requirements that permit selection among applicants of those least likely to create behavioral problems; it must take all convicted offenders sent to it. The college keeps its "good" students and rejects those who are undermotivated. The prison keeps its recalcitrants through denial of good-time rewards and paroles and, at least theoretically, expedites the release of "good" prisoners. A trend toward restricting imprisonment to the least promising or most aggressive convicted offenders would aggravate the safekeeping problems of the prison.

A fundamental question is whether a correctional institution can *emphasize* custody for the sake of social protection and still demonstrate high efficiency in achieving rehabilitation. Donald Cressey sees a conflict between these orientations. Individualized treatment requires concern for interests of the offender *and* protection of society. Since he views the inmate as "sick" rather than "bad," the treatment-oriented worker regards the inmate's rules infractions as symptoms of *inability* to conform. In contrast, custody orientation reflects the view that the inmate's violations of rules are *deliberate*.[12]

Johan Galtung sees other conflicts. If coercion is to deter potential criminals, the prison should have a negative public image; if the rehabilitated offender is to be accepted into the community after release, the public image should be either neutral or positive. Individualized treatment requires the staff to be alert to latent characteristics of the inmate for clues unlocking the riddle of his criminality; custodial responsibilities focus attention on those visible factors (age, recidivism, length of sentence, overt behavior, and so on) which lend themselves to standardized

[11] Richard N. Downey and E. I. Signori, "The Selection of Prison Guards," *Journal of Criminal Law, Criminology, and Police Science,* 49 (September–October 1958): 234.

[12] Donald R. Cressey, "Achievement of an Unstated Organizational Goal: An Observation on Prisons," *Pacific Sociological Review,* 1 (Fall 1955): 44–45.

reactions by keepers. The custodian usually avoids deviations from standardized rules and procedures; the therapist emphasizes differential handling of inmates in recognition of the variations among offenders and among causes of criminality.[13]

Another version of custody

Traditionally, the largest portion of staffs of most prisons has been given the tasks of maintaining internal order and protecting the outside community from inmates regarded as dangerous. The traditional version of custody is difficult to maintain because of the instability of any social system that depends on direct or indirect coercion to hold men against their will. This difficulty has been aggravated by the antiquity of many prisons, the reliance on even greater repressions to control prisoners when their rebellion demonstrates the failure of coercion, the role and goal conflicts between custodial and treatment staffs, the effects on inmate morale of a motivational system based essentially on denial of privileges, and the vulnerability of the control system to corruption by some custodians.

New conceptions of custody promise fuller recognition for the objective of preparing prisoners to be responsible citizens. The President's Crime Commission noted the emergence of a *collaborative regime* which emphasizes increased communication between custodial staff, inmates, and treatment staff.[14] Fuller use is made of the counseling potential in the close physical contact of correctional officers with all aspects of inmate life. Institution staff are encouraged to place less emphasis on surveillance and control for their own sake and to rely more on inmate morale and cooperation to maintain order. Some institutions have rewarded inmate residential or work groups for performance beyond minimal standards. Under this motivational system, the custodial role is less in the disciplinarian model and more in the coaching or counseling vein.

Custodial personnel as counselors

Because most correctional institutions lack enough trained counselors, one expedient is to employ custodial officers for this purpose. There are difficulties in this practice. Will the custodian-counselor be able to overcome the conflict between the policing and authoritative elements of his usual role and the free communication and mutual understanding re-

[13] Johan Galtung, "Prison: The Organization of Dilemma," in Donald R. Cressey (ed.), *The Prison* (New York: Holt, Rinehart, & Winston, Inc., 1960), pp. 122–23.

[14] President's Commission on Law Enforcement and Administration of Justice, *Task Force Report: Corrections* (Washington, D.C.: U.S. Government Printing Office, 1967), pp. 47–51.

quired of his role as counselor? To what extent can his personal qualities and unstructured previous experience qualify him for this hybrid role? Will he have the attitudinal flexibility to avoid extension of a punitive orientation into the therapeutic relationship? How can the sociocultural environment of a previously punitive-oriented institution be modified to win acceptance by correctional officer and inmate of the new role relationships?

Donald Clemmer describes such an experiment. Employees were prepared for the innovation by an in-service training program, publication of an administrative order, and article on counseling in the employee publication. The level of counseling technique was held to the "type in which one neighbor talks with another neighbor over the back fence." Clemmer says exploitation of one another by either employees or inmates was not a problem. Custodial supervisors gained insight and understanding through experience and study of the classification documents describing the personality and background of their charges. Fuller interest in the inmates was demonstrated, and the emotional atmosphere of the institutions improved. The aloofness between custodial and treatment staffs was reduced.[15]

Inmate participation in control

Four methods have been employed to share with inmates the responsibility of maintaining institutional order. First, guns have been placed in the hands of selected prisoners in three southern states. This technique holds escapes to a minimum. One of the secrets of its "success" is that the hostility of other prisoners toward the inmate guard forces him to maintain his allegiance to the officials. The operation of additional factors is indicated by William McWhorter's investigation of differential moral evaluations among armed trustees and other prisoners in Mississippi's Parchman Prison.[16] Isolation from previous peers and the expectation that armed trustees will enforce official norms act to move them toward value consensus with the staff. Unintentionally, this punitive-oriented setting provides support for the "retroflexive reformation" principle, which calls for alienation of a criminal from other criminals so that he identifies with prosocial values and ultimately becomes an active agent of reform for himself and other criminals.[17]

The second method is the unintended result of the accommodation

[15] Donald Clemmer, "Use of Supervisory Custodial Personnel as Counselors: An Expedient," *Federal Probation,* 20 (December 1956): 36–42.

[16] William L. McWhorter, "The Trusty: A Sociological Analysis of an Inmate Elite," Ph.D. dissertation, Southern Illinois University, Carbondale, 1972.

[17] Donald R. Cressey, "Changing Criminals: The Application of the Theory of Differential Association," *American Journal of Sociology,* 61 (September 1955): 119.

between the inmate and the formal systems of the maximum-security prison. By default or disuse some administrative responsibilities are turned over to selected inmate clerks. Under this arrangement, requests for cell or work reassignments can be handled expeditiously when clerks have personal reasons for being favorably inclined to them. Documents and reports can be "misfiled," "lost," or "delayed" mysteriously.

Inmate "self-government" has been the third approach. Development of constructive attitudes and habits is one of its purposes.[18] Thomas Mott Osborne credited the George Junior Republic of Freeville, New York, with inspiring his idea of a prisoner democracy, the Mutual Welfare League,[19] but Harold Helfman cited two antecedents. In the 1860s, Zebulon Brockway assigned selected prisoners to custodial and monitorial duties at the Detroit House of Correction in a manner similar to Maconochie's experiment at Norfolk Island.[20] Twenty years later, Warden Hiram F. Hatch formed The Mutual Aid League of Michigan State Prison at Jackson, with nine prisoners he appointed serving as an advisory board for preserving "good order."[21]

Inmate participation in the maintenance of order may be a means of encouraging self-discipline when inmates have a genuine voice in prison affairs, but the idea has little merit when tacked on to an essentially totalitarian prison. Under the latter circumstances, inmates are likely to suspect the motives of officials. The scheme becomes a thinly disguised spy system. Further, inmate leaders are likely to exploit the "inmate government" for personal advantage.[22]

The fourth approach, the traditional "honor grade" system, has been described as a form of inmate self-government. Selected prisoners are chosen to serve as trustees in work positions requiring trustworthiness. They are rewarded with good-time reductions in sentences and other privileges. Frequently, however, this system does not involve the selection of inmates according to criteria relevant to governing the prison as a democratic community. Instead, trustees are chosen to meet the demand for inmate workers at places and in jobs that are difficult to guard. The "honor grade" role demands passive subservience to official norms; it does not emphasize free expression or provide opportunities for demonstrating self-discipline.

---

[18] For a summary of issues involved, see J. E. Baker, "Inmate Self-Government," *Journal of Criminal Law, Criminology, and Police Science*, 55 (March 1964): 39–47.

[19] Thomas Mott Osborne, *Society and Its Prisons* (New Haven, Conn.: Yale University Press, 1916), p. 139.

[20] Zebulon R. Brockway, *Fifty Years of Prison Service* (New York: Charities Publication Committee, 1912), pp. 96–97.

[21] Harold M. Helfman, "Antecedents of Thomas Mott Osborne's 'Mutual Welfare League' in Michigan," *Journal of Criminal Law and Criminology*, 40 (January–February 1950): 597–600.

[22] Max Grünhut, *Penal Reform* (Oxford, England: Clarendon Press, 1948).

WORK PROGRAMS AS AN ADJUNCT TO TREATMENT

The history of prison industries has been marked by inconsistency of goals and the masking of genuine motives under the guise of prisoner "rehabilitation." Two trends have shaped prison labor programs. The first reflects the attitude that prison labor is somehow different from labor in general. In keeping with the punitive ideology, the prisoner is thought of as part of the abnormal world of repressive confinement. Work is seen as a punishment and an obligation imposed on the prisoner. "Hard labor while wearing stripes" is considered an efficient means of deterring future crime or of balancing the scales of retribution. It is also argued that the prisoner should work to pay for at least part of his keep as an obligation to taxpayers. Whereas the insane and mental defectives were formerly expected to help pay the expenses of custodial institutions, the imprisoned offender is currently the prime target of this argument.

The second trend has been toward improvement of prison labor conditions and increased concern that prison employment should play a part in the rehabilitation of character. The aim is to prepare the inmate for a constructive life after release, and prison labor is intended to reduce the alienation of the offender from society. Vocational instruction is used to develop occupational skills and work motivation in tasks related to the inmate's self-interest. The rhythm of work and rest and the conditions of employment are as similar as possible to those in the free world.

Quite separate from this approach is the argument that hard labor of any kind instills the commendable habits of the dedicated, efficient worker. Even menial drudgery is defended as a form of "therapy."

Sources of opposition to work programs

Correctional institutions have faced many impediments in realizing the diverse goals of work programs. Under the *principle of less eligibility,* the inmate is considered less worthy of satisfactory employment and training than the worst-paid noncriminal. This principle was supplanted by what Hermann Mannheim calls the *principle of nonsuperiority;* the earlier principle was slightly liberalized to contend that the condition of the criminal should not be superior to that of the worst-paid noncriminal. Consequently, the prison industry was restricted by a psychological perspective conflicting with the pure economics of reduced prison operational costs.[23]

When reformers sought to develop prison labor programs for purposes other than punishment, they encountered hostility from organized free labor and from some businessmen and industrialists. The development of group cohesiveness has been a major problem for organized labor in the

[23] Hermann Mannheim, *The Dilemma of Penal Reform* (London: George Allen & Unwin, Ltd., 1939), p. 56.

United States, where workers have been prone to identify themselves with the lower middle class and have lacked the spontaneous class solidarity upon which European unions were based psychologically. Selig Perlman describes the experimentation which culminated in the job-conscious unionism of the American Federation of Labor about 1890. Recognizing the strength of property rights in American society, unionism adapted the concept to justify the union's right to control jobs. With job opportunity viewed as limited, the worker's adherence to the union was won through establishing "rights" in the jobs for the individual and for the work group through agreements regulating priority and seniority in employment.[24] Since organized labor regards as exclusively its own the rights so painfully acquired, labor unions have been sensitive to the extension of job rights to nonmembers. Under the principle of less eligibility, the prison inmate was regarded as an inappropriate competitor for the jobs of free labor.

As labor unions were being organized, prison industries were operated under either the lease or the contract system. The *lease system* turned care and custody over to an entrepreneur for a stipulated fee. Under the *contract system,* the state retained control of inmates but sold their labor to an entrepreneur at a daily per capita fee. In an alternative form of the latter, the *piece-price system,* the entrepreneur furnished the raw materials and paid the prison for each finished item.[25]

Labor unions and employers' associations found a common cause in protesting the "competition" of prison labor. As early as 1801, a New York law required boots and shoes to be labeled with the words "State Prison."[26] The prosperous contract industries attracted major opposition in the northern industrial states. There was a series of investigations into the contract and lease systems in 11 states during the 1870s and 1880s, and manufacturers in certain industries organized a National Anti-Contract Association in 1886.[27] The piece-price system was proposed as an alternative to counter the growing opposition to the contract system. Contracting of federal criminals was made illegal in 1887.

From lease to state use

During the 1830–70 period, the lease and contract systems provided employment and the funds to establish American penitentiaries. In the

[24] Selig Perlman, *A Theory of the Labor Movement* (New York: Augustus M. Kelley, 1949), pp. 182–200.

[25] Definitions of the several systems were taken from Frank T. Flynn, "The Federal Government and the Prison—Labor in the States, I: The Aftermath of Federal Restrictions," *Social Science Review,* 24 (March 1950): 20–21.

[26] O. F. Lewis, *The Development of American Prisons and Prison Customs, 1776–1845* (Albany: Prison Association of New York, 1922), p. 48.

[27] Howard B. Gill, "The Prison Labor Problem," *Annals of the American Academy of Political and Social Science,* 157 (September 1931): 84.

zeal to make prisons self-supporting, the idea that prisoners should be denied opportunities to communicate with each other was necessarily set aside. Some prisons had been turned over to economic exploiters, jeopardizing security and treatment. The priority of profit making tended to jeopardize the parole of skilled prisoners, control of contraband, and the warden's authority. To keep production costs down, the contractor tended to discourage absenteeism, which was necessary for inmate participation in rehabilitation programs. Mass production of a limited variety of articles was favored over the diversity appropriate for vocational training on an individualized basis. Competition with free industry was direct. At the same time that many prisons were freeing themselves of the objectionable features of the contract and lease systems and achieving steady employment, the opponents of prison industry succeeded in barring sale of prison-made goods on the open market.[28]

As one major exception to the general trend, Minnesota established a model state account system in the early 1890s when it took over production and marketing of farm machinery and bindery twine from contractors.[29] In the *state account system,* the state becomes the manufacturer and sells its products on the open market. The political power of Minnesota farmers and the absence of private-enterprise production of farm machinery in the state explain the continued sale of prison-made farm machinery on the open market, a phenomenon today.

As legislation has struck at interstate commerce in prison-made goods, the state-use and public works and ways systems have become paramount. The *state-use system,* suggested in 1887 and endorsed in 1900 by the U.S. Industrial Commission,[30] produces goods and services for agencies of the state and their political subdivisions. *Public works and ways* involves road construction and repair, reforestation, soil-erosion control and the like. The Hawes-Cooper act of 1929 deprived prison-made goods of their interstate character and made them subject to state law. The Ashurst-Summers Act of 1935 prohibited transportation of goods into states forbidding their entry and required the labeling of prison-made goods shipped in interstate commerce. In the face of mass unemployment during the Great Depression, every state had passed legislation by 1940 to take advantage of this opportunity to ban prison-made goods of other states.[31]

---

[28] Attorney General's Survey of Release Procedures, *Prisons* (Leavenworth, Kans.: Federal Prison Industries, 1940), Vol. 5, pp. 29–30.

[29] Blake McKelvey, *American Prisons* (Chicago: University of Chicago Press, 1936), pp. 103–4.

[30] Ibid., pp. 98 and 105.

[31] Flynn, "Federal Government and Prison," pp. 20–21.

Conflict among work goals

The implied and stated objectives of work programs frequently conflict with one another. Labor as a punitive device stigmatizes labor for non-punitive purposes. It strengthens inmate resentment against the prison and its officials, complicating vocational training, which requires instructor-student rapport. "Hard labor" in prison as punishment deprives work of the dignity and incentives of labor in a free society, thereby distinguishing the inmate from the labor force he is supposed to rejoin ultimately. The punitive rationalization calls for labor at the lowest level of skill to remove the probability that the inmate will gain any personal satisfactions.

Conversely, employment for the sake of vocational training aborts the deterrent effect of punitive labor. Efforts to maximize economic return from industries require emphasis on output, rather than on correction of faulty attitudes of the prisoner-worker. Work pace must not be interrupted to counsel prisoners or to afford the personalized instruction necessary for on-the-job training. Industrial foremen usually are selected for their qualifications in meeting output quotas, rather than for their instructional skills. Maximum output usually demands concentration on a few products to exploit the possibilities of minimizing per unit costs. Cost factors favor the use of power machinery which reduces the economic advantage of prison labor and decreases the role of prison industries in overcoming prisoner idleness. The increased volume of output raises the issue of competition with free labor. To be in keeping with the objectives of individualized treatment, vocational training requires a wide variety of products to extend the range of skills taught.

Wardens agree that the most difficult prison to administer is the one in which prisoners languish in idleness. Absence of work leads to moral and physical degradation and corrupts institutional order. However, aimless drudgery is of little advantage. Consequently, official statements of industrial goals recognize the rehabilitation of prisoners to varying degrees. As Max Grünhut has noted, the attainment of rehabilitation through labor is supposed to be through *training for work* and *training by work*.[32] Work has the virtue of relieving boredom. Under the concept of training *by* work, it is assumed that habits developed through regular employment will persist automatically. In contrast, training *for* work would employ this more superficial and immediate motivation to work as the first stage of a more sophisticated process of stimulating the prisoner's interest in employment on a long-term basis. Inmate employment becomes only one aspect of a multifaceted effort to change the prisoner's attitudes and values. Wages and consideration of the inmate's individual qualities in job assignment can be inducements to work motivation.

[32] Grünhut, *Penal Reform*, p. 209.

Manuel López-Rey is one of those who hold the view that within certain limitations, prisoners should share the fundamental human rights to work and to earn equal pay for equal work. The limitations stem from the juridical situation of the prisoner, which denies him the right to select his work, to refuse a certain task without justification, or to change his place of work. Aside from these factors, López-Rey would organize prison labor to be as similar to free labor as circumstances would permit. He would bring private industry into the prison to provide the equipment and wage scales of free labor, arguing that self-respect and self-responsibility would emerge as basic elements in the rehabilitation of prisoners. Therefore, he contends, many of the existing psychological and psychiatric services would become unnecessary.[33]

His case has much merit under the sociological contention that a large share of the persons admitted to prison are psychologically normal and do not require deliberate therapeutic intervention. In any event, such intervention entails strong resistance from involuntary clients in the abnormal setting of the prison as an institution. If the inmates were employed at wage scales and under working conditions of the free community, they could be treated largely as members of that community but housed during nonworking hours in a correctional facility. They could be charged usual board and room costs and be responsible for obtaining their working clothes and equipment and for conducting the recreational programs otherwise sponsored by the institution. Thus they would be held responsible for the same matters as individual free citizens are. This largely normal setting would be able to avoid most of the usual costs of the total institution while meeting all the needs of its dependent residents.

In a similar vein, two other ideas have been noted as particularly promising. The United Nations has been the organizational framework for promotion of the integration of prison labor with the free economy under the moral principle that work and choices within its activities are rights.[34] Another encouraging trend in the United States is increased reliance on work release, in which prisoners are employed in the free community at regular paid jobs in the terminal phase of their sentences.[35]

Labor and rehabilitation

Four activities related to the training and employment of inmates can be differentiated. First, maintenance work activities are concerned with

[33] Manuel López-Rey, "Some Considerations of the Character and Organization of Prison Labor," *Journal of Criminal Law, Criminology and Police Science,* 49 (May–June 1958): 10–28.

[34] Ralph W. England, Jr., "New Departures in Prison Labor," *Prison Journal,* 21 (Spring 1961): 21–26.

[35] See Elmer H. Johnson and Kenneth E. Kotch, "Two Factors in Development of Work Release: Size and Location of Prisons," *Journal of Criminal Justice,* 1 (March 1973): 43–50.

the feeding and clothing of prisoners and with providing heat, power, light and other operational requirements of the institution. Second, farms reduce food costs while they afford employment. Third, the industrial department provides employment, opportunities for on-the-job training, and a means of reducing the costs to the taxpayer of prison operations and of government in general. Fourth, the educational department contributes to improvement of work skills to promote post-release employment and to upgrade the quality of prison industrial production.

In merging labor and rehabilitation purposes, a prime problem is to overcome conflicts among the four activities. Ideally, prison industries would be provided with well-trained and well-motivated workers through prisoner classification and vocational training programs that wed job requirements with inmate self-interest. Unfortunately, most prisons do not integrate vocational training, inmate vocational interests, and choice of industrial specialties with a vocational training program that is consistent with the job market for released offenders. Prison industries must even compete for the adequate workers among prisoners, because higher priority is usually given to maintenance activities.

Industrial supervisors customarily use excessive numbers of prisoners because their quality as workers depresses productivity. Another major problem is the high rate of turnover due to releases on parole or completion of sentence. This problem is most acute with prisoners most likely to be efficient workers, because their characteristics are consistent with those required for early release.

In many instances prison-made goods are inferior in design and workmanship to the products of private enterprise. The state-use industries have not been able to capture a significant share of the market offered by governmental institutions because of inferior quality and the stigma attached to prison-made goods. This failure has contributed to the small scale of industrial operations in prisons—too small to support cost reduction and continuity of production procedures that could give the inmate familiarity with work situations in the free community.

As a whole, prisoners have inadequate educational backgrounds, vocational skills, and work habits. To use the bulk of them for anything above unskilled labor, vocational and academic training is required. This preparation consumes a portion of the sentence, reducing the period when a skilled worker is available for full-time work assignment.

To make prison industrial work a real asset to vocational training, plants must be modernized by eliminating useless jobs, insisting that each shop be operated on the basis of present-day methods, emphasizing quality of products, and holding job training to rigid standards. Work programs must be designed to help inmates achieve self-development,

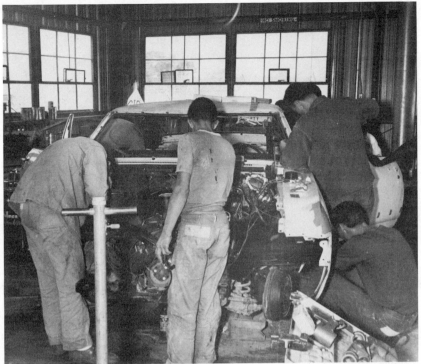

North Carolina Department of Correction (Hal E. Rericha)

Figure 18–2. Concurrent restoration of men and vehicles.

Inmate labor is utilized most frequently to help balance the prison budget. The Polk Youth Center at Raleigh purchases wrecked automobiles to train young offenders in mechanics. The sale of the restored vehicles on a bid basis through the State Surplus Property Agency provides means of purchasing additional wrecks and replacement parts. The interest of youth in automobiles stimulates inmate enthusiasm in a personality rehabilitation program.

while recognizing individual differences and acknowledging that some are incapable of training.[36]

If his labor is to contribute to production goals and his own long-term interest, the industrial program must motivate the prisoner, encourage development of good work habits, and fit him to tasks appropriate to his intelligence, educational potential, age, and ability. The training of industrial supervisors in orientation of new workers, constructive handling of grievances, and recurrent problems for counseling has been advocated.[37]

It is difficult to strike a proper balance between vocational training for prisoner rehabilitation and the achievement of high production for its own sake. However, even if prisoner rehabilitation were the only aim, the administration would encounter difficult problems: Should an inmate scheduled for early release be given priority in assignment to a wage-paying task so that he can gain funds to support himself and his dependents on the outside? What kinds of work should be given to the physically handicapped? What limitations should there be on the prisoner's expenditure of his earnings? Should a long-term prisoner be permitted to become so wedded to a particular job that he loses interest in other prison programs more in keeping with his needs?[38]

Trade advisory committees and councils provide the means for organized labor and management to participate in vocational and industrial training programs of prisons. A *trade advisory committee* may be set up for each vocational area, whereas a *trade advisory council* represents all trade training within a correctional institution. California has used this plan to obtain expert advice on training standards, procedures, equipment, trainee evaluation, postrelease placement, and instructor requirements. Increased support of prison industries by union and management has been an additional advantage.[39]

Wages for prisoners

When labor is forced and unrewarded, there is little incentive for diligence or skill development. Money is as effective an incentive and reward within an institution as it is in the free society. As part of the American cultural norms shaping the personality that the offender brings into the institution, it is a familiar incentive, one that will continue to

[36] John C. Burke, "A Warden's View on Vocational Education in Correctional Treatment," *Proceedings of American Prison Association, 1946,* p. 137.

[37] Wade K. Springsted, "Industries on the Treatment Team," *Progress Report,* 10 (April–June, 1962): 11.

[38] "Policies Relating to Inmate Industrial Assignments," *Progress Report,* 8 (April–June 1960): 10.

[39] Wesley O. Ash and Walter L. Barkdull, "California's Trade and Advisory Councils," *American Journal of Correction,* 23 (May–June 1961): 10.

operate after release. Money has great exchange power because the individual can convert it into the specific reward he values most among purchased goods and services. By using money, the institution skirts the difficult problem of fitting a reward to the interests of each inmate. It also serves as a bridge between self-interest and the ability to cooperate with others within a social organization.

Sufficient wages would allow the inmate to bear the financial burden of supporting his dependents, rather than adding them to the public welfare programs. He would have a "nest egg" to support himself during the crucial early period of release before he finds employment. With funds available to ease the released prisoner's adjustment, disintegration of families would be prevented. The inmate's sense of responsibility for his family would be nurtured during his confinement.

Wages symbolize the state's interest in the inmate's personal welfare.[40] Lack of money contributes to inmate subterfuge, disorder, and labor inefficiency. Leavenworth Penitentiary has rewarded prisoner-workers with a "paid vacation" after two years of good conduct, and wages have been continued during a period of absence from work. Improved worker morale and job tenure were reported.[41]

Among objections that have been raised to inmate wages is the belief that deprivation of earning capacity is a part of punishment. Easing the lot of the prisoner's family is seen by some as reducing the deterrent effect of imprisonment. It has also been argued that the cost of prison operations already is too great without the additional expense of paying wages.[42] To pay wages to convicted criminals has been opposed as a travesty on social justice when thousands of honest citizens are unable to find employment.[43]

In a national survey, 20 states, the District of Columbia, and the Federal Bureau of Prisons reported payment of wages to from 90 to 100 percent of their inmates. In five states, no more than 10 percent of prisoners earn money. Six states did not permit inmate earnings in prison. Of 33 states supplying such information in another survey, wages ranged from 4 cents a day to a high of $1.30 a day.[44]

SUMMARY

The formal organization of the prison is designed to implement custodial, industrial, and therapeutic programs. This chapter has concen-

---

[40] F. Emory Lyon, "Prison Labor and Social Justice," *Annals of the American Academy of Political and Social Science,* 46 (March 1913): 149–50.

[41] Springsted, "Industries on the Treatment Team," p. 12.

[42] Lyon, "Prison Labor and Social Justice," pp. 149–50.

[43] Louis N. Robinson, *Penology in the United States* (Philadelphia: John C. Winston Co., 1923), p. 181.

[44] Glaser, *Effectiveness of Prison and Parole System,* pp. 234–35.

trated on the first two types as a means of giving substance to the discussion in the previous chapter of the nature of the formal organization of correctional facilities. Each of these two programs make its own contributions to an effective, progressive correctional system. However, as a consequence of the growing recognition of the importance of preparing inmates for responsible conduct after return to society, the trend is toward integration of both custodial and industrial programs with treatment. Chapter 20 will be devoted to the nature and functioning of treatment programs, after consideration in the next chapter of the effects of confinement on inmates. Overcoming these effects constitutes the greatest challenge to the capacity of the formal organization of prisons to serve human and social needs.

FOR ADDITIONAL READING

Brown, Barry S., DuPont, Robert L., Kozel, Nicholas J., and Spevacek, John D. "Staff Conceptions of Inmate Characteristics: A Comparison of Treatment and Custodial Staffs at Two Differing Institutions." *Criminology,* 9 (August–November 1971): 316–29.

Chase, Paul. "Correlation of Vocational Education and Correctional Industries." In *Proceedings of American Correctional Association, 1963,* pp. 222–25.

Cooper, H. M., and King, R. D. "Social and Economic Problems of Prisoners' Work." In Paul Halmos (ed.), *Sociological Studies in the British Penal Services,* pp. 145–73. Keele, England: University of Keele, 1965.

Day, Robert C., and Hamblin, Robert L. "Some Effects of Closed and Punitive Styles of Supervision." *American Journal of Sociology,* 69 (March 1964): 499–510.

Edwards, Ralph D. "Correctional Industries and Inmate Training." In *Proceedings of American Correctional Association, 1963,* pp. 197–200.

Hazelrigg, Lawrence E. "An Examination of the Accuracy and Relevance of Staff Perceptions of the Inmate in the Correctional Institution." *Journal of Criminal Law, Criminology and Police Science,* 58 (June 1967): 204–10.

Hedblom, Jack H. "An Examination of Conflicting Ideologies," *Prison Journal,* 43 (Autumn 1963): 10–19.

Johnson, Elmer H. "Bureaucracy in the Rehabilitation Institution: Lower Level Staff as a Treatment Resource." *Social Forces,* 38 (May 1960): 355–59.

———. "Prison Industry." In Robert M. Carter, Daniel Glaser, and Leslie T. Wilkins (eds.), *Correctional Institutions,* pp. 356–64. Philadelphia: J. B. Lippincott Co., 1972.

Mechanic, David. "Sources of Power of Lower Participants in Complex Organizations." *Administrative Science Quarterly,* 7 (December 1962): 349–64.

Robinson, Louis N. *Should Prisoners Work?* Philadelphia: John C. Winston Co., 1931.

Street, David. "The Inmate Group in Custodial and Treatment Settings." *American Sociological Review,* 30 (February 1965): 40–55.

Van der Ryn, Sim. "Can Architecture Aid a Therapeutic Process?" *American Journal of Correction,* 31 (January–February 1969): 41–44.

19

Confinement and
the inmate social system

Late one night a telephone call from a released inmate awakened the
wife of the then Director of the U.S. Bureau of Prisons. Informed that the
Director was asleep, the ex-prisoner said: "Shine a flashlight in his face.
That's what the guards do to make sure a dummy is not in the bed."

In his autobiography James V. Bennett recalls he agreed with the caller
when his wife reported the incident. "I slept in as many cellblocks as
possible to get an inkling of what life in one of our penitentiaries was
like. . . . But I could never fully comprehend the prison experience. . . .
I was free . . . [and] could never really measure the men's resentment at
the petty details of regimentation."[1]

Humanitarian impulses have eased the severity that used to characterize imprisonment. The vindictive imposition of suffering has become the
exception, and belief in punishment for its own sake, where it persists,
is rationalized as a phase of "treatment." Indeed, many correctional institutions have moved toward genuine rehabilitation strategies, and prisoners' work is being seen as something to be oriented within the life of the
free community.

Nevertheless, the idea of restraint remains a major factor in the goals
of contemporary penological institutions. The persistent philosophic
legacy of punishment hampers efforts to implement the ideals of progressive correction, attainment of which often is blocked by administrative
lip service, obscure goals, and unqualified personnel.

This chapter considers the informal patterns of inmate response to the
experiences of confinement. Correctional establishments vary in the degree to which they conform to the custody model implied in our analysis.
Ideally, a correctional institution would resemble a school in orientation
of its programmed activities, attitudinal climate, relationships among staff
and clients, and communication with the world for which the clients are

---

[1] James V. Bennett, *I Chose Prison* (New York: Alfred A. Knopf, Inc., 1970),
pp. 19–20.

being prepared. However, the ideal can seldom be realized. Our emphasis on the custody model is justified because the dilemmas raised by confinement are present to a degree in all correctional establishments. In addition, the custody model is an apt description of the pathological consequences of confinement that correctional reformers are endeavoring to overcome.

Information on prisoner attitudes and behavior stems largely from observations of prison officials, confidences received by chaplains and counselors, studies by academic specialists, participant-observer studies by a few investigators who have had themselves imprisoned for this purpose, and the published narrations of prisoners. It is unlikely that the "tough" warden of earlier prisons had the sort of contact with inmates congenial to reliable estimates of the prisoners' inner feelings. Participant-observer studies vary in quality according to the objectivity and insights of the researcher, the length of time in observation, and the accidents of the observer's particular relationships within the institution. Two such studies were outcomes of Thomas Mott Osborne's week in Auburn in 1913 and Hans Riemer's three months in the Kansas State Penitentiary in 1946.[2] Accounts by prisoners are likely to be heavily subjective because of their need to justify their own behavior, their hostility against the society which rejected them, and the likelihood that their crimes reflect a lack of social insight. Either as staff members or in special research, sociologists and psychologists have made the most systematic studies.

SOCIAL PSYCHOLOGY OF CONFINEMENT

Confinement is an experience requiring major readjustments. To the newcomer, the world within gates of most prisons is strange and forbidding. Walls, steel bars, and guard towers dominate the scene. The clang of metal doors reverberates down long corridors. Chemical odors attest to the persistent struggle to maintain dehumanized sanitation. Uniforms symbolize the sharp division between the keepers and the kept. The mood of some prisons is one of hovering tension.

Prison as a total institution

The discerning observer may detect similarities between the prison and other social establishments such as custodial hospitals, military posts, boarding schools, or monasteries. In advancing the concept of total institutions, Erving Goffman points to the differences between the social environment of such establishments and the one previously experienced by inmates or enrollees. In a *total institution,* large groups live together

[2] Thomas Mott Osborne, *Within Prison Walls* (New York: D. Appleton Co., 1914); Hans Riemer, "Socialization in the Prison Community," *Proceedings of the American Prison Association, 1937,* pp. 151–55.

around the clock within a circumscribed space under a tightly scheduled sequence of activities imposed by a central authority. Most people are accustomed to sleep, play, and work in different places, with a different set of fellow participants and different schemes for organizing each of these sets of relationships. In total institutions, these spheres of life are not separated. The inmates carry out such sets of activities in one place, according to a schedule imposed by a single authority, in the immediate company of large blocks of others who are treated alike and subjected to a system of formal rules and officials under a rationale intended to achieve the organization's official aim.[3]

Certain key features of the prison as a form of social establishment would remain even if the maximum-security prison were to magically lose all the trappings of a punitive ideology. In this sense, the unintended consequences of the formal organization of prisons exist as a problem separate from the effects of the punitive ideology. As a domiciliary establishment, an institution created for treatment purposes would still have to overcome environmental features that differentiate it from the home community environment from which the inmate has come and to which he is supposed to adjust ultimately. The basic split between the managers and the managed in the total institution blocks communication between them. In many of these establishments, the usual manner of motivating work, a reasonable wage, is absent, and work tasks are inconsistent with the inmate's previous experience. Block living solely with members of one's own sex is a new experience for inmates habituated to family life.[4]

The prison contains hundreds of persons thrown together for a sufficient number of years to create regularities in behavior. These regularities reflect the efforts of the ruling group to achieve goals assigned by the society outside the walls. More informal patterns emerge as inmates try to meet the problems posed by the environment within which they work, eat, and live together. The inmate cannot become a salaried employee and thereby share in the authority granted to those having status in the formal organization. At least nominally, other organizations offer subordinates the opportunity to rise to higher status: The army private can hope to become a noncommissioned officer if he is a "good soldier." Motivation to rise into the upper strata of prison society, however, is denied the prisoner. But this denial also frees him of a moral obligation to the prison administration which might bind him to his keepers through a common set of values. The lack of moral consensus binding the entire population helps explain the reliance on coercion to systematize social relationships in prisons.

[3] Erving Goffman, "On the Characteristics of Total Institutions: The Inmate World," in Donald R. Cressey (ed.), *The Prison* (New York: Holt, Rinehart & Winston, Inc., 1960), pp. 16–17.

[4] Ibid., pp. 18–22.

Physical and psychological isolation

Upon admission, the offender is immediately subjected to such effects of compulsory confinement as restriction of physical space and relegation to a subordinate, even abject, status. Through an official and public procedure, outside society has rejected him. This may arouse feelings of guilt, remorse, resentment, or hostility. Compulsory isolation from outside society is maintained by social-psychological as well as physical means.

The maximum-security prison has guard towers, cell bars, walls, and other products of custodial technology which symbolize the protection of society against presumably dangerous criminals. Most inmates are not dangerous, but overcaution and failure to study inmates as unique individuals operate to inflate the number handled as though they were. Medium- and maximum-security prisons frequently differ only slightly; the physical restrictions of all such institutions symbolize the social-psychological gulf betwen prisoners and the free community. The walls of the medieval fortress kept dangerous strangers out; these walls are intended to keep them in.

Within prison walls the authorities impose restrictions, and the resultant conditions of confinement influence the attitudes of inmates. Regulations restrict the inmates' associations with one another, with the prison staff, and with outsiders. Daily life is routinized in dress, manner of carrying out tasks, eating arrangements, recreational activities, and a host of mundane details. Forced assignment to the group officially rated as outcasts is a blow to self-esteem. Psychological isolation may be maintained through staff and public attitudes implying that the inmate is unfit or somehow deficient simply because he has been confined. The fact of physical isolation symbolizes a psychological isolation from the world of "respectable" and "decent" people. The inmate may react by rejecting the "respectables."

An abnormal community

Inmate social relationships are conducted within a sharply circumscribed environment peopled by a strangely skewed population. The etiology of crime and the workings of the legal system operate selectively to produce a high number of maladjusted personalities among prisoners. A minority enters prison prepared to rebel or to behave in other ways so that those involved would become unsatisfactory members of any community.

The abnormal nature of the prison adds to the frustrations of the inmates. The prisoner is denied experiences taken for granted in free society: a wife's kiss on return from work, a choice of food, a leisurely cup of coffee, an opportunity to withdraw from unpleasant associations. Al-

Figure 19–1. Inmate crowd in prison yard.

Confinement places the offender in the abnormal world of the prison "yard," with its own culture and typical social relationships.

lowed only small, if any, economic compensation, prisoners usually are required to labor without the usual incentives of free industry. As a one-sex community, the prison encourages abnormal relationships. Shut away from friends and families that are part of normal life, inmates are denied the sympathetic contacts that soften the grossness of the sex drive. Contacts with the outside world are filtered through mail censorship and custodial surveillance.

Social debasement

Imprisoned intellectuals usually emphasize the prison's lack of concern for their personal dignity and their individuality. The prisoner becomes a number, a unit to be processed by the prison employees. Alfred Hassler describes the officials who assumed charge of him in the courtroom as being "not antipathetic or cruel as much as they were bored." He was seen as a job, rather than a person.[5]

Admission procedures impose a series of petty humiliations: fingerprinting, assignment of a number, deprivation of personal possessions, standardized haircuts, and issuance of drab prison garb.[6] The new prisoner is tested and queried on matters usually regarded as private. Information disappears into files. He does not know the specific nature of this information, the evaluations of him that it includes, the consequences it may have on his future, or the identity of the persons who will employ it in decision making of vital importance to him.

The inmate is expected to comply with a code of rules framed with only incidental interest in meeting his personal needs. The rules implement a control system which assigns him to the status of social inferior to his keepers. He must adjust to an etiquette of deference to guards. He must say "sir" to them but loses the dignity of "mister" before his own last name.

The inmate has storage space for few personal possessions, and these are subject to inspection. He must submit to "shakedowns." He has no privacy, even when engaged in the most personal activities. Arbitrary assignment to a cell or work group deprives him of much of his choice of associates. He may be repelled by the obscenity and personal habits of other prisoners. He may fear aggressive prisoners, but he cannot withdraw from unpleasant associations.

Social debasement and compulsory isolation contribute to strongly negativistic attitudes toward the administration. The typical prison-wise inmate assumes that others act out of selfishness, perversity, and other sinister motivations. Inmates who cooperate with the administration or

[5] Alfred Hassler, *Diary of a Self-Made Convict* (Chicago: Henry Regnery Co., 1954), p. 7.

[6] Erving Goffman, "On the Characteristics of Total Institutions: Staff-Inmate Relations," in Cressey, *The Prison*, pp. 23–48.

show enthusiasm about programmed activities are regarded with disapproval. In this shrunken world, trifling matters assume great importance, motivating subterfuge, "bootlicking," and perhaps violence. In Frank Tannenbaum's view, the inmate is forced to become a "closer neighbor to himself" and to feel emotions more intensely, more directly, and more overtly.[7]

Time and inmate adjustment

The exact time of release from prison is uncertain because of the discretion exercised by parole authorities and the possibility of good-time rewards. Time and uncertainty go together. Imprisonment disconnects the inmate from the patterns of his life outside the walls. It interferes with his vocational career, marital relationships, recreational habits, and associations within the free community.

The central problem is the "doing time" attitudes held by both staff and inmates.[8] The possibility of rehabilitating inmates is seen as hopeless. Prisoners stereotype staff as futile "head shrinkers" or political "hacks." Some employees regard inmates as shiftless, incorrigible, stupid, and unchangeable criminals. In prisons characterized by these attitudes, relationships are frozen into a system of accommodations for making time pass with minimum inconvenience.

Time is something to be overcome because it stretches from now to the moment of release. This moment usually rests on such obscure terms as "prisoner attitude," "parole board policies," and "readiness for release." Because the prisoner must rely largely on officials for word on his prospects, they can manipulate information to raise or dash hopes, to inflate or reduce the inmate's evaluation of the official's power over his fate, to destroy or improve the inmate's adaptation to the uncertainties of his situation, and to raise or lower the accuracy of the inmate's estimate of his chances for release. Johan Galtung argues that the prison official holds out hope because doing so helps provide release from tension; he prefers to avoid, if he can, witnessing the prisoner's disappointment and resentment, and he relishes an image of himself as a person with influence with higher officials.[9]

Activities within the prison can mitigate the sense of wasted time. Treatment programs can enhance personal skills and employability and offer hope of realizing the satisfactions of life after release. Even when progress is not made, these programs can be valuable for mental hygiene.

[7] Frank Tannenbaum, *Wall Shadows* (New York: G. P. Putnam's Sons, 1932), pp. 5–6.

[8] Lewis Yablonsky, "Corrections and the 'Doing-Time' Society," *Federal Probation,* 24 (March 1960): 55–60.

[9] Johan Galtung, "Prison: The Organization of Dilemma," in Cressey, *The Prison,* pp. 122–23.

Raleigh, N.C., News and Observer

Figure 19–2. Inmate reading in cell.

Behind bars, time is something to be overcome. Educational programs in prison promote the mental health of the prisoner. These programs also contribute to a more satisfactory adjustment of the prisoner to the community after release.

Time passes more quickly when reading, hobbycraft, academic study, and participation in sports and work are available. Gambling, alcoholic binges, and bull sessions about crime are unofficial and less constructive ways to accomplish the same thing.

The impact of time varies with inmates' attitudes. A study at Iowa State Penitentiary found greater suffering when the inmate regards his sentence as unjust, when he feels the time already served to be excessive, when he lacks knowledge concerning the probable length of his confinement, when he has lost hope of "getting a break," or when he sees the outside world as hostile or indifferent to his plight. Attitudes are influenced by the inmate's evaluation of his own guilt, comparison of his sentence with those of others convicted of the same crime, and the keeping of promises by the prosecutor or judge. Once he has served sufficient time to drain his guilt, the inmate is likely to feel growing bitterness and despair. Middle-aged prisoners appear to suffer most because they see their lives slipping away as they stagnate behind bars during their most vital years.[10]

One prisoner described his reaction to pronouncement of a life sentence as similar to that experienced when an elevator starts too suddenly. Physical and mental exhaustion from the trial had prevented a normal reaction to the prospect of a life behind bars. The prisoner recalled the notion that the sentence had been pronounced on someone else. After a week or two of "enchantment," the life prisoner slowly faces up to the implications of his situation. He adjusts to a target date set years ahead.[11] Another author serving a life sentence believes that hope is preserved by the sentence reductions and paroles granted to other prisoners. Someday, some way, somebody will help.[12]

Family relationships

Imprisonment is likely to have a disintegrating effect on marriages. The divorce laws recognize this; all but six states include conviction of a felony or imprisonment as grounds for divorce by the criminal's spouse.[13] Imprisonment of the breadwinner weakens the economic and psychological stability of the family, and frequently dependents are added to welfare rolls. However, the average prison sentence is not of sufficient length to justify the arbitrary conclusion that imprisonment dooms a marriage.

[10] Maurice L. Farber, "Suffering and Time Perspectives of the Prisoner," *University of Iowa Studies in Child Welfare,* 20 (1944): 170–74.

[11] J. M. Yeager, "The Lifer: A Peaceful Rebel," *Keystone* (Autumn 1959), p. 6.

[12] Tom Runyon, "Once—for a Lifetime," *Prison World,* 14 (September–October 1952): 27 ff.

[13] Morris Polscowe, *The Truth about Divorce* (New York: Hawthorne Books, Inc., 1955), pp. 265–94.

The chief means of preserving family ties is visiting. These contacts usually are infrequent, brief, and carried out under strained circumstances. Nevertheless, this is an improvement over the concept of shutting off all contacts with the outside world that was pursued by many early 19th-century prisons. The most frequent pattern is two-hour visits twice a month.[14] Conversations may be held through a mesh screen. Maximum-security institutions sometimes require that the persons be separated by glass and communicate by telephone. Some minimum-security institutions offer the more attractive environment of pleasantly furnished visiting rooms and outdoor picnic areas.

Home visits of prisoners have been restricted almost entirely to cases of death or serious illness in the family. More recently, many American correctional systems have expanded the use of home furloughs in the terminal period of the sentence.

Family visits ease sexual tensions and reduce homosexuality. Parchman, the Mississippi State Penitentiary, is the only American prison formally providing conjugal visits as a partial solution to the problem of sex adjustment. Each of the male camps on the 22,000-acre plantation has an adjacent "red house" with small rooms made available to the inmate and his wife during Sunday afternoon visiting hours. Mississippi prison officials claim that inmate morale has been raised, marital ties maintained, and prison homosexuality minimized. Inmates stress the preservation of marital ties rather than the reduction of homosexuality. Prisoners who benefited from conjugal visits were more likely to agree to cooperate with staff and felt that inmates should work hard. However, the practice has been objected to on the grounds that it violates American sex mores by lending official approval to long-term sexual unions outside formal marriage, overemphasizes the physical aspects of sex, aggravates the tensions of single male prisoners, and contributes to public welfare caseloads through pregnancy.[15]

Open institutions in Sweden permit selected unsupervised visits of husband and wife in a small visiting room with shades drawn to provide privacy.[16] Four prisons in Mexico permit conjugal visits. The Philippine Islands permit wives and families to live with prisoners in open colonies. The government pays the transportation of the family to the colony and provides land, a small house, farm tools, food, and clothing to start it toward self-support. The children attend school on the prison grounds. In a more restricted way, the same plan is followed in an island penal

[14] Eugene Zemans and Ruth S. Cavan, "Marital Relationships of Prisoners," *Journal of Criminal Law, Criminology, and Police Science,* 49 (May–June 1958): 51–52.

[15] Columbus B. Hopper, *Sex in Prison: The Mississippi Experiment with Conjugal Visiting* (Baton Rouge, La.: Louisiana State University Press, 1969).

[16] Based on author's observation of correctional facilities in Western Europe during spring of 1972.

colony of Mexico, some work camps in India, and a farm camp in Pakistan.[17]

REACTIONS TO PSYCHIC STRESS

Confinement creates pressures producing unusual reaction patterns. Anxiety is precipitated frequently by guilt and shame and aggravated by the sense of failure accompanying imprisonment. The emotional shock of loss of freedom and compulsory separation from relatives and friends turns the inmate toward introspection and self-preoccupation. In extreme cases all thought process may be blocked. Anxiety may increase to the point of maniacal outbursts, or there may be increasing apathy accompanied by mutism.[18] The one-sex quality of the prison population may precipitate homosexual panic. Inmates threatened by their fellows are subjected to fears. Tension accompanies the wait for decisions on petitions for executive clemency, for the setting aside of sentences, for parole, and for similar actions. To account creditably for his low estate, the inmate is likely to develop an elaborate apologia in which he presents himself as a victim of hard luck and/or treachery. Each crime has its typical rationalizations. Self-defense, fighting, accident, and revenge are claimed to justify homicide. Rapists frequently describe their victims as prostitutes. Drunkenness and need are favorite excuses for crimes against property.[19]

Psychoses and imprisonment

Modes of adjustment to the prospect of prolonged incarceration range from self-deception to desperate floundering, mental derangement, relatively passive acceptance, or attempts to escape. Self-deception involves exaggeration of one's chances for early release or denial that release is desirable.

Prison psychoses are less common than malingering, anxieties, depressions, conversion phenomena, and deterioration. Although persons already suffering psychoses are imprisoned, the examination of the effects of confinement focuses on the possibility that, for some inmates, mental breakdown would not have occurred without improvement. Situational factors may be present: helplessness in meeting family problems, homosexual conflicts aroused by enforced sexual abstinence, or fear of

[17] Eugene Zemans and Ruth S. Cavan, "Marital Relationships of Prisoners in Twenty-eight Countries," *Journal of Criminal Law, Criminology and Police Science*, 49 (July–August 1958): 137–38.

[18] Harry P. Lipton, "Stress in Correctional Institutions," *Journal of Social Therapy*, 6, No. 4 (1960): 216–23.

[19] Carl M. Rosenquist, "Differential Response of Texas Convicts," *American Journal of Sociology*, 38 (July 1932): 10–21.

physical punishments from officials and/or inmates. Minor personality disorders can blossom into major disorientation.[20]

Why, under the circumstances of confinement, is prison psychosis so rare? While it would appear that feigned insanity is an obvious technique for coping with imprisonment, this ruse exacts its price. The stigma of being "crazy" is felt by many prisoners. A psychiatric report can block parole. In any event, the inadequacy of psychiatric treatment in many prisons minimizes the likelihood that psychoses will be recognized within the abnormal environment of the prison.

Recently, military researchers have undertaken study of protracted confinement in relation to space travel and assignment of personnel to remote military posts. After a study of human adjustments to antarctic wintering, John Rohrer advanced hypotheses suggesting that group relationships can insulate accepted individuals against the psychiatric pressures of confinement. One was that when men are isolated as a group from the larger world, they tend to gain a sense of social equality which binds them to one another. Another stipulated that the greater the independence of members in the group, the less will be the hostility expressed toward one another. When each individual has a work function contributing to the work of his associates, tendencies to express hostility against associates are restricted. Other hypotheses suggest that adjustment to confinement is promoted by the individual's acceptance of his status as a confined person, a high degree of knowledge concerning the facts of his life under confinement, a high degree of work activity with variety in the social roles required, and a low degree of deprivations imposed on the individual.[21] These speculations suggest the importance of inmate peer groups in granting status, affording information, and exerting a degree of influence over the immediate environment.

Dependency

Some inmates adjust so successfully to the life of the prison that they cannot live outside it. Through maximum exploitation of those satisfactions procurable within the institution, the *dependent inmate* creates a stable existence which contents him sufficiently to counteract any temptations to risk the uncertainties of the world outside.

The environment of total institutions encourages any existing tendencies toward dependency through such factors as deindividuation, disculturation, psychological damage, estrangement, isolation, and stimulus deprivation.[22] The inmate becomes deindividuated because the routines

[20] Marion M. Estes and James S. New, "Some Observations on Prison Psychoses," *Journal of Medical Association of Georgia,* 37 (January 1958): 2–3.

[21] John H. Rohrer, "Human Adjustment to Antarctic Isolation," Office of Naval Research, Washington, D.C., 1960 (mimeo), pp. 23–24.

[22] Robert Sommer and Humphrey Osmond, "Symptoms of Institutional Care," *Social Problems,* 8 (Winter 1961): 87–90.

of institutional life and the deprivation of decision-making opportunities habituate him to regulation within a mass of humanity. Treated as though he were identical with blocks of inmates, he loses much of his capacity for spontaneous activity and independent thought. He is pressed to accept the special language, values, and attitudes of the institution and loses his concern for the problems of the world outside. He concentrates on the trivialities of eating, sleeping, and exercise. The interruptions to schooling, work experience, and the normal relationships of life in the free community, or well as the psychological correlates of confinement, may damage the released inmate's ability to carry on a mentally healthy life.

Generally, contacts with the outside world decline as the length of incarceration is increased. Renewed contact with home and community shocks the released prisoner into realization that confinement has estranged him from his preprison social world and that the outside world has undergone many changes in his absence. Wives have had to make readjustments. Children have grown. Friends have died or moved away. The old job is gone or is no longer the same. The retarded tempo and monotonous regime of institutional life have habituated him to stimulus deprivation. The quicker pace of life and greater heterogeneity of experience in the outside world create awe and fear among felons released after long confinement.

Preprison experience affects the likelihood that a dependency relationship will be sought. Some individuals have been in a series of institutions, such as orphanages, hospitals, jails, reformatories, and military establishments. They have never experienced family life and are immunized against the tensions created by differences between the home world and the institutional world. The correctional institution may offer some offenders their first experience at being an object of concern by others.[23] The prison may become a comforting haven.

Resistant prisoners

The "resister" is the inmate who deliberately refuses to cooperate with staff. His behavior and his influence on other prisoners make him a threat to institutional order. He has been defined as one who persists in recalcitrance toward the punishment which has been prescribed for him by law.[24] Penalized through imprisonment for lawbreaking in the community, the resister is subjected to additional penalties within the prison, where he continues to break rules and oppose authority.

Resistant behavior appears to stem both from personality qualities of the individual and the failure of the prison environment to provide op-

[23] Goffman, "Characteristics of Total Institutions," pp. 61–62.

[24] Jerome Gerald Sacks, *Troublemaking in Prison* (Washington, D.C.: Catholic University of America, 1942), p. 1.

portunities to channel aggressions into forms other than direct attacks on authority. In describing a "recidivism cycle," Vernon Fox suggested that repeated infractions arise from the inmate's inability to cope with the confinement situation. The resistant prisoner becomes involved in a series of regressive acts as an unrealistic substitute for satisfactory solutions to his dilemma.[25] Jerome Sacks reports resisters have a higher average intelligence than other prisoners and a greater tolerance for acts of cruelty. They had had more convictions as juvenile delinquents, poorer preprison employment records, and more memories of unpleasant early life experiences. In prison they had less interest in constructive leisure-time activities, made fewer contacts by visit and mail with their families, and demonstrated a greater tendency to malinger.[26]

A related pattern of revolt is intentional self-injury. A small minority of adult prisoners utilize self-mutilation to embarrass officials, to disqualify themselves physically for an undesirable work assignment, or to bring about transfer from a prison unit where they fear other inmates.[27] Caustic material may be placed under a wet cloth to burn an open sore. With a medicine dropper and hypodermic needle, a foreign substance may be injected under the skin to create a persistent infection. The forearm may be slashed in a feigned suicide attempt. An arm or leg may be deliberately broken. Fingers may be severed or the Achilles tendon cut.

Self-mutilations cannot be written off as simply the pathological behavior of a few individuals. The structure of the prison community itself is among the important factors contributing to this behavior. Under certain circumstances, the self-injuries are employed as a form of resistance to officials, including manipulation to gain rewards relatively unavailable to prisoners, such as reassignment to the hospital or to other prisons nearer home. They can be resorted to in order to escape punitive segregation, to escape threats from other prisoners, and to serve other immediate purposes. Certain inmates who lack firmness and elasticity of personality and are unable to accommodate to the inmate social system employ self-injury in response to the stresses imposed by imprisonment. A few inmates mutilate themselves as by-products of their severe mental disorder.[28]

25 Vernon Fox, "Analysis of Prison Disciplinary Problems," *Journal of Criminal Law, Criminology, and Police Science,* 49 (November–December 1958): 325.

26 Sacks, *Troublemaking in Prison,* pp. 129–30.

27 Rupert E. Koeninger, "What About Self-Mutilation?" *Prison World,* 13 (March–April 1951): 3–6 ff.

28 For further discussion, see Elmer H. Johnson and Benjamin Britt, *Self-Mutilation in Prison: Interaction of Stress and Social Structure* (Carbondale, Ill.; Center for Study of Crime, Delinquency and Corrections, Southern Illinois University, 1967). (Study sponsored by National Institutes of Mental Health, North Carolina Department of Correction, and North Carolina State University at Raleigh.)

Reactions to resistant prisoners

Official reactions to resistant prisoners range from stiffer punishment to efforts to eliminate rebellion through treatment. Some prison systems have developed special institutions, or units within a prison, to handle resisters. These specialized facilities stress maximum-security measures and architecture in isolating the resisters from the rest of the inmates.

Such a facility may be used only to isolate "troublemakers" to prevent contamination of other inmates and to safeguard the public and the prison population from the special risks the aggressive prisoner poses. This *maximum-confinement purpose* permits the use of privileges to motivate the prisoner to behave in an orderly manner within the immediate environment. Restriction of diet, total loss of mail and visiting privileges, and absence of work and recreation would cause persons confined for a long time to become desperate. A stringent regime in the long term invites rebellion and public sympathy for suffering captives.

The *"purgatory" purpose* would use the specialized facility to convince problem prisoners that alteration of conduct would be in their self-interest. Improved conduct is supposed to be promoted by: (1) minimization of opportunities for successful retaliation against institutional authority, (2) restriction of the inmate's opportunity for wish fulfillment by denial of privileges available in other prison units, (3) formal labeling of the inmate as a rebel who is unlikely to gain early release from prison, and (4) impressing the inmate with the fact that he has reached "the bottom" in a series of deprivatory stages. Because these pressures cannot be withstood indefinitely, the inmate must be transferred from the facility after he has adopted a more conforming attitude but before he reaches a point of desperation.

The *adjustment center* has been defined as "an area of the institution set aside and designed for intensive treatment of problem inmates with the objective of returning them to the rehabilitation program of the institution. It replaces the older concepts of isolation and segregation and is not a punishment unit."[29] Under conditions of maximum custody, a treatment staff is supposed to assist the resister in adopting socially approved methods of expressing or controlling his frustrations. The adjustment center differs from the "purgatory" facility in that treatment resources are mobilized, but the counselors, recreational therapists, and similar treatment workers encounter formidable obstacles in endeavoring to establish relationships with problem inmates in a facility designed for maximum security.

[29] Allen Cook, Norman Fenton, and Robert A. Heinze, "Methods of Handling the Severely Recalcitrant Inmate," *Proceedings of American Correctional Association, 1955*, p. 148.

THE PRISONER SOCIAL SYSTEM

Inmate groups emerge spontaneously from the stresses and deprivation of confinement. Spending extensive time together under the circumscribed environment of confinement, inmates with common interests are drawn into clusters on the basis of affective ties. The groups provide protection and assistance against being maligned and accused of wrongdoing by other inmates and against the power of officials. The group exerts influence also by restraining nonmembers. The leaders' knowledge of prison ways is useful for manipulating official procedures to serve prisoners' interests. The old hand shows the ropes to the newcomer. Through membership the inmate gains access to "grapevine" communication, which is doubly important when officials restrict information. The inmate gains satisfactions from membership among persons who understand him and listen to his complaints.

Processes of prisonization

Certain mechanisms maintain the inmate groups. Newcomers are screened for membership qualifications, and recruits are taught traditions and values transmitted through generations of prisoners. The traditions include institutional slang, secrets about illicit activities, and interpretations of the prison history that are unfavorable to the administration. Gradually the newcomer learns that his fellow prisoners are as varied as people in the outside world. Some are evil; most are essentially decent human beings. Bitterness against outsiders unites most inmates. Group ties are supported by sanctions ranging from gossip and ostracism to violence. Inmate commitment to these groups is encouraged by the fundamental split between officials and inmates, the custodial emphasis, and the inmate's bias against officials.[30]

To become a member of inmate groups, the newcomer must be accepted for membership, but he also must be willing to accommodate himself to the values and customs of the inmate groups. Donald Clemmer presents *prisonization* as the taking on by the inmate "in a greater or less degree of the folkways, mores, customs and general culture of the penitentiary." The newcomer adapts to the life of the prison, accepting the humble role of prisoner, new habits of eating and sleeping, and a new language. He makes the mores of the inmate groups his own.[31]

Certain factors favor the prisonization of the novice. A long sentence increases the period of exposure. Vulnerability is promoted by lack of any positive relationships with persons outside the walls, chance place-

[30] George H. Grosser, "The Role of Informal Inmate Groups in Change of Values," *Children,* 5 (January–February 1958): 26.

[31] Donald Clemmer, *The Prison Community* (New York: Rinehart & Co., 1958), pp. 298–300.

ment with cellmates or work groups who are integrated within the prisoner groups, a personal readiness to accept the mores of prisoners, a capacity for strong convictions and blind loyalty, and personal instability, as suggested by his prior associations with antisocial persons.[32]

The basic values of the inmate groups have been summarized by Gresham Sykes and Sheldon Messinger. The inmate should never betray his fellows to officials, even when he has been victimized or attacked by another inmate; talk too freely to officials; be too inquisitive about the background and affairs of other prisoners; or aggravate fellow prisoners. Feuds and arguments should be avoided. To "be right" implies payment of debts, respect for other prisoners' private property rights, and avoiding exploitation of others through force or chicanery. "Don't weaken" directs the inmate to withstand frustration and threats without complaint, admission of guilt, or subservience. The administration's indications of interest in the inmate's welfare are described as efforts to manipulate him for their own purposes only.[33]

A specialized and secret language identifies its users as members of a group, giving them a sense of unity and superiority over those ignorant of the argot and enabling them to communicate with one another without nonmembers understanding the message.[34] Sykes believes these to be secondary functions of prisoner argot, since both guards and inmates can use the language without necessarily being committed to the values the argot reflects. He sees its primary function in its utility for classifying prison experiences. The stream of events is given labels which reflect admiration or disapproval and influence the behavior of the user or the persons to whom the argot is applied.[35] Staff members, especially correctional officers, use the argot when talking to prisoners and to each other. Probably this begins as a means of semantic contact with prisoners, but eventually it becomes an occupational argot. This development illustrates acculturation of the prison staff by the inmates, a reverse twist on the usual conception of rehabilitation.

Collective teasing

Another means of solidifying inmate unity is the aggressive use of raillery, taunts, and trickery to direct hostility against inmates and officials.

[32] Donald Clemmer, "Observations on Imprisonment as a Source of Criminality," *Journal of Criminal Law and Criminology,* 41 (September–October 1950): 317–18.

[33] Gresham M. Sykes and Sheldon L. Messinger, "The Inmate Social System," in Richard A. Cloward *et al.* (eds.), *Theoretical Studies in Social Organization of the Prison* (New York: Social Science Research Council, 1960), pp. 5–9.

[34] Richard T. LaPiere, *Sociology* (New York: McGraw-Hill Book Co., 1946), p. 220.

[35] Gresham M. Sykes, *The Society of Captives* (Princeton, N.J.: Princeton University Press, 1958), pp. 85–86.

Unpopular food may be wrapped in paper by all inmates and dropped on the walk upon leaving the messhall. Cell doors may be jammed. Plumbing, lighting, and communication systems may be sabotaged.[36]

Poking fun at the officers reassures the inmates that their disadvantage role does not deprive them totally of power. The tables are turned when the dispossessed person makes fools of the masters. One death row inmate would keep guards busy taking newspapers to the cells of other doomed men according to an elaborate and ever-changing sequence of deliveries.[37] It seems reasonable that prisoners should exchange gifts, but security requirements necessitate control by the officers of such exchanges. The inmate was exploiting this situation to embarrass the officers by forcing them into the inferior role of errand boy. Because the traditional punishment-reward system breaks down before mass defiance and it is easier to conceal the tease within the anonymity of a mass of prisoners, teasing of officials is usually done collectively.[38]

One technique directed against other inmates is "signifying" whereby inmates will pretend to be talking about their victim, arousing his fear of some plot against him. "Playing the dozens" consists of obscene and insulting accusations of the inmate and the questioning of the morality of his wife, mother, sister, or daughter.[39]

The "rat" is a particularly easy target because officials share distaste for a traitor. The aggressive prisoner can vent his hostility against the rat with less risk of alienating other inmates because he poses as the champion of the inmate groups. One study found that the rat also serves as a "drain" for "free-floating" aggression stemming from the social deprivations of confinement.[40] Certain qualities of the particular prisoner determine whether he will be defined as a rat. His vocabulary, recreational interests, and personal tastes may cause him to stand out as a stranger among the inmates. His apparent aloofness may mark him as an appropriate target for hostility. However, the most important characteristics for such a target are personified in the *flaccid rat*. He is quick to fear and reluctant to retaliate because he is a dependent personality, lacking firmness and elasticity, and requiring emotional and intellectual support from others. His vulnerability to pressure makes him an appropriate "drain" for "free-floating" aggression. He is sent a note saying: "Be out of this cell block by tonight or your body will be passed out between the bars." His frantic floundering gives his tormentors a sense of power.

---

36 Clif Bennett, "Resistance in Prison," in Holley Cantine and Dachine Rainer (eds.), *Prison Etiquette* (Bearsville, N.Y.: Retort Press, 1950).

37 John Resko, *Reprieve* (New York: Bantam Books, Inc., 1958), p. 5.

38 Goffman, "Characteristics of Total Institutions," p. 56.

39 Hassler, *Diary of a Self-Made Convict*, pp. 126–27.

40 Elmer H. Johnson, "Sociology of Confinement: Assimilation and the Prison 'Rat,' " *Journal of Criminal Law, Criminology and Police Science*, 51 (January–February 1961): 528–33.

Inmate roles

The functioning of the inmate social system is reflected in its characteristic social roles. Each role is a fairly stable complex of behavior patterns. Presumably, an inmate's role describes his own personality and his mode of adjustment to the prison environment. He has either accepted the role, or evaluations of other inmates have pressed him into it.

Certain inmate types represent deviance from inmate norms. Some types center around violence. *Gorillas* deliberately employ violence to establish a satrapy based on coercion to intimidate fearful inmates into providing amenities of life, sexual favors, and gestures of deference. *Toughs* are swift to explode into violence against prisoners, not custodians, because of real or fancied insult. Exploitation of others is not their major goal, but the tough's "touchiness" makes him a constant hazard. *Hipsters* are bullies who choose victims of their aggression with caution in order to ingratiate themselves with other inmates through simulated physical bravery. Their "toughness" is a false front intended to win acceptance among inmates.[41] *Resisters,* as noted above, intentionally challenge the institution by flagrantly refusing to cooperate with staff.[42] They make officials the target of blatant disobedience, physical and verbal assault, and constant creation of disturbances. Because their futile individualistic insurrection brings greater surveillance and hostility from officers against all inmates, they usually are regarded with contempt by other inmates for disturbing prisoner-officer accommodations. Their intransigence usually reflects attitudes and conduct which make them troublemakers among inmates. However, when the resister is goaded beyond endurance by his lot or when he reacts after cool calculation of the adverse consequences upon himself, he is less likely to be regarded with contempt.[43]

Another role centers around violation of the inmate ban on exploitation of fellows through chicanery. *Merchants* exploit other inmates in sharp trading of goods stolen from prison supplies, in trickery in gambling, and in perverting routine practices of prison administrators to gain personal advantage at the expense of other prisoners.[44]

The rat and the square John violate prohibitions against too close intimacy with officialdom. The *rat* usually is one who betrays his fellows through communicating secrets to officials, but, as discussed above, he has some similarities to the *weak sister,* who violates the "don't weaken" dictum by his inability to withstand the pressures of confinement and other inmates. The *square John* allies himself with officials. This role centers around sincere self-identification with the rehabilitative goals of

[41] Sykes, *Society of Captives,* pp. 91, 103–5.
[42] Goffman, "Characteristics of Total Institutions," p. 58.
[43] Sykes, *Society of Captives,* p. 100.
[44] Sykes and Messinger, "Inmate Social System," pp. 9–10.

the officials, which is not approved by the inmate social system. Pretending to side with officials as a means of hoodwinking them *is* approved, but it is unthinkable to actually share the officials' point of view. Ironically, the square John frequently is rejected by officials as well.[45]

From the viewpoint of inmate groups, another deviant type is the *ding,* a catchall term applied to a variety of individuals placed in lowly and outcast status because of their inability to adjust to prisoner norms. Their erratic behavior may indicate mental deficiency, psychoses, religious fanaticism, or other behavior disruptive to predictable prison life.[46]

In the womanless world of the prison, the evaluation of homosexuality emphasizes masculinity. The *wolf,* who plays the active role in aberrant sex behavior, is viewed as masculine in the sense of aggression in sex relations, with a man as the rape victim. The wolf is judged to be a participant for the sake of physical release without connotations of love, thereby escaping the taint of effeminacy. Through personal preference, the *fag* accepts the passive role. He is believed to have the gestures, mannerisms, and guiles of women. The *punk* submits because of coercion without exhibiting feminine mannerisms, but his submission is nevertheless considered to be a sacrifice of manhood.[47]

The *right guy,* the inmate hero, endures confinement with dignity and self-control. His compliance with inmate norms can be trusted, but he does not abuse lesser inmates. He exploits every opportunity to gain personal advantages by fooling the officials, but not at the expense of inmate values.[48] He shares with his friends the food stolen from the mess hall, his cigarettes, and other valued items. He keeps his promises. He is neither aloof nor overeager in making friends. He neither looks for, nor runs from, a fight with other inmates. The traits of the right guy are essential to qualification as a prisoner leader. Other desired qualities for a leader are a large body of knowledge about criminal techniques, demonstrable sophistication in female companionship, participation in spectacular crimes or prison incidents, physical prowess, attitudes unfavorable to judicial and correctional authorities, cleverness in gambling, and possession of money with which luxuries can be dispensed generously to friends.[49] Clarence Schrag found leaders had served more years in prison; had been charged more frequently with violent crimes; were more likely to have been officially diagnosed as homosexual, psychoneurotic, or psychopathic; and had a greater number of serious rule violations.[50]

[45] Sommer and Osmond, "Symptoms of Institutional Care," pp. 87–90.

[46] Clarence Schrag, "Social Types in a Prison Community," Master's thesis, University of Washington, Seattle, 1944, pp. 91–96.

[47] Sykes, *Society of Captives,* pp. 95–99.

[48] Riemer, "Socialization in the Prison Community," pp. 152–53.

[49] Clemmer, *The Prison Community,* pp. 138–39.

[50] Clarence Schrag, "Leadership among Prison Inmates," *American Sociological Review,* 19 (February 1954): 37–42.

Reasons for the prevalence of the inmate social system

The explanation for the persistence and prevalence of the inmate social system can be framed in terms of the unification of inmates through a common hostility to officialdom engendered by the frustrations of confinement and the workings of the punitive-centered bureaucracy. Confinement threatens the masculinity of male prisoners through deprivation of heterosexual relationships, loss of the male role of economic provider, relegation to an inferior status, and loss of power to influence events crucial to the individual. Through acceptance of inmate norms, the prisoner protects himself against psychological devastation, fills the vacuum of prestige through peer relationships, and gains moral support in rejecting his rejecters. The structure and functioning of the official system operate both to create and to maintain the inmate social system. In addition to adding fuel to inmate hostility through custodial restrictions, the keepers accommodate themselves to the inmate social system as a means of maintaining a "quiet joint."[51]

But is there a unique and universally accepted inmate subculture? John Irwin and Donald Cressey question the insulation of inmate values from the outside world and the implication that inmates adhere to a subculture in a single way.[52] Believing that a variety of inmate groups is formed through the sharing of common understandings acquired from similar groups in the outside community, they have identified three subcultures in the prison community.

The *conventional subculture* within the prison is represented by inmates who continue to accept the values of legitimate society and rarely subscribe to an inmate code of behavior. Furthermore, among prisoners who do adhere to such a code, there are differences in responses to confinement.

The *thief subculture* emphasizes loyalty to the inmate ingroup in the style of the "right guy" described above. The career criminal has prestige among prisoners, and he prefers to do time with minimum inconvenience. Regarding his confinement as a temporary incident, he orients his values around his extraprison criminal status rather than his status as a prisoner.

Like the thief subculture, the convict subculture is oriented toward utilitarian methods of easing the immediate pains of confinement. Adherents of the *convict subculture* differ by striving to gain prestige in the status of prisoner and to obtain preferred inmate jobs and items forbidden by prison rules. This search for immediate goals is characteristic of some groups of inmates in total institutions generally, rather than being limited to prisons. This wide distribution of the utilitarian response sug-

[51] See Chapter 17, pp. 427–28.

[52] John Irwin and Donald R. Cressey, "Thieves, Convicts and the Inmate Culture," *Social Problems*, 10 (Fall 1962): 142–55. Also see John Irwin, *The Felon* (Englewood Cliffs, N.J.: Prentice-Hall, Inc., 1970), pp. 61–85.

gests that the characteristics of the total institution contribute to the rise and persistence of an inmate subculture.

BREACHES IN INSTITUTIONAL ORDER

Riots, escapes, and rebellious prisoners draw attention out of proportion to their prevalence among all the behaviors present in correctional institutions over the long run. Considering the abnormality of confinement as a human experience, there is remarkably little disorder. Nevertheless, as is the case for any social system, a correctional institution must pay special heed to breaches in its order. Extreme nonconformity suggests either a failure to achieve purposes assigned the facility or the need to reformulate those purposes.

Riots

The chemistry of the riot is a mixture of the inherent nature of imprisonment, the social psychology of crowd behavior, and faulty prison administration. To many prisoners incarceration is an unfamiliar experience. When a prison disturbance begins, these prisoners lack traditional ways of defining this unprecedented situation. Prison life has released them from the inhibitions of their previous life. Their accommodation to prison life is at too superficial a level to permit habitual response. Then, too, the prisoner population includes persons especially susceptible to crowd behavior because of chronic personal instability. The disturbance may bring welcome relief from regimented boredom. Excitement itself may serve as an intoxicant. Fear of punishment may be erased by the loss of personal identity in the mass of rioters. Repressed emotions and generalized hostilities are released in explosive behavior.

This tinderbox of emotions can be sparked into riots. A survey of newspaper files revealed three periods in which there were an unusual number of major prison disturbances in the United States: 1929–30, 1951–53, and 1968–72. G. David Garson has differentiated two major lines of reasoning employed by experts attempting to explain these upsurges. First, penal reform undermines the accommodative system whereby an inmate elite helps the custodial force to "keep the lid on." Second, riots are produced by rising expectations among inmates concerning their lot in prison. Using historical data, Garson found the distinctions between riot and nonriot eras to be insufficient to substantiate either explanation.[53] Probably he is correct in the sense that no single explanation can account for the multifaceted and highly emotional phenomena behind riots.

[53] G. David Garson, "The Disruption of Prison Administration: An Investigation of Alternative Theories of the Relationship among Administrators, Reformers, and Involuntary Service Clients," *Law & Society Review,* 6 (May 1972): 531–61.

An extensive literature on riots offers a number of explanations which have been summarized by the American Correctional Association Committee on Riots and Disturbances.[54] General causes stem from the emotional stress imposed by the unnatural environment of confinement and from the inclusion in the prisoner population of potentially aggressive personalities. The prison itself can contribute inept management, inadequate personnel practices and facilities, insufficient meaningful or constructive activities for inmates, and the general lack of the psychic and economic rewards available in the free world. Out of control of the prison administration are other sources of unrest. General turmoil and punitive attitudes in the community stimulate a greater incidence of inmate dissatisfactions. Social forces outside the confines of the prison produce the inequities of the criminal justice system, inadequate financing of prison programs, and the denial of opportunities to inmates during and after confinement.

Escapes

Fiction writers have found that the prison escape is likely to clutch the emotions of audiences and readers. Incorrigible and vicious criminals may be portrayed as breaking out to terrorize the citizenry, or prisoners may be shown struggling through swamps, bloodhounds baying in the distance, as "brutal guards" strive to return helpless captives to a "hell hole." In lieu of either of these hyperemotional evaluations, the criminologist is intrigued by three questions. What qualities distinguish escape-prone individuals from other prisoners? What situations are most likely to produce an escape? How are qualities of the prison itself associated with escapes?

Although penal confinement produces pressures which would appear to make escape attempts inevitable, they are relatively rare. Of the adjustments which can be made instead of illegal physical withdrawal from the prison, some would be considered "normal" by the standards of the free world and others would depart markedly from such standards. Escapes also are psychological and social events which come in too great variety to be classified under any single category. Motives range from consistency with expectations of the outside world, through "normality" according to standards of the peculiar world of the prison, to the most bizarre. While qualities of individuals differentiate escapists, escape incidents are all products of the socially structured situations of prison life.

Escape-prone individuals. Certain characteristics appear to distinguish escapists, according to William Morrow. First, some minimum

54 William D. Leeke, Chairman, American Correctional Association Committee on Riots and Disturbances, *Causes, Preventive Measures, and Methods of Controlling Riots and Disturbances in Correctional Institutions* (Washington, D.C., 1970), pp. 1–18.

competence is required in terms of physical, intellectual, and social characteristics. Indexes of this competence include relative youth, near-normal or higher intelligence, sixth-grade education or higher, and some minimal skill in relating to other persons. Second, a weak status anchorage in the legitimate community undermines incentive to complete the sentence. Evidence of this rootless status is found in these characteristics: single marital status, absence of positive family ties and financial dependents, and an unstable employment history. Third, some escapists exhibit defiance of prison authorities.[55]

One investigation reported clusters of variables distinguishing two escape-prone inmate types. "Transient criminality" was described as a combination of short-term residence in the state, considerable distance in mileage from the inmate's home state, prior penitentiary commitment in other states, and residence in places of less than 100,000 population. This type was described as a vagabond individual with weak home ties. The second escape-prone type ("early criminal history") was characterized by a record of juvenile institutionalization, first arrest at an early age, an absence of a family financially dependent on the inmate, and commission of property crimes.[56] Similarly, an earlier study reported a greater tendency to escape among inmates with weak or nonexistent home ties, a record of previous crimes, younger ages, a poor employment record, "inferior intelligence," and an aggressive personality.[57]

The urge for freedom may motivate violations of prison security by prisoners who could be properly evaluated as promising candidates for prosocial reintegration into the free community. A psychologically normal prisoner who reacts this way is negatively evaluated as a rebel when an escape is defined arbitrarily as a grossly antisocial act by a prison system placing high priority on security. American prisons rank high among the world's penal systems in this regard, as noted by Norman Hayner in a comparison of the correctional systems of a number of countries. He based his conclusion on the attitudes toward escape in the prisons of 13 of our western states, which include some of the most progressive American systems.[58] Evaluation of escape attempts should recognize that the problem is as much a barometer of the priorities assigned prison administrators as it is of the individual prisoner's personality. Escapes are unusual events and generally provide only short-term freedom. Because of the hue and cry raised by *any* escape and the heavy emphasis placed on

[55] William R. Morrow, "Escapes of Psychiatric Offenders," *Journal of Criminal Law, Criminology and Police Science,* 60 (December 1969): 471.

[56] W. S. Loving, F. E. Stockwell, and D. A. Dobbins, "Factors Associated with Escape Behavior of Prison Inmates," *Federal Probation,* 23 (September 1959): 50–51.

[57] Nelson M. Cochrane, "Escapes and Their Control: A Brief Study of Escape Data," *Prison World,* 10 (May–June 1948): 29.

[58] Norman S. Hayner, "Correctional Systems and National Values," *British Journal of Criminology,* 3 (October 1962): 163–70.

prison security, an essentially normal and promising personality may be labeled as incorrigible solely because of an escape attempt. This reaction to a prison escapist stands in sharp contrast to the diagnosis of a mental hospital walkaway as exhibiting favorable evidence of a desire to rejoin the normal world.[59]

Also among escape-prone personalities are prisoners who, within the strange and stressful environment of the prison, engage in behavior considered bizarre by standards of the free community. Galtung includes illegal physical withdrawal from the prison as among the psychological mechanisms employed in reaction to psychic stress which were discussed earlier in this chapter.[60] These mechanisms represent a broader definition of "escape" which includes affiliation with an inmate subculture, withdrawal into one's self, rebellion against officialdom, attracting punishment as a means of expiating one's own sense of guilt, and inflicting injuries on one's self as a means of qualifying as physically ill. Escape may be an aspect of any one of these psychological mechanisms. For example, research into the behavior of prisoners who injured themselves found that they had a greater proclivity for escape when compared with other inmates who did not do so.[61]

Situations conducive to escape. The fundamental dimension of the escape-provoking situation is the involuntary commitment to the penal environment. However, prisons vary in the intensity with which custodial precautions are taken. Some prisons lack observation towers, walls, and custodial technology such as the recent introduction of closed-circuit television. Custodial personnel are not always vigilant, and obsolete facilities undermine security. Industrial programs frequently make available devices useful to the escapist, and work settings such as agriculture provide opportunities for easy walkaway. Some locations offer access to means of rapid transportation, and a remote setting complicates evasion of authorities by an inmate unfamiliar with local geography. An inmate will be highly visible when he is of a different race than local inhabitants or if his demeanor marks him as a stranger.[62]

Temporal patterning also affects the situation. The majority of first escapes occur early in the prison career, in the afternoon or evening when detection is less likely, and during the warm months when the days are

[59] The excessive reaction to the escape is an example of types of operations in the criminal justice system which are negatively viewed by labeling theorists. See Chapter 10 above.

[60] Johan Galtung, "The Social Functions of a Prison," in Lawrence E. Hazelrigg (ed.), *Prison within Society: A Reader in Penology* (Garden City, N.Y.: Doubleday Anchor Books, 1968), pp. 36–40.

[61] Elmer H. Johnson, *Correlates of Felon Self-Mutilations* (Carbondale, Ill.: Center for the Study of Crime, Delinquency, and Corrections, Southern Illinois University, 1969), pp. 20–21.

[62] Richard J. Hildebrand, "The Anatomy of Escape," *Federal Probation,* 33 (March 1969): 58–66.

longer and the temperature more congenial.[63] These patterns are associated with the intensity of custodial supervision in the particular prison unit to which the inmate is assigned and the work tasks that are characteristic of a particular season. The frustrations of early imprisonment may coincide with the assignment of the apparently amenable first offender to a minimum-security facility. The hours and seasons of higher escape rates are associated with work rhythms that complicate surveillance.

Qualities of institutions.   Recognition of situational determinants is particularly relevant in comparing escape rates for various kinds of prison institutions. High escape rates are most often identified with the punishment-oriented prison, and penal reformers are embarrassed when they follow on the introduction of a therapeutic orientation. From another perspective, escapes are explained simply as the personal pathology of particular prisoners. Steven Lubeck and LaMar Empey put their fingers on the fundamental error of both of these interpretations, citing a failure to recognize that the personal characteristics distinguishing escapists operate within the context of a correctional system, and this context is subject to change. They argue that these personal characteristics of prisoners will differ among various kinds of prison institutions. Because the escape-prone personalities in one correctional institution will differ from escape-prone personalities in another, they question the efficacy of prediction devices that concentrate on the characteristics of prisoners as individuals. Instead of interpreting escapes as a means of comparing custodial prisons with treatment institutions, they see escapes as symptomatic of the control difficulties raised when any prison is undergoing structural change.[64]

Lubeck and Empey distinguish between *mediatory institutions,* those intended to move the offender into a nondelinquent status with minimum isolation from the free community, and *total institutions,* which they see as oriented toward total confinement and surveillance. Comparing an example of each type, the researchers analyzed runaways according to 30 measures of personal and background characteristics. The 10 best predictors for each program were grouped into four categories: personality characteristics, peer influence, offense history, and background factors. Peer influence had a markedly greater effect for the mediatory program than for the total institution. The total institution showed a markedly greater level of predictive efficiency for personality characteristics, as well as a greater level for both offense history and background factors.[65]

Both types of organization studied by Lubeck and Empey experienced drastic change. The mediatory institution encountered a high runaway

[63] Morrow, "Escapes of Psychiatric Offenders," p. 467.

[64] Steven G. Lubeck and LaMar T. Empey, "Mediatory vs. Total Institution: The Case of the Runaway," *Social Problems,* 16 (Fall 1968): 242–60.

[65] Ibid., pp. 243–48.

rate. To avoid adverse community reaction, the officials announced that *any* runaway would be automatically recommended for transfer to a total institution. For two months, there were no runaways, but then the rate increased. A significant result was the sharp decline in the effect of peer influence in preventing walkaways and a great increase in the predictive power of personality factors. Diminished tolerance of rule-breakers appeared to increase sharply the personal problems of boys, especially among those least able to handle strain and those newly admitted.

The total institution underwent several changes intended to improve the impact of treatment programs. More group-oriented strategies replaced the previous one-to-one relationships between staff and boys. Release from the institution was related more closely to constructive relationships with peers. Furloughs were based on merit rather than on set time intervals. These changes signaled the shift of power from custody to treatment staff. As in the mediatory setting, the predictive power of peer influence dropped and the predictive power of personality increased sharply. The runaway rate increased sharply, including both new admissions and boys who had had an established place in the earlier social system of the facility. Lubeck and Empey explain this development as an example of Durkheim's conception of anomie.[66] A drastic shift in organizational character produces a state of normlessness in which individuals lose the guidance of familiar norms and some previously adjusted individuals become deviants.

SUMMARY

Patterns of inmate behavior emerge in response to the pains of confinement and the rule of officials. Because the discussion in this chapter centered largely on the situation in maximum-security prisons, the analysis has tended to exaggerate the pains of confinement and the strength of the inmate social systems in particular institutions. However, these situations and problems exist to some degree in all correctional institutions, which vary greatly as to type. Thus the difficulties faced in making prisoners active participants in rehabilitative programs can be generalized from this discussion of the inmate social system.

FOR ADDITIONAL READING

Balogh, Joseph K. "Conjugal Visitations in Prisons: A Sociological Perspective." *Federal Probation,* 28 (September 1964) : 52–58.

Brodsky, Stanley L., and George V. Komaridis. "Military Prisonization." *Military Police Journal,* 16 (July 1966) : 8–9.

Davis, Alan J. "Sexual Assaults in the Philadelphia System and Sheriff's Van." *Trans-action,* 6 (December 1968) : 8–16.

[66] See Chapter 10.

Fisher, Sethard. "Informal Organization in a Correctional Setting." *Social Problems,* 13 (Fall 1965): 214–22.

Garabedian, Peter G. "Social Roles and Processes of Socialization in the Prison Community." *Social Problems,* 11 (Fall 1963): 139–52.

Giallombario, Rose. *Society of Women: A Study of a Women's Prison.* New York: John Wiley & Sons, 1966.

Griswold, Jack H.; Misenheimer, Mike; Powers, Art; and Tromanhauser, Ed. *An Eye for an Eye.* New York: Holt, Rinehart & Winston, 1970.

Grosser, George H. "External Setting and Internal Relations of the Prison." In Richard A. Cloward *et al.* (eds.), *Theoretical Studies in Social Organization of the Prison.* New York: Social Science Research Council, 1960.

Karpman, Benjamin. "Sex in Prison." *Journal of Criminal Law and Criminology,* 38 (January–February 1948): 475–86.

Mattick, Hans W. "Some Latent Functions of Imprisonment." *Journal of Criminal Law, Criminology and Police Science,* 50 (September–October 1959): 237–44.

Morris, Pauline. *Prisoners and Their Families.* London: George Allen & Unwin, 1965.

Morris, Terence, and Morris, Pauline. "The Experience of Imprisonment." *British Journal of Criminology,* 2 (April 1962): 337–60.

Roebuck, Julian. "A Critique of 'Thieves, Convicts and Inmate Culture,'" *Social Problems,* 11 (Fall 1963): 193–200.

Sheridan, William H., and Freer, Alice B. *Delinquent Children in Penal Institutions.* Washington, D.C.: U.S. Children's Bureau, 1964.

Thurrell, Richard J.; Halleck, Seymour L.; and Johnson, Arvid F. "Psychosis in Prison." *Journal of Criminal Law, Criminology and Police Science,* 56 (September 1965): 271–76.

Tittle, Charles R., and Tittle, Drollene P. "Social Organization of Prisoners: An Empirical Test." *Social Forces,* 43 (December 1964): 216–21.

Wilmer, Harry A. "The Role of the 'Rat' in the Prison." *Federal Probation,* 29 (March 1965): 44–49.

20

Treatment in
correctional institutions

Some 40 years ago Alexander Patterson, then commissioner of prisons for England and Wales, cited a paradox of penological development. In the 18th century the English gaol was used to hold the defendant until trial, and the aim of judges was to empty the gaols. The prison was derived from the gaol, but it was dedicated to long-term confinement as punishment, and the priority of emptying the places of confinement lost ground. As the institutions developed, some penologists, Patterson included, began to see the duty of the prison administration as returning to society a man less depraved than when he entered.[1]

PRISON ORGANIZATION AND TREATMENT

Progressive prison administrators in the United States and other countries today are engaged in efforts to convert the prison into a therapeutic institution. Criticisms of the negative effects of confinement are widespread, becoming established in the rhetoric of prison executives as well as penal reformers. At the same time, the standards of society have widened the discrepancy between prison precept and practice. Genuine progress has been made in eliminating the physical deprivations of confinement, but this kind of penal reform is only incidentally relevant to the objective of returning prisoners to the free community better equipped for socially approved behavior.

The integration of custodial and industrial programs with treatment programs already has been considered, in Chapter 18. This chapter concentrates on treatment programs as an aspect of the prison's formal organization. Because there are doubts that genuine treatment is feasible within the contemporary prison, major attention will be devoted to the qualities of the formal organization of prisons affecting treatment and

---

[1] Quoted in Fred E. Haynes, *The American Prison System* (New York: McGraw Book Co., 1939), pp. 335–36.

the factors in the treatment situation that complicate the work of the treatment staff.

While some penal reformers may urge the abolition of the prison as a social institution, a more likely prospect is that the prison will take on some new form. Public demands for protection against dangerous criminals may be expected to continue, although the range of convicted offenders defined as dangerous will probably be reduced. A minority of convicted offenders will always remain unreceptive to even the most effective treatment strategies. The substitution of persuasive controls for coercion in progressive correctional institutions rests in part on the inmate's awareness that gross misbehavior will result in his assignment to a closed prison. Similarly, increased reliance on probation, parole, and other community-based programs will require the continued existence of some version of the contemporary prison, if for no other purpose than as a threat. Because of the probable continued existence of the prison, several strategies for its reorganization will be proposed.

The prison and people changing

People-changing organizations, according to Robert Vinter, comprise *socialization agencies,* such as schools and youth-serving agencies, and *treatment agencies,* such as mental hospitals and prisons. Working with people to motivate them to develop their personalities and capacities in ways deemed "normal" by general cultural standards, the socialization agencies enjoy greater legitimation and accessibility to resources. They prepare socially approved clients for places in a world that can be expected to hold benign prospects. Treatment agencies, in contrast, specialize in deviant persons selected out from the general population through formal processing by medical and/or legal systems because their developmental history and overt behavior have somehow failed to meet approved standards. As a treatment institution, the prison must overcome peculiar obstacles in changing its clients: the past performance of clients, the involuntary nature of their admission to prison, less benign prospects for the graduates of their programs, and difficulties in gaining widespread public support.[2]

Vinter notes that as organizations, people-changing agencies deliberately structure staff-client relationships in the application of various kinds of operational strategies ranging from persuasive communication to the coercive imposition of negative sanctions. Treatment organizations differ at various points along this range, according to their relative emphasis on the standardized handling of categories of clients, the balance between personal gratifications provided clients and deprivations imposed on

[2] Robert D. Vinter, "Analysis of Treatment Organizations," *Social Work,* 8 (July 1963): 5.

them, and the complexity of the techniques employed to change the clients.[3]

The formal organization of the prison tends to favor characteristics of the custodial prison. Standardized handling is expedient when inmate population is large. Denial of personal gratifications is the norm when suppressive measures are emphasized. There is an apparent simplicity of techniques when control of overt behavior is the primary aim. These characteristics of the custodial prison simplify administration compared to the demands placed on treatment-oriented correctional institutions at the other end of the continuum. Mayer Zald finds truly treatment-oriented prisons have more complex departmental structures demanding the wider distribution of executive authority and practices which are less routinized and more individualized.[4]

Coercion and treatment

As a formal organization, the typical prison has essentially contradictory purposes. Officials may insist that men come to prison *as* a punishment, not *for* punishment, but safekeeping and continuity of prison operations continue to have priority over any organized reaction to the sources of misconduct reported in the histories of offenders. Most prisoners pose no more threat to the free community than the majority of people on the streets, but public fears of "dangerous" offenders continue to hinder the implementation of programs designed to reintegrate them into community life. Demands that prison operations place a minimum burden on taxpayers contribute to the scarcity of treatment resources and the diversion of prisoners from those that are available. A full report on how the time of prisoners is utilized will reveal that most energy is devoted to keeping the prison in operation by mopping floors, repairing plumbing, tending crops, and similar routine tasks.

Programmed activities must meet a peculiar issue of coerced confinement: enforcement of solitude, through punitive segregation as an extreme measure, versus denial of privacy, through surveillance and coerced congregate living. According to Paul Halmos, *solitude* is the lack of desired social contact. *Privacy* is desired freedom from social contact and observation.[5] Although cultural values see both concepts as favorable objectives for individuals, they can also be defined as proper subjects for therapy. At some point solitude opposes the sociability which is at the root of organized human activity and privacy insulates the antisocial deviant from social control.

[3] Ibid., pp. 6–8.

[4] Mayer N. Zald, "Organizational Control Structures in Five Correctional Institutions," *American Journal of Sociology*, 68 (November 1962): 335–45.

[5] Paul Halmos, *Solitude and Privacy: A Study of Social Isolation* (New York: Philosophical Library, 1953), p. 102.

Although it is difficult in any form of treatment to set the point when intervention is legitimate, the authoritarianism of correctional institutions and the legal imposition of penal confinement exaggerate the probability that the client's sphere of solitude and privacy will be invaded. The minimization of this invasion depends on the policies of the administration and the sensitivity of the staff to this issue in providing daily contacts with inmates in organized activities.

When operated as a total institution, the prison places the inmate in the same social setting 24 hours a day. He cannot withdraw from the role of inmate and become involved in the many other activities found in the free community. The patient on the outside finds it relatively easy to reveal intimate secrets to the therapist who does not have contacts with members of his other social groups. The intensity and frequency of contacts among the relatively small number in the prisoner population make it difficult to keep secrets. The prisoner cannot divorce the patient role from other roles he is expected to play. He cannot leave the treatment situation to gain relief through associations in other areas of his life where he is not regarded as a patient.[6]

Management and treatment

The formal organization of the usual correctional institution separates management and treatment functions. Management involves efforts to control the relationships of individual inmates and staff members within the prison as a means of achieving organizational goals. Efforts to change inmates usually are regarded as a particular sphere of the programmed activities, in the false belief that only a fraction of the inmate's current experiences are relevant to his success in meeting rehabilitation expectations. Management for the sake of custodial objectives ignores the fact that treatment entails the inmate's total experiences.

This divorce of management and treatment tends to develop role relationships that block the mobilization of the prison's official organization to achieve treatment goals. The separation also obstructs the involvement of the inmates in the social processes supposed to change them. The usual ordering of staff functions emphasizes custodial responsibilities and subordinates treatment functions, sometimes even among personnel tacitly assigned treatment duties. The rituals of "treatment" programs tend to become ends in themselves because the official decisions having greatest impact on inmates are made without real participation of the treatment division. Involvement of inmates in treatment processes is complicated by prohibitions against staff-inmate fraternalization and latent doubts

---

[6] Lloyd W. McCorkle and Richard R. Korn, "Resocialization within Walls," *Annals of American Academy of Political and Social Science*, 293 (May 1954): 536.

that treatment is feasible for inmates who are largely perceived as incorrigible.

Inmate resistance and treatment

In addition to organizational barriers to the utilization of treatment personnel and to the active involvement of inmates in treatment processes, qualities of the inmates themselves challenge the capabilities of treatment programs. The need for treatment varies among three kinds of prison inmates. For the first group, the crime was a symbolic release of persistent, deep-rooted mental conflict. Treatment modeled after that of mental hospitals is advocated for these offenders, but readmission rates among mental hospitals indicate the difficulties they pose. In a second group are offenders who are educationally "average" and psychologically "normal" but who have become committed to procriminal values. Their prognosis for rehabilitation is unfavorable. The third group consists of the large proportion of inmates who are deficient in vocational skills and educational attainment but who otherwise are essentially "normal" persons. Many have failed to respond positively to the efforts to socialize them made by family, school, church, probation agencies, and various character-building organizations.[7] Will they be able to reverse themselves and respond to similar overtures within the more artificial environment of the institution?

The majority of prisoners comes from the lower social classes. Educators have found that these classes lack strong interest in education.[8] Pupils in lower-class neighborhoods frequently regard school with indifference because of the attitudes of their parents and the middle-class orientation of the schools. As adults whose attitudes reflect their childhood distaste for school, the prisoners are not eager, at least initially, to participate in rehabilitation programs which are essentially educational in techniques and objectives.[9]

If rehabilitation is to take place, the inmate must possess intellectual and emotional capacity for change—qualities not characteristic of all prisoners. Many inmates are not convinced they require therapy, whereas clients of psychologists in outside practice are likely to recognize that

[7] George B. Vold, "Does the Prison Reform?" *Annals of the American Academy of Political and Social Science*, 293 (May 1954): 49.

[8] Robert J. Havighurst, W. Lloyd Warner, and Martin B. Loeb, *Who Shall Be Educated?* (New York: Harper & Bros., 1944), pp. 107–9.

[9] Proposals have been advanced to reorient the programs of schools in lower-class residential areas to bring them more in line with the needs of children and youth of these areas. These proposals suggest that the usual schools fail to stimulate children of the lower classes. For a review of findings on the relationships between schools and social classes, see Robert J. Havighurst and Bernice I. Neugarten, *Society and Education*, 2d ed. (Boston: Allyn & Bacon, Inc., 1962), pp. 228–48.

they do have a problem. The inmate sometimes volunteers for treatment because he recognizes his need for help, but others only seek relief from institutional boredom or an opportunity to gain special favors.

The inmate social system encourages negativism in attitudes toward officials and discourages sincere and active participation in treatment programs. The prison-wise inmate tends to suspect therapists of seeking to manipulate others for selfish motives, as he does himself. An inmate's frankness about his previous criminal behavior may be reflected in his official records. "Shakedowns," custodial rules, and other security measures inhibit inmate frankness. The experience of confinement itself is emotionally thwarting and heightens suspicion.[10]

The public image of "the convict" also impedes the prison official's efforts to win full inmate participation in therapy. The public stereotype persists sufficiently to sap the inmate's confidence that his own moral regeneration will win him acceptance in the free community.

CLASSIFICATION: ORGANIZATION FOR TREATMENT

Presumably, administration of any treatment strategy is based on diagnosis of the offender, development of a treatment plan deemed relevant to the diagnosis, implementation of the plan, and finally recheck of the outcome to reduce any discrepancies with expectations after implementation of the plan has proceeded far enough to reveal whether or not the diagnosis was accurate and how the offender has changed. *Classification* is the term applied to both the organization of treatment and the processes of its administration in the correctional institution.

Functions of classification

Underlying classification procedures is the principle of *progressive stages,* whereby the prisoner is granted fuller privileges and permissiveness as he demonstrates improvement in conduct and behavior. Theoretically, the uncooperative inmate would be placed in maximum security and the more tractable inmate in the lower security grades. As the maximum-security man showed greater trustworthiness and tractability, he would be moved through the close-, medium-, and minimum-security classifications and through the conduct grades to honor grade. Some correctional institutions have several types of quarters varying in degree of comforts, privileges, and permissiveness offered. The inmate is supposed to seek the individual rooms, freer movement, increased canteen privileges, and special recreational opportunities available in the honor unit. Max Grünhut warns that the progressive-stage principle encourages the

[10] Norman Johnston, "Sources of Distortion and Perception in Prison Interviewing," *Federal Probation,* 20 (March 1956): 43–44.

hypocrisy of overt compliance without internalized belief, but he agrees that this fault is characteristic of other prison methods.[11]

An effective classification system is the core of prison administration because most prison problems involve inmates. While debating the problems posed by inmates appearing before it, the classification committee becomes a seminar on the issues of penology. Information is exchanged in a mutual education of the representatives of all segments of staff serving on the committee. Friction between departments can be eased and a broader basis for organizational consensus developed. Because intelligent classification decisions require participation by all committee members, the sessions provide a training opportunity for development of staff.[12]

Classification is an asset to prison security and industrial programs. Accurate diagnosis permits the segregation of escape-prone and aggressive inmates to maximum- or close-custody facilities. Conversely, the high costs of maximum custody are reduced by referring more trustworthy prisoners to medium- and minimum-custody prisons where operating expenses are reduced by a lower prisoner-staff ratio and less costly custodial technology. The classification committee serves as a personnel office for prison industries in fulfilling its responsibility to assign each man to a job most appropriate to his skills and experience. The committee can feed inmates into vocational training classes to maintain a steady flow of apprentices into the industries.

Classification documents trace the official evaluations of the inmate, report his behavior, and summarize his past life. The record can provide a connecting link among administrative actions. When classification standards are high and reports are complete and accurate, each record permits an analysis of the inmate over a long period of time. Parole decisions and criminological research can be based on fuller information.

Styles of administrations

The switch from custodial to treatment orientation that has marked progressive prisons has placed emphasis on the quality of classification decisions and the effectiveness of attempted treatment programs. Ideally, these programs are based on some theoretical proposition about the causes of criminality and the proper strategy through which the period of confinement can be employed to deal with them. The classification decision relies on such propositions in placing the particular inmate in a program designed to correct the defects diagnosis has revealed.

It cannot be assumed that all classification decision makers have available a well-rounded and well-staffed treatment program that will provide

[11] Max Grünhut, *Penal Reform* (Oxford: Clarendon Press, 1948), p. 189.

[12] Frank Loveland, "Classification in the Prison System," in Paul W. Tappan (ed.), *Contemporary Correction* (New York: McGraw-Hill Book Co., 1951), pp. 101–2.

a reasonable range of alternatives for individual cases. If such a range of alternative programs actually exists, however, the classification board is expected to practice *discriminative administration,* defined as attempts to correlate the treatment problems posed by an inmate with a variety of treatment resources, within the framework of a theoretical basis for diagnosis and classification decisions. In practice, the board is likely to fall short of this ideal and to utilize one of two other kinds of administration. *Coactive administration* diverts attention away from changing inmates through treatment and toward the avoidance of a disorderly institution. It emphasizes security, internal order, and the continuity of prison maintenance and work programs. Although giving greater lip service to "rehabilitation," *diffusive administration* is characterized by a casual collection of "treatment programs" and an absence of underlying principles and objectives in classification decisions. Without serious study of the uniqueness of each case, the board prescribes a spoonful of education, a scoop of Dale Carnegie or Alcoholics Anonymous, a handful of recreation, or a dash of counseling.

The implementation of discriminative administration is advanced by the use of typologies through which the qualities of various clients are correlated with treatment programs based on theories related to behavioral change. Various typological approaches to offender classification have been identified by Marguerite Warren. First, research into subsequent behavior of previous clients can provide statistics on personal and social characteristics and on psychological test findings, and diagnosis of present clients produces base expectancy scores that relate their characteristics to probable outcomes for persons of similar type. Second, inmates can be distinguished according to the values of the group with whom they identify (reference group); one example would be degree of commitment to the various shadings of the inmate culture. Third, the behaviors of inmates in or outside of prison can be classified according to offense categories (such as armed robbery or "joyriding" automobile theft) or position in the conformity-nonconformity dichotomy. Fourth, personality structures can be analyzed in terms of psychiatric concepts (such as the "acting-out" neurotic or the unsocialized aggressive personality). Fifth, offenders can be differentiated according to psychological factors related to ego integration, level of interpersonal maturity, level of psychosocial development, and so on.[13]

Traditional organization

Traditionally, classification and treatment are handled independently of each other. Usually the institutionalized offender is studied and diag-

---

[13] Marguerite Q. Warren, "Classification of Offenders as an Aid to Efficient Management and Effective Treatment," *Journal of Criminal Law, Criminology and Police Science,* 62 (June 1971): 240–42.

nosed during the intial period of his confinement at a reception center and is sent to another institution for implementation of the treatment plan. Therefore, formal treatment does not begin until the initial classification has been completed at least two weeks after his admission to prison. Furthermore, the diagnoses and therapy are handled by different staff members.

Written reports are the major sources of information for the therapist on the inmate's background, characteristics, and conduct. Each treatment specialist experiences the inmate personally only through the relatively brief contacts of therapy. As Figure 20–1 illustrates, the treatment pro-

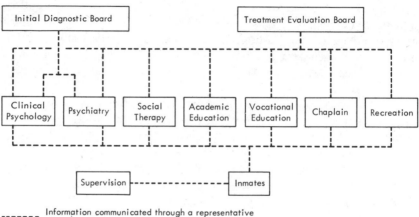

Figure 20–1. Traditional organization of classification and treatment.

gram deals with the inmate population as a whole. If relationships of inmates with treatment personnel were recorded sociometrically, there would be a snarl of lines. The teacher, recreation specialist, chaplain, or any other staff member would be able to regard certain inmates as individuals and have intimate knowledge of their background and behavior, but any evaluation board would lack intimate knowledge of the cases under discussion. Individuals on the board would be able to relay personal experiences, but the board would have to depend heavily on these reports, rather than being able to reach a joint decision representing an array of orientations. Written reports would be available, but this method imposes a heavy administrative load of report writing. A risk of inflexibility is inherent in routinized and formalized reports.

Treatment-team organization

To meet these disadvantages, the *treatment-team approach* immediately assigns the newly arrived inmate to a treatment team composed of specialists, including supervisory personnel. The inmate population is broken down into small groups. Figure 20–2 illustrates the organizational scheme.

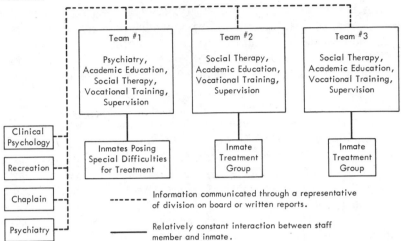

Figure 20–2. Team organization of classification and treatment.

When several staff members specialize in a particular activity, one is assigned to each team; examples of such specialties are clinical psychology, religion, recreation, and psychiatry. Because the supervisory or correctional officers have the most frequent contact with inmates, they too are placed on each team. If there are insufficient specialists of a type to be assigned to all teams, written reports are substituted for their presence on teams. Otherwise, the diagnostic study of the inmate will be part of the ongoing treatment process that is launched immediately upon admission to the institution. The inmate probably will participate in educational programs and other treatment activities not administered by members of his treatment team. However, all members of the team will include him among their caseloads.

The teams will find some inmates failing to respond to the general program of education, vocational training, and social therapy. These inmates are referred to Team No. 1, a "super team" composed of staff members with the most intensive training, including a psychiatrist. In this manner, the more expensive treatment resources, in short supply, are applied to those cases requiring intensive treatment, rather than being diluted by application to all cases.

The advantages of the treatment-team approach are varied. Compared to other approaches, inmate-staff interactions are more frequent and direct, of greater depth, and more continuous for the relatively brief period of treatment available in a short-term institution. Consequently, the inmate is more likely to identify himself with a staff group which conceives of him as a total person. Because of the range of specialties from which the team is recruited and because the team members experience and provide personal observations on each inmate, the diagnoses and evaluations of treatment progress are interdisciplinary. The team views the counselees under a variety of social situations. Team members can check the validity of their individual assessments of a particular case and gain the benefit of each other's observation of the inmate over a more continuous period of time than that available to a single staff member. The reduced reliance on written reports permits diversion of some of the time spent in report writing to face-to-face contacts with inmates. Direct involvement of teachers and correctional workers in the correctional process promotes identification of the total staff with rehabilitation. When adequately supported by treatment specialists, correctional workers are able to exploit their routine contacts with inmates as a therapeutic opportunity. Classification boards become less informal and impersonal as treatment teams because all members are prepared to contribute to the decisions. The inmate experiences treatment as a unity from the moment of admission, avoiding the relative lull of the usual reception procedures. The possibility of hostile and negative attitude development in the early period of imprisonment is reduced when the inmate engages in purposeful activity from the start, and the nature of his participation is a useful clue for diagnosis.[14]

THERAPEUTIC COMMUNITIES

The concepts of therapeutic community and open institution are prominent among proposals for restructuring the organization of the correctional institution. The objectives of these proposals are similar to those of team treatment in that they seek to make the organizational scheme an instrument through which treatment programs can be focused on the inmate's individualized qualities and his treatment needs. Reduction of the inadvertent consequences of the pains of confinement is sought, and excessive custodial reaction to resistance to treatment by inmates is discouraged. Both of these concepts rely on the capacity of prisoners to discipline their own behavior within a framework of psychological controls, rather than depending on external controls applied by an authoritarian bureaucracy.

Characteristics of the therapeutic community

The objective of the *therapeutic community* approach is to create an attitudinal climate in which all social relationships between staff and in-

[14] Leonard J. Hippchen, *Experience in Application of the Team Treatment Approach to Rehabilitation of Air Force Offenders* (Amarillo Air Force Base, Texas: 3320th Retraining Group, June 1963), pp. 10–12.

mate contribute to rehabilitation. Every activity within the institution is utilized to help the inmate realize a psychological state that will favor his early release to the outside community as a responsible citizen. When this goal cannot be achieved for a particular inmate, an effort is nevertheless made to help him live as nearly normal a life as possible within the institution.[15]

The inmate is given unusual opportunity to evaluate his own place and functioning within the social groups of his past and present life. The person is seen as a unified whole that is influenced by interacting social, psychological, economic, and physical forces. Any change in the environment creates a change in the person; any change in the person creates a change in the environment. A supporting, nonrejecting, and permissive environment is provided to encourage the inmate to uncover his inner feelings and uncertainties without risk of retaliation from other persons. He is given maximum opportunity to meet and experience life under controlled conditions in order that he may be more readily redirected and guided into behavior that will enhance both his feelings of self-worth and his social acceptance.[16]

The intention is to eliminate, as much as possible, the influences of the prison itself and the relationships in it as barriers to treatment. Communication between staff and inmates is opened, and spontaneity of relationships is encouraged. There are organized programs for education, work, clinical psychology, recreation, religion, individual and group counseling, and so on. Furthermore, within this external shell of organization, there is a spontaneity of relationships which permits the inmate to influence his relationships with other persons.

The spontaneity and permissiveness characterizing the therapeutic community approach create uncertainties for prisoners. "I'm supposed to adjust, but adjust to what?" many ask. The prison-wise and manipulative inmate prefers a formalized code of rules because, by outwitting officials, he can pervert it to his own ends. Without a clear-cut set of rules, the inmate must make his own adjustments on the basis of his own evaluation of his situation. His overt responses to social circumstances unfamiliar to him become diagnostic clues and raw material for treatment because they suggest his attitudes and personality makeup more accurately than the image of himself he presents to observers.

The therapeutic community approach creates new roles for staff and inmate. The specific division of labor between treatment and custody roles of the traditional prison is abandoned. Correctional workers operate in functions with more prestige than watchers of inmates and pro-

[15] Milton Greenblatt, Richard H. York, and Esther L. Brown, *From Custorial to Therapeutic Patient Care in Mental Hospitals* (New York: Russell Sage Foundation, 1955), p. 3.

[16] Leonard J. Hippchen, "The Air Force's 'Therapeutic Community' Concept," *American Journal of Correction,* 25 (January–February 1963): 16.

viders of creature necessities. Because they are in most continuous and frequent contact with inmates, custodial personnel have unusual opportunities to influence them, either positively or negatively, from a treatment point of view. Correctional workers are made positive influences in promoting treatment by defining their job slots as having treatment functions. The sharp division between treatment and custodial jobs is blurred; although the necessity of specialized training for treatment professionals continues to be recognized, the custodial staff is brought into the administration of treatment programs. Correctional workers are given access to official information necessary for therapy within the limits of client-professional secrecy. They are permitted to contribute their own observations on inmate behavior and suggestions for dealing with particular inmates. Staff training is employed to improve their skill in dealing with problem behavior.

The prisoner's role within the institution is oriented toward adjustment to the free community *after* release from the institution, rather than toward adjustment to life *within* the institution. His attention is directed to his problems within the context of real-life situations. Diagnostic and short-term treatment facilities appear to provide particularly appropriate settings for the therapeutic community.

Issues raised by the concept

The therapeutic community approach raises important issues.[17] The democratization of inmate-staff relationships strikes at the stratification of authority and the allocation of staff functions according to competence that characterize a formal organizational structure. Each member of the community is required to develop his personal style in fitting his own behavior into the informal social system which fills the vacuum created by the loss of formal structure. Bureaucracy lends itself to standardized, impersonal reactions to human clients, but it also gives continuity and stability to organization of the large volume and variety of relationships within a correctional institution. The unique contributions of various staff specialists can be mobilized for a total organizational effort, and each specialist thus can be freed to concentrate on those tasks he is best equipped to handle. Democratization of a previously custody-oriented facility creates confusion for staff caught in the contradictions between the rules of the old and new regimes.[18]

[17] Oliver T. Wertz, "Social Workers and the Therapeutic Community," *Social Work,* 11 (October 1966): 43–46; J. C. Spencer, "Problems in Transition: From Prison to Therapeutic Community," in Paul Halmos (ed.), *Sociological Studies in the British Penal Services* (Keele, England: University of Keele, 1965), pp. 13–30.

[18] Oscar Grunsky, "Role Conflict in Organization," *Administrative Science Quarterly,* 3 (March 1959): 452–72. Also see Mayer N. Zald, "Power Balance and Staff Conflict in Correctional Institutions," *Administrative Science Quarterly,* 7 (June 1962): 22–49.

The distinction between treatment and rehabilitation tends to become blurred. Correction of client deficiencies perceived by the staff is not necessarily relevant to the capacity of the client to cope with the realities he will confront in the free community after departing from the specialized environment of the therapeutic community.

The apparent permissiveness of the therapeutic community may only substitute the coercion of inmate-group norms for that of the official establishment. There is a latent assumption that inmates are susceptible to the same influences as self-disciplined members of a "normal" group in the free world, in spite of the selective factors at work in the appearance of deviant behavior and the operations of the criminal justice system.

Finally, the characteristics of the therapeutic community make it vulnerable to swings of mood in emotional climate and to dependence on a charismatic leader. These swings may produce cycles of equilibrium and disintegration of relationships which add to the uncertainty of outcomes. The efficacy of the therapeutic community may rest on the personality and unusual competencies of a charismatic leader, whose departure brings collapse of the program.

OPEN INSTITUTIONS

Walled prisons have been criticized for cutting inmates off from normal contacts with the community and for imposing a daily regime that promotes rebellion and parasitism. The *open institution* has been advocated as an answer to such criticisms. It is seen as a means of providing an environment more congenial to therapy, while it reduces construction and operational costs.

Emphasis on inner controls

The open institution is characterized by the absence of walls and the substitution of psychological controls for physical barriers against escape. If there is a fence, it is so low as to be easily surmountable. Authorities strive to make conditions within the institution resemble life in the free community as much as possible. Inmates are permitted free movement within the grounds. Work tasks and conditions are made similar to those of employment outside. Family visits and correspondence are encouraged.[19]

This type of institution is most likely to be located in the open country, to permit relative freedom of inmate movement. The dependence placed on intimacy of inmate-staff relationships for control and treatment pre-

---

[19] Charles Germain, "To What Extent Can Open Institutions Take the Place of the Traditional Prison?" *Proceedings of Twelfth International Penal and Penitentiary Congress, 1930,* Vol. IV, Sec. 2 (The Hague, 1951), pp. 11–12.

Figure 20–3. Design for community within an establishment.

Modeled after a village centered around a town square, the Vienna Correctional Center of the Illinois Department of Corrections is designed to encourage a sense of community among its residents. The "square" includes two chapels, a recreation building, hobby shop, canteen, and library as sites for adjustment to living. The residence units, resembling college dormitories, are grouped in "U" form to constitute neighborhoods. A vocational skill center, also providing basic education, provides economic compensation as well as training in welding, mechanical drafting, farm mechanics, office machine repair, production machinery, and water/waste treatment. Through Shawnee Community College, residents may obtain an associate of arts degree, and they can take more advanced courses through the Extension Division of Southern Illinois University. Students from the outside community also take the night vocational classes at Vienna Correctional Center.

supposes a small population. Selection of inmates for the facility emphasizes psychological qualities consistent with self-discipline.

Penologists generally agree that the open institution will not replace the closed prison. In order for open institutions to obtain properly selected inmates, the closed prison must serve as the source of population and afford a place for testing inmates for their possession of attitudes consistent with self-discipline. Furthermore, the possibility of reassignment to a closed prison serves as a deterrent against infractions in the open institution.

Applications and results

American correctional institutions for juveniles generally follow the open pattern. Medium-security institutions for adults include institutions which have some characteristics of the open institution. Examples are Wallkill Prison in New York, California Institution for Men at Chino, Bordentown State Reformatory in New Jersey, Norfolk Massachusetts Institution, and Seagoville, a federal institution near Dallas.

In Wisconsin's Fox Lake Correctional Institution, the architecture of the buildings, their distribution on the grounds, the minimization of arbitrary rules, and freedom of inmate movement are in the pattern of open institutions. One goal is to create an atmosphere of respect for the dignity of the individual and to provide maximum opportunity for positive behavior change. Grilles of textured, patterned stones are set approximately 3 feet from the walls of housing units to replace bars and to serve as sunshades. The 600 inmates have individual rooms with doors and windows. The occupant has his own key. The men are responsible for going to bed at a reasonable hour and are free to go to the dining room individually within meal periods. Catholic and Protestant chaplains provide religious programs in a unique chapel. The indoor visiting room is large and tastefully furnished, and the outdoor visiting area resembles a pleasant public park.

English borstals receive teen-age criminals sentenced to an indeterminate period between 9 and 36 months. The conditions of training are made as consistent with the inculcation of trust, personal decision, responsibility, and self-control as the different types of character of inmates will permit. The small units may be classified according to "closed" and "open" criteria. Classification procedures send the "better" offenders to the "open" borstals, which minimize custodial precautions and are intended to encourage young inmates to demonstrate self-control. The "closed" borstals rely to a greater extent on walls, guarding, and rules.

Hermann Mannheim and Leslie Wilkins question whether the open borstal system represents a better form of treatment than the closed. With "success" defined as absence of recommitment for a period averaging three and one half years, the open borstals had a success rate of 58 percent and the closed borstals of 36 percent. But was this because of superior treatment or because of efficiency in reception center diagnosis in sending the best cases to the open institutions? When the inmates are grouped according to prognosis, the success rates for open and closed institutions, respectively, are: good prognosis, 78 and 67 percent; average prognosis, 61 and 57 percent; and poor prognosis, 38 and 28 percent. Thus, open institutions showed a consistently better success rate.[20]

In certain districts of Israel, all offenders serving terms of three months or less were sent to the Maassiahu Camp, an open institution, with no other criteria of selection. A study of the first 100 prisoners so handled found that although 68 percent were multiple offenders (20 percent with more than six previous offenses), there were no escapes; only 3 percent had to be transferred for behavioral difficulties. The 100 inmates incurred 23 disciplinary proceedings, compared with 98 for 100 prisoners at the maximum-security prison for a like period. During the 12- to 18-month follow-up period, 20 of the 100 were recommitted.[21]

PERSONNEL IN TREATMENT PROGRAMS

Certain categories of personnel traditionally have been identified with treatment programs, and prison reform proposals emphasize the need for larger cadres of these professionals to make individualized treatment a reality. The opening of channels of communication with inmates is expected to increase the need for personnel with specialized competencies. Regardless of the particular strategy employed, correction is dependent on the quality of personnel applying it to human subjects. The tasks treatment professionals perform and how prison conditions test their performance are considered here.

The prison teacher

The establishment of Elmira Reformatory in New York in 1876 marked the beginning of correctional education.[22] In view of the remarkable faith Americans place in education, it is understandable that they believe prisoner rehabilitation and education to be closely related. The higher the attainment of education, the greater one's earning power and the greater the possibility of improving one's station in life. The school is viewed as a cure-all for social problems, including automobile accidents, sexual irregularity, and personality maladjustment. "Good parent-

---

[20] Hermann Mannheim and Leslie T. Wilkins, *Prediction Methods in Relation to Borstal Training* (London: Her Majesty's Stationery Office, 1958), pp. 108–13.

[21] Zvi Hermon, "The Advantage of Detaining Short-Term Prisoners in Open Institutions," *British Journal of Criminology*, 4 (July 1963): 83–84.

[22] Price Chenault, "Education," in Tappan, *Contemporary Correction*, p. 224.

hood" and high moral values are supposed to come from classroom experience.[23]

Since education deals with the development and change of human behavior, the faith in education as a treatment tool is well placed. Nevertheless, the number of crimes perpetrated by persons with above-average formal educations demonstrates that prison schooling and vocational training cannot provide simple, direct answers to recidivism.[24] In fact, prison schools often suffer because they are used only as means of merely keeping inmates busy for the sake of a "quiet joint."

The expression of faith in correctional education through administration and teaching should recognize that prisoners are a particular kind of pupil and that the teacher-pupil relationships take place within the prison setting. The prisoners have low average educational attainment and, for both sexes, are grossly underrepresented at educational levels beyond the 11th grade. The high proportion of inmates in grade levels below the eighth testifies to their inferior position in competing for employment and prestige in the community, but it also indicates a previous lack of scholarly interest. The prison teacher also must recognize that his work must be carried on in a total institution. When pupils confide inmate secrets, how can the teacher balance the objective of teacher-pupil educational rapport against the demands of institutional security? How can he cope with learning blocks stemming from social neglect in the outside community or from problems (such as drug abuse) outside his control? How should he respond to pupils' reports of "injustice" to inmates in the administration of the prison?[25]

The emotional tensions of imprisonment and the demonstrated inadequacies of the inmates call for social education, but latent suspicion is a challenge to the teacher seeking to create a classroom atmosphere favorable to learning. Prison teachers, unfortunately, include persons poorly prepared by training and personality to cope effectively with this special challenge.

A bona fide educational program in correctional institutions can provide a "second chance" for previously unmotivated students. The correctional institution fills a small portion of the gap in the community's educational system which results in failure to reach underprivileged youth.

Academic education concentrates on the core subjects common to public elementary and secondary schools, with college courses offered infrequently. Illiterates receive extra attention to overcome their handi-

[23] Wilbur B. Brookover, *A Sociology of Education* (New York: American Book Co., 1955), pp. 46–55.

[24] James M. Reinhardt, "Prison Education as an Aid to Therapy," *International Journal of Offender Therapy,* 12, No. 3 (1968): 113.

[25] Marguerite Wilson, "Strategies of Teaching in Corrections," *Social Casework,* 51 (December 1970): 618–24.

Figure 20–4. A second chance for an education.

Educational programs in correctional institutions represent a "second chance" for youths who either refused or were denied earlier opportunities to qualify themselves for a complex world. The teacher's personality and competence are crucial elements in this process.

caps. Improved skill in communication may enable the offender to reveal and express underlying misunderstandings and conflicts that have been conducive to deviant behavior. He may be able to comprehend more fully his personal problems and his relationships with other persons and to use his leisure more constructively during and after confinement. Through better understanding of government and society, he is expected to move toward responsible citizenship.

Ideally the total prison experience should prepare the inmate to be a more constructive participant in community life. *Social education* is the phase of formal education aimed primarily at this purpose. Social education is directed, first, to determining the inmate's attitudes toward his family, his community, and his work situation, and, second, to encouraging him to reorient those attitudes that handicap him in achieving responsible relationships with other persons while meeting his personal needs.

There are three methods of social education.[26] First, inmates may be given some measure of self-government and self-direction. Inmate councils in administration and recreation have been used with limited success because strong personalities are necessary to their effectiveness, making them vulnerable to shifts in inmate leadership. Furthermore, only a limited number of inmates is afforded actual practice. Second, inmate forums, visiting lecturers, inmate publications, and motion pictures with social content offer opportunities for inmate expression and for exposure to thoughts of others. However, inmate participation usually is limited to an articulate minority. Third, regular class work can be employed. Subjects in the realms of personality, social issues, and economic affairs permit exploration of human relationships, either directly or indirectly. An example of the indirect approach would be vocabulary development through such sentences as, "Going around with a chip on your shoulder has a figurative meaning, but often brings serious results." The course would be designed to improve the inmates' skill in the use of the English language, but the textbook would suggest socially constructive attitudes.

Prison educators advocate *vocational training* to prepare the inmate for more effective postrelease employment in work for which he is fitted and, secondarily, to promote more efficient use of labor in prison industries. Vocational preparedness is an essential element of full participation in community life. In an age of rapid technological change, such training enables the individual to obtain or maintain his place in the socioeconomic system. Gaining vocational competency gives a sense of personal purpose and a means of wish fulfillment. Steady employment is the mark of adulthood and manhood. When the male head of the family is not the chief breadwinner, his authority and status as a man are vulnerable.

If prison education is to be effective, systematic curriculum planning, counseling, and guidance are necessary. Courses may be offered because

[26] Glenn M. Kendall, "General and Social Education in Correctional Treatment," *Proceedings of American Prison Association, 1946,* p. 112.

they develop skills needed in prison work programs, but the curriculum should also include other trade subjects which prepare for postrelease employment. The training equipment and subject matter should be current with developments in employment in the community.

The psychiatrist

The relationship between psychiatry and institutionalized correction is colored by fundamental disagreements. Psychiatrists have been among the most ardent critics of the rigid controls and restrictions of the prison. They have disagreed among themselves concerning the proportion of inmates requiring psychotherapy. However, there is general agreement among correctional experts that psychiatric and psychological services are grossly inadequate in size of staff and opportunities offered for effective treatment, in light of the pains of confinement described in the previous chapter.

Prison psychiatrists make diagnostic examinations, write reports for parole and pardon boards, and advise on the disposition of problem prisoners. They serve as referring agents when psychotic prisoners are transferred to mental hospitals. In most prisons, psychiatrists have little time or hospital space to conduct a program of individual or group therapy, which should be their major function. After the prisoner is diagnosed as requiring psychiatric treatment, the absence or shortage of therapeutic resources frequently requires the assignment of regular prison work. Under these conditions psychiatry is perverted into lip-service support of a custodial regime. When the psychiatrist is given administrative authority within the structure of a program directed toward behavioral problems, he steps out of his usual diagnostic and advisory role. One such project employs the concept of therapeutic community discussed above.[27]

The psychiatrist also can be very useful in training prison personnel, especially custodial staff, to recognize and handle mental disturbances and emotional reactions to confinement. The public prestige of psychiatrists is instrumental in extending general knowledge of the mental health problems of prisons and prisoners.

The prison chaplain

With the possible exception of the physician, the chaplain was the first prison staff member to demonstrate a concern for inmates' welfare. Before the day of organized treatment, chaplains developed schools,

[27] Ludwig Fink, Wilfred N. Derby, and J. Peter Martin, "Psychiatry's New Role in Corrections," *American Journal of Psychiatry,* 126 (October 1969): 124–28.

wheedled gifts of books and recreation equipment, and worked with prisoners' families.[28]

The roles and functions of the prison chaplain vary. He may be a man with an eighth-grade education, preaching a religion of guilt and fear and serving as a court of last resort for prisoner grievances. In such circumstances the chaplain helps to keep the lid on potential inmate violence by using religion as an opiate. At the other extreme, he may have both a psychological and theological degree and work as an accepted member of the treatment team.[29]

Some inmates are more amenable to therapy when it is received from a chaplain under the guise of religion. The chaplain may serve as a bridge between the prison and the outside community through the assistance of religiously motivated citizens engaged in "good works" for inmates and their families before and after release from prison. Within the prison, grieving, fearful, or uncertain prisoners may receive solace if they "believe." Others turn to religion when their crime or imprisonment arouses a new concern for personal morality or they may use religion cynically for temporary advantage. Some prisoners abstain from religious activities in prison.

The prison chaplain is undergoing change in role and function because of developments both in society generally and in the prison specifically. Stuart Johnson notes that in society organized churches are being urged to act for social reform, to abandon traditional theologies based on supernaturalistic sanctions, and to rely on voluntary association to hold members. These developments have been felt in prisons, where compulsory attendance at religious services is declining. A shift from the idea of doing penance in prison toward participation in rehabilitation programs threatens the previous orientation of the chaplain. Librarians, teachers, and counselors have been added to staffs, so that the chaplain is no longer needed for the auxiliary functions he performed when treatment personnel were in short supply. Johnson suggests that clergymen should be trained as classification officers, counselors, or therapists so they could be living examples of the religious values of their churches. Otherwise, he believes, the role of chaplain will become residual.[30]

The recreation specialist

In a broad sense, *recreation* can be anything which does not involve activity for some specific economic purpose. It means "to create anew"

[28] Frederick C. Kuether, "Religion and the Chaplain," in Tappan, *Contemporary Correction*, pp. 255–56.

[29] Albert Morris (ed.), *What's New in the Work of the Church and the Chaplain in Correctional Institutions?* Correctional Research Bulletin No. 11 (Boston: United Prison Association of Massachusetts, 1961), pp. 17–18.

[30] Stuart D. Johnson, "The Correctional Chaplaincy: Sociological Perspectives

or "to refresh." The activity constitutes relief from everyday routine. Recreational activities have immediate value in releasing energies not dissipated in work, in relieving tensions created by confinement, in spurring the passage of time, and in promoting physical health. The failure to use leisure time in a constructive way may have contributed to criminal behavior in the first place.

Recreation programs have progressed from their situation in old-line prisons prior to World War II, when they usually consisted of men released into the "yard" for an hour, Saturday-night movies, Sunday-morning church services, and a few books in a storage closet. Now there is likely to be a schedule of many sports and gymnastics, an auditorium for various forms of entertainment, hobby and recreational clubs, and an enlarged library. Instead of regarding a recreation program as solely a means of preventing internal disorder and physical or mental deterioration among inmates, prison administrators recognize it as a treatment tool and a means of lending some degree of normalcy to prison life.[31]

Nevertheless, there is considerable doubt that most prison administrators perceive the potential therapeutic value of recreation and the necessity for trained recreational specialists if this potential is to be realized. The potential lies in the degree of personal choice and enjoyment these activities afford even within a prison, where the boundaries of free choice are sharply circumscribed. As a link to the generalized cultural values shaping interests in sports and recreational activities, this sphere of personal freedom offers unusual opportunity for revealing hidden interests and capacities of individual inmates and stimulating them into expression. Under the guise of recreation, personality problems may be approached through the back door of inmate-staff relationships to avoid the implications of involuntary, formalized treatment. Competence in sports or other recreational skills enables recreational specialists to gain rapport with some inmates, but training in psychological intervention and in understanding sociological implications of prison events is crucial to utilization of the therapeutic opportunities of recreation.

INVOLVEMENT OF INMATES IN TREATMENT PROGRAMS

The level of success in changing inmates depends to a great degree on whether or not the correctional institution is able to mobilize inmate-inmate relationships for this purpose. Raymond Adamek and Edward Dager cite three types of identification crucial to this mobilization. In *personal identification* the staff member becomes a model and the inmate

---

in a Time of Rapid Change," *Canadian Journal of Criminology and Corrections,* 14 (April 1972): 173–80.

[31] Mark S. Richmond, *Prison Profiles* (Dobbs Ferry, N.Y.: Oceana Publications, Inc., 1965), pp. 75–77.

takes on his norms and values in a context of positive affection and admiration. *Positional identification,* which results from one individual being placed in role relationships with one another, has possibilities for the deliberate use of organizational structure to advance treatment goals. Although relations are reciprocal, the teacher or other staff member has the superior status and control resources important to the inmate. Less dependent on a staff member as a specific model, *institutional identification* is characterized by positive attitudes toward the organization which are expressed in adoption of its goals, values, and norms.[32]

Is involvement feasible?

A study of a treatment-oriented, closed institution for delinquent girls found that identification with staff and institution is promoted by clear organizational structure and role expectations, long length of anticipated and actual stay, few alternative reference groups, high organizational participation, and readily available channels for the inmate to move up a ladder of prestige through such participation. Furthermore, if the resident perceives that the staff sees him as a prisoner, he is more likely to see himself that way.[33]

Opposing the general view that the inmate social system virtually dooms treatment programs to failure, David Street cites evidence from a study of two custodial and two treatment-oriented institutions. Inmates in the treatment-oriented institutions more often expressed positive attitudes toward the staff and institution, nonprisonized views on the best way to get along in prison, and positive views on whether their stay had helped them. They also showed close ties with fellow inmates who were positively associated with favorable attitudes toward staff and institution, regardless of length of stay. Stronger primary relations among inmates were also found in the treatment-oriented institutions.[34]

The sociologist tends to emphasize both the possibility and the desirability of involving inmates directly in the treatment process. Modification of the inmate culture is seen as a possibility because human behavior, as a product of a group interaction, entails the acceptance of group standards for the gaining of individual satisfactions. The inmate social system provides these standards when incentives are not offered for inmates to enlist themselves in support of the goals of prisons to which they have been committed involuntarily. The sociologist is likely to argue

[32] Raymond J. Adamek and Edward Z. Dager, "Social Structure, Identification and Change in a Treatment-Oriented Institution," *American Sociological Review,* 33 (December 1968): 931–44.

[33] See Charles R. Tittle and Drollene P. Tittle, "Structural Handicaps to Therapeutic Participation: A Case Study," *Social Problems,* 13 (Summer 1965): 80.

[34] David Street, "The Inmate Group in Custodial and Treatment Settings," *American Sociological Review,* 30 (February 1965): 40–55.

that the vacuum of inmate incentives offered by the official structure can be filled by an alternative to the inmate social system. Furthermore, he believes that because most of the inmates are not pathological beings, there is a genuine potential among inmates for participation in an alternative prosocial means of meeting their personal needs.

Officials already have granted certain inmates a function in maintaining order within prisons.[35] With the possible exception of inmate self-government, these inmate roles, designed by officials, have restricted inmate participation to relative subservience to custodial values without free interaction among inmates and staff members. The same deficiency is latent in naïve "treatment" strategies advocated as means of avoiding the expense of well-staffed programs. These include the use of inmate teachers and programs such as inmate discussion groups dominated by untrained staff and "Operation Teen-ager," in which inmate-speakers employ their own life histories in public speeches intended to deter teen-agers from a life of crime.[36]

A relevant experiment

As indicated above, positional identification and institutional identification are means of gaining inmate commitment to official goals. In positional identification the implication is that the official expectations of staff roles must be altered from those characteristic of the custodial prison. The concepts of therapeutic community and open institution are examples of organizational schemes designed for this purpose. Institutional identification requires drastic revision of correctional institutions into models radically different from the prison as a symbol of deterrence through punishment. A remarkable experiment, described below, attempted to create a new model congenial to involvement of inmates in therapeutic programs.

The C-Unit experiment at California's Deuel Vocational Institution (D.V.I.), reported by Elliot Studt, Sheldon Messinger, and Thomas Wilson, was an innovative attempt to establish conditions under which inmates could act as responsible members of a community and prepare themselves for release.[37] Incorporating the sociological premises stated above, the project saw the term "community" as denoting moral relationships derived from an ascription of dignity to individuals, respect for the rights and welfare of others in pursuing individual interests, and reliance on positive social controls rather than on force or manipulation of sub-

---

[35] See Chapter 18, pp. 443–44.

[36] Elmer H. Johnson, "Does Operation Teen-Ager Have a Place in Corrections?" *Police,* 11 (September–October 1966): 18–21.

[37] Elliot Studt, Sheldon L. Messinger, and Thomas P. Wilson, *C-Unit: Search for Community in Prison* (New York: Russell Sage Foundation, 1968), pp. 5–6, 10–11, 34–36, 165–68, 215–23.

ordinates. The general objective was to encourage maximum development of moral relationships among inmates and prison staff.

Selected at random and representing a cross section of the D.V.I. inmate population, the 130 inmates were housed in a single unit, with one man to a room. They were retained at the unit until release, even if their behavior warranted temporary segregation at times. All staff personnel were assigned to C-Unit throughout the life of the project, in contrast to the usual policy of rotating personnel, as a means of encouraging staff identification with these inmates through enduring face-to-face relationships in making classification, disciplinary, and counseling decisions. Finally, bridges to the community were promoted by assignment of parole agents from the three major metropolitan areas to which inmates were expected to return. As members of the C-Unit community, the parole agents would come to know those inmates who subsequently would be released in their jurisdictions.

Problem solving was conceived as the process by which the prison community would be created. The dynamics of problem solving were to involve the collaboration of all members of the community, inmates and staff, in seeking solutions to the problems they had together defined as being of immediate concern. Success in problem solving was evaluated against the objective of developing the characteristics identified above as being fostered by the concept of community. Through involvement of inmates and staff in the analysis and solution of problems, the structure of the community was to emerge from the necessity of agreed action. Action would be tested by the criterion of usefulness in accomplishing tasks essential to all community members.

In detail, the researchers reported the difficulties experienced by both staff and inmates in accommodating themselves to these principles within the realities of daily life. The complexities of penal reform were revealed when disagreements among executives at D.V.I. brought changes in the personnel and administrative patterns, to the detriment of realization of the project's principles. After the first year of the project, however, the inmate social system had moved in the direction sought by the staff and C-Unit residents were expressing concern about the welfare of others in mobilizing resources for "the good of the whole." C-Unit inmates had more contact with staff than did inmates in other D.V.I. units and came to rely on the official program in dealing with problems of daily life among inmates.

SUMMARY

Rehabilitation is accepted as a major objective of prisons without serious question, but achievement of its objectives depends on overcoming the resistance that stems from some inmates, from the inmate social system, and even from the prison organization itself. Most institutions emphasize treatment of inmates as individuals, rather than as members of groups. The therapeutic community and similar approaches hold promise as means of overcoming the barriers to successful treatment through utilization of group relationships. The major treatment programs in prisons operate in various ways to improve the probability of returning the prisoner to the free community as a capable, well-motivated citizen.

FOR ADDITIONAL READING

Adams, Stuart. *College-Level Instruction in U.S. Prisons.* Berkeley: School of Criminology, University of California, 1968.

Berker, Paul De. "Group Counselling in Penal Institutions." *British Journal of Criminology,* 4 (July 1963) : 62–68.

Bird, David T. "Discipline in the Therapeutic Community." *Corrective Psychiatry and Journal of Social Therapy,* 11 (September 1965) : 253–60.

Ferdinand, Theodore N. "An Evaluation of Milieu Therapy and Vocational Training as Methods for the Rehabilitation of Youthful Offenders." *Journal of Criminal Law, Criminology and Police Science,* 53 (March 1962) : 49–54.

Gibbons, Don C. *Changing the Lawbreaker.* Englewood Cliffs, N.J.: Prentice-Hall, 1965.

Grant, J. Douglas. "Delinquency Treatment in an Institutional Setting." In Herbert C. Quay (ed.), *Juvenile Delinquency: Research and Theory,* chap. 8. New York: D. Van Nostrand Co., 1965.

Greenblatt, Milton; York, Richard H.; and Brown, Esther Lucille. *From Custodial to Therapeutic Patient Care in Mental Hospitals.* New York: Russell Sage Foundation, 1955.

Griswold, H. Jack; Misenheimer, Mike; Powers, Art; and Tromanhauser, Ed. *An Eye for an Eye,* chaps. 3, 7, 8 and 10. New York: Holt, Rinehart & Winston, 1970.

Hart, Robert F., and Hippchen, Leonard J. "Team Treatment of Air Force Offenders." *American Journal of Correction,* 28 (September–October 1966) : 40–45.

Hindelang, Michael J. "A Learning Theory Analysis of the Correctional Process." *Issues in Criminology,* 5 (Winter 1970) : 43–58.

Johnson, Elmer H. "Realities of Prisoner Education." *Journal of Correctional Education,* 13 (July 1961) : p. 7 ff.

King, Daniel P. "Religious Freedom in the Correctional Institution." *Journal of Criminal Law, Criminology and Police Science,* 60 (September 1969) : 299–305.

Marnell, Gunnar. "The Prison Community." *International Annals of Criminology,* 8, No. 1 (1969) : 15–32.

Pacht, Asher R., and Halleck, Seymour L. "Development of Mental Health Programs in Corrections." *Crime and Delinquency,* 12 (January 1966) : 1–8.

Rose, Arnold M., and Weber, George H. "Change in Attitudes among Delinquent Boys Committed to Open and Closed Institutions." *Journal of Criminal Law, Criminology and Police Science,* 52 (July–August 1961): 166–77.

Soine, Valentin. "Finland's Open Institutions." *Federal Probation,* 28 (December 1964): 19–23.

Street, David; Vinter, Robert D.; and Perrow, Charles. *Organization for Treatment.* New York: Free Press, 1966.

Part VI

The offender in the community

By centering attention on the community, the final part of this book brings together for examination many of the ideas and problems analyzed in previous chapters. Social, economic and political forces operating within the community inspire the criminal behaviors which are the subject matter of criminological research and the focal concern of the system of criminal justice. The coercive power of criminal justice is brought to bear to safeguard the security of the community. The agents of criminal justice also are expected to work toward reintegration of former criminals into the community as a normative system. This reintegration involves access to education, jobs, medical care, and other services essential to the well-being of all participants in the complex order of the contemporary urban community. In terms of these multiple facets of the community, this concluding part of the book will examine crime prevention, correctional programs in the community, the issues involving the released prisoner, and prospects for criminal justice reform.

The community setting

As a community problem, crime usually is studied as behavior which must be controlled or corrected for the sake of the community. The community itself may be examined as both a source of criminality and the setting for various strategies intended to cope with the problem. In both senses, the concept of community must first be understood.

BASIS OF THE URBAN COMMUNITY

The term "community" has two interrelated facets. One, which sees the community as a locality, is that the sharing of a common territory evokes sentimental bonds among residents, and the structuring of human behavior is influenced by climate, topography, and natural resources. The second is that the residents are bound to one another in a social-psychological fashion because they share a common way of life. The sentimental bonds evoked by shared experiences are an important part of this facet.

Common bonds in a certain place

The social-psychological aspect is most germane to our immediate interest in the concept of community. Robert MacIver envisages communities as "areas of social living within which the threads of specific relationships are incessantly spun."[1] Men relate to one another in the activities of work; religion; education of children; recreation; buying and selling of goods and services; meeting the problems related to birth, illness, and death; safeguarding against disasters and criminals; maintaining roads and sewer systems; and a host of similar relationships. These activities involve the community to the extent that individuals must enter into relationships with one another in an organized fashion.

It is also important, however, to consider the community as a *place*

---

[1] Robert M. MacIver, *Society: A Textbook of Sociology* (New York: Farrar & Rinehart, 1945), p. 143.

on the earth's surface with a particular physical appearance and natural setting. "Common earth" alone is not sufficient to create a community, but the uniqueness of "community" as a concept is that the locality is its basis of social coherence. James Coleman points out that a resident in Los Angeles and a resident of Portland, Maine, have the same interest in protecting themselves from criminals, but efforts to prevent crime specifically in Los Angeles do not bind the Portland residents with those of Los Angeles in common interests.[2] The physical proximity of the residents of a community transforms their similar interests in self-protection into common interests.

The location of a community influences the size and nature of its population, as well as the proportion of nonresidents. A seaport, a resort city, or a town near a large military establishment have many transients who tend to increase crime rates either as offenders or victims of criminals attracted to the area by unusual opportunities for crime. The location also affects the availability of natural resources, access to markets, and other factors related to population growth. The larger the population within a given space, the more likely it is that it will include a diversity of subcultures based on occupation, ethnic or racial status, religion, and so on. As we have seen,[3] these differences among group members are conducive to the *gesellschaft* type of society, which is subject to social forces associated with a higher rate of deviance than that usually found in the *gemeinschaft* society, which is held together by similarities among group members.

The declining influence of locality

In earlier ages physical distance was a formidable barrier to social contacts outside the environs of the local community, and people were dependent on the immediate locality for goods and services. These effects of distance have been reduced considerably by technological developments—witness the effects of the automobile, airplane, telephone, radio, television, and the computer on human experience and commerce. Local job opportunities and the quality of services are increasingly dependent on decisions made by distant centers of power in government, business, industry, labor organizations, and professional associations. Such decisions, which have great impact on individual lives, are symptoms of issues which extend beyond local boundaries because of the implications of market changes, social trends, and political developments.

The impact of these developments is screened through bureaucracies designed to organize the complex activities of highly specialized workers

[2] James S. Coleman, "Community Disorganization and Conflict," in Robert K. Merton and Robert A. Nisbet (eds.), *Contemporary Social Problems,* 3d ed. (New York: Harcourt Brace Jovanovich, 1971), p. 661.

[3] See Chapter 10, pp. 229–30.

who frequently are distant from one another. These bureaucracies are managed from offices likely to be outside the local community, and they deal with issues and resources outside the control of local residents. Their activities must be broken down into smaller units to make them manageable and relevant to human beings. The local geographical area remains significant in setting boundaries on activities for the sake of management and to humanize the otherwise impersonal delivery of services.

The geographical aspect of the community can provide a basis for managing relationships among agencies comprising a service system, as well as for maintaining relationships between agencies and their clients. Features of the landscape (rivers and mountains, for example) are of historical importance in the fixing of state and county boundaries which continue to determine the jurisdictions of criminological and human service agencies. Because the features of the landscape may continue to affect patterns of social intercourse, they are relevant to the sentimental bonds which are the essence of the community as a social-psychological force. Thus jurisdictional boundaries among service agencies, the products of traditions derived partially from geographical features, continue to be consistent with the social-psychological bonds that transform an aggregate of residents into a sociological community.

Relationships in urban society are unlikely to be personal or to be based on long-term association with fellows. As the importance of territorial anchorage is reduced, there is, according to Maurice Stein, an "eclipse of community" through the weakening of the social-psychological bonds among residents of a given locale. Community ties, Stein says, have become "increasingly dispensable, finally extending even into the nuclear family."[4]

Opposing this evaluation, Don Martindale believes the community may properly be defined as a set of groups sufficient to solve all the basic problems encountered in ordinary life. This view emphasizes the group interactions incidental to problem solving rather than a fixed point on the earth's surface as the quality identifying a community.[5] Considered in this light, changes in the nature of the community as a social system may be interpreted as evidence of the need for a new basis for harmonizing groups to make them relevant to contemporary human requirements.

THE URBAN COMMUNITY AND CRIME

The question can be raised whether there is a bona fide need for a new basis for harmonizing groups to make the community a viable force

---

[4] Maurice R. Stein, *The Eclipse of Community* (Princeton, N.J.: Princeton University Press, 1960), pp. 107, 329.

[5] Don Martindale, "The Formation and Destruction of Communities," in George K. Zollschan and Walter Hirsch (eds.), *Explorations in Social Change* (Boston: Houghton Mifflin Co., 1964), pp. 61–87.

Figure 21–1. The problem neighborhood.

Delinquency prevention must operate within the sociological context of the community. In the problem neighborhood, the high rate of deviant behavior is a product of the deterioration of the informal controls of the community. Physical deterioration is significant largely because it reflects normative deterioration.

in meeting human requirements. Such a question suggests the importance of two themes to the final part of this book.

● By emphasizing "a set of groups sufficient to solve all of the basic problems encountered in ordinary life," Martindale's definition is consistent with the study of the community as a service system—a perspective to be explored later in this chapter.

● Particularly high crime rates are associated with urbanism, and the patterns of urban crime rates are interrelated with various indices of socioeconomic deprivation. Sociological theories take two differing perspectives in explaining these data. Order theories focus on the lack of or breakdown of social organization, weakened social control, inadequate socialization, and other evidences of a decline in the consensus on norms derived from a shared culture and common values. Conflict theories see society as the product of accommodations among contesting groups. Social stability is maintained by the influences of a succession of dominant groups that results from changes in the distribution of power, wealth, and status.[6]

The urban problem neighborhood

An earlier chapter noted that arrest rates for major crimes increase consistently with population size of cities and those in rural areas are comparatively lower.[7] Within American cities, studies have recorded fairly consistent patterns over the decades in crime and delinquency rates according to such variables as socioeconomic status, physical condition of neighborhoods, rate of population movement, percentage of minority groups in neighborhood populations, and so on.[8]

In explaining these differences in rates among the areas of a metropolis, ecological studies focus on the physical and social factors operating in the *problem neighborhood*. In Chicago, Clifford Shaw found these delinquency-prone areas to be located near the center of the city and to have certain characteristics: high rates of deviant behavior, great cultural diversity, high population mobility, socioeconomic deprivation, anonymity, and deterioration of buildings.[9] Ernest Burgess hypothesizes that the metropolis has developed into a series of concentric circles radiating out

[6] The order and conflict theories are discussed in Chapter 4, pp. 71–73.

[7] Chapter 2, pp. 38–39.

[8] See, for example, Clifford R. Shaw and Henry D. McKay, *Juvenile Delinquency and Urban Areas,* rev. ed. (Chicago: University of Chicago Press, 1969); Bernard Lander, *Toward an Understanding of Juvenile Delinquency* (New York: Columbia University Press, 1954); Ronald J. Chilton, "Continuity in Delinquency Area Research: A Comparison of Studies for Baltimore, Detroit, and Indianapolis," *American Sociological Review,* 29 (February 1964): 71–83.

[9] Clifford R. Shaw, *Delinquency Areas* (Chicago: University of Chicago Press, 1929).

from the central business district in this order: the zone of transition (problem neighborhood), working man's residential area, a more prosperous area of single-family dwellings, and the outer ring of suburbs.[10] The problem neighborhood is a zone of transition in that its proximity to the central business district holds prospects for future profits but reduces the owner's interest in maintaining residences. Thereby, it becomes the collection point for the less privileged segments of the population.

Perspective of order theories

The higher probability of delinquency and crime in problem neighborhoods may be explained as the consequence of social disorganization brought on by group breakdown or cultural conflict, the presence of deviant subcultures, or anomie.[11] In various ways, the theories representing these viewpoints relate the differences in crime and delinquency rates to the degree that residents comprise a social-psychological community. One investigation compared two areas of Cambridge, Massachusetts, which had similar socioeconomic characteristics but differences in juvenile delinquency rates. The area with the higher rate was found to be less integrated socially in that residents were more prone to dislike their neighborhood, to regard other residents as strangers, and to disagree with the value perspectives of other residents.[12]

The weak social cohesion is relevant to what Irving Spergel calls the *inauthentic community,* characterized by the distribution of social rewards to those who most readily conform to the normative expectations of the groups holding social, economic, and political power. Spergel sees mortal combat existing between social organizations and significant numbers of the persons they are supposed to serve. The inauthentic community is divided and divisive.[13] Such a community inspires anomie in many residents because there is a fundamental contradiction between the cultural goals it holds out and the means of attainment provided by the legitimate opportunity structure.

The inauthentic-community concept also is relevant in the mobilization of resources to cope with the underlying sources of delinquency and crime. When Michael Aiken surveyed studies of decision-making

[10] Ernest W. Burgess, "The Growth of the City," in Robert E. Park and Ernest W. Burgess, *The City* (Chicago: University of Chicago Press, 1925), pp. 50–51.

[11] The theories mentioned in these paragraphs are discussed in Chapter 10; implications of "conflict" and "order theories" for community-based corrections also are suggested in Chapter 24, pp. 592–94.

[12] Eleanor E. Maccoby, Joseph P. Johnson, and Russell M. Church, "Community Integration and Social Control of Juvenile Delinquency," *Journal of Social Issues,* 14, No. 3 (1958): 38–51.

[13] Irving A. Spergel, *Community Problem Solving: The Delinquency Example* (Chicago: University of Chicago Press, 1969), pp. 39–49.

processes in 31 American communities, he concluded that the greater the diffusion of the community power structure, the greater the degree of mobilization of community effort to deal with problems of housing, urban renewal, poverty, and slums.[14]

Perspective of conflict theories

Labeling theorists, as discussed earlier,[15] see the criminal justice system as an expression of the differential distribution of power among the groups composing the community. The interests of politically dominant groups are the basis of criminal laws. These laws are enacted and enforced when conflict among groups with differing social norms produces deviance that is regarded as threatening to the norms of the social order as it has been envisaged by the dominant groups. Conflict theorists argue that conflict among groups can serve other purposes than disruption, because aversions between contending parties can be a means of maintaining social stability when relationships among groups are changing in terms of economic and political power. Adversaries in yesterday's public issues can find common interests today in forming new coalitions for maintaining social stability.[16]

In their *conflict model of community*, Frederick Bates and Lloyd Bacon see various independent groups and organizations in conflict and competition with one another because the interests of one party oppose those of the others. These opposing groups are interdependent in that each requires the products or services of the others to achieve its own purposes. Conflicts and competition, therefore, must be managed if all parties are to gain the benefits of social stability.[17] The social structure of the community takes on its unique characteristics from the operation of the forces of conflict and accommodation.

From the perspective of ecology, this combination of competition and cooperation as a basis of the urban social system is compared to *symbiotic* relationships among differing species of plants and animals.[18] The tree

[14] Michael Aiken, "Community Power and Community Mobilization," *Annals of American Academy of Political and Social Science,* 385 (September 1969): 76–88.

[15] See Chapter 10, pp. 258–59.

[16] Lewis A. Coser, *The Functions of Social Conflict* (New York: Free Press, 1956), pp. 33–38, 121–37.

[17] Frederick L. Bates and Lloyd Bacon, "The Community as a Social System," *Social Forces,* 50 (March 1972): 373.

[18] The ecologists have had difficulty in applying their biological analogies to the sociocultural processes of life in human communities, but they have called attention to the competition for space among the groups making up the population of cities. Changes in population of various areas of the city and new uses of land constantly revise the social landscape of the community. For review of ecological studies, see Terence Morris, *The Criminal Area* (London: Routledge & Kegan Paul, 1957), pp. 1–18; Emma C. Llewelyn and Audrey Hawthorn, "Human Ecol-

shades plants near its trunk, and these plants preserve moisture for the tree. This mutual dependence is of mutual benefit, but the beneficiaries remain autonomous.

THE COMMUNITY AS A SERVICE SYSTEM

Urbanism has been instrumental in the development of the *service society,* which is characterized by the dependence of individuals and groups on the functions performed by a wide range of specialists. In this sense, "service" refers to a benefit other than some tangible product derived from labor. The United States became the first "service economy" following World War II, with more than half of the employed population engaged in work other than the production of food, clothing, housing, automobiles, or other tangible goods. The service economy includes wholesale and retail trade, finance, insurance, real estate, general government, and services of a professional, personnel, business, and repair nature. The dramatic development of the service economy is illustrated by the fact that the *increase* in employment in health services between 1950 and 1960 exceeded the total employees in automobile manufacturing in either year.[19]

Implications for criminological work

When the community is regarded as a *service system,* it is implied that the agencies providing services are integrated to an important degree. If the agencies do not somehow form a functional whole, they lack the coordination and complementarity suggested by the term "system." For the prevention, control, and correction of criminal behavior, the community is served by a network of private and public agencies engaged in law enforcement, probation and parole, adjudication of law violations, education, medical care, employment and family counseling, assistance to persons in financial need, and so on through the range of services required by individuals and groups in the complex urban community. Each of these agencies is an entity, but the work of all of them must comprise a *functional* whole if human needs are to be met and if this service network is to support a *community* strategy for dealing with social problems.

---

ogy," in Georges Gurvitch and Wilbert E. Moore (eds.), *Twentieth Century Sociology* (New York: Philosophical Library, 1945), pp. 466–99; Richard R. Korn and Lloyd W. McCorkle, *Criminology and Penology* (New York: Henry Holt & Co., 1959), pp. 282–92; and Judith A. Wilks, "Ecological Correlates of Crime and Delinquency," in President's Commission on Law Enforcement and Administration of Justice," *Task Force Report: Crime and Its Impact and Assessment* (Washington, D.C.: U.S. Government Printing Office, 1967), pp. 138–56.

[19] Victor R. Fuchs, *The Service Economy* (New York: Columbia University Press, 1968), p. 1.

The rise of the service society has increased demands that the criminal justice system engage in "people work" beyond the suppression of crime. There is increased emphasis on preventive and therapeutic models of criminal justice activities. The great demands placed on police agencies in the role of public servant and the growing recognition that law enforcement should operate within the informal control system of community institutions were discussed in Chapter 13. The juvenile court, analyzed in Chapter 14, is a predominant example of the judiciary's interest in using the processes of justice to combat the emotional and social sources of criminality. In the prison, custodial and industrial programs are claimed to be supportive of treatment programs manned by personnel qualified for people work, as was noted in Chapter 18. In chapters to follow, the fields of crime prevention, probation and parole, and prisoner aftercare will be identified with such services as education, vocational training, and mental health care, which are essential to a personally satisfying and socially productive life.

The increased recognition of the preventive and therapeutic ideologies has underlined the importance of integrating criminological work within the service delivery system of the community at large. Typically, the criminal justice system has been provincial in its outlook. The offender has been regarded only as an offender, with little regard for the fact that he, like other categories of clients, needs education, vocational training, medical care, family counseling, access to jobs, and other services provided by community agencies. Many agencies are reluctant to include offenders and former offenders with their noncriminal clients because of the social stigma attached to the criminal status.

Limited access to services

Delinquents suffer from a double failure of access to services, according to Spergel. They not only ordinarily have limited use or control of social resources and opportunities because they are members of underprivileged groups, but, once identified as delinquents, they are provided even less access to them.[20]

The lower social classes, from which the bulk of imprisoned offenders is drawn, receive comparatively fewer services in health care,[21] mental health care,[22] leisure-time activities,[23] and other people-oriented fields.

[20] Spergel, *Community-Problem Solving*, p. 49.

[21] See John A. Ross, "Social Class and Medical Care," *Journal of Health and Human Behavior*, 3 (Spring 1962): 35–40; Jules Henry, "Personality and Aged with Special Reference to Hospitals for the Aged Poor," in John C. McKinney and Frank T. DeVyver (eds.), *Aging and Social Policy* (New York: Appleton-Century-Crofts, 1966), pp. 281–97.

[22] See Marc Fried, "Social Differences in Mental Health," in John Kosa, Aaron Antonovsky, and Irving Kenneth Zola (eds.), *Poverty and Health: A Sociological*

Not only is the delivery of services distributed differentially among the social classes, but the underprivileged are likely to find access to the place of delivery difficult. Public assistance, employment, and medical care offices are often remote from lower-class residential areas. Whereas the well-to-do have private rooms in hospitals and can employ expert legal counsel, the poor occupy charity wards and receive no (or second-rate) legal assistance.[24]

It would be an oversimplification to explain the limited access of offenders to community services simply as a product of provincialism and the stigmatizing practices of agencies, which were noted above. Suggesting some of the other less obvious parameters of the difficulties, the President's Crime Commission stated:

> While in many respects the barriers to reintegration erected by the community are irrational, they do at base reflect, for example, the often severe disruption that delinquents can cause in school classes or recreational groups and the risks that an offender may present to employers. To some extent the community's exclusion of the offender is inevitable. Moreover, in a great many cases the services and community institutions that offenders need simply are not there in the first place—which may of course have contributed to their initial involvement in crime or delinquency. There is little sense in getting an offender readmitted to a slum school so poor that he will not profit from it; funds for the purchase of clinical services are useless if there are no clinics to go to. Mobilization of community institutions is a larger task than corrections alone can accomplish and it involves much broader interests than prevention of recidivism.[25]

The problem of mobilizing services

In the mobilization of community institutions in support of criminological programs, criminological workers must be able to establish colleagual relationships with personnel of other agencies and become familiar with their policies and procedures.[26] Such mobilization necessarily involves criminological agencies in the difficulties of interagency coordina-

Analysis (Cambridge, Mass.: Harvard University Press, 1969), pp. 113–67; James T. McMahon, "The Working Class Psychiatric Patient: A Clinical View," in Frank Reissman, Jerome Cohen, and Arthur Pearl (eds.), *Mental Health of the Poor* (New York: Free Press of Glencoe, 1964), pp. 283–302.

23 See Harold L. Wilensky, "The Uneven Distribution of Leisure: The Impact of Economic Growth of 'Free Time,' " in Erwin O. Smigel (ed.), *Work and Leisure* (New Haven, Conn.: College and University Press, 1963), pp. 107–45.

24 Adam Yarmolinsky, "The Service Society," *Daedalus,* 97 (Fall 1968): 1264–68.

25 President's Commission on Law Enforcement and Administration of Justice, *Task Force Report: Corrections* (Washington, D.C.: U.S. Government Printing Office, 1967), p. 12.

26 Implications for case management are discussed in Chapter 24, pp. 602–3.

tion and bureaucratic administration. Complaints against bureaucracies include "buck passing," giving the applicant "the runaround," and other symptoms of the failure to define clearly who is responsible for a given type of client or particular problem. Too frequently, a case is dropped before the client's needs have been met because an agency to whom he has been referred is not held accountable for final outcome.

The possibility of such failures is indicated by the *pinball machine model,* one of two descriptions of mental health care delivery systems offered by Elaine Cumming. In this model, a group of agencies is coordinated through generalized agreement rather than a central plan or organizational structure. The applicant for services approaches or is referred to one of the agencies according to how functions are distributed among the agencies, which are free to accept or reject him because centralized authority is absent. Each agency has its own policies and standards, and, because agencies overlap in services, the applicant is similar to a pinball as he ricochets among the "pockets." Cumming's suggestion for a second model for delivery of services recognizes the importance of planning. The *dispatcher model* postulates an overall plan and set of policies governing who shall be treated and which agency will provide a given service. "Traffic officers" with centralized authority coordinate the delivery of the services required by the particular client from among the various interdependent agencies, as a means of avoiding duplication of services and failures in agency responsibility and accountability.[27]

The vital importance of planning, coordination of component programs, allocation of responsibility for particular services among agencies, and fixing of accountability to ensure continuity of services for the individual client has been noted by Alfred Kahn.[28] Each agency contributes to a service *system* by relating its component activities to those of the others through planning. Intensive study of service needs and current delivery procedures precedes development of a plan to coordinate the activities to eliminate the waste of duplication and to fill the vacuum of unmet needs.

THE COMMUNITY CONCEPT AND THE PRISON

A theme of pessimism and frustrated hopes may have been conveyed by the analysis in previous chapters of the custodial prison, the primary model for implementation of the punitive ideology by the system of criminal justice. Chapter 17 described the prison "bureaucracy with a gun," which relies on coercion for conformity instead of inculcation of

[27] Elaine Cumming, "Care for the Mentally Ill, American Style," in Mayer N. Zald (ed.), *Organizing for Community Welfare* (Chicago: Quadrangle Books, 1967), pp. 125–33.

[28] Alfred J. Kahn, *Planning Community Services for Children in Trouble* (New York: Columbia University Press, 1963).

a sense of duty among inmates so that they come to identify with official prison goals. Although there are uniformities of behavior within the circumscribed boundaries of the prison, this is insufficient to qualify it as a genuine social-psychological community. Chapter 19 documented the pains of penal confinement, the continuous struggle between inmates and their keepers, and the formidable barriers the prison social structure raises to the development of sociocultural bonds.

In varying degrees, proposals to reorganize the custodial prison into a treatment model imply its transformation into a social-psychological community. Chapter 20 presented several strategies by which this could be accomplished: treatment teams, therapeutic communities, open institutions, and greater involvement of inmates in treatment processes. Whether the prison can become a genuine community is debatable at best, in light of the formidable barriers delineated in that chapter. Nevertheless, considerable progress toward that goal is possible.

The prison as a part of the community

Another application of the community concept, to be emphasized here, is the breaking down of the barriers which separate the prison from the community the prisoners leave involuntarily and to which most of them ultimately return. The general objective is to include correctional programs within societal processes by making the correctional institution a part of the life of the community. An associated goal is to give greater priority to correctional alternatives to confinement in institutions.

Issues concerning the bridging of prison experiences and life in the community after release from the correctional institution will be investigated in Chapter 24. Both crime prevention (Chapter 22) and probation and parole (Chapter 23) are alternative strategies to imprisonment as responses to crime which operate within the community. Prevention would circumvent the entire correctional system through various strategies designed to strengthen the vitality of community life, include a broader segment of the population in the benefits of an authentic community, and improve the delivery of human services. Expansion and improvement of probation and parole are means of making corrections a full participant among community institutions.

Means for accomplishing the inclusion of correctional institutions in the life of the community they are supposed to serve include local correctional centers, work-release programs, and an adaptation of the new-careers concept.

LOCAL CORRECTIONAL CENTERS

The *community-based institution* is envisaged as a new model, the architectural and methodological antithesis of the traditional fortress-like

Figure 21–2. Coordination in the community prison.

The community correctional center is located near the released prisoner's home. Here he can receive prerelease guidance, assistance in finding employment, and orientation to other services pertinent to his postrelease problems.

prison as a place of banishment. A small and informal structure, it would be located near the population center from which its inmates are drawn. Extensive screening and classification of inmates received from the courts would be the basis of alternative handling of sentenced offenders. Some would be placed immediately in community treatment programs. Others would be provided short-term, intensive treatment before being assigned to a community program. Diagnosis would result in a third category being referred to higher custody facilities required for long-term confinement of the more difficult or dangerous inmates. Eventually, these offenders would be returned to the local facility for reentry to the community.[29]

The *community prison,* according to Howard Gill, is the opposite of the traditional prison. Instead of mass housing, mass feeding, mass recreation, and so on, it is based on the small-group principle in size of living quarters, dining facilities, work programs, and leisure-time activities. Instead of physical isolation in cells, it promotes community contacts by bringing the community within its walls and taking the inmate to the outside world. Instead of regimentation, it promotes inmate participation in joint activity with staff, within legal and financial limits. Instead of life in a "monkey cage," it encourages normalcy in activities, interpersonal relations, and general climate.[30]

Interchange is a program of activities which take prisoners outside prison walls to participate selectively in community life. Community volunteers are also brought into the prison.[31] Such activities include attendance at athletic, cultural, and similar events, work-release assignments, entertainment by prisoners inside and outside the walls, prison art exhibits and fairs, athletic contests with teams from the outside community, and so on.

The community center holds potential for coordinating the aspects of society's reaction to offenders. Inmates scheduled for release could be moved near home for help in job guidance, home placement, and other attitudinal orientation to reentry into the community. Parole officers could initiate work with new cases. After release on parole, the parolee headed for difficulties could be reconfined briefly to determine whether renewal of conditional release is appropriate. As a sheltered workshop, the center could provide short-term employment for releasees unable to find jobs. It could employ work release to minimize the adverse effects of imprisonment and could utilize the final period of confinement to prepare the long-term prisoner for release.

[29] President's Commission on Law Enforcement, *Task Force Report: Corrections,* p. 11.

[30] Howard B. Gill, "What Is a Community Prison?" *Federal Probation,* 29 (September 1965): 15–18.

[31] Thomas R. Sard, "Contact with the Free Community Is Basic if Institutional Programs Are to Succeed," *Federal Probation,* 31 (March 1967): 3–8.

A problem is posed by the prisoner who would not be deemed fit for the local correctional center. There is the possibility that concern for "better" prisoners will result in continued neglect of those who are deemed incorrigible, long-term, or recidivistic. In these cases, the traditional prison may linger as an unsatisfactory solution.

WORK RELEASE

An adaptation of the open-institution idea is "day parole" or "work release." Under *work release,* selected prisoners are permitted to continue in their regular jobs in the community while spending daily after-work hours and unemployed weekends in confinement. If the prisoner approved for work release has no civilian job, the authorities endeavor to find one for him. Earnings are collected by the authorities, and after deductions for board and travel to and from work, the prisoner is given an allowance for his immediate personal needs. If directed by the court, funds are provided through a public welfare agency for support of his dependents. Any balance is paid the prisoner on his discharge from confinement.

Wisconsin's Huber Law of 1913 introduced work release officially for the first time in the United States, although earlier some female inmates in Massachusetts had been placed in the community under an indenture system. By 1971, the number of work-release programs had expanded among adult prison systems to include 41 states, the District of Columbia, and the Federal Bureau of Prisons in the United States.[32] Sweden has experimented with the approach since 1937. France, Scotland, Norway, Western Germany, and Great Britain also use it.[33]

As a form of disposition, work release is intermediate between probation and imprisonment. Its theoretical assumption is that there are offenders who require a period of supervision during off-work hours that is more strict than what the probation officer can provide. These particular offenders are not supposed to require full institutionalization, including the therapy which, theoretically at least, occurs concurrently with imprisonment. It is assumed that they are motivated to provide for their dependents through income-gaining activities and that they have sufficient work skills to generate enough income to do so after deductions for board, travel, and immediate personal needs.

[32] Elmer H. Johnson and Kenneth E. Kotch, "Two Factors in Development of Work Release: Size and Location of . Prisons," *Journal of Criminal Justice,* 1 (March 1973): 43–50.

[33] Stanley E. Grupp, "Work Release and the Misdemeanant," *Federal Probation,* 29 (June 1965): 7. During a visit in 1972 the author of the present text found Sweden moving away from work release and toward development of industrial programs within correctional institutions. The employment of short-sentence drunken drivers in highway and airport construction in Finland was particularly impressive.

Patterns of operation

There are three major patterns in recruitment of prisoners for work-release programs. Some retain their preconviction jobs because their skills are important to the employer and they are reliable workers. Others are given jobs by friends or members of their family to alleviate confinement or obtain work-release employment after being imprisoned.

The use of work release depends largely on the demand-supply relationship in the local labor market and the receptivity of employers, co-workers, and, in some cases, clients of the particular enterprise. The success of a work-release program rests upon the variety and level of skills available among prisoners, the quality of vocational training provided by the prison, and the degree of correlation between the job skills taught and the kinds of skills in demand in the free community. It also depends on the prisoners' attitudes toward work and discipline and their receptivity to the idea of supporting themselves and their dependents while prisoners.

Because of seasonal or other fluctuations in demand for workers employers may find the program useful as a reliable reservoir of labor. This function is most appropriate when wage scales are too low to attract sufficient free labor. The consequences are high job turnover and emphasis on low-income jobs.

Advantages claimed for work release center around humanitarian, economic, and rehabilitative themes: reduction of prison idleness, removal of dependents from public assistance rolls, increased responsibility of prisoners for dependents, preservation of family entity, avoidance of interruption in business and industrial operations in the free community caused by incarceration of skilled workers, reduction of the problem of finding jobs by released prisoners, increasing prisoners' job skills and employability, and encouragement of the prisoner to identify with the values and attitudes of the free community.

Administration of work release has its peculiar problems. Unless minimum-security jail or prison quarters are available locally, safe custody of less trustworthy inmates is made more difficult by the movement of work-release prisoners in and out of the facility. Measures against contraband smuggling are complicated. The night quarters must be located reasonably near the place of employment if transportation to and from work is to be practical. This tends to restrict the use of work release to urban areas of geographically concentrated employment. The sheriff or prison administration has additional duties in locating employment for some cases, maintaining records on disbursement of earnings, and providing transportation to and from work. The problems of selection of cases should not be underestimated for a program based on "half-free" prisoners who are not qualified for probation but must be trustworthy. Precautions must be taken against the possibility of employer exploita-

Figure 21–3a. The House of Glass.

In inaugurating a work-release program, the Illinois Department of Corrections leased from a private firm the above student dormitory adjacent to the Southern Illinois University campus at Carbondale. With the exception of modifications to provide office space, the facility retains much of the atmosphere of the free community, including an area (See Figure 21–3b) for receiving visitors. Residents are employed in local businesses or attend the educational institutions in the area. Recognizing the importance of model behavior in maintaining community goodwill, they named the facility "The House of Glass."

Figure 21–3b

tion of work-release prisoners because of the vulnerable status of individuals placed on the program. If a prison system uses the plan intensively, there is the possibility of competition with prison industries for well-motivated and skilled workers.

Work release as reform strategy

The potentiality of work release as a reform strategy lies in its implications for meeting the economic problems of the prison. Opposition to prisoner labor by private entrepreneurs and labor unions killed the industrial prison of earlier decades. Recent expansion of prison enterprises has been largely in terms of state use to avoid direct competition with local private enterprises. When such competition does occur in production exclusively for government agencies, the size of prison production has been minimized, thus relatively raising marginal costs of production and subverting opportunities to employ substantial numbers of prisoners. Prison industries operate without affording the prisoner, to a real extent, the economic incentives upon which the worker and breadwinner roles are based in free society. The discrepancy between the prison incentive system and that of free society creates fundamental problems for use of prisoner employment as a bridge toward approved postrelease behavior. The self-esteem of the offender is undermined by his loss of the wage-earner status, which is a major element of male adulthood. The erosion of the prisoner's status as a full-fledged adult indicates the importance of economic factors as limitations on correctional reform.[34]

Variants of work release are the extension of privileges for study release and for furloughs. Some state institutions and the federal pre-release guidance centers are experimenting with the release of inmates into the community to participate in educational programs.[35] The program has possibilities for permitting home furloughs for selected inmates. Among other advantages, furloughs are superior to conjugal visits in retaining family unity without undue emphasis on sexual relations.

THE NEW-CAREERS CONCEPT: THE SERVED BECOME SERVERS

Because automation and other technological changes have made great inroads on the demand for unskilled labor, there is a prospect of the growth of a "nonworking" class relegated to exile from meaningful functions in society. The *new-careers* concept would create new jobs normally allotted to professionals or technicians or would create entirely new jobs

---

[34] See Hermann Mannheim, *The Dilemma of Penal Reform* (London: George Allen & Unwin, Ltd., 1939), pp. 34–58.

[35] President's Commission on Law Enforcement, *Task Force Report: Corrections*, p. 11.

to meet an acknowledged need for service. In both instances the objective is to increase the number of jobs that can be performed by unskilled, inexperienced, and relatively untrained workers. The plight of the poor would be ameliorated by expanding their job opportunities and concurrently increasing the social services provided them. To assure that the job means a career, it would be incorporated into the organizational structure and provide for a degree of advancement through training.[36] Entry jobs would include teacher aides, community psychiatric aides, research aides, visiting homemakers, hospital aides, interviewers, community development workers, and case aides. This concept can be applied to utilization of inmates in prison staff roles as one aspect of the general effort to involve inmates in the affairs of prison life.[37]

Objectives of the strategy

The rationale of the new-careers concept is to provide new opportunities for the poor in job areas not likely to be automated and give them a social-psychological stake in the structure of the community. Such nonprofessionals would provide services for the poor to fill a void created by the reluctance of many professionals, social workers, and teachers to do so. Drawn largely from the neighborhoods or groups in which they would work, the nonprofessionals would be role models for their peers.[38] They would be more likely to identify with clients (and clients to identify with them) because they share cultural backgrounds and have experienced similar social circumstances.

By providing services such workers gain a sense of belonging and confidence to strengthen a feeling of personal worth.[39] The approach provides opportunity to undo an unanticipated consequence for individuals placed in the status of assistance recipient. The very process of assistance impairs the individual's previous identity, marking the quality of his intercourse with other persons. Because assistance is not an inherent right, the agency staff gains power over the client through control over the gateway to services. The status of assistance recipient entails surrender of the right to privacy. The individual's personal secrets may be probed in the name of diagnosis, treatment, and case investigation. His home, or equivalent social locale, may be invaded. His mode of income disposal is open to scrutiny. The greatest source of degradation, however, is his inability

---

[36] Arthur Pearl and Frank Riessman, *New Careers for the Poor* (New York: Free Press of Glencoe, 1965), pp. 13–14.

[37] The general effort was discussed in Chapter 20, pp. 506–9.

[38] Frank Riessman, "The Revolution in Social Work: The New Professional," *Trans-action,* 2 (November–December 1964): 13.

[39] J. Douglas Grant, "The Offender as Participant, Not Recipient, in the Correctional Process," *Canadian Journal of Corrections,* 9 (July 1967): 236–37.

to reciprocate for benefits received. The individual unable to contribute something to society is barred from full participation in that society.[40]

Application in correctional institutions

In correctional institutions, inmate participation in staff roles has received a modest degree of recognition as a device for changing inmate behavior. The prospects for the approach may be improved by the possibility that inmates themselves may be a means of meeting the critical manpower problem of the prisons.

The New Careers Development Project of California has trained inmates to be "program development assistants" in the community after release. They train high school dropouts to be change agents in the role of assistant teachers who direct volunteers tutoring slum children to reduce the cultural deprivation and thereby break the cycle of poverty.[41] The New York State Division for Youth has experimented with the hiring of trained ex-inmates to work with other released inmates in the community or for child care agencies.[42]

Problems in implementation

The selection of offenders for these roles raises issues. One view is that the major criterion should be ability to perform the job. This criterion assumes intellectual capacity, ability to relate to others, verbal communication skill, motivation to help others, and knowledge appropriate to the tasks. Another view rules out confirmed homosexuals and drug addicts, a criterion disputed on grounds that it employs stigmatization to select individuals for a program intended to undo the consequences of stigmatization. Selection is complicated because possession of desirable qualities does not guarantee success. The middle-class ex-prisoner may fail precisely because he has failed to use his advantages in a prosocial manner, whereas a lower-class offender, more deficient in such qualities, may respond favorably to new opportunities.[43]

[40] See Lewis Coser, "The Sociology of Poverty," *Social Problems,* 13 (Fall 1965): 144–47.

[41] Kenneth R. Jackson and Dennie L. Briggs, "Developing New Careers for Delinquents in Education: An Alternate to Confinement," *American Journal of Correction,* 28 (May–June 1966): 21–23.

[42] Milton Luger, "Selection Issues in Implementing the Use of the Offender as a Correctional Manpower Resource," in *The Offender: An Answer to the Correctional Manpower Crisis,* report of workshop sponsored by Institute for Study of Crime and Delinquency and National Institute of Mental Health, Asilomar, Calif., September 1966, pp. 9–10.

[43] See Gilbert Geis, "Summary of Discussion on Selection Issues," in ibid., pp. 19–27.

The pertinence and quality of training has crucial importance because a substantial proportion of offenders have histories of inferior learning and work motivation. Lower-status persons frequently are deficient in abstract thinking, verbal facility, capacity to relate themselves to a social structure, and self-esteem.[44] Training must come to grips with the difficulties of motivating the undermotivated. Ways must be sought to develop flexible responses among persons exposed to unfamiliar roles, fundamental understanding among persons with deficient academic experience, and social skills in a population generally not accomplished in this sphere.

Changes in existing status-role arrangements are the crux of the potentiality of this approach, but they also present the greatest difficulty. The granting of authority to former offenders threatens the social power of the occupants of leadership positions in the community or correctional system. Professionals control their occupational areas by selecting who will be given the opportunity to practice and determining the circumstances under which practice is conducted. The business and political sectors of the community include special-interest groups with a stake in preserving traditional arrangements whereby the underprivileged are denied access to leadership and economic opportunities sought under "the served become servers" approach. An equivalent situation exists in correctional institutions where new arrangements are intended to replace the inmate social system and traditional modes of interaction between staff and inmates. The potential clients include individuals reluctant to accept their peers in the new statuses. The selected offenders may lack the flexibility to assume new statuses and roles radically different from the expectations to which they have been socialized in the very environment they are expected to change.

SUMMARY

The social-psychological bonds of the community and its service system are important concepts in the goal of making criminological practice relevant to the prevention and correction of criminal and delinquent behavior. The "inauthentic community" describes conditions favorable to high rates of lawbreaking. The strategies of making the correctional institution more of a genuine community and moving it toward closer linkages with the outside community it is supposed to serve were examined in this chapter. In the chapters to follow, we shall see how prevention involves the strengthening of the community as an integrating force and probation and parole, as alternatives to imprisonment, must be integrated within the network of community institutions.

[44] See Orville R. Gursslin and Jack L. Roach, "Some Issues in Training the Unemployed," *Social Problems*, 12 (Summer 1964): 91–93.

FOR ADDITIONAL READING

Alix, Ernest K. "The Functional Interdependence of Crime and Community Social Structure." *Journal of Criminal Law, Criminology and Police Science,* 60 (September 1969) : 332–39.

Bernard, Jessie. *American Community Behavior.* Rev. ed. New York: Holt, Rinehart & Winston, 1962.

Chatterjee, Pranab, and Koleski, Raymond A. "The Concepts of Community and Community Organization: A Review." *Social Work,* 15 (July 1970) : 82–92.

Dentler, Robert A. *American Community Problems.* New York: McGraw-Hill Book Co., 1968.

Eriksson, Torsten. "The Swedish Furlough System for Prisoners." In Marvin E. Wolfgang (ed.), *Crime and Culture,* pp. 417–27. New York: John Wiley & Sons, 1968.

Grupp, Stanley E. "Work Furlough and Punishment Theory." *Criminology,* 8 (May 1970) : 63–79.

Hillery, George A., Jr. *Communal Organizations: A Study of Local Societies,* Appendix C. Chicago: University of Chicago Press, 1968.

Johnson, Elmer H. "Work Release: Conflicting Goals within a Promising Innovation." *Canadian Journal of Corrections,* 12 (January 1970) : 67–77.

Mays, John Barron. "Delinquency Areas—A Reassessment." *British Journal of Criminology,* 3 (January 1963) : 216–30.

Minar, David W., and Greer, Scott (eds.). *The Concept of Community: Readings with Interpretations.* Chicago: Aldine Publishing Co., 1969.

Moeller, H. G. "Corrections and the Community: New Dimensions." *Federal Probation,* 32 (June 1968) : 25–29.

Nelson, Elmer K., Jr. "Community-Based Correctional Treatment: Rationale and Problems." *Annals of American Academy of Political and Social Science,* 374 (November 1967) : 82–91.

Rein, Martin. "The Social Service Crisis." *Trans-action,* 1 (May 1964) : 3–6.

Skoler, Daniel L. "Future Trends in Juvenile and Adult Community Based Corrections." *Proceedings of American Correctional Association, 1970,* pp. 118–30.

22

Crime prevention

The term "prevention" implies that something evil, unpleasant, or destructive waits in the wings of the stage of life, but human ingenuity can foresee and therefore prevent it. To forestall the disagreeable eventualities of delinquency and crime, a broad range of action is undertaken to alleviate the personal and social difficulties contributing to criminal behavior. Some of these actions are merely expedient, consisting of short-sighted efforts to ward off immediate crises confronting the community. A premise common to all actions, however, is that prevention is less costly and more promising than subsequent efforts to halt a delinquent career.

ORIENTATIONS TOWARD PREVENTION

Criminologists consider prevention in two senses. The first, concerns the ability of criminal law enforcement to make citizens law-abiding.[1] In this sense, prevention includes all efforts to deter potential criminals and to prevent further offenses of apprehended criminals. The second refers to efforts to correct fundamental social conditions and personal maladjustments which are assumed to be the "seedbed" of crime. This approach to crime prevention involves efforts to forestall antisocial behavior by promoting healthy personality development in children and by eliminating environmental influences favorable to the emergence of antisocial behavior. Preventive efforts are directed toward strengthening the family, school, and other social institutions and toward eradication of mental and personality traits in the individual that are associated with criminal and delinquent behavior. Various approaches, including psychiatry, vocational education, sterilization, social work, recreation, and medicine, are used in these efforts.

[1] Johs. Andenaes, "General Prevention—Illusion or Reality?" *Journal of Criminal Law, Criminology, and Police Science*, 43 (July–August 1952): 179.

Targets of programs

Prevention is generally accepted as a major societal reaction to delinquency and crime, but there is less agreement on the approach and techniques to be employed.

Residents of a community may be differentiated into four groups along a continuum. The majority usually are so-called "normals" who do not become sufficiently maladjusted emotionally or behaviorally to need special attention. A second group does need special attention because the individuals in it do have maladjustments, but these have not progressed to the point where they would elicit official reactions to the individuals as delinquents or criminals. Individuals in the third group have been recognized officially as delinquents or criminals, but they are not committed to crime as a way of life. Finally, there are the confirmed criminals. Crime prevention is intended to forestall movement of an individual along the continuum in the direction of criminality.

Preventive agencies usually choose one or more of these groups as their primary target. Some agencies are concerned primarily with the first two groups, striving *to prevent antisocial behavior at its source.* Others deal indirectly with antisocial behavior in the source of promoting healthy personality development of all children or in taking action against other broad social problems. The "normals" are their primary target, and prevention is an incidental purpose in recreational, slum clearance, industrial development, educational, religious, and similar programs. Other agencies concentrate directly on antisocial behavior of the maladjusted group under the premise that prevention requires the reaching of potential delinquents before they get into trouble with the law. Examples are child guidance clinics, casework agencies, and street-gang workers, who concentrate on predelinquent children with personality problems.

Other programs are oriented toward the *prevention of recidivism.* Prevention is envisaged as lessening the likelihood of more serious offenses by individuals already in conflict with the law. The third group is to be kept from being recruited for the fourth group. Law enforcement, judicial, and correctional agencies become instruments for prevention.

The major approaches to delinquency and crime may be categorized roughly as those oriented toward individuals and those emphasizing the environment.

Individual-oriented prevention

Individualistic theories have been defined as those conceiving the individual as essentially autonomous and, in his natural state, free of group restrictions.[2] Delinquency and crime are attributed largely to mental, chemical, and organic qualities and processes within the individual. His transgressions are traced to such matters as emotional imbalance, asocial drives, and faults of his personality. The influence of the sociocultural environment is recognized in the development of such responses as faulty socialization and inferior educational background, but the focus of attention is on the individual. Preventive activities include child guidance clinics, special schools or educational programs for delinquents, some applications of street work with juvenile gangs, social work services, probation and parole services, and residential institutions.

Individual-oriented approaches to the prevention of delinquency and crime take the form of counseling, psychotherapy, and educational intervention. The physical presence of the client stands in sharp contrast to the abstract nature of the forces operating within the environment. At first glance he appears to be a simpler target for change than the complex, highly interrelated, and less apparent forces of the environment. In an individualistic culture it is easier to mobilize public support for prevention when the target is presented as individuals who are suffering or who pose a personalized threat to precious values. Prevention aimed at global and environmental factors is likely to require that "good, normal" people surrender some advantages afforded by the status quo—at least, they must question some familiar ideas which give comfort and a sense of order to life. Finally, compared with the heavy investments required by extensive attacks on environmental factors, individual-oriented programs can be directed toward particular segments of the problem population, thus bringing prevention within the scope of budgetary feasibility and available personnel resources.

The greatest justification for individual-oriented prevention, however, is that there *are* individuals who could benefit by such intervention. Hopefully, both the individual and the community would be benefited by the altering of self-defeating attitudes and perceptions, the redirection of energy toward more promising goals, and the strengthening of individual capacities. The weakness of individual-centered approaches lies in the failure to recognize that most offenders do not have emotional disturbances, and their law-breaking frequently reflects patterned deviancy in their neighborhoods. According to John Martin, practitioners generally work toward individual adjustment rather than change in the social conditions conducive to delinquency and crime. Public and private agencies allocate their resources to case-by-case treatment while largely ignoring community-centered programs of social prevention. He does not call for abandonment of individual-centered techniques, however, but points out

[2] See Chapter 9.

the error in the failure to include *both* individual treatment and social reorganization in programs for prevention.[3]

Environment-oriented prevention

Approaches emphasizing the environment encompass every relationship between man and the external conditions and influences affecting him as an organism and as a social creature. The geographical environment affects social patterns, and biological factors can be viewed in conjunction with both social and cultural factors.

The sociocultural environment is usually taken for granted as a set of constant factors. The environmental factors behind delinquency and crime are explained as deficiencies in the enthusiasm with which tried and true principles of child rearing, education, and economics are applied. Educational campaigns are devoted to making parents and the "average citizen" more aware of their "responsibilities." Law enforcement, welfare, educational, and other agencies are given greater financial support under the assumption that it is the lack of resources which blocks more effective prevention of crime, rather than any deficiencies in the fundamental principles and modes of organization upon which contemporary efforts are based.

Other environmental approaches are directed toward changing the context within which criminal behavior emerges. The objective may be *changing institutional relationships* in one of two general ways. First, there may be an attempt to *restructure the relationships* among the agencies and groups. Efforts are made to coordinate the organizations of the community in order to reduce inefficiency of duplicated services and, perhaps, conflict between the individual programs. The second way uses three strategies intended to create some *new form of relationship*. One strategy is to *create a lay leadership* to extend the base of public participation and to improve the coordination of programs. A second has as its target the *remotivation of delinquent groups* in an attempt to bring them within the scope of preventive programs which they have resisted. The detached-worker and aggressive-casework approaches employ this strategy. A third strategy is represented by the area-project approach, which would vitalize a *new sense of social solidarity* among the residents of delinquency areas.

The most sweeping attack on the environmental bases of social deviance calls for *institutional reorganization*. This ambitious approach would redesign the ideological basis of society and require reconstruction of society as a whole. In this view, the roots of delinquency are considered to

[3] John M. Martin, "Three Approaches to Delinquency Prevention: A Critique," in David Dressler (ed.), *Readings in Criminology and Penology*, 2d ed. (New York: Columbia University Press, 1972), pp. 726–27.

be too deeply intertwined in the fundamental values and traditions of contemporary society to be eradicated without major change in society itself. The final chapter will take up this approach.

Difficulties of prevention programs

Regardless of the approach, prevention programs have an inherent difficulty: delinquency and crime are not distinct behavioral entities as implied by conceptions which see them as some kind of "social disease." The "disease model" has been described as a set of beliefs, borrowed from medicine, that each undesirable condition is marked by a unique set of observable symptoms. A malign process within the organism supposedly persists over time to deprive the sick person of control over his behavior. Some pernicious agent—physical, chemical, genetic, interpersonal, or social—is seen as the source of difficulty.[4] For individual-oriented prevention, some form of therapy would be necessary to eliminate the delinquent behavior. For environment-oriented prevention, the rectification of undesirable social conditions—poverty, deteriorated housing, inferior education, and so on—would be the solution of delinquency.

Because delinquency and crime are not behavioral entities that can be sharply differentiated from nondelinquent behavior, the delineation of clear-cut, universal symptoms would be difficult. Delinquency is a status conferred upon some individuals, more as a reflection of administrative processes than of specific characteristics differentiating delinquents from nondelinquents. A single malign process and a single pernicious agent, running a particular course for all delinquents, cannot be identified. Behaviors defined as delinquent are only one of the various ways in which adolescents may respond to dilemmas faced in their lives, even if all face identical environmental adversities. Furthermore, individuals differ in how they perceive conditions and the particular aspirations they acquire.[5]

Because prevention entails forestalling future behaviors likely to be defined as lawbreaking, prediction and early identification of delinquent tendencies are often involved. The term "predelinquent" conveys the idea that, before any violation of legal norms, the presence of certain early symptoms indicates that a given youngster will move inexorably toward delinquency or crime. Although agreeing that cultural, social, or psychological deprivation has probable effects on later behavior, J. V. Fornataro objects to the concept of predelinquency on the grounds that attention is focused on only *one* possible expression of social inadequacy,

---

[4] Merlin Taber, *et al.*, "Disease Ideology and Mental Health Research," *Social Problems,* 16 (Winter 1969): 349–57.

[5] Thomas Gladwin, "Strategies in Delinquency Prevention," in Leonard J. Duhl (ed.), *The Urban Condition* (New York: Basic Books, 1963), pp. 268–69.

and this prediction carries social opprobrium in *advance* of delinquent behavior.[6]

Early identification of probable delinquents would be a useful product of science. Accurate predictions would permit economic administration and intelligent direction of treatment programs within the limits of scarce resources. Identification and early treatment need not be stigmatizing, but Jackson Toby warns of their possible boomerang effects. More intensive treatment will not be as effective as less intense but less discriminatory treatment. Toby raises a question as to how early identification and intensive programs can avoid "self-fulfilling prophecies." When treatment programs concentrate on youngsters who are especially vulnerable to delinquency, how can they avoid stigmatizing those youngsters and thereby increasing the motivation for delinquency to such a degree that it negates any beneficial effects of the treatment?[7]

Preventive measures sometimes are based on narrow monocausal explanations which oversimplify the etiology of crime. Delinquency and crime have been explained as evidence of the effects of parental neglect, comic books, crime and sex themes in television and movie productions, disreputable recreational establishments, empty churches, illiteracy, glandular imbalance, infected teeth, defective vision, insufficient recreation, jukeboxes, tobacco, inferior lighting of streets, and so on and on. Each explanation may promote understanding of a particular aspect of deviance, but the babel of explanations, usually untested, results in a chaos of diverse and often conflicting efforts.

Simple, direct methods frequently are more attractive than preventive measures requiring planning and complex explanation. Suppression of comic books and police raids on recreation centers of ill repute are dramatic actions compared with tortuously implemented, long-term attempts to reform social institutions. Even the well-planned program can be subverted by the appeal of direct action. A frequent procedure is to enact a law which "solves" a major problem in a most enlightened manner but fails to provide the resources and techniques essential for implementation. This deficiency transforms the laws into dead letters with no effect on the problems they were supposed to correct.

Fitting programs into a larger scheme

As indicated by earlier analysis of social institutions,[8] delinquency involves the operation of many variables in more complex fashion than

[6] J. V. Fornataro, "It's Time to Abolish the Notion of Pre-Delinquency!" *Canadian Journal of Corrections,* 7 (April 1965): 190.

[7] Jackson Toby, "An Evaluation of Early Identification and Intensive Treatment Programs for Predelinquents," *Social Problems,* 13 (Fall 1965): 160–75.

[8] Chapter 6.

that suggested by environmental theories based on poverty, inadequate parents, deficient education, and other simplistic explanations. Slum clearance, educational reform, income maintenance, and other programs directed against the effects of social disorganization can be useful in improving conditions for the underprivileged, and, in the course of helping a large segment of the population, they often serve to prevent delinquency. Martin sees the problem of delinquency prevention as basically one of social organization or reorganization; the merit of other approaches lies in their contribution to reorganization.[9]

The concept of social organization places the evaluation of prevention programs in the complicated context of the structure of society. Crime and delinquency prevention involve issues which at first glance appear to be irrelevant. For example, the functioning of human service bureaucracies is pertinent because delivery of welfare, educational, psychological, and other services crucial to prevention is determined by the quality of administration. The goals of agency policy include preservation of the agency, efficiency, and minimization of costs, especially through standardized procedures for services. The agencies thus tend to become habituated to particular strategies and schemes of interagency relationships, with the net result that higher priority is granted to administrative efficiency than to the delivery of services in ways most likely to be useful to the client.

Clients who come closest to middle-class "normality" are more likely to receive services. Of at least equal importance are the unintended consequences of agency administration in isolating clients from normal social intercourse as first-class citizens and complete personalities. In seeking funds, the agencies may exploit emotional appeals based on stereotyped views of offenders. Picturing the offender as psychologically inadequate reinforces public misconceptions of the offender as totally pathological; in this way, the agency stigmatizes its own clients. Because agencies tend to specialize in particular kinds of clients (such as the physically handicapped), and sometimes a particular subtype, they become vehicles for maintaining the isolation of offenders from "normals."

SOME PROGRAMS OF PREVENTION

Prevention of crime and delinquency entails every facet of human behavior. Certain components of the social structure, however, can be more obviously identified with programs designed to forestall law violations.

Education

Because virtually every child passes through the school system and because it is one of the principal socializing agencies of our culture, educa-

[9] Martin, "Three Approaches to Delinquency Prevention," p. 727.

tion is in a central position to facilitate programs of delinquency prevention. Our earlier discussion of the relevance of educational institutions to criminology placed heavy stress on delinquency prevention.[10] The relevance of education to the curbing of the problems of delinquency, and ultimately of crime, is one aspect of the special impact of deficient schooling on the individual's life chances in an urban society, where educational attainment is often seen as the gateway to vocational success and social opportunity. The issue of equal educational opportunity affects all aspects of contemporary life, including the probability of delinquent behavior.

If educational programs are to contribute effectively to the prevention of delinquency, it would seem necessary that they fit into long-term, comprehensive programs designed to lower the barriers against the participation of underprivileged groups in the activities and rewards of community life. William Amos suggests three general goals for education: (1) developing a new value system in which the school would be a force working against the discrimination and rejection experienced by pupils drawn from the lower classes; (2) making the school an instrument for fostering work attitudes, self-esteem, and job skills to improve the employability of graduates of schools in deprived areas; and (3) providing school experiences designed to improve the self-image of delinquency-prone children.[11]

Placing the school's contributions within a total community effort toward delinquency prevention, Robert MacIver conceives of the school as a neighborhood institution, cooperating with families and human service agencies in substandard, poverty-stricken urban areas and providing special services to equip children for effective use of schooling. He would train all teachers to identify problem children and to provide preliminary help and guidance through sympathetic understanding of needs.[12]

Psychiatric help

Psychiatric care comes in the form of treatment by psychiatrists, clinical psychologists, and psychiatric social workers in clinics. Persons of all ages have emotional problems requiring such care. Alleviation of frustrations may forestall adult crimes, but prevention of juvenile delinquency is usually emphasized because personality is more malleable in the early years. Some youngsters in conflict with the adult world exhibit

[10] Chapter 6, pp. 109–12.

[11] William E. Amos, "Prevention through the School," in William E. Amos and Charles F. Wellford (eds.), *Delinquency Prevention: Theory and Practice* (Englewood Cliffs, N.J.: Prentice-Hall, Inc., 1967), pp. 132–35.

[12] Robert M. MacIver, *The Prevention and Control of Delinquency* (New York: Atherton Press, 1967), pp. 122–23.

misbehavior beyond the tolerance of their parents and the community. Adolescents may act out their maladjustment through truancy, running away from home, aggression, and delinquencies which may bring them to the attention of the police and the courts. Early referral to psychiatric clinics can forestall more serious delinquencies.

Because clinical treatment for children usually assumes that parent-child relationships are at the core of the child's behavioral difficulties, the support of parents is especially important in the decision to take remedial action. For children designated as delinquent, authoritarian referrals from the juvenile court add to the problem. Parents often must be led to recognize that treatment is necessary, and their willingness to participate in the treatment processes must be cultivated.[13]

George Albee contends that psychiatric clinics in the United States have serious deficiencies requiring widespread overhaul. These clinics "are treating the wrong people; they are using the wrong methods; they are located in the wrong places; they are improperly staffed and administered." Albee cites evidence that little or no care is available for poor children, adolescents, multiproblem families, the aged, or discharged hospital cases. Individual psychotherapy is the usual method, although an excessive proportion of patients stop coming prematurely, and this method serves only a small fraction of the persons needing care. The clinics are heavily concentrated in northeastern states and at a distance from urban slums or rural areas. The staffs lack sufficient psychiatrists, psychologists, and social workers.[14]

Serious gaps exist between the professional staff of the orthodox municipal mental health service and the underprivileged persons who have special need for help. One study attributes this gap to the characteristics of the mental health system; fragmentation, complexity, and bureaucratization make services difficult to locate and lead to long waiting lists. Lower-class people have particular difficulty in communicating their needs or formulating them in ways acceptable to the formalized service structure. Neighborhood mental health centers are advocated as a means of closing this gap. Nonprofessional aides recruited from the neighborhood would be supervised by a professional mental health worker. They would work from storefront centers to bring people needing mental health care into the service delivery system.[15]

[13] Helen L. Witmer and Edith Tufts, *The Effectiveness of Delinquency Prevention Programs* (Washington, D.C.: U.S. Children's Bureau, 1954), p. 40.

[14] George W. Albee, "A Spectre Is Haunting the Outpatient Clinic," in Alan B. Tulipan and Saul Feldman (eds.), *Psychiatric Clinics in Transition* (New York: Brunner/Mazel, 1969), pp. 1–24.

[15] Harris B. Peck, Seymour R. Kaplan, and Melvin Roman, "Prevention, Treatment, and Social Action: A Strategy of Intervention in a Disadvantaged Urban Area," *American Journal of Orthopsychiatry*, 36 (January 1966): 57–69.

Recreation programs

Most organized recreation programs are directed toward improvement of the environment for children, although their use is expanding for other segments of the population, such as young adults and senior citizens. They are directed to all youngsters, regardless of proneness to delinquency, under the premise that delinquency will be reduced as an incidental effect of this use of recreation by abolishing idleness and offering an alternative channel for behavior likely to be judged delinquent. Studies suggest that delinquency is not halted by the mere provision of recreational facilities, that recreation is not the converse of delinquent activity, and that organized recreation should be employed in conjunction with other preventive approaches rather than as an autonomous program.

A less frequently used type of organized recreation is that directed toward those most likely to become delinquents. Through individual treatment, the predelinquent is induced to become a member of a recreational activity. These activities can be included under the general term *group work,* which is the application of individual casework principles within a group setting. Organized recreation can be a phase of a general attack on delinquency as a community problem through coordination of the work of several agencies.

A fundamental premise of the Scout and Big Brother and Big Sister movements and similar programs is that the presence of a wise, loving adult friend is sufficient to forestall delinquency. This friend serves potential delinquents by showing his interest in them, acting as an ego ideal, and generally guiding them.

The Cambridge-Somerville Youth Study tested the effectiveness of the "friendly-adult" approach through experimental and control groups, with a staff of nine trained counselors to work with boys in the experimental group. Friendship rather than a casework relationship was emphasized. Although working methods varied among the counselors, much emphasis was placed on taking trips, recreation, psychological and medical services, tutoring, and counseling.[16] Edwin Powers and Helen Witmer based their evaluation of this study on measurement of the extent to which the treated boys benefited by the work of the counselors, as indicated by reduction of delinquency or improvement of the boys' social adjustment. They found that only 21 percent of the boys definitely benefited, 10 percent received "slight benefit," and 6 percent received "temporary benefit."[17] The friendly-adult approach was most successful for

[16] Witmer and Tufts, *Effectiveness of Delinquency Prevention Programs,* pp. 26–28.

[17] Edwin Powers and Helen L. Witmer, *An Experiment in the Prevention of Delinquency* (New York: Columbia University Press, 1951), p. 441.

boys who were seriously maladjusted emotionally but relatively healthy in personality, and whose parents were somewhat dependent and immature. A boy likely to be benefited by the approach had to be the type who sought the friendship of adults, wanted to be aided in dealing with difficulties, and had parents whose inadequacies the counselor could offset. The police and court records of the experimental and control groups were nearly identical, with few of either group becoming seriously delinquent. The friendly-adult approach was especially ineffectual for chronic delinquents: slum boys with indifferent, neglectful parents; seriously neurotic boys from emotionally unfavorable homes; and feebleminded or neurologically handicapped boys from poor homes.[18]

Law enforcement

The policeman, as noted earlier, is conceived popularly in the guardian-of-society role, although the largest proportion of his work involves him in the public-servant role.[19] He is likely to see delinquency and crime prevention in terms of law enforcement and apprehension of violators. The realities of the urban environment, however, have increased the recognition of police executives that law enforcement must operate within the context of the total community system. Annual reports of police departments cite programs of "community relations" and work with juveniles as evidence that they conceive of law enforcement as encouraging law observance as well as providing direct reaction to offenses. Such reports often fail to demonstrate a sophisticated understanding of what "community relations" means, but there is evidence of a shifting of attitudes away from suppression and control as the only police strategies.

Among the representatives of the various human service agencies, the policeman is most likely to come in contact with the law violator or other disturber of community tranquility. His handling of the so-called "first offender" is of special importance because he influences the screening process whereby some juvenile delinquents are routed into the courts and correctional agencies and others are referred to social service agencies. Edwin Lemert notes the rise of spurious "social work" services by police agencies in the 1930s, the establishment of more competent youth bureaus, and the development in 1949 of a juvenile liaison scheme in Liverpool, England, in which special policemen work with school teachers, ministers, and so on for delinquency prevention. Criticisms of direct treatment of delinquents by police include the charges that officers are untrained for preventive work, police agencies are not in a position to

---

[18] Witmer and Tufts, *Effectiveness of Delinquency Prevention Programs,* pp. 29–30.

[19] Chapter 13, pp. 333–36.

Figure 22–1. Community relations in action.

As a phase of its community relations activities, the Honolulu Police Department conducts a "law and justice awareness" program. Officers teach regularly scheduled and accredited courses in elementary, intermediate, and high schools. Topics include the law and how it applies to citizens, the court system, constitutional rights, and the functions of law enforcement in society.

develop needed treatment facilities and the police station is an inappropriate setting for treatment. The charge is also made that police who treat delinquents waste taxpayers' money by duplicating services.[20]

An important element in delinquency prevention is the diversion of some offenders from further processing by the system of criminal justice. As gatekeepers for this system, the police have a central role in any diversion scheme. Lemert notes that the police are unlikely to tolerate any diversion that protects serious law violators or otherwise fundamentally undermines their primary duty to maintain community order.[21] Long-term development of an effective diversion system calls for bonds of colleagueship between members of law enforcement and other human service agencies, and the coordination of police departments and agencies to which selected delinquents are referred.

RESTRUCTURING RELATIONSHIPS

The diversity of approaches to crime prevention aggravates problems of coordinating the various preventive and treatment services within the community. Urbanization has changed the patterns of human relationships and social organization. As a consequence, programs designed for "reaching the unreached" and the related concept of "aggressive casework" have been proposed, and new organizational forms have been adopted.

Reaching the unreached

In recent developments in crime prevention, a basic theme has been *reaching the unreached*. Instead of waiting for people to present themselves for assistance and treatment, these programs are geared to reach out actively and aggressively to help those who do not voluntarily seek assistance, although they are in trouble or are approaching it.

Several premises are involved in reaching-out programs designed to prevent delinquency. First, families most likely to be involved in delinquency problems are comparatively untouched by the usual casework and recreational programs. Second, the community has the responsibility to take action to protect children when their behavior reflects a destructive process. To wait until court action is necessary would constitute community indifference. Third, if services are brought to bear early in the stages of development of maladjustments, the effectiveness of prevention will be enhanced. Fourth, the family is assumed to have some

---

[20] Edwin M. Lemert, *Instead of Court: Diversion in Juvenile Justice* (Chevy Chase, Md.: National Institute of Mental Health, Center for Studies of Crime and Delinquency, 1971), pp. 55–58.

[21] Ibid., p. 54.

capacity for change in spite of its inadequacies and its failure to volunteer for assistance.[22]

A concept closely related to reaching the unreached is *aggressive casework*. "Aggressive" here has the sense of vigorous, outgoing activity to achieve a purpose, rather than hostile behavior. A case is considered appropriate for aggressive casework to cope with delinquency when the referral unit determines that the child requires protection as evidenced by neglect or antisocial behavior, and that the parents are unable to meet the child's needs and will not seek help. The social worker writes the family that he will visit the home at a certain time. He persists in spite of such evidence of resistance as slammed doors, failure to answer, or verbal aggression. The sincerity of his offer of help is demonstrated by his continued physical presence and lack of resentment. Active social responsibility for the child's welfare is the basis of the authority he must exercise positively to give support to the clients in moving them toward acceptance of casework assistance.[23]

Under the concept of *intensive group-work services,* professionally trained workers are chosen for their skill in group therapy. As applied to delinquency, the work is with groups of children and youths and, sometimes, their parents. These groups have been referred to the workers by conventional programs, schools, police, and probation agencies as "hard-to-serve" cases. The objectives are to deal with the social behavior problems of the individuals rather than to provide wholesome leisure-time activity per se. Emphasis is given to helping group members to help one another.

For *intensive casework services,* special units are established to provide easily accessible, highly integrated counseling to individuals within the traditional programs of public or voluntary agencies. Case workers have small caseloads to free them for more intensive service.

New organizational schemes

Delinquency and crime prevention requires coordination of a "total community of effort" to increase the effectiveness of existing services and to bring a balanced growth of services through joint planning and action. Unfortunately, agencies usually operate in separate, specialized fields to such an extent that a particular family or individual with many problems may be dealing separately with several agencies at the same time. The procedures for case acceptance and assignment are slow. Workers from various agencies often are strangers to one another, breeding distrust.

[22] Bjarnes Romnes, *Coordination of the National Effort for Dealing with Juvenile Delinquency* (Washington, D.C.: U.S. Children's Bureau, 1960), p. 52.

[23] Alice Overton, "Aggressive Casework," in Sylvan S. Fuhrman (ed.), *Reaching the Unreached* (New York: New York City Youth Board, 1952).

Referral units in areas of high delinquency rates serve as detection centers for location of child problems in the incipient stages. Their functions are to study and diagnose behavior and personality problems, to locate community resources to treat individual problems, and to refer people to these services. Since existing youth guidance and family services may be overburdened with work, the detection of more cases through such referral units can increase the discrepancy between need and treatment resources. To support additional resources, a youth board could enter into contracts with treatment agencies specializing in family, youth, and vocational counseling, and in child guidance and group work. The board pays for the services of the agencies to which the children and families are sent by referral units. In keeping with their emphasis on prevention of delinquency and emotional disturbances, the units deal primarily with children of elementary school age. However, persons from 5 to 21 years of age are eligible when personality or behavior difficulties are involved.[24]

For similar purposes the *practitioner committee* has been employed to coordinate the law enforcement, health, welfare, and educational agencies serving an area with a high rate of delinquency. Each agency delegates a staff member to meet regularly with members designated by other agencies to serve on a practitioner committee. The committee's functions are to discuss coordinated planning, work with particular cases, suggest pertinent ways of referral from one agency to another, and explore new techniques that might be of help to families included in agency caseloads. The intimacy of working together increases mutual confidence and knowledge of one another's resources among specialists. New breadth and depth of services are gained. Committee discussions bring agencies that ordinarily would not have been involved into cases. By agreement, one person assumes responsibility for a case so that a network of relationships will not confuse the multiproblem family or individual. Pooling of information derived from various specialized contacts of the several agencies promotes conception of the client as a whole personality, whereas segmented contacts have limited insights into his personality. Administration is spurred through face-to-face contacts. Interagency discussions demonstrate the weaknesses of a segmented attack and stimulate revision of agency practices.[25]

Coordinating councils are neighborhood organizations intended to prevent law violations by coordinating existing services. The usual council is made up of representatives of government, parent-teacher organiza-

[24] Mary S. Diamond, "Reorienting Social Work Concepts in Referral Units," in Fuhrman, *Reaching the Unreached,* pp. 36–37.

[25] Gisela Konopka, "Coordination of Services as a Means of Delinquency Prevention," *Annals of the American Academy of Political and Social Science,* 322 (March 1959): 30–37.

tions, churches, social agencies, character-building organizations, and service clubs. Because coordinating councils have grown spontaneously without promotion from a national headquarters, there is a wide variation in names of organizations, sponsorship, and statement of objectives. They are sponsored by state youth commissions, universities, counties, and cities. Their activities include the improving of health conditions and services, recreation, education, housing, and traffic control.[26]

A useful device for intelligent planning and reliable research is the *central register,* a systematic gathering of facts on the number and characteristics of persons in the community whose behavior has, or could have, made them subject to the courts. Information also is obtained concerning their problems, who is providing services, and what type of services are being provided.

STRATEGIES FOR COMMUNITY PROGRAMS

As a strategy for initiating change in problem neighborhoods, community development has been defined as the improvement of the community through the cooperative efforts of the people immediately concerned. The idea is that the residents assume initiative for making changes in the area with maximum citizen participation and minimum professional leadership. Marshall Clinard[27] outlines the key assumptions:

1. Local people *will* participate in efforts to change neighborhood conditions,
2. Because they *do not* accept an adverse social and physical environment as natural and inevitable, and
3. Because self-imposed changes in the immediate environment will have real significance to the residents and consequently will have more permanent effect.

Furthermore, the work rests on assumptions that groups, rather than the individual, are the proper target for initiating change:

4. Because slum life is largely a product of group life and thus groups are the proper vehicle for change, and
5. Because change of local group values will radiate to change individuals.

[26] Kenneth S. Beam, "Organization of the Community for Delinquency Prevention," in Frank J. Cohen (ed.), *Youth and Crime* (New York: International Universities Press, Inc., 1957).

[27] Marshall B. Clinard, "The Organization of the Urban Development Services in the Prevention of Crime and Delinquency with Particular Reference to Less Developed Countries," *International Review of Criminal Policy* (United Nations), 19 (April 1962): 6.

Spiritual regeneration

The weak sense of community in urban problem areas reflects the inadequacies of communication among residents. Late in the 1930s Clifford Shaw and Jesse Jacobs called for a spiritual regeneration of residents through the utilization of indigenous leadership. They believed the reintegration of the problem community would become the means of eliminating the adverse environment when the people understood, wanted, and worked for a program of community betterment.[28]

Spiritual regeneration cannot be undertaken, however, until study of the nature and functioning of the community reveals the patterning of life. Every community has a variety of social institutions and agencies: churches, schools, recreation centers, places of employment, societies, and other social groupings. If the neighborhood has a relatively structured and stable community life, the objective of such a study is to lend coordination and a new sense of purpose to established institutions. If the community is less well structured and more unstable, the strategy is to stimulate the participation of residents in correcting physical, economic, and social conditions.

Community organizers study the history and culture of the local society, the indigenous power structure (including the illegitimate structure) whereby decisions are made and executed, and the sources of conflict among community groups.[29] The organizational strategies then are adapted to the conditions of the particular neighborhood.

A fundamental assumption is that a core of organized communal life exists in problem neighborhoods. In religious, economic, and political activities, some persons show social mobility aspirations even when they lack middle-class respectability. By encouraging these natural leaders toward organization and administration of a local program, this core can foster a campaign for spiritual regeneration.[30]

Fostering participation

In community development projects, indigenous leaders are encouraged to involve themselves in the planning and management of activities intended to foster community effectiveness. Financial support may come from outside the local community, but emphasis on local planning and management promotes a sense of self-reliance, preserves self-respect, enhances the prestige of local leaders among their neighbors, and stimu-

[28] Clifford R. Shaw and Jesse A. Jacobs, "The Chicago Area Project: An Experimental Community Program for the Prevention of Delinquency in Chicago," *Proceedings of American Prison Association, 1939*, pp. 43–44.

[29] Solomon Kobrin, "The Chicago Area Project—A 25-Year Assessment," *Annals of the American Academy of Social Science*, 322 (March 1959): 24.

[30] Ibid., p. 23.

lates the development of common interests and sentiments. Local people become both the servers and the served, and every effort is made to credit them for accomplishments. The salaried staff is drawn as much as possible from the local neighborhood. Having grown up in the neighborhood, these indigenous workers will have a more intimate understanding of the people with whom they work. They are less likely to arouse suspicion, and their appointment attests to confidence in the abilities of local people. They are encouraged to conceive of themselves as representatives of the neighborhood, not a centralized bureaucracy. The taint of humiliation associated with charity from sources outside the neighborhood is removed through local control of, and active participation in, a program of constructive changes.[31]

Individuals can be motivated to participate in such projects by a variety of factors. In many cases there is a universal interest and concern about children. Some people are motivated by affection for children; a few emphasize the need to develop ways of disciplining and supervising children who "run loose in the streets." There may be a desire to improve the physical appearance and normative climate of the neighborhood. Sensitivity regarding the adverse reputation of the neighborhood can cause some individuals to work to eliminate any justification for disparagement. Participation also can be motivated by desire for prestige among peers, personal accomplishment, power over others, or fellowship.[32]

Chicago Area Projects

Encouragement of participation per se has been a major element of the Chicago Area Projects. Started in the early 1930s by the late Clifford R. Shaw, the projects employ the local neighborhood as an active agent in reducing its own delinquency and youth crime. Programs are developed according to the particular interests of their leaders and the needs of the local situation. Each year the local committees raise money in the neighborhood to help finance their enterprises.

Chicago Area Projects programs are of several types. Recreation and sports are offered through volunteer residents. In abandoned stores, churches, or homes, volunteers and salaried workers may offer clubs, game room and library facilities, basketball, craft classes, music and dramatics, Girl and Boy Scouts, weekly "community fun nights" for adults, health lectures, holiday parties, monthly boxing and wrestling shows, talent shows, stage plays, weekly movies, or a mimeographed neighborhood newspaper. Campaigns for community improvement are

---

[31] Anthony Sorrentino, "The Chicago Area Project after 25 Years," *Federal Probation,* 23 (June 1959): 40.

[32] *Bright Shadows in Bronzetown* (Chicago: Southside Community Committee, Inc., 1949), pp. 63–66.

built around such issues as school improvement, traffic safety, sanitation, and law enforcement.

By creating primary group contacts between adults and adolescents, the projects have tempered the relationships between youth and the formal organizations created to control and correct deviant behavior. Courts, schools, police, probation and parole agencies, and correctional institutions rely on procedures which treat persons as members of generalized categories. The impersonality of these procedures reduces their efficiency in controlling or correcting deviance when a child's family and peers do not support the norms expressed by these agencies. The projects have tried to fill this gap between the individual adolescent and impersonal organizations. As committee members or paid staff, local residents are identified with the neighborhood by delinquents. Through regular contacts with the police, courts, and citywide welfare agencies, project personnel are able to present themselves as an alternative to the sentencing of delinquents to a correctional institution.

The Chicago Area Projects have encountered difficulties.[33] Local political leaders boycotted early organizational efforts in fear that their power was being challenged. Aggressive staff members and ambitious residents have undermined the democratic basis of organization. Because the principles of the projects emphasize indigenous leadership, local control, and lay participation, they have encountered the suspicions of traditional welfare organizations, which has handicapped solicitation of funds outside the neighborhood.

The volume of delinquency has declined in several communities where area projects have been in operation for a number of years, but reliable evaluation of the programs' influence, is difficult.[34] The community is a complex of many influences. Administrative procedures are changed by the police, courts, welfare agencies, and similar formal organizations operating in the slums. While the area projects probably have reduced delinquency, this conclusion has not been proved.

Detached-worker programs

An example of a program operating in a neighborhood setting rather than in agency confines is the detached worker. In this approach, social group workers or recreation leaders search out adolescent groups which include predelinquents or delinquents and do not use organized leisure-time programs. Such workers are usually associated with established social agencies, but they are detached from regular programs to operate

[33] See *Bright Shadows in Bronzetown*, pp. 71–73, and Sorrentino, "Chicago Area Project after 25 Years," pp. 44–45.

[34] Sorrentino, "Chicago Area Project after 25 Years," p. 45.

outside the agency walls as friendly adults providing assistance and guidance.[35]

The approach first presents a community *service,* not a membership program such as that of the recreation center which offers an adult-supervised and preplanned program to those juveniles and adolescents who become "members" by paying a fee. Instead of starting with a program, the detached worker brings the service to the place of greatest need because of a particular problem, often related to a street-corner group. The content of the service then is determined on the basis of that problem. Second, the approach either works or fails on the basis of the skills and knowledge of the worker and the network of relationships he develops with a particular street-corner group. Third, the service is carried outside the four walls of an agency building into the community. In building-centered programs the clientele are selected, directly or indirectly, thus enabling the worker to control such variables as the size and criteria of group membership. On the street, the detached worker can control few of the circumstances under which he operates. Fourth, the justification for this service is that it "reaches the unreached." The major objective is to bring services to persons and groups who have demonstrated a lack of interest in orthodox programs. The worker's key task is to open communication with people who have not sought his services. Fifth, the detached worker must deal with a *group* which existed before his appearance and which continues to function. He must offer his services within a framework of values which reflect the group's orientation to the world, frequently in conflict with that of the larger community. Instead of launching a frontal attack, the worker tries to create experiences which will modify these values indirectly.[36]

The detached worker's problem has three aspects, according to Irving Spergel. First, the values and activities of the street-corner group are related to the social and cultural processes of the community. Lack of access to legitimate opportunity and subcultural values in high-delinquency areas have been cited as explanations for gang delinquency.[37] Second, the street-corner gangs with which the worker deals are activating values found in the neighborhood or developed in the course of the gang's activities. Therefore, the worker should see his clients as subject to peer group influences[38] and the peer group as subject to the influences of its environment. In short, the worker operates within a *cultural* frame-

---

[35] Mary B. Novick, *Community Programs and Projects for Prevention of Juvenile Delinquency* (Washington, D.C.: U.S. Children's Bureau, 1960), p. 7.

[36] David M. Austin, "Goals for Gang Workers," *Social Work,* 2 (October 1947): 44–50.

[37] See Cloward-Ohlin and subcultural theories in Chapter 10, pp. 246–53.

[38] Reference group theory, Chapter 10, pp. 256–58, is relevant.

work rather than with a collection of diverse individuals.[39] He deals with individuals within a group context as a symbol of a moratorium on the rejection of group members by the larger society. His objective is to fit the gang member into the legitimate opportunity structure. Third, the detached worker recognizes the gang member as an individual who is a member of groups other than the street-corner gang. As a person with a unique personal and family history, the member becomes subject to the worker's intervention in family, work, and school settings as well as in the street-corner group. The worker's intervention is in building a bridge between appropriate community services and the problems of the client.[40]

The setting for detached work.   To the gang boy the world is a dangerous place, demanding hardness and toughness to survive. The "rep" of his gang for fighting is his protection and a prop for his own sense of importance. To show weakness in the face of insult is to be a "no-good punk." Adults are categorized as authorities, hoodlums, or suckers. Some parents and teachers and all policemen are seen as *authorities* who push boys around, moralize, threaten, condemn, and impose punishments. *Hoodlums* are "smart guys" who exploit, cheat, and outwit the other fellow. *Suckers* are weaklings who work for a living and always "keep their noses clean." They "fall" for any "line." Only suckers work, while hoodlums ride around in big cars.[41]

There are three stages in the detached worker's relationships with street-gang boys. First, the boys' distrust of adults must be overcome and their acceptance gained. Second, the worker concentrates on stimulating change in their attitudes and behavior. Third, he seeks to close his relationships with the group in a manner which does not negate the progress made.[42] Two interrelated approaches are used to develop relationships with the gangs. The worker might *"hang around"* the gathering place of the gang, frankly revealing his official affiliation. In the *social-introduction approach* the worker is brought to the gang by a friendly member of another gang or by a staff member known by the gang.

The detached worker first familiarizes himself with the socioeconomic characteristics, dominant attitudes, and customs of the slum area. He moves slowly to afford time for the boys to evaluate him. Dissimilarities between his dress, speech, and actions and those of the gang are deemphasized. Every effort is made to understand the feelings and thoughts of the boys. In initial contacts, antisocial conduct is regarded neutrally. The worker is alert to the interpretations of his behavior by the boys.

[39] Austin, "Goals for Gang Workers," p. 50.

[40] Irving Spergel, "Multidimensional Model for Social Work Practice; the Youth Worker Example," *Social Service Review,* 36 (March 1962): 62–71.

[41] Paul L. Crawford, Daniel I. Malamud, and James R. Dumpson, *Working with Teen-Age Gangs* (New York: Welfare Council of New York, 1950), pp. 14–20.

[42] Ibid., p. 127.

Specific services are provided when possible—assistance in finding a job or arranging for use of a gymnasium. The worker tries to develop closest relations with the gang leader and his clique to utilize their influence on the other members and to avoid threatening the leader's status. The gang tests the worker to determine whether he is some kind of policeman, sucker, or hoodlum. Gradually, he is seen as someone different, as an *adult helper* who knows the ins and outs but is easy to talk to and friendly without being a sucker. Some members see him as an *idealized father*— patient, understanding, trustworthy, and interested in them.[43]

In evaluating detached workers associated with the Hyde Park Youth Project in Chicago, John Gandy found little change in the frequency of antisocial activities among boys who had participated in such programs. There was some reduction of antisocial behavior by 46 percent of the youths, but only nine youths were moved from "frequent participation" in antisocial activities to no participation. He concludes that the project has its greatest success with youths who had little or no history of anti-social behavior.[44] Malcolm Klein regards the success of detached workers as pivoting on whether the approach weans the members away from gang participation. In his investigation of four Los Angeles juvenile gang clusters, he reports that, in the absence of this weaning process, the detached workers' efforts had three unanticipated results: the number of recorded offenses increased, more youngsters were recruited into the gangs, and the cohesiveness of delinquent gangs was strengthened.[45]

Another recent study compared three gangs: the Spartans, who received full service by detached workers; the Gavilanes, who received partial service; and the Valiants, who received no service. Records of gang members were followed for six years to determine exposure to probation, institutional, or parole programs before and after the treatment period. The financial costs per gang member were computed for the detached-worker service and the correctional programs received by all groups before and after treatment. Before treatment, the correctional costs per gang member were: Spartans, $3,944; Gavilanes, $3,695; and Valiants, $2,934. After treatment, the average costs were: Spartans, $2,345; Gavilanes, $2,601; and Valiants, $4,576. In addition to these overall savings, the younger siblings of gang members had similar differences among gangs in reducing correctional costs in their early correctional careers.[46]

[43] Ibid., pp. 27–34.

[44] John M. Gandy, "Preventive Work with Street-Corner Groups," *Annals of the American Academy of Political and Social Science,* 322 (March 1959): 114–16.

[45] Malcolm W. Klein, "Gang Cohesiveness, Delinquency, and a Street-Work Program," *Journal of Research in Crime and Delinquency,* 6 (July 1969): 135–66.

[46] Stuart Adams, "A Cost Approach to the Assessment of Gang Rehabilitation Techniques," *Journal of Research in Crime and Delinquency,* 4 (January 1967): 166–82.

A large share of delinquency in the lower-class community is related to peer-group membership. The conflict gang, however, is only one of the types of street-corner groups. The *nonproblem gang* hangs around street corners, but its activities are essentially innocent. The *problem gang* includes members with police records, but its chief threat to the community is the potentiality of its disturbed and maladjusted behavior patterns. These patterns emerge full-blown in the *conflict gang,* which has a reputation for violence.[47] The detached worker probably has the greatest chance for success in dealing with the first two types. Gandy sees the worker as having the most appeal in the role of a decisive, strong adult male for boys whose fathers are either absent or emotionally or financially dependent on the mother.[48]

SUMMARY

Prevention implies that delinquency and crime are undesirable, but their existence is not inevitable. It involves one of two targets: elimination of antisocial behavior at its source, or the forestalling of further offenses. The first target is sought by agencies interested in promoting healthy personality development of all children or in taking action against broad social problems. Agencies that serve persons with behavioral or emotional problems likely to lead to delinquency have the same target. Law enforcement, judicial, and correctional agencies focus on the second target.

Theories related to prevention tend to be oriented toward the individual and family or toward the environment to which the individual is exposed. Among preventive strategies related to the latter theories are restructuring of relationships and developing strategies for community programs.

FOR ADDITIONAL READING

Berleman, William C., and Steinburn, Thomas W. "The Value and Validity of Delinquency Prevention Experiments." *Crime and Delinquency,* 15 (October 1969): 471–78.

Bernstein, Saul. *Youth on the Streets: Work with Alienated Youth Groups.* New York: Association Press, 1964.

Brown, Gordon E. (ed.). *The Multi-Problem Dilemma: A Social Research Demonstration with Multi-Problem Families.* Metuchen, N.J.: Scarecrow Press, 1968.

[47] *Dealing with the Conflict Gang in New York City,* Interim Report No. 14, Juvenile Evaluation Project of the City of New York (New York: City College, May 1960), p. 2.

[48] Gandy, "Preventive Work with Street-Corner Groups," p. 111.

Grob, H. E., and Van Doren, E. E. "Aggressive Group Work with Teenage Delinquents." *Children,* 16 (May–June 1969) : 103–8.

Jeffery, Clarence Ray. *Crime Prevention through Environmental Design.* Beverly Hills, Calif.: Sage Publications, 1971.

Klein, Malcolm W., and Meyerhoff, Barbara G. (eds.). *Juvenile Gangs in Context: Theory, Research and Action.* Englewood Cliffs, N.J.: Prentice-Hall, 1967.

Kobetz, Richard W. *The Police Role and Juvenile Delinquency.* Gaithersburg, Md.: International Association of Chiefs of Police, 1971.

Morgan, John S., et al. *Changing Services for Changing Clients.* New York: Columbia University Press, 1969.

Platt, Anthony M. "Saving and Controlling Delinquent Youth: A Critique." *Issues in Criminology,* 5 (Winter 1970) : pp. 1–24.

Reid, William. "Interagency Coordination in Delinquency Prevention and Control." *Social Service Review,* 33 (December 1964) : 418–29.

Robin, Gerald D. "Anti-Poverty Programs and Delinquency." *Journal of Criminal Law, Criminology and Police Science,* 60 (September 1969): 323–31.

Robison, Sophia M. "Why Juvenile Delinquency Preventive Programs Are Ineffective." *Federal Probation,* 24 (December 1961) : 34–42.

Stream, Herbert S. "Role Theory, Role Models, and Casework: Review of Literature and Practice Applications." *Social Work,* 12 (April 1967): 77–88.

Wheeler, Stanton, and Cottrell, Leonard S., Jr. (eds.). *Juvenile Delinquency: Its Prevention and Control.* New York: Russell Sage Foundation, 1966.

23

Probation and parole

As the primary alternatives to imprisonment of convicted offenders, probation and parole have a great potential in meeting the problem of crime. Not only do they represent the major share of the community-based correctional programs that have been implemented in the past, but more systematic and more frequent employment of these techniques is to be expected in the future. Probation and parole are basic processes in moving the field of corrections toward greater efficiency in adding former criminals to the ranks of law-abiding, functioning citizens. This chapter will describe the nature and purposes of these extramural correctional programs—those external to correctional institutions—and will indicate some of the issues to be confronted in the course of realizing their potential.

ORIGINS OF PROBATION AND PAROLE

Methods of granting leniency to offenders have been known in all systems of criminal justice. From the time of Constantine until the beginning of the 12th century, Christian churches provided *sanctuary* from secular law. During the time of its widespread temporal power, the Roman Catholic Church demanded the right of immunity from secular law for clericals. The advantage was that the church employed less sanguinary penalties against offenders convicted by ecclesiastical courts. The *right of clergy* came to mean immunity for all who could read.[1] In another form of leniency, pardon has been used for the *"criminal-policeman."* The promise of a pardon was supposed to induce robbers, thieves, embezzlers, and murderers to betray their accomplices and to spy upon their companions. Under 14 major statutes enacted in the late 17th and 18th centuries in England, an offender could obtain a pardon by securing the conviction of one or more accomplices in the crime.[2]

[1] George Ives, *A History of Penal Methods* (London: Stanley Paul & Co., Ltd., 1914), pp. 34–35.
[2] Leon Radzinowicz, *A History of English Criminal Law and Its Administration from 1750* (London: Stevens and Sons, 1956), Vol. II, p. 40.

Probation and parole had different origins. Parole emerged when the decline of capital punishment and transportation brought a need for after-care of prisoners released into the community, and the public demanded protection against prisoners released without improved character. Probation arose from dissatisfaction with court procedures and a demand for a substitute for imprisonment.[3]

Probation and parole compared

Probation is a function of the court. The judge conditionally releases the convicted offender into the community under the supervision of an agent of the court. When a presentence investigation is the basis for sentencing, the probation officer will be familiar with the case when he assumes supervision. Parole involves release from a correctional institution and is controlled by an agency other than the court. Because parole and correctional institutions usually are separate administrative entities, the maintenance of continuity in treatment requires intensive effort.

Presumably, prison terms are imposed on the basis of a relatively unfavorable prognosis. Conversely, probation is granted when the offender is given a favorable prognosis. If it can be assumed that the courts employ probation in cases meriting it, the probation caseload would have a greater proportion of favorable prospects for rehabilitation when compared with the parolees selected from the prisoners. Confinement may have given the prisoner a degree of docility, causing many to accept supervision in the community more readily than probationers, but confinement experiences may impede the rehabilitative process. Furthermore, isolation from his family and community may aggravate the prisoner's adjustment problems, whereas the probationer is more likely to be able to resume relationships only briefly interrupted.

Probation and parole are advocated as substitutes for imprisonment. Probation is supposed to save the offender from the stigmatization and pains of confinement, thereby reducing the chances he will become hostile toward the norms it is hoped he will accept. Parole shortens his exposure to the possibly injurious effects of imprisonment; it is a device for timing the prisoner's release to coincide with the point in his prison career when he is most likely to become an effective member of the free community. By providing guidance, parole offers a partial answer to the readjustment problems of the released prisoner. Both probation and parole, but especially probation, enable the offender to support his dependents and maintain his family and community ties, which frees the taxpayers of some of the burden of providing for the prisoner's dependents. The probationer may be required to make restitution to the victim of his

[3] Charles H. Z. Meyer, "Differentiation in the Treatment of Probationers and Parolees," *National Probation Association Yearbook, 1945,* pp. 322–23.

crime, thus reducing the impact of his crime. The canceling out of the effects of his crime may have therapeutic value for the offender. The vast majority of prisoners is released eventually, and parole offers social protection and guidance through supervision not possible under outright discharge. Both probation and parole can utilize treatment resources in the community and incidentally correct some of the underlying difficulties in the offender's environment which could cause other members of his family also to turn to crime. Finally, probation and parole are less expensive than correctional institutions.

Beginnings of probation

Probation grew out of a number of early methods of alleviating severe punishment.[4] One of these was right of clergy. Early American courts were known to alleviate strict punishment by permitting the convicted minor offender to go free on condition of good behavior. Another method was to release offenders after guilty verdicts through technicalities. Victims of crimes might neglect to appear to give evidence at the trial or withhold evidence, and juries might reach compassionate verdicts in contradiction to the facts of the case.

The source of the practice of probation can be traced to Massachusetts in 1830, when Jerusha Chase pleaded guilty to stealing from a house. Upon application of her friends, the court permitted her to go at large on her recognizance for her appearance when called by the court. In 1831, she was acquitted before the same court of another charge of larceny. Thereafter she was sentenced on the basis of the 1830 crime. On appeal, the court's decision was upheld.[5]

In 1841, a spectator in the Boston police court asked the judge to permit him to be sponsor for an offender about to be imprisoned. In this fashion John Augustus, a bootmaker with a shop near the court, became the first probation officer. Augustus became involved because of his interest in the Washingtonian Total Abstinence Society, a reform group that tried to save the drunkard by understanding and moral suasion. In spite of opposition and misunderstanding from court officers and turn keys who lost fees because of his work, Augustus obtained contributions to make bail for more offenders than his slender means could provide. He used care in selecting cases on the basis of suitability in personality for probation.[6]

In 1878, the Massachusetts Legislature provided that the mayor of

---

[4] Frank W. Grinnel, "The Common Law History of Probation," *Journal of Criminal Law and Criminology*, 32 (May–June 1941): 17–21.

[5] Ibid., pp. 21–23.

[6] Donald W. Moreland, "John Augustus and His Successors," *National Probation Association Yearbook, 1941*, pp. 3–9.

Boston should annually appoint a probation officer as part of the police force. Probation spread from Boston throughout the United States, to Australia and New Zealand, and finally to Europe through the English Probation of Offenders' Act in 1907.[7]

Beginnings of parole

Parole developed from a number of independent measures: penal transportation to America and Australia, the English and Irish experiences with the ticket-of-leave system, and the work of 19th-century American reformatories. These historical precedents are described in detail in Chapter 16.

The British practice in the 18th century was to consign prisoners as laborers to contractors or shipmasters, who transported them to the colonies. After 1717 the British government gave the contractor or shipmaster "property in the service" of the prisoner until expiration of his term. The contractor or shipmaster sold the felon's services to the highest bidder, or on arrival in the colonies, and the criminal became an indentured servant under a contract. This procedure resembled later parole in that the prisoner, released conditionally, agreed to accept certain conditions in the release form.[8]

When transportation to Australia was undertaken, the government retained control of the prisoners. After 1790 the governors of Australia substituted for absolute pardons a conditional form known as tickets of leave, which resembled testimonials from the master to the servant who had lawfully terminated his employment, permitting him to seek work elsewhere. There was no provision for supervision during the period of conditional release. The English Penal Servitude Act of 1853 substituted imprisonment for transportation and specified the length of time prisoners were required to serve in prison before becoming eligible for a ticket of leave. It was assumed that correctional training in prisons had prepared the ticket-of-leave men for law-abiding behavior. The ticket specified that it could be forfeited for evil associations, idleness, and a dissolute life as well as for subsequent criminal behavior. However, supervision was not provided. Under the Irish system, Sir Walter Crofton provided improved prisoner rehabilitative programs, a procedure for preparing the prisoner for release through his stages of penal servitude, and a system of police supervision of released prisoners. In Dublin a civilian employee assisted the former prisoners to find employment, required them to report to him periodically, and visited their homes biweekly. After 1864 Pris-

[7] C. Bernaldo de Quiros, *Modern Theories of Criminality,* trans. Alfonso de Salvio (Boston: Little, Brown & Co., 1911), p. 155.

[8] Frederick A. Moran, "The Origins of Parole," *National Probation Association Yearbook, 1945,* pp. 71–75.

oner Aid Societies employed agents for supervision in England and Ireland, with the government contributing half of the costs.[9]

Under Zebulon Brockway, New York's Elmira Reformatory combined several known operating principles when it opened in 1876: the indeterminate sentence, relating privileges granted the prisoner to his conduct, compulsory education, and release of selected prisoners on parole.[10] A reaction against the classical school's assumption that punishments should be standardized and equated on the basis of the crime, these principles stem from the positive school's thesis that crimes are acts of men who differ in physical, psychological, and social backgrounds. Parole was seen as the culmination of a course of institutional training whereby the inmate's capacity for reform would be developed. Brockway also saw parole as a test period to determine whether the offender had absorbed the training.[11] Consequently, parole was perceived as part of the program of the correctional institution.

In subsequent development in the United States, parole administration has been separated from correctional institutions, although both are under a common higher executive in some states. Separation reduces the possibility that parole policies might reward the prison-wise inmate who conforms to institutional rules and penalize the offender who rebels against confinement because of personal qualities that would produce socially approved behavior in the free community. However, separation has complicated the integration of institutional and parole experiences into a consistent whole.

MODELS OF PROGRAMS

Any community-based criminological program relies heavily on public tolerance of offenders, in spite of the reservations that members of the community may hold about lawbreakers as the enemies of "decent" people. Tolerance is essential to gaining public acquiescence to the practices of foregoing imprisonment for probationers and shortening confinement for parolees. If probationers and parolees are to be included in the legitimate opportunity and human service systems of the community, however, their acceptance must go beyond public acquiescence. Extramural correctional programs vary in the balance they seek between two goals: protection of the community against further crimes by the convicted offenders released under community supervision, and rehabilitation of the offenders through their inclusion in the opportunity and human service systems.

[9] Ibid., pp. 77–92.
[10] Ibid., p. 93.
[11] Zebulon R. Brockway, *Fifty Years of Prison Service* (New York: Charities Publication Committee, 1912), p. 324.

Emphasis on community protection

Under the *policing conception* of extramural programs, the correctional worker maintains constant surveillance for the sake of community protection under the pessimistic expectation that the probationer or parolee is likely to violate the rules of his conditional release and there is a probability of additional crimes. Adherents of the punitive ideology believe that oversentimentality and undue leniency are exhibited when "dangerous criminals" are turned loose to prey on the community after policemen have labored to apprehend them.

A *social control conception* is also on the community-protection end of the protection-rehabilitation continuum, but compared with the policing model it gives greater recognition to the rehabilitation goal. T. George Street sees surveillance as an essential aspect of supervision and argues that the pressures placed on the convicted offender promote his constructive adjustment to community standards of regular employment, responsibility for dependents, avoidance of intoxicants, and so on. If supervision is punitive, Street says, it is at least punishment which should be beneficial to the offender.[12]

Concern for rehabilitation

At the "rehabilitation of the offender" end of the continuum of conceptions of extramural programs, protection of the community is sought incidentally, and the emphasis is on developing self-discipline and strengthening the capacity of the client to achieve personal goals through law-abiding behavior. The focus of attention is on the client because changes in his attitudes, behavior, and social relationships are seen as the product of effective supervision. When the case is terminated, it is hoped the client will have been changed from a person requiring surveillance and guidance to one who has the motivation and capacity to be a law-abiding citizen. Substitution of the term "client" for "criminal" implies that he is a total personality beyond the narrow, negativistic deviant status, that his willing participation in the events of supervision is essential to this change, and that he requires human services.

The *oversentimental conception* of extramural programs carries concern for the client to the extreme of rejecting the community-protection objective. Assignment of the convicted offender to a deviant status, we have noted,[13] tends to deny him access to the community services and opportunities provided the fully accepted citizen. Under any conception of rehabilitation, the community-based correctional worker is expected

[12] T. George Street, "Parole as a Social Control," *Canadian Journal of Corrections,* 7 (January 1965): 5–7.
[13] See Chapter 21, pp. 523–25.

to deal with such side effects of overpenalization on his client. In the oversentimental conception, the worker makes such strenuous efforts to counter categoric stigmatization and becomes so identified with the client on humanitarian grounds that he may fail to fulfill his function as an agent of a correctional organization. Exclusive attention to the self-interests of the client may go to the extreme of representing him *against* the correctional agency. On the other hand, exclusive attention to community protection from "dangerous criminals" carries the possibility that the worker will see himself as an agent of tough law enforcement dealing with "captured enemies" temporarily under his control.

From another perspective, the rehabilitative conceptions of extramural treatment may be subdivided in accordance with our earlier differentiation between individual-oriented and environment-oriented theories of treatment.[14] The *individual-oriented conception* of extramural programs relies on one-to-one relationships between client and supervisor in a clinical model that concentrates on the client as an individual requiring therapy. Civil service requirements for probation officers frequently call for a master of social work degree under the assumption that in-depth counseling or therapy is involved.[15] Probation is seen essentially as social casework based on psychiatric interpretations of lawbreaking as a symptom of personality maladjustments traced back to childhood experiences. In this conception, the correctional worker must come to grips with difficult issues: How can casework produce new insights and motives in the client? How can the clients' attitudes be changed and emotions be redirected to make him more effective in interpersonal relationships? How can the client's willing participation in a therapeutic process be gained when he is involuntarily placed under the authority of the correctional worker? How can deep-seated personality problems be handled in a supervision period which is relatively brief compared with the long history of personality development?

The *environment-oriented conception* places extramural programs within the network of human service agencies in the community. The community-based correctional worker becomes an intermediary between his client and the relevant services provided by the range of agencies operating in the given community. As a *community* worker, his expertise is derived from his knowledge of the operations of human service agencies and his acquaintance with the needs of his client. The worker is an advocate for his client, seeking to reduce the impact of the deviant status in shutting the client out from opportunities and services which are ger-

[14] Chapter 8, pp. 193–94.

[15] W. A. Goldberg, "Adult Probation in the United States, 1968," *Canadian Journal of Corrections*, 11 (April 1969): 101–2; also see Lewis Diana, "What Is Probation?" in Robert M. Carter and Leslie T. Wilkins (ed.), *Probation and Parole: Selected Readings* (New York: John Wiley & Sons, Inc., 1970), pp. 44–50.

mane to his rehabilitation. He is a case manager in that he implements a planned strategy utilizing such concrete measures as medical appointments, school transfers, and guided searches for employment. The development of a plan for a particular client can overcome the shortcomings of case "management" that constitutes expedient arrangements made in the fairly negative hope that *somehow,* keeping the client busy will forestall future crimes.[16]

SELECTION OF CASES

Regardless of what probation and parole are supposed to be under the conceptions delineated above, they are in reality what selection and supervision make them in community practice. "Selection" refers to the decision making by which some convicted offenders are placed on the extramural programs and others are rejected. By affecting the number and kinds of persons admitted to caseloads, selection largely determines the level of difficulty and kinds of problems workers will encounter. Supervision, to be discussed in the following section, entails the contacts of supervisors with the convicted offenders placed in their charge. The responsibilities are described variously as "surveillance," "guidance," "counseling," "case management," and "therapy," in keeping with the agency's conception of extramural programs. Within the limits shaped by this conception and the qualities of probationers or parolees produced by selection, the outcome of cases is determined in large measure by the relevant competence and task performance of correctional workers.

Investigation procedures

In selection for probation, the *presentence investigation* by the probation officer provides the court with facts necessary for an intelligent decision. These concern the background, current situation, and personality of the offender. Ideally, the report includes a history of family, personal, social, and economic factors in the offender's life; a statement of the circumstances of the offense; a description of his previous criminal record; copies of personal references, employer reports, clinical reports, and so on; an evaluation of the offender's personality; and a plan of treatment. Usually included also is a recommendation to the judge who has the authority to determine whether or not probation is granted and, if so, under what conditions beyond those specified by statute.

In selection for parole, the prisoner becomes eligible after serving a specified proportion of his sentence. Usually, a member of the parole board interviews the candidates to screen out those considered presently

---

[16] Diana, "What Is Probation?" pp. 41–42.

unworthy. Prisoners accepted for further consideration are expected to submit a plan for employment and place of residence if granted parole. Prisoners may refuse parole, usually because a relatively short period of further confinement is preferable to a longer period of supervision in the community. Parole officers investigate the employment-residence plan and the community conditions for parole. On the basis of the preparole investigation and letters of recommendation, the parole board makes its decision. Sometimes the consideration of a given prisoner will be announced publicly in his home community to permit residents to express their views to the parole board.

Factors affecting selection

The decision makers apply their judgments to a population of candidates which, through the operation of two sets of factors, differs from the total population of the community. The first set consists of the demographic, cultural, and socioeconomic characteristics of the community's population. As Chapter 5 demonstrated the statuses of age, sex, socioeconomic condition, and race influence the quality and volume of crime. The relationship between law violations and the social institutions of family, education, and religion were analyzed in Chapter 6, and Chapter 7 traced the linkages between patterns of crime and the sociocultural organization of the community. Communities differ in social class structure, kinds of employment, cultural heterogeneity, population mobility, and distribution of status variables. In these respects they will also differ in their reliance on the criminal law for social control, the volume of cases received by the system of criminal justice, and the qualities of the individuals received for processing by the system.

The second set of factors affecting selection involves the administrative accommodations practiced by police and court personnel. The informal process of decision making by police and court functionaries operates selectively to bring only some of the apprehended law violators to the stage of conviction in court. Because the nature of these accommodations is likely to change from time to time and to vary among jurisdictions, probation agencies are presented with differing populations of convicted offenders from which probation cases are selected.[17]

Parole agencies are exposed to a third set of selective factors if the sentencing court had considered probation before sentencing the offender to prison. To become a prisoner under these circumstances, the offender was either found an unlikely prospect for release into the community or he was unable to meet the test of probation supervision.

---

[17] The administrative accommodations are related to changes in community attitudes determining community tolerance of deviance (see Chapter 4, pp. 74–79). The police dilemma in arrest decisions is discussed in Chapter 13, pp. 324–25, and the accommodations in court procedures in Chapter 14, pp. 349–53.

Issues in decision making

Max Grünhut has proposed two vital questions in selection: Who *can* be put on extramural programs, and who *ought* to be put on them?[18] The first question refers to the objective of protecting the community against further lawbreaking and to the tolerance of the community for release of the particular kind of offender. The decision maker has to assess the *probability* of further crimes by the given candidate for conditional release, as well as the *probability* of an intensely adverse public reaction against the release of an offender judged to be a particularly notorious or dangerous criminal. The second question refers to the needs and prospects of the individual whom the extramural program hopefully can add to the ranks of law-abiding citizens, regardless of the risk of his failure under supervision in the community.

Within the population being considered, there are, first, offenders who identify themselves with law-abiding citizens and do not require supervision. In the second group are offenders who require a modest degree of guidance and supervision but are favorable prospects. A third group consists of questionable candidates requiring intensive help and highly competent efforts on the part of correctional officers. Offenders in a fourth group will fail almost inevitably because of gross personality deficits or a firm identification with criminal values.

How much risk of failure should be tolerated? If risk is to be all but eliminated, only the minority in the first group would be granted probation or parole, and the problems of supervision would be minor. If extramural treatment is taken seriously as a means of reducing the number of criminals, the second and third groups would be included among the selected cases, and problems of supervision would increase. The toleration of risk depends on the personal skills and specialized training of officers and the degree of faith placed in imprisonment as the most effective way of protecting society. When correctional institutions are overcrowded beyond reason, the level of toleration is likely to increase.

In which of the four groups does a particular offender belong? Prediction of human behavior is especially difficult when applied to a group of persons already selected from the total population of the community on the basis of demonstrated incapacity to handle personal problems in a socially approved manner. The issue is which offenders are *most likely* to succeed, not whether guaranteed prosocial behavior can be expected of all those released.

What factors should be considered in selection? First, the judges and parole boards appraise the risk to the community. Second, they decide the risk the state is willing to take with each person. Third, they ask

---

[18] Max Grünhut, *The Selection of Offenders for Probation* (New York: United Nations, Department of Economic and Social Affairs, 1959), p. 7.

whether his imprisonment would be beneficial or injurious to society's stake in his rehabilitation. Will his period of imprisonment, or continued imprisonment, be sufficiently long to outweigh the risk of making him a more dangerous criminal at the time of his discharge? Or will his period of confinement in a treatment-oriented institution be long enough to assure sufficient exposure to treatment? Is he now at the highest plateau of adjustment that can be expected of a person with his capabilities? Will release at this time give the offender superior opportunities for family readjustment, employment, and other factors related to his reintegration into the community? Would it be better to parole a poor-risk prisoner so that he will be under supervision in the community, or should he be held to the end of his sentence and discharged without supervision?

Fourth, probation and parole personnel attempt to determine how effective probation or parole supervision would be. If the workers lack skills and training and if their caseloads are too high for anything more than perfunctory supervision, the release of problem offenders would be questionable. Fifth, they consider what the effect of this particular decision will be on the morale of law enforcement officers, other offenders or prisoners, and correctional staff. Each decision is an object lesson to these third parties. The paroling of an incorrigible or resistant prisoner may undermine the desire of other prisoners to conform to institutional rules or respond to therapy. Sixth, the significance of release in modifying the offender's attitudes is considered. Perhaps he should be paroled as a means of reducing the overseverity of an original sentence.

The above questions imply that selection is a rational process concerned with balancing the goals of community protection and rehabilitation of the convicted offender. An essential ingredient of such a process would be a planned strategy for correcting the offender and/or his situation as a means of forestalling further criminal behavior. In reality, as James Devlin points out, the choice of an extramural program for a given offender results from the lack of any reasonable alternative—not rational decision making based on a planned strategy. This *solution by default* is arrived at because a fine would only take money from a needed family, the case does not justify imprisonment, or further penal confinement obviously would serve no constructive purpose.[19]

Means of making decisions

The decision maker's efficiency in predicting subsequent behavior depends on his skills, the techniques employed, and the reliability of the information available. Prediction may be based on intuitive prognosis,

[19] James M. Devlin, "Probation Is a Plan," in *Probation and Allied Services: Criminology in Action,* Vol. 1 (London: Association for the Psychiatric Treatment of Offenders, 1971), pp. 28–29.

"common sense," or analysis of previous experience. The experience and insights of a particular decision maker may insure the efficiency of the first two bases; there is evidence that decision makers tend to agree for given kinds of offenders.[20] Nevertheless, systematic analysis of previous experience with similar cases has at least one advantage: It avoids arbitrary decisions based on faulty intuitive judgments irrelevant to the offender's subsequent behavior. Several decision makers of this intuitive variety may make similar judgments because they share the faulty premises.

Prediction tables, as used in corrections, can be defined as any compilation of statistics on the postrelease behavior of different types of offenders.[21] The likelihood of success for a group of offenders is predicted on the basis of recorded behavior of similar offenders in past cases. For example, adult offenders placed on probation can be checked for subsequent violations of rules during probationary periods. Types of offense, marital status, age, and prior criminal record can be associated with the possibility of violation.

Prediction tables are intended to supplement the decision maker's judgment and experience, not to be a substitute for careful, individualized study of offenders as personalities. The decision to place an offender on probation or parole requires recognition of a number of factors which are interrelated in a unique fashion in each case. Human behavior is too complex and dynamic to be assessed accurately through the arbitrary application of statistics as the sole means of predicting the acts of a given individual. Because they are based on standardization of past experience with those variables found most predictive, tables underestimate the capacity of a specific individual to change as well as the possibility of change in his community environment.

The data are derived from presentence investigations, classification summaries of correctional staffs, and supervision reports. These data are only as sound as the insights, objectivity, and thoroughness of the persons making the reports. The competence of the staff is a prerequisite to effective development and use of prediction tables. Furthermore, prediction devices can be used improperly to eliminate the major justifications for extramural treatment. If only candidates not needing the guidance and therapeutic skills of supervisory staff are admitted to the program, there is no need for such a staff. The nonstatistical judgments of decision makers can be just as arbitrary, standardized, and unfounded.

One advantage of prediction tables is that the factors relevant to deci-

[20] Don M. Gottfredson and Kelley B. Ballard, Jr., "Differences in Parole Decisions Associated with Decision-Makers," *Journal of Research in Crime and Delinquency,* 3 (July 1966): 112–19.

[21] Daniel Glaser, "Prediction Tables as Accounting Devices for Judges and Parole Boards," *Crime and Delinquency,* 8 (July 1962): 240.

sion making are more likely to be considered in all cases. Tables check on intuitive hunches, which vary from case to case and create administrative inconsistencies. They screen out obviously inappropriate cases and free the decision maker to apply his judgment and experience in an individualized manner to the remaining cases. As records of past evaluations and performances, prediction tables offer a means of assessing the effectiveness of probation and parole programs.

SUPERVISION OF CASES

All people work carries the potential for either personal frustration or a great sense of accomplishment. As a form of people work, extramural correctional programs attempt to utilize an authoritative position to help selected persons solve problems which, presumably, have much to do with their previous criminal behavior. The helping purpose is congenial to the humanitarianism which attracts many people to this work but which is severely tested by characteristics inherent in the situation: clients resist efforts to change their habits, the client's problems derive from his established personality patterns, and the institutional arrangements of the community deprive underprivileged persons of opportunities and human services. There are also difficulties in using official authority without blocking the client's willing participation in the process of changing him and his situation. In urban society, the correctional worker as supervisor encounters these challenges to his humanitarian spirit within the context of a bureaucratic organization which ideally recognizes the individual qualities of each case, while in practice it takes advantage of standardized procedures to respond quickly to a great volume of similar cases.

The success or failure of extramural correctional programs rests in large measure on whether the supervisor can give dedicated enthusiasm to each client in spite of factors that test his endurance. Because people work comes down to the quality of contact between human beings, an important element is whether the supervisor sees his work as an unending string of frustrations or a series of challenges to his professional competence. Beyond this relationship between two persons (the officer-client dyad), supervision involves the application of one of the models of community programs described above, in which the supervisor represents the bureaucratic organizations as a flesh-and-blood symbol. Some combination of community protection and client rehabilitation goals is specified. Supervision also involves the complicated relationships between extramural treatment and the many groups in the community that are relevant to the operation of the program and the ultimate outcome of the case. The negotiations with this wide variety of third parties are the nub of *community* work in corrections.

Rules and supervision

Parole and probation are forms of *conditional release* in that the convicted offender avoids imprisonment but is required to live up to specified expectations. Failure to meet the conditions risks either the imposition of the prison sentence withheld for the probationer or the return of the parolee to the prison to complete his sentence. The conditions will vary among courts and parole agencies, but usually they entail avoidance of beverage alcohol and narcotics, "undesirable" associations, unapproved out-of-state travel, and possession of weapons. Periodic reports to the supervisor, permission for marriage and change of employment, and support of dependents are required. Parole conditions have increased in recent years because courts have become more concerned about the rights of parolees. A wide range of specific regulations simplifies the proving of parole violations in court.[22]

Two key questions are how far extramural programs should penetrate into the ordinary life of the convicted offender, and for what purpose. These questions reflect attempts to combine the objectives of protection of society and rehabilitation of the offender. Many conditions imposed on offenders are based on moral values held by only certain groups in the community. Enforcement of these conditions converts the officer into a defender of a narrow moral status quo.[23] The authority of the supervisor becomes an instrument of moral imperialism to be applied in attempts to control behavior beyond the province of criminal behavior; distinctions between public and private interests are blurred, and immorality becomes confused with illegality.[24] His status as a convicted offender exposes the probationer or parolee to the "moral entrepreneur," who attempts to apply legal norms to suppress any behavior that is considered deviant by the politically dominant group.[25]

Supervision: A fragile balance

There are three sets of interdependent factors in supervision, involving relations between (1) the dyad of the officer and his client, (2) the parole or probation agency, and (3) a number of third parties. Each has important effects on the client's experiences, and the interrelationships among the sets inflate the complexity of the supervisory task. From the perspective of the supervisor, case supervision is a complex, constantly

[22] Nat R. Arluke, "A Summary of Parole Rules—Thirteen Years Later," *Crime and Delinquency,* 15 (April 1969): 267–74.

[23] Eugene H. Czajkoski, "The Need for Philosophical Direction in Probation and Parole," *Federal Probation,* 29 (September 1965): 25–26.

[24] See Chapter 1, pp. 20–21.

[25] See discussion of labeling theory, Chapter 10, pp. 258–64.

changing process in which he must seek to maintain a fragile balance in the relationships of these separate but interdependent factors.

The two goals of community protection and offender rehabilitation are frequently in conflict with one another. As the person with primary responsibility in direct confrontations with the client, the supervisor experiences this conflict directly. Because his agency is properly concerned that adverse public reaction to a scandalous crime by a client will jeopardize the future of extramural treatment, it is likely to officially support the community-protection goal while urging on him the priority of the rehabilitation goal. As a community-based worker, the supervisor intervenes for his client in the client's relationships with third parties in the community: the police, human service agencies, employers, his family and neighbors, credit agencies, landlords, and so on. These third parties are likely to favor virtually exclusive attention to community protection, especially when a client is locally considered to be especially disreputable or it is known that he has been involved in a scandalous crime. Nevertheless, they are essential resources in making the community program meaningful for client rehabilitation.

In several respects, the supervisor is a *sociological stranger* in an alien land, away from his own people and consequently not subject to the informal controls exerted by the culture of the people among whom he finds himself. Because his migration from his "native land" has made him an exception to the personality-conditioning processes experienced by the orthodox members of the community, the stranger is objective in his attitudes toward their values. If his objectivity is coupled with personal ties with an indigenous individual, the stranger is fitted for the role of confidant. Unlike the wanderer, the stranger has a place in the community's social structure because of his economic, political, or social functions in some essential field of knowledge.[26]

The supervisor in probation or parole qualifies as a sociological stranger because he is the local representative of a central office that is physically remote from and out of intimate social contact with the environment of supervision. Assuming he has been highly trained in therapeutic or case-management techniques, the supervisor personifies the values of the educated elite and his own profession, which may run counter to the values of those with whom he works. He is likely to have been socialized in middle-class values, which also characterize the policies of his agency. This orientation stands in sharp contrast to the values prevalent in the neighborhood which the supervisor must enter in order to confront his client on the client's own social "turf." As an intermediary between the client and the local social system, the supervisor can act as an objective agent in transactions in which local citizens, police, employers, and various human service workers are likely to be prejudiced against

[26] Georg Simmel, *Soziologie* (Leipzig: Duncker & Humbolt, 1908), pp. 658–91.

Figure 23–1. Corrections on a street corner.

On an urban street corner, the supervisor strives to establish a relationship with the probationer which will balance the interests of the community with those of the probationer.

the deviant and may deny him the opportunities and services necessary to his rehabilitation.[27]

The supervisor may also be a stranger in the stance he takes toward his own agency. The interactions of the officer-client dyad are supposed to be consistent with the formal conditions established by the officer's remote central office. The fact that at the same time the office demands that rehabilitation be achieved does permit the officer to have, at least tacitly, a varying degree of freedom in the interpretation of rules. The ambivalence of the central office and the ambiguity of its interpretation of its own code of rules makes the officer vulnerable to retroactive evaluation if the case "blows up" on his client's native turf. If supervision is to be individualized, the officer must accommodate his rule interpretations to the situation. His vulnerability to censure by his superiors for the decisions he must make gives him the stance of a secretive stranger in his attitudes toward the central office.

The client evaluates the officer in terms of the intensity of supervision; willingness to condone or ignore deviance from formal rules or conventional morality; and "rightness" in keeping one's word, being dependable, and treating the client with respect, according to John Irwin. Because the officer cannot observe his clients at all times, the manipulative client has opportunities for deceit. He also has reasons, however, to maintain equilibrium in his relationships with the officer by reducing his deviant activities, at least temporarily. Other cases involve "problem persons" such as alcoholics, drug users, or the irregularly employed. Both manipulative clients and problem persons illustrate what Irwin calls a "fragile system" of relationships between the officer and client which can be shattered by a crisis. The officer may discover some event or may change his interpretation of the client's performance. A new officer may intensify supervision, be less tolerant of deviations, or be less "right."[28] The other two sets of factors mentioned above may also be a disruptive influence on the preexisting equilibrium between the officer and the client. The agency may veto a decision of the officer or alter its policies. Third parties in the community may become less tolerant of extramural treatment; the client may experience the effects of a general rise in local unemployment rates, a "law and order" crisis, a breakdown in race relations, or some other broad community problem.

Ideologies in supervision

The concept of "ideology" is useful in differentiating styles of working with offenders. The supervisor approaches his work with a set of explana-

[27] See Elmer H. Johnson, "The Parole Officer in the Role of Stranger," in Richard Quinney (ed.), *Crime and Justice in Society* (Boston: Little, Brown & Co., 1969), pp. 489–99.

[28] John Irwin. *The Felon* (Englewood Cliffs, N.J.: Prentice-Hall, Inc., 1970), pp. 166–72.

tions for the events he experiences, certain ideals and goals, and definite expectations concerning his own roles and statuses and those of the persons with whom he interacts.[29]

Familistic ideology is characterized by a feeling that the supervisor and the client constitute a "family" encompassing all activities and entailing reciprocal obligations in the pursuit of these activities. The supervisor regards the offender as an errant "son" who is supposed to share his frame of reference in the evaluation of social situations. The "son" is supposed to have a conscience molded by the same socialization experienced by the supervisor. Frequently the formal rules of the agency are regarded as barriers against a humanistic and personal relationship with the offender. The supervisor's authority stems from a "father" status.

The ideology has defects because it assumes the social intimacy of the bygone rural family in which personalities could be fused through long-term association. This is usually unattainable in extramural supervision, and the subcultural diversity of urban areas and the difficulties of resocialization are further handicaps. The officer who adheres to this ideology responds ambivalently to the application of formal sanctions against "his" offender. The rooting of the ideology in emotions obstructs a professional approach to the problem.

Paternalistic ideology assumes the life of subordinates should be regulated by the superior *for* them because they must be protected against their inadequacies. The supervisor is in the role of a "benevolent master" who has a personal concern for the offender in the spirit of "Christian charity." This concern extends to every aspect of the offender's moral life. The offender is considered akin to a "dependent child" with the duty of unquestioning compliance but the privilege of demanding services from his protector.

The policing strategy is favored by his ideology, wherein formal rules become an instrument for moral imperialism. The offender is encouraged to be dependent or manipulative in relationships with the officer, who is thrust into the role of all-wise authority. A mutuality of accommodation is aborted.

Contractual ideology assumes that the supervisor and the offender have *like,* not common, interests in that each wants the cooperation necessary for his own goals. The relationship is impersonal in that the requirements of the "contract" are applied regardless of the individuals holding the statuses of officer and client. The relationship is rational in that each party weighs his actions according to self-interest within the activities specified in the contract. Because the contract is based on impersonal re-

---

[29] Adapted from typology presented by John B. Knox, *The Sociology of Industrial Relations* (New York: Random House, 1955), chap. 9; extramural treatment is subject to various combinations of the therapeutic and punitive ideologies discussed in Chapter 8 above.

lationships, one officer can replace another in the interactive system. The contract can be terminated at a specific time and is limited to a specified area of responsibility.

This ideology recognizes that the offender has personal goals and a right to privacy in sectors outside the sphere of responsibility of the supervisor. It is consistent with the nature of social relationships in an urbanized society. The supervisor seeks rapport with the offender without attempting complete emotional identification. The relationship is impersonal in that the norms are not changed drastically for immediate convenience or because of factors in the situation or qualities of the offender that do not bear directly on the conditions of release. In keeping with therapeutic principles, the offender is permitted a degree of choice, increasing with demonstrated capacity for responsible decision making.

Qualities of the client

The outcome of extramural treatment is affected by the qualities the probationer or parolee brings to the program. Selection of cases always rests on the assumption of decision makers that successful outcome pivots on the personal and social characteristics of the client, apart from the energy and competence demonstrated by the supervisor. The risk of failure usually is assessed against the status characteristics of the candidate (age, sex, occupation, and race, for example), the nature of the offense, and the probable public reaction to the candidate's conditional release. The relevance of such statuses to the probability of criminal behavior and the particular types of offenses likely to be perpetrated has been demonstrated. Because statuses are important in determining the life chances and recurrent experiences of individuals within the social system of the community, they are useful predictors of probable behavior under supervision. The accuracy of predictions based on type of crime can be exaggerated, but crimes frequently do constitute behavior systems linked to sociocultural patterns of the community at large.[30] Community attitudes have crucial effects on the "fragile balance" of supervision, as indicated earlier in this section.

Enthusiasm for community-based programs as a strategy for treatment of personality deficits should be tempered by the formidable obstacles raised by the relative brevity of intervention, the complexity of factors operating within the dynamic community environment, the differing levels of competence among supervisors, and (to our immediate point) the varying qualities among clients. One study compared outcomes of four modes of treatment for 16- and 17-year-old delinquent boys: probation, a nonresidential guided group interaction center, a residential group interaction center, and a reformatory. Subsequent recidivism rates revealed

[30] See discussion of criminal behavior systems, Chapter 7.

that the boys posing most severe treatment problems, and thus likely to be assigned to an intensive treatment or punitive program, did not perform as well on probation. Probation was found to be most effective for less delinquent boys who came from fairly stable backgrounds.[31]

The judge's choice of probation is influenced by the status characteristics of offenders, the nature of their offense, and the absence of previous incarceration. Thus acceptance for probation usually produces a predominance of cases with preferred characteristics. Nevertheless, these characteristics also are associated with lower violation *rates* while under supervision. When violation rates of Wisconsin adult male probationers and parolees convicted for a first felony were compared according to married and unmarried status for various crimes, married men had lower violation rates with one exception—parolees convicted of nonsupport had a slightly higher rate. With the same exception, probationers had lower violation rates than parolees.[32]

Drawing on data of several states, Daniel Glaser and Vincent O'Leary summarized patterns in the relationships between parole outcome and certain personal characteristics. Parole violation rates tend to decrease as the age at parole increases. If criminality persists with age, the new offense is progressively likely to be a misdemeanor rather than a felony. Because of the transitional nature of adolescence, youthful prisoners are particularly difficult subjects for reliable prediction. Among offenders of approximately the same age, the earlier they first became subject to the processes of criminal justice, the more likely they are to continue in crime. Among types of offenses previously committed, the highest parole violation rates are associated with automobile theft (committed predominately by youths), other thefts, burglary, and forgery-fraud. The lowest violation rates are recorded for offenders previously convicted of rape, other sex offenses, felonious assault, or homicide—crimes likely to arouse public criticism if the offender is paroled. Although blacks exceed whites in arrest and imprisonment rates, racial differences in parole violation rates are small or inconsistent. Possibly a greater proportion of black prisoners is not dedicated to criminal values upon admission to prison. Females have a modest advantage over males in avoiding parole violations.[33]

---

[31] Frank R. Scarpitti and Richard M. Stephenson, "A Study of Probation Effectiveness," *Journal of Criminal Law, Criminology and Police Science,* 59 (September 1959): 361–69.

[32] Dean V. Babst and John W. Mannering, "Probation versus Imprisonment for Similar Types of Offenders," *Journal of Research in Crime and Delinquency,* 2 (July 1965): 60–71 (especially Table 5). Also see Judson R. Landis, James D. Mercer, and Carole E. Wolff, "Success and Failure of Adult Probationers in California," *Journal of Research in Crime and Delinquency,* 6 (January 1969): 34–40.

[33] Daniel Glaser and Vincent O'Leary, *Personal Characteristics and Parole Outcome* (Washington, D.C.: U.S. Department of Health, Education, and Welfare, Office of Juvenile Delinquency and Youth Development, 1966).

ASSESSMENT: STATUS AND PROSPECTS

Community-based corrections embraces probation, parole, community-based institutions, work-release programs, and fuller involvement of correctional institutions in the life of the community it serves. Chapter 21 considered the latter three aspects, and Chapter 24 will discuss the marginal position of released prisoners (including parolees) between the status of the inmate and that of the fully accepted participant in the life of the free world. It is the latter status that is the ultimate objective of rehabilitation.

The various components of community-based corrections ideally should function as an integrated social system. This system, in turn, should constitute a subsystem within the broader system of criminal justice, which is designed to restrict criminals with least promise for rehabilitative change and move those with a more promising prognosis toward effective functioning within the legitimate social order.

Probation and parole in the criminal justice system

As components of the system of community-based corrections, probation and parole should be evaluated in terms of their advancement of the system's goals. Probation is in the unique position of being an arm of the courts; as such, it links the work of the courts with that of corrections. Parole extends the authority and resources of corrections beyond the confines of correctional institutions and involves correctional authority and resources directly in the life of the free community. Correctional institutions are now developing new models (work release, community-based centers, and open institutions) to supplement parole.

Prospects are that probation will be adopted by courts that do not now use this approach and that probation will be extended to an increasing variety of offenders beyond the present criterion—those who raise few difficulties under supervision. Parole administration will have to adjust to trends in criminal justice, as noted by Donald Newman. He forecasts that shorter average sentences will require earlier granting of parole. The previous emphasis on rehabilitation through counseling, group therapy, or education will be replaced by the goal of reintegration of the offender into the community through guidance, case management, and other forms of assistance in the community. Imprisonment will be seen as a relatively brief "cooling-off" or diagnostic period for a large proportion of imprisoned offenders. Widespread concern over civil rights will inspire the court's increasing attention to procedural regularity in the granting and revocation of paroles.[34]

[34] Donald J. Newman, "Legal Model for Parole: Future Developments," *Proceedings of American Correctional Association, 1970*, pp. 300–307.

Bases for evaluation

Probation and parole may be evaluated from several perspectives. In the rectification model,[35] consideration of the negative effects of custodial imprisonment may result in extramural treatment being judged the best approach for offenders who do not constitute a threat to the security of the community, even if the therapeutic effectiveness of such programs cannot be demonstrated. At a minimum, a psychological payoff is gained by avoiding the adverse consequences of imprisonment that give casual offenders the self-image of confirmed criminals. Research indicates that the probability of parole success tends to decline with increasing length of confinement, although evidence is not conclusive and various characteristics of offenders must be considered.[36] Furthermore, as we shall elaborate below, probation and parole represent significant financial savings to the taxpayer.

Extramural treatment can also be evaluated as a strategy for reintegrating the convicted offender into the community, rather than as a collection of therapeutic tactics for changing his personality. As implied by our emphasis on community as a social-psychological entity and as a human service system, we regard the reintegration model as most promising. Instead of attempting to remold the client through individual-oriented treatment, the correctional worker would strive to fit him into the community's network of opportunities and human services, which would continue to serve the client after termination of supervision and guidance. In this case, the period of supervision, usually too brief for any semblance of profound treatment, becomes less of a disadvantage. The reintegration model requires evaluation of the extramural program in terms of knowledge of the network of opportunities and human services and competence in applying this knowledge to the needs and deficits of the client.

When the extramural program is evaluated according to the rehabilitation model, its effectiveness in dealing with the psychological, educational, vocational, and other deficits of the client are taken into account. Ideally, parole would be the capstone to therapeutic programs undertaken in the correctional institution, but research on the linkages between prisons and parole has not been promising.[37] In lieu of these linkages, the parole officer may undertake the formidable assignment of treating his client from scratch hoping that confinement experiences have not had

[35] Chapter 11 presents the rectification, rehabilitation, and reintegration models, pp. 280–88.

[36] Dorothy R. Jaman, Robert M. Dickover, and Lawrence A. Bennett, "Parole Outcome as a Function of Time Served," *British Journal of Criminology,* 12 (January 1972): 5–34.

[37] See Gene Kassebaum, David A. Ward, and Daniel M. Wilner, *Prison Treatment and Parole Survival: An Empirical Assessment* (New York: John Wiley & Sons, Inc., 1971). Chapter 3 above, pp. 51–52, summarizes several other relevant studies.

such adverse consequences that treatment in the relatively brief period of community supervision is impossible. Frequently, his central difficulty has been described as an excessive caseload, which necessitates superficial and fragmentary contacts. Whether this plea is appropriate remains an open question, as studies have failed to show superior results when small caseloads are provided. Outcome is affected by other variables concealed under caseload; for example, it is strongly influenced by the choice of the appropriate intervention strategy for the given client and by early detection of client problems.[38] Intensity of supervision alone does not determine the effectiveness of the therapeutic model.

Fiscal and other benefits

Apart from any superiority over imprisonment as a therapeutic strategy, probation and parole attract the interest of budget-minded legislators and administrators because they are the least costly correctional strategies. Growing prisoner populations give the state an incentive for expanding probation and parole cases, especially if the failure rate is not likely to increase substantially. Heavy investment in new correctional institutions, the expense of maintaining prison custodial forces and institutional programs, and the costs of providing domiciliary care can be avoided.

Facing this dilemma in the mid-1960s, California took the innovative approach of providing subsidies ranging from $2,000 to $4,000 a case to counties that reduced the number of offenders sent to the state's correctional institutions. Los Angeles County received $5,184,000 in fiscal year 1969–70 because it reduced its commital rate by 29.1 percent below the previous 63.5 per 100,000 of county population. Prior to the introduction of the parole subsidy, first commitments for the California Youth Authority had increased from 4,602 in 1960 to 6,190 in 1965. After the subsidy was introduced, first commitments declined from 5,470 in 1966 to 3,746 in 1970, in spite of increasing juvenile arrest rates. Total savings to California were estimated to be $186,000,000, minus the $60,000,000 in subsidy payments. In addition, extensive building programs could be cancelled.[39]

At least as important as the financial savings of this program are the qualitative benefits claimed. Caseloads of probation officers were reduced in spite of the increased numbers of individuals placed on probation; California requires that the absolute maximum caseload be 50 per officer. The retention of more difficult cases in the community under intensive supervision required more sophistication in treatment. Screening methods

[38] H. J. Vetter and Reed Adams, "Effectiveness of Probation and Caseload Sizes: A Review of the Empirical Literature," *Criminology*, 8 (February 1971): 333–43.

[39] Andrew Rutherford, "The California Probation Subsidy Programme," *British Journal of Criminology*, 12 (April 1972): 186–88.

and psychometric diagnoses were introduced as means of effectively relating client needs and treatment resources. In addition to the usual one-to-one counseling relationships, additional strategies such as group counseling and conjoint family therapy were introduced by a large proportion of the counties. A major advantage of the probation subsidy was the means it provided for giving organizational order to the state correctional system, in spite of the fractionalization of probation programs among the counties.

The probation subsidy strategy, however, creates new organizational strains because the staffs of state correctional facilities feel threatened by declining inmate populations, demands for improved work performance now that inmate-staff ratios have been lowered, or reductions in work forces if budgetmakers seize the opportunity for short-run economy. In the communities, the elevated standards and expectations of probation officers create tensions between the probation agency and other local agencies. Demands that they also raise the quality of detention facilities and services to probationers may be difficult for them to meet.[40]

Need for more research

The recommendation for further research has been used so frequently that it smacks of triteness, but it is most relevant to selection and supervision of candidates for extramural treatment. Because the behaviors of staff, clients, and community groups are patterned, they are proper subjects for research. Extramural programs, however, continue to be administered largely through intuition, on the basis of unsubstantiated faith in the "goodness" of emotionally inspired principles. Reluctance to question the workings of agencies as a major source of program failures and hesitation in making corrections a full-fledged participant in the institutional system of the community also govern the administration of these programs.

Research can offer action agencies considerable help, as pointed out in Chapter 3. However, there are serious deficits in the conditions encountered by research experts competent enough to make these contributions. In probation and parole, these deficits are suggested by the failure of prediction tables to be as useful to correctional decision makers as their advocates believe they can be. Charles Dean and Thomas Duggan point to the general lack of reliable, routinely gathered information about offenders. The data available often fail to incisively capture the essence of behavior or systematically provide comparable data over time. Their relevance to theoretical assumptions which could provide threads of meaning to correctional work is questionable. Without appropriate in-

[40] Robert L. Smith, *A Quiet Revolution: Probation Subsidy* (Washington, D.C.: U.S. Department of Health, Education, and Welfare, Youth Development and Delinquency Prevention Administration, 1972), pp. 63–71.

formation, more sophisticated statistical techniques are of little value.[41] Beyond the collection of more useful data and development of more usable predictive instruments for the selection of clients, probation and parole require evaluation of various strategies of supervision and research for guiding policy decisions among the rectification, reintegration, and rehabilitation models, as described above.

SUMMARY

Extramural treatment is a valuable correctional tool when selection and supervision of cases are competent. The tool is no better than the quality of the personnel employing it and the level of support it is given in the community, as evidenced by the granting of resources and acceptance of the offender who responds to this form of treatment. Program models vary as to relative emphasis on community protection and rehabilitation of the offender. In considering selection and supervision of clients, primary emphasis is on probation and parole as *community* programs. The strength of extramural treatment is also the force complicating the work of the officials implementing it: the strategy operates within the dynamic environment of the community.

FOR ADDITIONAL READINGS

Arnold, William R. *Juveniles on Parole: A Sociological Perspective.* New York: Random House, 1970.

Bassett, Joel. "Discretionary Power and Procedural Rights in the Granting and Revoking of Probation." *Journal of Criminal Law, Criminology and Police Science,* 60 (December 1969): 479–93.

Brown, Richard K. "Probation Work as a Career?" *Probation* (London), 12, No. 2 (1966): 65–70.

Burkhardt, Walter R. "The Parole Work Unit Programme: An Evaluation Report." *British Journal of Criminology,* 9 (April 1969): 125–47.

Carter, Robert M. "The Presentence Report and the Decision-Making Process." *Journal of Research in Crime and Delinquency,* 4 (July 1967): 203–11.

Fischer, Edward J., and Farber, Nathan. "The Psychologist in the Probation Department." *Crime and Delinquency,* 12 (January 1966): 55–57.

Gardner, Eugene J. "Community Resources: Tools for the Correctional Agent." *Crime and Delinquency,* 19 (January 1973): 54–60.

Gibbons, Don C. *Changing the Lawbreaker.* Englewood Cliffs, N.J.: Prentice-Hall, 1965, pp. 220–26.

Keve, Paul W. *Imaginative Programming in Probation and Parole.* Minneapolis: University of Minnesota Press, 1967.

---

[41] Charles W. Dean and Thomas J. Duggan, "Problems in Parole Prediction: A Historical Analysis," *Social Problems,* 15 (Spring 1968): 458–59.

Lee, Charles C. "The Concept of Authority in the Field of Probation and Parole." *American Journal of Correction,* 28 (March–April 1966): 26–27.

Martin, Gordon A., Jr.; Lewis, David C.; Guarino, Joseph; and Fishman, Robert. "Drug Abuse and the Court." *Crime and Delinquency,* 18 (April 1972): 192–203.

Parsloe, Phyllida. *The Work of the Probation and After-care Officer.* New York: Humanities Press, 1967.

Rogers, Joseph W., and Hayner, Norman S. "Optimism and Accuracy in the Perception of Selected Parole Prediction Items." *Social Forces,* 46 (March 1968): 388–400.

Scheier, Ivan H. "The Professional and the Volunteer in Probation: An Emerging Relationship." *Federal Probation,* 34 (June 1970): 12–18.

Spencer, Carol, and Berecochea, John E. *Recidivism among Women Parolees: A Long Term Survey.* Sacramento, Calif.: Research Division, California Department of Corrections, July 1972.

Stanton, John M. "Murderers on Parole." *Crime and Delinquency,* 15 (January 1969): 149–55.

Takagi, Paul, and Robison, James. "The Parole Violator: An Organizational Reject." *Journal of Research in Crime and Delinquency,* 6 (January 1969): 78–86.

24

Circumstances and problems of release

Return of the prisoner to the free community usually reveals a major lack of services which can assist the *former* offender to become an effective participant in the life of the community. Traditionally, society has been more willing to accept the expense of feeding, clothing, guarding and, to a lesser degree, treating the prisoner than the cost of providing him with a means for coping with the crisis of reentry into the community. This incongruity reflects a lack of coordination among the various segments of the system of criminal justice. At this point in the convicted offender's movement through the sequence of criminal justice procedures, the correctional institution has been released of its authority and responsibility but the assumption of responsibility by other agencies is problematic. This is especially true for the inmate discharged on completion of sentence without parole. When he lacks personal resources or support from family or friends, the discharged prisoner's prospects may be limited to seeking a handout soon after he goes out the prison gate.

REENTRY: A TIME OF TESTING

A crisis may be defined as a crucial turning point determining the outcome of earlier transactions. The inmate's reentry into the community qualifies as a crisis in this sense. A judge has made a sentencing decision, and a number of correctional workers have engaged in a wide variety of transactions involving the inmate. Meanwhile, the inmate has made his responses to the experiences of his penal career. The community he reenters constitutes an attitudinal climate and a system of socioeconomic opportunity. The willingness and capacity of the community to accept his reentry play a large part in determining the success or failure of reentry.

Three sets of factors affecting outcome

The crisis of reentry involves three interrelated sets of factors which influence the outcome of previous transactions. The first set of factors is the personal qualities of the released prisoner in terms of his attitudes, capacities, resourcefulness, and emotional flexibility. Assuming he entered prison with psychological, vocational, and other deficits, has the individual taken advantage of whatever resources the correctional institution offered to prepare him for more effective participation in community life? Does the released prisoner go into the reentry crisis psychologically prepared to cope with the difficulties of finding a useful and personally satisfying place for himself in the social system he is joining?

The second set of factors concerns the agencies of criminal justice, especially correctional workers. Now the wisdom of the sentencing judge is tested. Whether the sentencing decision was based on punitive or therapeutic grounds, correctional agencies are charged with the primary responsibility in carrying out its purpose. Did the courts and correctional agencies work together in this case in the coordinated way implied by the term "*system* of criminal justice"? Did the correctional workers justify the claim that imprisonment can increase the personal capacities of convicted offenders to cope with the contingencies of community life? Will community-based programs be coordinated with those of the correctional institutions?

The third set of factors involves the receiving community, which will be tested in terms of its willingness to accept its side of the *rehabilitation bargain*. This bargain implies that the offender's positive response to the call to change his attitudes and behavior will restore him to the good graces of the legitimate community and grant him access to its opportunity system. The "good graces" refer to the attitudinal climate within which he is received. Rehabilitation implies that the prisoner should strive to adopt the patterned ways of thinking, feeling, and behaving toward others which characterize the dominant culture of the receiving community. In other words, he is expected to have undergone *cultural assimilation,* in which he has accepted the norms of private property and abstinence from violence and has been led to abandon the particular deviant behavior that led to his imprisonment. If he has passed the test of cultural assimilation, the receiving community must now decide whether he will be granted *structural assimilation,* in which he can be absorbed into the intimate social life and opportunity system of the receiving community.[1]

These three sets of factors all bear on the question whether the reha-

---

[1] The differentiation of cultural and structural assimilation is presented by Milton M. Gordon in *Assimilation in American Life* (New York: Oxford University Press, 1964), pp. 67–78.

bilitative bargain will be carried out. From the point of view of the first set, which involves the released prisoner as an individual, an unsuccessful outcome will be attributed to his weaknesses or his inability (or unwillingness) to undergo cultural assimilation. As for the correctional institution, a primary agency in terms of the second set of factors, lack of success will cause it to be criticized for failures in its rehabilitation programs or for engendering hostility in former prisoners. Both of the first two sets of factors affecting outcome of reentry are concerned with inadequacies of cultural assimilation. Structural assimilation takes place in the environment of the receiving community, which in the final analysis will determine whether the reformed offender will be accepted as a participating member.

Adjustment in the reentry crisis

A crisis such as return to the free community should be examined from both personal and societal perspectives. David Mechanic points out that from the point of view of the person, the crisis involves the level of his skills and capacities in coping with the situation, as well as his motivation (Does the return arouse fears and other emotions related to deficient self-confidence and self-esteem?). From the societal perspective, Mechanic cites preparatory institutions (Has the correctional institution prepared the released inmate to deal with the challenges of post-release situations?), incentive systems (Do the rewards and punishments of prison programs and community organizations channel the released inmate's motivation toward effective coping?), and evaluative institutions (Does he receive approval and support or disapproval and dispargement from family, employing organizations, and other community institutions?).[2]

The released prisoner is supposed to adjust to the community, but, as Walter Eaton notes, the term "adjustment" has two different meanings.[3] *Attitudinal adjustment* refers to the individual's expression of satisfaction or dissatisfaction with the manner of life he has adopted. Does the returned prisoner like or dislike the situation in which he finds himself? To measure this aspect of the former prisoner's adjustment, the community-based worker encounters difficulties in determining precisely what the expression of satisfaction or dissatisfaction means in terms of behavior, whether or not the statement is sincere, and if the expression is relevant to the individual's living situation. *Functional adjustment* refers to the individual's conformity to the norms of the community. For the released

[2] David Mechanic, "Some Problems in Developing a Social Psychology of Adaption to Stress," in Joseph E. McGrath (ed.), *Social and Psychological Factors in Stress* (New York: Holt, Rinehart & Winston, Inc., 1970), pp. 113–14.

[3] Walter E. Eaton, "Alternative Meanings of Adjustment," *American Sociological Review,* 12 (February 1947): 75–81.

prisoner, this is a matter distinct from his attitudes toward his situation. Is he accepting responsibilities as a family head, employee, creditor, or occupant of other statuses in the community's social system? In a dynamic and complex society norms are difficult to describe precisely, and applications to convicted criminals run the special risk of demanding conformity more than abandonment of criminal behavior. Nevertheless, functional adjustment is the essence of the ultimate purpose of restoring the former offender to community life.

Adjustment as a goal of correctional work

The community-based worker is likely to emphasize attitudinal adjustment because humanitarian concerns motivate him to produce personal satisfactions ("happiness") for the client. Treatment success is related to rapport between client and worker, as expressed in the client's attitudes toward his current experiences. In spite of the pertinence of attitudinal adjustment to successful reentry to the community, the worker should recognize that as an ideal and exclusive goal it is beyond the grasp of a short-term intervention strategy. This is especially true in the light of the biography of most of his clients, his inability to control the multitude of factors operating in a community environment, and the extreme variability among individuals in how they undertake the search for the elusive values of "happiness."

Exclusive attention to the attitudinal adjustment of clients involves the worker in trying to create an ideal balance between personal aspirations and the demands of the environment. The individual must obtain the cooperation of other persons in the realization of his aspirations, which might include prestige, a sense of emotional mutuality with another human being, feelings of pleasurable excitement, or economic security. Such aspirations are difficult to gratify even for persons who are fully accepted in the community and have a reasonable degree of skill, knowledge, and material means for realizing them. Prospects are even more tenuous for the client of the community-based worker. The released prisoner is in a period of transition between his former status as inmate and a future status as accepted citizen. His biography usually indicates repeated failures in realizing aspirations or gaining means to do so. If, as is likely, he returns to a status in the community's social system which offers little promise for self-realization, he may see the community-based worker only as an agent of the criminal justice system that took away his freedom and aggravated his frustrations. The community-based worker challenges great odds when he undertakes the search for the "holy grail of happiness" for his client.

Attitudinal adjustment is an essential ingredient in any people-work intervention, but it is functional adjustment that holds promise for providing reasonably accessible goals in the face of realities. The community-based worker attempts to bring the client closer to conformity with the role norms germane to the problems of the given case. Attention is on expanding the client's resources to enable him to serve as an effective family breadwinner, reliable employee, physically healthy person, or in another appropriate community status. The worker serves as an intermediary between his client and the network of community human services as it bears on the client's problem. Under the premise that the worker is a professional who has been granted discretion to apply individualized interpretation to general rules, he becomes the implementing link between agency policies and the structuring of client behavior in the direction sought by agency policy makers.

Whereas attitudinal adjustment could entail widespread intervention in all aspects of the client's personality and behavior, with functional adjustment intervention can be isolated to key aspects, in keeping with the contractual ideology of parole supervision.[4] It can be assumed that attitudinal adjustment will be achieved in reasonable measure as a by-product of successful functional adjustment. Such side effects are an example of the virtue of considering correctional work at the reentry stage as preparation for the complete process of adjustment, which extends into the life of the client after he has left the intervention program.

Adjustment in the community setting of correctional work

Attitudinal adjustment assumes that the social order of the community is based on a virtually universal consensus. Imprisonment was ordered for a particular deviant because he violated the portion of the community's moral code that had been incorporated into criminal law. The released prisoner supposedly has learned that conformity to these norms must be his future life style. He is supposed to gain satisfaction (positive attitudinal adjustment) from such conformity.

The weaknesses of these assumptions already have been indicated. Because urban society is composed of many subcultures and its social structure includes groups with diverging self-interests, the contemporary community deviates from the *consensus model*, in which social order is seen as the derivative of the common socialization of all citizens in one set of norms. More descriptive of the basis of the urban order is the *conflict model*, in which conflicting special-interest groups are seen as promoting their own ends by alliances derived from a common need for social stability. In this model, community order is maintained through a constantly changing equilibrium among groups in conflict or competition with one another.[5]

---

[4] See Chapter 23, pp. 579–80.

[5] See discussion of order and conflict theories, Chapter 4, pp. 71–73, and Chapter 21, pp. 520–22, and of the urban community as a setting, Chapter 21, pp. 517–20.

Resort to criminal law suggests weak community consensus and, especially when official crime rates are high, an effort to prop up the faulty operation of social institutions. Under the consensus model, these institutions are supposed to maintain community stability through informal controls. Under the conflict model, community-based corrections could be charged with the responsibility of promoting the structural assimilation of the released prisoner by ensuring his access to the opportunity and human service systems of the community. This objective, which is consistent with the concept of functional adjustment, does not require the released offender to demonstrate the moral adherence implied in the concept of attitudinal adjustment.

An important aspect of the reentry crisis is that it may be conducted within what has been described above as an inauthentic community.[6] A fundamental dilemma of community-based corrections is that both the etiology of crime and the difficulties of the returned prisoner involve the faulty distribution of human services and the existence of environmental pressures toward deviance that characterize such communities.[7] The concept of functional adjustment both focuses on the vulnerability of community-based corrections to the poverty of human services in the inauthentic community and indicates the failures of such communities which result in inflation of the caseload of the criminal justice system.

Within the total community, the functional adjustment of the returned prisoner involves only those aspects of community organizations and social institutions that are directly and immediately relevant to his problem. The structural assimilation of the returned prisoner realistically can involve only those capacities and motivations he can present as qualifications for acceptance within the opportunity system of a particular community. If all effects of the ex-convict stigma were removed, the opportunity system could still be a determinant of his life chances as related to his community statuses (social class and race differentials, especially) and the range of services he can offer potential employers. In the latter instance, the vocational training, academic courses, and counseling programs of the correctional institution are of great importance, under Mechanic's concept of preparatory institutions. The evaluative institutions and incentive systems also involved in the societal perspective of the reentry crisis include not only employers but the client's family and other reference groups. These will subject his self-image and his level of skill in interpersonal relationships to intensive, personally meaningful challenges.

The community-based worker may be sharply aware of the deficiencies in the total community. In functional adjustment, however, only those

[6] Chapter 21, pp. 520–21.

[7] The "problem neighborhood" illustrates environmental pressures derived from the operation of the community as a social system; see Chapter 21, pp. 519–20.

segments of the community organization and institutions that affect a particular released prisoner are of concern. Thus community-based work with an individual in his reentry crisis can properly focus on the problem situations most relevant to him.

THE RELEASED PRISONER AS A DIMENSION OF THE REENTRY CRISIS

Offenders received by correctional institutions are not markedly dissimilar from average citizens at the socioeconomic levels from which most offenders are drawn. Both offenders and nonoffenders may have character and behavior disorders, defects in personality development, inferior work records, or inadequate skills in interpersonal relationships. Through probation, plea bargaining, and various dispositions before trial,[8] some offenders are diverted from imprisonment or receive relatively short exposure to penal confinement. Thus some portion of offenders is spared most of the difficulties of reentry to the community, to the ultimate benefit of society. We are concerned here with the remaining portion of convicted offenders who differ from other human beings in that they have recently experienced penal confinement.

Economic problems

The immediate problem of survival involves sufficient money for the purchase of food, shelter, and the other essentials in an urban society, where production for one's own use is rare. A frequent justification advanced for perpetration of a crime immediately after release is "I had to steal to eat." There is an obvious paradox when the released prisoner, after completing experiences intended to place him in the status of the law-abiding citizen, is placed in the free world without minimum resources. To avoid this, prisons usually provide *gate money,* a relatively modest gratuity, to released prisoners who are without funds, especially when a long sentence has been completed. Prison administrators prefer that inmates be required to earn such money through prison work because this provides an incentive for industrious labor. Some prisons require that a portion of earnings be saved against post-release needs, but wages are paid inmates in only a portion of the prisons, and the pay scale is low.[9] By writing books, painting, or, more frequently, making leather purses, furniture, toys, and other items for sale to visitors, some prisoners have earned large sums which are available on their release, but this is most unusual.

Provision also is usually made for transporting needy prisoners to

[8] See Chapter 14, pp. 350–53.

[9] Daniel Glaser, *The Effectiveness of a Prison and Parole System* (Indianapolis, Ind.: Bobbs-Merrill Co., Inc., 1964), pp. 316–20.

Figure 24–1. Will he come back?

With his belongings under his arm, the released prisoner walks through the prison gate. Will he find a place as a respected citizen in the outside community?

their homes. Issuance of transportation tickets may be encouraged by the desire of authorities to export former criminals out of the local or state jurisdiction, so that the probability of readmission is reduced. In this case, assistance in transportation is a side effect of a policy of banishment. Short-term prisoners are expected to wear the clothes they brought with them. Those who have served medium to long terms are entitled to a set of clothing at state expense because long-term storage of their civilian clothing is impractical.

While short-term economic needs are of obvious importance, if readjustment is to be successful a stable economic base must be established. Even when funds are sufficient for immediate needs, the released prisoner needs employment for dependable income so that economic insecurity will not paralyze his efforts to cope with the psychological and social problems that confront him. On the other hand, it is thought that relieving the former prisoner of impossible economic deprivation must be balanced against the need to cultivate the initiative and self-reliance prized in American culture as a mark of competent adulthood.

Private and public welfare agencies try to provide material assistance in ways that can overcome the underlying causes of the client's long-term difficulties. Louis Zeitoun would use the opportunity to help the discharged prisoner meet emotional and social problems of readjustment and progress toward independence. He believes the caseworker should distinguish between what the client requests and what he really needs, because the request may have no bearing on his employment, residence, or family problems. The request must also be evaluated relative to the agency's resources; it may be meritorious but beyond the funds presently available. The granting of assistance is related to the probability that the client will use the funds constructively. Will they be used to buy tools for a trade as the client promises, or will he use them to finance an alcoholic binge?[10]

Assistance from relatives and from welfare agencies is not the best solution. The need to accept such assistance deals a blow to the man's pride. The release of the prisoner will probably terminate any public assistance his family has been receiving. Reliance on relatives or welfare agencies for financial assistance usually will not solve the economic problem, and if there is nowhere else for him to turn, he may be thrust back into the criminalistic situation he is supposed to avoid.

Emotional problems

Sociological and psychological problems vary with the nature of the individual, length of incarceration, and circumstances of release. One

---

[10] Louis Zeitoun, "Material Assistance Given by After-Care Agencies in Canada," *American Journal of Correction*, 20 (January–February 1959): 17–18.

man may regard release with unjustified equanimity. Another has abnormal fears and requires reassurance. Still another has more modest fears, but they are not focused on the matters to which he should direct his attention.

Imprisonment always leaves some mark on the released inmate. Incarceration may weaken self-reliance and increase dependence on others. Compared with other applicants for jobs, he will suffer from a greater degree of defeatism, which is likely to sap his initiative and drive. The prison routine creates habits inconsistent with family and community life. Relationships with family, friends, and work associates are interrupted. In picking up the threads of his previous life, the releasee may have difficulty reducing the hostilities and frustrations aroused by life in prison and the loss of years of his life. The first flush of freedom may deprive him temporarily of self-control and release stored-up desires in a burst of license. At least initially, his reaction against the regimentation of prison life may interfere with his adjustment to the routines of daily work, supervision by others, and consistent work effort.

Prolonged incarceration can isolate the inmate from the community to such a degree that he finds the world into which he emerges strange. His family and friends have changed in his absence. Techniques of work have changed. He has to learn again such social skills as how to shop in stores use subways and buses, and order a meal in a restaurant. A married prisoner leaves prison to be confronted by family problems. The marital relationship has undoubtedly been weakened in his absence. If his family has been receiving public assistance during his confinement, his release may terminate this source of income. Old debtors, or those who have aided his family during his imprisonment, may press for payment, and his return may require a search for larger, more expensive living quarters.

Conditions placed upon behavior demonstrate to the parolee that he is not completely free. He must be wary of his associates, of drinking, choice of places of amusement, changes in job or residence, and long journeys. Because the parolee is exposed to standards not applied to non-criminals, his conformity to parole rules tends to make him a social eccentric among his friends.[11] Acutely self-conscious, burdened with anxieties, and aware of the possibility that his status in the community could be challenged, the former prisoner is likely to weigh the probable consequences of any behavior, no matter how innocuous. His sense of insecurity and uncertainty may cause him to question the behavior of family, friends, and business acquaintances. He may see slights and persecution where they do not exist. When he encounters rebuffs in his search for work or is frequently questioned by the police, his suspicions are given substance.

---

[11] Wayne K. Patterson, "Civil and Social Barriers to Treatment," *NPPA Journal,* 4 (July 1958): 269.

Expectations while in prison

In the final period of confinement before release, the inmate begins to realize the full impact of the consequences of his imprisonment. In his study of reformatory inmates, Stanton Wheeler found acceptance of the inmate culture insulated them against the pains of social rejection and status degradation. In delaying confrontation of such personal problems, this insulation only exaggerates the impact of confinement on inmates anticipating an impending return to the outside community.[12]

While still in prison, the prisoner may have expectations beyond the realities of his capacities and the situations he will encounter upon his release. Excessive hopes cultivated by enforced isolation from life in the outside world are a major element in later failures. Jerome Skolnick hypothesizes that, when the new parolee has high expectations that his personal wishes will be gratified on parole, he is more likely to display anger and resentment when the realities of parole experience prove these expectations to be unfounded. On the other hand, when the new parolee has extremely low expectations, he is likely to be apathetic in confronting the task of functional adjustment. It is when the parolee has moderate expectations that his adjustment to the realities of parole are most likely to be effective during the initial period of release. Success in functional adjustment depends upon the degree of deviation between the released prisoner's own norms and those of the group to which he is expected to adjust. If the norms of his immediate group and his own norms are in strong conflict with those of the legitimate world, he will not achieve functional adjustment. If his norms are in conflict with legitimate norms and if his immediate group rejects the offender's norms, functional adjustment is unlikely. Skolnick believes that parolees are more likely to be successful in reentry when the immediate group moderately accepts the former prisoner's norms, rather than completely accepting or rejecting them.[13]

The persistence of criminal behavior

The usual conception of a criminal career is that it unfolds consistently, continuously, and progressively. Daniel Glaser's data on federal prisoners challenge this conception. He reports that for at least 90 percent of imprisoned felons, the pattern is alternation between legitimate and criminal means of pursuing goals. Some men terminate early a cycle of crime to noncrime to crime. For others these fluctuations do not cease until late in life, and for a few, they never do. If the risk of crime is as-

[12] Stanton Wheeler, "Socialization in Correctional Institutions," *American Sociological Review,* 26 (October 1961): 697–712.

[13] Jerome H. Skolnick, "Toward a Developmental Theory of Parole," *American Sociological Review,* 25 (August 1960): 542–49.

sumed often enough, periodic failure is almost inevitable. Imprisonment usually brings some effort toward legitimacy, but when such efforts fail, further crime often is attempted.[14]

The aging process appears to influence persistence of criminal conduct. In a follow-up study of a thousand juvenile delinquents, Sheldon and Eleanor Glueck cited evidence that criminality tends to be abandoned in proportion to the passage of time from the point of first expression of definite delinquency. If delinquencies appear very early in life, they are more likely to be counteracted as maturation brings greater powers of reflection, inhibition, postponement of immediate desires, and learning from experience. If delinquencies begin in adolescence, the influence of maturation does not seem to appear until a later state of adulthood. The Gluecks see "various mental abnormalities" as the major factor counteracting the "natural maturation process,"[15] but their conception of mental abnormalities encompasses such a broad variety of behaviors that their explanation loses much of its significance.

Hermann Mannheim and Leslie Wilkins, studying borstal prisons in Britain, found that the earlier the career of crime was commenced, the less likely was reform of youths after borstal training.[16] Their conclusion conflicts with that of the Gluecks, perhaps because of the differences between the base populations employed. The Glueck study included all delinquents in its sample, whereas Mannheim and Wilkins considered only that portion of the offenders that had been institutionalized.

Aging is a more complex process than mere change in chronological age. It involves the individual's capacity to adjust to concurrent changes in relationships with others. In addition to physical development, increased chronological age brings changes in an individual's status within his social universe. Adolescence means acceleration of growth in height and weight and the onset of puberty. The wide variation in rate of physical change among adolescents of similar age creates psychological problems because new social demands are placed upon them. They are no longer regarded as children but may or may not be accorded full adult status. The degree of a teen-ager's physical development affects the possibility that he will be treated as an adult before he has the social maturity to handle this status. During this transitional period the judgments of his peers become more important to his self-evaluation; their expectations for him may conflict with those of his family or the larger community. The problems of courtship and selection of a vocation loom large.

Delinquencies may be symptomatic of the adolescent's inability to meet these adjustment problems in socially approved ways. With fuller

[14] Glaser, *Effectiveness of a Prison and Parole System*, p. 466.

[15] Sheldon and Eleanor T. Glueck, *Juvenile Delinquents Grown Up* (New York: Commonwealth Fund, 1940), pp. 103–4.

[16] Hermann Mannheim and Leslie T. Wilkins, *Prediction Methods in Relation to Borstal Training* (London: Her Majesty's Stationery Office, 1958), p. 65.

social experience, successful meeting of stressful situations, physical maturation, and the gaining of a more satisfactory social status, the individual may acquire forms of adjustment which remove him from the deviant group.

Among the factors demanding adjustment by young offenders is the nature of official intervention in response to a first delinquency attracting official notice. A study distinguishes three types of delinquents less than 16 years old. The *seasoned delinquent,* already a recidivist, operates with companions and displays serious propensities toward a criminal career. The *younger offender,* less than 14, commits solitary antisocial, acting-out offenses which are not serious and are situation-stimulated rather than patterned tendencies toward criminality. The *single-offense delinquent,* seldom a serious offender, gets into difficulty with the law because of a specific threat.[17] By ignoring the differences among these delinquent types, police and courts may press the latter two types toward the status of seasoned delinquent.

The relationship between age and recidivism may be explained by imagining two groups. The first consists of individuals who come in conflict with the law during their youth but abandon deviance after a relatively brief period. The second group persists in crime for a variety of reasons, one of which is failure to achieve a prosocial adjustment. This assessment is suggested by the failure of recidivism among prisoners to increase progressively with age to the degree that might be assumed because advancing age means more years in which the opportunity to commit crimes is presented.

For younger offenders, postinstitutional adjustment problems may be aggravated by difficulties incidental to status changes. Marriage, parenthood, psychological correlates of increasing chronological age, and medical problems are faced as the offender passes through the stages of life common to all human beings. Comfortable economic circumstances for the bachelor may be marginal at best for the husband-father. In their study of 454 reformatory inmates who were paroled, the Gluecks found 90.9 percent to be single previous to the reformatory sentence, 45.2 percent to be single 5 years after granting of parole, and 38.2 percent to be single after 10 years on parole. The need for assistance in managing personal affairs is suggested for such inmates, since 41 percent were clients of social service agencies during the second five-year period after parole. The Gluecks see "glaring" discrepancies between the services rendered by community agencies and the high incidence of social, economic, and medical problems.[18]

---

[17] Maude M. Craig and Laila A. Budd, "The Juvenile Offender: Recidivism and Companions," *Crime and Delinquency,* 13 (April 1967): 344–51.

[18] Sheldon and Eleanor T. Glueck, *Later Criminal Careers* (New York: Commonwealth Fund, 1937), pp. 40–42.

TESTING THE EFFECTIVENESS OF CORRECTIONS

Release from prison is an example of status passage which is particularly fraught with tensions. *Status passage* refers to the movement of an individual from one social position to another in a social system. Attached to each status are role norms guiding how the individual is expected to behave as an occupant of that status. The passage from childhood through adolescence to adulthood entails accommodation to differing roles attached to a sequence of age statuses. The occupational novice moves through the statuses of recruit, trainee, new practitioner, and master worker.

The individual brings his own capacities to the problems of accommodating his behavior to the expectations associated with an unfamiliar status. The social system can aggravate the individual's adjustment if its norms are ambiguous and it fails to cushion the tensions imposed upon the novice. These inadequacies of the social system are germane to the study of the released prisoner.

A difficult status passage

In applying the concept of status passage to parolees, Elliot Studt considers that the post-release period starts as a crisis (as we have noted) because the former inmate is subjected to sharp discontinuity between the inmate status and the statuses he is expected to assume in the free world. The inmate status was subservient and deprived within the highly structured life of the prison. The statuses he now is expected to assume are of greater variety and have little relationship to the inmate status. In attempting to cope with these discrepancies, the parolee is handicapped by his knowledge that failure is likely to bring his return to prison. Furthermore, there is an absence of positive rewards designed to encourage him to learn to handle his new statuses.[19] The released prisoner not on parole does not risk reimposition of confinement without a new crime, but, without support from parole supervision, he is expected to handle his new statuses while suffering the stigmatization of the "ex-convict." Unlike other status passage situations, the former status of prison inmate continues to permeate virtually every aspect of life in the ex-prisoner's new status.

The parolee differs from other released prisoners in one respect: parole rules regulate many aspects of his life.[20] This extensive intervention means that the parole agency shares the responsibility for the client's

---

[19] Elliot Studt, *The Reentry of the Offender into the Community* (Washington, D.C.: Office of Juvenile Delinquency and Youth Development, U.S. Department of Health, Education, and Welfare, 1969), pp. 3–6.

[20] Chapter 23, p. 575.

success and failure and has some degree of interest in guiding and assisting him. However, as Studt notes, ambiguous or inflexible agency rules can add uncertainties to status passage. The parole officer may undermine the family relationships when he asks the wife to inform on her husband. Prohibitions against using an automobile may interfere with employment opportunities or deny the use of a driver's license as an expected form of identification. The requirements of supervision may undermine the parolee's integration with the normal, legitimate patterns of social intercourse.[21]

Strain: Personal and societal

The difficulties of status passage reflect strain between the released prisoner and the correctional authorities, as well as strain among the public and private agencies that have an interest in his reentry into the community. In his quest for freedom, the prisoner encounters the authority of decision makers concerning the granting of "good time," commutation of sentence, pardon, or parole as means of reducing the time of confinement. While under control of the authorities, the prisoner has strong incentives to inhibit resentments, but what occurs when this control is removed? Then comes the crucial test of institutional treatment. Will he cut himself off from all agents of society whom he has come to identify with frustration and coercion? When he is unequipped to deal alone with the serious problems of release, such an attitude could cancel the benefits of institutionalized treatment. Will his "rehabilitation" persist, or is it a passing phase dependent on externalized control? The answer lies within the psychology of the offender and the circumstances of his release.

The release of the prisoner, presumably purged of his offense by his punishment, without thought or care for his future has been called morally indefensible.[22] The usual motivation for providing aftercare has been simple humanitarianism, but aftercare also protects society and its investment in institutionalized treatment by avoiding the results of special hardships imposed on released prisoners. In the correctional institution, the management of a case is simplified because the services are administered by a single authority, but the prison environment favors the development of dependency. If the inmate sought and received relevant treatment while in prison, the centralization of administration simplified his search for the counseling, instruction, and other services he required. After release, centralized case management disintegrates into a search for assistance in a network of community agencies that is loosely organized at best. Strains among community-based correctional workers and

21 Studt, *Reentry of the Offender*, pp. 5–6.

22 Lionel W. Fox, *The English Prison and Borstal System* (London: Routledge & Kegan Paul, 1952), p. 253.

these agencies are partially a spin-off of the tensions already existing among these agencies and the bureaucratic maze they present to would-be clients. The doubts many of these agencies have about accepting "criminals" as clients complicates relations with them for community-based correctional workers and released prisoners alike.

Case management requires knowledge of the varied operations among human service agencies and skill in fitting the individual's needs into the intricate organizational network. The releasee must qualify for services under definitions of client qualifications which may be complicated by the circumstances of release. For example, hospitalization may be denied because the case does not meet requirements for a certain period of residence in the community. Ideally, the parole officer or other specialist in postrelease cases becomes the intervening agent between the releasee and the agencies. Because he lacks knowledge of the ways of the programs, the releasee otherwise will usually not be able to find entry into the network of agencies. The erosion of his self-reliance in the protected environment of the correctional institution is poor preparation for independent action when an agent of intervention is not available.

Reducing the abnormality of confinement

Two general developments are underway to reduce the difficulties of status passage for the released inmate. The isolation of the prison from the outside world is being reduced, and correctional institutions are increasingly being oriented toward preparation of the inmate for his reentry into the free community.[23]

The open institution reduces the differences between the daily lives of institutionalized offenders and those of people in the free world. Minimum-security institutions fall short of this achievement, but tendencies in this direction include fewer restrictions on visiting, less routinization of activities and inmate movement within the confines of the institution, increased similarity with the working conditions of private enterprise, and fuller discussion of postrelease problems. A promising development has been experimentation with the inclusion of the inmate's family in the counseling program as a means of modifying the milieu to which the inmate will return.

Work release, which permits the inmate to continue, or reenter, civilian employment while serving his sentence, offers a means of retaining ties with the free community. His status as "part-time prisoner" may make him a marginal man in his civilian work associations; he is physically a part of his world of work, yet his peculiar role marks him as a person apart from the rest. Furthermore, his special status is apt to deprive him of the advantages of any organized treatment program offered

---

[23] These matters were considered in Chapter 21, pp. 525–26.

by the correctional system. Nevertheless, work release is of great value in minimizing the social isolation of the convicted offender from the world he is expected to reenter. It serves as a testing and adjustment period preliminary to granting of parole.

Another approach is to employ the terminal phase of the sentence as a transitional period within the institution between the confinement period proper and the initial period of return to the community. An "honor dormitory" or a special facility may be set aside to acclimate the prospective dischargee or parolee to a more normal community existence. Under this approach, the institution tries to counteract the negative influences of confinement and the organizational structure of the prison in isolating the inmate from the outside world. A *preparole camp* outside prison walls offers lectures by representatives of the clergy, colleges, governmental agencies, law enforcement organizations, personnel management, and the bar. Group discussion follows each lecture, under staff leadership. Specific topics include the alcohol problem, budgeting, family relationships, community resources for assistance, legal problems, tips for seeking employment, religion as a way of life, and parole practices and requirements.

THE COMMUNITY AS A DIMENSION OF THE REENTRY CRISIS

In community-based corrections, the word "community" may be interpreted as the focal point in programmed efforts to include the released inmate in the network of social-psychological bonds and to provide him with access to the delivery network of human services. These two networks are separate but interdependent aspects of the community as a social organization that can transform a collectivity of human beings into a social system that is superior to individual, unguided efforts to satisfy personal needs and aspirations. Study of the problems of the released prisoner should include consideration of the nature and functioning of the community as germane to his earlier involuntary withdrawal from it and the conditions under which he returns.

A target for prejudice

By resorting to the criminal law and imprisonment as responses to the transgression of a particular prisoner, the community told something about itself. The given offense was regarded as a threat to values held precious by the norm announcers of that community, and the threat was considered of sufficient intensity to justify the offender's penal incarceration. His offense may have implied the prisoner's lack of personal identification with these values and his unwillingness to be a social-psychological participant in the mutuality of community life. In any event, his official designation as a transgressor and his forced exile constituted a rejection of the prisoner as an accepted member of the community. Assuming that the former prisoner now wants this acceptance and is prepared to assume his obligations, the question is whether the community will assimilate him within its network of fellowships.

Presumably the prisoner's involuntary confinement has satisfied any retributive element in a punitive conception of criminal law; the balance between right and wrong has been restored. His experience of penal pain should have exceeded any pleasure he gained through his earlier crime, if we can believe the deterrent argument in defense of punishment. Now the question is whether or not the social rejection and physical isolation of this criminal is to be terminated. An issue considered earlier is relevant here: the blurring of the distinction between the definition of a given act as criminal and the evaluation of the total constellation of the behaviors of the individual to whom that definition is applied.[24] Has this individual been rejected and punished specifically for a given act of rape, theft, manslaughter, or other legally defined crime, or has he been relegated to an outcast status because of his *total* personality?

The criminal shares with members of other underprivileged groups the risk that relegation to a deviant status carries social penalties beyond the scope of the deviation itself. This risk entails *prejudice,* which includes the elements of unfounded judgment and innate feelings of scorn, dislike, fear, or aversion.[25] Criminals, racial or religious minorities, mentally ill or mentally subnormal persons, the poor, and other underprivileged groups are subjected to *stereotypes,* in which the individual is arbitrarily judged to possess characteristics *assumed* to be possessed by all members of a given group. A stereotype is a categoric judgment in which a given individual, regardless of his uniqueness and his differences in many respects from other members of a pertinent outgroup, is treated as though he were the personification of what the evaluator *believes* to be its behavior and values.

Hyperemotional public reactions to various images of crime and criminals are a part of the cost of the crime problem.[26] The released prisoner shares some of this cost as a member of one of the minority groups subjected to prejudice. There is evidence that the effects of hyperemotional reactions against some kinds of deviants have been reduced through greater recognition of alcoholism and mental disease as social problems requiring therapeutic reactions.[27] For such elements of society as racial

[24] See Chapter 1, pp. 18–19.

[25] Gordon W. Allport, *The Nature of Prejudice* (Reading, Mass.: Addison-Wesley Publishing Co., Inc., 1954), p. 7.

[26] See Chapter 2, pp. 34–38.

[27] In the case of mental disease, see Paul V. Lemkau and G. M. Crocetti, "An Urban Population's Opinion and Knowledge about Mental Illness," *American Journal of Psychiatry,* 118 (January 1962): 692–99; Bruce P. Dohrenwend and Edwin Chin-Shong, "Social Status and Attitudes toward Psychological Disorder:

minorities and released prisoners, however, these effects continue to be intensive.

The disengagement of prejudice

The impact of prejudice lies in the possibility of *discrimination* when attitudes based on stereotypes are expressed in categoric actions that deny members of the stigmatized minority access to those opportunities and privileges that our system of beliefs holds should be available to all. Through discrimination, prejudices are actualized in the exclusion of individuals from certain types of employment, educational and recreational opportunities, membership in organizations, political activities, or health services. The distinction between prejudice and discrimination is important because it holds the possibility of reducing the social consequences of prejudice, even though prejudiced attitudes are not eliminated.

Prejudiced attitudes are learned within the complex latent processes of personality development. They are maintained by the institutional practices that provide the social order that is essential to effective community life. Fundamental cultural change is required to eliminate prejudices; a campaign of public service announcements by the mass communication media or religious sermons on Sunday are not adequate means of achieving such a change. In any event, prejudice is not necessarily translated into action. A more promising reform strategy, therefore, would be to center attention on the prevention of evidences of discrimination against the released prisoner. Contrary to popular belief, prejudiced attitudes are *not* little mental packages tucked away in the corner of the brain, awaiting the proper stimulus to bring them to life in a predetermined way. A negative stereotype held by a given individual may not be hostile. Conversely, hostility may be present but a negative stereotype may be absent. The stereotype operates within complex social situations involving many other factors, and attitudes shape themselves to behavior.[28] Prejudices are formulated obscurely, and are likely to be expressed most frequently within the confines of the person's own group. Unless some concrete situation precipitates their expression, the prejudices remain disengaged.[29]

The Problem of Tolerance of Deviance," *American Sociological Review,* 32 (June 1967): 417–32; Kenneth Robinson, "The Public and Mental Health," in Hugh Freeman and James Farndale (ed.), *Trends in the Mental Health Service* (New York: Macmillan Co., 1963), pp. 13–16; Leonard J. Duhl, "The Changing Face of Mental Health," in Leonard J. Duhl (ed.), *The Urban Condition* (New York: Basic Books, Inc., 1963), pp. 66–67.

[28] Earl Raab and Seymour Martin Lipsett, "The Prejudiced Society," in Earl Raab (ed.), *American Race Relations Today* (Garden City, N.J.: Doubleday-Anchor Books, 1959), pp. 29–48.

[29] Robin M. Williams, Jr., *Strangers Next Door* (Englewood Cliffs, N.J.: Prentice-Hall, Inc., 1964), p. 77.

Anticonvict prejudices can be held without being expressed through discrimination against a particular released prisoner. The punitive concept of the dangerous, incorrigible criminal is being challenged by the therapeutic concept of the released prisoner as a deserving graduate of correctional programs which have imbued him with new attitudes and capacities. Crimes differ in the attention they draw and the degree to which they violate moral sensibilities or arouse fears of physical danger. Persons convicted of low-visibility crimes are less likely to encounter major resistance. The community status of the former offender also affects the nature of his reception. The very young and elderly, whites, members of the middle class, and persons in reputable occupations are more likely to escape the stigmatization applied to persons in their twenties and thirties, racial minorities, the underprivileged, and unskilled or unemployable groups.

The stigma of delinquency and crime depends on the evaluation of the illicit behavior made by members of the offender's reference groups. Technically, a person is a criminal when he has been convicted in court of an act prohibited by law. The real sting of stigmatization, however, comes through ostracism by the groups making up the immediate social universe of the offender. When traditions of delinquency persist in the neighborhood, there may be no such stigmatization. It is difficult for treatment to be effective when the discharged offender rejoins a community which supports the very values he is supposed to abandon in the course of his rehabilitation. On the other hand, if the offender *were* stigmatized by the neighborhood for behavior which is characteristic of an important segment of the population, the question becomes how the society which casts out the offender because he violated its laws can be induced to accept him.

The quest for employment

Securing a job looms large among the immediate problems encountered by many released prisoners. In an urban society income is crucial to meeting even minimal creature needs, and employment to gain income is an essential ingredient in a favorable self-image of adult males in a culture that emphasizes self-reliance. The difficulties encountered by a released prisoner in his job search are partially caused by his own defects and the inadequacies of the correctional facility as a preparatory institution, but conditions in the receiving community are also part of the problem.

The former prisoner frequently lacks qualities which would cause employers to be eager to employ him, especially when there is a surplus of workers. Those former prisoners who violate an employer's trust complicate the job hunt for future applicants. Others fail to perform work with even minimum dispatch and efficiency. Most releasees have had inferior work records before confinement, and their skills usually are at a low level. The applicant may fail to present his case effectively because he lacks social skills and self-confidence. The personal qualities of prisoners operate together with their employment characteristics in the effects they have on post-release outcome. For example, a study of parolees (all of whom had to have a job to qualify for parole) found that successful parole was greater for men who became married versus single men, for men over 23 years of age versus those younger, and for men with no other family member known to the police versus those with at least one other family member so known.[30]

When the correctional institution fails to prepare the otherwise qualified prisoner for the job market of his community, it contributes to the released-prisoner dilemma. We have analyzed the complex ideological and practical problems encountered by authorities in endeavoring to make the prison a means of strengthening the vocational competence of the offenders it receives, many of whom lack marketable job skills.[31] Beyond these difficulties, the prisons frequently are located in a region of the state remote from urban job markets, because citizens prefer that such institutions be at a considerable distance from their homes. The encouraging trend toward community-based corrections has the potential of increasing the relevance of prisoner employment to their aftercare, but the location of established prisons is a formidable obstacle to work-release programs.

While the job market of the receiving community raises barriers to successful reentry through rejection of the ex-convict, the frustrations many released inmates encounter also can be explained by the routine workings of economic institutions. Unless the community is experiencing a labor shortage, the applicant with a prison record carries an extra burden of suspicion which works against his interests when his competitor for a job has otherwise equivalent qualifications. This burden is unlikely to be imposed when the personnel office does not question the applicant's background. At a time of full employment, an English study found that nearly two thirds of the larger firms and about 40 percent of the smaller ones had some departments where men were recruited on a "no questions asked" basis. Firms in the insurance, banking and finance, professional, and scientific fields did not accept men on this basis, but as a whole, the majority of firms had hired offenders without knowing their criminal records. While it did not seem difficult for an English offender to get a job, there were difficulties in obtaining work at a level above the unskilled. Former prisoners were relegated largely to the less satisfying jobs. The barriers appeared to be related to the public image of the crime

---

[30] Robert Evans, Jr., "The Labor Market and Parole Success," *Journal of Human Resources,* 3 (Spring 1968): 205–6.

[31] See Chapter 18, pp. 445–53.

perpetrated. Rejection for employment declined in this order: sex offenses, stealing from fellow workers, stealing from customers, and stealing from the firm.[32]

Formidable barriers are erected against the released prisoner by some employers, but these barriers may be incidental to other purposes. Government, private enterprise, labor unions, and bonding companies cite the "risk" of giving jobs to former prisoners. Government usually fails to hire former inmates, even while parole and probation agencies are urging private employers to provide jobs. Prisons and parole agencies themselves are particularly unlikely to hire former felons for fear that, as employees, their loyalty to former associates may make them vulnerable to pressure from prisoners or parolees. Many men of fairly extensive training are forced into unskilled labor. Prison vocational training is not necessarily recognized for trade apprenticeship; labor unions tend to contrive a labor shortage as a means of protecting job opportunity for their present members and of preserving wage scales. Some jurisdictions curtail the licensing of trucks and issuing of certain business licenses to former prisoners because they fear infiltration of legitimate businesses by criminal syndicates.

Buffering agencies

Some private organizations have endeavored to ease the impact of reentry by serving as what John Irwin has called "buffering agencies." The family probably is the major buffering agency; initial residence, money, and other assistance is provided by relatives in many cases. We would prefer, however, to limit the term *buffering agency* to the private and public organizations which assume responsibilities for easing the status-passage problems of reentry as either primary or secondary functions. Irwin cites the halfway houses of the Allied Fellowship Service in Oakland and San Mateo, California, and of the American Friends Service Committee in San Francisco. The Seven Steps program, founded by Bill Sands and staffed primarily by other former prisoners, provides a series of inspirational talks to inmates shortly before their discharge from prison.[33]

Halfway houses, which serve a relatively small number of clients, require that members remain sober and seek employment. They afford the warm emotional climate appropriate for therapy. Other examples of halfway houses for released prisoners and parolees are the Parting of the Ways Home in Pittsburgh; the Isaac Hooper Home for Women and the Stuyvesant Residence Club in New York City; Norman House of Lon-

[32] J. P. Martin, *Offenders as Employees* (London: Macmillan & Co., Ltd., 1962), pp. 120–22, 111–12.

[33] John Irwin, *The Felon* (Englewood Cliffs, N.J.: Prentice-Hall, Inc., 1970), pp. 126–30.

don, England; Nusshof Home of Witzwill, Switzerland; Bruce House, operated in conjunction with New Jersey's Bordentown Reformatory; St. Leonard's House in Chicago; Creshaw House in Los Angeles; and "308 West Street" in Wilmington, Delaware.[34]

The idea of a halfway house is not new. In 1817, a commission of the Massachusetts Legislature recommended that a building be "erected of wood, at small expense" for discharged convicts who "are often entirely destitute." It was proposed that the releasees have "a lodging, rations from the prison at a cheap rate, and have a chance to occupy themselves in their trade, until some opportunity offers of placing themselves where they can gain an honest livelihood in society." The idea was ignored at the time, but in 1864, some citizens of Boston opened and operated for two decades a "Temporary Asylum for Discharged Female Prisoners" of jails and houses of correction.[35]

The therapeutic programs of halfway houses may combine several techniques: group and individual counseling, individual psychotherapy, social group work, personal counseling, religious and vocational counseling, Alcoholics Anonymous, and the use of Antabuse in aversion treatment. Generally, clients are discharged outright into the community on termination of the therapeutic programs, and subsequent contacts with the house are limited. The policy on length of stay ranges from five days to as much as two years.[36]

A promising development has been more systematic efforts by correctional agencies to bridge the gap between confinement and adjustment to the life of the free community. In one approach by the California Department of Corrections, the institutional treatment program is consciously coordinated with parole in the Increased Correctional Effectiveness Program. The intensity of parole supervision is related to the expectations of the parolee's behavior as derived from diagnosis and treatment within the institution that have been oriented toward his release. Provision is made for temporary return of the parolee to the institution without loss of parole status. Sharp administrative distinctions between the institution and parole programs are blurred to promote the reintegration of the offender within the community.

In another approach, the Federal Bureau of Prisons and an increasing proportion of state prison systems are developing halfway houses and programs based on the employment feature of work release.

[34] Richard W. Nice, "Halfway House Aftercare for the Released Offender," *Crime and Delinquency,* 10 (January 1964): 8–14; Robert C. Crosswhite and Maurice A. Breslin, Jr., "Bridging the Gap from Confinement to Freedom," *Federal Probation,* 23 (June 1959): 46–52.

[35] Edwin Powers, "Half-Way Houses: An Historical Perspective," *American Journal of Correction,* 21 (July–August 1959): 35.

[36] Edward Blocker and David Kantor, "Half-Way Houses for Problem Drinkers," *Federal Probation,* 24 (June 1960): 20–21.

In 1961, the Federal Bureau of Prisons launched a new program in which prerelease guidance centers were opened in New York City, Chicago, and Los Angeles for juvenile and youthful prisoners.[37] Subsequently, centers were established in other metropolitan areas, with greater emphasis on use of community resources to encourage offenders to acquire progressively greater self-sufficiency. Only youths who have homes or release plans approved by the U.S. probation officers in these metropolitan areas are accepted for the program at present. Most of the youths are granted parole with release dates approximately four months in the future but subject to change to meet individual needs.

Specific purposes of these federally sponsored centers are similar to those of a halfway house, while the offenders remain in the custody of the Attorney General. To an extent beyond that of the usual halfway house, a trained full-time staff is provided—a director, caseworker-researcher, employment placement specialist, and three correctional counselors. The director's primary function is to develop and maintain relationships with agencies and organizations in the community. The caseworker-researcher is in charge of intensive group and individual counseling, casework, and data collection for evaluation of this experimental project. The employment specialist coordinates the job hunt through familiarity with the local labor market and contacts with the U.S. Department of Labor, the state employment service, unions, and private employers. The counselors provide continuous supervision and guidance through close relationships with residents.

RECIDIVISM AND EVALUATION OF CORRECTIONS

Generally, recidivism is cited as evidence of the failure of correctional institutions. The *recidivist* usually is defined as a person who, having been convicted, imprisoned, and released, again commits a crime. Although recidivism frequently is defined in terms of number of previous prison sentences served, it also has been measured as the number of either previous arrests or prior convictions. Counting the number of arrests is the least accurate measurement of criminal behavior, because arrest is not equivalent to guilt. Conviction rates provide for an official finding of guilt before inclusion of the defendant among offenders; they also include offenders excluded from prison admissions because they have been fined or granted suspended sentences or probation. Imprisonment is the best measurement, according to some experts, because only the most serious and dedicated offenders end up in prison. In light of differential patterns of arrest and court decisions in extending leniency,[38] however, prison

---

[37] "Pre-Release Guidance Center Demonstration Project," *Progress Reports,* 10 (July–September 1962): 2–5.

[38] See Chapter 14, pp. 350–53.

Figure 24–2. Coffee break after a day of job hunting.

In a recently introduced program of prerelease guidance centers, the Federal Bureau of Prisons is attempting to close the gap between the correctional institution and outright release into the community. Here the residents of a center in Detroit, Michigan, share their experiences in hunting jobs as they drink coffee.

admission is an unreliable basis for distinguishing dedicated criminals from casual offenders.

Criticism of usual estimates

Some observers and prison officials maintain that approximately two thirds of released prisoners return again to prison. These estimates are derived from examination of the prior imprisonment of a particular group of inmates in a particular prison. Daniel Glaser cites basic errors in this method of estimating. Recidivists usually receive longer sentences and are concentrated in certain prisons because first offenders are placed in institutions where they are less likely to be "contaminated" by experienced criminals. The counting of previous prison terms among inmates will inflate rates when a prison receiving long-term inmates is used as an example on which to base estimates of recidivism rates for all kinds of prisons. Short-term prisoners are underrepresented in prison population statistics taken at a given time because the longer tenure of long-termers increases the possibility of their presence at the time statistics are compiled. Together, the accumulation of prisoners with long sentences and the association of recidivism with longer sentences add up to an inflation of recidivism estimates for a given inmate population in a correctional system.[39] Further, the range of sentences imposed and the proportion of prisoners released each year can be related to demonstrate that a recidivist rate of two thirds is statistically impossible.[40]

Examining data of several state prison systems, Glaser concluded that only a third of all men released from an entire prison system are returned in the first two to five years after release. His estimate reflects his contention that reliable recidivism rates based on imprisonment can be obtained only through an expensive and time-consuming cohort study in which a sample of released prisoners is traced over the years to determine whether or not they are imprisoned for new crimes.[41]

Premises in the concept of recidivism

The evaluation of prisons as failures on the basis of recidivism is rather unusual when compared with other people-processing institutions. The medical patient's later appendectomy is not viewed as a failure of medical treatment for a broken arm, although the sources of criminal behavior are at least as varied as the forms of illness and injury requiring medical attention. In fact, recurrence of a skin rash can be interpreted as evidence

[39] Glaser, *Effectiveness of a Prison and Parole System,* pp. 13–14.

[40] Sol Rubin, "Recidivism and Recidivism Statistics," *NPPA Journal,* 4 (July 1958): 236.

[41] Glaser, *Effectiveness of a Prison and Parole System,* pp. 19–24.

of the need for continued treatment or of the resistance of the patient's condition to treatment.[42]

It has been argued that success or failure in the treatment of criminals should be defined more specifically.[43] When an offender resumes his criminality, statistics could show whether the new crimes stemmed from new problems which arose after release from treatment or reflected failure to solve the problems that stimulated the earlier crime. This would bring us closer to determining whether a failure of treatment was involved. On the other hand, nonrecidivism is not proof of treatment success. The offender may have adjusted through his own efforts or because of other factors unrelated to the correctional program. Perhaps he became rehabilitated *in spite of* the program.

Recidivism rates as a measure of correctional effectiveness have important defects. Even assuming that correctional institutions are in a position to offer genuine therapeutic experiences, the low amenability of some prisoners to treatment would produce recidivists. The failures of correctional institutions to prevent recidivism in offenders should be evaluated against the background of earlier failures of the family, school, church, and other character-building institutions, which had greater resources, received the individuals earlier in life when personality is more malleable, and usually had more time to handle them. The successes of correctional treatment are less available for counting in follow-up studies than are its failures, because successes do not attract the attention of criminal justice agents. Recidivism rates vary not only because of varying qualities of offenders but because changes in administration practices, such as stricter enforcement by police and less willingness of courts to grant probation, will affect the numbers of offenders returned to prisons. Such policies differ among jurisdictions, making reliable comparison of recidivism rates among state systems impracticable.

SUMMARY

The reentry crisis challenges the qualities of the individual, but this especially difficult status passage also reveals the inadequacies of the prison as a preparatory institution and the importance of the willingness and capacity of the receiving community to assimilate the returning prisoners in fulfillment of the rehabilitation bargain. In assessing these three major dimensions of the released prisoner's problems, this chapter has attempted to demonstrate again that solution of the crime problem lies

[42] Edward Glover, "Prognosis or Prediction: A Psychiatric Examination of the Concept of 'Recidivism,' " *British Journal of Delinquency,* 6 (September 1955): 116–25.

[43] C. J. Beck, "A Reconsideration of Labels in Penology," *ETC: A Review of General Semantics,* 17 (Autumn 1959): 84.

as much in societal factors as in the qualities of the individual offender, who usually is the center of attention in explanations for recidivism.

FOR ADDITIONAL READING

Benson, Margaret. "A Whole-Hearted Look at Half-Way Houses." *Canadian Journal of Corrections*, 9 (July 1967): 198–226.

Blumstein, Alfred, and Larson, Richard C. "Problems in Modeling and Measuring Recidivism." *Journal of Research in Crime and Delinquency*, 8 (July 1971): 124–32.

Clemmer, Donald. "The Prisoner's Pre-Release Expectations in the Free Community." *Proceedings of American Correctional Association, 1959*, pp. 244–48.

Empey, LaMar T. *Alternatives to Incarceration*. Washington, D.C.: Office of Juvenile Delinquency and Youth Development, U.S. Department of Health, Education, and Welfare, 1967.

Finestone, Harold. "Reformation and Recidivism among Italian and Polish Criminal Offenders." *American Journal of Sociology*, 72 (May 1967): 575–88.

Freeman, Howard E., and Simmons, Ozzie G. *The Mental Patient Comes Home*. New York: John Wiley & Sons, 1963.

Hammond, W. H., and Chayen, Edna. *Persistent Criminals*. London: Her Majesty's Stationery Office, 1963.

Haskell, Martin R., and Weeks, H. Ashley. "Role Playing as Preparation for Release from a Correctional Institution." *Journal of Criminal Law, Criminology, and Police Science*, 50 (January–February 1960): 441–47.

Laulicht, Jerome. "A Study of Recidivism in One Training School." *Crime and Delinquency*, 8 (April 1962): 161–71.

Levin, Martin A. "Policy Evaluation and Recidivism." *Law & Society Review*, 6 (August 1971): 17–46.

Morris, Pauline. *Prisoners and Their Families*. London: George Allen & Unwin, 1965.

Parker, Tony. *The Unknown Citizen*. London: Hutchinson & Co., 1963.

Pearl, Arthur. "The Halfway House: The Focal Point of a Model Program for the Rehabilitation of Low Income Offenders." In Frank Riessman, Jerome Cohen, and Arthur Pearl (eds.), *Mental Health of the Poor*, pp. 497–508. New York: Free Press of Glencoe, 1964.

Sinclair, Ian. *Hostels for Probationers*. London: Her Majesty's Stationery Office, 1971.

Turner, Merfyn. "The Lessons of Norman House." *Annals of American Academy of Political and Social Science*, 381 (January 1969): 39–46.

Uusitalo, Paavo. "Recidivism after Release from Closed and Open Penal Institutions." *British Journal of Criminology*, 12 (July 1972): 211–29.

West, Donald J. *The Habitual Criminal*. New York: St. Martin's Press, 1963.

25

Reform and criminal justice

Among community problems, crime ranks high as an object of concern. There is nothing new in the existence of this concern, but there are reasons to believe the nature of the societal reactions to crime is undergoing such a degree of change that we can properly describe this as an era of criminological reform. The consideration of these reasons is the subject of this chapter.

THE SOCIAL STRUCTURE AS A TARGET OF REFORM

Crime is frequently explained as the failure of a given individual to "adjust" to the norms (the substance of social institutions) which are supposed to lend direction to behavior that will facilitate the maintenance of community order. In this view, the word "reform" refers to the objective of various forms of intervention in bringing the deviant into line with standards that have been accepted as proper and essential to the community order. We will use "reform" in a different sense, to divert attention away from the deviant per se and toward the possibility that social  arrangements, including the organizations implementing criminal justice, contribute to criminological problems, criminal behavior, and recidivism. Rather than reform of the individual offender, we will be concerned with reform of the social structure and the criminal justice system.

Limited objectives in seeking change

In social reform, deliberate efforts are undertaken to reduce perceived discrepancies between the outcomes of institutionalized practice and the expectations derived from the values of a given society. Reform entails an optimistic view that these discrepancies can be reduced because man is regarded as a plastic being capable of change and social institutions, as human creations, also are believed to be subject to modification. Reform

616

is directed toward strengthening the contemporary social structure rather than uprooting it, because reformers continue to have faith in the principles upon which it is based.[1]

Similarly criminological reform does not seek to uproot the contemporary justice system and replace it with an entirely new set of principles and practices. Instead the objective is likely to be modification of selected practices or revision of some portion of the organizational framework. There are instances, such as occasional calls for elimination of the prison, when proposals go beyond reform, but by definition criminological reform seeks goals short of the extreme and thoroughgoing changes identified as "radical."

The mobilization of broad-based support for criminological reform is more likely when the given issue involves other groups than adjudicated offenders or the members of the criminal justice establishment. If influential groups are to be enlisted in the movement, the reform message must appeal to public groups as well as those most immediately and directly affected. In the past the values of such groups have motivated them to push for penal reform because they viewed prisoners as one of several categories of persons who shared specific problems. Prisoners have been identified as "sinners" symbolizing a widespread "immorality," victims of alcohol, mental defectives or psychotics, products of broken homes, or participants in other broad social problems. More recently, the prospects for criminological reform have lain in the increased recognition of crime as a societal problem.

Reform is more than a moral and humanitarian endeavor undertaken by altruistic members of power-holding groups who are willing to surrender their immediate advantages in the status quo because of sympathies for underprivileged groups. Prospects for significant change can be anticipated when the conditions for which reform is sought qualify as a societal problem that imposes burdens on all segments of the population. Crime is a collection of private "troubles" for victims and subsequently for criminals who reap the legal penalties, but the community as a whole experiences the financial losses and erosion of trust caused by crime and must underwrite the costs of supporting the criminal justice system. The seeming intractability of the crime problem cannot be separated from social causes for the rise and persistence of law violations.[2]

Reform: A series of accommodations

Reform has been pictured as a rational and deliberate process proceeding through stages of careful, objective analysis of causal factors and relevant conditions, the framing of a corrective strategy, the mobilization

---

[1] The nature of reform was considered in Chapter 11, pp. 268–70.

[2] See Chapter 11, p. 268.

of necessary resources, and the implementation of a deliberately organized program of correction. In practice, the reform process is more complex, less orderly, and more unpredictable. A reform movement does have typical patterns in the initial recognition by some individual or group of a need for change, the spread of this consciousness through agitation and propaganda, the emergence of leadership and concerted action by additional converts, the introduction of new patterns, and the institutionalization of these patterns into the social organization in forms which probably will meet only a portion of the original goals.

The process of reform operates through a series of accommodations whereby relationships between groups within a system are recast in a new form that presumably will be more suited to solving the problem that has stimulated the reform effort. The ultimate nature of these accommodations is not predictable because the change agents do not control other participating groups and probably do not initially realize all the ramifications of the problem. The original goal may have been relatively narrow and short range—alleviation of an immediate problem—which could not take into account the complex interdependence of the many factors affecting the conditions for which change is sought.[3]

Because of this unpredictability and lack of complete control, change agents often employ what has been called a "sounding-out process."[4] When one of the interacting parties wishes to alter characteristic relationships but is uncertain of the reaction of the other party to the proposed change, it makes initial overtures in ambiguous terms. If it is rebuffed by the second party, the proposal can be reformulated in more acceptable terms. A series of actions and reactions leads the parties to a new clearcut relationship and reveals a common concern as a basis for implementing reform.

Knowledge: Stimulant of change

The growth and widespread distribution of knowledge is important to a growing awareness of undesirable conditions, increasing demand for their correction, and mobilization of efforts to overcome them. The extension of formal education and the development of mass communications have increased the proportion of the population that is aware of society's conditions outside the range of direct observation by the average person. Concurrently, contemporary technology has made remarkable progress in overcoming space limitations, the impact of disease, and the previous economic inaccessibility of certain goods. A larger share of the

[3] See Robert M. MacIver, *Social Causation* (Boston: Ginn & Co., 1942), pp. 295–96.

[4] James D. Thompson and William J. McEwen, "Organizational Goals and Environment: Goal-Setting as an Interactive Process," *American Sociological Review,* 23 (February 1958): 23–31.

population has become aware of and acquired faith in the potentialities of technology for significant gains against such evils as poverty and disease. As underprivileged groups have reacted more openly to undesirable conditions, all elements of the social organization have been made subject to vigorous criticism and protest. Thus criminal justice agencies find themselves dealing with a clientele that is increasingly less passive and more vocal. Further, their work is more subject to public and judicial examination.

Along with the wider distribution of knowledge has come growing recognition among men of the influence of the social systems created by man. There is also growing consciousness, especially in recent decades, that these contrived systems can be *changed* by man.[5] The application of knowledge to the improvement of human organizations, Warren Bennis believes, has been particularly prevalent in the United States because of the growing disenchantment of scientists with a morally neutral stance, the increased respectability of action research, a larger volume of research, and new demands that the performance of bureaucracies be improved.[6] These developments have been instrumental in reducing the marginal status of theoretical criminology among the sciences[7] and in increasing awareness of the defects of criminal justice organizations.

Another significant development has been the recent trend in industry, business, and government to organize the innovating processes by establishing research bureaus, planning groups, and programs to reward workers for innovative ideas. The criminal justice system has lagged in following this trend, but the President's Crime Commission has called for substantial research and development to improve police capability in apprehension, management of court cases, and operation of correctional agencies.[8]

Effects of emotionalism

Whether prompted by fears of the criminal as some kind of monster or concern for the continuing failure to provide equal justice under the law, criminological issues are fraught with emotionalism. Reform movements stir emotions because they confront vested interests, challenge the reluctance of most groups to change familiar habits, and inspire honest differences of opinion concerning the existence of a given problem and

[5] Kenneth E. Boulding, *The Impact of the Social Sciences* (New Brunswick, N.J.: Rutgers University Press, 1966), pp. 4–7.

[6] Warren G. Bennis, "Theory and Method in Applying Behavioral Science to Planned Organizational Change," *Journal of Applied Behavioral Science,* 1 (October–December 1965): 337–39.

[7] Chapter 1, pp. 8–9.

[8] See Chapter 3 and President's Commission on Law Enforcement and Administration of Justice, *Task Force Report: Science and Technology* (Washington, D.C.: U.S. Government Printing Office, 1967).

Interpreter, July–September 1972 (Colorado State Penitentiary); Charles Broussard, artist

Figure 25–1. The prisoner's view on penal reform.

This cover illustration of an inmate-edited magazine shows the walls of the closed prison breached by a force coming from the outside community.

what to do about it. Although it complicates thoughtful analysis of issues, emotionalism provides impetus to reform because it produces a sense of crisis that can mobilize public concern and overcome resistance to change.

When conceived as "enemies of society" or "abnormal" beings, those processed by criminal justice agencies are in no position to exert pressure for change. The prisoner usually is voteless and unappealing to the politician, except as a symbol for the need for "law and order." Convicted offenders are drawn disproportionately from groups that are deficient in political and social power. Under the principle of less eligibility, the convicted offender is considered less worthy than the most underprivileged law-abiding citizen.[9] This principle, coupled with the belief that punishment of criminals should entail suffering, accounts in part for the low level of citizen attention usually given to criminological issues.

Inmates are frequently emotional in their protests against the prison as a social institution and the conditions of penal confinement, but their writings include well-reasoned arguments for citizen participation in penal reform. The lead editorial in an issue of *Interpreter,* an inmate-edited journal at Colorado State Penitentiary, that was devoted to prison reform said, in part:

> If crime, violence, and drug abuse are national problems, then the issue of prison reform should be of concern to every citizen in the nation; because these problems cannot possibly be resolved so long as the prison system continues to function as a major cause of them. . . . Almost everyone, convicts included, agrees that the primary function of a prison system should be protection of the public; and almost everyone, convicts especially, realizes that the present system not only fails in that function, but also that it works against the interests of the public. . . . In calling for prison reform, convicts aren't forgetting that they've violated the law nor asking to be "coddled." We are simply asserting that it is in the mutual interests of ourselves and society that the nature and purpose of these penalties be constructively and humanely defined.[10]

Paradoxically, as George Bernard Shaw has observed, the work of previous reformers can create conditions requiring reform today. "The neglect, oppression, corruption of the old common gaol" aroused reformers of the past so that they created the contemporary prison, which Shaw indicts as "that diabolic den of torment, mischief, and damnation."[11] The zeal of the reformer must persist in the face of institutional immobility and stubborn resistance from vested interests. Because of this persistent

---

[9] Chapter 18, p. 445.

[10] "Editorial," *Interpreter,* 8 (July–September 1972): 2.

[11] George Bernard Shaw, *The Crime of Imprisonment* (New York: Citadel Press, 1961), p. 13.

zeal, the reformer is likely to be the type who will disturb the peace, trespass on forbidden ground, and assault complacency.[12] The zeal of some reformers can be traced to truculence and self-righteousness which are more productive of conflict than long-term solution of problems.

A more optimistic appraisal of penal history is that of Norval Morris, who interprets it as a trend toward the reduction of gratuitous suffering —that which fails to produce the social good of decreased incidence or seriousness of crime and delinquency. The deficiency of this development, Morris says, is that accomplishments are limited to uneasy compromises between punitive and therapeutic objectives. Penal reform still must confront the task of developing correctional systems that actually protect society from crime and recidivism.[13]

CRIMINAL JUSTICE AND THE SYSTEMS CONCEPT

The term "system" has several uses relevant to criminological reform. Generally, it suggests an orderly combination or arrangement of parts, elements, ideas, or functions into a whole. For reform, "system" implies that if the orderly arrangement is not efficient in producing anticipated outcomes, at some point it will instigate a demand for reform. Internally induced reform, discussed below, tends to be derived from this implication.

"System" also implies that categories of factors operate in relationship with one another to produce outcomes. Therefore, reform requires recognition of these interrelationships rather than simplistic confrontation of only certain factors. This conception of system is applicable to all reform endeavors, but it is particularly pertinent to the inclusion of criminal justice within the larger social system of the community.

Improving outcomes of transactions

The problems of each of the several components of the criminal justice system have been discussed in earlier chapters, implying that the police, courts, and correctional agencies operate as largely independent systems. This approach has the advantage of narrowing the scope to concentrate on the conflicts and strains existing among the units comprising a particular component. A fundamental defect of American criminal justice, however, is that the work of the various components is insufficiently coordinated to produce an acceptable rate of successful outcomes. The

[12] Arthur M. Schlesinger, *The American as Reformer* (Cambridge, Mass.: Harvard University Press, 1951), p. 66.

[13] Norval Morris, "Impediments to Penal Reform," in Robert M. Carter, Daniel Glaser, and Leslie T. Wilkins (eds.), *Correctional Institutions* (Philadelphia: J. B. Lippincott Co., 1972), pp. 462–64.

loose confederation of offices and agencies fails to qualify as a genuine system, in spite of the interrelationships portrayed in Figure 12–1.[14]

The reform campaign may be directed toward improving the speed of transactions, the relevance of the decision-making processes to problem solutions, and the consistency of each of a series of transactions as the client moves through a number of related agencies. An alternative approach is to focus on a given issue, such as congested court calendars or jail overcrowding. Whether attention is concentrated on the sequence of transactions or on a particular issue, single-purpose reform tends to deal more with symptoms than with the common causes latent in the overall administration of justice. Congested court calendars may be corrected by additional personnel and improved management of courts, but the heavy caseloads of police and correctional agencies also are involved in the reliance on punishment as the urban response to deviance. Jail overcrowding may be eliminated by building larger facilities, but bail practices are also involved in the same problem.

Administrators are likely to try to lift the agency by its own bootstraps without significant change in relationships with the external community. Garrett Heyns, Executive Director of the Joint Commission on Correctional Manpower and Training, believes that penal reform is the responsibility of correctional executives, although he recognizes that relationships with outside parties are crucial. He has lamented the serious deficiencies in coordination and communication among a number of factors: correctional agencies, college education and in-service training for careers, training in management, working conditions, community-based programs, and operational research.[15] This approach is committed to the rehabilitation model, which relies on one-to-one relationships between therapist and client and usually employs the identification method of influencing behavior.[16] The emphasis is on replacing outmoded facilities and equipment; for example, correctional institutions would provide more commodious sleeping quarters, improved sanitary facilities, better equipped schoolrooms and workshops, and more pleasant dining arrangements. Counseling and medical services would be expanded, and the impact of treatment would be strengthened by reducing caseloads.

This approach is a continuation of a 20th-century trend toward mitigation of the harshness of prisons, but the reform effort is directed toward what Don Gibbons calls the "bread and butter" problems of administrators who are compelled to operate agencies on shoestring budgets. When additional funds are allocated, they are likely to be devoted to expanding cell space, patching obsolete facilities, or propping up programs of doubt-

---

[14] Chapter 12, pp. 298–99.
[15] Garrett Heyns, "The Road Ahead in Corrections," *American Journal of Corrections,* 30 (November–December 1968): 6–8, 10.
[16] Chapter 11, pp. 282–83.

ful effectiveness.[17] Rejecting the continued reliance on confinement as the primary measure against crime, Manuel López-Rey sees a bureaucratic myopia converting medico-psychological services and other forms of treatment into "patch" remedies.[18] Tom Hadden warns that the outcome is likely to be a few showplace prisons which serve to divert attention from the continued inadequacies of most such facilities.[19]

Internally induced reform

Reform of the criminal justice system is usually seen as a movement initiated by outsiders who establish a public issue by arousing interest and seeking to impose changes. Another strategy is *internally induced reform,* in which changes are implemented by individuals and groups occupying roles and statuses within the criminal justice system.

Certain advantages accrue to the second approach. Changes induced within the agency are more likely to become part of practice, and objectives are likely to be limited and, therefore, more concentrated in impact. Change agents are more likely to be acquainted with the parameters of the environment, and, as residents of the agency structure, they are more apt to persist in the reform effort than would outsiders with only segmental or superficial interest in the organization. The concept of internally induced reform calls attention to the importance of restructuring the organization itself if reform, however induced, is to have long-range impact. The outcome of any change program can be determined by the intensity of the resistance it engenders among agency personnel. This varies with the degree of threat to cherished beliefs and entrenched behavioral patterns, the scope of proposed changes, the resources and prestige available to the reformers, and their choice of strategies.[20]

The concept of reform as an accommodative process is consistent with the political bargaining process through which administrators endeavor to acquire resources and authorization of programs from superiors and legislators.[21] Nevertheless, administrators usually prefer to limit the number of parties participating in the accommodative transactions of reform.

[17] Don C. Gibbons, *Changing the Lawbreaker* (Englewood Cliffs, N.J.: Prentice-Hall, Inc., 1965), pp. 190–96.

[18] Manuel López-Ray, "Analytical Penology," in Manuel López-Rey and Charles Germain (eds.), *Studies in Penology Dedicated to Sir Lionel Fox* (The Hague: Martinus Mijhoff, 1964), pp. 138–39.

[19] Tom Hadden, "The Other Side of Penal Reform," *New Society,* 453 (June 3, 1971): 952–54.

[20] George A. Brager, "Effecting Organizational Change through a Demonstration Project: The Case of the Schools," in George A. Brager and Francis P. Purcell (eds.), *Community Action against Poverty* (New Haven, Conn.: College and University Press, 1967), pp. 104–5.

[21] For an insider's report on the trials and tribulations of this bargaining process by the internal change agent, read Part II of Russell G. Oswald, *Attica: My Story* (Garden City, N.Y.: Doubleday & Co., Inc., 1972).

Many favor public disinterest, believing that laymen cannot understand the technical content of criminological work and full relevation would only produce adverse political reactions. Administrators are apt to argue that they are charged with responsibilities in dealing with public issues as defined by a public opinion which is unlikely to see the nature or the moral dimensions of some "crisis" with the objectivity and historical perspective of the criminological scientist.

Doubting that the correctional administrator has exclusive competence, Richard Korn argues that the denial of official information makes the average citizen unduly dependent on offenders for information about law enforcement and corrections. The administrator loses the opportunity for massive public support, which is essential to reform. Although officials may recognize their dependence on the participation or support of ordinary citizens, they continue to be reluctant to include them in the problem-solving processes.[22] They also are in need of the reliable evaluation and interpretation of problems that can be provided by objective scientific investigation.

Attitudinal prerequisites for internal reform

The deterioration of reform movements is most often attributed to the brief span of public interest in an issue and the failure of politicians to honor campaign promises once they assume power. Recognition should also be given, however, to the corrosive effects of the ingrained habits and the self-interests of the rank-and-file workers who man bureaucracies through a succession of administrations. Once assured their jobs are safe, they fall into the bureaucratic pattern of maintaining traditional practices and the equilibrium of their administrative units. In the course of acquainting superiors with details, these workers are able to stifle needed changes by their efforts to preserve what they regard as organizational efficiency.[23] Reform as an accommodative process, therefore, also involves the restructuring of organizations and the resocialization of their staffs.

Restructuring is a helpful means of converting an innovation-resisting organization into an innovation-producing one. This process usually entails decentralization, teams of change experts free to move about the organization, and the creation of temporary units. An essential element of the process, according to Herbert Shepard, is an adaptable, creative outlook by personnel which will counter inherent tendencies to preserve contemporary status and to exploit opportunities for power and personal

[22] Richard R. Korn, "Correctional Innovation and the Dilemma of Change-From-Within," *Canadian Journal of Corrections,* 10 (July 1968): 450–51.

[23] Seymour M. Lipset, "Bureaucracy and Social Reform," in Amitai Etzioni (ed.), *Complex Organizations: A Sociological Reader* (New York: Holt, Rinehart & Winston, Inc., 1961), pp. 260–67.

rewards. Reeducation in self-concepts and interpersonal relations is a prerequisite to producing the capacities for independent action and autonomous interdependence that are characteristic of the innovator.[24]

The emergence of a change agent from among agency personnel is inhibited by long-term exposure to the routines, traditions, and values to which employees have been socialized and to which they are expected to be loyal. The internal change agent has the advantages of familiarity with agency history and practices and acceptance as a member of the organization. To qualify as a change agent, however, he must also have the capacity to objectively evaluate the ideology and the practices to which he has been socialized.[25] He must be able to question ideas held sacred by his colleagues and, probably, some of his superiors. He must be capable of withstanding the pressures of colleagues who identify organizational loyalty with conformity to established norms and practices. The organization itself may try to neutralize the change agent by promoting him into a position where he is obligated to maintain the established system or lacks significant influence on agency policies.[26]

The fact that there are executives and employees ready to break with traditions suggests several possibilities. The internal change agent may be a carrier of ideas that previously were not characteristic of agency practice —ideas gained through education, training, or experience in other settings. A second possibility is that the agency has been exposed to drastically revised conditions because of changes underway in the larger system of which it is a segment. For example, a prison system may be experiencing a heavy influx of new inmates because of a "law and order" crisis in the community, a more aggressive law enforcement policy, or a disproportionate representation in the community population of young adults with the highest crime rates. Such revised conditions aggravate the usual discrepancy between available resources and agency requirements and gives administrators reason to press for changes in the conditions under which the agency operates.

CRIMINAL JUSTICE AS A PART OF THE COMMUNITY SYSTEM

The final part of this book has been organized around the community because criminal justice cannot be divorced from the organizational structure of the community. Further, the law observance supposedly induced by criminal law entails the social-psychological bonds that characterize the community. The components of the system of criminal justice are included in the structure of government developed to maintain community order and to deliver services vital to the needs and aspirations of citizens.

[24] Herbert A. Shepard, "Innovation-Resisting and Innovation-Producing Organizations," *Journal of Business,* 40 (October 1967): 477.

[25] Ideologies are discussed in Chapter 8, pp. 186–91.

[26] Korn, "Correctional Innovation," p. 455.

As a part of the governmental structure, criminological agencies are subject to problems that have been broadly defined as the urban crisis.

Reintegrating the offender

The usual justification for the penologist's interest in the community is that the overwhelming majority of adjudicated offenders return eventually to their homes. As explained below, more compelling reasons are the community's role in the appearance of criminal behavior and in the delivery of services essential to crime prevention and the reduction of recidivism. For these reasons, the reintegration model[27] is becoming increasingly characteristic of correctional practice.

Emphasis on preparing the inmate for reentry into the community implies that prison programs will be made relevant to the conditions and problems he will encounter on his return. The community-worker role assumes the capacity and willingness of the community to absorb the released offender into its structure of opportunity and services, in keeping with the rehabilitation bargain.[28] Further, the reintegration model implies that the prison will take on the form of a community providing a place for the inmate as a genuine participant. Minimum resistance will be offered to influences from the outside community, and the prison will be less dominant as an official reaction to criminals.[29] The number of inmates has increased in the United States, but not in proportion to the growth of the civilian population. In 1940, for every 100,000 Americans 14.6 adult felons were in federal correctional institutions and 117.3 in state institutions. In 1970 the equivalent rates were 9.8 and 86.8, respectively.[30]

Rather than concentrating change strategies on the individual offender, the reintegration strategy strives to enter into partnership with the human service agencies of his home community. The goal is to remedy the deficits in the relationships between the prisoner and available community services. As this partnership implies, changes in the community environment are of as much interest to the correctional worker as changes in the offender. The focus of attention is on the interactions of the individual and the environment.

The community as a criminogenic setting

The criminal behaviors that are the concern of the criminal justice system are derived from the forces operating within the community. The

[27] The reintegration model is presented in Chapter 11, pp. 284–87.

[28] Chapter 24, p. 589.

[29] Chapter 21, pp. 525–26.

[30] *National Prisoner Statistics: Prisoners in State and Federal Institutions for Adult Felons* (Washington, D.C.: Federal Bureau of Prisons, April 1972), Table 1.

dimensions and nature of the contemporary crime problem are related to urban society's particular reliance on formal controls to supplement traditions and mores. These informal means of control operate ineffectively in an urban society, which is characterized by cultural homogeneity, population mobility, impersonal relations, and a high rate of social change. Such conditions are conducive to discrepancies between cultural goals and the institutionalized means of realizing opportunities. They also create conflicts among the subcultures that are characteristic of a highly differentiated society with a pluralistic culture.[31]

In various ways, the urban society generates contradictions in the norms which are supposed to guide individual behavior in conformity with the social order. The problem neighborhood is a prime example of how physical and social factors converge in the metropolis to produce high delinquency and crime rates.[32] Problems of crime control are interrelated with the difficulties of maintaining a sense of community among divergent interests and subcultures. Problem neighborhoods are populated by such numbers of people that the interpersonal contacts which generate informal controls are difficult to maintain.

Case histories of adjudicated offenders are frequently cited in support of claims that criminal behavior is an effect of particular conditions, such as deficient family life or unwholesome recreation. These simplistic explanations emphasize symptoms of more profound causes latent in what Irving Spergel has called the inauthentic community.[33] In such a community, rewards are distributed largely on the basis of conformity to the norms of politically and socioeconomically dominant groups, rather than according to professed ideals. The operation of the system for delivering services that are essential to individuals in the contemporary urban community fails to justify the claims of those charged with administering it. Further, in the inauthentic community social institutions are deficient in orienting individuals to socially effective and personally satisfying adult roles and statuses.[34]

Criminal justice and the delivery of services

Criminological agencies today are expected to cope with forms of deviance that formerly were governed by informal control mechanisms. This is due to the greater scale of deviance in a mass society and the belief that law enforcement can be an effective substitute for moral controls that

[31] See Chapter 10.

[32] See Chapter 21, pp. 519–20.

[33] Irving A. Spergel, *Community Problem-Solving: The Delinquency Example* (Chicago: University of Chicago Press, 1969), pp. 39–49. See Chapter 21, p. 520.

[34] The relevance of the social institutions of family, school, church, and mass communications was discussed in Chapter 6; economic institutions were considered in Chapter 8, pp. 198–203.

rely on the rewards or denial of fellowship and the sting of conscience.

To a degree, the criminal justice system has been pressed to fill a vacuum of community services. It is expected to deal with the violence and property crimes that partially stem from earlier failures of the community system to deliver the services vital to the "good life" promised by an affluent society. Further, criminal justice has assumed the function of providing human services outside the province of which are not filled by other agencies. The major share of police work is in the public-servant role,[35] juvenile courts are deeply involved in social work,[36] the jail is the dumping ground for various human problems,[37] and the prison is expected to be a place of both treatment and coercion.[38]

Community-based corrections is increasingly adopting the reintegration model, which includes the former offender in the opportunity and service delivery systems of the community. To increase chances that former criminals will become legitimate members of the community, the agents of criminal justice are expected to work toward reintegration of former criminals into the community's normative system. Reintegration also must provide access to education, jobs, medical care, and other services essential to the well-being of the individual participant in the complex order of the contemporary urban community.

Relevance of local government

Issues of criminal justice reform are intimately related to reform of local government, as suggested in the data of Table 25–1. Analysis of expenditures for the criminal justice system tends to overlook the dominance of local government because in proportion to numbers of offenders, relatively greater revenues are available to federal and state governments. Nevertheless, local government dominates total expenditures, especially for police and the courts. Another key pattern is the differential distribution of the three components of criminal justice (police, courts, and corrections) among the levels of government. The varying functions of the levels of government are indicated by the heavy investment of states in corrections and relatively high expenditures of the federal government in prosecution as an attempt to cope with nationwide social problems. Greater federal expenditures for defense of indigent defendants suggest the lag of local government in reforming the inequities of the legal system. The "other criminal justice" category includes expenditures on criminal justice curricula in educational institutions, criminal justice planning agencies, crime commissions, and so on. The investment in these essential prerequisites to reform is exceptionally low by local government.

[35] Chapter 13, p. 333.
[36] Chapter 14, pp. 367–70.
[37] Chapter 15, p. 380.
[38] Chapter 20, pp. 486–87.

TABLE 25–1.
Expenditures for the criminal justice system by level of government,
fiscal years 1969–70

| | Levels of government | | | |
	Federal	State	Local	Percent*
Total criminal	Thousands of dollars			
justice system	$1,031,700	$2,267,549	$5,505,472	—
	Percentage distribution			
Police protection	11.6	13.5	74.9	59.3
Judicial	10.8	23.7	65.5	13.9
Prosecution	23.1	18.8	58.1	5.2
Indigent defense	54.6	9.2	36.2	1.2
Correction	4.9	61.6	33.5	19.9
Other criminal justice	41.0	47.5	11.5	.5
Average	11.4	25.0	63.6	100.0

Source: *Expenditure and Employment Data for the Criminal Justice System, 1969–70* (Washington, D.C.: U.S. Department of Justice—U.S. Department of Commerce, February 1972), Table 1.
* Percent of total expenditures for all government represented by each category.

Attempts to change local government are impeded by a number of factors.[39] The Jeffersonian faith in grass-roots government has imbued American culture with the belief that a small community of educated yeomen is the core of democracy, in the style of the New England town meeting which provided each citizen with a direct voice in government. When Jacksonian democracy extended this concept of local self-rule to the urban masses, it was assumed that any intelligent citizen could hold governmental office, that rotation of office and popular election would assure qualified officials, and that distribution of offices among members of the victorious political party was justified. Political reforms intended to mitigate the corruption produced by the Jacksonian "spoils system" have not touched the fundamental principle of local self-rule, which is vigorously defended by a political establishment with a vested interest in local offices. The relatively low rate of participation by citizens in political affairs reflects an apathy which shelters this status quo from reform, in spite of the declining influence of the physical locality in human affairs.[40]

The fragmentation of local government complicates the formation of a public consensus on criminological issues and exposes reform issues to diverse local interpretations. The political processes of a metropolitan

[39] See John C. Bollens and Henry J. Schmandt, *The Metropolis: Its People, Politics and Economic Life* (New York: Harper & Row, 1965), pp. 493–98; and Scott Greer, *Governing the Metropolis* (New York: John Wiley & Sons, Inc., 1962), pp. 124–25.

[40] The declining importance of the immediate physical locale is discussed in Chapter 21, pp. 516–17.

area are not those of a unified community, because there is a split between the central city and the suburbs, which are fragmented into hundreds of separate governments. The central-city electorate has the major
voice in city government, but suburbanites have a great economic, social,
and cultural investment in the government of a city's economic enterprises and social institutions.[41] Criminological issues of the entire area
are deeply involved in how the city government manages law enforcement, jails, and courts and what resource priorities are granted these services. Metropolitan criminological reform suffers from the low visibility
of its problems, the effect of the dichotomy of central-city government
and suburbia on management, and the overall discrepancy between demand for services and revenues.

LEGALIZATION AND CONTROL

The complexity of urban society and its special need for a high degree
of public order have increased reliance on *legalization,* the process by
which selected norms are translated into the abstract language of laws and
made subject to official enforcement. Modern states qualify as what
Allan Silver calls "policed societies," in which a criminal justice bureaucracy is capable of diffusing centralized power throughout civil society
by small, discretionary, and rapidly concentrated operations. Differing
from totalitarian police states, the policed society has been produced by
an extension of the need to safeguard the moral community by legal
norms. Tightly woven political and economic systems have become dependent on organized protection against criminality, casual violence, and
riotous protest, to an unprecedented degree.[42]

Law as social engineering

Man's relationships with others are patterned into a meaningful whole
because the individual largely conforms to the rules characteristic of his
group. Behaviors of individuals and groups are fitted together to comprise
the social order that lends predictability to social transactions and a state
of peace and tranquility to the community. The criminal law is part of the
structure of formal controls to which the community resorts to remedy
breeches in the social order. These breeches result when the informal controls derived from a sense of conscience and socialization to appropriate
norms are insufficient to achieve compliance to norms that are deemed
essential to the community.

[41] Greer, *Governing the Metropolis,* pp. 107–17.
[42] Allan Silver, "The Demand for Order in Civil Society: A Review of Some
Themes in the History of Urban Court, Police, and Riot," in David J. Bordua (ed.),
The Police: Six Sociological Essays (New York: John Wiley & Sons, Inc., 1967),
pp. 6–13.

Identifying the legal order as a part of the total order, Roscoe Pound sees the law as an aspect of social engineering in that it has been contrived deliberately to serve a consciously implemented system of formal control. The legal order applies a system of rules and procedures to harmonize and reconcile controversies. Further, it restrains and deters antisocial acts threatening the general safety, health, peace, and economic order.[43] The primary function of such an order is to provide guidelines for mitigating conflict and integrating the community through meaningful, socially constructive intercourse.

The law may be conceived in either passive or active terms, as William Evan points out. As a passive social force, the law would be viewed as a codification of existing customs or mores which have taken root in the behavior of citizens. In this case the function of the law is reinforcement of the mores through uniform, predictable administration of sanctions against deviants. The conception of law as a passive social force can be seen in criticism of the law as a prop for entrenched special interests. In the conception of the law as an active social force the law is still seen as reflecting existing customs and mores but it is also regarded as a potential force for influencing behavior and beliefs through the institutionalization of new norms and their enforcement. The law ultimately facilitates the incorporation of new attitudes and beliefs by those who are expected to comply with newly legalized norms.[44]

The conception of law as an active social force implies that legalization is a tool for social reform which can reshape attitudes in support of a new moral order. Criminal sanctions are conceived as means for public education rather than as reactions to specific criminal acts. The conception is consistent with the compliance model, discussed below, which encourages taking into account the predispositions of the target populations in the framing of laws. This use of legalization also implies that the effectiveness of existing legal norms should be reassessed continually for evidence of outmoded and possibly counterproductive sanctions. The compliance model is relevant here in its emphasis on the study of feedback effects.

If the law is to serve an educational function, certain conditions must be met. Evan has specified some of these. The lawmakers (legislative, executive, administrative, or judicial) must enjoy prestige and authority in the minds of the citizens, especially when the probability of resistance is high. The rationale of the new law should be consistent and compatible

[43] Roscoe Pound, "Criminal Justice in the American City—A Summary," *Crime and Delinquency,* 10 (October 1964): 419–21.

[44] William M. Evan, "Law as an Instrument of Social Change," in Alvin W. Gouldner and S. M. Miller (eds.), *Applied Sociology: Opportunities and Problems* (New York: Free Press, 1965), pp. 286–87. Also see Edwin M. Lemert, "Social Structure, Social Control, and Deviation," in Marshall B. Clinard (ed.), *Anomie and Deviant Behavior* (New York: Free Press, 1964), pp. 88–96.

with existing institutionalized values. There should be groups in the community whose preexisting conformity to the new law may be cited to illustrate its efficacy. Time should be provided for transition from previous behavior to the new expectations. Enforcement agents must be committed in their own behavior to the new expectations, even if they are not committed to its implicit values. Rewards for compliance are more likely to produce learning than reliance on negative punishments, and the likelihood of compliance is increased when effective protection is provided for the victims of the prohibited behavior.[45]

Law as a source of problems

The substance and administration of criminal law become appropriate targets for reform when the legal system loses effectiveness as a means of resolving disputes and reconciling conflicts. The usefulness of the legal system in integrating the activities of community groups requires its continued relevance to these activities, in spite of changes underway in the community. Otherwise, the law becomes an inertial body of outmoded traditions.

Hermann Mannheim describes the "crisis in values" resulting from the failure to relate criminal sanctions to the priority of values requiring the support of legal norms under contemporary social conditions.[46] The rapid development of science and modern technology in an urban society has produced an unprecedented emphasis on collectivities (such as business corporations) instead of individuals as the central concern of the law.[47] In practice, however, the law continues to concentrate on individual crimes, such as thievery, rather than the impact of collective crimes such as bogus bankruptcies and stock swindles. Punishment after an offense continues to be the dominant strategy, in spite of the widespread advocacy of prevention as a more promising course of action.

The substantive criminal law defines criminal conduct, authorizes punishment, and directs the state's use of the criminal sanction. As the basic source of authority, the contents of criminal law are of crucial importance to reform of law enforcement and corrections as well as of the courts. The President's Crime Commission reported:

The absence of substained legislative consideration of criminal codes has resulted in the perpetuation of anomalies and inadequacies which have complicated the duties of police, prosecutor, and court and have hindered the attainment of a rational and just penal system. Some examples of these sub-

[45] Evan, "Law as an Instrument of Social Change," pp. 288–92.

[46] Hermann Mannheim, *Criminal Justice and Social Reconstruction* (New York: Oxford University Press, 1946), pp. 2, 195–96.

[47] Arthur S. Miller, "Science Challenges Law: Some Interactions between Scientific and Legal Changes," *American Behavioral Scientist,* 13 (March–April 1970): 586–87.

stantive inadequacies are the failure in most cases to treat as crimes highly dangerous conduct which does not produce injury, whether the conduct is undertaken negligently or recklessly; the unsatisfactory delineation of the line that separates innocent preparation from criminal attempt; the absence of laws that make criminal the solicitation to commit crimes; the amorphous doctrines of conspiracy that have grown unguided by considered legislative direction; the inconsistent and irrational doctrines of excuse and justification that govern the right to use force, including deadly force, self-defensively or in the prevention of crime, or in the apprehension of criminals; and the confusion that surrounds the definition of the intent or other culpable mental states required for particular crimes. . . . The whole problem of sentencing structure, the laws governing judicial sentencing alternatives, the range of authorized imprisonment for particular crimes, and the distribution of authority between courts and correctional agencies, is also in need of legislative consideration.[48]

Modern society, which is characterized by varied and often opposing subcultures, is likely to produce situations in which legal norms do not coincide with the social norms of some groups and may fail to be defined as binding on individual conduct. Social differentiation also creates disparities in the capacity of groups to enlist the criminal law in protection of their particular interests and values. Further, changes in social conditions continually modify norms, making some laws so obsolete their effective enforcement is unlikely.[49]

Law innovators have been known to create new problems by the formulation of laws intended to solve existing ones. Juvenile courts were developed to protect children from the stigma of being convicted in an adult criminal court, but they have been severely criticized for denying the protection of due process. The application of criminal sanctions to control homosexuality, alcohol abuse, and other moral deviations has involved criminal justice in medical problems and interfered with the use of appropriate therapies.[50]

Overcriminalization and diversion from the system

A "crisis of overcriminalization" exists, Sanford Kadish thinks, because of excessive reliance upon the criminal law to enforce morals, provide social services, and sidestep legal restraints on law enforcement. Examples of social services are the use of police and jails to handle public drunks, enforcement of bad-check laws for the sake of creditors, and

[48] President's Commission on Law Enforcement and Administration of Justice, *Task Force Report: The Courts* (Washington, D.C.: U.S. Government Printing Office, 1967), p. 97.

[49] Richard Quinney, *The Problem of Crime* (New York: Dodd, Mead & Co., 1970), pp. 29–31.

[50] Arnold M. Rose, "Law and the Causation of Social Problems," *Social Problems,* 16 (Summer 1968): 33–43.

prosecution of deserting husbands under family nonsupport laws. Disorderly conduct and vagrancy laws are not administered to prevent specific behavior but to hold suspects, control beggars and other indigent persons, and otherwise provide police discretion outside the bounds of due process. Kadish warns that these practices erode the criminal law's claim to legitimacy, impose a special burden on the poor, generate cynicism and indifference to the law, and divert resources from the control of serious crime.[51]

The difficulties of the juvenile court also have been cited as an example of the use of the power and authority of law to achieve ends that are unlikely to be achieved by legal means. The wide variety of misconduct defined as delinquency, the evasion of due process, the delegation of intangible authority to workers of doubtful therapeutic competence, and the burden of cases are among the weaknesses of the juvenile court.

Diversion of some delinquent cases from the juvenile courts, and of adult moral offenses from criminal courts, is the major proposed remedy. As Edwin Lemert points out, however, this solution requires that other agencies assume the tasks left when the problem domain of the juvenile court (or the criminal court) is made smaller and more specialized.[52]

Diversion of persons from the criminal justice system is a common practice in the United States, but it is doubtful that it successfully screens out the less serious offenders.[53] Informal processes may be abused through inconsistent administration and decision-making practices for the sole purpose of staff convenience. Civil commitment and transfer to welfare or health agencies are frequent means of diversion, but the use of these facilities for control purposes raises issues. The lack of adequate procedural safeguards, the justification of involuntary commitment on the grounds that treatment is available, and the possibility of longer confinement than under a prison sentence have all been questioned.[54]

COMPLIANCE AS A METHOD OF CONTROL

The criminal justice system has the responsibility of reducing the volume of crime. Formal sanctions, however, are merely one means of

[51] Sanford H. Kadish, "The Crisis of Overcriminalization," *Annals of American Academy of Political and Social Science,* 374 (November 1967): 157–70. Also see Francis A. Allen, *The Borderline of Criminal Justice* (Chicago: University of Chicago Press, 1964); Edwin Schur, *Crimes without Victims* (Englewood Cliffs, N.J.: Prentice-Hall, Inc., 1965); and Gilbert Geis, *Not the Law's Business?* (Rockville, Md.: National Institute of Mental Health, Center for Studies of Crime and Delinquency, 1972).

[52] Edwin M. Lemert, *Instead of Court: Diversion in Juvenile Justice* (Chevy Chase, Md.: National Institute of Mental Health, Center for Studies of Crime and Delinquency, 1971), pp. 5–7, 18.

[53] See Chapter 14, pp. 350–53.

[54] Eleanor Harlow, J. Robert Weber, and Fred Cohen, *Diversion from the Criminal Justice System* (Rockville, Md.: National Institute of Mental Health, Center for Studies of Crime and Delinquency, 1971), pp. 1–4.

inducing loyalty. They must be supported by the socialization of personality and the conferring of legitimacy on legal norms by members of the community. The compliance model,[55] defined below, provides an appropriate means for administering the law in ways likely to gain this support. This model is consistent with the reintegration approach which, we have seen, directly involves corrections in the processes of community life.

Impact and compliance models

Criminal justice policies have usually been based on the *impact model,* in which measures designed to control deviance, including the criminal law, are evaluated in terms of narrowly defined relationships ("impact") between the causes of deviance and the outcome of measures taken against it.[56] The analysis of the effects of a measure regards the measure itself as the crucial variable in determining either obedience or nonobedience, rather than the overall sociocultural context within which the deviant evaluates the sanctions threatening him. Some set of events (such as a rash of skyjacking episodes) causes policy makers to take a certain action (such as electronic monitoring of airline passengers and their luggage), which is evaluated in terms of its effects in reducing the incidence of the events (decline of skyjacking episodes).

The *compliance model* broadens the sphere of concern to include predispositioning processes and the feedback effects of the obedience or nonobedience outcomes of the measure taken against deviance. Upon entering the event, the targets of the measure have varying predispositions to conform to the norms that have been legalized. These predispositions have been shaped by socialization of the individuals' personalities, the effects of learning in determining whether a given policy will serve as positive or negative reinforcement, and the relevance of the norms of the individuals' reference groups to the achievement of the policy's goals. The compliance model is concerned with the process of acceptance of a given measure, largely prior to its point of "impact." This acceptance must be self-generating to some degree if law enforcement is to be meaningful. Through feedback, acceptance presumably will influence the predispositioning processes to favor the insertion of new norms into socialization, as well as affecting the relationship between learning and reinforcement, and the culture of reference groups. In this process,

---

[55] The term "compliance" is used here to refer to behavioral conformity with norms, rather than the narrower definition in Chapter 11 which involves the manipulation of rewards and punishments to induce preferred behavior.

[56] The impact and compliance models are discussed by Jerry N. Clark *et al.,* "Compliance, Obedience, and Revolt: An Overview," in Samuel Krislov *et al.,* (eds.), *Compliance and the Law* (Beverly Hills, Calif.: Sage Publications, 1972), pp. 11–12.

formal controls become a means of introducing informal control mechanisms to promote future compliance.

Policy makers also are involved in these predispositioning processes and feedback effects. Their analysis of the particular control problem and their choice among alternatives are related to perceptions and values shaped by their own socialization, learning, and reference groups. Their tolerance of various forms of deviance varies over time and place, suggesting the possibility that previous experience with unproductive penal measures will alter the predispositions in some new criminological crisis. There is evidence that the predispositions of policy makers are changing: the near elimination of capital punishment, the sharp revision of policies on abortion, and the trend toward decriminalization of alcohol abuse are examples.

We assume that these trends indicate a tendency among policy makers to recognize the shortcomings of arbitrary punishments in effecting conformity, but this tendency should not be exaggerated because existing law continues to diverge from the community's moral conceptions. Traditions are more persistent in legal institutions than in the dynamic environment of community mores. Lawmakers usually are subject to only modest pressure to recognize the need for changes, and they have difficulty in ascertaining the contemporary moral sense of the community.[57]

Major defects in the arbitrary imposition of punishment have been cited: overlooking the unique aspects of each individual's personality, isolation of the offender from legitimate society, the negativism of punishment, and underestimation of the complexity of deterrence.[58] The compliance model provides an opportunity to remedy these defects by proposing that policy makers fit their measures to the psychological and sociological forces which either reinforce or oppose conformity. Feedback effects can be applied to avoid counterproductive use of coercion and substitute more promising methods of control.

Labeling theorists have called particular attention to the importance of analysis of the criminal justice system, taking into account the values of the framers and enforcers of the law and the differential distribution of power within the social structure.[59] By emphasizing the place of criminal law within the total control system of the community, the compliance model sees the exercise of power in terms of mutual social interactions between groups with varying degrees of power. Such a conception is consistent with widespread participation in community decision making. Implying the study of feedback effects of control measures, it identifies

[57] Julius Cohen, Reginald A. H. Robson, and Alan Bates, *Parental Authority: The Community and the Law* (New Brunswick, N.J.: Rutgers University Press, 1958), pp. 195–98.

[58] Chapter 8, pp. 172–78.

[59] Chapter 10, pp. 258–61.

the self-interests of politically dominant groups with the development of at least partial common interests among all groups in the community.

Exchange and the strategy of conflict

Criminal law is an application of social power[60] that is usually seen in terms of an elitist, leader-centered struggle among groups to exercise power over authorities as a goal in itself. The state's monopoly over legitimate coercion becomes a means of maintaining the advantageous position of elites. It reenforces their unidirectional dominance of subordinate groups in maintaining predictable superordinate-subordinate relationships. Samuel Krislov, who regards this description as departing from the real play of power, believes the factors producing compliance with norms more properly emphasize the mutual social interaction between the decision makers and those to whom the decisions are applied. Differences in power among groups fall along a continuum rather than presenting "concentrated, instant omnipotence." Similarly, "antisocial" behavior is seen as the product of an ongoing social system, and compliance is seen as psychosocial behavior distributed throughout the population.[61]

In stressing the importance of mutuality in gaining compliance to group norms, the concept of *exchange* calls attention to the intrinsic rewards human beings gain in associations with one another. The joy of winning a football game, the gratifications of family life, and the pleasures of love inhere in the associations themselves. These rewards, however, tend to entail a cost to other persons. The pleasures of the child require some yielding of narrow self-interests and perhaps financial sacrifice by the parents. The football victory was possible because the supporters of the other team were disappointed. "Exchange" implies that a person for whom another has done a service is expected to express his gratitude and return a service when the occasion arises. This reciprocity of service also induces individuals to accept the costs of self-discipline to group norms because social bonds are created by the promise of future rewards through mutual exchange of services. These rewards include affection, approval, and respect—sentiments which are intrinsic in associations with other persons and which provide a note of altruism that is absent in the concept of the play of power as unidirectional and concentrated in the hands of an elite.[62]

[60] The relationship between criminal law and power was discussed in Chapter 4, pp. 71–73; Chapter 5, pp. 93–95; and Chapter 10, pp. 258–59.

[61] Samuel Krislov, "The Perimeters of Power: The Concept of Compliance as an Approach to the Study of Legal and Political Processes," in Krislov *et al., Compliance and the Law;* pp. 333–36.

[62] Peter M. Blau, *Exchange and Power in Social Life* (New York: John Wiley & Sons, Inc., 1964), pp. 4, 7, 112–14.

As Thomas Schelling points out, deterrence, an important concept in criminal law, works only because of what the potential violator expects the responses to his choices to be. A threat can be made only in anticipation of its influence on his choice. Further, the deterrence concept requires that there be *both* conflict and a potential common interest between the parties involved; neither pure common interest nor pure antagonism of interest is a proper target for deterrence. By placing the deviant in a position where he shares potential common interests to be acquired through compliance with the law, deterrence couples the course of criminal justice with the individual's course of action. Changing his behavior involves tacit bargaining through which each party strives to gain ends which are dependent on the participation of the other party. He is supposed to be confronted with evidence that the responses to his behavior will be determined by his behavior. The deterrent threat becomes credible to the deviant because it is based on the other party's knowledge of his value system. His ability to perceive alternatives and to calculate probable outcomes and the need for tailoring the behavior of agents of criminal justice to the deviant's own behavior are also taken into account. Defining "threat" as not necessarily aggressive or hostile, Schelling sees deterrence as a strategy of conflict based on interdependent decisions in which the deviant is capable of choosing those actions that will maximize the probability of outcomes he finds desirable.[63]

Differential influences of legal sanctions

The deterrent influence of punishment, William Chambliss explains, is dependent on the criminal's level of commitment to crime as a way of life and on whether the criminal act is "expressive" or "instrumental." Persons with high commitment perceive their law violation as receiving group support, see themselves as criminals, and pattern their way of life around involvement in crime.[64] *Expressive crimes* are impulsive and less responsive to punishment. *Instrumental crimes* are perpetrated to serve some calculated purpose for the offender. The criminal's calculated motivation provides an opportunity to employ punishment as a means of convincing him that he shares, at least partially, the community interest in avoiding such contemplated crimes. Chambliss contends that instrumental crimes are more likely to be deterred by punishment than expressive crimes. Among both types, low commitment of the individual to crime as a way of life is associated with his greater responsiveness to punishment.[65]

[63] Thomas C. Schelling, *The Strategy of Conflict* (Cambridge, Mass.: Harvard University Press, 1960), pp. 10–17.

[64] Differential commitment is an important variable among criminal behavior systems, especially for professional crime; see Chapter 7 above.

[65] William J. Chambliss, *Crime and the Legal Process* (New York: McGraw-Hill Book Co., 1969), pp. 368–69.

Murder is a crime highly likely to be expressive and low on commitment; therefore, most murders are unlikely to be deterred by criminal sanctions. Even specific acts of murder vary in their positions along the continuums of Chambliss's typologies, however, and the highly generalized legal categories (murder, rape, petty theft, and so on) are ineffective criteria for gauging the deterrent impact of punishment. As Schelling noted above, regardless of the legal category, deterrence is applicable only when both conflict and a potential common interest exist between the agent of justice and the population comprising the target for penal policies. Punishment is more likely to be counterproductive when extended to expressive offenses such as drug abuse, psychic abnormality, and nonviolent sexuality, in which a commitment to criminal values is absent. Austin Turk believes legal sanctions have been more effective in coping with sexual and nonsexual violence and petty misappropriation of goods and services.[66] Chambliss cites the irony in the application of most of the criminal-legal efforts to the processing and sanctioning of those who are least likely to be deterred by legal sanctions.[67]

Extension of the boundaries of legal sanctions invites counterproductive effects unless the probable reactions of offenders are considered and feedback effects are studied. Individualized justice is thus applicable to both crime control and correction. The sanctions are more likely to achieve compliance when they are consistent with the predispositions of the persons to whom they are applied and when they enjoy the support of the community's norms. These predispositions and the community norms are relevant to the development of a sense of mutuality—a mutuality identified with social sentiments under the concept of "exchange"— which is the means of enlisting the deviant in the achievement of the ultimate purposes of the framers of criminal law. Instead of employing the criminal law solely to apply superior power through coercion, "the strategy of conflict" would use power in a series of bargaining relationships with the deviant as a means of gaining his recognition that his own interests can be advanced through compliance.

SUMMARY

The study of criminology continues in a state of ferment, making our presentation of crime, corrections, and society comparable to a photograph which artificially freezes one moment of a dynamic happening. This dynamism provides a remarkable opportunity for criminological reform—the parameters, difficulties, and prospects of which we have re-

[66] Austin T. Turk, *Legal Sanctioning and Social Control* (Rockville, Md.: National Institute of Mental Health, Center for Studies of Crime and Delinquency, 1972), pp. 28–68.

[67] Chambliss, *Crime and the Legal Process,* p. 370; see Chapter 2 above for data supporting this conclusion.

viewed in this chapter. It is derived from the community, because the crime problem is interwoven with many other societal problems requiring reform of the social structure.

The present unsettled state of criminology also has affected our search for reliable answers to the questions raised by the appearance of criminal behavior and the defects revealed in the administration of criminal justice. The outcome of this search has probably been a disappointment to those expecting pat, final, or simple answers. Some may be highly pessimistic about ever meeting the crime problem; Émile Durkheim has declared that crime will always be with us because it is a normal symptom of the conditions of collective life.[68]

Nevertheless, this book has been dedicated to the proposition that the dimensions of the crime problem can be reduced significantly. One of the reasons for this optimism is that the bankruptcy of facile explanations has been demonstrated by the relevation of unanticipated issues in the normal course of scientific inquiry. Our pursuit of these issues has prepared the way for understanding criminology as a facet of the broader studies of man as an individual and a sociocultural creature. If the reader began this investigation with the intention of understanding what makes the criminal "tick," he ended up, we trust, with greater insights into himself and the environment he shares with the offender in many respects.

FOR ADDITIONAL READING

Abel-Smith, Brian, and Stevens, Robert. *In Search of Justice,* pp. 352–68. London: Penguin Press, 1968.

Bates, Sanford. "Anglo American Progress in Penitentiary Affairs." In Manuel López-Rey and Charles Germain (eds.), *Studies in Penology Dedicated to Memory of Sir Lionel Fox,* pp. 30–41. The Hague: Martinus Nijhoff, 1964.

Bennis, Warren. *Changing Organizations.* New York: McGraw-Hill Book Co., 1966.

Berkowitz, Leonard, and Walker, Nigel. "Laws and Moral Judgments." *Sociometry,* 30 (December 1967): 410–22.

Corwin, Roger G. "Strategies for Organizational Innovation: An Empirical Comparison." *American Sociological Review,* 37 (August 1972): 441–54.

Hage, Jerald, and Aiken, Michael. *Social Change in Complex Organizations.* New York: Random House, 1970.

Haurek, Edward, and Clark, John P. "Variants of Integration of Social Control Agencies." *Social Problems,* 15 (Summer 1967): 46–60.

Janchill, Mary Paul. "Systems Concepts in Casework Theory and Practice." *Social Casework,* 50 (February 1969): 74–82.

Jeffery, C. Ray. "Social Change and Criminal Law." *American Behavioral Scientist,* 13 (March–April 1970); 523–34.

[68] Chapter 4, p. 77.

Jobson, K. B. "Commitment and Release of the Mentally Ill under Criminal Law." *Criminal Law Quarterly*, 11 (February 1969): 186–203.

Jones, Garth N. *Planned Organizational Change*. London: Routledge & Kegan Paul, 1969.

Lerman, Paul (ed.). *Delinquency and Social Policy*. New York: Frederick A. Praeger, 1970.

Little, Alan. "Penal Theory, Penal Reform and Borstal Practice." *British Journal of Criminology*, 3 (January 1963): 225–75.

Livermore, Joseph M.; Malmquist, Carl P.; and Meehl, Paul E. "On the Justifications for Civil Commitment." *University of Pennsylvania Law Review*, 117 (November 1968): 75–96.

Morris, Albert. *Correctional Reform: Illusion and Reality*. Bulletin 22, Massachusetts Correctional Association. Boston, 1972.

Rose, Gordon. "Penal Reform as History." *British Journal of Criminology*, 10 (October 1970): 348–71.

Rubin, Sol. "Illusions of Treatment in Sentences and Civil Commitments." *Crime and Delinquency*, 16 (January 1970): 79–92.

Schur, Edwin M. *Law and Society*. New York: Random House, 1968.

Skoler, Daniel L. "Comprehensive Criminal Justice Planning—A New Challenge." *Crime and Delinquency*, 14 (July 1968): 197–206.

Index of names

Subject index

This book has been set in 10 and 9 point Times Roman, leaded 2 points. Chapter numbers are in 36 point Optima and part numbers are in 24 point Optima Semibold. Part and chapter titles are in 24 point Optima. The size of the type page is 26 x 46½ picas.

D